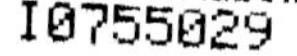

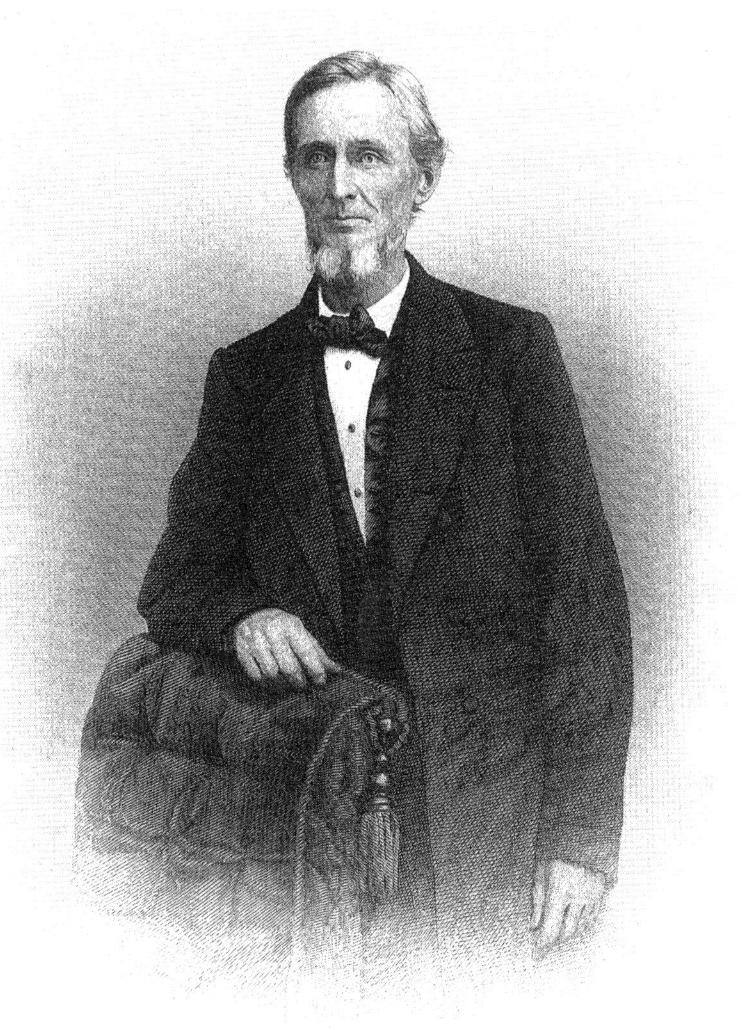

Engd by J. C. Buttre New York.

Jeffn Davis

From a recent Photograph taken from Life.

THE LIFE

OF

JEFFERSON DAVIS.

BY FRANK H. ALFRIEND,

Late Editor of The Southern Literary Messenger.

CINCINNATI AND CHICAGO:

CAXTON PUBLISHING HOUSE.

PHILADELPHIA, RICHMOND, ATLANTA AND ST. LOUIS:

NATIONAL PUBLISHING CO.

BALDWYN, MISS.: P. M. SAVERY & COMPANY.

SAN FRANCISCO, CAL.: J. LAWS & CO.

1868.

PREFACE.

In offering this volume to the public, the occasion is embraced to avow, with unfeigned candor, a painful sense of the inadequate manner in which the design has been executed. Emboldened rather by his own earnest convictions, than by confidence in his capacity, the author has undertaken to contribute to American History, an extended narration of the more prominent incidents in the life of Jefferson Davis. Whatever may be the decision of the reader upon the merits of the performance, the author has the satisfaction arising from a conscientious endeavor to subserve the ends of truth. In pursuit of the purpose to write *facts* only, to the aid of familiar acquaintance with many of the topics discussed, and to information derived from the most accurate sources, has been brought laborious investigation of numerous interesting papers, which his avocation made accessible. It is therefore claimed that no statement is to be found in this volume, which is not generally conceded to be true, or which is not a conclusion amply justified by indisputable evidence.

Nor is it to be fairly alleged that the work exhibits undue sectional bias. As a Southern man, who, in common with his countrymen of the South, was taught to believe the principles underlying the movement for Southern independence, the only possible basis of Republicanism, the author has regarded, as a worthy incentive, the desire to vindicate, as best he might, the motives and conduct of the South and its late leader.

Disclaiming the purpose of promoting sectional bitterness, or of a wholesale indictment of the Northern people, he deems it needless to dwell upon the obvious propriety of discrimination. Holding in utter abhorrence the authors of those outrages, wanton barbarities and petty persecutions, of which her people were the victims, the South yet feels the respect of an honorable enemy for those distinguished soldiers, Buell, Hancock, McClellan and others, who served efficiently the cause in which they were employed, and still illustrated the practices of Christian warfare. To fitly characterize the remorseless faction in antagonism to the sentiments of these honorable men, it is only necessary to recall the malice which assails a "lost cause" with every form of detraction, and aspires to crown a triumph of arms with the degradation and despair of a conquered people.

In his especial solicitude for a favorable appreciation of his efforts, by his Southern countrymen, the author has striven to avoid affront to those considerations of delicacy which yet affect many incidents of the late war. He has not sought to revive, unnecessarily, questions upon which Southern sentiment was divided, and has rarely assailed the motives or capacity of individuals in recognized antagonism to the policy of President Davis. Perhaps a different course would have imparted interest to his work, and have more clearly established the vindication of its subject. But besides being wholly repugnant to the tastes of the author, it would have been in marked conflict with the consistent aim of Mr. Davis' career, which was to heal, not to aggravate, the differences of the South.

A large part of the labor, which would otherwise have devolved upon this enterprise, if adequately performed, had already been supplied by the writings of Professor Bledsoe. To the profound erudition and philosophical genius of that eminent writer, as conspicuously displayed in his work entitled, "Is Davis a Traitor?" the South may, with confidence, intrust its claims upon the esteem of posterity.

The author heartily acknowledges the intelligent aid, and generous encouragement, which he has received from his publishers.

JANUARY, 1868.

CONTENTS.

INTRODUCTION.

CHAPTER I.

CHAPTER II.

CHAPTER V.

CHAPTER VI.

CHAPTER VII.

CHAPTER VIII.

CHAPTER IX.

CHAPTER X.

CHAPTER XI.

CHAPTER XII.

CHAPTER XIII.

CHAPTER XIV.

CHAPTER XV.

CHAPTER XVIII.

CHAPTER XIX.

CHAPTER XX.

CHAPTER XXI.

CHAPTER XXII.

LIFE OF JEFFERSON DAVIS.

INTRODUCTION.

ATTRACTIONS OF THE LATE WAR TO POSTERITY—MR. LINCOLN'S REMARK—DISADVANTAGES OF MR. DAVIS' SITUATION—SUCCESS NOT SYNONYMOUS WITH MERIT—ORIGIN OF THE INJUSTICE DONE MR. DAVIS—REMARK OF MACAULAY—REMARK OF MR. GLADSTONE—THE EFFECT THAT CONFEDERATE SUCCESS WOULD HAVE HAD UPON THE FAME OF MR. DAVIS—POPULAR AFFECTION FOR HIM IN THE SOUTH—HIS VINDICATION ASSURED.

TO future generations the period in American history, of most absorbing interest and profound inquiry, will be that embracing the incipiency, progress, and termination of the revolution which had its most pronounced phase in the memorable war of 1861. Historians rarely concur in their estimates of the limits of a revolution, and usually we find quite as much divergence in their views of the scope of its operations, as in their speculations as to its origin and causes, and their statements of its incidents and results. If, however, it is difficult to assign, with minute accuracy, the exact limits and proper scope of those grand trains of consecutive events, which swerve society from the beaten track of ages, divert nations from the old path of progress into what seems to be the direction of a new destiny, and often transform the aspect of continents, it is comparatively an easy task to reach a reliable statement of their more salient and conspicuous incidents. It is in this aspect that the Titanic conflict, which had its beginning with the booming of the guns in Charleston harbor in April, 1861, and its crowning catastrophe at Appomattox Court-house in April, 1865, will be chiefly attractive to the future student. As a point of departure from the hitherto unbroken monotony of American history, the beginning of a new order of things, the extinction of important elements of previous national existence, embracing much that was consecrated in the popular affections; in short, as a complete political and social transformation, an abrupt, but thorough perversion of the government from its original purposes and previous policy, this period must take its place, with important suggestions of theory and illustration, among the most impressive lessons of history.

The profound interest which shall center upon the period that we have under consideration, must necessarily subject to a rigid investigation the lives, characters, and conduct of those to whom were allotted conspicuous parts in the great drama. It is both a natural and reasonable test that the world applies in seeking to solve, through the qualities and capacities of those who direct great measures of governmental policy, the merits of the movements themselves. The late President of the United States, Mr. Lincoln, avowed his inability to escape the judgment of history, and the bare statement sufficiently describes the inevitable necessity, not only of his own situation, but of all who bore a prominent part on either side of the great controversy.

JEFFERSON DAVIS confronts posterity burdened with the disadvantage of having been the leader of an unsuccessful political movement. "Nothing succeeds like success," was the pithy maxim of Talleyrand, to whose astute observation nothing was more obvious than the disposition of mankind to make success the touchstone of merit. It is, nevertheless, a vulgar and often an erroneous criterion. What could be more absurd than to determine by such a test the comparative valor, generalship, and military character of the two contestants in the late war? Concede its applicability, however, and we exalt the soldiership of the North above all precedent, and consign the unequaled valor of the Southern soldiery to reproach, instead of the deathless fame which shall survive them. To such a judgment every battle-field of the war gives emphatic and indignant contradiction. History abounds with evidence of the influence of accident and of extraneous circumstances, in the decision of results, which, if controlled by the question of merit, as understood by the predominant sense of mankind, would have borne a vastly different character.

But, in addition to the disparaging influence of the failure of the cause which he represented, Mr. Davis has encountered an unparalleled degree of personal hate, partizan rancor, of malignant and gratuitous misrepresentation, the result, to a great extent, of old partizan rivalries and jealousies, engendered in former periods of the history of the Union, and also of the spirit of domestic disaffection and agitation which inevitably arises against every administration of public affairs, especially at times of unusual danger and embarrassment.* The

*A pertinent remark of Macaulay is, "It is the nature of parties to retain their original enmities far more firmly than their original principles. During many years, a generation of Whigs, whom Sydney would have spurned as slaves, continued to wage war with a generation of Tories whom Jeffries would have hanged."

almost fanatical hatred of the Northern masses against Mr. Davis, as the wicked leader of a causeless rebellion against the Government of his country, as a conspirator against the peace and happiness of his fellow-citizens, and as a relentless monster, who tortured and starved prisoners of war, springs from the persistent calumnies of such leaders of Northern opinion, as have an ignoble purpose of vindictive hatred to gratify by the invention of these atrocious charges. Yet this feeling of the North hardly exceeds in violence, the resentment with which it was sought to inflame the Southern people against him, at critical stages of the war, as an unworthy leader, whose incapacity, pragmatism, nepotism, and vanity were rushing them into material and political perdition. Of popular disaffection to the Confederate cause, or dislike of Mr. Davis, there was an insignificantly small element, never dangerous in the sense of attempted revolt against the authorities, but often hurtful, because it constituted the basis of support to such prominent men as fancied their personal ambition, or *amour propre,* offended by the President. A misfortune of the South was that there were not a few such characters, and their influence upon certain occasions was as baleful to the public interests as their *animus* was malignant against Mr. Davis. Hoping to advance themselves by misrepresentations of him, during the war they persistently charged upon him every disaster, and do not scruple to impute to his blame those final failures so largely traceable to themselves. A patriotic regard for the public safety imposed silence upon Mr. Davis while the war continued, and a magnanimity which they have neither deserved nor appreciated, coupled with a proper sense of personal dignity, have impelled him since to refrain from refutation of misstatements utterly scandalous and inexcusable.

The distinguished English statesman,* who, during the progress of the late war, declared that "Mr. Jefferson Davis had created a nation," stated more than the truth, though he hardly exaggerated the flattering estimate which the intelligent public of Europe places upon the unsurpassed ability and energy with which the limited resources of the South, as compared with those of her enemies, were, for the most part, wielded by the Confederate administration. Nor, indeed, would such an estimate have been too extravagant to be entertained by his own countrymen, had the South achieved her independence by any stroke of mere good fortune, such as repeatedly favored her adversaries at critical moments of the war, when, apparently, the most trifling incidents regulated the balance. More than once the South stood upon the very threshold of the full fruition of her aspirations for independence and nationality. Had Jackson not fallen at Chancellorsville, the Federal Army of the Potomac, the bulwark of the Union in the Atlantic States, would have disappeared into history under circumstances far different from those which marked its dissolution two years later. At Gettysburg the Confederacy was truthfully said to have been "within a stone's-throw of peace." If at these fateful moments the treacherous scales of fortune had not strangely turned, and in the very flush of triumph, who doubts that now and hereafter there would have come from Southern hearts, an ascription of praise to Jefferson Davis, no less earnest than to his illustrious colaborers? At all events, it is undeniable that, as the Confederate arms prospered, so the affection of the people for Mr. Davis was always more enthusiastic and demonstrative. Only in moments of extreme public depression could the malcontents obtain even a patient

*Mr. Gladstone.

audience of their assaults upon the chosen President of the Confederacy.

The people of the late Confederate States, whose destinies Jefferson Davis directed during four years, the most momentous in their history, are competent witnesses as to the fidelity, ability, and devotion with which he discharged the trust confided to him.

Their judgment is revealed in the affectionate confidence with which, during their struggle for liberty, they upheld him, and in the joyful acclaim, which echoed from the Potomac to the Rio Grande upon the announcement of his release from his vicarious captivity. As he was the chosen representative of the power, the will, and the aspirations of a chivalrous people, so they will prove themselves the jealous custodians of his fame. Be the verdict of posterity as it may, they will not shrink from their share of the odium, and will be common participants with him in the award of eulogy. There is more than an unreasoning presentiment, something more tangible than vague hope, in the calm and cheerful confidence with which both look forward to that ample vindication of truth which always follows candid and impartial inquiry.

That time will triumphantly vindicate Mr. Davis is as certain, as that it will dispel the twilight mazes which yet obscure the grand effort of patriotism which he directed. The rank luxuriance of prejudice, asperity, and falsehood must eventually yield to the irresistible progress of reason and truth. Bribery, perjury, every appliance which the most subtle ingenuity of eager and unscrupulous malice could invent, have been exhausted in the vain effort to make infamous, in the sight of mankind, a noble cause, by imputation of personal odium upon its most distinguished representative. Day by day he rises beyond the reach of calumny, and his character expands into the fair proportions of the grandest ideals of excellence. An adamantine heroism of the *antique* pattern; purity exalted to an altitude beyond conception even of the vulgar mind; devotion which shrank from no sacrifice and quailed before no peril, were qualities giving tone to the genius, which, wielding the inadequate means of a feeble Confederacy, for years, withstood the shock of powerful invasion, baffled and humiliated a nation, unlimited in resources, and in spite of disastrous failure, lends unexampled dignity to the cause in which it was employed.

CHAPTER I.

BIRTH—EDUCATION—AT WEST POINT—IN THE ARMY—RETIREMENT—POLITICAL TRAINING IN AMERICA—MR. DAVIS NOT EDUCATED FOR POLITICAL LIFE AFTER THE AMERICAN MODEL—BEGINS HIS POLITICAL CAREER BY A SPEECH AT THE MISSISSIPPI DEMOCRATIC CONVENTION—A GLANCE PROSPECTIVELY AT HIS FUTURE PARTY ASSOCIATIONS—HIS CONSISTENT ATTACHMENT TO STATES' RIGHTS PRINCIPLES—A SKETCH OF THE DEVELOPMENT OF THE QUESTION OF STATES' RIGHTS—MR. CALHOUN NOT THE AUTHOR OF THAT PRINCIPLE—HIS VINDICATION FROM THE CHARGE OF DISUNIONISM—MR. DAVIS THE SUCCESSOR OF MR. CALHOUN AS THE STATES' RIGHTS LEADER.

JEFFERSON DAVIS was born on the third day of June, 1808, in that portion of Christian County, Kentucky, which, by subsequent act of the Legislature, was made Todd County. His father, Samuel Davis, a planter, during the Revolutionary war served as an officer in the mounted force of Georgia, an organization of local troops. Subsequently to the Revolution Samuel Davis removed to Kentucky, and continued to reside in that state until a few years after the birth of his son JEFFERSON, when he removed with his family to the neighborhood of Woodville, Wilkinson County, in the then territory of Mississippi. At the period of his father's removal to Mississippi, Jefferson was a child of tender years. After having enjoyed the benefits of a partial academic training at home, he was sent, at an earlier age than is usual, to Transylvania University, Kentucky, where he remained until he reached the age of sixteen. In 1824 he was appointed, by President Monroe, a cadet at the West Point Military Academy.

Among his contemporaries at the academy were Robert E. Lee, Joseph E. Johnston, Albert Sidney Johnston, Leonidas Polk, John B. Magruder, and others who have since earned distinction. Ordinary merit could not have commanded in such an association of talent and character the position which Davis held as a cadet. A fellow-cadet thus speaks of him: "Jefferson Davis was distinguished in the corps for his manly bearing, his high-toned and lofty character. His figure was very soldier-like and rather robust; his step springy, resembling the tread of an Indian 'brave' on the war-path." He graduated in June, 1828, receiving the customary appointment of Brevet Second Lieutenant, which is conferred upon the graduates of the academy. Assigned to the infantry, he served with such fidelity in that branch of the service, and with such especial distinction as a staff officer on the North-western frontier in 1831–32, that he was promoted to the rank of First Lieutenant and Adjutant of a new regiment of dragoons in March, 1833.

About this period the Indians, on various portions of the frontier, stimulated by dissatisfaction with the course of the Government concerning certain claims and guarantees, which had been accorded them in previous treaties, were excessively annoying, and the Government was forced to resort to energetic military measures to suppress them. Lieutenant Davis had ample opportunity for the exhibition of his high soldierly qualities, cool courage, and admirable self-possession, in the Black Hawk war, during which he was frequently employed in duties of an important and dangerous character. During the captivity of Black Hawk, that famous Indian chieftain and warrior is said to have conceived a very strong attachment for Lieutenant Davis, whose gallantry and pleasing amenities of bearing greatly impressed the captive enemy. After his transfer to the dragoons, Lieutenant Davis saw two years of very active service in the various expeditions against the Pawnees, Camanches, and other Indian tribes, and accompanied the first expedition which successfully penetrated the strongholds of the savages, and conquered a peace by reducing them to subjection.

Though attached to the profession of arms, for which he has on repeated occasions, during his subsequent life, evinced an almost passionate fondness and a most unusual aptitude, Lieutenant Davis resigned his commission in June, 1835, and returning to Mississippi devoted his attention to the cultivation of cotton and to the assiduous pursuit of letters. Not long after his resignation, he had married the daughter of Col. Zachary Taylor, under whose eye he was destined, in a few years, to win such immortal renown upon the fields of Mexico. Living upon his plantation in great seclusion, he devoted himself with zeal and enthusiasm to those studies which were to qualify him for the eminent position in politics and statesmanship which he had resolved to assume. In that retirement were sown the seed, whose abundant fruits were seen in those splendid specimens of senatorial and popular eloquence, at once models of taste and exhibitions of intellectual power; in the pure, terse, and elegant English of his matchless state papers, which will forever be the delight of scholars and the study of statesmen, and in that elevated and enlightened statesmanship, which scorning the low ambition of demagogues and striving always for the ends of patriotism and principle, illumines, for more than a score of years, the legislative history of the Union.

The period of Mr. Davis' retirement is embraced within the

interval of his withdrawal from the army, in 1835, and the beginning of his active participation in the local politics of Mississippi, in 1843, a term of eight years. The diligent application with which he was employed during these years of seclusion constituted a most fortunate preparation for the distinguished career upon which he at once entered. There is not, in the whole range of American biography, an instance of more thorough preparation, of more ample intellectual discipline, and elaborate education for political life.

The *trade* of politics is an avocation familiar to Americans, and in the more ordinary maneuvers of party tactics, in that lower species of political strategy which, in our party vocabulary, is aptly termed "wire-pulling," our politicians may boast an eminence in their class not surpassed in the most corrupt ages of the most profligate political establishments which have ever existed. Statesmanship, in that broad and elevated conception which suggests the noblest models among those who have adorned and illustrated the science of government, combining those higher attributes of administrative capacity which are realized equally in a pure, sound, and just polity, and in a free, prosperous, and contented community, is a subject utterly unexplored by American politicians at the outset of their career, and is comparatively an after-thought with those intrusted with the most responsible duties of state.

The political training of Mr. Davis was pursued upon a basis very different from the American model. It has been more akin to the English method, under which the faculties and the tastes are first cultivated, and the mind qualified by all the light which theory and previous example afford for the practical labors which are before it. The tastes and habits formed during those eight years of retirement have adhered to

Mr. Davis in his subsequent life. When not engrossed by the absorbing cares of state, he has, with rare enthusiasm and satisfaction, resorted to those refining pleasures which are accessible only to intellects which have known the elevating influences of culture.

Emerging from his seclusion in 1843, when the initiatory measures of party organization were in course of preparation for the gubernatorial canvass of that year and the Presidential campaign of the next, he immediately assumed a prominent position among the leaders of the Democratic party in Mississippi. At this time, probably, no state in the Union, of equal population, excelled Mississippi in the number and distinction of her brilliant politicians. Especially was this true of Vicksburg, and of the general neighborhood in which Mr. Davis resided.* The genius of Seargent S. Prentiss was then in its meridian splendor, and his reputation and popularity were coëxtensive with the Union. Besides Prentiss were Foote, Thompson, Claiborne, Gholson, Brown, and many others, all comparatively young men, who have since achieved professional or political distinction. The appearance of Mr. Davis was soon recognized as the addition of a star of no unworthy effulgence to this brilliant galaxy.

The Democratic State Convention, held for the purpose of organization for the gubernatorial canvass, and for the appointment of delegates to the National Convention, assembled at Jackson in the summer of 1843. From the meeting of this convention, which Mr. Davis attended as a delegate, may be dated the beginning of his political life. In the course of its

*Mr. Davis has, since his withdrawal from the army until the breaking out of the war, resided on his plantation in Warren County, a few miles from Vicksburg.

deliberations he delivered his first public address, which immediately attracted toward him much attention, and a most partial consideration by his party associates. The occasion is interesting from this circumstance, and as indicating that consistent political bias which, beginning in early manhood, constituted the controlling inspiration of a long career of eminent public service. The undoubted preference of the convention, as of an overwhelming majority of the masses of the Southern Democracy, was for Mr. Van Buren, and its entire action in the selection of delegates, and formal expressions of feeling, was in accordance with this well-ascertained preference. To a proposition instructing the delegates to the National Convention, to support the nomination of Mr. Van Buren so long as there was a reasonable hope of his selection by the party, Mr. Davis proposed an amendment instructing the delegates to support Mr. Calhoun as the *second choice* of the Democracy of Mississippi, in the event of such a contingency as should render clearly hopeless the choice of Mr. Van Buren. In response to an inquiry from an acquaintance if his amendment was meant in good faith, and did not contemplate detriment to the interests of Mr. Van Buren, Mr. Davis rose and addressed the convention in explanation of his purpose, and in terms of such earnest and appropriate eulogy of Mr. Calhoun and his principles as to elicit the most enthusiastic commendation.

So favorable was the impression which Mr. Davis made upon his party, and so rapid his progress as a popular speaker, that in the Presidential campaign of 1844, the Democracy conferred upon him the distinction of a place upon its electoral ticket. In this canvass he acquired great reputation, and established himself immovably in the confidence and admiration of the people of Mississippi.

This seems an appropriate point from which to glance prospectively at the political principles and party associations of Mr. Davis in his after career. Until its virtual dissolution at Charleston, in 1860, he was an earnest and consistent member of the Democratic party. To those who are familiar with the party nomenclature of the country, no inconsistency with this assertion will appear involved in the statement, that he has also been an ardent disciple of the doctrine of States' Rights. The Democratic party and the States' Rights party were indeed identical, when a profession of political faith in this country was significant of something ennobling upon the score of principle, something higher than a mere aspiration for the spoils of office. When, in subsequent years, to the large majority of its leaders, the chief significance of a party triumph, consisted in its being the occasion of a new division of the spoils, many of the most eminent statesmen of the South became in a measure indifferent to its success. Its prurient aspiration for the rewards of place provoked the sarcasm of Mr. Calhoun, that it "was held together by the cohesive power of the public plunder," and the still more caustic satire of John Randolph, of Roanoke, that it had "seven principles: five loaves and two fishes."

Nevertheless, in its spirit thoroughly national, catholic in all its impulses, for many years shaping its policy in harmony with the protection of Southern institutions, and with few features of sectionalism in its organization, it worthily commanded the preference of a large majority of the Southern people. To this organization Mr. Davis adhered until the inception of the late conflict, supporting its Presidential nominations, in the main favoring such public measures as were incorporated in the policy of the party, and he was, for several years prior to the war, by no means the least prominent of those named in connection with its choice for the Presidency in 1860.

It is no part of the task which has been undertaken in these pages to sketch the mutations of political parties, or to trace the historical order and significance of events, save in their immediate and indispensable connection with our appropriate subject. So closely identified, however, has been the public life of Mr. Davis with the question of States' Rights, so ardent has been his profession of that faith, and so able and zealous was he in its advocacy and practice, that his life virtually becomes an epitome of the most important incidents in the development of this great historical question. His earliest appearance upon the arena of politics was at a period when the various issues which were submitted to the arbitrament of arms in the late war began to assume a practical shape of most portentous aspect. The address which first challenged public attention, and that extensive interest which has rarely been withdrawn since, was an emphatic indorsement of the political philosophy of Mr. Calhoun and a glowing panegyric upon the character and principles of that immortal statesman and expounder. Unreservedly committing himself, then, he has steadfastly held to the States' Rights creed, as the basis of his political faith and the guide of his public conduct.

If it be true that the decision of the sword only establishes facts, and does not determine questions of principle, then the principle of States' Rights will be commemorated as something more valuable, than as the mere pretext upon which a few agitators inaugurated an unjustifiable revolt for the overthrow of the Government of the Union. Nothing is more likely than that many who recently rejoiced at its suppression by physical force, may mourn its departure as of that one vital inspiration, which alone could have averted the decay of the public liberties. Practically a "dead letter" now in the partizan slang of the demagogues who rule the hour, since its prostration by military power in the service of the antipodal principle of consolidation, it will live forever as the motive and occasion of a struggle, unparalleled in its heroism and sacrifices in behalf of constitutional liberty.

There is little ground for wonder at the total ignorance and persistent misconception in the mind of Europe, at the commencement of the war, of the motives and purposes of the Confederates in seeking a dissolution of the Union, when we consider the limited information and perverted views of the Northern people and politicians respecting the nature of the Federal Government and the intentions of its authors. Naturally enough, perhaps, the North, seeing in the Union the source of its marvelous material prosperity, and with an astute appreciation of its ability, by its rapidly-growing numerical majority, to pervert the Government to any purpose of sectional aggression agreeable to its ambition or interests, refused to tolerate, as either rational or honest, any theory that contemplated disunion as possible in any contingency. In their willful ignorance and misapprehension most Northern orators and writers denounced the doctrines of States' Rights as *new inventions*—as innovations upon the faith of the fathers of the Republic—and professed to regard the most enlightened and patriotic statesmen of the South, the pupils and followers of illustrious Virginians and Carolinians of the Revolutionary era, as agitators, conspirators, and plotters of treason against the Union. Upon the score of antiquity, States' Rights principles have a claim to respectability—not for a moment to be compared with the wretched devices of expediency or the hybrid products of political atheism, to which the brazen audacity and hypocrisy of the times apply the misnomer of "principles."

They are, in fact, older than the Union, and antedate, not only the present Constitution, but even the famous Articles of Confederation, under which our forefathers fought through the first Revolution. The Congress which adopted the Declaration of Independence emphatically negatived a proposition looking to consolidation, offered by New Hampshire on the 15th of June, 1776, that the Thirteen Colonies be declared a "free and independent State," and expressly affirmed their separate sovereignty by declaring them to be "free and independent States." The declaration of the Articles of Confederation was still more explicit—that "each State retains its sovereignty, freedom, and independence, and every power, jurisdiction, and right, which is not by this Confederation expressly delegated to the United States in Congress assembled." The Convention of 1787 clearly designed the present Constitution to be the instrument of a closer association of the States than had been effected by the Articles of Confederation, but the proof is exceedingly meager of any general desire that it should establish a consolidated nationality.

At this early period the antagonism of the two schools of American politics was plainly discernible. The conflict of faith is easily indicated. The advocates of States' Rights regarded the Union as a *compact between the States*—something more than a mere league formed for purposes of mutual safety, but still a strictly *voluntary* association of Sovereignties, in which certain general powers were specifically delegated to the Union; and all others not so delegated were reserved by the States in their separate characters. The advocates of Consolidation considered the Union a *National* Government—in other words, a centralized power—to which the several States occupied the relation of separate provinces.

The famous resolutions of '98, adopted respectively by the Virginia and Kentucky Legislatures, were the formal declarations of principles upon which the States' Rights party was distinctly organized under Mr. Jefferson, whom it successfully supported for the Presidency against the elder Adams at the expiration of the term of the latter. With the progress of time the practical significance of these opposing principles became more and more apparent, and their respective followers strove, with constantly-increasing energy, to make their party creed paramount in the policy of the Government. A majority of the Northern people embraced the idea of a perpetual Union, whose authority was supreme over all the States, and regulated by the will of a numerical majority, which majority, it should be observed, they had already secured, and were yearly increasing in an enormous ratio. The South, in the course of years, with even more unanimity, clung to the idea of State Sovereignty, and the interpretation of the Government as one of limited powers, as its shield and bulwark against the Northern majority in the collision which it was foreseen the aggressive spirit of the latter would eventually occasion.

A common and totally erroneous impression of the Northern mind is that John C. Calhoun *invented* the idea of State Sovereignty for selfish and unpatriotic designs, and as the pretext of a morbid hatred to the Union. That eminent statesman and sincere patriot never asserted any claim to the paternity of the faith which he professed. It is true that, in a certain sense, he was the founder of the States' Rights party as it existed in his day, and which survived him to make a last unsuccessful struggle to save first the Union, and, failing in that, to rescue the imperiled liberties of the South. During the eventful life of Mr. Calhoun the question of the relative powers of the Federal and State Governments assumed a more practical bearing than before, and his far-reaching sagacity was illustrated in his efforts to avert the impending evils of consolidation. He was the authoritative exponent and revered leader of the votaries of those principles which he advocated, but did not originate or *invent*, and sought to apply as the legitimate and safe solution of the circumstances by which he was surrounded.

Equally absurd and unfounded with the pretense, asserted at the North, of the novelty of the idea of State Sovereignty and its incompatibility with the spirit of the Constitution, was the charge so persistently iterated against Mr. Calhoun and his followers, of disunionism; of a restless, morbid discontent, which sought continually revenge for imaginary wrongs in a dissolution of the Union. To the contrary we have the irrefutable arguments of Mr. Calhoun himself in favor of the superior efficacy of the States' Rights interpretation, as an agency for the preservation of the Union as it was designed to exist by its authors. So far from having an anarchical or disorganizing tendency, he, on all occasions, maintained that his theory was "the only solid foundation of our system and the Union itself."

To this faith the public life of Jefferson Davis has been dedicated. For more than twenty years he sought to illustrate it in the realization of a splendid but barren vision of a time-honored and time-strengthened Union, consecrated in the common affections and joint aspirations of a people, now, alas! united only in name.

During the period of their public service together, Mr. Davis received a large share of the confidence and regard of Mr. Calhoun, and when the death of the latter deprived the South of the counsels of an illustrious public servant, Mr. Davis, though comparatively a young man, stood foremost as heir to the mantle of the great apostle of States' Rights.*

* Dr. Craven relates the following incident, which is an impressive illustration of the depth and intensity of Mr. Davis' veneration for the character of Mr. Calhoun:

"General Miles observed, interrogatively, that it was reported that John C. Calhoun had made much money by speculations, or favoring the speculations of his friends, connected with this work (the Rip-Raps, near Fortress Monroe).

"In a moment Mr. Davis started to his feet, betraying much indignation by his excited manner and flushed cheek. It was a transfiguration of friendly emotion. The feeble and wasted invalid and prisoner, suddenly forgetting his bonds—forgetting his debility, and ablaze with eloquent anger against this injustice to the memory of one he loved and reverenced. Mr. Calhoun, he said, lived a whole atmosphere above any sordid or dishonest thought—was of a nature to which even a mean act was impossible. It was said in every Northern paper that he (Mr. Davis) had carried with him five millions in gold when quitting Richmond—money pilfered from the treasury of the Confederate States; and that there was just as much truth in that as in these imputations against Calhoun. . . . . Calhoun was a statesman, a philosopher, in the true sense of that grossly-abused term—an enthusiast of perfect liberty in representative and governmental action."—*Prison Life of Jefferson Davis. Library edition, pages* 206, 207.

CHAPTER II.

RESULTS OF PRESIDENTIAL ELECTION IN 1844—MR. DAVIS ELECTED TO CONGRESS—HIS FIRST SESSION—PROMINENT MEMBERS OF THE HOUSE—DOUGLAS, HUNTER, SEDDON, ETC.—DAVIS' RAPID ADVANCEMENT IN REPUTATION—RESOLUTIONS OFFERED BY HIM—SPEECHES ON THE OREGON EXCITEMENT, AND ON THE RESOLUTION OF THANKS TO GENERAL TAYLOR AND HIS ARMY—NATIONAL SENTIMENTS EMBODIED IN THESE AND OTHER SPEECHES—A CONTRAST IN THE MATTER OF PATRIOTISM—MASSACHUSETTS AND MISSISSIPPI IN THE MEXICAN WAR—DEBATE WITH ANDREW JOHNSON—JOHN QUINCY ADAMS' ESTIMATE OF JEFFERSON DAVIS.

THE Presidential canvass of 1844 was one of the most memorable and exciting in the annals of American politics. By its results the popular verdict was rendered upon vital questions involved in the administrative and legislative policy of the Government. The Democratic party was fully committed to the annexation of Texas, with the prospect of war with Mexico as an almost inevitable condition of the acquisition of that immense territory, desirable to the Union at large, but especially popular with the South, for obvious and sufficient reasons. But apart from the signal victory achieved by the Democracy, in favor of this and other leading measures of that party, the election of 1844 had an incidental significance, which the country generally recognized, in its final and irrevocable disappointment of the Presidential aspirations of Henry Clay. This canvass, too, has a peculiar historical interest in the demonstration which it gave of the real popular strength of the respective parties which had so long divided the country. Comparatively few temporary issues, of a character to excite strong popular feeling respecting either party or its candidates, were made, and there was a square and obstinate battle of Democracy against Whiggery, of what Governor Wise called the old-fashioned "Thomas-Jefferson-Simon-Snyder-red-waistcoat-Democracy," against Henry Clay and his "American System."

The canvass was remarkable not only for its duration and the ardor with which it was conducted, but for its unsurpassed exhibitions of "stump oratory." The best men of both parties were summoned to the fierce conflict; and many were the youthful paladins, hitherto unknown to fame, who won their golden spurs upon this their first battle-field. Mr. Davis had borne a leading part in support of Polk and Dallas and Texas annexation in Mississippi. His services were not of a character to be forgotten by his party, nor did an intelligent and appreciative public fail to discover in the young man whose eloquence and manly bearing had so enlisted their admiration, such abilities and acquirements as qualified him to represent the honor of his State in any capacity which they might intrust to his keeping.

Of Mississippi it might have been said, as of Virginia, that "the sun of her Democracy knew no setting." If possible, however, the State was more closely than ever confirmed in her Democratic moorings by the decisive results of the election in 1844. When Mr. Davis received the appropriate acknowledgment of popular appreciation in his election to the House of Representatives, in November, 1845, Mississippi sent an unbroken Democratic delegation to Washington. His associates were Messrs. Roberts and Jacob Thompson (afterward Secretary of the Interior under Mr. Buchanan) in the House, and Messrs. Foote and Speight in the Senate.

On Monday, December 8, 1845, Mr. Davis was qualified as a member of the House of Representatives, and from that day dates his eventful and brilliant legislative career. The Twenty-ninth Congress was charged with some of the gravest duties of legislation. The questions of the tariff, the Oregon excitement, during which war with England was so imminent, and the settlement of important details pertaining to the Texas question, were the absorbing concerns which engaged its attention until the provisions and appropriations necessary to the successful prosecution of the Mexican war imposed still more serious labors. The records of this Congress reveal many interesting facts concerning individuals who have since figured prominently in the history of the country. The fact to which we have alluded of the unusual interest which had been exhibited in the recent Presidential contest, doubtless had a considerable influence in the choice of members of Congress in the various States, and largely contributed to its elevated standard of ability.

The debates in the House of Representatives of the Twenty-ninth Congress, are unsurpassed in ability and eloquence by those of any preceding or subsequent session of that body, and upon its rolls are to be found many names, now national in reputation, which were then but recently introduced to public attention. Stephen A. Douglas, the most thoroughly representative American politician of his time, uniting to a more than average proportion of the respectability of his class, his full share of its vicious characteristics, politic, adroit, and ambitious, was comparatively a new member, and, at this time, in the morning of his reputation. R. M. T. Hunter, of Virginia, a statesman of sound judgment and accurate information, who based his arguments upon the facts, and reduced the complicated problems of governmental economy to the conditions of a mathematical demonstration, had not yet been transferred to the Senate. James A. Seddon, the safe theorist, whose study, like Edmund Burke's, was "*rerum cognoscere causas,*" the acute dialectician, who, in his mental characteristics, no less than in his principles, was so closely allied to Mr. Calhoun, was, like Jefferson Davis, for the first time a member of Congress. Andrew Johnson was then a member of the House and at the outset of his remarkable career; and in addition to these were Brinkerhoff, Washington Hunt, Dromgoole, George S. Houston, and a score of others, whose names recall interesting reminiscences of the day in which they figured.

To a man of ordinary purpose, or doubtful of himself, the prospect of competition with such men, at the very outset of his public career, would not have been encouraging. But there are men, designed by nature, to rejoice at, rather than to shrink from those arduous and hazardous positions to which their responsibilities summon them. An attribute of genius is the consciousness of strength, and that sublime confidence in the success of its own efforts, which doubly assures victory in the battle of life. It was with an assurance of triumph, far different from the harlequin-like effrontery which is often witnessed in the political arena, that Jefferson Davis advanced to contest the awards of intellectual distinction. With the activity and vigor of the disciplined gladiator, with the *gaudia certaminis* beaming in every feature, with the calm confidence of the trained statesman, and yet with all the radiant *elan* of a youthful knight contending for his spurs at Templestowe, he pursued his brief but impressive career in the lower house of Congress.

As a member of the House of Representatives Mr. Davis rapidly and steadily won upon the good opinion of his associates, and the favorable estimate of him, entertained by his constituents and friends, was confirmed by his greatly advanced reputation at the period of his withdrawal from Congress in the ensuing summer. He became prominent, less by the frequency with which he claimed the attention of the House, than by the accuracy of his information, the substantial value of his suggestions and the easy dignity of his demeanor. His speeches, though not comparable with his senatorial efforts, were characterized by great perspicuity, argumentative force, and propriety of taste, and frequently rose to the dignity of true eloquence. They, in every instance, gave promise of that rhetorical finish, power of statement, unity of thought and logical coherence, which, in subsequent years, were so appropriately illustrated on other theaters of intellectual effort. Mr. Davis participated prominently in the debates upon the Oregon excitement, Native Americanism, and the various other contemporary topics of interest, which were then before Congress, but was especially prominent in the discussion of military affairs, the interests and requirements of the army, and the measures devised for the prosecution of the Mexican war. Upon the latter subjects his experience was of great practical value.

On the 19th of December, 1845, he offered the following resolutions: "*Resolved,* That the Committee on Military Affairs be instructed to inquire into the expediency of converting a portion of the forts of the United States into schools for military instruction, on the basis of substituting their present garrisons of enlisted men, by detachments furnished from each State of our Union, in the ratio of their several representation in the Congress of the United States."

"*Resolved*, That the Committee on the Post-office and Post-roads be required to inquire into the expediency of establishing a direct daily mail route from Montgomery, Alabama, to Jackson, Mississippi."

The occasion of these motions was the first upon which he occupied the floor of the House.

On the 29th of December, Mr. Davis spoke in a very earnest and impressive manner upon Native Americanism, which he strongly opposed, and on subsequent occasions addressed the House in favor of the bill to receive arms, barracks, fortifications, and other public property, the cession of which to the Federal Government, by Texas, had been provided to take place upon its admission to the Union; in favor of the proposition to raise additional regiments of riflemen; in opposition to appropriations for improvement of rivers and harbors; upon the Oregon question, and in favor of a resolution of thanks to General Taylor and his army.

The extracts from his speech on the Oregon question, and the speech in favor of thanks to General Taylor and his army, which is here given in full, are taken from the reports of the *Congressional Globe*. The intelligent reader will appreciate their real value, as to accuracy, without any suggestion from us.

On February 6, 1846, the House, having resolved itself into Committee of the Whole, and having under consideration the joint resolution of notice to the British Government concerning the abrogation of the Convention between the United States and Great Britain respecting the territory of Oregon, Mr. Davis spoke at some length, and in an attractive and instructive style, upon the subject before the House. A great portion of the speech consists of interesting historical details, evincing a most accurate acquaintance with the subject, and giving a clear and valuable analysis of facts. We have space for only brief extracts, which are sufficient to reveal Mr. Davis' position upon this important question:

. . . . . . "Sir, why has the South been assailed in this discussion? Has it been with the hope of sowing dissensions between us and our Western friends? Thus far, I think, it has failed. Why the frequent reference to the conduct of the South on the Texas question? Sir, those who have made reflections on the South as having sustained Texas annexation from sectional views have been of those who opposed that great measure and are most eager for this. The suspicion is but natural in them. But, sir, let me tell them that this doctrine of the political balance between different portions of the Union is no Southern doctrine. We, sir, advocated the annexation of Texas from high national considerations. It was not a mere Southern question; it lay coterminous to the Western States, and extended as far north as the forty-second degree of latitude. Nor, sir, do we wish to divide the territory of Oregon; we would preserve it all for the extension of our Union. We would not arrest the onward progress of our pioneers; we would not, as has been done in this debate, ask why our citizens have left the repose of civil government and gone to Oregon? We find in it but that energy which has heretofore been characteristic of our people, and which has developed much that has illustrated our history. It is the onward progress of our people toward the Pacific which alone can arrest their westward march, and on the banks of which, to use the language of our lamented Linn, the pioneer will sit down to weep that there are no more forests to subdue. . . . . . It is, as the representative of a high-spirited and patriotic people, that I am called on to resist this war clamor. My constituents need no such excitements to prepare their hearts for all that patriotism demands. Whenever the honor of the country demands redress; whenever its territory is invaded—if, then, it shall be sought to intimidate by the fiery cross of St. George—if, then, we are threatened with the unfolding of English banners if we resent or resist—from the gulf shore to the banks of that great river, throughout the length and breadth—Mississippi will come. And whether the question be one of Northern or Southern, of Eastern or Western aggression, we will not stop to count the cost, but act as becomes the descendants of those who, in the war of the Revolution, engaged in unequal strife to aid our brethren of the North in redressing their injuries. . . . . We turn from present hostility to former friendship—from recent defection to the time when Massachusetts and Virginia, the stronger brothers of our family, stood foremost and united to defend our common rights. From sire to son has descended the love of our Union in our hearts, as in our history are mingled the names of Concord and Camden, of Yorktown and Saratoga, of Moultrie and Plattsburgh, of Chippewa and Erie, of Bowyer and Guildford, and New Orleans and Bunker Hill. Grouped together, they form a monument to the common glory of our common country; and where is the Southern man who would wish that monument were less by one of the Northern names that constitute the mass? Who, standing on the ground made sacred by the blood of Warren, could allow sectional feeling to curb his enthusiasm as he looked upon that obelisk which rises a monument to freedom's and his country's triumph, and stands a type of the time, the men and event that it commemorates; built of material that mocks the waves of time, without niche or molding for parasite or creeping thing to rest on, and pointing like a finger to the sky, to raise man's thoughts to philanthropic and noble deeds."

It is well known that, upon this subject, there was considerable division among the Democracy. The effort to commit the party, as a unit, to a position which would have inevitably produced war with England signally failed. The country had not then reached its present pitch of arrogant inflation, which emboldens it to seek opportunity for exhibition in the vainglorious role of braggadocio. Mr. Davis, upon this and other occasions, significantly rebuked the demagogical clamor which would have precipitated the country into a calamitous war. His reply, on the 17th of April, 1846, to Stephen A. Douglas, who was among the leading instigators of the war-feeling in the House, is exceedingly forcible and spirited.

The following speech in favor of the resolution of thanks to General Taylor, the officers and men of his army, for their recent successes on the Rio Grande, was delivered May 28, 1846:

"As a friend to the army, he rejoiced at the evidence, now afforded, of a disposition in this House to deal justly, to feel generously toward those to whom the honor of our flag has been intrusted. Too often and too long had we listened to harsh and invidious reflections upon our gallant little army and the accomplished officers who command it. A partial opportunity had been offered to exhibit their soldierly qualities in their true light, and he trusted these aspersions were hushed—hushed now forever. As an American, whose heart promptly responds to all which illustrates our national character, and adds new glory to our national name, he rejoiced with exceeding joy at the recent triumph of our arms. Yet it is no more than he expected from the gallant soldiers who hold our post upon the Rio Grande—no more than, when occasion offers, they will achieve again. It was the triumph of American courage, professional skill, and that patriotic pride which blooms in the breast of our educated soldier, and which droops not under the withering scoff of political revilers.

"These men will feel, deeply feel, the expression of your gratitude. It will nerve their hearts in the hour of future conflicts, to know that their country honors and acknowledges their devotion. It will shed a solace on the dying moments of those who fall, to be assured their country mourns their loss. This is the meed for which the soldier bleeds and dies. This he will remember long after the paltry pittance of one month's extra pay has been forgotten.

"Beyond this expression of the nation's thanks, he liked the *principle* of the proposition offered by the gentleman from South Carolina. We have a pension system providing for the disabled soldier, but he seeks well and wisely to extend it to all who may be wounded, however slightly. It is a reward offered to those who seek for danger, who first and foremost plunge into the fight. It has been this incentive, extended so as to cover all feats of gallantry, that has so often crowned the British arms with victory, and caused their prowess to be recognized in every quarter of the globe. It was the sure and high reward of gallantry, the confident reliance upon their nation's gratitude, which led Napoleon's armies over Europe, conquering and to conquer; and it was these influences which, in an earlier time, rendered the Roman arms invincible, and brought their eagle back victorious from every land on which it gazed. Sir, let not that parsimony (for he did not deem it economy) prevent us from adopting a system which in war will add so much to the efficiency of troops. Instead of seeking to fill the ranks of your army by increased pay, let the soldier feel that a liberal pension will relieve him from the fear of want in the event of disability, provide for his family in the event of death, and that he wins his way to gratitude and the reward of his countrymen by periling all for honor in the field.

"The achievement which we now propose to honor richly deserves it. Seldom, sir, in the annals of military history has there been one in which desperate daring and military skill were more happily combined. The enemy selected his own ground, and united to the advantage of a strong position a numerical majority of three to one. Driven from his first position by an attack in which it is hard to say whether professional skill or manly courage is to be more admired, he retired and posted his artillery on a narrow defile, to sweep the ground over which our troops were compelled to pass. There, posted in strength three times greater than our own, they waited the approach of our gallant little army.

"General Taylor knew the danger and destitution of the band he left to hold his camp opposite Matamoras, and he paused for no regular approaches, but opened his field artillery, and dashed with sword and bayonet on the foe. A single charge left him master of their battery, and the number of slain attests the skill and discipline of his army. Mr. D. referred to a gentleman who, a short time since, expressed extreme distrust in our army, and poured out the vials of his denunciation upon the graduates of the Military Academy. He hoped now the gentleman will withdraw these denunciations; that now he will learn the value of military science; that he will see, in the location, the construction, the defenses of the bastioned field-works opposite Matamoras, the utility, the necessity of a military education. Let him compare the few men who held that with the army who assailed it; let him mark the comparative safety with which they stood within that temporary work; let him consider why the guns along its ramparts were preserved, whilst they silenced the batteries of the enemy; why that intrenchment stands unharmed by Mexican shot, whilst its guns have crumbled the stone walls in Matamoras to the ground, and then say whether he believes a blacksmith or a tailor could have secured the same results. He trusted the gentleman would be convinced that arms, like every occupation, requires to be studied before it can be understood; and from these things to which he had called his attention, he will learn the power and advantage of military science. He would make but one other allusion to the remarks of the gentleman he had noticed, who said nine-tenths of the graduates of the Military Academy abandoned the service of the United States. If he would take the trouble to examine the records upon this point, he doubted not he would be surprised at the extent of his mistake. There he would learn that a majority of all the graduates are still in service; and if he would push his inquiry a little further, he would find that a large majority of the commissioned officers who bled in the action of the the 8th and 9th were graduates of that academy.

"He would not enter into a discussion on the military at this time. His pride, his gratification arose from the success of our arms. Much was due to the courage which Americans have displayed on many battle-fields in former times; but this courage, characteristic of our people, and pervading all sections and all classes, could never have availed so much had it not been combined with military science. And the occasion seemed suited to enforce this lesson on the minds of those who have been accustomed, in season and out of season, to rail at the scientific attainments of our officers.

"The influence of military skill—the advantage of discipline in the troops—the power derived from the science of war, increases with the increased size of the contending armies. With two thousand we had beaten six thousand; with twenty thousand we would far more easily beat sixty thousand, because the general must be an educated soldier who wields large bodies of men, and the troops, to act efficiently, must be disciplined and commanded by able officers. He but said what he had long thought and often said, when he expressed his confidence in the ability of our officers to meet those of any service—favorably to compare, in all that constitutes the soldier, with any army in the world; and as the field widened for the exhibition, so would their merits shine more brightly still.

"With many of the officers now serving on the Rio Grande he had enjoyed a personal acquaintance, and hesitated not to say that all which skill, and courage, and patriotism could perform, might be expected from them. He had forborne to speak of the general commanding on the Rio Grande on any former occasion; but he would now say to those who had expressed distrust, that the world held not a soldier better qualified for the service he was engaged in than General Taylor. Trained from his youth to arms, having spent the greater portion of his life on our frontier, his experience peculiarly fits him for the command he holds. Such as his conduct was in Fort Harrison, on the Upper Mississippi, in Florida, and on the Rio Grande, will it be wherever he meets the enemy of his country.

"Those soldiers, to whom so many have applied depreciatory epithets, upon whom it has been so often said no reliance could be placed, they too will be found, in every emergency renewing such feats as have recently graced our arms, bearing the American flag to honorable triumphs, or falling beneath its folds, as devotees to our common cause, to die a soldier's death.

"He rejoiced that the gentleman from South Carolina (Mr. Black) had shown himself so ready to pay this tribute to our army. He hoped not a voice would be raised in opposition to it—that nothing but the stern regret which is prompted by remembrance of those who bravely fought and nobly died will break the joy, the pride, the patriotic gratulation with which we hail this triumph of our brethren on the Rio Grande."

A striking feature of these two speeches, as, indeed, of all Mr. Davis' Congressional speeches, is the strong and outspoken *national* feeling which pervades them. It is a part of the history of these times, that while Jefferson Davis eloquently avowed a noble and generous sympathy with his heroic compatriots in Mexico, a prominent Northern politician bespoke for the American army, "a welcome with bloody hands to hospitable graves." When, a few months afterwards, the names of Jefferson Davis and his Mississippi Rifles were baptized in blood amid those frowning redoubts at Monterey, and when, upon the ensanguined plain of Buena Vista, he fell stricken in the very moment of victory, just as his genius and the valor of his comrades had broken that last, furious onset of the Mexican lancers, New England and her leaders stood indifferent spectators of the scene.* Yet the same New

* Massachusetts even refused military honors to the remains of a gallant son of her own soil, (Captain Lincoln,) and a descendant of one

England bounded eagerly to the conquest and spoliation of their countrymen, and the same leaders clamored valiantly for the humiliation, for the blood even, of Jefferson Davis, *as a traitor and a rebel. Quosque tandem.*

An interesting sequel of this speech was the debate, which it occasioned two days afterwards, between Mr. Davis and Andrew Johnson, now President of the United States. Mr. Johnson, who boasts so proudly of his plebeian origin, and is yet said to be morbidly sensitive of the slightest allusion to it by others, excepted to Mr. Davis' reference to the "tailor and blacksmith," warmly eulogized those callings and mechanical avocations in general, and took occasion to expatiate extensively upon the virtue and intelligence of the masses. Mr. Davis, whose language is clearly not susceptible of any interpretation disparaging to "blacksmiths and tailors," disclaimed the imputation, saying that he had designed merely to illustrate his argument, that the profession of arms, to be understood, must be studied, and that a mechanic could no more fill the place of an educated soldier, than could the latter supply the qualifications of the former. Mr. Johnson, however, was resolved to seize the opportunity for a panegyric upon the populace, and no explanations could avail. The *Globe* reports this debate as, "in all its stages, not being of an entirely pleasant nature."

As an appropriate conclusion to this sketch of Mr. Davis' career in the House of Representatives, we quote the following extract from an interesting work,* published some years

of her most eminent families, who was killed at Buena Vista. Her fanatical intolerance would not forget that he had fallen in a war which she did not approve.

* "Our Living Representative Men," by Mr. John Savage.

since: "John Quincy Adams had a habit of always observing new members. He would sit near them on the occasion of their Congressional *debut*, closely eyeing and attentively listening if the speech pleased him, but quickly departing if it did not. When Davis first arose in the House, the Ex-President took a seat close by. Davis proceeded, and Adams did not move. The one continued speaking and the other listening; and those who knew Mr. Adams' habits were fully aware that the new member had deeply impressed him. At the close of the speech the 'Old Man Eloquent' crossed over to some friends and said, 'That young man, gentlemen, is no ordinary man. He will make his mark yet, mind me.'"

CHAPTER III.

THE NAME OF JEFFERSON DAVIS INSEPARABLE FROM THE HISTORY OF THE MEXICAN WAR—HIS ESSENTIALLY MILITARY CHARACTER AND TASTES—JOINS GENERAL TAYLOR'S ARMY ON THE RIO GRANDE, AS COLONEL OF THE FAMOUS "MISSISSIPPI RIFLES"—MONTEREY—BUENA VISTA—GENERAL TAYLOR'S ACCOUNT OF DAVIS' CONDUCT—DAVIS' REPORT OF THE ACTION—NOVELTY AND ORIGINALITY OF HIS STRATEGY AT BUENA VISTA—INTERESTING STATEMENT OF HON. CALEB CUSHING—RETURN OF DAVIS TO THE UNITED STATES—TRIUMPHANT RECEPTION AT HOME—PRESIDENT POLK TENDERS HIM A BRIGADIER'S COMMISSION, WHICH HE DECLINES ON PRINCIPLE.

THE name of Davis is inseparable from those lettered glories of the American Union, which were the brilliant trophies of the Mexican war. In those bright annals it was engraven with unfading lustre upon the conquering banners of the Republic, and his genius and valor were rewarded with a fame which rests securely upon the laurels of Monterey and Buena Vista.

Jefferson Davis is a born soldier. Even if we could forget the glories of the assault upon Teneria and El Diablo, and banish the thrilling recollection of that movement at Buena Vista, the genius, novelty, and intrepidity of which electrified the world of military science, and extorted the enthusiastic admiration of the victor of Waterloo, we must yet recognize the impress of those rare gifts and graces which are the titles to authority. The erect yet easy carriage, the true martial dignity of bearing, which is altogether removed from the supercilious *hauteur* of the mere martinet, the almost fascinating expression of *suaviter in modo*, which yet does not for an instant conceal the *fortiter in re*, constitute in him that imperial semblance, to which the mind involuntarily concedes the right to supreme command. It is impossible, in the presence of Mr. Davis, to deny this recognition of his intuitive soldiership. Not only is obvious to the eye the commanding mien of the soldier, but the order, the discipline of the educated soldier, whose nature, stern and unflinching, was yet plastic to receive the impressions of an art with which it felt an intuitive alliance. This military precision is characteristic of Mr. Davis in every aspect in which he appears. There is the constant fixedness of gaze upon the object to be reached, and the cautious calculation of the chances of success with the means and forces ready at hand; a constant regard for bases of supply and a proper concern for lines of retreat, and, above all, the prompt and vigorous execution, if success be practicable and the attack determined upon. Even in his oratory and statesmanship are these characteristics evinced. In the former there is far more of rhetorical order, harmony, and symmetry, than of rhetorical ornament and display; and in the latter there is purpose, consistency, and method, with little regard for the shifts of expediency and the suggestions of hap-hazard temerity.

The attachment of Mr. Davis for the profession of arms is little less than a passion—an inspiration. True, he voluntarily abandoned the army, at an age when military life is most attractive to men, but the field of politics was far more inviting to a commendable aspiration for fame, than the army at a season of profound peace. But a more potent consideration, of a domestic nature, urged his withdrawal from military life.

He was about to be married, and preferred not to remain in the army after having assumed the responsibilities of that relation. His speeches in the House of Representatives, indicating his earnest interest in military affairs, his solicitude in behalf of the army, his enthusiastic championship of the Military Academy, and his thorough information respecting all subjects pertaining to the military interests of the country, show his ambitious and absorbing study of his favorite science.

In common with an overwhelming majority of the Southern people, he had favored the annexation of Texas, and cordially sustained Mr. Polk's Administration, in all the measures which were necessary to the triumphant success of its policy. While in the midst of his useful labors, as a member of Congress, in promoting the war policy of the Government, he received, with delight, the announcement of his selection to the command of the First Regiment of Mississippi Volunteers. He immediately resigned his seat in Congress and started to take command of his regiment, after obtaining for it, with great difficulty, the rifles which were afterwards used with such deadly effect upon the enemy. Overtaking his men, who were already *en route* for the scene of action, at New Orleans, by midsummer he had reinforced General Taylor on the Rio Grande.

The incidents of the Mexican war are too fresh in the recollection of the country to justify here a detailed narrative of the operations of the gallant army of General Taylor in its progress toward the interior from the scenes of its splendid exploits at Palo Alto and Resaca de la Palma. For several weeks after the arrival of Colonel Davis and his Mississippians, active hostilities were suspended. When the preparations for the campaign were completed, the army advanced, and reached Walnut Springs, about three miles from Monterey, on the 19th of September, 1846. Two days afterwards began those series of actions which finally resulted in the capitulation of a fortified city of great strength, and defended with obstinate valor. Of the part borne in these brilliant operations which so exalted the glory of the American name, and immortalized the heroism of Southern volunteers, by Colonel Davis and his "Mississippi Rifles," an able and graphic pen shall relate the story:

"In the storming of Monterey, Colonel Davis and his riflemen played a most gallant part. The storming of one of its strongest forts (Teneria) on the 21st of September was a desperate and hard-fought fight. The Mexicans had dealt such death by their cross-fires that they ran up a new flag in exultation, and in defiance of the assault which, at this time, was being made in front and rear. The Fourth Infantry, in the advance, had been terribly cut up, but the Mississippians and Tennesseeans steadily pressed forward, under a galling fire of copper grape. They approached to within a hundred yards of the fort, when they were lost in a volume of smoke. McClung,* inciting a company which formerly had been under his command, dashed on, followed by Captain Willis. Anticipating General Quitman, Colonel Davis, about the same time, gave the order to charge. With wild desperation, his men followed him. The escalade was made with the fury of a tempest, the men flinging themselves upon the guns of the enemy. Sword in hand, McClung has sprung over the ditch. After him dashes Davis, cheering on the Mississippians, and then Campbell, with his Tennesseeans and others, brothers in the fight, and rivals for its honors. Then was wild work. The assault was irresistible. The Mexicans, terror-stricken,

*Lieutenant-Colonel A. K. McClung.

fled like an Alpine village from the avalanche, and, taking position in a strongly-fortified building, some seventy-five yards in the rear, opened a heavy fire of musketry. But, like their mighty river, nothing could stay the Mississippians. They are after the Mexicans. Davis and McClung are simultaneously masters of the fortifications, having got in by different entrances. In the fervor of victory the brigade does not halt, but, led on by Colonel Davis, are preparing to charge on the second post, (El Diablo,) about three hundred yards in the rear, when they are restrained by Quitman. This desperate conflict lasted over two hours. The charge of the Mississippi Rifle Regiment, without bayonets, upon Fort Teneria, gained for the State a triumph which stands unparalleled.

"Placed in possession of El Diablo, on the dawn of the 23d Colonel Davis was exposed to a sharp fire from a half-moon redoubt, about one hundred and fifty yards distant, which was connected with heavy stone buildings and walls adjoining a block of the city. Returning the fire, he proceeded, with eight men, to reconnoitre the ground in advance. Having reported, he was ordered, with three companies of his regiment and one of Tennesseeans, to advance on the works.

"When they reached the half-moon work a tremendous fire was opened from the stone buildings in the rear. Taking a less-exposed position, Davis was reinforced, and, the balance of the Mississippians coming up, the engagement became general in the street, while, from the house-tops, a heavy fire was kept up by the Mexicans. 'The gallant Davis, leading the advance with detached parties, was rapidly entering the city, penetrating into buildings, and gradually driving the enemy from the position,' when General Henderson and the Texan Rangers dismounted, entered the city, and, through musketry and grape, made their way to the advance. The conflict increased, and still Davis continued to lead his command through the streets to within a square of the Grand Plaza, when, the afternoon being far advanced, General Taylor withdrew the Americans to the captured forts."*

Thus, in their first engagement, the Mississippians and their commander achieved a reputation which shall endure so long as men commemorate deeds of heroism and devotion. Veteran troops, trained to despise death by the dangers of a score of battles, have been immortalized in song and story for exploits inferior to those of the "Mississippi Rifles" at Monterey. Colonel Davis became one of the idols of the army, and took a prominent place among the heroes of the war. The nation rang with the fame of "Davis and his Mississippi Rifles;" the journals of the day were largely occupied with graphic descriptions of their exploits; and the reports of superior officers contributed their proud testimony to the history of the country, to the chivalrous daring and consummate skill of Colonel Davis. A becoming acknowledgment of his conduct was made by General Taylor in assigning him a place on the commission of officers appointed to arrange with the Mexicans the terms of capitulation. The result of the negotiations,

*For this spirited account of the operations of the Mississippi regiment at Monterey, the author is indebted to a sketch of Mr. Davis in Mr. John Savage's "Living Representative Men," which was published a year or two prior to the war. Though having several other accounts, possibly more complete, I have selected this as the most graphic. The author readily acknowledges the assistance which he has derived from the work of Mr. Savage.

though approved by General Taylor, was not approved by the Administration, which ordered a termination of the armistice agreed upon by the commissioners from the respective armies and a speedy resumption of hostilities. The terms of capitulation were assailed by many, who thought them too lenient to the Mexicans; among others, by General Quitman, the warm, personal, and political friend of Colonel Davis. A very important portion of the history of the war consists of the latter's defense of the terms of surrender and his memoranda of the incidents occurring in the conferences with the Mexican officers.

To sustain the proud prestige of Monterey—if possible to surpass it, became henceforth the aspiration of the Mississippians. But the name of Mississippi was to be made radiant with a new glory, beside which the lustre of Monterey paled, as did the dawn of Lodi by the full-orbed splendor of Austerlitz. All the world knows of the conduct of Jefferson Davis at Buena Vista. How he virtually won a battle, which, considering the disparity of the contending forces, must forever be a marvel to the student of military science; how like Dessaix, at Marengo, he thought there was "still time to win another battle," even when a portion of our line was broken and in inglorious retreat, and acting upon the impulse rescued victory from the jaws of defeat; saving an army from destruction, and flooding with a blaze of triumph a field shrouded with the gloom of disaster, are memories forever enshrined in the Temple of Fame. Americans can never weary of listening to the thrilling incidents of that ever-memorable day. By the South, the lesson of Buena Vista and kindred scenes of the valor of her children, can never be forgotton. In these days of her humiliation and despair, their proud memories throng upon her, as do a thousand noble emotions upon the modern Greek, who stands upon the sacred ground of Marathon and Plætea.

The following vivid and powerful description of the more prominent incidents of the battle is from the pen of Hon. J. F. H. Claiborne, of Mississippi:

"The battle had been raging sometime with fluctuating fortunes, and was setting against us, when General Taylor, with Colonel Davis and others, arrived on the field. Several regiments (which were subsequently rallied and fought bravely) were in full retreat. O'Brien, after having his men and horses completely cut up, had been compelled to draw off his guns, and Bragg, with almost superhuman energy, was sustaining the brunt of the fight. Many officers of distinction had fallen. Colonel Davis rode forward to examine the position of the enemy, and concluding that the best way to arrest our fugitives would be to make a bold demonstration, he resolved at once to attack the enemy, there posted in force, immediately in front, supported by cavalry, and two divisions in reserve in his rear. It was a resolution bold almost to rashness, but the emergency was pressing. With a handful of Indiana volunteers, who still stood by their brave old colonel (Bowles) and his own regiment, he advanced at double-quick time, firing as he advanced. His own brave fellows fell fast under the rolling musketry of the enemy, but their rapid and fatal volleys carried dismay and death into the adverse ranks. A deep ravine separated the combatants. Leaping into it, the Mississippians soon appeared on the other side, and with a shout that was heard over the battle-field, they poured in a well-directed fire, and rushed upon the enemy. Their deadly aim and wild enthusiasm were irresistible. The Mexicans fled in confusion to their reserves, and Davis seized the commanding position they had occupied. He next fell upon a party of cavalry and compelled it to fly, with the loss of their leader and other officers. Immediately afterwards a brigade of lancers, one thousand strong, were seen approaching at a gallop, in beautiful array, with sounding bugles and fluttering pennons. It was an appalling spectacle, but not a man flinched from his position. The time between our devoted band and eternity seemed brief indeed. But conscious that the eye of the army was upon them, that the honor of Mississippi was at stake, and knowing that, if they gave way, or were ridden down, our unprotected batteries in the rear, upon which the fortunes of the day depended, would be captured, each man resolved to die in his place sooner than retreat. Not the Spartan martyrs at Thermopylæ—not the sacred battalion of Epaminondas—not the Tenth Legion of Julius Cæsar—not the Old Guard of Napoleon—ever evinced more fortitude than these young volunteers in a crisis when death seemed inevitable. They stood like statues, as frigid and motionless as the marble itself. Impressed with this extraordinary firmness, when they had anticipated panic and flight, the lancers advanced more deliberately, as though they saw, for the first time, the dark shadow of the fate that was impending over them. Colonel Davis had thrown his men into the form of a reëntering angle, (familiarly known as his famous V movement,) both flanks resting on ravines, the lancers coming down on the intervening ridge. This exposed them to a converging fire, and the moment they came within rifle range each man singled out his object, and the whole head of the column fell. A more deadly fire never was delivered, and the brilliant array recoiled and retreated, paralyzed and dismayed.

"Shortly afterwards the Mexicans, having concentrated a large force on the right for their final attack, Colonel Davis was ordered in that direction. His regiment had been in action all day, exhausted by thirst and fatigue, much reduced by the carnage of the morning engagement, and many in the ranks suffering from wounds, yet the noble fellows moved at double-quick time. Bowles' little band of Indiana volunteers still acted with them. After marching several hundred yards they perceived the Mexican infantry advancing, in three lines, upon Bragg's battery, which, though entirely unsupported, held its position with a resolution worthy of his fame. The pressure upon him stimulated the Mississippians. They increased their speed, and when the enemy were within one hundred yards of the battery and confident of its capture, they took him in flank and reverse, and poured in a raking and destructive fire. This broke his right line, and the rest soon gave way and fell back precipitately. Here Colonel Davis was severely wounded."

The wound here alluded to was from a musket ball in the heel, and was exceedingly painful, though Colonel Davis refused to leave the field until the action was over. For some time grave apprehensions were entertained lest it should prove dangerous by the setting in of erysipelas.

General Taylor, who was deeply impressed with the large share of credit due to Colonel Davis, in his official report of the battle, says: "The Mississippi Riflemen, under Colonel Davis, were highly conspicuous for their gallantry and steadiness, and sustained throughout the engagement, the reputation of veteran troops. Brought into action against an immensely superior force, they maintained themselves for a long time, unsupported and with heavy loss, and held an important part of the field until reinforced. Colonel Davis, though severely wounded, remained in the saddle until the close of the action. His distinguished coolness and gallantry, at the head of his regiment on this day, entitle him to the particular notice of the Government."

The report of Colonel Davis, of the operations of his regiment, is highly important as a description of the most important features of the action, and as an explanation of his celebrated strategic movement. We omit such portions as embrace mere details not relevant to our purpose.

"SALTILLO, MEXICO, 2d March, 1847.

"SIR: In compliance with your note of yesterday, I have the honor to present the following report of the service of the Mississippi Riflemen on the 23d ultimo:

"Early in the morning of that day the regiment was drawn out from the head-quarters encampment, which stood in advance of and overlooked the town of Saltillo. Conformably to instructions, two companies were detached for the protection of that encampment, and to defend the adjacent entrance of the town. The remaining eight companies were put in march to return to the position of the preceding day, now known as the battle-field of Buena Vista. We had approached to within about two miles of that position, when the report of artillery firing, which reached us, gave assurance that a battle had commenced. Excited by the sound, the regiment pressed rapidly forward, manifesting, upon this, as upon other occasions, their more than willingness to meet the enemy. At the first convenient place the column was halted for the purpose of filling their canteens with water; and the march being resumed, was directed toward the position which had been indicated to me, on the previous evening, as the post of our regiment. As we approached the scene of action, horsemen, recognized as of our troops, were seen running, dispersed and confusedly from the field; and our first view of the line of battle presented the mortifying spectacle of a regiment of infantry flying disorganized from before the enemy. These sights, so well calculated to destroy confidence and dispirit troops just coming into action, it is my pride and pleasure to believe, only nerved the resolution of the regiment I have the honor to command.

"Our order of march was in column of companies, advancing by their centers. The point which had just been abandoned by the regiment alluded to, was now taken as our direction. I rode forward to examine the ground upon which we were going to operate, and in passing through the fugitives, appealed to them to return with us and renew the fight, pointing to our regiment as a mass of men behind which they might securely form.

"With a few honorable exceptions, the appeal was as unheeded, as were the offers which, I am informed, were made by our men to give their canteens of water to those who complained of thirst, on condition that they would go back. General Wool was upon the ground making great efforts to rally the men who had given way. I approached him and asked if he would send another regiment to sustain me in an attack upon the enemy before us. He was alone, and, after promising the support, went in person to send it. Upon further examination, I found that the slope we were ascending was intersected by a deep ravine, which, uniting obliquely with a still larger one on our right, formed between them a point of land difficult of access by us, but which, spreading in a plain toward the base of the mountain, had easy communication with the main body of the enemy. This position, important from its natural strength, derived a far greater value from the relation it bore to our order of battle and line of communication with the rear. The enemy, in number many times greater than ourselves, supported by strong reserves, flanked by cavalry and elated by recent success, was advancing upon it. The moment seemed to me critical and the occasion to require whatever sacrifice it might cost to check the enemy.

"My regiment, having continued to advance, was near at hand. I met and formed it rapidly into order of battle; the line then advanced in double-quick time, until within the estimated range of our rifles, when it was halted, and ordered to 'fire advancing.'

"The progress of the enemy was arrested. We crossed the difficult chasm before us, under a galling fire, and in good order renewed the attack upon the other side. The contest was severe—the destruction great upon both sides. We steadily advanced, and, as the distance diminished, the ratio of loss increased rapidly against the enemy; he yielded, and was driven back on his reserves. A plain now lay behind us—the enemy's cavalry had passed around our right flank, which rested on the main ravine, and gone to our rear. The support I had expected to join us was nowhere to be seen. I therefore ordered the regiment to retire, and went in person to find the cavalry, which, after passing round our right, had been concealed by the inequality of the ground. I found them at the first point where the bank was practicable for horsemen, in the act of descending into the ravine—no doubt for the purpose of charging upon our rear. The nearest of our men ran quickly to my call, attacked this body, and dispersed it with some loss. I think their commander was among the killed.

"The regiment was formed again in line of battle behind the first ravine we had crossed; soon after which we were joined upon our left by Lieutenant Kilbourn, with a piece of light artillery, and Colonel Lane's (the Third) regiment of Indiana volunteers. . . . We had proceeded but a short distance when I saw a large body of cavalry debouche from his cover upon the left of the position from which we had retired, and advance rapidly upon us. The Mississippi regiment was filed to the right, and fronted in line across the plain; the Indiana regiment was formed on the bank of the ravine, in advance of our right flank, by which a reëntering angle was presented to the enemy. Whilst this preparation was being made, Sergeant-Major Miller, of our regiment, was sent to Captain Sherman for one or more pieces of artillery from his battery.

"The enemy, who was now seen to be a body of richly-caparisoned lancers, came forward rapidly, and in beautiful order—the files and ranks so closed as to look like a mass of men and horses. Perfect silence and the greatest steadiness prevailed in both lines of our troops, as they stood at shouldered arms waiting an attack. Confident of success, and anxious to obtain the full advantage of a cross-fire at a short distance, I repeatedly called to the men not to shoot.

"As the enemy approached, his speed regularly diminished, until, when, within eighty or a hundred yards, he had drawn up to a walk, and seemed about to halt. A few files fired without orders, and both lines then instantly poured in a volley so destructive that the mass yielded to the blow and the survivors fled. . . . . At this time, the enemy made his last attack upon the right, and I received the General's order to march to that portion of the field. The broken character of the intervening ground concealed the scene of action from our view; but the heavy firing of musketry formed a sufficient guide for our course. After marching two or three hundred yards, we saw the enemy's infantry advancing in three lines upon Captain Bragg's battery; which, though entirely unsupported, resolutely held its position, and met the attack with a fire worthy the former achievements of that battery, and of the reputation of its present meritorious commander. We pressed on, climbed the rocky slope of the plain on which this combat occurred, reached its brow so as to take the enemy in flank and reverse when he was about one hundred yards from the battery. Our first fire—raking each of his lines, and opened close upon his flank—was eminently destructive. His right gave way, and he fled in confusion.

"In this, the last contest of the day, my regiment equaled—it was impossible to exceed—my expectations. Though worn down by many hours of fatigue and thirst, the ranks thinned by our heavy loss in the morning, they yet advanced upon the enemy with the alacrity and eagerness of men fresh to the combat. In every approbatory sense of these remarks I wish to be included a party of Colonel Bowles' Indiana regiment, which served with us during the greater part of the day, under the immediate command of an officer from that regiment, whose gallantry attracted my particular attention, but whose name, I regret, is unknown to me. When hostile demonstrations had ceased, I retired to a tent upon the field for surgical aid, having been wounded by a musket ball when we first went into action. . . . . Every part of the action having been fought under the eye of the commanding General, the importance and manner of any service it was our fortune to render, will be best estimated by him. But in view of my own responsibility, it may be permitted me to say, in relation to our first attack upon the enemy, that I considered the necessity absolute and immediate. No one could have failed to perceive the hazard. The enemy, in greatly disproportionate numbers, was rapidly advancing. We saw no friendly troops coming to our support, and probably none except myself expected reinforcement. Under such circumstances, the men cheerfully, ardently entered into the conflict; and though we lost, in that single engagement, more than thirty killed and forty wounded, the regiment never faltered nor moved, except as it was ordered. Had the expected reinforcement arrived, we could have prevented the enemy's cavalry from passing to our rear, results more decisive might have been obtained, and a part of our loss have been avoided. . . . .

"I have the honor to be, very respectfully, your obedient servant. "JEFFERSON DAVIS,

"*Colonel Mississippi Rifles.*

"MAJOR W. W. S. BLISS, *Assistant Adjutant-General.*"

The reputation earned by Colonel Davis at Buena Vista could not fail to provoke the assaults of envy. An effort, equally unwarranted and unsuccessful, has since been made to deprive him of a portion of his merited fame of having conceived and executed a movement decisive of the battle. It has been pretended, in disparagement of the strategy of Colonel Davis, that his celebrated V movement (for so it is, and will always be known) had not the merit of originality, and besides was forced upon him by the circumstances in which he was placed, and especially by the conformation of the ground, which would not admit of a different disposition of his troops. Such a judgment is merely hypercritical. There is no account in military history, from the campaigns of Cæsar to those of Napoleon, of such a tactical conception, unless we include a slightly-analogous case at Waterloo. The movement in the latter engagement, however, differs essentially from that executed by Davis at Buena Vista. A party of Hanoverian cavalry, assailed by French huzzars, at the intersection of two roads, by forming a salient, repulsed their assailants almost as effectually as did the reëntrant angle of the Mississippians at Buena Vista. As to the second criticism, it is certainly a novel accusation against an officer, that he should, by a quick appreciation of his situation, avail himself of the only possible means by which he could not only extricate his own command from imminent peril of destruction, but also avert a blow delivered at the safety of the entire army.

In a lecture on "The Expatriated Irish in Europe and America," delivered in Boston, February 11, 1858, the Hon. Caleb Cushing thus alludes to this subject: "In another of the dramatic incidents of that field, a man of Celtic race (Jefferson Davis) at the head of the Rifles of Mississippi, had ventured to do that of which there is, perhaps, but one other example in the military history of modern times. In the desperate conflicts of the Crimea, at the battle of Inkermann, in one of those desperate charges, there was a British officer who ventured to receive the charge of the enemy without the precaution of having his men formed in a hollow square. They were drawn up in two lines, meeting at a point like an open fan, and received the charge of the Russians at the muzzle of their guns, and repelled it. Sir Colin Campbell, for this feat of arms, among others, was selected as the man to retrieve the fallen fortunes of England in India. He did, however, but imitate what Jefferson Davis had previously done in Mexico, who, in that trying hour, when, with one last desperate effort to break the line of the American army, the cavalry of Mex-

5

ico was concentrated in one charge against the American line; then, I say, Jefferson Davis commanded his men to form in two lines, extended as I have shown, and receive that charge of the Mexican horse, with a plunging fire from the right and left from the Mississippi Rifles, which repelled, and repelled for the last time, the charge of the hosts of Mexico."

These puerile criticisms, however, were unavailing against the concurrent testimony of Taylor, Quitman, and Lane, and the grateful plaudits of the army, to shake the popular judgment, which rarely fails, in the end, to discriminate between the false glare of cheaply-earned glory and the just renown of true heroism.

The term of enlistment of his regiment having expired, Colonel Davis, in July, 1847, just twelve months after the resignation of his seat in the House of Representatives, returned to the United States. His progress toward his home was attended by a series of congratulatory receptions, the people every-where assembling *en masse* to do honor to the "Hero of Buena Vista." Mississippi extended a triumphant greeting to her soldier-statesman, who, resigning the civic trust which she had confided to his keeping, had carried her flag in triumph amid the thunders of battle and the wastes of carnage, carving the name of Mississippi in an inscription of enduring renown.

During his journey homeward, there occurred a most impressive illustration of that strict devotion to principle which, above all other considerations, is the real solution of every act of his life, public and private. While in New Orleans, Colonel Davis was offered, by President Polk, a commission as Brigadier-General of Volunteers, an honor which he unhesitatingly declined, on the ground that no such commission could be conferred by Federal authority, either by appointment of the President or by act of Congress. As an advocate of States' Rights, he could not countenance, even for the gratification of his own ambition, a plain infraction of the rights of the States, to which respectively, the Constitution reserves the appointment of officers of the militia.* The soldier's pride in deserved promotion for distinguished services, could not induce the statesman to forego his convictions of Constitutional right. The declination of this high distinction was entirely consistent with his opinions previously entertained and expressed. Before he resigned his seat in the House of Representatives, the bill authorizing such appointments by the President was introduced, and rapidly pressed to its passage. Mr. Davis detected the Constitutional infraction which it involved, and opposed it. He designed to address the House, but was suddenly called away from Washington, and before leaving had an understanding with the Chairman of the Committee from which the bill had come, that it would not be called up before the ensuing Monday. On his return, however, he found that the friends of the measure had forced its passage on the previous Saturday.

This is but one in a thousand evidences of an incorruptible loyalty to his convictions, which would dare face all opposition and has braved all reproach. It is an attribute of true greatness in the character of Jefferson Davis, which not even his enemies have called in question, to which candor must ever accord the tribute of infinite admiration.

* This Constitutional question was again raised by Mr. Davis, while President of the Confederacy, and his action with reference to similar legislation by the Confederate Congress, was in entire accordance with the reason assigned for declining Mr. Polk's appointment.

CHAPTER IV.

MR. DAVIS IN THE UNITED STATES SENATE, FIRST BY EXECUTIVE APPOINTMENT, AND SUBSEQUENTLY BY UNANIMOUS CHOICE OF THE LEGISLATURE OF HIS STATE—POPULAR ADMIRATION NOT LESS FOR HIS CIVIC TALENTS THAN HIS MILITARY SERVICES—FEATURES OF HIS PUBLIC CAREER—HIS CHARACTER AND CONDUCT AS A SENATOR—AS AN ORATOR AND PARLIAMENTARY LEADER—HIS INTREPIDITY—AN INCIDENT WITH HENRY CLAY—DAVIS THE LEADER OF THE STATES' RIGHTS PARTY IN CONGRESS—THE AGITATION OF 1850—DAVIS OPPOSES THE COMPROMISE—FOLLY OF THE SOUTH IN ASSENTING TO THAT SETTLEMENT—DAVIS NOT A DISUNIONIST IN 1850, NOR A REBEL IN 1861—HIS CONCEPTION OF THE CHARACTER OF THE FEDERAL GOVERNMENT—LOGICAL ABSURDITY OF CLAY'S POSITION EXPOSED BY DAVIS—THE IDEAL UNION OF THE LATTER—WHY HE OPPOSED THE COMPROMISE—THE NEW MEXICO BILL—DAVIS' GROWING FAME AT THIS PERIOD—HIS FREQUENT ENCOUNTERS WITH CLAY, AND WARM FRIENDSHIP BETWEEN THEM—SIGNAL TRIUMPH OF THE UNION SENTIMENT, AND ACQUIESCENCE OF THE SOUTH.

WITHIN less than two months from his return to Mississippi, Colonel Davis was appointed by the Governor of the State to fill the vacancy in the United States Senate occasioned by the death of General Speight. At a subsequent session of the Legislature, the selection of the Governor was confirmed by his unanimous election for the residue of the unexpired term. Seldom has there been a tender of public honor more deserved by the recipient, and more cheerfully accorded by the constituent body. It was the grateful tribute of popular appreciation to the hero who had risked his life for the glory of his country, and the worthy recognition of abilities which had been proven adequate to the responsibilities of the highest civic trust. Doubtless Colonel Davis owed much of the signal unanimity and enthusiasm which accompanied this expression of popular favor to his brilliant services in Mexico. The military passion is strong in the human breast, and the sentiment of homage to prowess, illustrated on the battle-field and in the face of danger, is one of the few chivalrous instincts which survive the influence of the sordid vices and vulgarisms of human nature. In all ages men have declaimed and reasoned against the expediency of confiding civil authority to the keeping of soldiers, and have cautioned the masses against the risk of entrusting the public liberties to the stern and dictatorial will educated in the rugged discipline and habits of the camp. Yet the masses, in all time, will continue their awards of distinction to martial exploits with a fervor not characteristic of their recognition of any other public service.

But the tribute had a higher motive, if possible, than the generous impulse of gratitude to the "Hero of Buena Vista," in the universal conviction of his eminent fitness for the position. His service in the House of Representatives, brief as it was, had designated him, months before his Mexican laurels had been earned, as a man, not only of mark, but of promise; of decided and progressive intellectual power; of pronounced mental and moral individuality.

Of all the public men of America, Jefferson Davis is the least indebted for his long and noble career of distinction to adventitious influences or merely temporary popular impulses. The sources of his strength have been the elements of his character and the resources of his genius. Never hoping to *stumble* upon success, by a stolid indifference amid the fluctuations of fortune, nor engaged in the role of the trimmer, who adjusts his conduct conformably with every turn of the popular current, his hopes of success have rested upôn the merits of principle alone. He has succeeded in all things *where success was possible*, and failed, at last, in contradiction of every lesson of previous experience, with the light of all history pleading his vindication, and to the disappointment of the nearly unanimous judgment of disinterested mankind.

A peculiar feature in the public career of Mr. Davis was its steady and consecutive development. He has accepted service, always and only, in obedience to the concurrent confidence of his fellow-citizens in his peculiar qualifications for the emergency. From the beginning he gave the promise of those high capacities which the fervid eulogy of Grattan accorded to Chatham—to "strike a blow in the world that should resound through its history." His first election to Congress was the spontaneous acknowledgment of the profound impression produced by his earliest intellectual efforts. The consummate triumph of his genius and valor at Buena Vista did not exceed the anticipations of his friends, who knew the ardor and assiduity of his devotion to his cherished science, and now in the noble arena of the American Senate his star was still to be in the ascendant.

At the first session of the Thirtieth Congress, Jefferson Davis took his seat as a Senator of the United States from the State of Mississippi. The entire period of his connection with the Senate, from 1847 to 1851, and from 1857 to 1861, scarcely comprises eight years; but those were years pregnant with the fate of a nation, and in their brief progress he stood in that august body the equal of giant intellects, and grappled, with the power and skill of a master, the great ideas and events of those momentous days. Mr. Davis could safely trust, whatever of ambition he may cherish for the distinguished consideration of posterity, to a faithful record of his service in the Senate. His senatorial fame is a beautiful harmony of the most pronounced and attractive features of the best parliamentary models. He was as intrepid and defiant as Chatham, but as scholarly as Brougham; as elegant and perspicuous in diction as Canning, and often as profound and philosophical in his comprehension of general principles as Burke; when roused by a sense of injury, or by the force of his earnest conviction, as much the incarnation of fervor and zeal as Grattan, but, like Fox, subtle, ready, and always armed *cap a pie* for the quick encounters of debate.

Among all the eminent associates of Mr. Davis in that body, there were very few who possessed his peculiar qualifications for its most distinguished honors. His character, no less than his demeanor, may be aptly termed senatorial, and his bearing was always attuned to his noble conception of the Senate as an august assemblage of the embassadors of sovereign States. He carried to the Senate the loftiest sense of the dignity and responsibility of his trust, and convictions upon political questions, which were the result of the most thorough and elaborate investigation. Never for one instant varying from the principles of his creed, he never doubted as to the course of duty; profound, accurate in information, there was no question pertaining to the science of government or its administration that he did not illuminate with a light, clear, powerful, and original.

It has been remarked of Mr. Davis' style as a speaker, that it is "orderly rather than ornate," and the remark is correct so far as it relates to the mere statement of the conditions of the discussion. For mere rhetorical glitter, Mr. Davis' speeches afford but poor models, but for clear logic and convincing argument, apt illustration, bold and original imagery, and genuine pathos, they are unsurpassed by any ever delivered in the American Senate. Though the Senate was, undoubtedly, his appropriate arena as an orator, and though it may well be doubted whether he was rivaled in senatorial eloquence by any contemporary, Mr. Davis is hardly less gifted in the attributes of popular eloquence. Upon great occasions he will move a large crowd with an irresistible power. As a popular orator, he does not seek to sway and toss the will with violent and passionate emotion, but his eloquence is more a triumph of argument aided by an enlistment of passion and persuasion to reason and conviction. He has less of the characteristics of Mirabeau, than of that higher type of eloquence, of which Cicero, Burke, and George Canning were representatives, and which is pervaded by passion, subordinated to the severer tribunal of intellect. It was the privilege of the writer, on repeated occasions, during the late war, to witness the triumph of Mr. Davis' eloquence over a popular assemblage. Usually the theme and the occasion were worthy of the orator, and difficult indeed would it be to realize a nobler vision of the majesty of intellect. To a current of thought, perennial and inexhaustible, compact, logical and irresistible, was added a fire that threw its warmth into the coldest bosom, and infused a glow of light into the very core of the subject. His voice, flexible and articulate, reaching any compass that was requisite, attitude and gestures, all conspired to give power and expression to his language, and the hearer was impressed as though in the presence of the very transfiguration of eloquence. The printed efforts of Mr. Davis will not only live as memorials of parliamentary and popular eloquence, but as invaluable stores of information to the political and historical student. They epitomize some of the most important periods of American history, and embrace the amplest discussion of an extended range of subjects pertaining to almost every science.

The development in Mr. Davis of the high and rare qualities, requisite to parliamentary leadership, was rapid and decisive. His nature instinctively aspires to influence and power, and under no circumstances could it rest contented in an attitude of inferiority. Independence, originality, and intrepidity, added to earnest and intelligent conviction; unwavering devotion to principle and purpose; a will stern and inexorable, and a disposition frank, courteous, and generous, are features of character which rarely fail to make a representative man. After the death of Mr. Calhoun, he was incomparably the ablest exponent of States' Rights principles, and even during the life of that great publicist, Mr. Davis, almost equally with him, shared the labors and responsibilities of leadership. His personal courage is of that knightly order, which in an age of chivalry would have sought the trophies of the tourney, and his moral heroism fixed him immovably upon the solid rock of principle, indifferent to the inconvenience of being in a minority and in no dread of the storms of popular passion. His faith in his principles was no less earnest than his confidence in his ability to triumphantly defend them. In the midst of the agitation and excitement of 1850, Henry Clay, the Great Compromiser, whose brilliant but erring genius so long and fatally led estray, from the correct understanding of the vital issue at stake between the North and the South, a numerous party of noble and true-hearted Southern gentlemen, furnished the occasion of an impressive illustration of this quality. Turning, in debate, to the Mississippi Senator, he notified the latter of his purpose, at some future day, to debate with him elaborately, an important question of principle. "Now is the moment," was the reply of the intrepid Davis, ever eager to champion his beloved and imperiled South, equally against her avowed enemies, and the not less fatal policy of those who were but too willing to compromise upon an issue vital to her rights and dignity. And what a shock of arms might then have been witnessed, could Clay have dispelled thirty years of his ripe three-score and ten! Each would have found a foeman worthy of his steel. In answer to this bold defiance, Clay, like Hotspur, would have rushed to the charge, with visor up and lance *couchant;* and Davis, another Saladin, no less frank than his adversary, but far more dexterous, would have met him with a flash of that Damascus scymetar, whose first blow severed the neck of the foeman.

That would have been a bold ambition that could demand a formal tender of leadership from the brilliant array of gallant gentlemen, ripe scholars, distinguished orators and statesmen, who, for twenty years before the war, were the valiant champions in Congress of the principles and aspirations of the South. Yet few will deny the preëminence of Mr. Davis, in the eye of the country and the world, among States' Rights leaders. Equally with Mr. Calhoun, as the leader of a great intellectual movement, he stamped his impress upon the enduring tablets of time.

Like Mr. Calhoun, too, Mr. Davis gave little evidence of capacity or taste for mere party tactics. Neither would have performed the duties of drill-sergeant, in local organizations, for the purposes of a political canvass, so well as hundreds of men of far lighter calibre and less stability. Happily, both sought and found a more congenial field of action.

The unexpired term, for which Mr. Davis had been elected in 1847, ended in 1851, and, though he was immediately reëlected, in consequence of his subsequent resignation his first service in the Senate ended with the term for which he had first been elected. A recurrence to the records of Congress will exhibit the eventful nature of this period, especially in its conclusion. In the earlier portion of his senatorial service, Mr. Davis participated conspicuously in debate and in the general business of legislation. Here, as in the House of Representatives, his views upon military affairs were always received with marked respect, and no measure looking to the improvement of the army failed to receive his cordial coöperation.

The extensive conquests of the army in Mexico, and the necessity of maintaining the authority of the Federal Government in the conquered country until the objects of the war could be consummated, created considerable embarrassment. Upon this subject Mr. Davis spoke frequently and intelligently. His sagacity indicated a policy equally protective of the advantages which the valor of the army had achieved, and humane to the conquered. In a debate with Mr. John Bell, in February, 1848, he defined himself as favoring such a military occupation as would "prevent the General Government of Mexico, against which this war had been directed, from reëstablishing its power and again concentrating the scattered fragments of its army to renew active hostilities against us." He disclaimed the motive, in this policy, of territorial acquisition, and earnestly deprecated interference with the political institutions of the Mexicans. The estimate entertained by the Senate, of his judgment and information upon military subjects, was indicated by his almost unanimous election, (thirty-two for Mr. Davis, and five for all others,) during the session of the Thirty-first Congress, as Chairman of the Committee on Military Affairs. His speeches on the subject of offering congratulations to the French people upon their recent successful political revolution, resulting in the establishment of a republican form of government, the proposed organization of the territorial government of Oregon, upon various subjects of practical and scientific interest, and his incidental discussions of the subject of slavery, were able, eloquent, and characteristic.

The session of Congress in 1849 and 1850 brought with it a most angry and menacing renewal of sectional agitation. Previous events and innumerable indications of popular sentiment had clearly revealed to candid minds, every-where, that the increasing sectional preponderance of the North, and its growing hostility to slavery, portended results utterly ruinous to the rights and institutions of the South. To the South it was literally a question of vitality, to secure some competent check upon the aggressive strength of the North. To maintain any thing like a sectional balance, the South must necessarily secure to her institutions, at least, a fair share of the common domain to be hereafter created into States. The immense territorial acquisitions resulting from the Mexican war were now the subjects of controversy. After a contest, protracted through several months, and eliciting the most violent exhibitions of sectional feeling, a plan of adjustment, under the auspices chiefly of Henry Clay, whose fatal gift was to preserve, for a time, the peace of the country by the concession of the most precious and vital rights of his section to an insolent and insatiate fanaticism, was finally reached. This settlement, known, by way of distinction, as the "Compromise of 1850," averting for the time the dangers of disunion and civil war, met the approval of the advocates of expediency, but was opposed, with heroic pertinacity, by Mr. Davis and his associates of the States' Rights party. They saw the hollowness of its pretended justice, its utter worthlessness as a guarantee to the South, and sought to defeat it—first in Congress, and afterwards by the popular voice. But the sentiment of attachment to the Union triumphed over every consideration of interest, principle, even security, and the snare succeeded. Again the South receded, again received the stone instead of the asked-for loaf, and again did she *compromise* her most sacred rights and dearest interests, receiving, in return, the reluctant and insincere guarantee of the recovery of her stolen slaves.

The folly of the South in assenting to this adjustment is now obvious to the dullest understanding, and subsequent events were swift to vindicate the wisdom, patriotism, and foresight of Mr. Davis and those who sustained him in opposition to the much-vaunted Union-saving compromise. Yet, they were no more disunionists in 1850 than rebels and traitors in 1861. The charge of disunionism was freely iterated against them, and not without effect, even in their own section, where the sentimental attachment to the Union was stronger, just as its sacrifices in behalf of the Union were greater, than those of the North. Jefferson Davis never was a disunionist, not even in his subsequent approval of secession, in the sense of a wanton and treasonable disposition to sever the bonds of that association of co-equal sovereignties which the founders of the Federal Government bequeathed to their posterity.

His action, at all times, has been thoroughly consistent with his declared opinions, and with the earnest attachment to the Union, avowed in his congressional speeches and in his public addresses every-where. In 1850 and in 1861 his course was the logical sequence of his opinions, maintained and asserted from his introduction to public life. To save the Union, upon the only basis upon which it could rest as a guarantee of liberty, —the basis of absolute equality among the States; to blend Federal power and States' Rights, was the grand, paramount object to which all his aspirations and all his investigations of political science were directed. Repudiating the power of a State to nullify an act of Congress, and yet not surrender its normal relations as a member of the Union, he always asserted the right of secession, in the last resort, as an original, inherent, and vital attribute of State Sovereignty. The Federal Government, to his mind, was a mere agent of the States, created by them for a few general and intestate purposes, but having in it no principle subversive of the paramount sovereignty of the States. Rapidly extending its power by enactments of Congress and judicial constructions, he foresaw, and sought to counteract, its tendency to obliterate all State individuality, and ultimately absorb into its own keeping the liberties of the people. With dread and indignation, he contemplated its progress towards that *monstrum horrendum*, a consolidated democracy—the Union of to-day, in which we see that the *will of the majority is the sole measure of its powers.*

Such was his consistency, and such his sagacity, as vindicated in the light of subsequent events, and patent to the eyes of the world to-day. Who can now doubt which was the better and more logical theory? Clay said: "I owe allegiance to two sovereignties, and only two: one is to the sovereignty of this Union, and the other is to the sovereignty of the State of Kentucky." Thus he held to the paradox of an *imperium in imperio,* that obvious absurdity in our system of government, a divided sovereignty. In his ardent Unionism, the great exponent of expediency disavowed allegiance to the *South,* though still holding to his allegiance to Kentucky. But suppose Kentucky asserts her sovereignty, and chooses to unite with the South, what, then, becomes of State Sovereignty and State allegiance? Just here was the *hiatus* in Clay's logic, and, closely pressed by Davis, he emphatically declared his *first* allegiance to the Union as the supreme authority; and the State Sovereignty of Clay's conception was seen to be as intangible and unreal as the "baseless fabric of a vision."

Far more fair in its semblance, noble in its proportions, and beautiful in its harmonies, was the ideal of Davis. In his speech on the compromise measures, July 31, 1850, he said:

> "Give to each section of the Union justice; give to every citizen of the United States his rights as guaranteed by the Constitution; leave this Confederacy to rest upon that basis from which it arose—the fraternal feelings of the people—and I, for one, have no fear of its perpetuity; none that it will not survive beyond the limits of human speculation, expanding and hardening with the lapse of time, to extend its blessings to ages unnumbered, and a people innumerable; to include within its empire all the useful products of the earth, and exemplify the capacity of a confederacy, with general, well-defined powers, to extend illimitably without impairing its harmony or its strength."

The grounds of Mr. Davis' opposition to the so-called "Compromise" programme of Mr. Clay were far otherwise than a factious and impracticable hostility to an amicable adjustment of sectional differences. He conscientiously doubted the disposition of the North to abstain from all future interference with Southern institutions, and he detected and exposed the utter want of efficacy of the compromise measures as an assurance of protection against future aggression. He abhorred the substitution of expediency for principle; could see no *compromise* where one side simply *surrendered* what the other had no right to demand, and correctly estimated this settlement, like those which had preceded it, as but an invitation to still more intolerable exactions by an implacable sectional majority. While discussing, in private conversation with Mr. Clay, the merits of Mr. Webster's memorable speech of the 7th of March, 1850, a few days after its delivery, he briefly, but sufficiently defined his position. "Come," said Mr. Clay, "my young friend; join us in these measures of pacification. Let us rally Congress and the people to their support, and they will assure to the country thirty years of peace. By that time" (turning to John M. Berrien, who was a party to the conversation) "you and I will be under the sod, and my young friend may then have trouble again." "No," said Davis, "I can not consent to transfer to posterity a question which is as much ours as theirs, when it is evident that the sectional inequality, as it will be greater then than now, will render hopeless the attainment of justice."

His clear, penetrating glance discovered, under the guise of a friendly and pacific purpose, the insidious presence so mischievous to Southern interests, just as George Mason, more than fifty years before, had seen the "poison under the wing of the Federal Constitution." While the bill for the organization of the Territory of New Mexico was pending, the vigilance and sagacity of Mr. Davis elicited the most flattering commendation from his Southern associates. In this bill there was a general grant, in loose and ambiguous phraseology, of legislative power, with a reservation that no law should be passed "in respect to African slavery." Strangely enough, this provision, though obviously involving an inhibition against the enactment of laws for the protection of Southern property, escaped general detection. Mr. Davis promptly exposed its purpose, and offered an amendment, striking out the restraint against legislation "in respect to African slavery," and prohibiting the enactment of any law interfering "with those rights of property growing out of the institution of African slavery as it exists in any of the States of this Union." To meet the concurrence of other Senators, the amendment was variously modified, until, as explained by Mr. Davis, it embodied "the general proposition that the Territorial Legislature should not be prevented from passing the laws necessary for the protection of the rights of property of every kind which might be legally and constitutionally held in that territory." It is needless to say that so just a proposition, affording equal protection to Southern with Northern institutions, was defeated.

While there was little in Mr. Clay's plan of pacification to recommend it to Southern support, beyond the merely temporary staving off of a dissolution of the Union and civil war, it embodied propositions utterly incompatible with the security of the South. Mr. Davis especially and persistently combated its provision for the abolition of the slave-trade in the District of Columbia, and the concession that slavery did not legally exist in the newly-acquired territory. His position upon the general issues involved can not be more clearly and forcibly stated than in his own language:

"But, sir, we are called upon to receive this as a measure of compromise!—as a measure in which we of the minority are to receive something. A measure of compromise! I look upon it as a modest mode of taking that, the claim to which has been more boldly asserted by others; and that I may be understood upon this question, and that my position may go forth to the country in the same columns that convey the sentiments of the Senator from Kentucky, I here assert that never will I take less than the Missouri Compromise line to the Pacific Ocean, with specific right to hold slaves in the territory below that line; and that before such territories are admitted into the Union as States, slaves may be taken there from any of the United States, at the option of the owners. I can never consent to give additional power to a majority to commit further aggression upon the minority in this Union; and I will never consent to any proposition which will have such a tendency without a full guarantee or counteracting measure is connected with it."

The parliamentary annals of the Union embrace no period more prolific of grand intellectual efforts than the debates incident to this gigantic struggle. The prominence of Mr. Davis, with his extreme ardor in behalf of the rights and interests of his section, brought him constantly into conflict with the most eminent leaders of both the great political parties, who had cordially agreed to ignore all minor issues and unite in the paramount purpose of saving the Union. Cass, Douglas, Bright, Dickinson, and King, earnestly coöperated with Clay, Webster, and other Whig champions, in the advocacy of the measures of compromise. That Davis, younger in years and experience than most of these distinguished men, amply sustained his honorable and responsible role as the foremost champion of the South, contemporary public opinion and the Congressional records give abundant testimony. The great compromise chieftain, between whom and Davis occurred such obstinate and protracted encounters in debate, delighted to testify his respect for the talents and intrepidity of his "young friend," which was his habitual salutation to Davis. Despite the pronounced antagonism between them, on all measures of public policy, and their comparatively brief acquaintance, Mr. Clay repeatedly evinced, in a most touching manner, his warm regard for one who had been the companion-in-arms and cherished friend of a noble son,* who lost his life on the same field, upon which Davis won such deathless distinction. "My poor boy," were his words to the latter, upon his return from Mexico, "usually occupied about one-half of his letters home in praising you." A still more touching incident, illustrative of his friendly regard, at the moment not understood by those present, occurred, in the heat of discussion during the exciting period, which we have had under consideration. Replying to Davis, said Mr. Clay: "My friend from Mississippi—and I trust that he will permit me to call him my friend, for between us there is a tie, the nature of which we both well understand." At this moment the utterance of the aged statesman became tremulous with emotion, and, bowing his head, his eyes were seen to fill with tears. This friendship was warmly reciprocated by Mr. Davis, and its recollections are among those the most highly-cherished of his public life.

With the defeat of those who had opposed the compromise, terminated, for the present, Southern resistance in Congress, though it did not for an instant check Northern aggression. Yet many prominent public characters at the South, and, as the

* Henry Clay, Jr., a graduate of West Point, and at the time of his death, Lieutenant-Colonel of volunteers. He fell at Buena Vista.

sequel demonstrated, indorsed by popular sentiment, avowed themselves fully satisfied with a mere show of triumph and pretense of justice—a few paltry concessions, not worth the parchment upon which they were written. In the meantime, upon another arena, Mr. Davis entered upon a gallant struggle, in opposition to a policy from which he foresaw and predicted a fruitful yield of disaster in the future.

CHAPTER V.

OPPOSITION TO THE COMPROMISE IN SOUTH CAROLINA AND MISSISSIPPI—DAVIS A CANDIDATE FOR GOVERNOR—HIS DEFEAT REALLY A PERSONAL TRIUMPH—IN RETIREMENT, SUPPORTS GENERAL PIERCE'S ELECTION—DECLINES AN APPOINTMENT IN PIERCE'S CABINET, BUT SUBSEQUENTLY ACCEPTS SECRETARYSHIP OF WAR—REMARKABLE UNITY OF PIERCE'S ADMINISTRATION, AND HIGH CHARACTER OF THE EXECUTIVE—DAVIS AS SECRETARY OF WAR—KANSAS-NEBRASKA BILL AND THE EXCITEMENT WHICH FOLLOWED—DAVIS AGAIN ELECTED TO THE SENATE—SPEECHES AT PASS CHRISTIAN AND OTHER POINTS WHILE ON HIS WAY TO WASHINGTON.

BUT, though the battle had been fought and won in Congress, and it was evident, at an early date, that the weight of great names in favor of the Compromise, aided by the ever-timid counsels of capital and commerce, would command for that measure the overwhelming support of the country, the States' Rights men were resolved upon a test of popular sentiment. Accordingly, in South Carolina and Mississippi, States at all times the most advanced in Southern feeling, the opponents of the Compromise organized, as did its friends also. The issue, though substantially the same, was presented in a somewhat different form in these two States.

In South Carolina, where public sentiment was always singularly unanimous, upon all questions affecting the honor and interests of the South, and in entire accord as to the mode and measure of redress for the grievances of the States, the propriety of resistance was a foregone conclusion. The only question was, whether South Carolina should act separately, or await the coöperation of other Southern States. The party of coöperation triumphed in the election of members to a State convention, by the decisive popular majority of seven thousand votes.

In Mississippi the issue was one of *resistance* or *acquiescence.* The States' Rights, or resistance party, embraced four-fifths of the Democracy of the State and a small accession of States' Rights Whigs; while the Union, or Compromise party, was composed of the Clay Whigs and a fraction of the Democracy.

The Legislature provided an election for members of a State convention to consider the subject of Federal aggressions, to be held in September, 1851, and, in the ensuing November the regular election of Governor occurred. Much interest centred upon the gubernatorial contest, and the State was for months previous to the election the scene of great excitement. General John A. Quitman, one of the most distinguished officers of the army, during the Mexican war, a man of the loftiest character, a reliable statesman, and sterling patriot, was nominated by the States' Rights Convention. Mr. Henry S. Foote, then a Senator from Mississippi, and an active supporter of the Compromise measures, was the candidate of the Union party. While an exceedingly animated canvass between these candidates was still in progress, the election for members of the convention resulted in an aggregate majority of seven thousand five hundred votes for the Union candidates. General Quitman, disappointed by such an unexpected and decisive exhibition of public sentiment, and viewing it as the forerunner of the result of the gubernatorial election in November, withdrew from the contest.

Mr. Davis, who had already been elected for a second term

to the Senate, was now looked to as almost the sole dependence of the States' Rights men, and they summoned him to take the field as the adversary of Mr. Foote. There was little inducement, had he consulted selfish considerations, to relinquish a high position, already secured, and become the leader of a forlorn hope. Though greatly enfeebled in health, and at that time an acute sufferer, he accepted the nomination. His sense of duty and devotion to his principles triumphed even over his physical infirmities, and, resigning his seat in the Senate, he entered upon the canvass.

The result was, as had been foreseen, the defeat of Mr. Davis. Mr. Foote, a man of more than average ability, and of varied and extensive attainments, whose excessive garrulity and total want of discretion disqualified him for usefulness as a member of a legislative body, or for any practical end of statesmanship, was, nevertheless, an adroit party tactician. With great dexterity he had conducted the canvass with General Quitman, by skillfully evading the real issue, introducing side questions, and thus breaking the force of the plain and statesman-like arguments of his more open and less dexterous adversary. When Mr. Davis entered the field, under all the disadvantages to which we have alluded, the election of Foote was almost universally conceded. Had the canvass lasted a few weeks, however, the result, in all probability, would have been different. The popularity of Mr. Davis was indicated by the paltry majority (nine hundred and ninety-nine votes) given against him, as compared with the Union majority at the election in September, for members of the convention. Under all the circumstances, his friends rightly viewed it as a personal triumph, and he emerged from the contest with increased reputation and public regard.

The results of these appeals to popular judgment were scarcely less decisive, in favor of the Compromise, than had been its congressional victory. It was evident that the Southern people were yet far from being ready for organized and practical resistance, and were not likely to be, until some flagrant outrage should arouse their resentment.

Mr. Davis was now in retirement, and, though abiding the decision of Mississippi, he was yet avowedly determined to devote his energies to the efficient organization of the States' Rights party for future struggles. Yet nothing was farther from his purpose than a factious agitation. His aim was to secure for the States' Rights principle a moral and numerical support in the ranks of the Democracy, which should enable its friends to wield an appropriate influence upon the policy of that party. He contemplated no organization outside of the Democracy, for the promotion of disunionism *per se;* and, in the Presidential canvass of 1852, separated himself from many of his closest personal and political friends, who had nominated the Presidential ticket of Troup and Quitman, upon the distinctive platform of States' Rights and separation.

The nomination of Franklin Pierce, upon the Baltimore platform, met his cordial approbation, and received his active support. With General Pierce, Mr. Davis held the most friendly relations, and in his constitutional opinions he had entire confidence. His support of the platform was quite as consistent as his advocacy of the nominee. Both indorsed, with emphasis, the Compromise, which he had opposed, but which Mississippi had ratified, and both avowed their acceptance of it, as a *finality,* beyond which there was to be no farther agitation of the slavery question. In Mississippi, Louisiana, and Tennessee he participated actively in the canvass, and rendered most efficient service to his party, especially in the two latter States.

General Pierce indicated his estimate of Davis, by a prompt tender of a position in his Cabinet. Considering himself committed to the fortunes of his principles in Mississippi, he preferred to "remain and fight the issue out there," and reluctantly declined. Subsequently the President-elect addressed him a letter expressing a desire that, upon personal grounds at least, Mr. Davis should be present at his inauguration. After he had reached Washington the tender of a Cabinet appointment was repeated. The obvious advantages to the States' Rights party of representation in the Government, an argument earnestly urged upon him by prominent Southern statesmen, at length overcame his personal preference, and he accepted the position of Secretary of War.

With the policy of President Pierce's administration, Secretary Davis was, of course, fully identified. Whatever of influence and sympathy he could command, were employed in promoting its success, and between the President and himself there was an uninterrupted harmony of personal and official intercourse. Indeed the glory of this administration and the explanation of its title to that high award which it earned from impartial criticism, for its courageous pursuit of an upright, constitutional policy, was the characteristic unity which prevailed between its head and his advisers. During the four years of its existence the Cabinet of President Pierce continued unchanged, at its close the head of each department surrendering the seals of office which he had received at its inauguration. The history of no other administration is adorned with such an instance of cordial and unbroken coöperation, and the fact is equally creditable to the sagacity of General Pierce in the selection of his advisers, and his consummate tact in the reconciliation of those antagonisms, which are hardly to be avoided in the operations of the complicated machinery of Government.

A common statement of its enemies, that the administration must eventually break down by disorganization, in consequence of the utterly discordant elements which composed it, was never realized. At one time Mr. Marcy, the Secretary of State, was the wily Macchiavelli, against whose intrigues the rest of the Cabinet was in arms, while Mr. Davis was charged with playing alternately the roles of Richelieu and Marplot.

Of all American executives, Franklin Pierce is preëminently entitled to the designation of the constitutional President. The great covenant of American liberty, so ruthlessly despoiled in these degenerate days, when opportunity and pretext are the sufficient justification of flagrant violations of justice, was the guide whose precepts he followed without deviation. His Northern birth and training did not swerve from his obligations to extend an equal protection to the interests of other sections, the patriotic executive, whom posterity will delight to honor, for his wisdom, purity, and impartiality, just in proportion as those qualities provoke the clamor of the dominant ignorance and passion of to-day.

In a Cabinet, noted for its ability, of which William L. Marcy was the Premier, and Caleb Cushing the Attorney-General, Secretary Davis occupied a position worthy of his abilities and his previous reputation, and peculiarly gratifying to his military tastes. It is no disparagement of his associates to say that his strongly-marked character commanded a constant and emphatic recognition in the policy of the Government.

Under his control the department of war was greatly advanced in dignity and importance, receiving a character far more distinctive and independent of other branches of the Government than it had previously claimed. He infused into all its operations an energy till then unknown, introducing improvements so extensive and comprehensive as to occasion apprehension of an almost too powerful and independent system of military organization. It is a fact universally conceded that his administration of the War Office was incomparably superior to that of any official who has filled that position—contributing more to the promotion of efficiency in the army, to the advancement of those great national establishments so vital to the security of the nation, and to the systematic, practical management of the details of the office. In reviewing Mr. Davis' conduct of this important department of the Government, the splendid improvements which he inaugurated, his earnest and unceasing labors in behalf of the efficiency of the army, it is impossible to overestimate his eminent services to the Union, which even at that time his traducers and those of the South would pretend he was plotting to destroy. In the Cabinet, as in the Senate, there was no measure of national advantage to which he did not give his cordial support, no great national institution which he would not have fostered with generous and timely sympathy; nothing to which he was not zealously committed, promising to redound to the glory, prosperity, and perpetuity of that Union, in whose service he had been trained, whose uniform he had proudly worn, and beneath whose banner he had braved a soldier's death.

Secretary Davis made many recommendations contemplating radical alterations in the military system of the Union. One of his first measures was a recommendation for the thorough revision of the army regulations. He opposed the placing of officers, at an early period of service, permanently upon the staff, and advocated a system, which, he contended, would improve the discipline and efficiency of officers, "whereby the right of command should follow rank by one certain rule." The increase of the medical corps; the introduction of camels; the introduction of the light infantry or rifle system of tactics, rifled muskets, and the Minie-ball were all measures advocated by Secretary Davis, and discussed in his official papers with a force and intelligence that make them highly valuable to the military student. He urged a thorough exploration of the Western frontier, and important changes in the arrangement of defenses against the Indians, demonstrating the inefficiency of the system of small forts for the purposes of war with the savages. To obviate, in a measure, the expense, and almost useless trouble, of locating military posts in advance of settlement, he suggested the plan of maintaining large garrisons at certain points, situated favorably for obtaining supplies and accessible by steamboat or railway. From these posts strong detachments could be supplied and equipped for service in the Indian country. His efforts were most strenuous to obtain an increase of pay to officers of the army, and pensions to the widows and orphans of officers and men, upon a basis similar to that of the navy.

During the Crimean war, Secretary Davis sent a commission, of which Major-General McClellan, then a captain of cavalry, was a member, to study and report upon the science of war and the condition of European armies, as illustrated in the operations incident to that struggle. At his suggestion four new regiments—two of cavalry—were added to the army, and numerous appropriations made for the construction of new forts, improvements in small arms, and the accumulation of munitions of war.

The Presidential term of Pierce expired on the 4th of March, 1857, and with it terminated the connection of Mr. Davis with the executive branch of the Government. He retired with the hearty respect of his associates, and in the enjoyment of the most confiding friendship with the late head of the Government, a feeling which is cherished by both, with unabated warmth, at this day. All parties concurred in pronouncing Mr. Davis' conduct of his department successful, able, and brilliant, and in the midst of the tide of misrepresentation, with which, during and since the war, it has been sought to overwhelm his reputation, the least candid of his accusers have been compelled to this reluctant confession.

Incidental to the late administration, but by no means traceable to its influence, had been legislation by Congress of a most important character, which was to give a powerful impulse to agencies long tending to the destruction of the Union. The election of Pierce had been carried with a unanimity unprecedented, upon the distinct pledge of the acceptance of the Compromise as a *finality*. The country, for months subsequently, reposed in profound quiet, produced by its confidence in an approaching season of unequaled prosperity, and exempt from all danger of political agitation. This hallucination was destined to be speedily and rudely dispelled by events, which afford striking evidence of how completely the peace and happiness of the American people have always been at the mercy of aspiring and unscrupulous demagogues. Mr. Stephen A.

Douglas must ever be held, equally by both sections, responsible for the disastrous agitation, which followed his introduction of certain measures, under the pretense of a sentimental justice, or a concession of principle to the South, but in reality prompted by his personal ambition, and which greatly aided to precipitate the catastrophe of disunion.

Upon the application of the Territory of Nebraska for admission into the Union, Senator Douglas, from the Committee on Territories, submitted a bill creating the two Territories of Nebraska and Kansas, and affirming the supersession of the Missouri restriction of 1820, which prohibited slavery north of 36° 30′, by the Compromise of 1850. It declared the Missouri restriction inconsistent with the principle of *non-intervention* by Congress with territorial affairs, which had been adopted in the settlement of 1850, and therefore inoperative.

This bill was apparently a mere concession of principle to the South, not likely to be of much practical value, but still gratifying, as it gave to her citizens the right to carry their property into districts from which it had been hitherto inhibited. Passing both houses of Congress, in 1854, it was approved by the Pierce administration,* sanctioned by the

* The repeal of the Missouri Compromise has been commonly alluded to as the special and leading measure of the Pierce administration. It was, in reality, not an administration measure. The well-known cordiality of Mr. Davis' relations with President Pierce induced a number of Senators to call upon Mr. Davis, on the Sunday morning previous to the introduction of the Kansas-Nebraska Bill, and ask his aid in securing them the pledge of the President's approval. They represented the measure as contemplating merely the assertion of the rights of property, slavery included, in the Territories. Mr. Davis objected, at first, to an interruption of the President, on the Sabbath, for such a purpose, but finally yielded. The President promptly signified his approbation of a measure contemplating such a purpose. It is not necessary to say that the legislation of Congress embraced a far greater scope than that indicated. The

Democracy generally, and greeted by the South as a triumph. It was not imagined that a victory, so purely sentimental and intangible, could be accepted by the North, as a pretext for violent eruptions of sectional jealousy, and least of all did the South believe its author capable of the subsequent duplicity with which, by specious arguments and verbal ingenuity, he claimed for the measure, a construction far more insidious, but not less fatal to her interests, than the designs of proclaimed Abolitionists. The immediate result was a tempest of excitement in the Northern States, in the midst of which the so-called Republican party, for the first time, appeared as a formidable contestant in political struggles, and defeated the Democracy in almost every State election. The latter, with extreme difficulty, elected Mr. Buchanan to the Presidency two years afterwards.

In the meantime, while his term of office as Secretary of War was still unexpired, Mr. Davis had been elected, by the Legislature of Mississippi, to the Senate, for the term beginning March 4, 1857. On his return home, he was received by the Democracy of the State with distinguished honors. Dinners, receptions, and public entertainments of various kinds were tendered him; and, during the summer and autumn, previous to his departure for Washington, he addressed numerous large popular gatherings with his accustomed force and boldness upon pending issues. These addresses commanded universal attention, and were highly commended for their able, dispassionate, and statesman-like character.

administration indorsed the Kansas-Nebraska Bill in full, because the principle was correct, though its assertion then was wholly unnecessary, unprofitable, and likely to lead to mischievous results. This was the real connection of the Pierce administration with a measure for whose consequences the ambition of Judge Douglas was almost solely responsible.

His speech at Pass Christian, while on his journey to Washington, was a masterly and eloquent review of the condition of the country, with its causes and remedies. He attributed the national difficulties chiefly to the puritanical intolerance and growing disregard of constitutional obligations of the North. These influences seriously menaced the safety of the Union, for which he had no hope, unless in the event of a reaction in Northern sentiment, or of such resolute action by a united South as should compel her enemies to respect their constitutional duties. To the latter policy he looked as the best guarantee of the security of the South and the preservation of the Union. Interference by one State with the institutions of another could not, under any circumstances, be tolerated, even though resistance should eventually result in a dissolution of the Union. The latter event was possible—indeed, might become necessary—but should never be undertaken save in the last extremity. He would not disguise the profound emotion with which he contemplated the possibility of disunion. The fondest reminiscences of his life were associated with the Union, into whose military service, while yet a boy, he had entered. In his matured manhood he had followed its flag to victory; had seen its graceful folds wave in the peaceful pageant, and, again, its colors conspicuous amid the triumphs of the battle-field; he had seen that flag in the East, brightened by the sun at its rising, and, in the West, gilded by his declining rays—and the tearing of one star from its azure field would be to him as would the loss of a child to a bereaved parent.

This speech—one of the most eloquent he has ever made—was received by his audience with unbounded enthusiasm, and was approvingly noticed by the press of both sections.

At Mississippi City he delivered an address in explanation of his personal course, and in vindication of the administration of which he had lately been a member. He had obeyed the will of Mississippi, respecting the legislation of 1850, though against his convictions, and, in the present disorders in Kansas, he saw the fruits of the unwise substitution of expediency for principle. Of President Pierce he could speak only in terms of eulogy, defended his vetoes of bills "for internal improvements and eleemosynary purposes," depicting, in passages of rare and fervent eloquence, his heroic adherence to the Constitution, elevated patriotism, and distinguished virtues. Contrasting the conduct of the Fillmore and Pierce administrations concerning the Cuban question, he avowed his belief that Cuba would then be in possession of the United States had Congress sustained General Pierce in his prompt and decided suggestions as to the Black Warrior difficulty.

Mr. Davis expressed his approbation of the course pursued by the late administration with reference to Nicaragua. "Unlawful expeditions" should be suppressed, though he should rejoice at the establishment of American institutions in Central America, and maintained the right of the United States to a paramount influence in the affairs of the continent, with which European interference should be, at all times, promptly checked.

When the Thirty-fifth Congress assembled in December, 1857, the Kansas question had already developed a difficult and critical phase. The rock upon which Mr. Buchanan's administration was to split had been encountered, and the wedge prepared, with which the Democratic party was destined to be torn asunder.

CHAPTER VI.

RETURN OF MR. DAVIS TO THE SENATE—OPENING EVENTS OF MR. BUCHANAN'S ADMINISTRATION—TRUE INTERPRETATION OF THE LEGISLATION OF 1854—SENATOR DOUGLAS THE INSTRUMENT OF DISORGANIZATION IN THE DEMOCRATIC PARTY—HIS ANTECEDENTS AND CHARACTER—AN ACCOMPLISHED DEMAGOGUE—DAVIS AND DOUGLAS CONTRASTED—BOTH REPRESENTATIVES OF THEIR RESPECTIVE SECTIONS—DOUGLAS AMBITION—HIS COUP D'ETAT, AND ITS RESULTS—THE KANSAS QUESTION—DOUGLAS' TRIUMPHS OVER THE SOUTH AND THE UNITY OF THE DEMOCRATIC PARTY LOST—"SQUATTER SOVEREIGNTY"—PROPERLY CHARACTERIZED—DAVIS' COURSE IN THE KANSAS STRUGGLE—DEBATE WITH SENATOR FESSENDEN—PEN-AND-INK SKETCH OF MR. DAVIS AT THIS PERIOD—TRUE SIGNIFICANCE OF POLITICAL EVENTS TO THE SOUTH—SHE RIGHTLY INTERPRETS THEM—MR. DAVIS' COURSE SUBSEQUENT TO THE KANSAS IMBROGLIO—HIS DEBATES WITH DOUGLAS—TWO DIFFERENT SCHOOLS OF PARLIAMENTARY SPEAKING—DAVIS THE LEADER OF THE REGULAR DEMOCRACY IN THE THIRTY-SIXTH CONGRESS—HIS RESOLUTIONS—HIS CONSISTENCY—COURSE AS TO GENERAL LEGISLATION—VISITS THE NORTH—SPEAKS IN PORTLAND, BOSTON, NEW YORK, AND OTHER PLACES—REPLY TO AN INVITATION TO ATTEND THE WEBSTER BIRTH-DAY FESTIVAL—MR. SEWARD'S ANNOUNCEMENT OF THE "IRREPRESSIBLE CONFLICT"—MR. DAVIS BEFORE MISSISSIPPI DEMOCRATIC STATE CONVENTION—PROGRESS OF DISUNION—DISSOLUTION OF THE DEMOCRATIC PARTY—SPEECHES OF MR. DAVIS AT PORTLAND AND IN SENATE.

MR. DAVIS returned to the Senate at a period marked by agitation, no less menacing to the Union than that which had so seriously threatened it in 1850. His health at this time was exceedingly infirm, and for several months he was so much prostrated by his protracted sufferings, that a proper regard for the suggestions of prudence would have justified his entire abstinence from the labors and excitements of this stormy period. Again and again, however, did his heroic devotion carry him from his sick bed to the capitol, to engage in the death-struggle of the South, with her leagued enemies, for safety in the Union, which she was still loath to abandon, even under the pressure of intolerable wrong. Frequently, with attenuated frame and bandaged eyes, he was to be seen in the Senate, at moments critical in the fierce sectional conflict; and at the final struggle upon the Kansas question, not even the earnest admonitions of his physician, that to leave his chamber would probably be followed by the most dangerous results, were availing to induce his absence from the scene.

The opening events of the first session of the Thirty-fifth Congress, (the first incidental to the administration of Mr. Buchanan,) were far from being auspicious of the continued unity of the Democratic party, which, for several years past, the intelligence of the country had correctly appreciated as an essential condition to the preservation of the Union.

Mainly through the undivided support given him by the South, Mr. Buchanan was elected upon the Cincinnati platform of 1856, which was a re-affirmation of the cardinal tenets of the Democratic faith, involving also emphatic approval of the Kansas-Nebraska legislation two years previous. Not until months after his inauguration were there any indications of hostility to his administration within the ranks of his own party. Nor had there been any avowed difference of construction as to the end and effect of the legislation of 1854. The rare unanimity with which the South had been rallied to the support of the Democracy was based upon the unreserved admission, by all parties, that the Kansas-Nebraska act was designedly friendly in its *spirit*, at all events, to Southern interests. No Southern statesman, for a moment, dreamed that it was capable of an interpretation unfriendly to his section. That the plain purpose of the bill was to remove the subject of slavery outside the bounds of congressional discussion, and to place it in the disposition of the States separately, and in the *Territories, when organizing for admission as States*, was regarded by the South as the leading vital principle which challenged her enthusiastic support. Such, indeed, was the doctrine asserted by the entire Democratic party of the South, enunciated by the administration, and tacitly approved by the Northern Democracy. Very soon, however, after the meeting of Congress, the action of Senator Douglas revealed him as the instrument of disorganization in his party. To a proper understanding of his motives and conduct at this conjuncture, a brief statement of his antecedents is essential.

Stephen A. Douglas was now in the meridian of life and the full maturity of his unquestionably vigorous intellectual powers. For twenty-five years he had been prominent in the arena of politics, and as a member of Congress his course had been so eminently politic and judicious as to make him a favorite with the Democracy, both North and South. To an unexampled degree his public life illustrated the combination of those characteristics of the demagogue, a fertile ingenuity, facile accommodation to circumstances, and wonderful gifts of the *ad captandum* species of oratory, so captivating to the populace, which in America peculiarly constitute the attributes of the "rising man." Douglas was not wanting in noble and attractive qualities of manhood. His courage was undoubted, his generosity was princely in its munificence to his personal friends, and he frequently manifested a lofty magnanimity. In his early youth, deprived of the advantages of fortune and position, the discipline of his career was not propitious to the development of the higher qualities of statesmanship—with which, indeed, he was scantily endowed by nature. It is as the accomplished politician, subtle, ready, fearless, and indefatigable, that he must be remembered. In this latter character he was unrivaled.

Not less than Davis was Douglas a representative man, yet no two men were more essentially dissimilar, and no two lives ever actuated by aspirations and instincts more unlike. Douglas was the representative of expediency—Davis the exponent of principles. In his party associations Douglas would tolerate the largest latitude of individual opinion, while Davis was always for a policy clearly defined and unmistakable; and upon a matter of vital principle, like Percy, would reluctantly surrender even the "ninth part of a hair." To maintain the united action of the Democratic party on election day, to defeat its opponents, to secure the rewards of success, Douglas would allow a thousand different constructions of the party creed by as many factions. Davis, on the other hand, would, and eventually did, approve the dissolution of the party, when it refused an open, manly enunciation of its faith. For mere party success Douglas cared every thing, and Davis nothing, save as it ensured the triumph of Constitutional principles. Both loved the Union and sought its perpetuity, but by different methods; Douglas by never-ending compromises of a quarrel, which he should have known that the North would never permit to be amicably settled; by staving off and ignoring issues which were to be solved only by being squarely met. Davis, too, was not unwilling to compromise, but he wearied of perpetual concession by the South, in the meanwhile the

North continuing its hostility, both open and insidious, and urged a settlement of all differences upon a basis of simple and exact justice to both sections.

Douglas was preëminently the representative politician of his section, and throughout his career was a favorite with that boastful, bloated, and mongrel element, which is violently called the "American people," and which is the ruling element in elections in the Northern cities. In character and conduct he embodied many of its materialistic and socialistic ideas, its false conception of liberty, its pernicious dogmas of equality, and not a little of its rowdyism.

Davis was the champion of the South, her civilization, rights, honor, and dignity. He was the fitting and adequate exponent of a civilization which rested upon an intellectual and æsthetical development, upon lofty and generous sentiments of manhood, a dignified conservatism, and the proud associations of ancestral distinction in the history of the Union. Always the Senator in the sense of the ideal of dignity and courtesy which is suggested by that title, he was also the *gentleman* upon all occasions; never condescending to flatter or soothe the mob, or to court popular favor, he lost none of that polished and distinguished manner, in the presence of a "fierce Democracie," which made him the ornament of the highest school of oratory and statesmanship of his country.

The ambition of Douglas was unbounded. The recognized leader, for several years, of the Northern Democracy, his many fine personal qualities and courageous resistance of the ultra Abolitionists secured for him a considerable number of supporters in the Southern wing of that party. The Presidency was the goal of his ambition, and for twenty years his course had been sedulously adjusted to the attainment of that most coveted of prizes to the American politician. On repeated occasions he had been flattered by a highly complimentary vote in the nominating conventions of the Democracy. Hitherto he had been compelled to yield his pretensions in favor of older members of his party or upon considerations of temporary availability. It was evident, however, that in order to be President, he must secure the nomination in 1860. The continued ascendancy of the Democracy was no longer, as heretofore, a foregone conclusion, and, besides, there were others equally aspiring and available. His Presidential aspirations appeared, indeed, to be without hope or resource, save through the agency of some adroit *coup d'etat*, by which the truculent and dominant free-soil sentiment of the North, which he had so much affronted by his bid for Southern support in the introduction of the Kansas-Nebraska bill, could be conciliated. In Illinois, his own State, the Abolition strength was alarmingly on the increase, and to secure his return to the Senate at the election to be held in 1858, an object of prime importance in the promotion of his more ambitious pretensions, he did not scruple to assume a position, falsifying his previous record, wantonly insulting and defiant to his Southern associates, and in bold antagonism to a Democratic administration. The sequel of this rash and ill-judged course was the overthrow of his own political fortunes, the disintegration of his party, and the attempted dissolution of the Union.

The earliest recommendations of Mr. Buchanan, respecting the Kansas controversy, which, several months since, had developed in that Territory into a species of predatory warfare, marked by deeds of violence and atrocity, between the Abolition and Pro-slavery parties, were signalized by a coalition of the followers of Douglas with the Abolitionists and other opponents of the administration. The speedy pacification of the disorders in Kansas, by the prompt admission of that Territory, was the condition essential to the success of Mr. Buchanan's entire policy. He accordingly recommended the admission of Kansas into the Union, with the "Lecompton" constitution, which had been adopted in September, 1857, by the decisive vote of six thousand two hundred and twenty-six in favor of that constitution, with slavery, and five hundred and nine for it, without slavery. A rival instrument, adopted by an election notoriously held exclusively under the control of Abolitionists, prohibiting slavery, was likewise presented.

For months the controversy was waged in Congress between the friends of the administration and its enemies, and finally resulted in a practical triumph of the Free-soil principle. The Anti-Lecompton coalition of Douglas and the Abolitionists, aided by the defection of a few Southern members, successfully embarrassed the policy of the administration by defeating its recommendations, and eventually carried a measure acceptable to Northern sentiments and interests.

Mr. Douglas thus triumphed over a Democratic administration, at the same time giving a shock to the unity of the Democratic party, from which it has never recovered, and effectually neutralized its power as a breakwater of the Union against the waves of sectional dispute. The alienation between himself and his former associates was destined never to be adjusted, as indeed it never should have been, in consideration of his inexcusable recreancy to the immemorial faith of his party. Mr. Douglas simply abandoned the South, at the very first moment when his aid was seriously demanded. Nay, more; he carried with him a quiver of Parthian arrows, which he discharged into her bosom at a most critical moment in her unequal contest.

It is not to be denied that Mr. Douglas' new interpretation of the Kansas-Nebraska act was urged by himself and his advocates as having a merit not to be overlooked by the North, in its suggestion of a method of restricting slavery, presenting superior advantages. "Squatter sovereignty," as advocated by Mr. Douglas, proposing the decision of the slavery question by the people of the Territories, while yet unprepared to ask admission as States, was far more effectual in its plans against slavery, and only less prompt and open, than the designs of the Abolitionists. It would enable the "Emigrant Aid Societies," and imported janizaries of Abolition to exclude the institutions of the South from the Territories, the joint possessions of the two sections, acquired by an enormously disproportionate sacrifice on the part of the South, with a certainty not to be realized, for years to come, perhaps, from the Abolition policy of congressional prohibition.* According to Mr. Douglas' theory, the existence of slavery in all the Territories was to depend upon the verdict of a few hundred settlers or "squatters" upon the public lands. It practically conceded to Northern interests and ideas every State to be hereafter admitted, and under the operation of such a policy it was not difficult to anticipate the fate of slavery, at last even in the States.

From the inception of this controversy until its close Mr. Davis was fully committed to the policy of Mr. Buchanan, and his position was in perfect harmony with that of all the leading statesmen of the South. Less prominent, perhaps, in

* Governor Wise, of Virginia, characterized "squatter sovereignty" as a "short cut to all the ends of Black Republicanism."

debate, from his constant ill-health during the first session, than at any other period of his public life, he was still zealous and influential.

An interesting incident of the session was a discussion between Mr. Davis and Mr. Fessenden, of Maine, a Senator second only to Mr. Seward among Abolition leaders, in point of intellect, and behind none in his truculent animosity to Southern institutions. Reviewing the message of Mr. Buchanan with great severity, Fessenden took occasion to discuss elaborately the slavery question, with all its incidental issues. Mr. Davis replied, not at great length, but with much force and spirit. The discussion terminated with the following colloquy, which is interesting chiefly in its personal allusions:

"Mr. Fessenden. . . . . . . Sir, I have avowed no disunion sentiments on this floor—neither here nor elsewhere. Can the honorable gentleman from Mississippi say as much?

"Mr. Davis. Yes.

"Mr. Fessenden. I am glad to hear it, then.

"Mr. Davis. Yes. I have long sought for a respectable man who would allege the contrary.

"Mr. Fessenden. I make no allegation. I asked if he could say as much. I am glad to hear him say so, because I must say to him that the newspapers have represented him as making a speech in Mississippi, in which he said he came into General Pierce's cabinet a disunion man. If he never made it, very well.

"Mr. Davis. I will thank you to produce that newspaper.

"Mr. Fessenden. I can not produce it, but I can produce an extract from it in another paper.

"Mr. Davis. An extract! then that falsifies the text.

"Mr. Fessenden. I am very glad to hear the Senator say so. I made no accusation—I put the question to him. If he denies it, very well. I only say that, with all the force and energy with which he denies it, so do I. The accusation never has been made against me before. On what ground does the Senator now put it? . . .

"MR. DAVIS. Does the Senator ask me for an answer?

"MR. FESSENDEN. Certainly, if the Senator feels disposed to give one.

"MR. DAVIS. If you ask me for an answer, it is easy. I said your position was fruitful of such a result. I did not say you avowed the object—nothing of the sort, but the reverse. . . .

"MR. FESSENDEN. That is a matter of opinion, on which I have a right to entertain my view as well as the Senator his. . . .

"MR. DAVIS. Mr. President, I rise principally for the purpose of saying that I do not know whence springs this habit of talking about intimidation. I am not the first person toward whom a reply has been made, that we are not to carry our ends by intimidation. I try to intimidate nobody; I threaten nobody; and I do not believe—let me say it once for all—that any body is afraid of me—and I do not want any body to be afraid of me.

"MR. FESSENDEN. I am. [Laughter.]

"MR. DAVIS. I am sorry to hear it; and if the Senator is really so, I shall never speak to him in decided terms again.

"MR. FESSENDEN. I speak of it only in an intellectual point of view. [Laughter.]

"MR. DAVIS. Then, sir, the Senator was in a Pickwickian sense when he began; there were no threats, no intimidations, and he is just where he would have been if he had said nothing." [Laughter.] . . . .

While the Kansas question was pending in Congress, a sketch of Mr. Davis, in connection with two other prominent Southern Senators, which appeared in the correspondence of a leading journal, was extensively copied in the newspapers of the day. We extract that portion which relates specially to Mr. Davis. The portrait is from the pen of one who had no sympathy with his political views:

DAVIS, HUNTER, AND TOOMBS,

THE SOUTHERN TRIUMVIRATE.

[Correspondence of the Missouri Democrat.]

"WASHINGTON CITY, January 21.

"Yesterday, when Hale was speaking, the right side of the chamber was empty, (as it generally is during the delivery of an anti-slavery speech,) with the exception of a group of three who sat near the centre of the vacant space. This remarkable group, which wore the air if not the ensigns of power, authority, and public care, was composed of Senators Davis, Hunter, and Toombs. They were engaged in an earnest colloquy, which, however, was foreign to the argument Hale was elaborating; for though the connection of their words was broken before it reached the gallery, their voices were distinctly audible, and gave signs of their abstraction. They were thinking aloud. If they had met together, under the supervision of some artist gifted with the faculty of illustrating history and character by attitude and expression, who designed to paint them, in fresco, on the walls of the new Senate chamber, the combination could not have been more appropriately arranged than chance arranged it on this occasion. Toombs sits among the opposition on the left, Hunter and Davis on the right; and the fact that the two first came to Davis' seat—the one gravitating to it from a remote, the other from a near point—may be held to indicate which of the three is the preponderating body in the system, if preponderance there be; and whose figure should occupy the foreground of the picture if any precedence is to be accorded. Davis sat erect and composed; Hunter, listening, rested his head on his hand; and Toombs, inclining forward, was speaking vehemently. Their respective attitudes were no bad illustration of their individuality. Davis impressed the spectator, who observed the easy but authoritative bearing with which he put aside or assented to Toomb's suggestions, with the notion of some slight superiority, some hardly-acknowledged leadership; and Hunter's attentiveness and impassibility were characteristic of his nature, for his profundity of intellect wears the guise of stolidity, and his continuous industry that of inertia; while Toomb's quick utterance and restless head bespoke his nervous temperament and activity of mind. But, though each is different from either of the others, the three have several attributes in common. They are equally eminent as statesmen and debaters; they are devoted to the same cause; they are equals in rank, and rivals in ambition; and they are about the same age, and none of them—let young America take notice—wears either beard or mustache. I come again to the traits which distinguish them from each other. In face and form, Davis represents the Norman type with singular fidelity, if my conception of that type be correct. He is tall and sinewy, with fair hair, gray eyes, which are clear rather than bright, high forehead, straight nose, thin, compressed lips, and pointed chin. His cheek bones are hollow, and the vicinity of his mouth is deeply furrowed with intersecting lines. Leanness of face, length and sharpness of feature, and length of limb, and intensity of expression, rendered acute by angular, facial outline, are the general characteristics of his appearance."

The controversy, excited by the question of the admission of Kansas, can not be viewed as having terminated with the mere practical decision of her status, as a State tolerating or prohibiting slavery. Southern men had freely admitted the improbability of the permanent abiding of the institution in that Territory, or elsewhere, north of the line of 36° 30′, and their defeat had a far more alarming significance than the exclusion of slavery from soil where the laws of nature opposed its location. Important conclusions were deducible from the lesson of Kansas, which the South must have been smitten with voluntary blindness not to have accepted. Of the purpose of the Republican party, never to consent to the admission of additional slave States, there was added to constantly accumulating proof from other sources, the bold declarations of Abolition members of Congress. Recent experience clearly demonstrated that the South could no longer rely upon the Northern Democracy in support of the plainest guarantees of the Constitution, for the protection of her property, when they were in conflict with the dominant fanaticism of that section. Accordingly, the Southern Democracy, wisely and bravely resolved, and the unfortunate issue should not prejudge their action, to require of their Northern associates, as the condition of continued cooperation, a pledge of better faith in the future.

It was in the progress of events, which may be justly called the sequel of the Kansas controversy, that Mr. Davis was most conspicuous during his second service in the Senate. His course was such as might have been anticipated from his zealous and vigilant regard for constitutional principles, and the rights and interests of his section. His feeble health had prevented his frequent participation in the struggles incidental to the Kansas question, but in those subsequent struggles, which marked the dissolution of the Democratic party, he was the constant, bold, and able adversary of Douglas. The ingenious sophistries of the latter were subjected to no more searching and scathing refutations than those with which Davis met his every attempt at their illustration.

At this period the position of Mr. Davis was no less prominent than in 1850, though his speeches were less frequent and voluminous. Upon both occasions his elevation was an ample reward to honorable ambition, but would have been perilous in the extreme had he been deficient in those great and rare qualities which were necessary to its maintenance. Among his numerous contests with the distinguished exponents of the sentiment in opposition to the South, none are more memorable than his collisions with Douglas.

Of these the most striking occurred on the 23d of February, 1859, and on the 16th and 17th of May, 1860. To have matched Douglas with an ordinary contestant, must always have resulted in disaster; it would have been to renew the contest of Athelstane against Ivanhoe. Douglas was accustomed to testify, cheerfully, to the power of Davis, as evinced in their senatorial struggles; and it is very certain that at no other hands did he fare so badly, unless an exception be made in favor of the remarkable speech of Senator Benjamin, of Louisiana. The latter was an adept in the strategy of debate, a parliamentary Suchet.

The 23d of February, 1859, was the occasion of a protracted battle between Davis and Douglas, lasting from midday until nearly night. This speech of Mr. Davis is, in many respects, inferior to his higher oratorical efforts, realizing less of the forms of oratory which he usually illustrated so happily, and is wanting somewhat in that symmetry, harmony, and comeliness in all its features, with which his senatorial efforts are generally wrought to the perfection of expression. The circumstances under which it was delivered, however, fully meet this criticism, and show a most remarkable readiness for the instantaneous and hurried grapple of debate, and this latter quality was the strong point of Douglas' oratory. The latter had replied at great length, and with evident preparation, to a speech made by Mr. Davis' colleague (Mr. Brown), who was not present during Douglas' rejoinder. Without hesitation Mr. Davis assumed the place of his absent colleague, and the result was a running debate, lasting several hours, and exhibiting on both sides all the vivacious readiness of a gladiatorial combat.

In their ordinary and characteristic speeches there was an antithesis, no less marked than in their characters as men. Douglas was peculiarly *American* in his style of speaking. He dealt largely in the *argumentum ad hominem;* was very adroit in pointing out immaterial inconsistencies in his antagonists; he rarely discussed general principles; always avoided questions of abstract political science, and struggled to force the entire question into juxtaposition with the practical considerations of the immediate present.

In nearly all of Davis' speeches is recognized the pervasion of intellect, which is preserved even in his most impassioned passages. He goes to the very "foundations of jurisprudence," illustrates by historical example, and throws upon his subject the full radiance of that noble light which is shed by diligent inquiry into the abstract truths of political and moral science. Strength, animation, energy without vehemence, classical elegance, and a luminous simplicity, are features in Mr. Davis' oratory which rendered him one of the most finished, logical, and effective of contemporary parliamentary speakers.

During the Thirty-sixth Congress, which assembled in December, 1859, Mr. Davis was the recognized leader of the Democratic majority of the Senate. His efforts, during this session, were probably the ablest of his life, and never did his great powers of analysis and generalization appear to greater advantage. On the second of February, 1860, Mr. Davis presented a series of seven resolves, which embodied the views of the administration, of an overwhelming majority of the Democratic members of the Senate, and of the Southern Democracy, and were opposed by Mr. Douglas (though absent from the Senate by sickness), Mr. Pugh, and by the Abolition Senators. They are important as the substantial expression of the doctrines upon which the Southern Democracy were already prepared to insist at the approaching National Convention.

The *first* resolution affirms the sovereignty of the States and their delegation of authority to the Federal Government, to secure each State against *domestic* no less than foreign dangers. This resolution was designed with special reference to the recent outrages of John Brown and his associate conspirators, several of whom had expiated their crimes upon the gallows, at the hands of the authorities of Virginia.

Resolution *second* affirms the recognition of slavery as property by the Constitution, and that all efforts to injure it by citizens of non-slaveholding States are violations of faith.

Third insists upon the absolute equality of the States.

The *fourth* resolution of the series, which embodied the material point of difference between Mr. Douglas and the majority of Democratic Senators, was modified, as stated by Mr. Davis, "after conference with friends," and finally made to read thus:

"*Resolved*, That neither Congress nor a Territorial Legislature, whether by direct legislation, or legislation of an indirect and unfriendly character, possesses power to annul or impair the constitutional right of any citizen of the United States to take his slave property into the common Territories, and there hold and enjoy the same while the territorial condition remains."

Fifth declares it the duty of Congress to supply any needed protection to constitutional rights in a Territory, provided the executive and judicial authority has not the adequate means.

The *sixth* resolution was an emphatic repudiation of what Mr. Douglas, by an ingenious perversion of terms, and a bold array of sophisms, was pleased to designate "popular sovereignty"—reading thus:

"*Resolved*, That the inhabitants of a Territory of the United States, when they rightfully form a constitution to be admitted as a State into the Union, may then, for the first time, like the people of a State when forming a new constitution, decide for themselves whether slavery, as a domestic institution, shall be maintained or prohibited within their jurisdiction; and 'they shall be admitted into the Union, with or without slavery, as their constitution may prescribe at the time of their admission.'"

The *seventh* and last of the series affirmed the validity and sanctity of the Fugitive Slave Law, and denounced all acts, whether of individuals or of State Legislatures, to defeat its action.

The struggle upon these resolutions lasted more than three months, the Senate not reaching a vote upon the first of the series until May 24, 1860. They constituted substantially the platform presented by the South at the Charleston Democratic Convention, in April, and upon which, after the withdrawal of the Southern delegations, the Presidential ticket of Breckinridge and Lane was nominated, and supported in the ensuing canvass, receiving the electoral votes of eleven States of the South.

It was alleged against these resolutions, and the general principle of protection to Southern property in the Territories, which their advocates demanded should be asserted in the Democratic creed, that they involved a new issue, raised for factious purposes, and were not sanctioned by any previous action of the party. This, even if it had been true, which assuredly it was not, constituted no sufficient reason for denying a plain constitutional right.

But, however sustained might have been this charge of inconsistency against other Southern leaders, it had no application to Davis. Indeed, Douglas unequivocally admitted that the position assumed by Davis in 1860 was precisely that to which he had held for twenty years previous. While the Oregon Bill was pending in the Senate, on the 23d of June, 1848, Mr. Davis offered this amendment:

> "*Provided*, That nothing contained in this act shall be so construed as to authorize the prohibition of domestic slavery in said Territory whilst it remains in the condition of a Territory of the United States."

Eleven years afterwards, in his address before the Mississippi Democratic Convention, July 5, 1859, he said:

> "But if the rules of proceeding remain unchanged, then all the remedies of the civil law would be available for the protection of property in slaves; or if the language of the organic act, by specifying chancery and common-law jurisdiction, denies to us the more ample remedies of the civil law, then those known to the common law are certainly in force; and these, I have been assured by the highest authority, will be found sufficient. If this be so, then we are content; if it should prove otherwise, then we but ask what justice can not deny—the legislation needful to enable the General Government to perform its legitimate functions; and, in the meantime, we deny the power of Congress to abridge

or to destroy our constitutional rights, or of the Territorial Legislature to obstruct the remedies known to the common law of the United States."

In 1848 he advocated General Cass' election *in spite* of the Nicholson letter, and not because he either approved or failed to detect the dangerous heresies which it contained. As a choice of evils, he preferred Cass, even upon the Nicholson letter, to General Taylor, his father-in-law, both because Cass was the choice of his own party, and he distrusted the influences which he foresaw would govern the administration of Taylor.

The attention of Mr. Davis was far from being confined to the slavery question and the issues which grew out of it during the important period which we have sketched. His extensive acquaintance with the practical labors of legislation, and his uniformly thorough information upon all questions of domestic economy, foreign affairs, the finances, and the army, were amply exemplified, to the great benefit of the country.

During the debate in the Thirty-fifth Congress, on the bill proposing the issue of $20,000,000 of Treasury notes, which he opposed, he avowed himself in favor of the abolition of custom-houses, and the disbanding of the army of retainers employed to collect the import duties. Free trade was always an important article of his political creed. He valued its fraternizing effects upon mankind, its advantages to the laboring classes; and held that, under a system of free trade, the Government would not be defrauded. He traced the financial distress of the country, in the "crisis" of 1857, to its commercial dependence on New York, whose embarrassments must, so long as that dependence continued, always afflict the country at large. The army, as on previous occasions, received a large share of his attention, and he advocated its increase on a plan similar to that of Mr. Calhoun, when Secretary of War under President Monroe, providing a skeleton organization in peace, capable of expansion in the event of war. The fishing bounties he opposed, as being obnoxious to the objections urged against class legislation.

In the summer of 1858, during the recess of Congress, Mr. Davis visited the North, with a view to the recuperation of his health. Sailing from Baltimore to Boston, he traversed a considerable portion of New England, and sojourned for some time in Portland, Maine. His health was materially benefited by the bracing salubrity of that delightful locality, and, both here and at other points, he was received with demonstrations of profound respect. Upon several occasions he was persuaded to deliver public addresses, which were largely read and criticized. They were every-where commended for their admirable catholicity of sentiment, and not less for their bold assertions of principles than for their emphatic avowals of attachment to the union of the States. His speech at Portland, Maine,* was especially admired for its statesman-like dignity, and was singularly free from partisan or sectional temper. In his journey through the States of Massachusetts and New York, he was tendered distinguished honors, and addressed the people of the leading cities. On the 10th of October, he spoke in Faneuil Hall, Boston, and, on the 19th, he addressed an immense Democratic ratification meeting in New York.

The following is an extract from his address upon the latter occasion:

* To be found at the conclusion of this chapter.

"To each community belongs the right to decide for itself what institutions it will have—to each people sovereign in their own sphere. It belongs only to them to decide what shall be property. You have decided it for yourselves, Mississippi has done so. Who has the right to gainsay it? [Applause.] It was the assertion of the right of independence—of that very right which led your fathers into the war of the Revolution. [Applause.] It is that which constitutes the doctrine of State Rights, on which it is my pleasure to stand. Congress has no power to determine what shall be property anywhere. Congress has only such grants as are contained in the Constitution; and it conferred no power to rule with despotic hands over the independence of the Territories."

The second session of the Thirty-fifth Congress was comparatively uneventful. Mr. Davis was an influential advocate of the Pacific Railroad by the Southern route. His most elaborate effort during this session was his argument against the French Spoliation Bill—denying that the failure of the Government, in its earlier history, to prosecute the just claims of American citizens on the Government of France, made it incumbent upon the present generation to satisfy the obligations of justice incurred in the past.

In reply to an invitation to attend the Webster Birthday Festival, held in Boston, in January, 1859, Mr. Davis wrote as follows:

"At a time when partisans avow the purpose to obliterate the landmarks of our fathers, and fanaticism assails the barriers they erected for the protection of rights coeval with and essential to the existence of the Union—when Federal offices have been sought by inciting constituencies to hostile aggressions, and exercised, not as a trust for the common welfare, but as the means of disturbing domestic tranquillity—when oaths to support the Constitution have been taken with a mental reservation to disregard its spirit, and subvert the purposes for which it was established—surely it becomes all who are faithful to the compact of our Union, and who are resolved to maintain and preserve it, to compare differences on questions of mere expediency, and, forming deep around the institutions we inherited, stand united to uphold, with unfaltering intent, a banner on which is inscribed the Constitutional Union of free, equal, and independent States.

"May the vows of 'love and allegiance,' which you propose to renew as a fitting tribute to the memory of the illustrious statesman whose birth you commemorate, find an echo in the heart of every patriot in our land, and tend to the revival of that fraternity which bore our fathers through the Revolution to the consummation of the independence they transmitted to us, and the establishment of the more perfect Union which their wisdom devised to bless their posterity for ever!

"Though deprived of the pleasure of mingling my affectionate memories and aspirations with yours, I send you my cordial greeting to the friends of the Constitution, and ask to be enrolled among those whose mission is, by fraternity and good faith to every constitutional obligation, to insure that, from the Aroostook to San Diego, from Key West to Puget's Sound, the grand arch of our political temple shall stand unshaken."

In the meantime a variety of events measurably added to the vehemence of the sectional dispute, which never, for a moment, had exhibited any abatement since the opening of the Kansas *imbroglio.* The antagonism between the two sections, becoming more and more pronounced each day, rapidly developed the true character of the struggle, as one for existence on the part of the South, against the revolutionary designs of the North. Mr. Seward, the Ajax of Black Republicanism, the founder and leader of the party organized for the destruction of Southern institutions, in the fall of 1858, at the city of Rochester, for the first time proclaimed his revolutionary doctrine of an "irrepressible conflict" between the civilizations of the two sections. This announcement, from such a source, could only be accepted by the South as a menace to her peace and security. Such was her construction of it.

In his address before the Mississippi Democratic Convention, in July, 1859, from which we have already quoted, Mr. Davis said:

"We have witnessed the organization of a party seeking the possession of the Government, not for the common good, not for their own particular benefit, but as the means of executing a hostile purpose against a portion of the States."

Approaching more directly the doctrine of Mr. Seward, he said:

"The success of such a party would indeed produce an 'irrepressible conflict.' To you would be presented the question, Will you allow the Constitutional Union to be changed into the despotism of a majority? Will you become the subjects of a hostile Government? or will you, outside of the Union, assert the equality, the liberty and sovereignty to which you were born? For myself I say, as I said on a former occasion, in the contingency of the election of a President on the platform of Mr. Seward's Rochester speech, let the Union be dissolved. Let the 'great, but not the greatest, evil' come; for, as did the great and good Calhoun, from whom is drawn that expression of value, I love and venerate the Union of these States, but I love liberty and Mississippi more."

When Congress assembled, in December, 1859, the lawless

expedition of John Brown had greatly accelerated the inevitable climax of disunion. Thenceforward the incipient revolution was, to a great extent, transferred from the hands of Congress, whose action was but lightly regarded in comparison with the animated scenes which marked the State conventions and popular assemblages, held with reference to the approaching presidential nominations.

Mr. Davis approved the test made at the Charleston Convention, by the Southern Democracy, as to the construction of the Cincinnati platform, and the demand for a more explicit announcement of the position of the party concerning slavery in the Territories. His speech, in reply to Judge Douglas, on the 16th and 17th of May, 1860, is a vindication of Southern action at Charleston, and an exhaustive discussion of all the phases of the issue upon which the Democracy had divided.

Events soon demonstrated the irreconcilable nature of the antagonism which had severed this giant organization. It had simply realized the destiny of political parties. In one generation they rise, as a virtue and a necessity, to remedy disorders and reform abuses; in another generation, they are themselves the apologists of corruption and the perpetrators of wrong. The Democratic party became insensible to the appeals of principle, and its fifty years' lease of power terminated, not speedily to be recovered.

HON. JEFFERSON DAVIS AT PORTLAND, MAINE.

[From the Eastern Argus.]

We are gratified in being able to offer our readers a faithful and quite full report of the speech of Hon. Jefferson Davis, of Mississippi, on the occasion of the serenade given him by the citizens of Portland, without distinction of party, on Friday evening last. It will be read with interest and pleasure, and we can not doubt that every sentiment, uttered by the distinguished Mississippian, will find a hearty response and approval from the citizens of Maine. The occasion was indeed a pleasing, a hopeful one. It was in every respect the expression of generous sentiments, of kindness, hospitality, friendly regard, and the brotherhood of American citizenship. Prominent men of all parties were present, and the expression, without exception, so far as we have heard, has been that of unmingled gratification; and the scene was equally pleasant to look upon. The beautiful mansion of Rensallaer Cram, Esq., directly opposite to Madame Blanchard's, was illuminated, and the light thrown from the windows of the two houses revealed to view the large and perfectly orderly assemblage with which Park and Danforth Streets were crowded. We regret that our readers can get no idea of the musical voice and inspiring eloquence of the speaker from a report of his remarks; but it is the best we can do for them. After the music had ceased, Mr. Davis appeared upon the steps, and as soon as the prolonged applause with which he was greeted had subsided, he spoke in substance as follows:

FELLOW-CITIZENS: Accept my sincere thanks for this manifestation of your kindness. Vanity does not lead me so far to misconceive your purpose as to appropriate the demonstration to myself; but it is not the less gratifying to me to be made the medium through which Maine tenders an expression of regard to her sister, Mississippi. It is, moreover, with feelings of profound gratification that I witness this indication of that national sentiment and fraternity which made us, and which alone can keep us, one people. At a period but as yesterday, when compared with the life of nations, these States were separate, and, in some respects, opposing colonies, their only relation to each other was that of a common allegiance to the Government of Great Britain. So separate, indeed almost hostile, was their attitude, that when General Stark, of Bennington memory, was captured by savages on the headwaters of the Kennebec, he was subsequently taken by them to Albany, where they went to sell furs, and again led away a captive, without interference on the part of the inhabitants of that neighboring colony to demand or obtain his release. United as we now are, were a citizen of the United States, as an act of hostility to our country, imprisoned or slain in any quarter of the world, whether on land or sea, the people of each and every State of the Union, with one heart and with one voice, would demand redress, and woe be to him against whom a brother's blood cried to us from the ground. Such is the fruit of the wisdom and the justice with which our fathers bound contending colonies into confederation, and blended different habits and rival interests into a harmonious whole, so that, shoulder to shoulder, they entered on the trial of the Revolution, and step with step trod its thorny paths until they reached the height of national independence, and founded the constitutional representative liberty which is our birthright.

When the mother country entered upon her career of oppression, in disregard of chartered and constitutional rights, our forefathers did not stop to measure the exact weight of the burden, or to ask whether the pressure bore most upon this colony or upon that, but saw in it the infraction of a great principle, the denial of a common right, in defense of which they made common cause—Massachusetts, Virginia, and South Carolina vieing with each other as to who should be foremost in the struggle, where the penalty of failure would be a dishonorable grave. Tempered by the trials and sacrifices of the Revolution, dignified by its noble purposes, elevated by its brilliant triumphs, endeared to each other by its glorious memories, they abandoned the Confederacy, not to fly apart when the outward pressure of hostile fleets and armies were removed, but to draw closer their embrace in the formation of a more perfect Union.

By such men, thus trained and ennobled, our Constitution was framed. It stands a monument of principle, of forecast, and, above all, of that liberality which made each willing to sacrifice local interest, individual prejudice, or temporary good to the general welfare and the perpetuity of the republican institutions which they had passed through fire and blood to secure. The grants were as broad as were necessary for the functions of the general agent, and the mutual concessions were twice blessed, blessing him who gave and him who received. Whatever was necessary for domestic government—requisite in the social organization of each community—was retained by the States and the people thereof; and these it was made the duty of all to defend and maintain. Such, in very general terms, is the rich political legacy our fathers bequeathed to us. Shall we preserve and transmit it to posterity? Yes, yes, the heart responds; and the judgment answers, the task is easily performed. It but requires that each should attend to that which most concerns him, and on which alone he has rightful power to decide and to act; that each should adhere to the terms of a written compact, and that all should coöperate for that which interest, duty, and honor demand.

For the general affairs of our country, both foreign and domestic, we have a national Executive and a national Legislature. Representatives and Senators are chosen by districts and by States, but their acts affect the whole country, and their obligations are to the whole people. He who, holding either seat, would confine his investigations to the mere interests of his immediate constituents, would be derelict to his plain duty; and he who would legislate in hostility to any section, would be morally unfit for the station, and surely an unsafe depository, if not a treacherous guardian, of the inheritance with which we are blessed. No one more than myself recognizes the binding force of the allegiance which the citizen owes to the State of his citizenship, but that State being a party to our compact, a member of the Union, fealty to the Federal Constitution is not in opposition to, but flows from the allegiance due to one of the United States. Washington was not less a Virginian when he commanded at Boston, nor did Gates or Greene weaken the bonds which bound them to their several States by their campaigns in the South. In proportion as a citizen loves his own State, will he strive to honor by preserving her name and her fame free from the tarnish of having failed to observe her obligations and to fulfill her duties to her sister States. Each page of our history is illustrated by the names and deeds of those who have well understood and discharged the obligation. Have we so degenerated that we can no longer emulate their virtues? Have the purposes for which our Union was formed lost their value? Has patriotism ceased to be a virtue, and is narrow sectionalism no longer to be counted a crime? Shall the North not rejoice that the progress of agriculture in the South has given to her great staple the controlling influence of the commerce of the world, and put manufacturing nations under bond to keep the peace with the United States? Shall the South not exult in the fact that the industry and persevering intelligence of the North has placed her mechanical skill in the front ranks of the civilized world—that our mother country, whose haughty Minister, some eighty odd years ago, declared that not a hob-nail should be made in the colonies, which are now the United States, was brought, some four years ago, to recognize our preëminence by sending a commission to examine our workshops and our machinery, to perfect their own manufacture of the arms requisite for their defense? Do not our whole people, interior and seaboard, North, South, East and West, alike feel proud of the hardihood, the enterprise, the skill, and the courage of the Yankee sailor, who has borne our flag far as the ocean bears its foam, and caused the name and character of the United States to be known and respected wherever there is wealth enough to woo commerce and intelligence to honor merit? So long as we preserve and appreciate the achievements of Jefferson and Adams, of Franklin and Madison, of Hamilton, of Hancock, and of Rutledge, men who labored for the whole country, and lived for mankind, we can not sink to the petty strife which would sap the foundations and destroy the political fabric our fathers erected and bequeathed as an inheritance to our posterity forever.

Since the formation of the Constitution a vast extension of territory, and the varied relations arising therefrom, have presented problems which could not have been foreseen. It is just cause for admiration, even wonder, that the provisions of the fundamental law should have been so fully adequate to all the wants of government, new in its organization, and new in many of the principles on which it was founded Whatever fears may have once existed as to the consequences of territorial expansion must give way before the evidence which the past affords. The General Government, strictly confined to its delegated functions, and the State left in the undisturbed exercise of all else, we have a theory and practice which fits our Government for immeasurable domain, and might, under a millennium of nations, embrace mankind.

From the slope of the Atlantic our population, with ceaseless tide, has poured into the wide and fertile valley of the Mississippi, with eddying whirl has passed to the coast of the Pacific; from the West and the East the tides are rushing toward each other, and the mind is carried to the day when all the cultivable land will be inhabited, and the American people will sigh for more wildernesses to conquer. But there is here a physico-political problem presented for our solution. Were it purely physical your past triumphs would leave but little doubt of your capacity to solve it. A community which, when less than twenty thousand, conceived the grand project of crossing the White Mountains, and unaided, save by the stimulus which jeers and prophecies of failure gave, successfully executed the Herculean work, might well be impatient if it were suggested that a physical problem was before us too difficult for mastery. The history of man teaches that high mountains and wide deserts have resisted the permanent extension of empire, and have formed the immutable boundaries of States. From time to time, under some able leader, have the hordes of the upper plains of Asia swept over the adjacent country, and rolled their conquering columns over Southern Europe. Yet, after the lapse of a few generations, the physical law, to which I have referred, has asserted its supremacy, and the boundaries of those States differ little now from those which were obtained three thousand years ago.

Rome flew her conquering eagles over the then known world, and has now subsided into the little territory on which the great city was originally built. The Alps and the Pyranees have been unable to restrain imperial France; but her expansion was a feverish action, her advance and her retreat were tracked with blood, and those mountain ridges are the reëstablished limits of her empire. Shall the Rocky Mountains prove a dividing barrier to us? Were ours a central consolidated Government, instead of a Union of sovereign States, our fate might be learned from the history of other nations. Thanks to the wisdom and independent spirit of our forefathers, this is not the case. Each State having sole charge of its local interests and domestic affairs, the problem, which to others has been insoluble, to us is made easy. Rapid, safe, and easy communication between the Atlantic and the Pacific will give co-intelligence, unity of interest, and coöperation among all parts of our continent-wide Republic. The net-work of railroads which bind the North and the South, the slope of the Atlantic and the valley of the Mississippi, together testify that our people have the power to perform, in that regard, whatever it is their will to do.

We require a railroad to the States of the Pacific for present uses; the time no doubt will come when we shall have need of two or three, it may be, more. Because of the desert character of the interior country the work will be difficult and expensive. It will require the efforts of a united people. The bickerings of little politicians, the jealousies of sections must give way to dignity of purpose and zeal for the common good. If the object be obstructed by contention and division as to whether the route shall be Northern, Southern, or Central, the handwriting is on the wall, and it requires little skill to see that failure is the interpretation of the inscription. You are practical people, and may ask, How is that contest to be avoided? By taking the question out of the hands of politicians altogether. Let the Government give such aid as it is proper for it to render to the company which shall propose the most feasible plan; then leave to capitalists with judgment, sharpened by interest, the selection of the route, and the difficulties will diminish, as did those which you overcame when you connected your harbor with the Canadian provinces.

It would be to trespass on your kindness and to violate the proprieties of the occasion were I to detain the vast concourse which stands before me by entering on the discussion of controverted topics, or by further indulging in the expression of such reflections as circumstances suggest. I came to your city in quest of health and repose. From the moment I entered it you have showered upon me kindness and hospitality. Though my experience has taught me to anticipate good rather than evil from my fellow-man, it had not prepared me to expect such unremitting attention as has here been bestowed. I have been jocularly asked in relation to my coming here, whether I had secured a guarantee for my safety, and lo! I have found it. I stand in the midst of thousands of my fellow-citizens. But, my friends, I came neither distrusting nor apprehensive, of which you have proof in the fact that I brought with me the objects of tenderest affection and solicitude, my wife and my children; they have shared with me your hospitality, and will alike remain your debtors. If, at some future time, when I am mingled with the dust, and the arm of my infant son has been nerved for deeds of manhood, the storm of war should burst upon your city, I feel that, relying upon his inheriting the instincts of his ancestors and mine, I may pledge him in that perilous hour to stand by your side in the defense of your hearth-stones, and in maintaining the honor of a flag whose constellation, though torn and smoked in many a battle by sea and land, has never been stained with dishonor, and will, I trust, forever fly as free as the breeze which unfolds it.

A stranger to you, the salubrity of your location, and the beauty of its scenery were not wholly unknown to me, nor were there wanting associations which busy memory connected with your people. You will pardon me for alluding to one whose genius shed a lustre upon all it touched, and whose qualities gathered about him hosts of friends wherever he was known. Prentiss, a native of Portland, lived from youth to middle age in the county of my residence; and the inquiries which have been made show me that the youth excited the interest which the greatness of the man justified, and that his memory thus remains a link to connect your home with mine. A cursory view, when passing through your town on former occasions, had impressed me with the great advantages of your harbor, its easy entrance, its depth, and its extensive accommodations for shipping. But its advantages and its facilities, as they have been developed by closer inspection, have grown upon me, until I realize that it is no boast, but the language of sober truth, which, in the present state of commerce, pronounces them unequaled in any harbor of our country.

And surely no place could be more inviting to an invalid who sought refuge from the heat of Southern summer. Here waving elms offer him shaded walks, and magnificent residences, surrounded by flowers, fill the mind with ideas of comfort and rest. If, weary of constant contact with his fellow-men, he seeks a deeper seclusion, there, in the background of this grand amphitheater, lie the eternal mountains, frowning with brow of rock and cap of snow upon smiling fields beneath, and there in its recesses may be found as much wildness and as much of solitude as the pilgrim, weary of the cares of life, can desire. If he turn to the front, your capacious harbor, studded with green islands of ever-varying light and shade, and enlightened by all the stirring evidences of commercial activity, offer him the mingled charms of busy life and nature's calm repose. A few miles further, and he may sit upon the quiet shore to listen to the murmuring wave until the troubled spirit sinks to rest; and in the little sail that vanishes on the illimitable sea we find the type of the voyage which he is soon to take, when, his ephemeral existence closed, he embarks for that better state which lies beyond the grave.

Richly endowed as you are by nature in all which contributes to pleasure and to usefulness, the stranger can not pass without paying a tribute to the much which your energy has achieved for yourselves. Where else will one find a more happy union of magnificence and comfort? Where better arrangements to facilitate commerce? Where so much of industry with so little noise and bustle? Where, in a phrase, so much effected in proportion to the means employed? We hear the puff of the engine, the roll of the wheel, the ring of the ax and the saw, but the stormy, passionate exclamation so often mingled with the sounds are nowhere heard. Yet neither these nor other things which I have mentioned, attractive though they be, have been to me the chief charm which I have found among you. Far above all these, I place the gentle kindness, the cordial welcome, the hearty grasp which made me feel truly and at once, though wandering afar, that I was still at home. My friends, I thank you for this additional manifestation of your good-will.

REPLY OF HON. JEFFERSON DAVIS, OF MISSISSIPPI, TO THE SPEECH OF SENATOR DOUGLAS, IN THE UNITED STATES SENATE, MAY 16 AND 17, 1860.

[The Senate resumed the consideration of the resolutions submitted by Mr. Davis on the first of March, relative to State rights, the institution of slavery in the States, and the rights of citizens of the several States in the Territories.]

MR. DOUGLAS having concluded his speech—

MR. DAVIS arose and said:

Mr. President: When the Senator from Illinois commenced his speech, he announced his object to be to answer to an arraignment, or, as he also termed it, an indictment, which he said I had made against him. He therefore caused extracts to be read from my remarks to the Senate. Those extracts announce that I have been the uniform opponent of what is called squatter sovereignty, and that, having opposed it heretofore, I was now, least of all, disposed to give it quarter. At a subsequent period, the fact was stated that the Senator from Illinois and myself had been opposed to each other, on those questions which I considered as most distinctly involving Southern interests in 1850. He has not answered to the allegation. He has not attempted to show that he did not stand in that position. It is true he has associated himself with Mr. Clay, and, before closing, I will show that the association does not belong to him; that upon those test questions they did not vote together. He then, somewhat vauntingly, reminded me that he was with the victorious party, asserted that the Democracy of the country then sustained his doctrine, and that I was thus outside of that organization. With Mr. Clay! If he had been with him, he would have been in good company; but the old Jackson Democracy will be a little surprised to learn that Clay was the leader of our party, and that a man proves his allegiance to it by showing how closely he followed in the footsteps of Henry Clay.

When the Senator opened his argument, by declaring his purpose to be fair and courteous, I little supposed that an explanation made by me in favor of the Secretary of State, and which could not at all disturb the line of his argument, would have been followed by the rude announcement that he could not permit interruption thereafter. A Senator has the right to claim exemption from interruption if he will follow the thread of his argument, direct his discourse to the question at issue, and confine himself to it; but if he makes up a medley of arraignments of the men who have been in public life for ten years past, and addressing individuals in his presence, he should permit an interruption to be made for correction as often as he misrepresents their position. It would have devolved on me more than once, if I had been responsible for his frequent references to me, to correct him and show that he misstated facts; but as he would not permit himself to be interrupted, I am not responsible for any thing he has imputed to me.

The Senator commenced with a disclaimer of any purpose to follow what he considered a bad practice of arraigning Senators here on matters for which they stood responsible to their constituents; but straightway proceeded to make a general arraignment of the present and the absent. I believe I constitute the only exception to whom he granted consistency, and that at the expense of party association, and, he would have it, at the expense of sound judgment. He not only arraigned individuals, but even States—Florida, Alabama, and Georgia—were brought to answer at the bar of the Senate for the resolutions they had passed; Virginia was held responsible for her policy; Mississippi received his critical notice. Pray, sir, what had all this to do with the question? Especially, what had all this to do with what he styled an indictment against him? It is a mere resort to a species of declamation which has not been heard to-day for the first time; a pretext to put himself in the attitude of a persecuted man, and, like the satyr's guest, blowing hot and cold in the same breath, in the midst of his complaint of persecution, vaunts his supreme power. If his opponents be the very small minority which he describes, what fear has he of persecution or proscription?

Can he not draw a distinction between one who says: "I give no quarter to an idea," and one who proclaims the policy of putting the advocates of that idea to the sword? Such was his figurative language. That figure of the sword, however, it seemed, as he progressed in his development, referred to the one thought always floating through his brain—exclusion from the spoils of office, for, at last, it seemed to narrow down to the supposition that no man who agreed with him was, with our consent, to be either a Cabinet officer or a collector. Who has advanced any such doctrine? Have I, at this or any other period of my acquaintance with him, done any thing to justify him in attributing that opinion to me? I pause for his answer.

Mr. Douglas. I do not exactly understand the Senator. I have no complaint to make of the Senator from Mississippi of ever having been unkind or ungenerous towards me, if that is what he means to say.

Mr. Davis. Have I ever promulgated a doctrine which indicated that if my friends were in power, I would sacrifice every other wing of the Democratic party?

Mr. Douglas. I understood the making of a test on this issue against me would reach every other man that held my opinions; and, therefore, if I was not sound enough to hold office, no man agreeing with me would be; and hence, every man of my opinions would be excluded.

Mr. Davis. Ah, Mr. President; I believe I now have caught the clue to the argument; it was not before apprehended. I was among those who thought the Senator, with his opinions, ought not to be chairman of the Committee on Territories. This, I suppose, then, is the whole imposition. But have I not said to the

Senator, at least once, that I had no disposition to question his Democracy; that I did not wish to withhold from him any tribute which was due to his talent and his worth? Did I not offer to resign the only chairmanship of a committee I had if the Senate would confer it upon him? Then, where is this spirit of proscription, the complaint of which has constituted some hours of his speech? If others have manifested it, I do not know it; and as the single expression of "no quarter to the doctrine of squatter sovereignty" was the basis of his whole allegation, I took it for granted his reference to a purpose to do him and his friends such wrong must have been intended for me.

The fact that the Senator criticised the idea of the States prescribing the terms on which they will act in a party convention recognized to be representative, is suggestive of an extreme misconception of relative position; and the presumption with which the Senator censured what he was pleased to term "the seceders," suggested to me a representation of the air of the great monarch of France when, feeling royalty and power all concentrated in his own person, he used the familiar yet remarkable expression, "the State, that's me." Does the Senator consider it a modest thing in him to announce to the Democratic Convention on what terms he will accept the nomination; but presumptuous in a State to declare the principle on which she will give him her vote? It is an advance on Louis Quatorze.

Nothing but the most egregious vanity, something far surpassing even the bursting condition of swollen pride, could have induced the Senator to believe that I could not speak of squatter sovereignty without meaning him.

Towards the Senator, personally, I have never manifested hostility—indeed, could not, because I have ever felt kindly. Many years of association, very frequent coöperation, manly support from him in times of trial, are all remembered by me gratefully. The Senator, therefore, had no right to assume that I was making war upon him. I addressed myself to a doctrine of which he was not the founder, though he was one of the early disciples; but he proved an unprofitable follower, for he became rebellious, and ruined the logic of the doctrine. It was logical in Mr. Cass's mind; he claimed the power to be inherent in the people who settled a new Territory, and by this inherent power he held that they might proceed to form government and to exercise its functions. There was logic in that—logic up to the point of sovereignty. Not so with the Senator. He says the inhabitants of the Territories derive their power to form a government from the consent of Congress; that when we decide that there are enough of them to constitute a government, and enact an organic law, then they have power to legislate according to their will. This power being derived from an act of Congress—a limited agency tied down to the narrow sphere of the constitutional grant—is made, by that supposition, the bestower of sovereignty on its creature.

I had occasion the other day to refer to the higher law as it made its first appearance on earth—the occasion when the tempter entered the garden of Eden. There is another phase of it. Whoever attempts to interpose between the supreme law of the Creator and the creature, whether it be in the regions of morals or politics, proclaims a theory that wars upon every principle of government. When Congress, the agent for the States, within the limits of its authority, forms, as it were, a territorial constitution by its organic act, he who steps in and proclaims to the settlers in that Territory that they have the right to overturn the Government, to usurp to themselves powers not delegated, is preaching the higher law in the domain of politics, which is only less mischievous than its other form, because the other involves both politics and morals in one ruinous confusion.

The Senator spoke of the denial of Democratic fellowship to him. After what has been said and acknowledged by the Senator, it is not to be supposed that it could have any application to me.

It may be proper to add, I know of no such denial on the part of other Democratic Senators. Far be it from me to vaunt the fact of being in a majority, and to hold him to the hard rule he prescribes to us, of surrendering an opinion where we may happen to have been in a minority. Were I to return now to him the measure with which he metes to us, when he assumes that a majority in the Charleston Convention has a right to prescribe what shall be our tenets, I might, in reply to him, say, as a sincere adherent of the Democratic party, how can you oppose the resolutions pending before the Senate? If twenty-seven majority in a body of three hundred and three constituent members had, as he assumes, the power to lay down a binding law, what is to be said of him who, with a single adherent, stands up against the whole of his Democratic associates? He must be outside of the party, according to his enunciation; he must be wandering in the dark regions to which he consigns the followers of Mr. Yancey.

The Senator said he had no taste for references to things which were personal, and then proceeded to discuss that of which he showed himself profoundly ignorant—the condition of things in Mississippi. It is disagreeable for me to bring before the Senate matters which belong to my constituents and myself, and I should not do so but for the fact of their introduction into the Senator's elaborate speech, which is no doubt to be spread over all parts of the country. The Senator, by some means or other, has the name of very many citizens of Mississippi, and as there is nothing in our condition to attract his special attention, his speech is probably to be sent over a wide field of correspondence; and it is, therefore, the more incumbent on me to notice his attempt to give a history of affairs that were transacted in Mississippi. He first announces that Mississippi rebuked the idea of intervention asserted in 1850; then that Mississippi rejected my appeal; that Mississippi voted on the issue made up by the compromise measure of 1850, and vaunts it as an approval of that legislation of which he was the advocate and I the opponent. Now, Mississippi did none of these things. Mississippi instructed her Senators, and I obeyed her instructions. I introduced into this body the resolutions which directed my course. On that occasion I vindicated Mississippi, and especially the Southern rights men, from the falsehood of that day, and reiterated now, of a purpose to dissolve the Union. I vindicated her by extracts from the proceedings as well of her convention as of her primary assemblies; and my remarks on that occasion, as fully as the events to which he referred in terms of undeserved compliment, justified the Senator in saying to-day that he knew I had always been faithful to the Government of which I was a part.

Acting under the instructions from Mississippi—not merely voting and yielding reluctant compliance; but, according to my ideas of the obligation of a Senator, laboring industriously and zealously to carry out the instructions which my State gave me, I took and maintained the position I held in relation to the measures of 1850. As it was with me a cordial service, I went home to vindicate the position which was hers, as well as my own. Shortly after that a canvass was opened, in which a distinguished gentlemen of our party, who had not been a member of Congress, was nominated for Governor. Questions other than the compromise measures of 1850 arose in that canvass; they were discussed in a great degree to the exclusion of a consideration of the merits of the action of Congress in 1850; and, at the election in September, for delegates to a convention, we had fallen from a party majority of some eight thousand to a minority of nearly the same number. It was after the decision of the question involved in calling a convention—after our party was defeated—after the candidate for Governor had retired, that the Democracy of Mississippi called upon me to bear their standard. It was esteemed a forlorn hope, therefore an obligation of honor not to decline the invitation. But so far as the action in the Senate in 1850 was concerned, if it had any effect, it must have been the reverse of that assumed, as, in the subsequent election for State officers on the first Monday in November, this majority of nearly eight thousand against us was reduced to about one thousand.

But when this convention assembled, though a large majority of the members belonged to the party which the Senator has been pleased to term the "Submissionists"—a name which they always rejected—this convention of the party most adverse to me, when they came to act on the subject said, after citing the "compromise" measures of the Congress of 1850:

"And connected with them, the rejection of the proposition to exclude slavery from the Territories of the United States, and to abolish it in the District of Columbia; and, *while they do not entirely approve*, will abide by it as a permanent adjustment of this sectional controversy, so long as the same, in all its features, shall be faithfully adhered to and enforced."

Then they go on to recite six different causes, for which they will resort to the most extreme remedies which we had supposed ever could be necessary. The case only requires that I should say that the party to which I belonged did not then, nor at any previous time, propose to go out of the Union, but to have a Southern convention for consultation as to future contingencies, threatened and anticipated. It was at last narrowed down to the question, whether we should meet South Carolina and consult with her. Honoring that gallant State for the magnanimity she had manifested in the first efforts for the creation of the Government, in the preliminaries to the struggle for independence, when she, a favored colony, feeling no oppression, nursed by the mother country, cherished in every method, yet agreed with Massachusetts, then oppressed, to assert the great principle of community independence, and to carry it to the extent of war—honoring her for her unvarying defense of the Constitution throughout her whole course—believing that she was true to her faith, and would redeem all her pledges—feeling that a friendly hand might restrain, while, if left to herself, her pride might precipitate her on the trial of separation, I did desire to meet South Carolina in convention, though nobody but ourselves should be there to join her.

But, to close the matter, this convention, in its seventh resolution, after stating all those questions on which it would resist, declared:

> "That, as the people of Mississippi, in the opinion of this convention, desire all further agitation of the slavery question to cease, and have acted upon and decided the foregoing questions, thereby making it the duty of this convention to pass no act in the perview and spirit of the law under which it is called, this convention deems it unnecessary to refer to the people, for approval or disapproval, at the ballot-box, its action in the premises."

So that when the Senator appealed to this as evidence of what the people of Mississippi had done, he was ignorant of the fact that the delegates of the people of Mississippi did not agree with him; that their resolutions did not sustain the view which he took, and that the people of Mississippi never acted on them. If, then, there had been good taste in the intervention of this local question, there was certainly very bad judgment in hazarding his statements on a subject of which he was so little informed.

The Senator here, as in relation to our friends at Charleston, takes kind care of us—supposes we do not know what we are about, but that he, with his superior discrimination, sees what must necessarily result from what we are doing; he says that, at Charleston, they—innocent people—did not intend to destroy the Government; but he warns them that, if they do what they propose, they will destroy it; and so he says we of Mississippi, not desiring to break up the Union, nevertheless pursued a course which would have had that result if it had not been checked. Where does he get all this information? I have been in every State of the Union except two—three now, since Oregon has been admitted—but I have never seen a man who had as much personal knowledge. It is equally surprising that his facts should be so contrary to the record.

We believed then, as I believe now, that this Union, as a compact entered into between the States, was to be preserved by good faith, and by a close observance of the terms on which we were united. We believed then, as I believe now, that the party which rested upon the basis of truth; promulgated its opinions, and had them tested in the alembic of public opinion, adopted the only path of safety. I can not respect such a doctrine as that which says, "You may construe the Constitution your way, and I will construe it mine; we will waive the merit of these two constructions, and harmonize together until the courts decide the question between us." A man is bound to have an opinion upon any political subject upon which he is called to act; it is skulking his responsibility for a citizen to say, "Let us express no opinion; I will agree that you may have yours, and I will have mine; we will coöperate politically together; we will beat the opposition, divide the spoils, and leave it to the court to decide the question between us."

I do not believe that this is the path of safety; I am sure it is not the way of honor. I believe it devolves on us, who are principally sufferers from the danger to which this policy has exposed us, to affirm the truth boldly, and let the people decide after the promulgation of our opinions. Our Government, resting as it does upon public opinion and popular consent, was not formed to deceive the people, nor does it regard the men in office as a governing class. We, the functionaries, should derive our opinions from the people. To know what their opinion is, it is necessary that we should pronounce, in unmistakable language, what we ourselves mean.

My position is, that there is no portion of our country where the people are not sufficiently intelligent to discriminate between right and wrong, and no portion where the sense of justice does not predominate. I, therefore, have been always willing to unfurl our flag to its innermost fold—to nail it to the mast, with all our principles plainly inscribed upon it. Believing that we ask nothing but what the Constitution was intended to confer—nothing but that which, as equals, we are entitled to receive—I am willing that our case should be plainly stated to those who have to decide it, and await, for good or for evil, their verdict.

For two days, the Senator spoke nominally upon the resolutions, and upon the territorial question; but, like the witness in the French comedy, who, when called upon to testify, commenced before the creation, and was stopped by the judge, who told him to come down, for a beginning, to the deluge, he commenced so far back, and narrated so minutely, that he never got chronologically down to the point before us.

What is the question on which the Democracy are divided? Are we called upon to settle what every body said from 1847 down to this date? Have the Democracy divided on that? Have they divided on the resolutions of the States in 1840, or 1844, or 1848? Have the Democracy undertaken to review the position taken in 1854, that there should be a latitude of construction upon a particular point of constitutional law while they did await the decision of the Supreme Court? No, sir; the question is changed from before to after the event; the call is on every man to come forward now, after the Supreme Court has given all it could render upon a political subject, and state that his creed is adherence to the rule thus expounded in accordance with previous agreement.

The Senator tells us that he will abide by the decision of the Supreme Court; but it was fairly to be inferred, from what he said, that, in the Dred Scott case, he held that they had only decided that a negro could not sue in a Federal Court. Was this the entertainment to which we were invited? Was the proclaimed boon of allowing the question to go to judicial decision, no more than that, one after another, each law might be tested, and that, one after another, each case, under every law, might be tried, and that after centuries should roll away, we might hope for the period when, every case exhausted, the decision of our constitutional right and of the federal duty would be complete? Or was it that we were to get rid of the controversy which had divided the country for thirty years; that we were to reach a conclusion beyond which we could see the region of peace; that tranquillity was to be obtained by getting a decision on a constitutional question which had been discussed until it was seen that, legislatively, it could not or would not be decided? If, then, the Supreme Court has judicially announced that Congress can not prohibit the introduction of slave property into a Territory, and that no one deriving authority from Congress can do so, and the Senator from Illinois holds that the inhabitants derive their power from the organic act of Congress, what restrains his acknowledgment of our right to go into the Territories, and his recognition of the case being closed by the opinion of the court? I can understand how one who has followed to its logical consequences the original doctrine of squatter sovereignty might still stand out, and say this inherent right can not be taken away by judicial decision; but is not one who claims to derive the power of the territorial legislation from a law of Congress, and who finds the opinion of the court conclusive as to Congress, and to all deriving their authority from it, estopped from any further argument?

Much of what the Senator said about the condition of public affairs can only be regarded as the presentation of his own case, and repuires no notice from me. His witticism upon the honorable Senator, the Chairman of the Committee on the Judiciary [Mr. Bayard], who is now absent, because of the size of the State which he represents, reminds one that it was mentioned as an evidence of the stupidity of a German, that he questioned the greatness of Napoleon because he was born in the little island of Corsica. I know not what views the Senator entertained when he measured the capacity of the Senator from Delaware by the size of that

State, or the dignity of his action at Charleston by the number of his constituents. If there be any political feature which stands more prominently out than another in the Union, it is the equality of the States. Our stars have no variant size; they shine with no unequal brilliancy. A Senator from Delaware holds a position entitled to the same respect, as such, as the Senator from any other State of the Union. More than that, the character, the conduct, the information, the capacity of that Senator might claim respect, if he was not entitled to it from his position.

Twice on this occasion, and more than the same number of times heretofore, has the Senator referred to the great benefit derived from that provision which grants a trial in the local court, an appeal to the Supreme Court of the Territory, and an appeal from thence to the Supreme Court of the United States, on every question involving title to slaves. I wish to say that whatever merit attaches to that belongs to a Senator to whom the advocates of negro slavery have not often been in the habit of acknowledging their obligations—the Senator from New Hampshire [Mr. Hale], who introduced it in 1850 as an amendment to the New Mexico Bill. We adopted it as a fair proposition, equally acceptable upon one side and the other. On its adoption, no one voted against it. That proposition was incorporated in the Kansas Bill, but unless we acknowledge obligations to the Senator from New Hampshire, how shall they be accorded for that to the Senator from Illinois?

I am asked whether the resolutions of the Senate can have the force of law. Of course not. The Senate, however, is an independent member of the Government, and from its organization should be peculiarly watchful of State rights. Before the meeting of the Charleston Convention, it was untruly stated that these resolutions were concocted to affect the action of the Charleston Convention. Now we are asked if they are to affect the Baltimore Convention. They were not designed for the one; they are not pressed in view of the other. They were introduced to obtain an expression of the opinion of the Senate, a proceeding quite frequent in the history of this body. It was believed that they would have a beneficial effect, and that they were stated in terms which would show the public the error of supposing that there was a purpose on the part of the Democracy, or of the South, to enact what was called a slave code for the Territories of the United States. It was believed that the assertion of sound principles at this time would direct public opinion, and might be fruitful of such reuniting, harmonizing results as we all desire, and which the public need. Whether it is to have this effect or not; whether at last we are to be shorn of our national strength by personal or sectional strife, depends upon the conduct of those who have it in their power to control the result. The Democratic party, in its history, presents a high example of nationality; its power and its usefulness has been its co-extension with the Union. The Democrats of the Northern States who vote for these resolutions, but affirm that which we have so often announced with pride, that there was a political opinion which pervaded the whole country; there was a party capable to save the Union, because it belonged to all the States. If the two Democratic Senators who alone have declared their opposition should so vote, to that extent the effect would be impaired, and they will stand in that isolation to which the Senator points as a consequence so dreadful to the Southern men at Charleston.

[Here Mr. Davis gave way for a motion to adjourn, and on the 17th resumed.]

MR. DAVIS. At the close of the session of yesterday, I was speaking of the hope entertained that the Democratic party would yet be united; that the party which had so long wielded the destinies of the country, for its honor, for its glory, and its progress, was not about to be checked midway in its career—to be buried in a premature grave; but that it was to go on, with concentrated energy, toward the great ends for which it has striven since 1800, by a long pull, and a strong pull, and a pull altogether, to bring the ship of State into that quiet harbor where

"Vessels safe, without their hawsers, ride."

This was a hope, however, not founded on any supposition that we were to escape from the issues which are presented—a hope not based on the proposition that every man should have his own construction of our creed, and that we should unite together merely for success; but that the party, as heretofore, in each succeeding quadrennial convention, would add to the resolutions of the preceding one such declarations as passing events indicated, and the exigencies of the country demanded.

In the last four years a division has arisen in the Democratic party, upon the construction of one of the articles of its creed. It behooves us, in that state of the case, to decide what the true construction is; for, if the party be not a union of men upon principle, the sooner it is dissolved the better; and if it be such a union, why shall not those principles be defined, so as to remove doubt or cavil, and be applied in every emergency to meet the demands of each succeeding case? Thus only can we avoid division in council and confusion in action.

The Senator from Illinois, who preceded me, announced that he had performed a pleasing duty in defending the Democratic party. That party might well cry out, Save me from my defender. It was a defense of the party by the arraignment of its prominent members. It was the preservation of the body by the destruction of its head—for the President of the United States is, for the time being, the head of the party that placed him in position; and the head of the party thus in position can not be destroyed without the disintegration of the members and the destruction of the body itself. I suppose the Senator, however, was at his favorite amusement of "shooting at the lump." The "lump" heretofore has been those Democratic Senators who dissented from him: this time he involved Democrats all over the country. Not even the presiding officer, whose position seals his lips, could escape him. And here let me say that I found nothing in the extract read from that gentleman's address, which, construed as was no doubt intended, does not meet my approval; but if tried by the modern lexicon of the Senator, it might be rendered a contradiction to his avowed opinions, and by the same mode of expounding, non-intervention would be a sin of which the whole Democracy might be convicted, under the indictment of squatter sovereignty. The language quoted from the address of the Vice-President is to be construed as understood at the time, at the place, and by men such as the one who used it.

With that force which usually enters into his addresses—with even more than his usual eloquence—the Senator referred to the scene which awaited him upon his return to Chicago, when, as represented, he met an infuriated mob, who assailed him for having maintained the measures of 1850—those compromises which, in the Northern section, it was urged had been passed in the interest of the South. But, pray, what one of those measures was it which excited the mob so described? Only one, I believe, was put in issue at the North—the fugitive slave law; that one he did not vote for. But it was the part of manliness to say that, though absent and not voting for it, he approved of it. Such, I believe, was his commendable course on that occasion. I give him, therefore, all due credit for not escaping from a responsibility to which they might not have held him. Are we to give perpetual thanks to any one because he did not yield to so senseless a clamor, but conceded to us that small measure of constitutional right—because he has complied with a requirement so plain that my regret is that it ever required congressional intervention to enforce it? It belonged to the honor of the States to execute that clause of the Constitution. They should have executed it without congressional intervention; congressional action should only have been useful to give that uniformity of proceeding which State action could not have secured.

Concurring in the depicted evil of the destruction of the Democratic organization, it must be admitted that such consequence is the inevitable result of a radical difference of principle. The Senator laments the disease, but instead of healing, aggravates it. While pleading the evils of the disruption of the party, it is quite apparent that, in his mind, there is another still greater calamity; for, through all his arraignment of others, all his self-laudation, all his complaints of persecution, like an air through its variations, appears and re-appears the action of the Charleston Convention. That seemed to be the beginning and the end of his solicitude. The oft-told tale of his removal from the chairmanship of the Committee on Territories had to be renewed and connected with that convention, and even assumed as the basis on which his strength was founded in that convention. I think the Senator did himself injustice. I think his long career and distinguished labors, his admitted capacity for good hereafter, constitute a better reason for the support which he received, than the fact that his associates in the Senate had not chosen to put him in a particular position in the organization of this body. It is enough that that fact did not divert support from him; and I am aware of none of his associates here who have forced it upon public attention with a view to affect him.

He claims that an arraignment made against his Democracy has been answered by the action of a majority of the Convention at Charleston; and then proceeds to inform the minority men that he would scorn to be the candidate of a party unless he received a majority of its votes. There was no use in making that declaration; it requires not only a majority, but, under our ruling, a vote of two-thirds, for a nomination. It was unnecessary for any body to feel scorn toward that which he could not receive. Other unfortunate wights might mourn the event; it belonged to the Senator from Illinois to scorn it. The remark of Mr. Lowndes, which has been so often quoted, and which, beautiful in itself, has acquired additional value by time, that the Presidency was an office neither to be sought nor declined, has no application, therefore, to the Senator, for, under certain contingencies, he says he would decline it. It does not devolve on me to decide whether he has sought it or not.

But, sir, what is the danger which now besets the Democratic party? Is it, as has been asserted, the doctrine of intervention by Congress, and is that doctrine new? Is the idea that protection, by Congress, to all rights of person or property, wherever it has jursdiction, so dangerous that, in the language employed by the Senator, it would sweep the Democratic party from the face of the earth? For what was our Government instituted? Why did the States confer upon the Federal Government the great functions which it possesses? For protection—mainly for protection beyond the municipal power of the States. I shall have occasion, in the progress of my remarks, to cite some authority, and to trace this from a very early period. I will first, however, notice an assault which the Senator has thought proper to make upon certain States, one of which is, in part, represented by myself. He says they are seceders, bolters, because they withdrew from a party convention when it failed to announce their principles. There can be no tie to bind me to a party beyond my will. I will admit no bond that holds me to a party a day longer than I agree to its principles. When men meet together to confer, and ascertain whether or not they do agree, and find that they differ—radically, essentially, irreconcilably differ—what belongs to an honorable position except to part? They can not consistently act together any longer. It devolves upon them frankly to announce the difference, and each to pursue his separate course.

The letter of Mr. Yancey—acknowledged to be a private letter, an unguarded letter, but which, somehow or other, got into the press—was read to sustain this general accusation against what are called the Cotton States. I do not pretend to judge how far the Senator has the right here to read a private letter, which, without the authority of the writer, has gone into the public press. It is one of those questions which every man's sense of propriety must, in his own case, decide. Whether or not the use of that letter was justifiable, how is it to be assumed that the Southern States are bound by any opinion there enunciated? How to be asserted that we, the residents in those States, have pinned our faith to the sleeve of any man, and that we will follow his behest, no matter whither he may go? But was this the only source of information, or was the impression otherwise sustained? Did Mr. Yancey, in his speech delivered at Charleston, justify the conclusions which the Senator draws from this letter? Did he admit them to be correct? There he might have found the latest evidence, and the best authority. Speaking to that point, Mr. Yancey said:

"It has been charged, in order to demoralize whatever influence we might be entitled to, either from our personal or political characteristics, or as representatives of the State of Alabama, that we are disruptionists, disunionists *per se;* that we desire to break up the party in the State of Alabama—to break up the party of the Union, and to dissolve the Union itself. Each and all of these allegations, come from what quarter they may, I pronounce to be false. There is no disunionist, that I know of, in the delegation from the State of Alabama. There is no disruptionist that I know of; and if there are factionists in our delegation, they could not have got in there, with the knowledge upon the part of our State Convention that they were of so unenviable a character. We come here with two great purposes: first, to save the constitutional rights of the South, if it lay in our power to do so. We desire to save the South by the best means that present themselves to us; and the State of Alabama believes that the best means now in existence is the organization of the Democratic party, if we shall be able to persuade it to adopt the constitutional basis upon which we think the South alone can be saved."

He further says:

"We have come here, then, with the twofold purpose of saving the country and saving the Democracy; and if the Democracy will not lend itself to that high, holy, and elevated purpose; if it can not elevate itself above the mere question of how perfect shall be its mere personal organization, and how wide-spread shall be its mere voting success, then we say to you, gentlemen, mournfully and regretfully, that, in the opinion of the State of Alabama, and, I believe, of the whole South, you have failed in your mission, and it will be our duty to go forth, and make an appeal to the loyalty of the country to stand by that Constitution which party organizations have deliberately rejected." [Applause.]

Mr. Yancey answers for himself. It was needless to go back to old letters. Here were his remarks delivered before the convention, speaking to the point in issue, and answering both as to his purposes and as to the motives of those with whom he conferred and acted.

The Senator next cited the resolutions of the State of Alabama; and here he seemed to rest the main point in his argument. The Senator said that Alabama, in 1856, had demanded of the Democratic convention, non-intervention, and that, in 1860, she had retired from the convention because it insisted upon non-intervention. He read one of the resolutions of the Alabama Convention of 1856; but the one which bore upon the point was not read. The one which was conclusive as to the position of Alabama then, and its relation to her position now, was exactly the one that was omitted—I read from the resolutions of this year—was as follows:

"*Resolved, further*, That we re-affirm so much of the first resolution of the platform adopted in the convention by the Democracy of this State, on the 8th of January, 1856, as relates to the subject of slavery, to-wit."

It then goes on to quote from that resolution of 1856, as follows:

"The unqualified right of the people of the slaveholding States to the protection of their property in the States, in the Territories, and in the wilderness, in which territorial governments are as yet unorganized."

That was the resolution of 1856; and like it was one of February, 1848:

"That it is the duty of the General Government by all proper legislation, to secure an entry into those Territories to all the citizens of the United States, together with their property, of every description; and that the same shall be protected by the United States, while the Territories are under its authority."

So stands the record of that State which is now held responsible for retiring, and is alleged to have withdrawn because she received now what, in former times, she had demanded as the full measure of her rights. Did she receive it? The argument could only be made by concealing the fact that her resolutions of 1848 and 1856 asserted the right to protection, and claimed it from the General Government. What, then, is the necessary inference? That, in the Cincinnati platform, they believed they obtained that which they asserted, or that which necessarily involved it. So much for the point of faith; so much for the point of consistency in the assertion of right. But if it were otherwise; if they had neglected to assert a right; would that destroy it? If they had failed at some time to claim this protection, are they to be estopped, in all time to come, from claiming it? Constitutional right is eternal—not to be sacrificed by any body of men. A single man may revive it at any period of the existence of the Constitution. So the argument would be worthless, if the facts were as stated. That they are not so stated, is shown by the record.

Here allow me to say, in all sincerity, that I dislike thus to speak about conventions; it does not belong to the duties of the Senate; we did not assemble here to make a President, except in the single contingency of a failure by the people and by the House of Representatives to elect. When that contingency arrives, the question will be before us. I am sorry that it should have been prematurely introduced. But since the action of the recent convention at Charleston is presented as the basis of argument, it may be as well to refer to it, and see what it is. The majority report, presented by seventeen States of the Union, and those the States most reliable to give Democratic votes—the States counted so certain to give Democratic votes that they have been regarded as a fixed basis, a nucleus to which others were to be attracted—these seventeen States reported to the convention a series of resolutions, one of which asserted the right to protection. A minority of States reported another series, excluding the avowal of the right—not exactly denying it, but not avowing it—and a second minority report was submitted, being the Cincinnati platform, pure and simple. It is true that a majority of delegates adopted the minority report, but not a majority of States, nor does it appear, by an analysis of the votes, and the best evidence I have been able to obtain, that it was by a majority of delegates, if each had been left to his own choice; but that, by one of those ingenious arrangements—one of those incidents which, among jurists, is described as the favor the vigilant receives from the law—it so happened that, in certain States, the delegates were instructed to vote as a unit; in other States they were not; so that, wherever they were instructed to vote as a unit, the vote must so be cast, and wherever they were not, they might disintegrate. Thus minorities were bound in one instance, and released in another; and, by a comparison made by those who had an opportunity to know, it appears that the minority report could not have got a majority of the delegates, if each delegate had been permitted to cast his own vote in the Convention. Neither could it have obtained, as appears by the action of the committee, in a majority of the States, if they had been spoken as such. So that this vaunt as to the effect of the adoption of the platform by a majority, seems to have very little of substance in it. Again, I find that, after this adoption of a platform, a delegate from Tennessee offered a resolution:

> "That all the citizens of the United States have an equal right to settle, with their property, in the Territories of the United States; and that, under the decision of the Supreme Court of the United States, which we recognize as a correct exposition of the Constitution of the United States, neither their rights of person or property can be destroyed or impaired by congressional or territorial legislation."

It does not appear that a vote was taken on it. There is a current belief that it would have been adopted. If it had been, it would have been an acknowledgment by the Democracy, in convention assembled, that the question had been settled by the decisions of the Supreme Court. But in the progress of the convention, when they came to balloting, it appears, by an analysis of the vote for candidates, that the Senator from Illinois received from seventeen undoubted Democratic States of the Union, casting one hundred and twenty-seven electoral votes, but eleven votes. It is not such a great triumph, then, in the Democratic view, as is claimed. It does not suffice to add up the number of votes where they do not avail. It is not fair to bring the votes of Vermont, where I believe nobody expects we shall be successful, and count them for a particular candidate. The electoral votes—and these alone, tell upon the result; and it appears that in those States which have been counted certain to cast their electoral votes for the candidate who might have been nominated at that convention, the Senator received but eleven. This is but meagre claim to bind us to his car as the successful champion of the majority. This is but small basis for the boast that his hopes were gratified, that he would not receive the nomination unless sustained by a majority of the party, and that his opinions had received the indorsement of the Democracy.

My devotion to the party is life-long. If the assertion be allowable, it may be said that I inherited my political principles. I derive them from a revolutionary father—one of the earnest friends of Mr. Jefferson; who, after the revolution which achieved our independence, bore his full part in the civil revolution of 1800, which emancipated us from federal usurpation and consolidation. I therefore have all that devotion to party which belongs to habitual reverence and confidence. But, sir, that devotion to party rests on the assumption that it is to maintain sound principles; that it is to strive hereafter, as heretofore, to carry out the great cardinal creed in which the Democratic party was founded. When the resolutions of 1798 and 1799 are discarded; when we fly from the extreme of monarchy to land in the danger to republics, anarchy, and the Democratic party says its arm is paralyzed—can not be raised to maintain constitutional rights, my devotion to its organization is at an end. It fails thenceforward in the purposes for which it was established; and if there be a constitutional party in the land which, in the language of Mr. Jefferson, would find in the vigor of the Federal Government the best hope for our liberty and security, to that party I should attach myself whenever that sad contingency arose.

The resolutions of 1798 and 1799, though directed against usurpation, were equally directed against the dangers of anarchy. Their principles are alike applicable to both. Their cardinal creed was a Federal Government, according to the grants conferred upon it, and these righteously administered. It is not fair to the men who taught us the lessons of Democracy that they should be held responsible for a theory which leaves the Federal Government, as one who has abdicated all authority, to stand at the mercy of local usurpations. Least of all does their teaching maintain that this Government has no power over the Territories; that this Government has no obligation to protect the rights of person and property in the Territories; for, among the first acts under the Constitution, was one which both asserted and exercised the power.

After the adoption of the Constitution, in 1789, an act was passed, to which reference is frequently made as being a confirmation of the ordinance of 1787; and this has been repeated so often that it has received general belief. There was a constitutional provision which required all obligations and engagements under the confederation to hold good under the Constitution. If there was an obligation or an engagement growing out of the ordinance of 1787, out of the deed of cession by Virginia, it was transmitted to the Government established under the Constitution; but that Congress under the Constitution gave it no vitality—that they added no force to it, is apparent from the fact which is so often relied upon as authority. It was in view of this fact, in full remembrance of this and of other facts connected with it, that Mr. Madison said, in relation to passing regulations for the Territories, that "Congress did not regard the interdiction of slavery among the needful regulations contemplated by the Constitution, since, in none of the territorial governments created by them, was such an interdict found." I am aware that Justice McLean has viewed this as an historical error of Mr. Madison. I shall not assume to decide between such high authorities. The act is as follows:

"*An Act to provide for the government of the Territory north-west of the Ohio River.*

"WHEREAS; In order that the ordinance of the United States in Congress assembled, for the government of the territory north-west of the river Ohio, may continue to have full effect, it is requisite that certain provisions should be made so as to adapt the same to the present Constitution of the United States.

"SECTION 1. *Be it enacted by the Senate and House of Representatives of the United States of America in Congress assembled*, That, in all cases in which, by the said ordinance, any information is to be given, or communication made, by the governor of the said Territory to the United States in Congress assembled, or to any of their officers, it shall be the duty of the said governor to give such information, and to make such communication, to the President of the United States; and the President shall nominate, and, by and with the advice and consent of the Senate, shall appoint all officers which, by the said ordinance, were to have been appointed by the United States in Congress assembled; and all officers so appointed shall be commissioned by him; and in all cases where the United States in Congress assembled might, by the said ordinance, make any commission, or remove from any office, the President is hereby declared to have the same powers to revocation and removal.

"SEC. 2. *And be it further enacted*, That in the case of the death, removal, resignation, or necessary absence of the governor of the said Territory, the secretary thereof shall be, and he is hereby authorized and required to execute all the powers and perform all the duties of the governor during the vacancy occasioned by the removal, resignation, or necessary absence of the said governor.

"Approved August 7, 1789."

All that is to be found in this act which favors the supposition and frequent assertion that, under the Constitution, the ordinance of 1787 was ratified and confirmed is to be found in the preamble, and that preamble so vaguely alludes to it that the idea is refuted by reference to an act which followed soon afterwards—the act of 1793—from which I will read a single section:

"SEC. 3. *And be it further enacted*, That when a person held to labor in any of the United States, or in either of the Territories on the north-west or south of the river Ohio, under the laws thereof, shall escape into any other of the said States or Territories, the person to whom such service or labor may be due, his agent, or attorney, is hereby empowered to seize or arrest such fugitive from labor," etc.

Is it not apparent that, when the Congress legislated in 1793, they recognized the existence of slavery and protected that kind of property in the territory north-west of the river Ohio, and is it not conclusive that they did not intend, by the act of 1789, to confirm, ratify, and give effect to the ordinance of 1787, which would have excluded it?

This doctrine of protection, then, is not new. It goes back to the foundation of the Government. It is traceable down through all the early controversies; and they arose at least as early as 1790. It is found in the messages of Mr. Jefferson and Mr. Madison, and in the legislation of Congress; and also in the messages of the elder Adams. There was not one of the first four Presidents of the United States who did not recognize this obligation of protection, who did not assert this power on the part of the Federal Government; and not one of them ever attempted to pervert it to a power to destroy. If division in the Democratic party is to arise now, because of this doctrine, it is not from the change by those who assert it, but of those who deny it. It is not from the introduction of a new feature in the theory of our Government, but from the denial of that which was recognized in its very beginning.

As I understood the main argument of the Senator, it was based upon the general postulate that the Democratic Convention of 1848 recognized a new doctrine, a doctrine which inhibited the General Government from interfering in any way, either for the protection of property or otherwise, with the local affairs of a Territory; he held the party responsible for all the opinions entertained by the candidate in 1848, because the party had nominated him, and he quoted the record to show what States, by voting for him, had committed themselves to the doctrine of the "Nicholson letter." He even quoted South Carolina, represented by that man who became famous for a single act, and, as South Carolinians said, without authority at home to sustain it. But this was cited as pledging the faith of South Carolina to the doctrine of the "Nicholson letter;" and, worse than all, the Senator did this, though he knew that the doctrine of the "Nicholson letter" was the subject of controversy for years subsequently; that, what was the true construction of that letter, entered into the canvass in the Southern States; that the construction which Mr. Cass himself placed upon it at a subsequent period was there denied; and the Senator might have remembered, if he had chosen to recollect so unimportant a thing, that I once had to explain to him, ten years ago, the fact that I repudiated the doctrine of that letter at the time it was published, and that the Democracy of Mississippi had well-nigh crucified me for the construction which I placed upon it; there were men mean enough to suspect that the construction I gave to the Nicholson letter was prompted by the confidence and affection I felt for General Taylor. At a subsequent period, however, Mr. Cass thoroughly reviewed it. He uttered, for him, very harsh language against all who had doubted the true construction of his letter, and he construed it just as I had done during the canvass of 1848. It remains only to add that I supported Mr. Cass, not because of the doctrine of the Nicholson letter, but in despite of it; because I believed a Democratic President, with a Democratic cabinet and Democratic counselors in the two houses of Congress, and he as honest a man as I believed Mr. Cass to be, would be a safer reliance than his opponent, who personally possessed my confidence as much as any man living, but who was of and must draw his advisers from a party, the tenets of which I believed to be opposed to the interests of the country as they were to all my political convictions.

I little thought at that time that my advocacy of Mr. Cass, upon such grounds as these, or his support by the State of which I am a citizen, would at any future day be quoted as an indorsement of the opinions contained in the Nicholson letter, as those opinions were afterwards defined. But it is not only upon this letter, but equally upon the resolutions of the convention as constructive of that letter, that he rested his argument. I will here say to the Senator that if, at any time, I do him the least injustice, speaking as I do from such notes as I could take while he progressed, I will thank him to correct me.

But this letter entered into the canvass; there was a doubt about its construction; there were men who asserted that they had positive authority for saying that it meant that the people of a Territory could only exclude slavery when the Territory should form a constitution and be admitted as a State. This doubt continued to hang over the construction, and it was that doubt alone which secured Mr. Cass the vote of Mississippi. If the true construction had been certainly known he would have had no chance to get it. Our majority went down from thousands to hundreds, as it was. In Alabama the decrease was greater. It was not that the doctrine was countenanced, but the doubt as to the true meaning of the letter, and the constantly reiterated assertion that it only meant the Territories when they should be admitted as States, enabled him to carry those States.

But if I mistook the Senator there, I think probably I did not on another point: that he claimed the support of certain Southern men for Mr. Richardson as Speaker of the House to be by them an acknowledgment of the doctrine of squatter sovereignty.

I suppose those Southern men who voted for Mr. Richardson voted for him as I did for Mr. Cass, in despite of his opinions on that question, because they preferred Mr. Richardson to Mr. Banks, even with squatter sovereignty. They considered that the latter was carrying an amount of heresies which greatly exceeded the value of squatter sovereignty. It was a choice of evils—not an indorsement of his opinions. Neither did they this year indorse the opinions on that point of Mr. McClernand when they voted for him. According to the Senator's argument I could show him that Illinois was committed to the doctrine of federal protection to property in the Territories and the remedy of secession as a State right; committed irrevocably, unmistakably, with no right to plead any ignorance of the political creed of the individual, or the meaning of his words.

In 1852—I refer to it with pride—Illinois did me the honor to vote consistently for me for the Vice-Presidency, up to the time of adjournment; though in 1850, and in 1851, I had done all these acts which have been spoken of, and the Senator has admitted my consistency, in opinions which were avowed with at least such perspicuity as left nobody in doubt as to my opinion. Did Illinois then adopt my theory of protection in the Territories, or of the right of State secession? No, sir. I hold them to no such consequences. Some of the old inhabitants of Illinois may have remembered me when their northern frontier was a wilderness, when they and I had kind relations in the face of hostile Indians. Some of them may have remembered me, and, I believe, kindly, as associated with them, at a later period, on the fields of Mexico. The Senator himself, I know, remembered kindly his association with me in the halls of Congress. It was these bonds which gave me the confidence of the State of Illinois. I never misconstrued it. I never pretended to put them in the attitude of adopting all my opinions. Never required it, never desired it, save as in so far as wishing all men would agree with me, confidently believing my position to be true. At a later period, and when these questions were more important in the public mind, when public attention has been more directed to them, when public opinion has been more matured, at the very time when the Senator claims that his doctrine culminated, the State of Illinois voted for a gentleman for Vice-President at Cincinnati who held the same opinions with myself, or, if there was a difference, held them to a greater extreme—I mean General Quitman.

Mr. Douglas. We made no test on any one.

Mr. Davis. Then, how did the South become responsible for the doctrine of General Cass, by consenting to his nomination in 1848, and supporting his election? But at a later period, down to the present session, what is the position in which the Senator places his friends—those sterling Democrats, uncompromising Anti-Know-Nothings; men who give no quarter to the American party, and yet who voted this year for Mr. Smith, of North Carolina, to be Speaker of the House of Representatives. Is the Senator answered? Does he not see that there is no justice in assuming a vote for an individual to be the entire adoption of his opinions?

He cited, in this connection, a resolution of 1848, as having been framed to cover the doctrines of the Nicholson letter; and he claimed thus to have shown that the convention not only understood it, but adopted it, and made it the party creed, and that we were bound to it from that period forward. He even had that resolution of 1848 read, in order that there should be, at no future time, any question as to the principle which the party then avowed; that it should be fixed as a starting point in all the future progress of Democracy. I was surprised at the importance the Senator attached to that resolution of 1848, because it was not new; it was not framed to meet the opinions of the Nicholson letter, but came down from a period as remote as 1840; was copied into the platform of 1844, and again into that of 1848, being the expression which the condition of the country in 1840 had induced—a declaration of opinion growing out of the agitation in the two houses of Congress at that day, and the fearful strides which antislavery was making, and which Mr. Calhoun had labored to check by the declaration of constitutional truths, as set forth in his Senate resolutions of 1837–'8.

That there may be no mistake on this point, and particularly as the Senator attached special importance to it, I will turn to the platform of 1840, and read from it, so that it shall be found to be—

Mr. Douglas. It is conceded.

Mr. Davis. The Senator concedes the fact, that the resolution of 1848 was a copy of that of 1840, and with the concession falls his argument. The platforms of 1840 and 1844 were re-affirmed in 1848; and, consequently, the resolution of '48 being identical with that of '40, was not a construction of the letter written in 1847.

True to its instincts and to its practices, the Democratic party, from time to time, continued to add to their "platform" whatever was needful for action by the Government in the condition of the country. Thus, in 1844, they re-asserted the platform of 1840; and they added thereto, because of a question then pending, that—

"The re-annexation of Texas, at the earliest practicable period, is a great American measure, which the convention recommend to the cordial support of the Democracy of the Union."

In 1848 they re-adopted the resolutions of 1844; and were not a little laughed at for keeping up the question of Texas after it had been annexed. In 1852 a new question had arisen; the measures of 1850 had presented, with great force to the public mind, the necessity for some expression of opinion upon the disturbing questions which the measures of 1850 had been designed to quiet. Therefore, in 1852, the party, true to its obligation to announce its principles, and to meet issues as they arise, said:

"*Resolved*, That the foregoing proposition (referring to the resolution of 1848) covers, and was intended to embrace, the whole subject of slavery agitation in Congress; and, therefore, the Democratic party in the Union, standing on this national platform, will abide by and adhere to a faithful execution of the act known as the compromise measure, settled by the last Congress, the act for reclaiming fugitives from labor included; which act, being designed to carry out an express provision of the Constitution, can not, with fidelity thereto, be repealed, or so changed as to destroy or impair its efficacy.

"*Resolved*, That the Democratic party will restrain all attempts at renewing, in Congress or out of it, the agitation of the slave question, under whatever shape or color the attempt may be made.'

This was the addition made in 1852, and it was made because

of the agitation which then prevailed through the country against the fugitive slave act, and it was because the fugitive slave act, and that alone, was assailed, that the Democratic convention met the issue on that measure specifically, and for the same reason it received the approbation of the Southern States. Had this been considered as the indorsement of the slave trade bill for the District of Columbia, it would not have received their approval. The agitation was in relation to recovering fugitive slaves, and the Democratic party boldly and truly met the living issue, and declared its position upon it.

In 1856 other questions had arisen. It was necessary to meet them. The convention did meet them, and met them in a manner which was satisfactory, because it was believed to be full. I will not weary the Senate by reading the resolutions of 1856; they are familiar to every body. I only quote a portion of them:

> "The American Democracy recognize and adopt the principles contained in the organic laws establishing the Territories of Kansas and Nebraska as embodying the only sound and safe solution of the 'slavery question' upon which the great national idea of the people of this whole country can repose in its determined conservatism of the Union—non-interference by Congress with slavery in State and Territory, or in the District of Columbia.
>
> "That, by the uniform application of this Democratic principle to the organization of Territories, and to the admission of new States, with or without domestic slavery, as they may elect, the equal rights of all States will be preserved intact, the original compacts of the Constitution maintained inviolate, and the perpetuity and expansion of this Union insured to its utmost capacity of embracing, in peace and harmony, every future American State that may be constituted or annexed with a republican form of government."

Pray, what can this mean? Squatter sovereignty? Incapacity of the Federal Government to enact any law for the protection of slave property anywhere? Could that be in the face of a struggle that we were constantly carrying on against the opponents of the fugitive slave law? Could that be, in the face of the fact that a majority had trodden down our constitutional rights in the District of Columbia, by legislating in relation to that particular character of property, and that they had failed to redeem a promise they had sacredly made to pass a law for the protection of slave property, so as to punish any one who should seduce, or entice, or abduct it from an owner in this District?

With all these things fresh in mind, what did they mean? They meant that Congress should not decide the question, whether that institution should exist within a Territory or not. They did not mean to withdraw from the inhabitants of the District of Columbia that protection to which they were entitled, and which is almost annually given by legislation; and yet States and Territories and the District of Columbia are all grouped together, as the points upon which this idea rests, and to which it is directed. It meant that Congress was not to legislate to interfere with the rights of property anywhere; not to attempt to decide what should be the institutions maintained anywhere; but surely not to disclaim the right to protect property, whether on sea or on land, wherever the Federal Government had jurisdiction and power. But some stress has been laid upon the resolution, which says that this principle should be applied to

"The organization of the Territories, and to the admission of new States, with or without domestic slavery, as they may elect."

What does "may elect" mean? Does it refer to organization of the Territory? Who may elect? Congress organizes the Territories. Did it mean that the Territories were to elect? It does not say so. What does it say?

"That by the uniform application of this Democratic principle to the organization of Territories, and to the admission of new States, with or without domestic slavery, as they may elect."

And here it met a question which had disturbed the peace of the country, and well-nigh destroyed the Union—the right of a State holding slaves to be admitted into the Union. It was declared here that the State so admitted should elect whether it would or would not have slaves. There is nothing in that which logically applies to the organization of a Territory. But if this be in doubt, let us come to the last resolution, which says:

"We recognize the right of the people of all the Territories, including Kansas and Nebraska, acting through the legally and fairly-expressed will of a majority of actual residents—"

Does it stop there? No—

"and whenever the number of their inhabitants justifies it, to form a constitution, with or without domestic slavery, and be admitted into the Union upon terms of perfect equality with the other States."

If there had been any doubt before as to what "may elect" referred to, this resolution certainly removed it. It is clear they meant, that when a Territory had a sufficient number of inhabitants, and came to form a constitution, then it might decide the question as it pleased. From that doctrine, I know no Democrat who now dissents.

I have thus, because of the assertion that this was a new idea attempted to be interjected into the Democratic creed, gone over some portion of its history. Important by its connection with the existing agitation, and last in the series, is an act with the ushering in of which the Senator is more familiar than myself, and on which he made remarks, to which, it is probable, some of those who acted with him, will reply. I wish merely to say, in relation to the Kansas-Nebraska act, that there are expressions in it which seem to me not of doubtful meaning, such as, "in all cases involving title to slaves, or involving the question of personal freedom," there should be a trial before the courts, and without reference to the amount involved, an appeal to the Supreme Court of the Territory, and from thence to the Supreme Court of the United States. If there was no right of property there; if we had no right to recognize it there; if some sovereign was to determine whether it existed or not, why did we say that the Supreme Court of the United States, in the last resort, should decide the question? If it was an admitted thing, by that bill, that the Territorial Legislature should decide it, why did we provide for taking the case to the Supreme Court? If it had been believed then, as it is asserted now, that a Territory possessed all the power of a State; that the inhabitants of a Territory could meet in convention and decide the question as the people of a State might do, there was nothing to be carried to the Supreme Court. You can not appeal from the decision of a constitutional convention of a State to the Supreme Court of the United States, to decide whether slave property shall be prohibited or admitted within the limits of a State; and if they rest on the same footing, what is the meaning of that clause of the bill?

But this organic law further provides, just as the resolution of the convention had done, that when a legal majority of the residents of either Territory formed a constitution, then, at their will, they might recognize or exclude slavery, and come into the Union as co-equal States. This fixes the period, defines the time at which the territorial inhabitants may perform this act, and clearly forbids the idea that it was intended, by those who enacted the law, to acknowledge that power to be existent in the inhabitants of a Territory during their territorial condition. If I am mistaken in this; if there was a contemporaneous construction of it differing from this, the Senators who sit around me and who were then members of the body, will not fail to remember it.

The Senator asserts that, in relation to this point, those who acted with him have changed, and claims for himself to have been consistent. If this be so, it proves nothing as to the present, and only individual opinions as to the past. I do not regard consistency as a very high virtue; neither, it appears, does he; for he told us that if it could be shown to him that he was in error on any point, he would change his opinion. How could that be? Who would undertake to show the Senator that he was in error? Who would undertake to measure the altitude of the Colossus who bestrides the world, and announces for, and of, and by himself, "We, the Democracy," as though, in his person, all that remained of the party was now concentrated! Other men are permitted to change, because other men may be mistaken; and if they are honest, when convicted of their error, they must change, but how can one expect to convince the Senator, who, where all is change, stands changeless still?

In the course of his reply to me—if indeed it may be called such; it seemed to be rather a review of every thing except what I had said—he set me the bad example of going into the canvass in my own State. It is the first, I trust it will be the last time, I shall follow his example; and now only to the extent of the occasion, where criticism was invited by unusual publicity. In the canvass which the Senator had with his opponent, Mr. Lincoln, and the debates of which have been published in a book, we find much which, if it be consistent with his course as I had known it, only proves to me how little able I was to understand his meaning in former times.

The Kansas-Nebraska Bill having agreed the right for which I contend to be the subject of judicial decision; it having specially provided the mode and facilitated the process by which that right should be brought to the courts and finally decided; not allowing any check to be interposed because of amount, that bill having continued the provision which had been introduced into the New Mexico Bill, how are we to understand the Senator's declarations, that, let the Supreme Court decide as they may, the inhabitants of a Territory may lawfully admit or exclude slavery as they please?

What a hollow promise was given to us in the provision referring this vexed question to judicial decision, in order that we might reach a point on which we might peacefully rest, if the inhabitants of the Territories for which Congress had legislated could still decide the question and set aside any decision of the Supreme Court, and do this lawfully. I ask, was it not to give us a stone, when he promised us bread; to incorporate a provision in the organic act securing the right of appeal to the courts, if, as now stated, those courts were known to be powerless to grant a remedy?

Here there is a very broad distinction to be drawn between the power of the inhabitants of a Territory, or of any local community, lawfully to do a thing, and forcibly to do it. If the Senator had said, that whatever might be the decision of the Supreme Court, whatever might be the laws of Congress, whatever might be the laws of the Territories, in the face of an infuriated mob, such as he described on another occasion, it would be impossible for a man to hold a slave against their will, he would but have avowed the truism that in our country the law waits upon public opinion. But he says that they can do it lawfully. If his position had been such as I have just stated, it would have struck me as the opinion I had always supposed him to entertain. More than that, it would have struck me as the opinion which no one could gainsay; which, at any time, I would have been ready to admit. Nothing is more clear than that no law could prevail in our country, where force, as a governmental mean, is almost unknown, against a pervading sentiment in the community. Every body admits that; and it was in that view of the case that this question has been so often declared to be a mere abstraction. It is an abstraction so far as any one would expect in security to hold against the fixed purpose and all-pervading will of the community, whether territorial or other, a species of property, ambulatory, liable, because it has mind enough to go, to be enticed away whenever freed from physical restraint, and which would be nearly valueless if so restrained. It may be an abstraction as a practical question of pecuniary advantage, but it is not the less dear to those who assert the constitutional right. It would constitute a very good reason why no one should ever say there was an attempt to force slavery on an unwilling people, but no reason why the right should not be recognized by the Federal Government as one belonging to the equal privileges and immunities of every citizen of the United States.

But the main point of the Senator's argument—and it deserved to be so, because it is the main question now in the public mind—was, what is the meaning of non-intervention? He defined it to be synonymous with squatter sovereignty, or with popular sovereignty. . . . . .

The Senator and myself do not seem to be getting any nearer together; because the very thing which he describes constitutes the only case in which I would admit the necessity, and, consequently, the propriety of the people acting without authority. If men were cast upon a desert island, the sovereignty of which was unknown, over which no jurisdiction was exercised, they would find themselves necessitated to establish rules which should subsist between themselves; and so the people of California, when the Congress failed to give them a government; when it refused to enact a territorial law; when, paralyzed by the power of contending factions, it left the immigrants to work their own unhappy way; they had a right—a right growing out of the necessity of the case—to make rules for the government of their local affairs. But this was not sovereignty. It was the exercise, between man and man, of a social function necessary to preserve peace in the absence of any controlling power—essential to conserve the relations of person and property. The sovereignty, if it existed in any organization or government of the world, remained there still; and whenever that sovereignty extended itself over them, whether shipwrecked mariners, or adventurous Americans—whether cast off by the sea, or whether finding their weary way across the desert plains which lie west of the Mississippi—whenever the hand of the Government holding sovereign jurisdiction was laid upon them, they became subject; their sovereign control of their own affairs ceased. In our case, the directing hand of the Government is laid upon them at the moment of the enactment of an organic law Therefore, the very point at which the Senator begins his sovereignty, is the point at which the necessity, and, in my view, the claim ceases.

But suppose that a territorial legislature, acting under an organic law, not defining their municipal powers further than has been general in such laws, should pass a law to exclude slave property, would the Senator vote to repeal it?

MR. DOUGLAS. I will answer. I would not, because the Democratic party is pledged to non-intervention; because, furthermore, whether such an act is constitutional or not is a judicial question. If it is unconstitutional, the court will so decide, and it will be null and void without repeal. If it is constitutional, the people have a right to pass it. If unconstitutional, it is void, and the court will ascertain the fact; and we pledged our honors to abide the decision. . . . . . .

MR. DAVIS. If it will not embarrass the Senator, I would ask him if, as Chief Executive of the United States, he would sign a bill to protect slave property in State, Territory, or District of Columbia—an act of Congress?

MR. DOUGLAS. It will be time enough for me, or any other man, to say what bills he will sign, when he is in a position to exercise the power.

MR. DAVIS. The Senator has a right to make me that answer. I was only leading on to a fair understanding of the Senator and myself about non-intervention. . . . . . .

I think it now appears that, in the minds of the gentlemen, non-intervention is a shadowy, unsubstantial doctrine, which has its application according to the circumstances of the case. It ceased to apply when it was necessary to annul an act in Kansas in relation to the political rights of the inhabitants. It had no application when it was necessary to declare that the old French laws should not be revived in the Territory of Kansas after the repeal of the Missouri Compromise; but it rose an insurmountable barrier when we proposed to sweep away the Mexican decrees, usages, or laws, and leave the Constitution and laws of the United States unfettered in their operation in the Territory acquired from Mexico. It thus seems to have a constantly varying application, and, as I have not yet reached a good definition, one which quite satisfies me, I must take it as I find it in the Senator's speech, in which he says Alabama asserted the doctrine of non-intervention in 1856. The Alabama resolutions of 1856 asserted the right to protection, and the duty of the Federal Government to give it. So, if he stands upon the resolutions of Alabama in 1856, non-intervention is very good doctrine, and exactly agrees with what I believe—no assumption, by the Federal Government, of any powers over the municipal territorial governments which is not necessary; that the hand of Federal power shall be laid as lightly as possible upon any territorial community; that its laws shall be limited to the necessities of each case; that it shall leave the inhabitants as unfettered in the determination of their local legislation as the rights of the people of the States will permit, and the duty of the General Government will allow. But when non-intervention is pressed to the point of depriving the arm of the Federal Government of its one great function of protection, then it is the doctrine which we denounce—which we call squatter sovereignty; the renunciation by Congress, and the turning over to the inhabitants a sovereignty which, rightfully, it does not belong to the one to grant or the other to claim, and, further and worse, thus to divest the Federal Government of a duty which the Constitution requires it to perform.

To show that this view is not new—that it does not rest singly on the resolutions of Alabama, I will refer to a subject, the action upon which has already been quoted in this debate—the Oregon Bill. During the discussion of the Oregon Bill, I offered in the Senate, June 23, 1848, an amendment which I will read:

"*Provided*, That nothing contained in this act shall be so construed as to authorize the prohibition of domestic slavery in said Territory, whilst it remains in the condition of a Territory of the United States."

Upon this, I will cite the authority of Mr. Calhoun, in his speech on the Oregon Bill, June 27, 1848:

"The twelfth section of this bill is intended to assert and maintain this demand of the non-slaveholding States, while it remains a Territory, not openly or directly, but indirectly, by extending the provisions of the bill for the establishment of the Iowa Territory to this, and by ratifying the acts of the informal and self-constituted government of Oregon, which, among others, contains one prohibiting the introduction of slavery. It thus, in reality, adopts what is called the Wilmot proviso, not only for Oregon, but, as the Bill now stands, for New Mexico and California. The amendment, on the contrary, moved by the Senator from Mississippi, near me [Mr. Davis], is intended to assert and maintain the position of the slave-holding States. It leaves the Territory free and open to all the citizens of the United States, and would overrule, if adopted, the act of the self-constituted Territory of Oregon, and the twelfth section, as far as it relates to the subject under consideration. We have thus fairly presented the grounds taken by the non-slaveholding and the slave-holding States, or as I shall call them, for the sake of brevity, the Northern and Southern States, in their whole extent, for discussion."—*Appendix to Congressional Globe, Thirtieth Congress, first Session*, p. 868.

I will quote also one of the speeches which he made near the close of his life, at a time when he was so far wasted by disease that it was necessary for him to ask the Senator from Virginia, who sits before me [Mr. Mason], to read the speech which his tameless spirit impelled him to compose, but which he was physically unable to deliver; and once again he came to the Senate chamber, when standing yet more nearly on the confines of death; he rose, his heart failing in its functions, his voice faltered, but his will was so strong that he could not realize that the icy hand was upon him, and he erroneously thought he was oppressed by the weight of his overcoat. True to his devotion to the principles he had always advocated, clinging, to the last hour of his life, to the duty to maintain the rights of his constituents, still he was here, and his honored, though feeble, voice was raised for the maintenance of the great principle to which his life had been devoted. From the speech I read as follows:

"The plan of the administration can not save the Union, because it can have no effect whatever towards satisfying the States composing the Southern section of the Union, that they can, consistently with safety and honor, remain in the Union. It is, in fact, but a modification of the Wilmot proviso. It proposes to effect the same object—to exclude the South from all territory acquired by the Mexican treaty. It is well known that the South is united against the Wilmot proviso, and has committed itself, by solemn resolutions, to resist should it be adopted. Its opposition *is not to the name*, but that which it *proposes to effect.* That, the Southern States hold to be unconstitutional, unjust, inconsistent with their equality as members of the common Union, and calculated to destroy irretrievably the equilibrium between the two sections. These objections equally apply to what, for brevity, I will call the executive proviso. There is no difference between it and the Wilmot, except in the mode of effecting the object; and in that respect, I must say that the latter is much the least objectionable. It goes to its object openly, boldly, and distinctly. It claims for Congress unlimited power over the Territories, and proposes to assert it over the territories acquired from Mexico by a positive prohibition of slavery. Not so the executive proviso. It takes an indirect course, and, in order to elude the Wilmot proviso, and thereby avoid encountering the united and determined resistance of the South, it denies, by implication, the authority of Congress to legislate for the Territories, and claims the right as belonging exclusively to the inhabitants of the Territories. But to effect the object of excluding the South, it takes care, in the meantime, to let in immigrants freely from the Northern States, and all other quarters, except from the South, which it takes special care to exclude by holding up to them the danger of having their slaves liberated under the Mexican laws. The necessary consequence is to exclude the South from the Territories, just as effectually as would the Wilmot proviso. The only difference, in this respect, is, that what one proposes to effect directly and openly, the other proposes to effect indirectly and covertly.

"But the executive proviso is more objectionable than the Wilmot in another and more important particular. The latter, to effect its object, inflicts a dangerous wound upon the Constitution, by depriving the Southern States, as joint partners and owners of the Territories, of their rights in them; but it inflicts no greater wound than is absolutely necessary to effect its object. The former, on the contrary, while it inflicts the same wound, inflicts others equally great, and, if possible, greater, as I shall next proceed to explain.

"In claiming the right for the inhabitants, instead of Congress, to legislate for the Territories, the executive proviso assumes that the sovereignty over the Territories is vested in the former, or, to express it in the language used in a resolution offered by one of the Senators from Texas [General Houston, now absent], they 'have the same inherent right of self-government as the people in the States.' The assumption is utterly unfounded, unconstitutional, without example, and contrary to the entire practice of the Government, from its commencement to the present time, as I shall proceed to show."—*Calhoun's Works*, vol. 4, p. 562.

Mr. Davis. I find that I must abridge, by abstaining from the reading of extracts. When this question arose in 1820, Nathaniel Macon, by many considered the wisest man of his day, held the proposed interference to be unauthorized and innovative. In arguing against the Missouri Compromise, as it was called—the attempt by Congress to prescribe where slaves might or might not be held—the exercise, by the Federal Government north of a certain point, of usurped power by an act of inhibition, Mr. Macon said our true policy was that which had thus far guided the country in safety: the policy of non-intervention. By non-intervention he meant the absence of hostile legislation, not the absence of governmental protection. Our doctrine on this point is not new, but that of our opponents is so.

The Senator from Illinois assumes that the congressional acts of 1850 meant no legislation in relation to slave property; while, in the face of that declaration, stand the laws enacted in that year, and the promise of another, which has not been enacted—laws directed to the question of slavery and slave property; one even declaring, in certain contingencies, as a penalty on the owner, the emancipation of his slave in the District of Columbia. If no action upon the question was the prevailing opinion, what does the legislation mean? Was it non-action in the District of Columbia? Be it remembered, the resolution of the Cincinnati platform says, "Non-interference, by Congress, with slavery in State and Territory, or in the District of Columbia." They are all upon the same footing.

Again, he said that the Badger amendment was a declaration of no protection to slave property. The Badger amendment declares that the repeal of the Missouri Compromise shall not revive the laws or usages which preëxisted that compromise; and the history of the times, so far as I understand it, is, that it intended to assure those gentlemen who feared that the laws of France would be revived in the Territories of Kansas and Nebraska, by the repeal of the act of 1820, and that they would be held responsible for having, by congressional act, established slavery. The Southern men did not desire Congress to establish slavery. It has been our uniform declaration that we denied the power of the Federal Government either to establish or prohibit it; that we claimed for it protection as property recognized by the Constitution, and we claimed the right for it, as property, to go, and to receive federal protection wherever the jurisdiction of the United States is exclusive. We claim that the Constitution of the United States, in recognizing this property, making it the basis of representation, put it, not upon the footing which it holds between foreign nations, but upon the basis of the compact or union of the States; that, under the delegated grant to regulate commerce between the States, it did not belong to a State; therefore, without breach of contract, they can not, by any regulation, prohibit transit, and the compact provided that they should not change the character of master and slave in the case of a fugitive. Could Congress surrender, for the States and their citizens, the claim and protection for those or other constitutional rights, against invasion by a State? If not, surely it can not be done in the case of a Territory, a possession of the States. The word "protecting," in that amendment, referred to laws which preëxisted—laws which it was not designed, by the Democrats, to revive when they declared the repeal of the Missouri Compromise; and, therefore, I think, did not affect the question of constitutional right and of federal power and duty.

In all these territorial bills we have the language "subject to the Constitution;" that is to say, that the inhabitants are to manage their local affairs in their own way, subject to the Constitution; which, I suppose, might be rendered thus: "In their own way, provided their own way shall be somebody else's way;" for "subject to the Constitution" means, in accordance with an instrument with which the territorial inhabitants had nothing to do; with the construction of which they were not concerned; in the adoption of which they had no part, and in relation to which it has sometimes been questioned whether they had any responsibility. My own views, as the Senator is aware from previous discussions, (and it is needless to repeat,) are that the Constitution is co-extensive with the United States; that the designation includes the Territories, that they are necessarily subject to the Constitution. But if they be subject to the Constitution, and subject to the organic act, that is the language used; that organic act being the law of Congress, that Constitution being the compact of the States—the territorial inhabitants having no lot or part in one or the other, save as they are imposed upon them—where is their claim to sovereignty? Where is their right to do as they please? The States have a compact, and the agent of the States gives to the Territories a species of constitution in the organic act, which endures and binds them until they throw off what the Senator on another occasion termed the minority condition, and assume the majority condition as a State. The remark to which I refer was on the bill to admit Iowa and Florida into the Union. The Senator then said:

"The father may bind the son during his minority, but the moment that he (the son) attains his majority, his fetters are severed, and he is free to regulate his own conduct. So, sir, with the Territories; they are subject to the jurisdiction and control of Congress during infancy, their minority; but when they attain their majority, and obtain admission into the Union, they are free from all restraints and restrictions, except such as the Constitution of the United States imposes upon each and all of the States."

This was the doctrine of territorial sovereignty—perhaps that is the phrase—at that period. At a later period, in March, 1856, the Senator said:

"The sovereignty of a Territory remains in abeyance, suspended in the United States in trust for the people, until they shall be admitted into the Union as a State. In the meantime, they are admitted to enjoy and exercise all the rights and privileges of self-government, in subordination to the Constitution of the United States, and in obedience to the organic law passed by Congress in pursuance of that instrument."

If it be admitted—and I believe there is no issue between the Senator and myself on that point—that the Congress of the United

12

States have no right to pass a law excluding slaves from a Territory, or determining in the Territory the relation of master and slave, of parent and child, of guardian and ward; that they have no right anywhere to decide what is property, but are only bound to protect such rights as preëxisted the formation of the Union—to perform such functions as are intrusted to them as the agent of the States—then how can Congress, thus fettered, confer upon a corporation of its creation—upon a territorial legislature, by an organic act, a power to determine what shall be property within the limits of such Territory?

But, again, if it were admitted that the territorial inhabitants did possess this sovereignty: that they had the right to do as they pleased on all subjects, then would arise the question, if they were authorized, through their representatives, thus to act, whence came the opposition to what was called the Lecompton Constitution? How did Congress, under this state of facts, get the right to inquire whether those representatives in that case really expressed the will of the people. Still more; how did Congress get the right to decide that those representatives must submit their action to a popular vote in a manner not prescribed by the people of the Territory, however eminently it may have been advisable, convenient, and proper in the judgment of the Congress of the United States? What revisory function had we, if they, through their representatives, had full power to act on all such subjects whatsoever?

I have necessarily, in answering the Senator, gone somewhat into the *argumentum ad hominem*. Though it is not entirely exhausted, I think enough has been said to show the Senate in what the difference between us consists. If it be necessary further to illustrate it, I might ask how did he propose to annul the organic act for Utah, if the recognition by the Congress of a sufficient number of inhabitants to justify the organization of a territorial government transferred the sovereignty to the inhabitants of the Territory? If sovereignty passed by the recognition of the fact, how did he propose, by congressional act, to annul the territorial existence of Utah?

It is this confusion of ideas, it is this confounding of terms, this changing of language, this applying of new meanings to words, out of which, I think, a large portion of the dispute arises. For instance, it is claimed that President Pierce, in using the phrase "existing and incipient States," meant to include all Territories, and thus that he had bound me to a doctrine which precluded my strictures on what I termed squatter sovereignty. This all arises from the misuse of language. An incipient State, according to my idea, is the territorial condition at the moment it changes into that of a State. It is when the people assemble in convention to form a constitution as a State, that they are in the condition of an incipient State. Various names were applied to the Territories at an earlier period. Sometimes they were called "new States," because they were expected to be States; sometimes they were called "States in embryo," and it requires a determination of the language that is employed before it is possible to arrive at any conclusion as to the differences of understanding between gentlemen. Therefore, it was, and, I think, very properly, (but not, as the Senator supposed, to catechise him,) that I asked him what he meant by non-intervention, before I commenced these remarks.

In the same line of errors was the confusion which resulted in his assuming that the evils I described as growing out of his doctrine on the plains of Kansas, were a denunciation, on my part, of the bill called the Kansas-Nebraska Bill. At the time that bill passed, I did not foresee all the evils which have resulted from the doctrine based upon it, but which I do not think the bill sustains. I am not willing now to turn on those who were in a position which compelled them to act, made them responsible, and to divest myself of any responsibility which belongs to any opinion I entertained. I will not seek to judge after the fact and hold the measure up against those who had to judge before. Therefore I will frankly avow that I should have sustained that bill if I had been in the Senate; but I did not foresee or apprehend such evils as immediately grew up on the plains of Kansas. I looked then, as our fathers had looked before, to the settlement of the question of what institutions should exist there, as one to be determined by soil and climate, and by the pleasure of those who should voluntarily go into the country. Such, however, was not the case. The form of the Kansas-Nebraska Bill invited to a controversy—not foreseen. I was not charging the Senator with any responsibility for it, but the variation of its terms invited contending parties to meet on the plains of Kansas, and had well-nigh eventuated in civil war. The great respect which even the most lawless of those adventurers in Kansas had for the name and the laws of the United States, served, by the timely interposition of the Federal force and laws, to restrain the excited masses and prevented violence from assuming larger proportions than combats between squads of adventurers.

This brings me in the line of rejoinder, to the meaning of the phrase, "the people of a Territory, like those of a State, should decide for themselves," etc., the language quoted against the President in the remarks of the Senator. This, it was announced, was squatter sovereignty in its broadest sense; and it was added, that the present Executive was elected to the high office he holds on that construction of the platform. Now, I do not know how it is that the Senator has the power to decide why the people voted for a candidate. I rather suppose, among the many millions who did vote, there must have been a variety of reasons, and that it is not in the power of any one man to declare what determined the result. But waiving that, is it squatter sovereignty in its broadest sense? Is it a declaration that the inhabitants of a Territory can exercise all the powers of a State? It says that, "like the people of a State," they may decide for themselves. Then how do the people of a State decide the question of what shall be property within the State? Every one knows that it is by calling a convention, and that the people, represented in convention, and forming a constitution their fundamental law, do this. Every one knows that, under the constitutions and bills of rights which prevail in the republican States of this Union, no legislature is invested with that power. If this be the mode which is prescribed in the States—the modes which the States must pursue—I ask you, in the name of common sense, can the language of the President be construed to mean that a territorial legislature may do what it is admitted the legislature of a State can not; or that the inhabitants of a Territory can assemble a convention, and form a fundamental law overriding the organic act, to which the Senator has already acknowledged they stand subject until they be admitted as a State?

We of the South, I know, are arraigned, and many believe justly, for starting a new question which distracts the Democratic party. I have endeavored, therefore, to show that it is not new. I have also asserted, what I think is clear, that if it were new, but yet a constitutional right, it is not only our province, but our duty to assert it—to assert it whenever or wherever that right is controverted. It is asserted now with more force than at a former period, for the simple reason that it is now denied, to an extent which has never been known before. We do not seek, in the cant language of the day, to force slavery on an unwilling people. We know full well there is no power to do it; and our limited observation has not yet made us acquainted with the man who was likely to have a slave forced upon him, or who could get one without paying a very high price for him. He must first have the will, and, secondly, he must put money in his purse to enable him to get one. They are too valuable among those by whom they are now owned, to be forced upon any body. Not admitting the correctness of the doctrine which the Senator promulgated in his magazine article in relation to a local character of slave property, I recognize the laws of nature, and that immigration will follow in the lines where any species of labor may be most profitably employed; all, therefore, we have asked—fulfillment of the original compact of our fathers—was that there should be no discrimination; that all property should be equally protected; that we should be permitted to go into every portion of the United States save where some sovereign power has said slaves shall not be held, and to take with us our slave property in like manner as we would take any other; no more than that. For that, our Government has contended on the high seas against foreign powers. That has entered into our negotiations, and has been recognized by every government against whom a claim has been asserted. Where our property was captured on the land during the period of an invasion, Great Britain, by treaty, restored it, or paid for it. Wherever it has suffered loss on the high seas, down to a very recent period, we have received indemnity; and where we have not, it was only because the power and duty of the Federal Government was sacrificed to this miserable strife in relation to property, with the existence of which, those making the interference had no municipal connection, or moral responsibility.

I do not admit that sovereignty necessarily exists in the Federal Government or in a territorial government. I deny the Senator's proposition, which is broadly laid down, of the necessity which must exist for it in the one place or the other. I hold that sovereignty exists only in a State, or in the United States in their associated capacity, to whom sovereignty may be transferred, but that their agent is incapable of receiving it, and, still more, of transferring it to territorial inhabitants.

I was sorry for some of the remarks which he thought it necessary to make, as to the position of the South on this question, and for his assertion that the resolutions of the convention of

1848 put the pro-slavery men and the Abolitionists on the same ground. I think it was altogether unjust. I did not think it quite belonged to him to make it. I was aware that his opponent, in that canvass to which I referred, had made a prophecy that he was, sooner or later, to land in the ranks of the Republicans. Even if I had believed it, I would not have chosen—and it is due to candor to say I do not believe—— . . . . . .

MR. DAVIS. Well, it is unimportant. I feel myself constrained, because I promised to do it, to refer to some portion of the joint record of the Senator and myself in 1850, or, as I have consumed so much time, I would avoid it. In that same magazine article, to which I have referred, the Senator took occasion to refer to some part which I had taken in the legislation of 1850; and I must say he presented me unfairly. He put me in the attitude of one who was seeking to discriminate, and left himself in the position of one who was willing to give equal protection to all kinds of property. In that magazine article the Senator represents Mr. Davis, of Mississippi, as having endeavored to discriminate in favor of slave property, and Mr. Chase, of Ohio, as having made a like attempt against it; and he leaves himself, by his argument, in the attitude of one who concurred with Mr. Clay in opposition to both propositions.

I offered an amendment to the compromise bill of 1850, which was to strike out the words "in respect to," and insert "and introduce or exclude," and after the word "slavery" to insert the following:

"*Provided*, That nothing herein contained shall be construed to prevent said territorial legislature passing such laws as may be necessary for the protection of the rights of property of any kind which may have been or may be hereafter, conformably to the Constitution and laws of the United States, held in, or introduced into, said Territory."

Mr. Chase's amendment is in these words:

"*Provided further*, That nothing herein contained shall be construed as authorizing or permitting the introduction of slavery, or the holding of persons as property within said Territory."

Whilst the quotation in the magazine article left me in the position already stated, the debates which had occurred between us necessarily informed the Senator that it was not my position, for I brought him in that debate to acknowledge it.

On that occasion, I argued for my amendment as an obligation of the Government to remove obstructions; to give the fair operation to constitutional right; and so far from the Senator having stood with Mr. Clay against all these propositions, the fact appears, on page 1134 of the *Globe*, that, upon the vote on Chase's amendment, Douglas voted for it, and Davis and Clay voted against it; that upon the vote on Davis' amendment, Clay and Davis voted for it, and Douglas voted against it.

MR. DOUGLAS. The Senator should add, that that vote was given under the very instructions to which he referred the other day, and which are well known to the Senate, and are on the table.

MR. DAVIS. I was aware that the Senator had voted for Mr. Seward's amendment, the "Wilmot proviso," under these instructions, but I receive his explanation. Mr. Berrien offered an amendment to change the provision, which said there should be no legislation in respect to slavery, so as to make it read, "there shall be no legislation establishing or prohibiting African slavery." Mr. Clay voted for that; so did Mr. Davis. Mr. Douglas voted against it. Mr. Hale offered an amendment to Mr. Berrien's amendment, to add the word "allowing." Here Mr. Douglas voted for Mr. Hale's amendment, and against Davis and Clay. Then a proposition was made to continue the Mexican laws against slavery until repealed by Congress. I think I proved—at least I did to my own satisfaction—that there was no such Mexican law; that it was a decree, and that the legislation which occurred under it had never been executed. But that proposition by Mr. Baldwin, which was to continue the Mexican laws in force, was brought to a vote, and again Mr. Douglas voted for it, and Mr. Davis and Mr. Clay voted against it. When another proposition was brought forward to amend by "removing the obstructions of Mexican laws and usages to any right of person or property by the citizens of the United States in the Territories aforesaid," I do not find the Senator's name among those who voted, though, by reference to the Appendix, I learned he was present immediately afterwards, by his speaking to another amendment.

Thus we find the Senator differing from me on this question, as was stated; but we do not find him concurring with Mr. Clay, as was stated; and we do not find the proposition which I introduced, and which was mentioned in the magazine article, receiving the joint opposition of himself and Mr. Clay; and yet his remarks in the Senate the other day went upon the same theory, that Mr. Clay and himself had been coöperating. Now, the fact of the case is, that they agreed in supporting the final passage of the bill, and I was against it. I was one of the few Southern men who resisted, in all its stages, what was called the compromise, or omnibus bill. I have consumed the time of the Senate by this reference, made as brief as I could, on account of the remarks the Senator had made.

Coupled with this arraignment of myself, at a time when he says he had leisure to discuss the question with the Attorney-General, but when there was nothing in my position certainly to provoke the revision of my course in Congress, is his like review of it in the Senate. As I understood his remarks, for I did not find them in the *Congressional Globe* the next morning, he vaunted his own consistency and admitted mine, but claimed his to be inside and mine outside of the Democratic organization. Is it so? Will our votes on test questions sustain it? The list of yeas and nays would, on the points referred to, exhibit quite the reverse. And it strikes me that, on the recent demonstrations we have had, when the Democratic administration was, as it were, put on its trial in relation to its policy in Kansas, the Senator's associations, rather than mine, were outside of the Democratic organization. How is it, on the pending question—the declaration of great principles of political creed—the Senator's position is outside of the Senate's Democracy, and mine in it, so that I do not see with what justice he attempts that discrimination between him and me? That the difference exists, that it involves a division greater or less in Democratic ranks, is a personal regret, and I think a public misfortune. It gives me, therefore, no pleasure to dwell upon it, and it is now dismissed.

Mr. President, after having for forty years been engaged in bitter controversy over a question relating to common property of the States, we have reached the point where the issue is presented in a form in which it becomes us to meet it according to existing facts; where it has ceased to be a question to be decided on the footing of authority, and by reference to history. We have decided that too long had this question been disturbing the peace and endangering the Union, and it was resolved to provide for its settlement by treating it as a judicial question. Now, will it be said, after Congress provided for the adjustment of this question by the courts, and after the courts had a case brought before them, and expressed an opinion covering the controversy, that no additional latitude is to be given to the application of the decision of the court, though Congress had referred it specially to them; that it is to be treated simply and technically as a question of *meum et tuum*, such as might have arisen if there had been no such legislation by Congress? Surely it does not become those who have pointed us to that provision as the peace-offering, as the means for final adjustment, now to say that it meant nothing more than that the courts would go on hereafter, as heretofore, to try questions of property.

The courts have decided the question so far as they could decide any political question. A case arose in relation to property in a slave held within a Territory where a law of Congress declared tha such property should not be held. The whole case was before them; every thing, except the mere technical point that the law was not enacted by a territorial legislature. Why, then, if we are to abide by the decision of the Supreme Court in any future case, do they maintain this controversy on the mere technical point which now divides, disturbs, distracts, destroys the efficiency and the power of the Democratic party? To the Senator, I know, as a question of property, it is a matter of no consequence. I should do him injustice if I left any one to infer that I treated his argument as one made by a man prejudiced against the character of property involved in the question. That is not his position; but I assert that he is pursuing an *ignis fatuus*—not a light caught from the Constitution—but a vapor which has arisen from the corrupting cess-pools of sectional strife, of faction, and individual rivalry. Measured by any standard of common sense, its magnitude would be too small to disturb the adjustment of the balance of our country. There can be no appeal to humanity made upon this basis. Least of all could it be made to one who, like the Senator and myself, has seen this species of property in its sparse condition on the north-western frontier, and seen it go out without disturbing the tranquillity of the community, as it had previously existed without injury to any one, if not to the benefit of the individual who held it. He has no apprehension, he can have none, that it is to retard the political prosperity of the future States—now the Territories. He can have no apprehension that in that country, to which they never would be carried except for domestic purposes, they could ever so accumulate as to constitute a great political element. He knows, and every man who has had experience and judgment must admit, that the few who may be so carried there have nothing to fear but the climate, and that living in that close connection which belongs to one or half a dozen of them in a family, the kindest relations which it is possible to exist between master and dependent, exist between these domestics and their owners.

There is a relation belonging to this species of property, unlike that of the apprentice or the hired man, which awakens whatever there is of kindness or of nobility of soul in the heart of him who owns it; this can only be alienated, obscured, or destroyed by collecting this species of property into such masses that the owner is not personally acquainted with the individuals who compose it. In the relation, however, which can exist in the north-western Territories, the mere domestic connection of one, two, or, at most, half a dozen servants in a family, associating with the children as they grow up, attending upon age as it declines, there can be nothing against which either philanthropy or humanity can make an appeal. Not even the emancipationist could raise his voice, for this is the high road and the open gate to the condition in which the masters would, from interest, in a few years, desire the emancipation of every one who may thus be taken to the north-western frontier.

Mr. President, I briefly and reluctantly referred, because the subject had been introduced, to the attitude of Mississippi on a former occasion. I will now as briefly say, that in 1851, and in 1860, Mississippi was, and is, ready to make every concession which it becomes her to make to the welfare and the safety of the Union. If, on a former occasion, she hoped too much from fraternity, the responsibility for her disappointment rests upon those who fail to fulfill her expectations. She still clings to the Government as our fathers formed it. She is ready to-day and to-morrow, as in her past, and though brief, yet brilliant history, to maintain that Government in all its power, and to vindicate its honor with all the means she possesses. I say brilliant history; for it was in the very morning of her existence that her sons, on the plains of New Orleans, were announced, in general orders to have been the admiration of one army and the wonder of the other. That we had a division, in relation to the measures enacted in 1850, is true; that the Southern rights men became the minority in the election which resulted, is true; but no figure of speech could warrant the Senator in speaking of them as subdued; as coming to him or any body else for quarter. I deemed it offensive when it was uttered, and the scorn with which I repelled it at the instant, time has only softened to contempt. Our flag was never borne from the field. We had carried it in the face of defeat, with a knowledge that defeat awaited it; but scarcely had the smoke of the battle passed away which proclaimed another victor, before the general voice admitted that the field again was ours; I have not seen a sagacious, reflecting man, who was cognizant of the events as they transpired at the time, who does not say that, within two weeks after the election, our party was in a majority; and the next election which occurred showed that we possessed the State beyond controversy. How we have wielded that power it is not for me to say. I trust others may see forbearance in our conduct—that, with a determination to insist upon our constitutional rights, then and now, there is an unwavering desire to maintain the Government, and to uphold the Democratic party.

We believe now, as we have asserted on former occasions, that the best hope for the perpetuity of our institutions depends upon the coöperation, the harmony, the zealous action of the Democratic party. We cling to that party from conviction, that its principles and its aims are those of truth and the country, as we cling to the Union for the fulfillment of the purposes for which it was formed. Whenever we shall be taught that the Democratic party is recreant to its principles; whenever we shall learn that it can not be relied upon to maintain the great measures which constitute its vitality, I, for one, shall be ready to leave it. And so, when we declare our tenacious adherence to the Union, it is the Union of the Constitution. If the compact between the States is to be trampled into the dust; if anarchy is to be substituted for the usurpation and consolidation which threatened the Government at an earlier period; if the Union is to become powerless for the purposes for which it was established, and we are vainly to appeal to it for protection, then, sir, conscious of the rectitude of our course, the justice of our cause, self-reliant, yet humbly, confidingly trusting in the arm that guided and protected our fathers, we look beyond the confines of the Union for the maintenance of our rights. A habitual reverence and cherished affection for the Government will bind us to it longer than our interests would suggest or require; but he is a poor student of the world's history who does not understand that communities at last must yield to the dictates of their interests. That the affection, the mutual desire for the mutual good, which existed among our fathers, may be weakened in succeeding generations by the denial of right, and hostile demonstration, until the equality guaranteed, but not secured within the Union, may be sought for without it, must be evident to even a careless observer of our race. It is time to be up and doing. There is yet time to remove the causes of dissension and alienation which are now distracting, and have for years past divided the country.

If the Senator correctly described me as having, at a former period, against my own preferences and opinions, acquiesced in the decision of my party; if when I had youth, when physical vigor gave promise of many days, and the future was painted in the colors of hope, I could thus surrender my own convictions, my own prejudices, and coöperate with my political friends, according to their views, as to the best method of promoting the public good; now, when the years of my future can not be many, and experience has sobered the hopeful tints of youth's gilding; when, approaching the evening of life, the shadows are reversed, and the mind turns retrospectively, it is not to be supposed that I would abandon lightly, or idly put on trial, the party to which I have steadily adhered. It is rather to be assumed that conservatism, which belongs to the timidity or caution of increasing years, would lead me to cling to—to be supported by, rather than to cast off, the organization with which I have been so long connected. If I am driven to consider the necessity of separating myself from those old and dear relations, of discarding the accustomed support, under circumstances such as I have described, might not my friends who differ from me pause and inquire whether there is not something involved in it which calls for their careful revision?

I desire no divided flag for the Democratic party, seek not to depreciate the power of the Senator, or take from him any thing of that confidence he feels in the large army which follows his standard. I prefer that his banner should lie in its silken folds to feed the moth; but if it unrestrainedly rustles, impatient to be unfurled, we who have not invited the conflict, shrink not from the trial; we will plant our flag on every hill and plain; it shall overlook the Atlantic and welcome the sun as he rises from its dancing waters; it shall wave its adieu as he sinks to repose in the quiet Pacific.

Our principles are national; they belong to every State of the Union; and though elections may be lost by their assertion, they constitute the only foundation on which we can maintain power, on which we can again rise to the dignity the Democracy once possessed. Does not the Senator from Illinois see in the sectional character of the vote he received, that his opinions are not acceptable to every portion of the country? Is not the fact that the resolutions adopted by seventeen States, on which the greatest reliance must be placed for Democratic support, are in opposition to the dogma to which he still clings, a warning that if he persists and succeeds in forcing his theory upon the Democratic party, its days are numbered? We ask only for the Constitution. We ask of the Democracy only from time to time to declare, as current exigencies may indicate, what the Constitution was intended to secure and provide. Our flag bears no new device. Upon its folds our principles are written in living light; all proclaiming the constitutional Union, justice, equality, and fraternity of our ocean-bound domain, for a limitless future.

CHAPTER VII.

ELECTION OF ABRAHAM LINCOLN—HISTORICAL IMPORTANCE OF THE EVENT—THE OBJECTS AIMED AT BY HISTORY AND BIOGRAPHY IDENTICAL IN THE DISCUSSION OF EVENTS OF THE LATE WAR—NORTHERN EVASION OF THE REAL QUESTION—THE SOUTH DID NOT ATTEMPT REVOLUTION—SECESSION A JUSTIFIABLE RIGHT EXERCISED BY SOVEREIGN STATES—BRIEF REVIEW OF THE QUESTION—WHAT THE FEDERALIST SAYS—CHIEF-JUSTICE MARSHALL—MR. MADISON—COERCION NOT JUSTIFIED AT THE NORTH PREVIOUS TO THE LATE WAR—REMARKS OF JOHN QUINCY ADAMS—OF ABRAHAM LINCOLN—OF HORACE GREELEY—SUCCESSFUL PERVERSION OF TRUTH BY THE NORTH—PROVOCATIONS TO SECESSION BY THE SOUTH—AGGRESSIONS BY THE NORTH—ITS PUNIC FAITH—LOSS OF THE BALANCE OF POWER—PATIENCE OF THE SOUTH—REMARKS OF HON. C. C. CLAY—WHAT THE ELECTION OF MR. LINCOLN MEANT—HIS ADMINISTRATIVE POLICY—REVELATIONS OF THE OBJECTS OF THE REPUBLICAN PARTY—WENDELL PHILLIPS—NO SECURITY FOR THE SOUTH IN THE UNION—MEETING OF CONGRESS—MR. DAVIS' ASSURANCE TO PRESIDENT BUCHANAN—CONCILIATORY COURSE OF MR. DAVIS—HIS CONSISTENT DEVOTION TO THE UNION, AND EFFORTS TO SAVE IT—FORESEES WAR AS THE RESULT OF SECESSION, AND URGES THE EXHAUSTION OF EVERY EXPEDIENT TO AVERT IT—THE CRITTENDEN AMENDMENT—HOPES OF ITS ADOPTION—DAVIS WILLING TO ACCEPT IT IN SPITE OF ITS INJUSTICE TO THE SOUTH—REPUBLICAN SENATORS DECLINE ALL CONCILIATORY MEASURES—THE CLARKE AMENDMENT—WHERE RESTS THE RESPONSIBILITY OF DISUNION?—STATEMENTS OF MESSRS. DOUGLAS AND COX—SECESSION OF THE COTTON STATES—A LETTER FROM JEFFERSON DAVIS TO R. B. RHETT, JR.—MR. DAVIS' FAREWELL TO THE SENATE—HIS REASONS FOR WITHDRAWING—RETURNS TO MISSISSIPPI—MAJOR-GENERAL OF STATE FORCES—ORGANIZATION OF THE CONFEDERATE GOVERNMENT—MR. DAVIS PRESIDENT OF THE CONFEDERATE STATES.

AS had been foreseen, and, indeed, as was the inevitable sequence of the disruption of the Democratic party, Abraham Lincoln, the candidate of the Republican party, was, in November, 1860, elected President of the United States. This was the supreme and sufficient incitement to the adoption of the dreaded resort of disunion. As the *occasion* which finally brought the South to the attitude of resistance, the event acquires vast historical importance.

When it is conceded that Mr. Lincoln was elected in accordance with the *forms* of the Constitution, having received a majority of electoral votes; that the mere ceremony of election was attended by no unusual circumstances, we concede every possible ground upon which can be based an argument denying its ample justification of the course pursued by the South. Such an argument, however, leads to a wholly untenable conclusion, and may be easily exposed in its hypocritical evasion of the real question. We are here required to note the distinction between *cause* and *occasion.* As the final consummation of tendencies, long indicating the result of disunion, this event has an appropriate place in the recapitulation of those influences, and can be rightly estimated only in connection with their operation.

Trite observations upon the influence of passion and prejudice, over contemporary judgment, are not necessary to a due conception of the obstacles which, for the present, exclude candor from the discussion of the late movement for Southern independence. In the face of the disastrous overthrow of that movement, the wrecked hopes and fortunes of those who participated in it, discussion is chiefly serviceable, as it throws additional light upon the development of those eternal principles in whose ceaseless struggles men are only temporary agents.

History and biography are here most intimately blended;

beginning from the same stand-point, they encounter common difficulties, and aim to explore the same general grounds of observation. So far as a verdict—from whatever tribunal, whether rendered at the bar of justice or in the award of popular opinion, when the embers of recent strife are still fiercely glowing—can affect the dispassionate judgment of History, the Southern people can not be separated, either in fact or in sentiment, from Jefferson Davis. He was the illustrious compatriot of six millions of freemen, who struck for nationality and independence, and lost—as did Greece and Poland before them; or he and they were alike insurgents, equally guilty of the crime of treason.

With an adroitness which does credit to the characteristic charlatanism of the North, an infinite variety of special questions and side issues have been interwoven with the narrative of the late war, for the obvious purpose of confounding the judgment of mankind regarding the great question which really constitutes the gravamen of the controversy. Conspicuous among these efforts, from both audacity and plausibility, are appeals to the sympathies of the world, in consideration of the abolition of slavery, which it is well known was merely an incident, and not the avowed design of the war.

Persistent in its introduction of the *moral* question of slavery, the North seeks to shield itself from the reproach justly visited upon its perpetration of an atrocious political crime, by an insolent intrusion of a false claim to the championship of humanity. Whatever may be the decision of Time upon the merits of slavery, it is in vain for the North to seek escape from its responsibility for an institution, protected and sustained by a government which was the joint creation of Southern and Northern hands.

The attempted dissolution of the Union by the South was a movement involving moral and political considerations, not unlike those incidental to revolutions in general, yet presenting certain peculiar characteristics, traceable to the inherent and distinctive features of the American political system. These latter considerations constitute a vital part of its justification. The South did not appeal only to the inalienable right of revolution, which is the natural guarantee of resistance to wrong and oppression. Nor did the States, severally, as they assumed to sever their connection with the Union, announce a purpose of constitutional revolution, or adopt a course inviting or justifying violence. Mr. Davis and those who coöperated with him, neither by the acts of secession, nor the subsequent confederation of the States under a new government, could have committed *treason* against Mr. Lincoln, since they were not his subjects. Nor yet were they traitors to the Government of the United States, since the States of which they were citizens had rescinded the grant of powers voluntarily made by them to that Government, and begun to exercise them in conjunction with other powers which they had withheld by express reservation.

It is impossible to conceive a movement, contemplating such important political changes, more entirely unattended by displays of violence, passion, and disorder. A simple assertion, with due solemnity, by each State, of its sovereignty—a heritage which it had never surrendered, but which had been respected by innumerable forms of recognition in the history of the Union—and the exercise of those attributes of sovereignty, which are too palpable to require that they shall be indicated, was the peaceable method resorted to of terminating a political alliance which had become injurious to the highest interests of one of the parties. Could there have been a more becoming and dignified exercise of the vaunted right of self-government? It is that right to which America is so conspicuously committed, and which has been such an inexhaustible theme for the tawdry rhetoric of Northern eloquence.

Even in the insolence of its triumph, the North feels the necessity of at least a decent pretext for its destruction of the cardinal feature in the American system of government—the sovereignty of the States. With habitual want of candor, Northern writers pretend that the Constitution of the United States does not affirm the sovereignty of the States, and that, therefore, secession was treason against that Constitution to which they had subscribed; in other words, the created does not give authority to the creator—*i. e.*, the Constitution, which the States created, does not accredit sovereignty to the States, and, therefore, the States are not sovereign. It is not pretended that the States were not, each of them, originally independent powers, since they were so recognized by Great Britain, in the plainest terms, at the termination of the first revolution. Nor is it asserted that the union of the States, under the title of United States, was the occasion of any surrender of their individual sovereignty, as it was then declared that "each State retains its sovereignty, freedom, and independence." A conclusive demonstration of the retention of sovereignty by the States is seen in the entire failure of the Constitution, either by direct assertion or by implication, to claim its surrender to the Union.

If the sovereignty of the States be conceded, the South stands justified as having exercised an unquestionable right. It was never formally denied, even at the North, until Mr. Webster, in his debate with Mr. Calhoun, affirmed the doctrine of the supremacy of the Union, to which conclusion the Northern masses sprung with alacrity, as an available justification for compelling the submission of the South to the outrages which they had already commenced.

Volumes of testimony have been adduced, proving the theory of State sovereignty to have been the overwhelmingly predominant belief among the statesmen most prominent in the establishment of the Union, and in shaping the policy of the Government in its earlier history. Argument proved an unavailing offset to the stern decrees of the sword, and is quite unnecessary so long as the unanswerable logic of Calhoun, Davis, and a score of Southern statesmen remains upon the national records—a perpetual challenge, as yet unaccepted, to the boasted intellect of the North, and a significant warning of the final adjudication of the centuries. We shall intrude no argument of our own in support of State sovereignty, upon which rests the vindication of the South and her leaders. Before us are the apposite and conclusive assumptions of men who have been the revered sources of political inspiration among Americans.

The *Federalist*, that most powerful vindication of the Constitution, and earnest plea for its adoption by the States, assumes that it was a "compact," to which "the States, as distinct and independent sovereigns," were the parties. Yet this doctrine, the basis upon which rests the august handiwork of Madison and Hamilton, the "architects of the Constitution," when applied by Davis and his compatriots, becomes treason! Such is the extremity to which despotism, in its wretched plea of expediency, is driven; and the candid, enlightened American of to-day realizes, in his country, a land in which "truth is treason, and history is rebellion."

Chief-Justice Marshall, the great judicial luminary of America, and an authority not usually summoned to the support of doctrines hostile to the assumptions of Federal power, gave most emphatic testimony to the propriety of the States' Rights view of the relations of State and Federal authority. In the Virginia Convention which ratified the Constitution, he said: "The State governments did not derive their powers from the General Government. But each government derived its powers from the people, and each was to act according to the powers given it. Would any gentleman deny this? He demanded, if powers not given were retained by implication? Could any man say, no? Could any man say that this power was not retained by the States, since it was not given away?" The view so earnestly urged by Marshall, was not only avowed generally, but Virginia, Massachusetts, and Pennsylvania insisted upon a written declaration, in the Constitution, of the principle that certain attributes of sovereignty, which they did not delegate to the Union, were retained by the States.

Mr. Madison, whose great abilities were taxed to the utmost to secure the ratification of the Constitution by Virginia, vigorously and earnestly defended it against the allegation that it created a consolidated government. With the utmost difficulty, he secured a majority of ten votes, in the Virginia Convention, in favor of the Constitution, which his rival, Patrick Henry, denounced as destructive of State sovereignty.

Defining the expression, "We, the people," Mr. Madison said: "The parties to it were the people, but not the people as composing one great society, but the people as composing '*thirteen sovereignties.*'" To quote Mr. Madison again: "If it were a consolidated government, the assent of a majority of the people would be sufficient to establish it. But it was to be binding on the people of a State only by their own separate consent." Under the influence of these arguments, and others of the same import from Mr. Madison, whom she thought, from his close relations to the Constitution, high authority upon all questions pertaining to its character, Virginia finally acceded to the Union. It is especially noteworthy, however, that Virginia, when becoming a party to the Constitution, expressly affirmed, in the most solemn manner, the right to "resume" her grants of power to the Federal Government.

In deference to the accumulated evidence upon this subject, came the unqualified statement, from eminent Northern authority,* that, "This right [of secession] must be considered an ingredient in the original composition of the General Government, which, though not expressed, was mutually understood."

But whatever may be thought of the prescriptive and inherent right of sovereignty, exercised by the South in withdrawing from the Union, as deducible from the peculiar nature of the American system, and as expounded by the founders of that system, there can be no question as to its entire accordance with the *spirit* of American polity. Authority is abundant in support of the assertion that, not even in the North, previous to the inception of the present revolu-

*William Rawle, of Philadelphia, an able lawyer and constitutional expounder. Mr. Buchanan, in his history of his own administration, thus mentions him: "The right of secession found advocates afterwards in men of distinguished abilities and unquestioned patriotism. In 1825, it was maintained by Mr. William Rawle, of Philadelphia, an eminent and universally-respected lawyer. . . . . . His biographer says that, 'in 1791, he was appointed District Attorney of the United States,' and 'the situation of Attorney General was more than once tendered to him by Washington, but as often declined,' for domestic reasons."

tion, was the idea of a constrained connection with the Union entertained. From every source of Northern opinion has come indignant repudiation of a coerced association of communities, originally united by a common pledge of fealty to the right of self-government.

Upon this subject Mr. John Quincy Adams spoke in language of characteristic fervor: "The indissoluble link of union between the people of the several States of this confederated nation is, after all, not in the *right,* but in the *heart.* If the day should ever come (may heaven avert it!) when the affections of the people of these States shall be alienated from each other—when the fraternal spirit shall give way to cold indifference, or collision of interest shall fester into hatred, the bands of political association will not long hold together parties no longer attracted by the magnetism of conciliated interests and kindly sympathies; and far better will it be for the people of the disunited States to part in friendship from each other than to be held together by constraint."

Even Mr. Lincoln, whose statesmanship is not likely to be commemorated for its profundity or scholarship, fully comprehended the exaggerated reverence of the American mind for the "sacred right of self-government." Now that his homely phrases are dignified by the Northern masses with the sanctity of the utterances of Deity, assuredly there should be no apprehension that his opinions may not be deemed conclusive. In 1848, Mr. Lincoln said: "Any people whatever have the right to abolish the existing government, and form a new one that suits them better. This is a most valuable, a most sacred right."

A brave affirmation was this of the doctrine of the Declaration of Independence, that "Governments derive their just powers from the consent of the governed;" and one which would have commanded the united applause of the North, then and now, had the application concerned Hungary, Poland, Greece, or Mexico. But, with reference to the South, there was a most important modification of this admirable principle of equity and humanity. When asked, "Why not let the South go?" Abraham Lincoln, *the President*, in 1861, said: "*Let the South go! Where, then, shall we get our revenue?*" And the united North reëchoed: "*Let the South go! Where, then, shall we look for the bounties and monopolies which have so enriched us at the expense of those improvident, unsuspecting Southerners? Where shall we find again such patient victims of spoliation?*"

Mr. Horace Greeley frequently and emphatically, previous to the war, affirmed the right of changing its political association asserted by the South. Three days after the election of Mr. Lincoln, in November, 1860, his paper, the New York *Tribune*, said: "If the Cotton States shall become satisfied that they can do better out of the Union than in it, we insist on letting them go in peace. . . . . . We must ever resist the right of any State to remain in the Union, and nullify or defy the laws thereof. *To withdraw from the Union is quite another matter; and whenever any considerable section of our Union shall deliberately resolve to go out, we shall resist all coercive measures designed to keep it in.* We hope never to live in a Republic whereof one section is pinned to another by bayonets." On the 17th of December, 1860, the *Tribune* said: "If it [the Declaration of Independence] justifies the secession of three millions of colonists in 1776, *we do not see why it would not justify the secession of five millions of Southerners from the Federal Union in* 1861."

Such are a few illustrations, to which might be added innumerable quotations, of the same import, from the most prominent sources of Northern opinion. Never has there been a question so capable of positive solution and easy comprehension, when subjected to the test of candid investigation, and never so successful a purpose to exclude the illumination of facts by persistent and ingenious misrepresentation. The North has reason for its extravagant exultation at the skill and audacity with which the brazen front of hypocrisy, for a time, at least, has successfully sustained, in the name of humanity and liberty, the most monstrous imposition and transparent counterfeit of virtue ever designed upon an intelligent age.

To the triumphant historical vindication of the South, there remains only the essential condition of a clear and truthful statement of the provocations which impelled her to adopt that long-deferred remedy, which is the last refuge of a people whose liberties are imperiled. Secession, however strong in its prescriptive or implied justification as a principle, was not to be undertaken from caprice, or trivial causes of dissatisfaction.

Abuses, numerous, serious, and consecutive, were required before disunion became either desirable or acceptable to the South. The native conservatism of the Southern character renders it peculiarly averse to agitation ; to this were added social features, the safety of which would be greatly imperiled by civil war, and thus a train of influences tended to make Southern soil, of all others, the least favorable to the growth of revolutionary principles.

In the development of this volume, we have glanced at the progress of those sectional differences, at various periods precipitated by the insolent aggressions of Abolitionism, which steadily depreciated the value of the Union in Southern estimation. Continued aggressions by her enemies; their Punic faith, illustrated in a series of violated pledges, and habitual disregard of the conditions of the covenant which bound South and North together; petty outrages, taunts and insults, emanating from every possible source of public expression at the North, for many years had banished fraternal feeling and precluded those interchanges of comity between the sections which were the indispensable requisites to national harmony. It is undeniable, that for years previous to secession, the sentimental attachment to the Union, which was the distinctive characteristic of Southern patriotism—unlike the coarse, utilitarian estimate of the Union as a source of pecuniary profit, which constituted its value to the North—had been greatly impaired. Since 1850, and to a considerable extent during the preceding decade, the most sagacious statesmen of the South contemplated disunion as an event almost inevitable, unless averted by a contingency of very improbable occurrence. There must be an awakening by the North to a more just appreciation of its constitutional and patriotic obligations, or an unmanly submission by the South, to a condition of degrading inferiority, in a government to whose construction, prosperity, and distinction, she had contributed more than a proportionate share of influence.

Chief among the considerations which admonished the South of the perils which environed her situation in the Union, was the total destruction of that sectional balance, which had been wisely adjusted by its founders, as the safeguard of the weaker against the stronger influence. Having in mind the wise saying of Aristotle, that "the weak always desire what is equal and just, but the powerful pay no regard to it," the statesmen of 1787 designedly shaped the chart of government with a view to the preservation of equality. The struggle between the weaker element, naturally contending in behalf of the equilibrium, and the stronger striving for its overthrow, was, at an early period, distinctly foreshadowed. With characteristic prevision, Alexander Hamilton, probably the foremost statesman of his day, foretold the nature of this contest over the principle of equality. Said that sagacious publicist: "The truth is, it is a contest for power, not for liberty."

This contest, indeed, so long waged, was, many years since, decided overwhelmingly against the South. In 1850, the Northern majority in the House of Representatives, the popular branch of the government, had increased from a majority, in 1790, of five votes, to fifty-four. Years before, the legislation of Congress assumed that sectional bias, which was undeviatingly adhered to for the purpose, and with ample success, of the material depression of the South. Under the baleful influences of hostile legislation, of tariffs aimed directly at her commercial prosperity, of bounties for fostering multifarious Northern interests, her position in the Union was helpless and deplorable in the extreme. Yet, like a rock-bound Prometheus, with the insidious elements of destruction gnawing at her vitals, the South suffered herself to be chained by an influence of sentiment, of association, and reminiscence to the Union, fully conscious of the growing rapacity of her despoiler and of her own hopeless decline. Her infatuation was indeed marvelous, in trusting to the dawning of justice and generosity in a fierce, vindictive, and remorseless sectional majority.

The alarming portents of ultimately complete material prostration, to be consummated by these perversions of the purposes of the Union, were terribly significant, in view of the venom which actuated the enemies of the South. The sectional balance was hopelessly gone; Southern material prosperity destroyed by sectional legislation; not a check, originally provided by the Constitution for the protection of the weaker section, but had been virtually obliterated; Northern perfidy illustrated in the violation of every compact which, in operation, proved favorable to the South, while the latter was held to a rigid fidelity in all agreements favorable to her enemies; the nullification, by the legislatures of half the Northern States, of Federal laws for the protection of Southern property, are a few of those grievances which presented to the South the hard and inexorable alternative of resistance, or abject submission to endless insult and outrage.

A Southern Senator,* announcing the secession of his State, and his own consequent withdrawal from the Senate, stated the question in a form, which even then had the authority of history.

"Not a decade, nor scarce a lustrum, has elapsed (since Alabama became a State) that has not been strongly marked by proofs of the growth and power of that antislavery spirit of the Northern people, which seeks the overthrow of that domestic institution of the South, which is not only the chief source of her prosperity, but the very basis of her social order and State polity. It is to-day the master-spirit of the Northern States, and had before the secession of Alabama, of Mississippi, of Florida, or of South Carolina, severed most of the bonds of the Union. It denied us Christian communion, because it could not endure what it calls the moral leprosy of slave-holding; it refused us permission to sojourn, or even to pass through the North with our property; it claimed freedom for the slave, if brought by his

* Hon. C. C. Clay, of Alabama.

master into a Northern State; it violated the Constitution, and treaties, and laws of Congress, because designed to protect that property; it refused us any share of lands acquired mainly by our diplomacy, and blood, and treasure; it refused our property any shelter or security beneath the flag of a common government; it robbed us of our property, and refused to restore it; it refused to deliver criminals against our laws, who fled to the North with our property or our blood upon their hands; it threatened us by solemn legislative acts, with ignominious punishment, if we pursued our property into a Northern State; it murdered Southern men when seeking the recovery of their property on Northern soil; it invaded the borders of Southern States, poisoned their wells, burnt their dwellings, and murdered their people; it denounced us by deliberate resolves of popular meetings, of party conventions, and of religious, and even legislative assemblies, as habitual violators of the laws of God and the rights of humanity; it exerted all the moral and physical agencies that human ingenuity can devise, or diabolical malice can employ, to heap odium and infamy upon us, and to make us a by-word of hissing and of scorn throughout the civilized world."

There was no room for uncertainty as to the significance of the election of Abraham Lincoln to the Presidency, in 1860, by a party exclusively sectional in organization, and upon a platform, which virtually declared the Union, as then constituted, in opposition to justice, humanity, and civilization.

The real danger to the South, involved in this election, was that it was a *sectional* triumph—a victory of North over South, in a contest where the South risked every thing, the North nothing. From time immemorial sincere patriots of both sections had deprecated the formation of sectional parties, organized upon geographical interests, or upon ideas confined to limited portions of the Union. Washington, in his farewell injunction, admonished his countrymen of the deplorable results which must follow the presentation of such issues.

The Chicago platform was more than a menace to the South; it was a defiance of law, a declaration of war upon the Constitution. The election of Lincoln was both a legal and moral severance of the bonds of Union. While he received the united vote of the North, save New Jersey, he did not receive one electoral vote from the South. His shaping of his administration was consistent with the character of the party which elected him. All his constitutional advisers were Northern men or Southern Abolitionists; social outlaws in their own section, in consequence of their notorious personal depravity, and infidelity to their immediate fellow-citizens. Of like character were the subordinate appointments of the Federal Government in Southern communities.

Nor was there reason to doubt the policy of the Government under its new management. Mr. Lincoln had been sufficiently communicative of his own bitter hostility to Southern institutions. In fact, with much show of justice, his admirers claimed for him the original suggestion of the idea of an "irrepressible conflict," afterwards so elaborately pronounced by William H. Seward. Public announcements, from prominent speakers of the successful party, amply revealed the feast to which the South was invited. Wendell Phillips, the most able, eloquent, and sagacious of the original Abolitionists, thus pointedly defined the situation: "No man has a right to be surprised at this state of things. It is just what we have attempted to bring about. It is the first sectional party ever organized in this country. It does not know its own face, and calls itself national; but it is not national—it is sectional.

The Republican party is a party of the North pledged against the South."

Such was the complexion to which political affairs were brought by the election of Abraham Lincoln. There remained hardly a hope, even for future security or domestic tranquillity to the South, except in withdrawal from an association, in which she had become an inferior and an outcast—an object of oppression, outrage, and contumely. From a relentless Abolition majority she could expect no favors; and the Northern Democracy, so long her ally, for common purposes of party, had cowered before the storm of fanaticism, and repudiated the first demand made upon its fidelity to principle.

Congress assembled on the first Monday of December, 1860, a few weeks subsequent to the Presidential election. Never had that body met under circumstances of such gravity. Universal foreboding of peril to the nation was mingled with hope of such action, as would avert the impending calamities of disunion and civil war. There were few indications, at the opening of the session, of conciliatory sentiments; from the representatives of both sections came open defiance, and Northern members of both houses were more than ever bold in the utterance of insult and menace. Before the opening of the session, President Buchanan received from Mr. Davis the most satisfactory assurances of his coöperation with the administration in a pacific policy, having for its object the settlement of the national difficulties upon terms promotive of the peace of the country, and assuring the security of the South.* To such a

* It is not to be understood that Mr. Davis approved Mr. Buchanan's policy in the winter of 1861. The message of the President disappointed the South, and was offensive to many of his most attached supporters, in consequence of its denial of the right of secession. Denying the right of

settlement the efforts of Mr. Davis were addressed so long as there was the slightest ground for the indulgence of hope.

This session of Congress, the last which was held previous to the commencement of civil war, is chiefly interesting as the historical record of those patriotic efforts which were made to save the Union, and as furnishing incontestible proof of the guilt of those who, by their persistent refusal of all conciliatory propositions, are justly responsible for the calamities which were to befall the country. Happily for the reputation of Mr. Davis, the proof is authentic and conclusive in his favor upon these important questions. There is no portion of his career in which statesmanship, patriotism, and a noble appreciation of the claims of humanity shine forth more conspicuously. So overwhelming is the evidence that, in these last days of the Union, he was false to none of these high considerations, that the most mendacious assailants of himself and the cause he lately represented have not yet ventured to call it in question.

A disposition is frequently evinced to plead for him immunity from the responsibility of his position, as the leader of the Confederate movement, upon the score of his consistent Unionism, manifested in the prevailing conservatism of his course as a politician. He needs no such palliation. His devotion to the Union of the American fathers was as unquestionable as was that of Washington. His patriotism was illustrated by every mode of exemplification in the service of country. To

secession, Mr. Buchanan yet denied, also, the power of coercing the States, but subsequently lent himself to the latter policy. Mr. Davis freely testified his disappointment at certain positions taken in the Message, and criticised them with emphasis, but great courtesy. Mr. Buchanan indicates the special message of January, 1861, as the occasion of the termination of all friendly relations between himself and those whom he terms the "secession Senators."

substantiate his attachment to that association of States, designed by the fathers, sublime in its objects of mutual fidelity, generous sympathies, justice, and equality, no elaborate statement is required, nor could formal vindication strengthen its defenses.* He never arrayed himself against such a Union, but, abhorring that perverted instrument of sectional aggression, which the Government had become, he did accompany and lead his fellow-citizens in their exercise of the highest privilege of freemen.

He was always prepared to follow the principles of States' Rights to their logical consequences, and was yet consistent in his attachment to the Union. Thus he was a firm believer in the absolute sovereignty of the States, and of the enjoyment, by the States, of all the attributes of sovereignty, including, necessarily, the right of secession. He had never urged the expediency of secession, though, upon repeated occasions, he had foreshadowed its probable necessity in the future, as the only remedy remaining to the South in certain contingencies. In the Senate, in 1850, he thus alluded to the possibility of a successful organization of a sectional party: "The danger is one of our own times, and it is that sectional division of the people which has created the necessity of looking to the question of the balance of power, and which carries with it, when disturbed, the danger of disunion."

In 1859, again, he proclaimed, in unequivocal terms, his course in the event of the success of a party indorsing the Rochester pronunciamento of Mr. Seward. Yet his course,

* It is a notable fact that, years ago, the strong and avowed attachment of Mr. Davis for the Union, was habitually sneered at by some Southern men, who are now seeking to gratify their lust for place by "crooking the pregnant hinges of the knee," to those who persecute him and his countrymen.

subsequent to the election of Mr. Lincoln, was directed entirely in the interest of moderation. Having little hope of concession from the enemies of the South, in the moment of their overwhelming victory, he yet anxiously, earnestly entered that last struggle for the Constitution, before it passed into the keeping of iconoclasts, who were pledged to its destruction.

His zeal in behalf of pacification was actuated by considerations of humanity, no less ennobling than his impulse of disinterested patriotism. Regarding a long and bloody war as the certain result of dissolution, he anxiously sought to avert that calamitous result, and stood pledged to the acceptance of any basis of settlement which should guarantee the safety and honor of the South. At no time, however, did he advocate submission. His language in the Senate is explicit. Speaking of the secession of Mississippi, he said: "I, however, may be permitted to say, that I do think she has justifiable cause, and I approve of her act. I conferred with her people before that act was taken, counseled them then that, if the state of things which they apprehended should exist when the convention met, they should take the action which they have now adopted."

During the session, numerous efforts at compromise were made, in every instance emanating from Southern Representatives or Northern Democrats, the dominant party of the North declining all tenders of pacification, and offering no terms of conciliation in return. It is unnecessary to trace the progress of these abortive efforts, which, in the main, received the support of feeble minorities, and had, from their inception, no prospect of adoption.

There was one proposition, and probably only one, which embodied a competent basis of settlement, and was entitled to favor. This was called the "Crittenden Compromise," and originated with the venerable Kentucky Senator, by whose name it is designated. For a time it seemed that the demonstrations of popular sentiment in its favor, especially the well-ascertained readiness of a large majority of the Southern people to accept it, and its exceedingly practical nature, as a *final* settlement of the slavery question, would eventually secure its adoption by Congress. The result was a disappointment of this patriotic expectation, and a conclusive demonstration of the purpose of the Republican party to consent to no settlement which the South could accept.

An examination of the Crittenden proposition will reveal a most striking illustration of the ever-present spirit of accommodation, in matters affecting the safety of the Union, which, even in its last hours, was characteristic of the leaders and people of the South, and of the narrow, selfish, and exacting sectionalism of the North. In reality, it was little short of a surrender, in its ample concessions, to the encroachments of Abolitionism.

The resolutions introduced by Mr. Crittenden, in the Senate, on the 18th of December, 1860, contemplated amendments to the Constitution having the following objects: The prohibition of slavery in all Territories north of the old Missouri Compromise line, and providing protection for it south of that line; a denial of the power of Congress to abolish slavery in the District of Columbia, or in ports, arsenels, dock-yards, or wherever else the Federal Government exercised jurisdiction; remuneration to owners of escaped slaves by communities in which the Federal laws, providing rendition of slaves, might be violently obstructed. Such were the material features of the "Crittenden Compromise."

It will be seen at a glance how absurd was the misnomer of "compromise" applied to so one-sided a settlement. The South was required, by its provisions, to abandon the sacred right of protection to her property, guaranteed by the Constitution and unequivocally re-affirmed by the highest judicial tribunal in the land. The Supreme Court, in the Dred Scott case, had already decided the right to take slaves into all the Territories, while the Crittenden proposition prohibited it entirely in the major portion of the common Territory, and merely tolerated it in the residue. The Constitution, as expounded by the Supreme Court, guaranteed the right of introduction and protection of slavery in all the Territories, in whatever latitude, as the common property of the States. The Crittenden amendment proposed to confine this right to Territory south of 36° 30′, prohibiting, in the meanwhile, slavery *forever* north of that line, and in regions where its legal existence had been emphatically affirmed by that august tribunal, the Supreme Court. If adopted, it would have yielded every thing to Abolition rapacity, save a mere abstraction. Of all the vast territory yet remaining to be hereafter divided into States, only in New Mexico did it propose even to tolerate slavery, and in that locality the laws of nature precluded its permanent establishment.

A few days after its introdution in the Senate, the Crittenden amendment was proposed by its author to a special committee of thirteen, created on motion of Senator Powell, of Kentucky, for the consideration of all questions pertaining to the pending national difficulties. This committee was composed of the most eminent and influential Senators, embracing five leading Republicans, five Southern Senators, and Messrs. Bright, Bigler, and Douglas, on behalf of the Northern Democracy. Mr. Davis, originally appointed, at first declined to serve, but finally consented, in compliance with the urgent requests of other Senators. At the first meeting of the committee, 21st December, it was "resolved that no proposition shall be reported as adopted, unless sustained by a majority of each of the classes of the committee; Senators of the Republican party to constitute one class, and Senators of the other parties to constitute the other class."

This resolution was necessary, in consequence of the obvious futility of any settlement which did not meet the approval of a majority of the Republican Senators. In this Committee the Crittenden proposition was defeated. Not one of the Republican Senators voted for it, and Messrs. Davis and Toombs likewise voted against it when it was ascertained that it would not receive the sanction of a majority of the Republican Senators.

Despite its unfairness as a measure of settlement, and its great injustice to the South, Mr. Davis would have accepted it, as would a large majority of Southern Senators, as a *finality*, if the Republican Senators had tendered it. This, however, the latter were determined not to do, nor did a single Republican Senator, at any time during the session, express even a desire that any action, conciliatory to the South, should be adopted.* Insolent, dictatorial, and defiant, they proclaimed their purpose, at all hazards, to assert the authority of the Government, and their acts clearly indicated their stern

* Mr. Crittenden, whose supreme devotion to the Union, can not be called in question, since he continued to cling to the shadow long after the substance had departed, and in the midst of actual war continued to hope for a final pacific settlement, was greatly incensed at the unpatriotic course of the Republican Senators. His gray hairs, his eloquence, his

purpose to refuse every proposition contemplating concession or compromise. In substitution of the Crittenden adjustment, they voted solidly for the amendment of Senator Clarke, of New Hampshire, which denied the necessity of amendments to the Constitution, which ought to be obeyed rather than amended, and declared that the remedy for present difficulties was to be sought in a stern enforcement of the laws, rather than in assurances to peculiar ideas and guarantees to peculiar interests. This palpable defiance, and emphatic avowal of a purpose to concede nothing to Southern demands, was indorsed by the action of Republican caucusses of both houses of Congress, by resolutions of State Legislatures, and by tenders of men and means to compel the submission of the South. The entire Republican party were clearly committed to the purpose, avowed by Mr. Salmon P. Chase, in a letter from the Peace Congress, to Portsmouth, Ohio, to "use the power while they had it, and prevent a settlement." *

On the 31st December, 1860, the Committee of Thirteen reported to the Senate their inability to "agree upon any general plan of adjustment," and thus, with the arrival of the new year, had vanished the last hope of preserving the peace of the country. The failure of the Crittenden proposition was decisive of the question of pacification; no other plan of adjustment, that was presented, having either its merits or its practical features.

Southern resistance came none too soon for Northern power,

unquestioned Unionism, were all unavailing. He was frequently hotly denunciatory, of what, equally with Mr. Davis, he regarded a purpose to prevent any adjustment which could have a pacifying effect upon the country.

* Statement of Hon. S. S. Cox.

hate, and lust, but far too late for the precious goal of independence. Delay had been fatal, and the golden opportunity long since lost. But there was still time to emulate the glorious examples of the past. With marvelous calmness and dauntless intrepidity, a heroic race prepared an exhibition of noble devotion and willing sacrifice, the contemplation of which revives the memories of Thermopylæ.

Comparatively of little moment, now, is the question, whether the acceptance of this basis of adjustment by the South would have been consistent with discretion. In the end the result, in all likelihood, would have been the same. Had a settlement been reached in 1861, Southern liberties must eventually have perished, through the influences of corruption and the demoralization engendered by continued submission to wrong, no less effectually than by their overthrow in that gallant struggle of arms, which terminated with such fatal results. But there still remains the question of responsibility for those horrors of civil strife, which the failure of the Crittenden amendment soon precipitated upon the country. Those crimson spots which stain the subsequent history of the Republic, are traceable to no parricidal hand raised by the South. No historical question has received more satisfactory decision than this; and the South is acquitted even by the testimony of her enemies. It is unnecessary to give the evidence of Southern men, when there is such ample testimony from those who deprecated and condemned the subsequent course of the South.

Senator Douglas, on the 3d January, 1861, only three days after the report of the Committee of Thirteen had been submitted, and within hearing of its members, thus expressed himself in the course of an address to the Senate:

"If you of the Republican side are not willing to accept this [a proposition of his own] nor the proposition of the Senator from Kentucky [Mr. Crittenden,] pray tell us what are you willing to do? I address the inquiry to the Republicans alone, for the reason, that in the Committee of Thirteen, a few days ago, every member from the South, including those from the Cotton States [Messrs. Toombs and Davis,] expressed their readiness to accept the proposition of my venerable friend from Kentucky [Mr. Crittenden] as a final settlement of the controversy, if tendered and sustained by the Republican members. Hence, the sole responsibility of our disagreement, and the only difficulty in the way of an amicable adjustment, is with the Republican party."

Again, on the 2d March, 1861, Mr. Douglas re-affirmed this important statement. Said he:

"The Senator has said that if the Crittenden proposition could have been passed early in the session, it would have saved all the States except South Carolina. I firmly believe it would. While the Crittenden proposition was not in accordance with my cherished views, I avowed my readiness and eagerness to accept it, in order to save the Union, if we could unite upon it. No man has labored harder than I have to get it passed. I can confirm the Senator's declaration that Senator Davis himself, when on the Committee of Thirteen, was ready at all times to compromise on the Crittenden proposition. I will go further, and say that Mr. Toombs was also ready to do so."

Hon. S. S. Cox, for several years an able and eloquent member of Congress from Ohio, has made a most interesting statement upon this subject:

The vote on the Crittenden proposition was well defined, but is not so well understood. From the frequency of inquiries since the war as to this latter vote, the people were eager to know upon whom to fix the responsibility of its failure. It may as well be stated that all other propositions, whether of the Peace Convention or the Border State *project*, or the measures of the committees, were comparatively of no moment; for the Crittenden proposition was the only one which could have arrested the struggle. It would have received a larger vote than any other. It would have had more effect in moderating Southern excitement. Even Davis, Toombs, and others of the Gulf States, would have accepted it. I have talked with Mr. Crittenden frequently on this point. Not only has he confirmed the public declarations of Douglas and Pugh, and the speech of Toombs himself, to this effect, but he said it was so understood in committee. At one time, while the committee was in session, he said: "Mr. Toombs, will this compromise, as a remedy for all wrongs and apprehensions, be acceptable to you?" Mr. Toombs, with some profanity, replied: "Not by a good deal; but my State will accept it, and I will follow my State to ——." And he did.

I will not open the question whether it was wise then to offer accommodations. It may not be profitable now to ask whether the millions of young men whose bodies are maimed, or whose bones are decaying under the sod of the South, and the heavy load of public debt under which we sweat and toil, have their compensation in black liberty. Nor will I discuss whether the blacks have been bettered by their precipitate freedom, passing, as so many have, from slavery, through starvation and suffering, to death. There is no comfort in the reflection that the negroes will be exterminated with the extermination of slavery. The real point is, could not this Union have been made permanent by timely settlement, instead of cemented by fraternal blood and military rule? By an equitable partition of the territory this was possible. We had then 1,200,000 square miles. The Crittenden proposition would have given the North 900,000 of these square miles, and applied the Chicago doctrines to that quantity. It would have left the remaining fourth substantially to be carved out as free or slave States, at the option of the people when the States were admitted. This proposition the radicals denounced. It has been stated, to rid the Republicans of the odium of not averting the war when that was possible, that the Northern members tendered to the Southern the Crittenden compromise, which the South rejected. This is untrue. It was tendered by Southern Senators and Northern Democrats to the Republicans. It was voted upon but once in the House, when it received eighty votes against one hundred and thirteen. These eighty votes were exclusively Democrats and Southern Americans, like Gilmer, Vance, and others. Mr. Briggs, of New York, was the only one not a Democrat who voted for it. He had been an old Whig, and never a Republican. The Republican roll, beginning with Adams and ending with Woodruff, was a unit against it. Intermingled with them was one Southern extremist (General Hindman) who desired no settlement. There were many Southern men who did not vote, believing that unless the Republicans, who were just acceding to power, favored it, its adoption would be a delusion.

The plan adopted by the Republican Senators to defeat it was by amendment and postponement. On the 14th and 15th of January they cast all their votes against its being taken up; and on the 16th, when it came up, Mr. Clark, of New Hampshire, moved to strike it out, and insert something which he knew would neither be successful nor acceptable. The vote on Clark's amendment was 25 to 23; every "aye" being a Republican, and every "no," except Kennedy and Crittenden (Americans), being Democrats.

When this result was announced universal gloom prevailed. The people favored this compromise. Petitions by thousands of citizens were showered upon Congress for its passage. Had it received a majority only, they would have rallied and sustained those who desired peace and union. One more earnest appeal was made to the Republicans. General Cameron answered it by moving a reconsideration. His motion came up on the 18th, when he voted against his own motion. It was carried, however, over the votes of the Republicans, although Wigfall voted with them. When it was again up on the second of March, 1861, the Southern States were nearly all gone. Even then it was lost by one vote only. But on that occasion all the Democrats were for, and all the Republicans against it. The truth is, there was nothing but sneers and skepticism from the Republicans at any settlement. They broke down every proposition. They took the elements of conciliation out of the Peace Convention before it assembled. Senators Harlan and Chandler were especially active in preparing that convention for a failure. If every Southern man and every Northern Democrat had voted for this proposition, it would have required some nine Republicans for the requisite two-thirds. Where were they? Dreaming with Mr. Seward of a sixty days' struggle, or arranging for the division of the patronage of administration. The only Southern Senators who seemed against any settlement were Iverson and Wigfall; that no man will challenge if he will refer to the *Globe* (1st part, Thirty-fifth Congress, page 270) for the testimony of Douglas and Pugh, and to Mr. Bigler's Bucks County speech, September 17, 1863. The latter knew it to be true when he said that—

"When the struggle was at its height in Georgia, between Robert Toombs for secession, and A. H. Stephens against it, had those men in the Committee of Thirteen, who are now so blameless in their own estimation, given us their votes, or even three of them, Stephens would have defeated Toombs, and secession would have been prostrated. I heard Mr. Toombs say to Mr. Douglas that the result in Georgia was staked on the action of the Committee of Thirteen. If it accepted the Crittenden proposition, Stephens would defeat him; if not, he would carry the State out by 40,000 majority. The three votes from the Republican side would have carried it at any time; but union and peace in the balance against the Chicago platform were sure to be found wanting."

If other testimony were wanting, I would ask a suspension of judgment until those facts, better known to Southern men, transpire. The intercourse about to be reëstablished between the sections will cumulate the proof. It will also bring to the light many facts showing that, while President Buchanan was working for the Peace Conference, while Virginia had been gained to our side with her ablest men, there were even then in the Cabinet those who not only encouraged revolt, but foiled by letter and speech the efforts of the Unionists at Washington and Richmond. These letters and acts are referred to in the recent speech of General Blair. They will be, and should be brought into the sunshine, if only to vindicate the true Union men of that dark hour, and to condemn those who have since made so much pretension with so much zealotry, coupled with unexampled cruelty and tyranny.

In the light of subsequent events that policy was developed. It was the destruction of slavery at the peril of war and disunion; or, as Senator Douglas expressed it, "a disruption of the Union, believing it would draw after it, as an inevitable consequence, civil war, servile insurrections, and finally the utter extermination of slavery in all the Southern States."

While these fruitless efforts at compromise were in progress at Washington, public sentiment in the South, especially in the Cotton States, was rapidly reaching a point of exasperation, which refused to brook longer delay in the vain hope of justice from the exultant and unyielding North. In several of the States, so excited was popular feeling, that within a few weeks what was originally merely a purpose of resistance, intensified into a determination of absolute national independence and permanent separation. South Carolina, on the 20th December, 1860, adopted her ordinance of secession, and thus bravely gave the example, which other States speedily followed.

The work of secession, so thoroughly started by the opening

of the new year, was not accomplished without a severe struggle in several of the Cotton States, in which contest, those who advocated unconditional separation were greatly assisted by the defiant position of the Republican party. The more sagacious Southern leaders foresaw the inevitable failure of the movement of separation, unless it should be sustained by an extensive coöperation among the Southern States. To secure the united action of the Cotton States, at least, was essential to give the movement strength and dignity. Mr. Davis, who advocated secession only in the event of the failure to obtain reasonable guarantees, and had never proposed to abandon the Union without an effort to save it, was a most earnest and influential advocate of the policy of coöperation. Of great historical importance is the fact, that the counsels of himself and those who acted with him, were adopted in preference to a more hasty policy, which, however ample the provocation to immediate action, would have deprived the South of the potent justification of having forborne until "endurance ceased to be a virtue."

In a letter written a few days after the election of Mr. Lincoln, he thus expressed his views:

WARREN COUNTY, MISS., Nov. 10, 1860.

HON. R. B. RHETT, JR.—*Dear Sir:* I had the honor to receive, last night, yours of the 27th ult., and hasten to reply to the inquiries propounded. Reports of the election leave little doubt that the event you anticipated has occurred, that electors have been chosen, securing the election of Lincoln, and I will answer on that supposition.

My home is so isolated that I have had no intercourse with those who might have aided me in forming an opinion as to the effect produced on the mind of our people by the result of the recent election, and the impressions which I communicate are founded upon antecedent expressions.

1. I doubt not that the Governor of Mississippi has convoked the Legislature to assemble within the present month, to decide upon the course which the State should adopt in the present emergency. Whether the Legislature will direct the call of a convention of the State, or appoint delegates to a convention of such Southern States as may be willing to consult together for the adoption of a Southern plan of action, is doubtful.

2. If a convention of the State were assembled, the proposition to secede from the Union, independently of support from neighboring States, would probably fail.

3. If South Carolina should first secede, and she alone should take such action, the position of Mississippi would not probably be changed by that fact. A powerful obstacle to the separate action of Mississippi is the want of a port; from which follows the consequence that her trade, being still conducted through the ports of the Union, her revenue would be diverted from her own support to that of a foreign government; and being geographically unconnected with South Carolina, an alliance with her would not vary that state of the case. [*Sic.*]

4. The propriety of separate secession by South Carolina depends so much upon collateral questions that I find it difficult to respond to your last inquiry, for the want of knowledge which would enable me to estimate the value of the elements involved in the issue, though exterior to your State. Georgia is necessary to connect you with Alabama, and thus to make effectual the cooperation of Mississippi. If Georgia would be lost by immediate action, but could be gained by delay, it seems clear to me that you should wait. If the secession of South Carolina should be followed by an attempt to coerce her back into the Union, that act of usurpation, folly, and wickedness would enlist every true Southern man for her defense. If it were attempted to blockade her

ports and destroy her trade, a like result would be produced, and the commercial world would probably be added to her allies. It is probable that neither of those measures would be adopted by any administration, but that Federal ships would be sent to collect the duties on imports outside of the bar; that the commercial nations would feel little interest in that; and the Southern States would have little power to counteract it.

The planting States have a common interest of such magnitude, that their union, sooner or later, for the protection of that interest, is certain. United they will have ample power for their own protection, and their exports will make for them allies of all commercial and manufacturing powers.

The new States have a heterogeneous population, and will be slower and less unanimous than those in which there is less of the Northern element in the body politic, but interest controls the policy of States, and finally all the planting communities must reach the same conclusion. *My opinion is, therefore, as it has been, in favor of seeking to bring those States into coöperation before asking for a popular decision upon a new policy and relation to the nations of the earth.* If South Carolina should resolve to secede before that coöperation can be obtained, to go out leaving Georgia, and Alabama, and Louisiana in the Union, and without any reason to suppose they will follow her, there appears to me to be no advantage in waiting until the Government has passed into hostile hands, and men have become familiarized to that injurious and offensive perversion of the General Government from the ends for which it was established. I have written with the freedom and carelessness of private correspondence, and regret that I could not give more precise information.

Very respectfully, yours, etc.,

JEFFERSON DAVIS.

Mr. Davis remained in the Senate, a friend of peace, and,

until the last moment, laboring for adjustment, when he received the summons of Mississippi, forbidding the longer exercise of the trust which she had given to his keeping. Mississippi seceded on the 9th of January, 1861. Mr. Davis, receiving formal announcement of the event, withdrew on the 21st, after pronouncing an impressive valedictory to the Senate. Its dignified, courteous, and statesman-like character has challenged the unqualified eulogy of the enlightened world.

SPEECH OF HON. JEFFERSON DAVIS, ON WITHDRAWING FROM THE U. S. SENATE. JAN. 21, 1861.

Mr. Davis. I rise, Mr. President, for the purpose of announcing to the Senate that I have satisfactory evidence that the State of Mississippi, by a solemn ordinance of her people, in convention assembled, has declared her separation from the United States. Under these circumstances, of course, my functions are terminated here. It has seemed to me proper, however, that I should appear in the Senate to announce that fact to my associates, and I will say but very little more. The occasion does not invite me to go into argument; and my physical condition would not permit me to do so, if otherwise; and yet it seems to become me to say something on the part of a State I here represent, on an occasion so solemn as this.

It is known to Senators who have served with me here, that I have, for many years, advocated, as an essential attribute of State sovereignty, the right of a State to secede from the Union. Therefore, if I had not believed there was justifiable cause; if I had thought that Mississippi was acting without sufficient provocation, or without an existing necessity, I should still, under my theory of the Government, because of my allegiance to the State of which I am a citizen, have been bound by her action. I, however, may be permitted to say that I do think she has justifiable cause, and I approve of her act. I conferred with her people before that act was taken, counseled them then that if the state of things which they apprehended should exist when the convention met, they should take the action which they have now adopted.

I hope none who hear me will confound this expression of mine with the advocacy of the right of a State to remain in the Union, and to disregard its constitutional obligations by the nullification of the law. Such is not my theory. Nullification and secession, so often confounded, are, indeed, antagonistic principles. Nullification is a remedy which it is sought to apply within the Union, and against the agent of the States. It is only to be justified when the agent has violated his constitutional obligations, and a State, assuming to judge for itself, denies the right of the agent thus to act, and appeals to the other States of the Union for a decision; but when the States themselves, and when the people of the States, have so acted as to convince us that they will not regard our constitutional rights, then, and then for the first time, arises the doctrine of secession in its practical application.

A great man, who now reposes with his fathers, and who has often been arraigned for a want of fealty to the Union, advocated the doctrine of nullification because it preserved the Union. It was because of his deep-seated attachment to the Union—his determination to find some remedy for existing ills short of a severance of the ties which bound South Carolina to the other States, that Mr. Calhoun advocated the doctrine of nullification, which he proclaimed to be peaceful—to be within the limits of State power, not to disturb the Union, but only to be a means of bringing the agent before the tribunal of the States for their judgment.

Secession belongs to a different class of remedies. It is to be justified upon the basis that the States are sovereign. There was a time when none denied it. I hope the time may come again, when a better comprehension of the theory of our Government, and the inalienable rights of the people of the States, will prevent any one from denying that each State is a sovereign, and thus may reclaim the grants which it has made to any agent whomsoever.

I, therefore, say I concur in the action of the people of Mississippi, believing it to be necessary and proper, and should have been bound by their action if my belief had been otherwise; and this brings me to the important point which I wish, on this last occasion, to present to the Senate. It is by this confounding of nullification and secession, that the name of a great man, whose ashes now mingle with his mother earth, has been evoked to justify coercion against a seceded State. The phrase, "to execute the laws," was an expression which General Jackson applied to the case of a State refusing to obey the laws while yet a member of the Union. That is not the case which is now presented. The laws are to be executed over the United States, and upon the people of the United States. They have no relation to any foreign country. It is a perversion of terms—at least it is a great misapprehension of the case—which cites that expression for application to a State which has withdrawn from the Union. You may make war on a foreign State. If it be the purpose of gentlemen, they may make war against a State which has withdrawn from the Union; but there are no laws of the United States to be executed within the limits of a seceded State. A State, finding herself in the condition in which Mississippi has judged she is—in which her safety requires that she should provide for the maintenance of her rights out of the Union—surrenders all the benefits (and they are known to be many), deprives herself of the advantages (and they are known to be great), severs all the ties of affection (and they are close and enduring), which have bound her to the Union; and thus divesting herself of every benefit—taking upon herself every burden—she claims to be exempt from any power to execute the laws of the United States within her limits.

I well remember an occasion when Massachusetts was arraigned before the bar of the Senate, and when the doctrine of coercion was rife, and to be applied against her, because of the rescue of a fugitive slave in Boston. My opinion then was the same that it is now. Not in a spirit of egotism, but to show that I am not influenced, in my opinion, because the case is my own, I refer to that time and that occasion, as containing the opinion which I then entertained, and on which my present conduct is based. I then said that if Massachusetts, following her through a stated line of conduct, choose to take the last step which separates her from the Union, it is her right to go, and I will neither vote one dollar nor one man to coerce her back; but will say to her, God speed, in memory of the kind associations which once existed between her and the other States.

It has been a conviction of pressing necessity—it has been a belief that we are to be deprived, in the Union, of the rights which our fathers bequeathed to us—which has brought Mississippi into her present decision. She has heard proclaimed the theory that all men are created free and equal, and this made the basis of an attack upon her social institutions; and the sacred Declaration of Independence has been invoked to maintain the position of the equality of the races. The Declaration of Independence is to be construed by the circumstances and purposes for which it was made. The communities were declaring their independence; the people of those communities were asserting that no man was born, to use the language of Mr. Jefferson, booted and spurred, to ride over the rest of mankind; that men were created equal—meaning the men of the political community; that there was no divine right to rule; that no man inherited the right to govern; that there were no classes by which power and place descended to families; but that all stations were equally within the grasp of each member of the body politic. These were the great principles they announced; these were the purposes for which they made their declaration; these were the ends to which their enunciation was directed. They have no reference to the slave; else, how happened it, that, among the items of arraignment against George III, was, that he endeavored to do just what the North has been endeavoring of late to do, to stir up insurrection among our slaves. Had the Declaration announced that the negroes were free and equal, how was the prince to be arraigned for raising up insurrection among them? And how was this to be enumerated among the high crimes which caused the colonies to sever their connection with the mother country? When our Constitution was formed, the same idea was rendered more palpable; for there we find provision made for that very class of persons as property; they were not put upon the footing of equality with white men—not even upon that of paupers and convicts; but, so far as representation was concerned, were discriminated against as a lower caste, only to be represented in the numerical proportion of three-fifths.

Then, Senators, we recur to the compact which binds us together; we recur to the principles upon which our Government was founded; and when you deny them, and when you deny to us the right to withdraw from a government, which, thus perverted, threatens to be destructive of our rights, we but tread in the path of our fathers when we proclaim our independence, and take the hazard. This is done, not in hostility to others—not to injure any section of the country—not even for our own pecuniary benefit; but from the high and solemn motive of defending and protecting the rights we inherited, and which it is our duty to transmit unshorn to our children.

I find in myself, perhaps, a type of the general feeling of my constituents toward yours. I am sure I feel no hostility toward you, Senators from the North. I am sure there is not one of you, whatever sharp discussion there may have been between us, to whom I can not now say, in the presence of my God, I wish you well; and such, I am sure, is the feeling of the people whom I represent toward those whom you represent. I, therefore, feel that I but express their desire, when I say I hope, and they hope, for peaceable relations with you, though we must part. They may be mutually beneficial to us in the future, as they have been in the past, if you so will it. The reverse may bring disaster on every portion of the country; and if you will have it thus, we will invoke the God of our fathers, who delivered them from the power of the lion, to protect us from the ravages of the bear; and thus, putting our trust in God, and in our firm hearts and strong arms, we will vindicate the right as best we may.

In the course of my service here, associated, at different times, with a great variety of Senators, I see now around me some with whom I have served long; there have been points of collision, but whatever of offense there has been to me, I leave here—I carry with me no hostile remembrance. Whatever offense I have given, which has not been redressed, or for which satisfaction has not been demanded, I have, Senators, in this hour of our parting, to offer you my apology for any pain which, in the heat of discussion, I have inflicted. I go hence unincumbered of the remembrance of any injury received, and having discharged the duty of making the only reparation in my power for any injury offered.

Mr. President and Senators, having made the announcement which the occasion seemed to me to require, it only remains for me to bid you a final adieu.

A frequent accusation alleged against Mr. Davis and other Southern Senators who adopted his course of a formal withdrawal from the Senate, is that they thus gave the Republican party control of the Senate, and voluntarily surrendered its power to the hostile administration soon to be inaugurated. It is a sufficient answer to this statement that the mere admission that the administration was hostile to Southern interests, and menacing to Southern safety and honor, or even that the South had good reason for so believing, is to fix the responsibility of disunion elsewhere than upon the Southern leaders.

To have retained his seat under such circumstances would have been altogether inconsistent with Mr. Davis' conception of the nature of the position. He was committed, by public announcement, to a very different view of the obligations of the representative of a State in the Federal Congress. Holding it to be a point of honor not to occupy such a relation, with the object of hostility to the Government, years ago he announced, in connection with an allusion to a calumnious insinuation, that he would answer in monosyllables the man who would charge him with being a disunionist.

Entertaining his view of the character of the American political system, of which the foundation was the doctrine of a paramount allegiance of the citizen to his State, when Mississippi withdrew from the Union, he had no other alternative than to vacate the position which he held by her commission, and which was, at once, the sign of the equality and sovereignty of the States, and of the adherence of each to the league by which she was united to the others. To represent a State adhering to the Union, and use the position to make war upon the Government, or to retain a seat in Congress when the State had, by its sovereign fiat, revoked its grants, and withdrawn from the league, were offenses belonging to the last stage of decadence in political morality and personal honor.

Retiring from the Senate, Mr. Davis returned, within a few days thereafter, to his residence in Mississippi. The State was not unmindful of the necessity of preparations for a war which, though not deemed inevitable, was yet extremely probable. Mr. Davis was honored by an appointment to the command of the militia of the State, with the rank of Major-General. His retirement upon his plantation thus promised to be of short duration, but before he could assume the responsibilities which Mississippi, in this reiteration of her confidence, had conferred, the voice of millions invoked his guidance of their destinies in the hazardous experiment of independent national existence.

Secession, in its rapid progress, confirmed the threadbare theory of the progressive tendency of revolutionary movements. Acquiring impetus as it advanced, before the first of February, 1861, six States had declared themselves no longer members of the Union.* Representatives from these States met, in convention, at Montgomery, Alabama, on 4th February, 1861, for the purpose of forming a provisional government. On the 8th February, this body adopted a constitution, and proclaimed an addition to the family of nations, under the title of THE CONFEDERATE STATES OF AMERICA.

The next day the Congress of the Confederate States announced its choice of the two highest constitutional officers of the new Government:

President, JEFFERSON DAVIS, of Mississippi.
Vice-President, ALEXANDER H. STEPHENS, of Georgia.

* Acts of secession were adopted by the various States as follows:

South Carolina, December 20, 1860.
Florida, January 7, 1861.
Mississippi, January 9, 1861.
Alabama, January 11, 1861.
Georgia, January 20, 1861.
Louisiana, January 26, 1861.
Texas, February 1, 1861.

CHAPTER VIII.

THE CONFEDERACY ESTABLISHED AND IN OPERATION—CALMNESS AND MODERATION OF THE SOUTH—THE MONTGOMERY CONSTITUTION—THE IMPROVEMENTS UPON THE FEDERAL INSTRUMENT—POPULAR DELIGHT AT THE SELECTION OF MR. DAVIS AS PRESIDENT—MOTIVES OF HIS ACCEPTANCE—HIS PREFERENCE FOR THE ARMY—DAVIS THE SYMBOL OF SOUTHERN CHARACTER AND HOPES—ON HIS WAY TO MONTGOMERY—A CONTRAST—INAUGURATION AND INAUGURAL ADDRESS—THE CONFEDERATE CABINET—TOOMBS—WALKER—MEMMINGER—BENJAMIN—MALLORY—REAGAN—HISTORICAL POSITION OF PRESIDENT DAVIS—THE TWO POWERS—EXTREME DEMOCRACY OF THE NORTH—NOBLE IDEAL OF REPUBLICANISM CHERISHED BY THE SOUTH—DAVIS' REPRESENTATIVE QUALITIES AND DISTINGUISHED SERVICES—THE HISTORIC REPRESENTATIVE OF THE CONFEDERATE CAUSE—EARLY HISTORY OF THE GOVERNMENT AT MONTGOMERY—CONFIDENCE IN PRESIDENT DAVIS UNLIMITED—PRESIDENT DAVIS' ADMINISTRATIVE CAPACITY—HIS MILITARY ADMINISTRATION—THE CONFEDERATE ARMY—WEST POINT—NEGOTIATIONS FOR SURRENDER OF FORTS SUMTER AND PICKENS—MR. BUCHANAN'S PITIABLE POLICY—THE ISSUE OF PEACE OR WAR—PERFIDIOUS COURSE OF THE LINCOLN ADMINISTRATION—MR. SEWARD'S DALLIANCE WITH THE CONFEDERATE COMMISSIONERS—HIS DECEPTIONS—THE EXPEDITION TO PROVISION THE GARRISON OF SUMTER—REDUCTION OF THE FORT—WAR—GUILT OF THE NORTH—ITS RESPONSIBILITY FOR THE WAR.

THUS, without the disorder of anarchy, and without the violence of armed conflict, a new and imposing structure of state was speedily erected from the separated fragments. The event was indeed unparalleled, and, to the mind of the world, unused to the novel spectacle of the dismemberment of an empire, except as the consummation of years of bloodshed, its philosophy was difficult of comprehension.

The sixth of November, 1860, was the ominous day upon which the revolution, so long threatened, and so often deferred by Southern concession and sacrifice, was inaugurated. Upon that day, with the election of Abraham Lincoln, was opened a new volume in American history. Upon that day, the American Union, "formed to establish justice," resting upon the principle of equality as its foundation-stone, passed under the control of an arrogant majority, pledged to its perversion, to the oppression of nearly one-half its members. From the profession of fraternity, and the outward pretense of comity, it passed under the domination of principles whose origin was discord and whose logical result was dissolution.

The answer of those who were threatened most seriously by this subversion of the Government of their fathers, though well considered, neither debated with passion, nor concluded with rashness, was worthy of men—the descendants of the authors of American Independence, and educated in that political school which teaches the assertion of the rights of the few against the power of the many. A manly resistance, such as only threatened degradation inspires in the bosoms of freemen, which the insolence of faction had long defied and a conscious physical superiority had haughtily derided, was, at length, thoroughly aroused. Within a few months, the revolutionary movement, begun in November, and pressed, by its authors, to its inevitable consequences, had reached the important result of a withdrawal of nearly one-fourth of the States constituting the American Union.

The new government, in the incidents attending its construction and setting in operation, fully vindicated the earnest and conscientious convictions of the people who had called it into existence. The absence of tumult and of all passionate display, at Montgomery, was in marked contrast with the indecent exultation witnessed at Washington from the adherents of the incoming administration. The calmness, moderation, and evident earnestness of purpose which prevailed at the South, and was thus manifested by those who were intrusted with the framing of the new government, impressed the world to an extent that prepared it to entertain a sympathy for the Southern cause not to have been expected from the prevalent, though erroneous, impressions of foreigners respecting the merits of the sectional quarrel in America.

That secession was not a revolutionary movement, but merely the necessary defense of a people threatened with material ruin and political degradation, by a revolution which had already been consummated, was amply demonstrated by its immediate consequences. The Confederate leaders, at Montgomery, exhibited an almost religious veneration for the spirit, forms, and associations of the government which they had abandoned. The strict adherence of the Montgomery Constitution to the features of the Federal instrument, indicates the absurdity of the impression that it was a proclamation of revolution; and the circumstances of its adoption are totally inconsistent with a correct conception of the conduct of an insurgent body.

It was a signal improvement upon the original American Constitution, and the few alterations made were commended by enlightened and conservative intellects every-where, as necessary changes in the perfection of the American polity. The object sought, and successfully consummated, was to embody every valuable principle of the old Constitution with certain remedial provisions for the correction of obvious evils, which experience had fully indicated. Among these changes, which were universally recognized as of the utmost value, were provisions making the Presidential term six years, instead of four, as under the old system, and precluding reëlection; permitting cabinet ministers to participate in the debates of Congress, and the virtual abolition of the pernicious system of removing all officials, of whatever degree, upon each advent of a new administration. The Confederate Constitution positively prohibited the African slave-trade, which the Federal Constitution had failed to do. A striking provision, and one never before avowed in any similar instrument, was the prohibition of duties for the purpose of protection. There was, indeed, nothing whatever in the Montgomery instrument which a candid and enlightened public sentiment, even at the North, might not have fully approved, excepting the ample and avowed protection to property in slaves. This, it was claimed, was not an alteration of the old Constitution, but merely a formal interpretation of its obvious purpose.

In no respect was the action of the new Confederacy deemed more fortunate than in the selection of its leader. That, in the choice of Mr. Davis as President, the Congress only responded to the preconceived choice of the Southern people, was attested by the spontaneous acclamation with which the announcement was received. Even those who had been in doubt as to the proper personage to endow with the powers and responsibilities of a position, at once the most onerous, and, looking to the contingencies of the early future, a long and sanguinary war, with the chances of a disastrous termination, the most precarious of modern times, yielded hearty recognition of the wise selection of the Congress.

The responsibilities and difficulties of the trust, did not suggest to Mr. Davis hesitation as to its acceptance. If this, the highest distinction which public appreciation had yet tendered him should prove a forlorn hope, his sense of duty would no more permit hesitation than in the assumption of more cheaply-earned honors. Entertaining no purpose of inglorious ease, amid the trials and perils, which, with a prevision, rare, indeed, at that period, he already anticipated, his own preference was for a different station of public service. Months subsequently he indicated the post of danger as the post of duty to which he had aspired in that gigantic struggle through which his country must pass to the assurance of independence. "I then imagined," said he, "that it might be my fortune again to lead Mississippians in the field, and to be with them where danger was to be braved and glory won. I thought to find that place which I believed to be suited to my capacity—that of an officer in the service of the State of Mississippi."*

Of the public conviction as to his preëminent fitness, there could not be a question. His character, his abilities, his military education and experience, had long been recognized throughout the Union, and his exalted reputation was a source of just pride to the South. No Southern statesman presented so admirable a combination of purity, dignity, firmness, devotion, and skill—qualities for which there is an inexorable demand in revolutionary periods. William Tell, with his cross-bow and apple, to the rustic simplicity of the Swiss, was the very embodiment of the genius of liberty. Far beyond any influence of fiction was the magic potency of the red shirt and felt hat of Garibaldi to imaginative Italy; and Washington, as Lamartine said, with his sword and the law, was the symbol standing erect at the cradle of American liberty. Equally with

* Extract from President Davis' address before the Mississippi Legislature, December, 1862.

the greatest of these prototypes was Jefferson Davis, the symbol of the noble aspirations of the proud, impulsive, chivalrous race which confided to him the conduct of its destinies through the wilderness of revolution to the goal of independence and nationality beyond. He did not seek the position; had not been conspicuous in flaming exhortations to popular assemblies; had not employed any of the arts of the demagogue—of flattery or cajolery of the masses into a false and extravagant estimate of his qualities; but before the world were his character, fame, and services, in unadorned simplicity, painted only in the severe colors of truth. It was the tribute to virtue, most to be valued when unsought; the award of honor, only appropriate when merited and becomingly worn.

Mr. Davis' assumption of his trust was characterized by a dignity, absence of ostentation, and profound appreciation of its delicate nature, in the highest degree imposing. From it was augured such a worthy administration of public affairs as would secure for the Confederacy, if permitted the blessings of peace, an enviable position among the nations of the earth. But his first announcement of its policy indicated his appreciation of the danger of war, in which its utmost exertions would be required to vindicate the independence which the States had declared. To the heroic maintenance of that position he committed himself by the most emphatic avowals; and in whatever contingency, whether of peace or war, his purpose was one of deathless resistence to any denial of the right of self-government, which his fellow-citizens had exercised.

Informed of his election, Mr. Davis immediately left his home for the seat of government. Along the route to Montgomery he was greeted, by the people, with every possible demonstration of patriotic enthusiasm and personal regard.

In response to these demonstrations, he at several points addressed the people in terms of characteristic eloquence, dignity and moderation.

Proud, indeed, must ever be, to the Southern people, the contrast of the noble bearing of their chosen ruler with the display of vulgarity attending the journey of Mr. Lincoln from Springfield to Washington. These two men—the one with the calm dignity of the statesman and the polished bearing of the gentleman; the other with coarse jests and buffoonery, upon the eve of the most important event in their individual history, and pregnant with significance to millions—were no bad indices of the civilization of their respective sections.

Arriving in Montgomery, Mr. Davis was inaugurated on the 18th February, with a simplicity of ceremony, an absence of personal inflation, and a degree of popular enthusiasm, which well befitted the formal assertion of true republican liberty, equally protected against the license of mobs and the usurpations of tyrants. The ceremonies of inauguration were little more than the taking of the oath of office and the delivery of the inaugural address. The inaugural of President Davis is unquestionably of the highest order of state papers. As a model of composition, it is rarely equaled; and its statement of the position of the South, the grievances which had led to the assumption of that position, her hopes, aspirations, and purposes, has never been surpassed in power and perspicuity, by any similar document.

INAUGURAL ADDRESS OF PRESIDENT DAVIS, DELIVERED AT THE CAPITOL, MONDAY, FEB. 18, 1861.

Gentlemen of the Congress of the Confederate States of America;
Friends and Fellow-Citizens:

Called to the difficult and responsible station of Chief Executive of the Provisional Government which you have instituted, I approach the discharge of the duties assigned to me with an humble distrust of my abilities, but with a sustaining confidence in the wisdom of those who are to guide and aid me in the administration of public affairs, and an abiding faith in the virtue and patriotism of the people.

Looking forward to the speedy establishment of a permanent government to take the place of this, and which, by its greater moral and physical power, will be better able to combat with the many difficulties which arise from the conflicting interests of separate nations, I enter upon the duties of the office, to which I have been chosen, with the hope that the beginning of our career, as a Confederacy, may not be obstructed by hostile opposition to our enjoyment of the separate existence and independence which we have asserted, and, with the blessing of Providence, intend to maintain. Our present condition, achieved in a manner unprecedented in the history of nations, illustrates the American idea that governments rest upon the consent of the governed, and that it is the right of the people to alter or abolish governments whenever they become destructive of the ends for which they were established.

The declared purpose of the compact of union from which we have withdrawn, was "to establish justice, insure domestic tranquillity, provide for the common defense, promote the general welfare, and secure the blessings of liberty to ourselves and posterity;" and when, in the judgment of the sovereign States now composing this Confederacy, it had been perverted from the purposes for which it was ordained, and had ceased to answer the ends for which it was established, a peaceful appeal to the ballot-box, declared, that so far as they were concerned, the government created by that compact should cease to exist. In this they merely asserted a right which the Declaration of Independence of 1776 had defined to be inalienable. Of the time and occasion for its exercise, they, as sovereigns, were the final judges, each for itself. The impartial and enlightened verdict of mankind will vindicate the rectitude of our conduct, and He, who knows the hearts of men, will judge of the sincerity with which we labored to preserve the government of our fathers in its spirit. The right solemnly proclaimed at the birth of the States, and which has been affirmed and re-affirmed in the bills of rights of States subsequently admitted into the Union of 1789, undeniably recognizes in the people the power to resume the authority delegated for the purposes of government. Thus the sovereign States, here represented, proceeded to form this Confederacy, and it is by abuse of language that their act has been denominated a revolution. They formed a new alliance, but within each State its government has remained, and the rights of person and property have not been disturbed. The agent, through whom they communicated with foreign nations, is changed; but this does not necessarily interrupt their international relations.

Sustained by the consciousness that the transition from the former Union to the present Confederacy, has not proceeded from a disregard on our part of just obligations, or any failure to perform any constitutional duty; moved by no interest or passion to invade the rights of others; anxious to cultivate peace and commerce with all nations, if we may not hope to avoid war, we may at least expect that posterity will acquit us of having needlessly engaged in it. Doubly justified by the absence of wrong on our part, and by wanton aggression on the part of others, there can be no cause to doubt that the courage and patriotism of the people of the Confederate States will be found equal to any measures of defense which honor and security may require.

An agricultural people, whose chief interest is the export of a commodity required in every manufacturing country, our true policy is peace and the freest trade which our necessities will permit. It is alike our interest, and that of all those to whom we would sell and from whom we would buy, that there should be the fewest practicable restrictions upon the interchange of commodities. There can be but little rivalry between ours and any manufacturing or navigating community, such as the North-eastern States of the American Union. It must follow, therefore, that a mutual interest would invite good will and kind offices. If, however, passion or the lust of dominion should cloud the judgment or inflame the ambition of those States, we must prepare to meet the emergency, and to maintain, by the final arbitrament of the sword, the position which we have assumed among the nations of the earth. We have entered upon the career of independence, and it must be inflexibly pursued. Through many years of controversy with our late associates, the Northern States, we have vainly endeavored to secure tranquillity, and to obtain respect for the rights to which we were entitled. As a necessity, not a choice, we have resorted to the remedy of separation; and henceforth our energies must be directed to the conduct of our own affairs, and the perpetuity of the Confederacy which we have formed. If a just perception of mutual interest shall permit us peaceably to pursue our separate political career, my most earnest desire will have been fulfilled; but if this be denied to us, and the integrity of our territory and jurisdiction be assailed, it will but remain for us, with firm resolve, to appeal to arms and invoke the blessings of Providence on a just cause.

As a consequence of our new condition, and with a view to meet anticipated wants, it will be necessary to provide for the speedy and efficient organization of branches of the Executive Department, having special charge of foreign intercourse, finance, military affairs, and the postal service.

For purposes of defense, the Confederate States may, under ordinary circumstances, rely mainly upon the militia; but it is deemed advisable, in the present condition of affairs, that there should be a well-instructed and disciplined army, more numerous than would usually be required on a peace establishment. I also suggest that, for the protection of our harbors and commerce on the high seas, a navy adapted to those objects will be required. These necessities have doubtless engaged the attention of Congress.

With a Constitution differing only from that of our fathers, in so far as it is explanatory of their well-known intent, freed from the sectional conflicts which have interfered with the pursuit of the general welfare, it is not unreasonable to expect that States, from which we have recently parted, may seek to unite their fortunes with ours under the government which we have instituted. For this your Constitution makes adequate provision; but beyond this, if I mistake not the judgment and will of the people, a reunion with the States from which we have separated is neither practicable nor desirable. To increase the power, develop the resources, and promote the happiness of the Confederacy, it is requisite that there should be so much of homogeneity that the welfare of every portion shall be the aim of the whole. Where this does not exist, antagonisms are engendered which must and should result in separation.

Actuated solely by the desire to preserve our own rights and promote our own welfare, the separation of the Confederate States has been marked by no aggression upon others, and followed by no domestic convulsion. Our industrial pursuits have received no check; the cultivation of our fields has progressed as heretofore; and even should we be involved in war, there would be no considerable diminution in the production of the staples which have constituted our exports, and in which the commercial world has an interest scarcely less than our own. This common interest of the producer and consumer can only be interrupted by an exterior force, which should obstruct its transmission to foreign markets—a course of conduct which would be as unjust toward us as it would be detrimental to manufacturing and commercial interests abroad. Should reason guide the action of the Government from which we have separated, a policy so detrimental to the civilized world, the Northern States included, could not be dictated by even the strongest desire to inflict injury upon us; but if otherwise, a terrible responsibility will rest upon it, and the suffering of millions will bear testimony to the folly and wickedness of our aggressors. In the meantime, there will remain to us, besides the ordinary means before suggested, the well-known resources for retaliation upon the commerce of an enemy.

Experience in public stations, of subordinate grade to this which your kindness has conferred, has taught me that care, and toil, and disappointment, are the price of official elevation. You will see many errors to forgive, many deficiencies to tolerate, but you shall not find in me either a want of zeal or fidelity to the cause that is to me highest in hope and of most enduring affection. Your generosity has bestowed upon me an undeserved distinction—one which I neither sought nor desired. Upon the continuance of that sentiment, and upon your wisdom and patriotism, I rely to direct and support me in the performance of the duty required at my hands.

We have changed the constituent parts but not the system of our Government. The Constitution formed by our fathers is that of these Confederate States, in their exposition of it; and, in the judicial construction it has received, we have a light which reveals its true meaning.

Thus instructed as to the just interpretation of the instrument, and ever remembering that all offices are but trusts held for the people, and that delegated powers are to be strictly construed, I will hope, by due diligence in the performance of my duties, though I may disappoint your expectations, yet to retain, when retiring, something of the good-will and confidence which welcomed my entrance into office.

It is joyous, in the midst of perilous times, to look around upon a people united in heart, where one purpose of high resolve animates and actuates the whole—where the sacrifices to be made are not weighed in the balance against honor, and right, and liberty, and equality. Obstacles may retard—they can not long prevent—the progress of a movement sanctified by its justice, and sustained by a virtuous people. Reverently let us invoke the God of our fathers to guide and protect us in our efforts to perpetuate the principles which, by his blessing, they were able to vindicate, establish, and transmit to their posterity, and with a continuance of His favor, ever gratefully acknowledged, we may hopefully look forward to success, to peace, and to prosperity.

Working in great harmony between its executive and legislative departments, the new government, within a very few weeks, presented an extraordinary spectacle of compact organization, though in all its parts it was yet purely provisional. The Cabinet announced by the President, embraced, for the most part, names well known to the country in connection with important public trusts. It may not be inappropriate to speak briefly here of those who sustained to President Davis the close relations of constitutional advisers.

Mr. Robert Toombs, the Secretary of State, was indebted for his appointment not less to the position of his State, the first in rank in the Confederacy, than to the public appreciation of his abilities. For several years he had represented Georgia in the United States Senate, and in that body his reputation was very high as a debater and orator. His oratory, however, was a good index of his mind and disposition, strong and impassioned, but desultory, vehement and blustering. Mr. Toombs had contributed largely to prepare the people of Georgia for secession, and his fierce and persistent eloquence had greatly accelerated the movement. His capacity for agitation and destruction was indeed immeasurably superior to any qualification that he may have had for reconstructing the broken and scattered fragments of the governmental column. Restless, arrogant, and intolerant—a born destructive and inveterate agitator—Mr. Toombs speedily demonstrated his deficiency in statesmanship. His connection with the Confederate Cabinet was of brief duration, and his subsequent military service undistinguished. The War Department—the second post of distinction in the Cabinet—was given to Alabama, the second State of the Confederacy, in the person of Mr. Leroy P. Walker. His connection with the Government, like that of Mr. Toombs, was brief, and wholly unmarked by evidence of fitness. Mr. Memminger, of South Carolina, the Secretary of the Treasury, made an exceedingly unpopular officer; and, as the sequel demonstrated, was incompetent to the delicate task of financial management. The Attorney-General, Mr. Benjamin, of Louisiana, an eminent lawyer and a prominent Senator, was, beyond all question, the ablest of Mr. Davis' Cabinet. He was a man of marvelous intellectual resources, an orator, a lawyer, and gifted, to an unexampled degree, in the varied attributes, entering into the *savior faire* of politics and diplomacy. Mr. Benjamin continued the trusted counselor of President Davis during the whole period of his authority. Mr. Mallory, of Florida, was the Secretary of the Navy—a gentleman of excellent sense, unpretending manners, who probably conducted his department as successfully as was possible, with the limited naval resources of the South. The Post-office Department was given to Mr. Reagan, of Texas, noted for his fidelity, industry, and good sense.

The Cabinet of President Davis was destined to many changes in the progress of subsequent events. Of those originally appointed, Messrs. Benjamin, Mallory, and Reagan continued their connection with the Confederate Government during the entire period of its existence. The brief experiment of Confederate independence was fruitful in illustrations of the important truth that political distinction achieved in the ordinary struggles of parties, in times of profound peace, is not the sure guarantee of the possession of those especial and peculiar qualifications which befit the circumstances of revolution. That President Davis, in the selection of some of his advisers, was at fault, is to be ascribed rather to the novelty and necessities of the public situation than to errors of his judgment. Not only must public sentiment respecting men be to some extent consulted, but the test of experience must, necessarily, after all, determine the question of fitness, where all were untried.

Jefferson Davis now occupied a position in the highest sense historical. It was plain that his name was destined to be indelibly associated with a series of incidents forming a most thrilling and instructive episode in political history. As the exponent of a theory of constitutional principles never asserted, and unknown save through the inspiration of the genius of American Liberty, and as the head of a Government whose birth and destiny must enter conspicuously into all future questions of popular government, he stood, in a double sense, the central figure in a most striking phase of the drama of human progress. Splendid as had been American history until that day, it was now to contribute, still more generously, to the illumination of the great truths of political science.

The issue was again to be joined between constitutional freedom and the odious despotism of an enthroned mob. On the one side were asserted the principles of regulated liberty, without which free government can never be stable—order, allegiance, and reverence for law and authority. On the other, the wild passions of an infuriated populace, hurling down the restraints of law, shattering constitutions; and when its frenzied lust had been satiated by the destruction of every accessible image of virtue and order, transferring supreme power from its polluted grasp to the hands of demagogues—capable agents of the depraved will which invests them with authority.

Such was really a faithful contrast of the two powers which were now inaugurated in what had been the United States. It was still the old Greek question of the "few or the many," the "King Numbers" of the North against the conservatism of the South. The old contest was to be revived, of Cleon and Nicias, in the Athenian Agora, and struggling on through the political battle-fields of free governments in all ages.

It is not an abuse of language to characterize the North as realizing the *ultra* theory of popular government. Its political fabric rests exclusively upon the Utopian conception of an intelligence and integrity in the masses which they have never been known to possess. Carrying out its pernicious construction of the doctrine of the Declaration of Independence, that "all men are born free and equal," it professes to hold in light esteem the obvious distinctions of race, property, and color. Earnestly devoted to the successful illustration of the experiment of Democracy, it has sedulously directed its social and political development to the overthrow of caste, the oblit-eration of necessary social distinctions, and the practical asser-tion of the principle of absolute social, political, and personal equality among all men. The election of Lincoln was the grand, decisive triumph of these tendencies. He went into power as the avowed champion of the interests of the poor and laboring classes, which he declared to be in conflict with those of the slave-holding aristocrats of the South. Entirely undistinguished, with no political record, his popularity was based upon his vulgar antecedents—no slight recommendation to the populace, gratified at the prospective promotion of one of its own class.

A free society, politically, in which wealth and distinction were debarred to none, the aristocratic influences of slavery were the propitious inducements in the South, to the cultiva-tion of that personal dignity which marks the refinement of rank, in contradistinction to the vulgar pretensions and affecta-tion of a mere aristocracy of money. The patrician society of the South sought the noblest type of republicanism—regulated liberty—beyond the influence of ignorant and fanatical mobs, that perfect order which reposes securely upon virtue, intelli-gence, and interested attachment, which all human experience teaches are the only reliable safeguards of freedom.

The noblest achievement of constitutional liberty would have been the realization of the Southern ideal of republican-ism. The success and beneficence of such a government would have been in perfect accord with the philosophy of history. Every nation to which has been guaranteed a free constitution is indebted for its liberal features to its educated, patrician classes, while all the decayed republics of history owed their downfall to the corruption and excesses of an "unbridled Democracy."

Of such a government, Jefferson Davis was the appropriately chosen head. An ardent republican, in the truest and noblest sense of that abused term, a foe to absolutism and radicalism in every shape, he was the noblest product of a conservatism in which the elements of distinction were ability, intelligence, refinement, and social position. When, added to this representative quality, are considered his splendid career of public service, and his varied talents, exemplified on almost every field of exertion, it must be conceded that no ruler was ever more worthily invited to the head of a nation, and assuredly none ever was invited with such unanimity of popular acclaim.

We have said that Jefferson Davis must ever appear to the eye of mankind the historic representative of the Confederate cause. The North can not, assuredly, reject this decision, since it made him the vicarious sufferer for what it affected to consider the sins of a nation. Through him, it actually accomplished that from which the great abilities of Edmund Burke recoiled in confession of impotent endeavor, the indictment of an entire people. Those Southern men who have rashly and ungenerously assailed him as responsible for the failure of the South to win its independence, can not complain if the verdict of history shall be that the genius of its leader was worthy of a noble cause, whose fate the laws of nature, not the resources or the impotence of one man, determined. The star of Napoleon went down upon the disastrous field of Waterloo, and the millions that he had liberated passed again under the domination of tyrants whom they despised. But would the most stupid Bourbon partisan, therefore, call in question the mighty genius of Napoleon? It is a glorious memory to France, that her illustrious sovereign, aided by the valor of her children, defied for twenty years, the arms of combined Europe, but she has no blush that those energies were not equal to an indefinite resistance. That the South, struggling against mortal odds, with her comparatively feeble resources constantly diminishing with each prodigious effort, finally succumbed to an enemy inexhaustible in strength and reinforced by the world, is no testimony against either the valor or the skill with which her struggle was directed. Like Washington, Davis was embarrassed, in a hazardous cause, with defection, distrust, and discontent. But, unlike Washington, Davis did not receive the assistance of a powerful ally at the moment when aid could be most serviceably employed.

Recurring to the early history of the Confederacy, during the brief season when Montgomery was its seat of government, and especially to its unwritten details, there seems wanting no auspicious omen to presage for it future security and renown. The cause and its leader equally challenged the enthused sympathies of a patriotic people, and all that patriotism was ready to sacrifice for the one was cheerfully confided to the other. Hopefully, almost joyously, the young Confederacy began its short-lived career. Those were the halcyon days of that cheap patriotism and ferocious valor which delights to vaunt itself beyond the sound of "war's rude alarms." Every aspect of the situation appears tinged with the *couleur de rose*. In fancied security of certain independence, achieved without the harsh resort of arms, demagogues boasted that they courted a trial of strength with the North, as an opportunity for the display of Southern prowess. Men who subsequently were noted for unscrupulous assaults upon the Confederate administration, and, since the war, for their ready prostration before the Northern juggernaut, were then loud in "never surrender" proclamations of eternal separation from the North.

Such was not an appropriate season for expressing grave and painful doubts of the President's fitness for his high trust. No whisper was then heard of his want of appreciation of his situation. There was no intimation then that he failed to discern the future, or refused to provide against the perils that menaced the Confederacy, and were so obvious to more sagacious minds. Sensational newspaper correspondents, professing to base their accounts upon reliable hints from the executive quarter, were profuse in their panegyrics upon his indefatigable industry, his vigilance, penetration, and marvelous intuition of Yankee designs. They vied with each other in telling the world, especially the North, of the stupendous preparations which the Government was making in anticipation of a possible attempt at coercion by the Lincoln government. It was evident, from the outgivings of every source of opinion, that the Confederates trusting much to the merits of their cause and their own valor, yet largely depended for the successful issue of their assertion of independence upon the soldier-statesman, who, charged with many public duties, had never proven either unwilling or incapable in any trust. The time for censure was not yet at hand. Incompetent generals and recreant politicians were not yet in want of a scape-goat upon which to throw their own delinquencies. Harsh and censorious criticism was reserved for a more opportune period, when the Confederacy, like a wearied gladiator, whose spirit was invincible, reeled under the exhaustion of a dozen successive combats, with as many fresh adversaries.

The high administrative capacity of Mr. Davis had received

a most fortunate discipline in his brilliant conduct of the Federal War Department. That service was a valuable auxiliary to his efficiency as the executive head of a new government, whose safety was, from its incipiency, to depend upon the resources of that rarest phase of genius, the combined capacity for civil and military administration. The complex machinery of government, even when moving smoothly in the accustomed grooves, imposes not only severe labor, but is frequently a painful tax upon the faculties of those most familiar with its workings. When to the labor of comprehension is added the task of construction and organization from comparative chaos, such as prevailed at Montgomery, and as prevails every-where, as the result of political change, the difficulties are increased tenfold. Creation must then precede order. Organization is to be perfected before administration can be successfully attempted. It is this task of organization which has invoked some of the most splendid displays of genius, and interposed the obstacles which have occasioned its severest disappointments. Universal testimony awards to Napoleon, for his wonderful ingenuity in penetrating social necessities and meeting civil emergencies, a merit not inferior to his unrivaled genius for war. Frederick the Great, in times of peace, exhibited a vicious pragmatism which rendered his civil rule contemptible when contrasted with his military success.

The underlying secret of all successful administration is the union of the advantages flowing from unity of purpose, and those resulting from division of labor—so necessary to exact and intelligent execution. President Davis, throughout his administration, sought the attainment of this aim. Confiding the various departments to men of at least reputed talents and integrity, he yet exercised that constant supervision which was inseparable from his responsibilities, and exacted by public expectation, and this without arrogance or dictation. Disingenuous criticism has alleged that, by an assumption of autocracy, he united in himself all the powers and prerogatives of government, and thus professes to hold him alone responsible for the loss of his country's liberties. A score of years, or even a decade hence, and he will be exalted as the all-informing mind which directed, vitalized, and inspired the noblest struggle of republicanism known to ancient or modern story.

At the organization of the Confederate Government, his individual taste, capacity and experience, were fortunately coincident with the necessities of the situation in urging upon President Davis a thorough and efficient military establishment upon a war footing. The necessity of thorough preparation for war with the United States was never lost sight of by him. Whatever his efforts to avert that calamity, its probabilities were too menacing not to challenge unremitting precautions. In the War Department and military legislation of the Confederacy was felt the infusion of his energy and system, and were realized the fruits of his labors. There can be no more splendid monument of his genius than that superb specimen of scientific mechanism, the army of the Confederate States. Its nucleus was prepared in those few weeks' respite from actual war, passed by the Confederate Government, at Montgomery; and the framework then established was subsequently enlarged upon, until it was developed into a model of military anatomy—of complex, yet harmonious organism—seldom rivaled and never surpassed in the history of war. Whatever may be said of defective features exhibited in the Confederate military organization, in the numerous and varied campaigns of the war, those defects are not to be attributed to the original system. Whatever may be alleged against its lax discipline—that morbid influence which so fearfully enervated its efficiency, neutralized valor and strategy, and made the war a series of magnificent but valueless successes, the shadow without the substance of victory—the fault was in the execution, not in the original conception. However admirably tempered the blade, that must be a skillful hand which would efficiently wield it.

A graduate of West Point and a practical as well as theoretical soldier, President Davis naturally and, as the war demonstrated, wisely inclined in his military administration to those theories which regard war as a science difficult and laborious of mastery. His marked and judicious partiality for *educated soldiers* was often the ground of censorious comment during the war, but this will hardly be adjudged a fault now. "West Point" was amply vindicated by the experience of both armies, against the sneers of those who affected such extreme admiration for the "native genius" of citizen-soldiers. With a few notable exceptions in the Confederate army (and here is to be considered the peculiar genius for war of the South), and scarcely one worth mention in the armies of the North, the achievements of educated officers, and those of officers from civil life, are so utterly disproportionate as to forbid comparison.

The paramount object of all Confederate diplomacy was to secure a recognition of the new Government by the Government of the United States. If war with the United States could be averted, the Confederacy was, for all time, a fixed fact. At an early period President Davis instituted efforts to secure by negotiation possession of certain fortifications and other property of the Federal Government located within the limits of the seceded States. Arsenals, located in the interior, had, in many instances, been seized by the State troops previous to the formation of the Confederate Government. Happily, those in authority at these places, appreciating the folly of resistance in a situation utterly helpless, had avoided a needless shedding of blood, by a prompt compliance with the demands of the State authorities.

When the Confederate Government went into operation, there were but two fortifications within the limits of its jurisdiction in the possession of Federal garrisons: Fort Sumter, in Charleston Harbor, and Fort Pickens, off Pensacola, Florida. These two positions were of the utmost value to the Confederacy, viewed as to location, and their peaceable acquisition was of increased importance in consideration of the obstinate defense of which they were capable. The continued occupation of these positions by Federal forces was, in the highest degree, inconsistent with the dignity of the Confederacy after it had proclaimed a distinct and independent nationality. Moreover, in the present temper of the dominant party in the United States, a large majority of which favored coercion of the South back into the Union, Federal occupancy of these forts was a menace to the safety of the Confederacy.

It is easy to appreciate the delicate character of the diplomacy now required by the situation of the Confederacy. Without at all acquiescing in the Federal possession of Sumter and Pickens—on the contrary, asserting the right of the Confederacy to those places, and avowing its willingness to give adequate compensation whenever they should be surrendered—it was yet necessary to avoid affront to a respectable minority at the North, influenced, apparently, by pacific intentions. In short, it became the settled policy of the Confederate Government to postpone collision with the Federal Government until the latest possible moment—until obvious considerations of public safety should impel a resort to hostile measures.

President Buchanan, whose term of office expired March 4, 1861, after numerous badly disguised attempts at duplicity with the Confederate authorities, or more properly, with the authorities of some of the States constituting the Confederacy, and after a contemptibly weak and driveling policy of evasion, had left the negotiations between the two Governments in a most unsatisfactory and confused condition. A brief summary of Mr. Buchanan's conduct affords a most singular exhibition of mingled imbecility, timidity, and disingenuousness. His course, until the meeting of Congress, in December, 1860, was understood to be in thorough accord with that of the States' Rights party of the South. In that party were his most trusted advisers, both in and out of the Cabinet, and it had given to his administration a consistent and cordial support. Like them, he was pledged to the preservation of a *constitutional Union*, and also to a full recognition of the perils which menaced the South, resulting from the late sectional triumph. In his opening message he condemned the exercise of secession as unauthorized and illegal, but denied emphatically the right of coercion. Yet, in the sequel, he proved, equally with the Republican party, an enemy to peaceable secession.

When South Carolina was preparing for secession, Mr. Buchanan entered into a solemn understanding with a delegation of several of her most prominent citizens, that, upon condition that the people and authorities of that State should refrain from hostile demonstrations, no reinforcements should be sent to the forts in Charleston harbor, and that *"their relative military status should remain as at present."* Yet, when Major Anderson, in positive violation of this agreement, removed his forces from the weaker forts to Fort Sumter, Mr. Buchanan refused to order him back. Having broken one stipulation, he now determined to disregard the other, and, under the pretense of "provisioning a starving garrison," Mr. Buchanan attempted to send troops to Sumter.*

But the conduct of Mr. Buchanan, weak, offensive, and disgusting, as it was to both North and South, becomes simply pitiable, when contrasted with the greater magnitude of the perfidy of the Lincoln government.

The two Presidents, Davis and Lincoln, were inaugurated within a fortnight of each other—the first on the 18th of February, the latter on the 4th of March. Between them the question of peace or war must, after all, depend—for, however pacific might have been Mr. Buchanan's policy, it would fail, should Lincoln adopt a belligerent course. Considerable hope was, at times, indulged, that the negotiations with Mr. Lincoln and his Cabinet would at least be marked with a better display of candor than had commemorated the policy of his predecessor. These negotiations, as fruitless as those attempted in Congress during the preceding winter, for the prevention of secession, were to involve a question of even more moment. The direct issue of peace or war was now pending. It is confidently and successfully maintained by the South, that in the grave question of responsibility for actual bloodshed, her vindication is as clear and incontestable as

* By the steamer "Star of the West," which was driven back by the South Carolina batteries.

must ever be her acquittal of the responsibility of disunion. War with the United States was deprecated by official declaration of the Confederate States as "a policy detrimental to the civilized world." Most impressive is the declaration of President Davis' inaugural: "Sustained by the consciousness that the transition from the former Union to the present Confederacy has not proceeded from a disregard, on our part, of just obligations, or any failure to perform any constitutional duty—moved by no interest or passion to invade the rights of others—anxious to cultivate peace and commerce with all nations, *if we may not hope to avoid war, we may at least expect that posterity will acquit us of having needlessly engaged in it.*"

President Davis was at all times most solicitous for peace, and adopted every expedient of negotiation that could promote that end. Heartily responding to the wishes of the Congress and people of the Confederacy, he appointed, in February, an embassy to the Government at Washington. The resolution of Congress, asking that the embassy should be sent, explains its object to be the "negotiating friendly relations between that Government and the Confederate States of America, and for the settlement of all questions of disagreement between the two governments upon principles of right, justice, equity, and good faith."

Two of these commissioners, Messrs. Crawford and Forsyth, arrived in Washington on the 5th of March, the day succeeding Mr. Lincoln's inauguration. Wishing to allow the President abundant opportunity for the discharge of the urgent official duties necessarily crowding upon him at such a season, the Confederate commissioners did not immediately press their mission upon his attention. At first giving merely an informal announcement of their arrival, they waited until the

12th of March before making an official presentation of their mission. On that day they addressed a formal communication to the Secretary of State, Mr. Seward, announcing their authority to settle with the Federal Government all claims of public property arising from the separation of the States from the Union, and to negotiate for the withdrawal of the Federal forces from Forts Sumter and Pickens.

Here begins a record of perfidy, the parallel of which is not to be found in the history of the world. Mr. Seward, while declining to recognize the Confederate commissioners officially, yet frequently held confidential communication with them, by which the faith of the two Governments was fully pledged to a line of policy, by what should certainly be the strongest form of assurance—the personal honor of their representatives. In verbal interviews, the commissioners were frequently assured of a pacific policy by the Federal Government, that Fort Sumter would be evacuated, that the *status* at Fort Pickens should not be changed, and that no departure from these pacific intentions would be made without due notice to the Confederate Government.

The commissioners, conformably to the spirit of their Government, to avoid, if possible, collision with the United States, made an important concession in these interviews in consenting to waive all questions of form. It was alleged that formal negotiations with them, in an official capacity, would seriously jeopardize the success of Mr. Lincoln's manipulation of public sentiment at the North, which, it was further confidentially alleged, he was sedulously educating to concurrence with his own friendly purposes toward the Confederates. By this cunning device and the unscrupulous employment of deception and falsehood in his interviews with the commissioners, Mr.

Seward accomplished the double purpose of successful imposition upon the credulity of the commissioners and evasion of official recognition of the Confederate embassy.

In the meantime, while these negotiations were pending, and in the midst of these friendly assurances, the Lincoln administration was secretly preparing hostile measures, and, as was clearly demonstrated by subsequent revelations, had never seriously entertained any of the propositions submitted by the Confederate Government. Resolved not to evacuate Fort Sumter, the Federal Government, while amusing the Confederate commissioners with cunning dalliance, had for weeks been meditating the feasibility of reënforcing it. To pass the numerous batteries erected by the Confederates in Charleston harbor was clearly a task of the utmost difficulty, if, indeed, possible. So complete was the cordon of Confederate batteries which had been in course of preparation for many weeks, that the beleaguered fortress was evidently doomed whenever the Confederates were provoked to fire upon it. The evacuation of Fort Sumter was clearly a military necessity, so pronounced by the highest military authority in the United States, and so regarded by the intelligent public of the North. Never had a Government so auspicious an opportunity to save the needless effusion of blood, and to avert indefinitely, if not finally, the calamity of war.

Such a result was, however, farthest from the wishes of Mr. Lincoln and the majority of his Cabinet. Reinforcement of Fort Sumter being out of the question, it became the study of the Federal authorities to devise a convenient and effective pretext by which the North could be united in a war of subjugation against the South, and for the extermination of slavery. To this end an expedition was ordered to Charleston, for the purpose of supplying the garrison of Sumter with provisions, *peaceably or forcibly*, as events might decide. As it was well known that the Confederate authorities would not permit the execution of the object of this expedition, it was clearly a measure of hostility, prepared and conducted, too, under the most dishonorable circumstances of secrecy and falsehood as to its destination.

In the meantime the Federal authorities continued to practice the base policy of deception with the Confederate commissioners. Upon one occasion Mr. Seward declared that Fort Sumter would be evacuated before a letter, then ready to be mailed, could reach President Davis at Montgomery. Five days afterward, General Beauregard, commanding the Confederate forces in Charleston harbor, telegraphed the commissioners at Washington the ominous intelligence that the Federal commandant was actively strengthening Fort Sumter. The commissioners were again soothed with Mr. Seward's renewed assurances of the positive intention of his government to evacuate the fort. As late as the 7th of April Mr. Seward gave the emphatic assurance: "Faith as to Sumter fully kept: wait and see." *This was the date of the sailing of the Federal fleet with a strong military force on board.** The just characterization, by

*It was not until the 8th of April that the commissioners obtained a reply to their official communication of March 12th. From this reply, it appeared that "during the whole interval while the commissioners were receiving assurances calculated to inspire hope of the success of their mission, the Secretary of State and the President of the United States had already determined to hold no intercourse with them whatever; to refuse even to listen to any proposals they had to make, and had profited by the delay created by their own assurances, in order to prepare secretly the means for effective hostile operations."—*President Davis' Message, April 29th*, 1861.

President Davis, of these deceptions, was, that "the crooked paths of diplomacy can scarcely furnish an example so wanting in courtesy, in candor, and directness, as was the course of the United States Government toward our commissioners in Washington." *

The expedition was some hours on its way,† when its purpose to provision the fort was announced to the Governor of South Carolina by an agent of the United States. This announcement was telegraphed to Montgomery by General Beauregard, who also asked for instructions. His government replied, that if the message was authentic, a demand should be made for the surrender of the fort to the Confederate forces; and in the event of refusal, its reduction should be undertaken. On the 11th of April the demand was made and refused.‡ In obedience to the orders of his government General Beauregard

* Message to Confederate Congress.

† This expedition, ostensibly "for the relief of a starving garrison," consisted of eleven vessels, with two hundred and eighty-five guns and twenty-four hundred men.

‡ Before instructing General Beauregard to fire upon the fort, President Davis made another effort to prevent hostilities, which he thus explains: "Even then" (after Beauregard had applied for instructions), "under all the provocation incident to the contemptuous refusal to listen to our commissioners, and the treacherous course of the Government of the United States, I was sincerely anxious to avoid the effusion of blood, and directed a proposal to be made to the commander of Fort Sumter, who had avowed himself to be nearly out of provisions, that we would abstain from directing our fire at Fort Sumter, if he would promise not to open fire on our forces unless first attacked. This proposal was refused. The conclusion was, that the design of the United States was to place the besieging force at Charleston between the simultaneous fire of the fleet and fort. The fort should, of course, be at once reduced. This order was executed by General Beauregard with skill and success."—*Message, 29th Avril*, 1861.

opened fire upon Fort Sumter early on the morning of the 12th April. On the 13th the fort surrendered.

The calculations of Mr. Lincoln and his cabinet, as to the result to be produced by the attack on Fort Sumter, provoked by their deliberate and dishonest design, were not disappointed. A furious and instantaneous rush to arms by the North followed the intelligence of the surrender of the fort, and revealed the ferocious lust with which it had awaited the signal to begin the crusade against the liberties and property of the South. As no possible trait of guilt had been wanting in the means employed to precipitate hostilities, so no conceivable feature of atrocity was to be wanting in the conduct of a war by the North, produced by its own avarice, perfidy, and lust of dominion.

The brief recapitulation which we have given sufficiently exposes the pretexts upon which the North began the war of coercion. Assuming that the national dignity had been insulted, and the national honor violated, by an attack upon the flag of the Union, under the impious profession of vindicating the law, the North drew its sword against the sovereignty of the States. It had procured the assault upon Sumter—that essential step to the desired frenzy of the masses. By a shallow device, the South had been provoked to initiate resistance—that long-sought pretext which should justify the most barbaric invasion of modern times. Yet, under this flimsy imposition, the North cloaks its crime, and exults in its anticipated immunity from those execrations which have been the reward of similar examples of turpitude. The spirit of inquiry is not to be thus deftly eluded, nor the avenging sentence of history so easily perverted. The question shall not be, who fired the first shot? but, *who offered the first aggression? who first indicated the purpose of hostility?* We are not required to await the bursting forth of the flames over our heads, when the fell intent of the incendiary is revealed to our sight. The menace of the murderer justifies his intended victim in eluding the blow while the steel is uplifted.

Jefferson Davis signed the order for the reduction of Fort Sumter, but he did not thereby invoke the calamities of war. That act was simply the patriot's defiance to the menace of tyranny. It was the choice of the freeman between resistance and shame.

CHAPTER IX.

EVENTS CONSEQUENT UPON THE BOMBARDMENT OF FORT SUMTER—MR. LINCOLN BEGINS THE WAR BY USURPATION—THE BORDER STATES—CONTINUED DUPLICITY OF THE FEDERAL GOVERNMENT—VIRGINIA JOINS THE COTTON STATES—AFFAIRS IN MARYLAND, MISSOURI, AND KENTUCKY—UNPROMISING PHASES OF THE SITUATION, AFFECTING THE PROSPECTS OF THE SOUTH—DIVISIONS IN SOUTHERN SENTIMENT—THE NORTHERN DEMOCRACY—PRESIDENT DAVIS' ANTICIPATIONS REALIZED—HIS RESPONSE TO MR. LINCOLN'S PROCLAMATION OF WAR—PUBLIC ENTHUSIASM IN THE SOUTH—PRESIDENT DAVIS' MESSAGE—VIRGINIA THE FLANDERS OF THE WAR—REMOVAL OF THE CONFEDERATE CAPITAL TO RICHMOND—POLICY OF THAT STEP CONSIDERED—POPULAR REGARD FOR MR. DAVIS IN VIRGINIA—ACTION OF THE VIRGINIAN AUTHORITIES—NORTH CAROLINA; HER NOBLE CONDUCT, AND EFFICIENT AID TO THE CONFEDERACY—MILITARY PREPARATIONS IN VIRGINIA—GENERAL LEE—HIS SERVICES IN THE EARLY MONTHS OF THE WAR—MINOR ENGAGEMENTS—PREPARATIONS FOR THE GREAT STRUGGLE IN VIRGINIA—AN IMPORTANT HISTORICAL QUESTION—CHARGES AGAINST MR. DAVIS CONSIDERED—HIS STATESMAN-LIKE PREVISION—DID HE ANTICIPATE AND PROVIDE FOR WAR?—WHEN MR. DAVIS' RESPONSIBILITY BEGAN—HIS ENERGETIC PREPARATION—THE PREVAILING SENTIMENT AT MONTGOMERY AS TO THE WAR—QUOTATIONS FROM GENERAL EARLY AND GENERAL VON MOLKTE.

EVENTS quickly followed the surrender of Fort Sumter, foreshadowing the violence and magnitude of the strife about to be joined between the sundered sections of America. If the North showed itself prompt and enthusiastic to recognize the signal of conquest and spoliation, the South was tenfold more resolute and confident in its triple armor of right. If the adroit appeals of Mr. Lincoln's adherents, in behalf of an "insulted flag," and an "outraged national dignity," broke down the barriers of party, and united the Northern masses in an imagined crusade of patriotism for the rescue of the Union, the occasion brought to the Confederacy accessions of strength, which, if they did not ensure a successful defense, established the fact of protracted resistance.

Mr. Lincoln and his advisers promptly seized upon the favorable opportunity presented by the fanatical excitement prevalent throughout the North. Within forty-eight hours after the intelligence of the bloodless encounter of Sumter was flashed over the land, his proclamation of war against the seceded States was read by thousands of excited people.* A flimsy and indefensible perversion of an act, passed by Congress, in 1795, which simply provided the raising of armed *posses* "in aid of the civil authorities," was the shallow pretext, under which was masked the real design of a war which was to terminate in the destruction of the sovereignty of the States. Beginning with this clear usurpation of the power of Congress, which is alone authorized to declare war, and proclaiming a purpose to "maintain the honor, the integrity, and existence" of the Union, "and the perpetuity of popular government," the work of conquest was begun.

The *role* undertaken by the Federal government was embarrassed by many difficulties. It had not yet relinquished the hope of retaining the Border States firm in their adhesion to the Union. As yet the action of those States had indicated no purpose of separation from the North, unless in the event of direct interference by the Federal authorities with their domestic concerns, or in the event of a war of subjugation against the seceded States. Popular feeling in all the Border States was unmistakably resolved against the policy of coer-

* Mr. Lincoln's proclamation was dated April 15, 1861.

cion, and in several instances State Legislatures had declared a purpose to make common cause with the seceded States, whenever the Federal authorities should appeal to force against them. It was difficult indeed for the latter to reconcile their hostile purposes against the Confederate States with the professions of peaceful intentions which they so freely tendered to the Border States. Well pleased, however, with the uniform success of its policy of duplicity, the Federal administration adhered to its "treacherous amusement of double and triple negotiations," hoping to amuse the Border States, by pacifying assurances, until its schemes of coercion could be thoroughly prepared.* But the sham was too transparent to deceive. Friendly assurances and protestations of a desire to avoid the effusion of blood were not to be accepted in the face of gigantic martial preparations.

An immediate consequence of Mr. Lincoln's proclamation of war, and invocation of an army of seventy-five thousand men, for the subjugation of the Cotton States, was to throw the mighty energies and heroic spirit of Virginia, hitherto neutral and hesitating, into hearty sympathy with the Confederacy. The sublime courage and devotion of this noble State, manifested by the circumstances of her accession to the cause of her sister States, have been the theme of repeated, but not extravagant eulogy. With a full conviction of her own peculiar perils in a war which she had zealously striven to prevent; from which, whatever its eventualities, she had

* On the day of the surrender of Fort Sumter, Mr. Lincoln protested to the Virginia commissioners the pacific purposes of his government. When giving these assurances to Virginia he had heard of the surrender of the fort, and knew that for two days Beauregard had been firing upon the "sacred flag."

little to hope, and with a perfect prevision of the ruin which was to ravage her bosom, Virginia proudly assumed the post of leadership and of peril in the struggle for those immortal principles, of which her soil was the nursery and her illustrious sons the foremost champions. The historic *prestige* of Virginia was heightened by this act of supreme devotion, and the value of her influence was speedily demonstrated by the enthusiastic accession of other States to the cause which she had espoused. The ordinance of secession, adopted by the Virginia Convention, was followed immediately by a temporary alliance* with the Confederate States, and in a few weeks afterward the Confederacy embraced, in addition to its original members, Virginia, North Carolina, Tennessee, and Arkansas, each of which, by formal State action, ratified the Confederate constitution.

The arbitrary acts of the Federal government, in Maryland and Missouri, not only vindicated the course of those States which had interpreted its policy as one of subjugation, but greatly strengthened the already preponderant Southern sympathies of those two commonwealths. Increasing by consecutive proclamations his demands for troops, Mr. Lincoln soon had nearly two hundred thousand men under arms. These troops assembled under false pretenses at different points, were used for purposes of glaring despotism; overawing the pronounced Southern feeling of the people by military arrests, by licentious and violent demonstrations of the soldiery. Missouri was soon in open revolt against the Federal authorities, and in Maryland a general uprising was prevented by the thorough precautions which had been adopted, rendering clearly hopeless

*April 24, 1861. Virginia joined the Confederacy as a member May 6, 1861.

such an undertaking. The Legislature of Missouri, unquestionably representing a large majority of her citizens, eventually adopted an ordinance of secession and ratified the constitution of the Confederate States. Kentucky, vainly attempting a policy of neutrality, was divided in sentiment and in strength between the contestants. A portion of her citizens, residing within the Confederate lines, several months after the beginning of the war, declared the State out of the Union, and associated Kentucky with the Confederacy.

Such were the immediate consequences resulting from the capture of Fort Sumter. All hopes of peace vanished in the rush of events which daily contributed new elements to the incipient strife, and with constant reinforcements of strength and feeling to each of the contending parties, there was wanting no omen of a struggle bloody and exhaustive beyond all previous example.

There were phases of the situation not to be lightly appreciated by so thoughtful a statesman as President Davis, which did not encourage that sanguine conviction, so extravagantly indulged in by many popular leaders, of an overwhelming and immediate triumph of the Southern cause. The immense disparity of physical resources, as was abundantly shown by the lessons of history, could be neutralized by a wise public administration, by superior valor, and by that high sense of public virtue, in its original Roman sense of fortitude, endurance, and willing sacrifice in the cause of country, which is the last and sure defense of a nation's liberties. Nor were those important advantages of the South, to the value of which historical precedents have so conclusively testified—a conscious rectitude of purpose—a supreme conviction that theirs was the better cause, and that, besides, it was a war for home and family, to be fought mainly upon their own soil—to be overlooked in an intelligent estimate of the relative strength of the belligerents.

It was not a failure to recognize these great advantages which forbade wise and reflective Southern statesmen to indulge in those grotesque exhibitions of braggadocio, with which demagogues amused excited crowds at railway stations and upon street-corners. There was an element of weakness in the South, which, looking to the contingencies of the future, and remembering the incertitude of war, might prove the source of serious danger. This was the absence of that unity in the South, to which all her statesmen had looked forward, whenever actual battle should be joined between the defenders and assailants of Southern liberties. To see a "UNITED SOUTH," had been for years the dream of Calhoun's noble intellect. Davis, with equal energy and ability, had striven for such united action by the South as would command peace and security in the Union, or independence beyond its limits. But now the battle was joined, and the dream was not to be realized.

Kentucky was hopelessly divided, and though, from the overwhelming majority of her people in sympathy with the South, were to come thousands of gallant soldiers, the Confederacy was to be denied the powerful aid which the brave heart and mighty resources of united Kentucky should have thrown into the scale. Missouri, in consequence of her geographical position, peculiarly assailable by the North-western States, and by divisions among her population, was similarly situated; while Maryland, a gallant and patriotic State, not less than South Carolina devoted to the independence of the South, was securely shackled at the first demonstration, by her people, of sympathy with their invaded countrymen.

But not only was there a failure to realize united action by those States, which, by geographical contiguity, no less than by identity of political institutions, constituted what was designated as THE SOUTH. There was by no means a thoroughly harmonious sentiment among the people of those States which had joined the Southern alliance. This was conspicuously the case in Western Virginia and Eastern Tennessee.* Though apparently insignificant in the midst of the general enthusiasm which prevailed in the early months of the war, these and other instances of local disaffection were to prove, at more than one critical period, fruitful of embarrassment. Intelligence of Confederate disasters was always the signal for exhibitions of that covert disloyalty which Confederate success compelled to concealment. Always ready to assist the invaders of their country, the so-called "Union men" of the South were valuable auxiliaries to the Federal armies as spies, and as secret enemies to the cause of the patriots; but they were not more hurtful and insidious in these capacities than as the nucleus around which crystallized, under the direction of disappointed demagogues, the various elements of discontent which were subsequently developed.

Yet in both sections was the outward seeming at least of an undivided war sentiment. The Union party of the South, as it had previously existed—a powerful political organization, embracing a majority of the people of the Border States—did not more immediately disappear, as the certainty of war was developed, than did the party of peace at the North. The Northern Democracy did not, for a moment, strive to breast the popular current, but its leaders, the life-long allies of the

* "East Tennessee" was a perpetual "fire in the rear" to the Confederacy.

South, committed, by a thousand declarations to the cause of States' Rights, eagerly vied with the Republican leaders in threats of vengeance against the South. The Dickinsons, Everetts, Cochranes, Logans, and Butlers—hitherto the professed friends and advocates of the South—with that pliant accommodation to circumstances, so befitting the instincts of the demagogue, in their harangues to howling mobs, proclaimed themselves the advocates of a ruthless and indiscriminate warfare upon a people who had been driven, by intolerable wrongs, into patriotic resistance.

We have already described the attitude and condition of the Confederate Government at Montgomery previous to the attack upon Fort Sumter. The honorable exertions of President Davis, cordially approved by Congress and the people, to avoid a collision of arms, were disappointed, and events had now verified his life-long conviction, that the exercise of their sovereignty, by the States, would be attended by a war involving their existence. Sustained by an unlimited popular confidence, with a comparatively perfected organization, and with every possible preparation that the difficulties of its situation would permit, the Government met, with commendable composure, the shock of arms which its chief had foreseen to be inevitable.

The proclamation of President Lincoln, declaring war upon the Confederate States, was promptly responded to by President Davis, in official announcements, appropriately recognizing the condition of public affairs, and inviting energetic preparations for immediate hostilities. He at once called upon the various States for quotas of volunteers for the public defense. By public proclamation, he invited applications for privateering service, in which armed vessels might assist in the public defense on the high seas, under letters of marque and reprisal granted by Congress.*

In every instance, and by all classes of citizens, an enthusiastic response was given to the demands of the Government. Individuals and corporations entered into a generous and patriotic rivalry in the tender of aid to the cause. Wealthy citizens donated large sums of money or supplies, while railroad and transportation companies tendered valuable assistance in the conveyance of troops and stores. An enthusiastic desire to enter the public service was manifested in every community. Men decrepit from age, or infirm from disease, were importunate in demanding any service suitable to their condition. Volunteering progressed so actively that a few weeks only sufficed to show that the Confederacy—for the present at least—would not want soldiers. In all the States the responses to the call for volunteers exceeded the quotas.

Congress assembled in special session, in obedience to a

* President Davis appreciated the immense value to the South of privateering. The Federal Government employed all the naval force at their command to blockade the South, recalled the squadrons stationed in foreign waters, and made extensive purchases of vessels for purposes of war. The South, of course, had no navy, since there had been no time to prepare or purchase one within the brief space between the organization of the Confederate Government and the beginning of hostilities. Under these circumstances there remained only the resort to private armed ships, under letters of marque, to assault the floating commerce of the enemy, and, to some extent, neutralize the blockade. Doubting the constitutional power of the executive in the premises, he, with characteristic regard for law, determined not to commission privateers until duly authorized by the legislation of Congress. The authority to issue commissions, and letters of marque and general reprisal, to privateers, was given by act of Congress, passed 6th of May.

proclamation of the President, on the 29th of April. The message was an eminently characteristic document, and made a profound impression both in Europe and the United States. Its calm and clear statements were in marked contrast with the wild elements of war convulsing the country. Europe was not less amazed and delighted with its dignity and force, than was the North impressed with the earnest terms in which the purpose of resistance was announced. He reviewed and established the doctrine of secession, detailed the facts showing the bad faith of the Northern government about Fort Sumter, and the necessity for its capture; spoke in terms of keen, yet dignified satire of Lincoln's proclamation, which attempted to treat seven sovereign States united in a confederacy, and holding five millions of people and a half million of square miles of territory, as "combinations," which he proposed to suppress by a *posse comitatus* of seventy-five thousand men; congratulated the Congress on the probable accession of other slave States; informed them that the State Department had sent three commissioners to England, France, Russia and Belgium, to seek the recognition of the Confederate States; advised legislation for the employment of privateers for measures of defense, and for perfecting the government organization; and concluded with these impressive words: "We feel that our cause is just and holy; we protest solemnly in the face of mankind that we desire peace at any sacrifice save that of honor and independence; we seek no conquest, no aggrandizement, no concession of any kind from the States with whom we were lately confederated. All we seek is to be let alone; that those who never held power over us shall not now attempt our subjugation by arms. This we will, this we must resist to the direst extremity. The moment that this pretension is abandoned, the sword will drop from our grasp, and we shall be ready to enter into treaties of amity and commerce that can not but be materially beneficial. So long as this pretension is maintained, with firm reliance on that divine power which covers with its protection the just cause, we will continue the struggle for our inherent right to freedom, independence, and self-government."

The geographical position of Virginia clearly indicated that State as the Flanders of the war. Within her boundaries was necessarily to be located the first line of Confederate defense, and also to be found more than one favorable *point d'appui* for the invading forces. To the aid of important geographical and physical considerations, moral and political necessities were superadded, to urge a prompt and vigorous assistance to Virginia, in the heroic effort which she was preparing for her deliverance. With the eye of the soldier and the appreciation of the statesman, President Davis urged the immediate removal of the seat of government to the neighborhood of the seat of war. On the 20th of May the seat of the Confederate Government was transferred from Montgomery to Richmond, the capital of Virginia, and within a few days afterward Mr. Davis reached the latter city.*

*A recent work (*Richmond During the War*) thus mentions the arrival of Mr. Davis in Richmond:

"He was received with an outburst of enthusiasm. A suite of handsome apartments had been provided for him at the Spotswood Hotel, until arrangements could be made for supplying him with more elegant and suitable accommodations. Over the hotel, and from the various windows of the guests, waved numerous Confederate flags, and the rooms destined for his use were gorgeously draped in the Confederate colors. In honor of his arrival, almost every house in the city was decorated with the 'Stars and Bars.'

The transfer of the Confederate capital to Richmond was an event affecting the direction, character, and destinies of the war to such an extent as entitles it to be considered one of its salient incidents. As a measure of policy, it has been variously viewed, and has involved some interesting discussion of military and strategic considerations. In the progress of events during the war, its wisdom was generally recognized, and in the calmer judgment of the present there is scarcely a dissenting voice to the prevailing opinion that it was a master-stroke of political sagacity and military forecast.

High military authority has been quoted in support of the opinion opposed to locating the Confederate capital at Richmond. Ingeniously enough it was alleged that such a step involved fighting on the exterior of the circle instead of the centre, and that thus the great advantage to the party conducting operations upon an interior line would be surrendered. It was also tolerably certain that the North would aim, in its invasion, at the Confederate capital as the vital objective point of its campaigns; and to transfer the capital to a point so far

"An elegant residence for the use of Mr. Davis was soon procured. It was situated in the western part of the city, on a hill, overlooking a landscape of romantic beauty. This establishment was luxuriantly furnished, and there Mr. and Mrs. Davis dispensed the elegant hospitalities for which they were ever distinguished. Mrs. Davis is a tall, commanding figure, with dark hair, eyes and complexion, and strongly-marked expression, which lies chiefly in the mouth. With firmly-set yet flexible lips, there is indicated much energy of purpose and will, but beautifully softened by the usually sad expression of her dark, earnest eyes. Her manners are kind, graceful, easy, and affable, and her receptions were characterized by the dignity and suavity which should very properly distinguish the drawing room entertainments of the Chief Magistrate of a Republic."

north as Richmond, greatly diminished the enemy's difficulties —first, as to space; and secondly, by shortening his line of transportation and supply.

But these views were the conclusions of a purely strategic judgment, overlooking entirely moral and political considerations involved, nor are they by any means exhaustive of the argument as to the military aspects of the situation. The courageous and unselfish action of Virginia deserved a response of similar spirit from the Confederacy. Virginia had voluntarily become the outpost of the South, and her people needed the presence among them of that authority which was to wield her great resources, organize her energies, and give counsel to her courage. Her people invited the Government to join them and make the battle for the common deliverance of the South around their homesteads. To accept this invitation was a step no less characteristic of President Davis than was his prompt, decisive action in the crisis at Buena Vista. It had the combined advantage of bold defiance and prudent calculation. This bold courting of the issue by the infant power, at the very outset of hostilities, was the foundation of that brilliant *prestige* which marked its earlier history. To an adversary intoxicated with an overweening sense of numerical superiority, and a brutal reliance upon his superior strength, this defiant planting of the standard in front of his first line was a significant warning of the difficulties of the task which he had undertaken.

President Davis has never seen reason to regret the transfer of the Government to Richmond. It bound Virginia, by indissoluble ties to the fortunes of the Confederacy, and was the beginning of an affection for himself, among her citizens, which it was their pride to exhibit in the face of calamities common to him and to themselves. Not even in his own gallant State of Mississippi are the genius, virtues, and fame of Jefferson Davis cherished with a more tender association than in Virginia.

A brief résumé of events will now assist to a clear understanding of the situation of affairs when President Davis reached Richmond in the latter part of May. Virginia, a week previously, had, by formal vote of her people, ratified the ordinance of secession adopted by her convention. When the convention passed the ordinance of secession on the 17th of April, the State authorities, with commendable discretion, prepared to make important seizures of arms, stores, etc., the property of the Federal Government within the limits of the State. Governor Letcher—well known for his steadfast devotion to the Union, and for his honorable zeal to preserve it—in this trying crisis of the State, was nobly faithful to his Virginian instincts, and mindful of the honorable part which devolved upon Virginia's Governor.

The capture of two places of special importance was sought by expeditions arranged with secrecy and ingenuity, but resulting, in both instances, in only partial success. These places were Gosport Navy-yard—famous for its dry-dock, shops, ammunition, arms, timber, rope-walks, and other appurtenances of an extensive naval establishment—and Harper's Ferry, on the Potomac, with its extensive armory and arsenal, large collection of arms, and valuable machinery. At the latter place, the Federal commander, by an unworthy subterfuge, obtained a delay in the attack which the Virginians were about to make, and took advantage of a parley, to attempt the destruction, by fire, of the buildings and machinery. Much valuable property was destroyed, but the State secured machinery, which was afterward turned to most important account, and many excellent arms for her rapidly gathering volunteers. The attempted destruction, by the Federals, at Gosport, was imperfectly executed. Among the prizes captured here was the steam frigate Merrimac, nearly finished, but greatly damaged by fire. Within a very few months this vessel was destined to a performance, conspicuous for all time in the annals of naval warfare.

The authorities of North Carolina—a State which had clung with unsurpassed fidelity to the Federal Union—acted with a vigor which well befitted a community conspicuous, in the first American revolution, for the fidelity of its patriotism. Slow to reach her conclusions, North Carolina was fully up to the demands of the occasion, in her preparation for a struggle, during which her revolutionary fame was to be excelled by a second dedication of her blood and energies to the cause of liberty. On the 21st of May, North Carolina, by unanimous vote of her convention, adopted an ordinance of secession. Her brave Governor (Ellis) whose services were too soon lost to his State and country, had previously caused the seizure of Forts Macon and Caswell, and the arsenal at Fayetteville, with nearly sixty thousand arms, of which half were of the most approved construction.

On the 19th of April occurred a collision between citizens of Baltimore and Massachusetts soldiers, *en route* to the Federal capital, followed by such a stringent policy as made clearly hopeless the open coöperation of Maryland, unless by successful invasion of the Confederate forces.

Missouri, under the guidance of Jackson, Price, and other able and resolute leaders, was preparing a heroic resistance, but under difficulties greater than were experienced in any other Southern State, against the domination established upon her soil.

When President Davis reached Richmond he found Virginia in an advanced state of preparation. Thirty thousand troops were in camps of instruction, or upon duty at Norfolk, upon the peninsula of James and York Rivers, and at different points upon the northern boundary of the State. In supreme command was General Robert E. Lee, the friend and former classmate of the President at West Point; and, under him, Colonel John B. Magruder, also his associate at West Point, and other officers of promise and ability, seeking service in defense of their native State and the South. As the several States acceded to the Confederacy, their troops, arms, stores, etc., were turned over to the Confederate authorities, and officers were assigned rank in the Confederate service by a rule, regulated by the rank which they had held in the Federal army.

In accordance with this rule, General Lee was third on the list of full generals appointed by President Davis—General Cooper being first, and General Albert Sydney Johnston being second. General Lee had been first commissioned, after the tender of his resignation in the Federal service, a Major-General of Virginia forces. Until he was commissioned full general, by President Davis, in June, 1861, he continued to act as the general commanding the Virginia forces, and was invested also with the direction of the Confederate troops which were arriving daily from the States south. His authority was as follows:

"MONTGOMERY, May 10, 1861.

"*To Major-General R. E. Lee:* To prevent confusion, you will assume control of the forces of the Confederate States in

Virginia, and assign them to such duties as you may indicate, until further orders; for which this will be your authority.

"L. P. WALKER, *Secretary of War.*"

It would be impossible to overestimate the services of General Lee in the preparation of the Virginia troops for the field, and in preparing the general defense of the State by the location and disposition of the Confederate forces as they arrived in Virginia. His distinguished services afterwards are hardly better evidence of his genius as a soldier, than the results of his arduous labor at this trying period, and in a position of comparative obscurity. President Davis fully indicated his confidence in the counsels of Lee by his constant retention of him at his side. The South has probably not yet appreciated the extent to which the genius of Lee, in coöperation with that of Davis, aided in those earlier achievements of the war, which secured the immediate preservation of the Confederacy, and earned so flattering a reputation for others.

With the establishment of the Confederate authority in Virginia, reinforcements from other States were constantly added to her own levies, and by the middle of June, more than fifty thousand men were in arms for her defense. As yet, collisions between the opposing forces had been rare, and totally indecisive. A force of raw volunteers, unorganized and imperfectly armed, was surprised in Western Virginia, by a movement of considerable vigor on the part of the Federal commander, and the patriots, under Colonel Porterfield, compelled to retreat. At Great Bethel, near Fortress Monroe, a few hundred Virginians and North Carolinians, under Colonel

Magruder, handsomely repulsed a large column of Federal troops, attempting to advance up the peninsula. In the then uneducated popular idea of military operations, the fight at Bethel was magnified to an extent greatly beyond its real importance. It had, nevertheless, a timely significance, in its evidence of the spirit of the Confederate soldiery. President Davis was pleased to recognize this fact in a congratulatory letter to Governor Ellis, commending the conduct of the North Carolinians who were engaged in the fight.

These minor affairs were preliminary incidents to the thrilling events, upon a more extended scale of operations, and upon a more important theatre, which were to make memorable the approaching midsummer. Pending the preparations, active and extensive on both sides, for the coming grand encounter, there was a marked pause in military operations, attended by an agreeable subsidence of the feverish excitement of which war is so productive. The struggle for the mastery in Virginia, which it was plain would decide the present fate of the Southern movement, was destined also to decide, in a large measure, the extent and duration of the war. Viewed in its historical significance, it becomes chiefly important as a stage of the revolution indicating a new departure, and an altered direction of events. Preparation was now to be displaced by action. Skirmishes were to be followed by heavy engagements, and the high prestige of the South was now to be subjected to its first test, in that long series of cruel encounters, between valor and endurance on one side, and mere weight of numbers on the other.

Preliminary to the narrative of these important events, appropriately arises one phase of that historical question which involves the statesmanship, the forecast, and the general fitness of Jefferson Davis in the position which he now occupied, and under the circumstances by which he was surrounded.

It would be a superfluous and unprofitable task to consider in detail the numerous allegations, trivial and serious, made against President Davis by his assailants, in support of their professed belief in his responsibility for the failure of the Confederate cause. When facts are perverted, history distorted, and prejudice, rather than truth, is the governing influence, such allegations will be sufficiently numerous, even though they be not well sustained. Nor yet is it maintained that President Davis committed no errors in the long and trying term of his administration. It is very certain that no such defense, asserting his infallibility, would be approved by him. But the real historical significance of the question of Mr. Davis' capacity for his office may be reduced to very simple dimensions. Conceding him to be mortal, we concede that he is fallible. Then the question arises, Were his errors sufficiently numerous and serious, unaided by other and greater causes, to have occasioned the failure of the South in the late war? Again, conceding still more liberally to his assailants, were those errors the chief causes of a failure, which might have been avoided, despite all other adverse influences, disadvantages, and obstacles, if a different administrative policy had prevailed?

The subject now has no value, save in its historical sense, and in that sense its value must be determined from the standpoint just indicated. At least it is in that aspect that we propose to consider it, whenever its discussion shall be appropriate in these pages. The consideration will be modified by many collateral questions which must incidentally arise. It may be necessary to ask if no other Southern leader, entrusted with great responsibilities, and enjoying uninterrupted popular favor, during and since the war, committed mistakes quite as serious and frequent as did the President, in proportion to the multiplicity of his cares? It may be appropriate, too, to consider the influence that these mistakes of others exerted upon those final disasters for which he alone is held responsible. These questions we propose to consider, each in its appropriate place, and with becoming candor. If we shall not meet the arguments and allegations employed against Mr. Davis with a spirit more ingenuous than has seemed to actuate his assailants, our success must be poor, indeed.

Those who profess to consider President Davis wanting in the necessary qualifications for his position, dwell with especial emphasis upon what they are pleased to characterize his failure in the early months of the war, to foresee its character, duration and magnitude, and the consequent imperfect preparation of the Confederate Government. It is asserted that he was utterly blind to all the indications of a long and obstinate struggle, urged upon his attention by a more sagacious statesmanship than his own; that he was persistent and arrogant in his prophecies of a struggle, short, brilliant, and overwhelming in favor of the South, even after the war had commenced; and that before the bombardment of Sumter he was no less positive in his convictions that there would be no war; that he was, in short, stupidly unreasoning and inactive, deaf alike to entreaties, arguments, and facts.

If, indeed, it could be established that during the era of secession (the interval between November, 1860, and April, 1861), Mr. Davis had cherished expectations of peaceable separation, and that during that portion of his presidential term embraced before the assault upon Sumter, relying upon this prospect of peace, he had failed to prepare for war, then, indeed, would his responsibility be great; but it would be shared by every contemporary statesman of the South, almost, if not quite, without an exception. History may palliate the amazing infatuation of the Southern masses at this period, but surely its verdict must be a contemptuous condemnation of that vaunted statesmanship which scouted war as the result of secession, as an impossibility, and its anticipation as the product of timidity. But President Davis is not driven to the extremity of seeking so poor a refuge as the common and universal blindness and weakness of that critical period. Recognizing the justice of that test which demands of the true statesman a prescience beyond the average vision, it is believed that his defense may be made easy and triumphant.

Candid investigation will demonstrate the fact that Davis, among Southern statesmen, was an almost solitary exception in his rejection of the dominant sentiment of the times. The remarkable consistency of his public life is in no respect better sustained than in his oft-repeated apprehensions of eventual war between the sections. His dread of disunion arose from his dread of civil war, and the latter he always urged to be the necessary consequence of the former. Striving to save the Union upon a just and constitutional basis, he yet habitually admonished the South of the inevitable result of disunion, and coupled his admonitions with earnest exhortations of thorough preparation for the most serious emergency in its history. His speeches, addresses, and letters, furnish irrefutable testimony of his apprehension of civil war as an inevitable concomitant of disunion. *Not one line, or one sentence, written or uttered by him in the entire period of his public career, can be so construed as to indicate a different conviction.* Believing that he foresaw the impending conflict, he strove with indefatigable energy and incomparable ability, in company with Calhoun, in 1850, to place the South in a position which would then have rescued her liberties. If the warning voice of the South, proclaiming the inexorable decree of disunion, unless her constitutional rights were fully and forever secured, had then been disregarded, at least her *resistance* must have been more effectual than it could become by postponement. In innumerable passages of rare eloquence, he has left an imperishable record of patriotic devotion to a constitutional union, and touching proofs of the emotion with which he contemplated the evils which were to follow its destruction. The words of his farewell address to the Senate, ("putting our trust in God, and in our firm hearts and strong arms, we will vindicate the right as best we may") do not more clearly indicate the calm determination with which he would meet the peril, than his appreciation of its serious nature.

When it is alleged that the inadequate preparation of the South, during the period which we have characterized as the era of secession, enters as a most important feature in the explanation of her failure, a proposition is boldly asserted, which is, at least, debatable; but its discussion does not devolve upon us.* Mr. Davis is assuredly not to be held

* We intentionally waive the discussion of this question as to the extent of the preparation made by the States, severally, for actual war. It is not incumbent upon us here to examine the action of the individual States. We do not desire to be understood, however, as assenting to the proposition that all the States were inadequately prepared. It is a singular commentary upon the wisdom and sagacity of the leaders of secession in its earlier stages (by the various States), that Virginia and North Carolina were each better able to arm their troops than were some of the Cotton States. The latter may have made as much preparation as was

justly accountable for what the various States failed to do while he was at his post of duty in the Senate, and in no manner controlling their action. No responsibility can attach to him beyond the action of the Confederate Government, save in the case of his own State, and whatever preparation Mississippi made was at his instance. By what law of justice or logic can Mr. Davis be made accountable for the inadequate preparation of Georgia, (assuming that Georgia *was* unprepared, or had omitted any preparation that was possible under the circumstances), which then had the full benefit of the counsels of reputed statesmen like Messrs. Toombs, Stephens, and Brown? or of South Carolina, under the counsels of Messrs. Rhett and Orr, and the *Charleston Mercury?* Of Alabama, led by the brilliant genius of Mr. Yancey? Yet, upon the aggregate resources and means of defense of these and the other States must depend the safety of the Confederacy. While Mr. Davis was yet in Washington, striving against hope to avert the dreaded issue, many of the States, under the guidance of their leading men, were passing ordinances of secession. Assuredly, then, he is not to be censured for any lack of preparation at this period. Yet no very close examination of the record is necessary to establish the fact, that those who have since been most forward in denying the prevision of statesmanship to Davis, were then, by their own showing, precipitating their several States into

possible under the circumstances. When Mr. Davis reached Mississippi, after his withdrawal from the Senate, the Legislature had appropriated $150,000 for military purposes. As Major-General commanding the forces of the State, he was consulted as to additional appropriations. He immediately recommended an appropriation of *three millions of dollars.* It is needless to say that such a recommendation, at that period, was deemed little less than extravagant folly.

secession, totally unprepared for a war, the very possibility of which they derided.

The responsibility of Mr. Davis can date only from his inauguration as President of the Confederate States, on February 18, 1861. Between that date and the actual breaking out of war was an interval of *less than two months.* Within this period the results accomplished were certainly all that could have been anticipated, and all that ever were accomplished by any government yet in its infancy, within the same space of time. The organization of the Government had been perfected, efforts made to secure intercourse with foreign nations, and the civil administration completed in all important features. With the aid of that master genius for organization, General Samuel Cooper, Adjutant and Inspector-General of the Confederate army, the basis of a military organization, upon which the most splendid armies of modern history were speedily created, was prepared; troops were called into the field; and the Confederacy, in proportion to its means, was actually placed, *in two months,* upon a war footing, not inferior to that of the enemy at the outbreak of hostilities.

The unprejudiced Northern or European reader, whose admiration has been freely expressed for the valor and endurance of the South, and for the skillful use of its comparatively limited resources, may well be amazed at the censures of Mr. Davis, from Southern sources.

But what was his error after assumption of the Presidency? More important still, what is the evidence? So far as we have been able to gather the evidence, it consists in the fact that President Davis did not urge the indiscriminate purchase of arms in Europe, or wherever else they might have been obtained. The intelligent foreign reader can only be amazed

19

that, upon this single fact—for it is the only *fact* alleged—rests the charge that President Davis did not make adequate preparation for war. The answer is very simple, and indisputable. First, the Confederate Government, from the date of its organization, endeavored constantly to purchase *serviceable* arms wherever they could be obtained. Second, the Confederate Government had given extensive orders to Northern manufactories (because they were nearest) at Chickopee and elsewhere, some of which were filled and the arms received, while, in other cases, they were seized by the Federal authorities after the commencement of hostilities while *en route* South. Third, there were very few serviceable arms to be purchased in Europe; and in support of this assertion we have only to recall the enormous swindles practised on the Federal Government in its purchase of arms in Europe at this period. Arms were offered, in some instances, to the Government, and rejected, because President Davis, while Secretary of War, had become acquainted with their worthlessness; and thus, while certain speculations were disappointed, the means of the Government were not squandered. An examination of the records will demonstrate the fact that the Confederate Ordnance Bureau, under Colonel Gorgas, was conducted with signal judgment and ability. From the beginning to the end, it was managed with a success which entitles it to be considered probably the most ably conducted bureau of the Government.

But not only do the recorded events of the period vindicate Mr. Davis from the accusations of a tardy and delinquent policy in providing for the threatened emergency of war; they are fully conclusive as to the energetic provision made when hostilities were opened. Nothing can be more emphatic in its enunciation of a bold, vigorous policy than President Davis' message to the Confederate Congress, assembled by special convocation, on the 29th of April:* "There are now in the field at Charleston, Pensacola, Forts Morgan, Jackson, St. Philip, and Pulaski, nineteen thousand men, and sixteen thousand are now *en route* for Virginia. *It is proposed to organize and hold in readiness for instant action, in view of the present exigencies of the country, an army of one hundred thousand men.*" Surely we must look elsewhere than to such an announcement as this, for evidence in support of this pretended absence of foresight, and inappreciation of the extent and character of the approaching struggle. This, be it remembered, was in Davis' first response to the Federal declaration of war, only two weeks after the fall of Sumter, and when President Lincoln had, as yet, called for but seventy-five thousand men. This was the spirit in which President Davis began the contest, and the results which immediately followed, in months of brilliant and consecutive triumphs, demonstrated the ample provision made for the emergency.†

In marked contrast with this vigorous policy were the silly vaporings of demagogues, prating of Southern invincibility against a world in arms, protesting that the North, under no circumstances, could be induced to fight, and scouting a longer

* It should be observed that Mr. Lincoln did not call upon the Federal Congress to assemble until July 4th, two months after the meeting of the Confederate Congress.

† In this connection, we quote from a remarkably faithful and careful chronicle of events during a portion of the war: "On the morning of the 29th of May, President Davis arrived in Richmond. . . . . . . He found the military preparations in a state requiring instant energy, and, within a few hours after his arrival, he telegraphed and wrote messages to every State in the South, urging that troops should be sent forward with increased speed."—*Howison's History of the War.*

duration of a war with "Yankees," than six months at the farthest. That such was the dominant conviction at Montgomery, no contemporary authority will deny. An eminent Virginian, a commissioner from his own State to the Confederate Congress, was amazed to hear laughed at as an excellent joke, his congratulations to that body, upon the wise determination to locate the seat of government at Richmond, in close proximity to the seat of war. The grave legislators at Montgomery, at least, had not yet comprehended that there was to be war.

But perhaps we are in fault, in thus offering the evidence of uncontradicted facts and obvious conclusions, where only vague inferences and unsupported allegations are urged to the contrary. There are graver questions yet to be encountered, far better justifying difference of opinion, and affording better ground for discussion of the philosophy of the Southern failure. Censure of those who have had the conduct of a ruined cause is as inevitable as the criticism which ever waits upon history; but it is not, therefore, always just. A great soldier,* who has but recently contributed a chapter to history, thrilling in interest and inestimable in importance, when congratulated since upon his brilliant triumphs, touchingly replied: "How would it have been if success—this unexampled success—had not crowned our undertaking? Would not this undeserved exaltation have been so much unreasonable criticism and undeserved blame?"

To a certain class of Southern critics, we commend the magnanimous sentiment of an illustrious fellow-countryman,†

* General Von Molkte, who planned the Prussian campaign in Bohemia.

† General Jubal A. Early.

now mourning, in exile, the afflictions of his country: "As for myself, I have not undertaken to speculate as to the causes of our failure, as I have seen abundant reason for it in the tremendous odds brought against us. Having had some means of judging, I will, however, say that, in my opinion, both President Davis and General Lee, in their respective spheres, did all for the success of our cause which it was possible for mortal men to do; and it is a great privilege and comfort for me so to believe, and to have been able to bring with me, into exile, a profound love and veneration for those great men."

CHAPTER X.

CHARACTERISTICS OF THE WAR IN 1861—THE TWO GOVERNMENTS MORE DIRECTLY CONNECTED WITH RESULTS IN THE FIELD THAN AT SUBSEQUENT PERIODS—MR. DAVIS' CONNECTION WITH THE MILITARY POLICY OF THE CONFEDERACY—THE CONFEDERATE GOVERNMENT ADOPTS, IN THE MAIN, THE DEFENSIVE POLICY OF THE VIRGINIAN AUTHORITIES—FEDERAL PREPARATIONS —GENERAL SCOTT—DEFENSIVE PLANS OF THE CONFEDERATES—DISTRIBUTION OF THEIR FORCES—THE CONFEDERATE CAMPAIGN OF 1861 JUSTIFIED—DISTRIBUTION OF THE FEDERAL FORCES—PROGRESS OF THE CAMPAIGN—GENERALS PATTERSON AND JOHNSTON—JUNCTION OF BEAUREGARD AND JOHNSTON—MANASSAS—PRESIDENT DAVIS ON THE BATTLE-FIELD—HIS DISPATCH—HIS RETURN TO RICHMOND—A SPEECH NEVER PUBLISHED BEFORE—REFLECTIONS UPON THE RESULTS OF MANASSAS—MR. DAVIS NOT RESPONSIBLE FOR THE ABSENCE OF PURSUIT—STONEWALL JACKSON'S VIEWS—DAVIS IN FAVOR OF PURSUIT OF THE FEDERALS—MISREPRESENTATIONS—MILITARY MOVEMENTS IN VARIOUS QUARTERS—THE "TRENT AFFAIR"—RESULTS OF THE FIRST YEAR OF THE WAR.

WHATEVER crudities may appear in the general plans of warfare, adopted by the American belligerents in 1861, when tested by the maxims which have obtained in other wars, waged upon different theatres of action, and for different purposes, at least there was not wanting a palpable and definitive shape. With remarkable rapidity and precision, the military situation was adjusted to the attainment of certain general objects, which continued, during the successive stages of the war, to be pursued, with varying fortune, by the respective contestants.

The incipient campaign of the war was peculiarly regulated

and determined by the paramount aims which had impelled the respective parties to arms. Of necessity, the campaign, on the part of the North, must be offensive, while the South, in a defensive attitude, must prepare to parry the blows of her assailant. The pretext of the North was to assert the "national authority" over what it was pleased to term "rebellious" territory. The *animus* of the South was to repel an invasion which menaced her liberties and firesides. Whatever advantages may have belonged to the position of the South were not overlooked by those who were charged with her defense; and it may safely be claimed, in view of the immediate and overwhelming result in her favor, that whatever compensation, for obvious disadvantages, she had anticipated from the resources of skillful leadership, was fairly rendered.

The two Governments, at Washington and at Richmond, were then more directly chargeable with the actual results in the field than at subsequent periods. The army had then become less independent of the Government. Its organic structure was undeveloped, and it had not yet become identified with those commanders whose history was hereafter to be so interwoven with its own. In a general sense, it may be remarked, that the connection of President Davis with all the campaigns of the Confederate army, was that which the country designed it should be, when, in consequence of his military aptitude and experience, it placed him in charge of the public administration. Moreover, it was consistent with that inevitable responsibility which attached to the office of chief executive. Ignorant and intemperate partisans have labored to prove his responsibility for those casualties of war, which are utterly beyond human calculations, and to trace to his influence disasters of the battle-field, with which he could by no possibility have been connected. As is usual in such cases, these criticisms are made with a total forgetfulness of the unintentional tribute, which is accorded to Mr. Davis, in ascribing to him the chief responsibility for a military administration, which the world declares to have had few parallels in its history.

When President Davis reached Richmond, from Montgomery, the military situation had already assumed a well-defined shape. The plans of defense, adopted by the Virginian authorities, mainly under the direction of General Lee, and carried into partial execution before the alliance with the Confederacy had been formally consummated, were adhered to by the Confederate Government. President Davis, as we have seen, fully impressed with the demands of the exigency, immediately upon his arrival, addressed himself, with characteristic vigor and promptitude, to such measures as would secure a successful campaign. In the meantime, the preparations of the Federal Government were equally vigorous, and by no means indefinite in their aims.

Whatever may be the comparative merits, when placed in antithetical juxtaposition, of the plans of campaign adopted by the two Governments in 1861, or whatever may be alleged of the blunders and mishaps of the Federal scheme of warfare, there could be no question of the full comprehension of the necessities of the situation by the veteran commander of the Federal armies. We are not called upon here to give an opinion of General Scott in his personal or political relations, but that combination of sagacious military minds, upon which devolved the defense of Southern liberties, was not likely to commit the error of a disparaging estimate of his abilities.

General Scott, far in advance of the prevailing opinion at the North, dreamed of no holiday enterprise. He well knew that Southern valor, directed by leaders whose names were identified with the proudest *prestige* of America, and enlisted in the defense of principles which were the dearest convictions and traditions of the Southern heart, was not to be crushed in a "three-months'" wrestle of arms. Accordingly, his preparations were for *war* in its broadest and most terrible sense; a war between powerful nationalities; a war in which, though sustained by inexhaustible resources and popular enthusiasm, he had yet to contend with a race essentially military in its instincts, earnest in conviction, led by men whose capacities he had amply tested, and aided by defensive position, vast extent of territory, and by those numerous obstacles in the way of conquest, which must have been apparent to the eye of an experienced soldier.

The attitude of the Confederate Government was necessarily defensive. History would be searched in vain for examples justifying an invasion by a people entirely agricultural in habits and resources, weak in numbers, and with a government not yet organized three months, of a powerful manufacturing and commercial nation, of dense population, and great wealth and resources. Without supplies, equipment and transportation, and without the time or opportunity to obtain them, successful invasion of the North, however attractive to the popular imagination, was clearly impossible. Viewed from the more educated stand-point, furnished by the later developments of the war, the crude ideas, from which arose the popular aspiration of at once "carrying the war into Africa," are ludicrous in the extreme. Indeed, there can be little doubt that the defensive, subjected to such modifications as the casualties of war render proper and necessary in all plans, whether offensive or defensive, was at all times the true policy of the

South. Certain it is, that, upon two occasions, essaying the offensive under the most favorable circumstances, and under their greatest commander, the Confederates were overtaken by disaster. There can be no just criterion, furnished by European wars, by which to test the Confederate military policy in the main. Parallels between the American civil war and those waged by Frederick the Great and Napoleon are inadmissable. Not only were circumstances entirely dissimilar, but able military critics have indicated physical peculiarities, forbidding the unexceptional application to American warfare, of maxims which, elsewhere, are undisputed.

Nevertheless, war as a science must be worse than useless, unless its underlying principles have universal application. Nor is it maintained that there were no circumstances which would have justified a departure from the usually defensive policy of the Confederates. Upon two occasions the main army of the South, having successfully encountered upon its own soil the most prodigious efforts of the enemy's strength, sought to follow him in the moment of his recoil. The Confederate invasion of 1862, culminating at Antietam, and that of 1863, culminating at Gettysburg, were undertaken with the purpose of destroying, upon his own soil, an enemy already defeated. Each of these endeavors was based upon sound principles; and there is no little palliation for the disaster, in either case, in reflecting how great would have been the results of success. Much of the philosophy of the war in Virginia is to be explained by the fact of the thoroughly aggressive character, as soldiers, of President Davis and General Lee. These two directing minds, by whose combined genius and will, the fortunes of the Confederacy were so long upheld, in full and cordial coöperation during the entire war, were in nothing more harmonious, than in the desire for an aggressive campaign, whenever it could be undertaken with a reasonable promise of success. Hence, the history of the army of Northern Virginia develops, throughout, that military policy which is known as the "defensive with offensive returns."

After the conclusion of the alliance between Virginia and the Confederate States, which placed all "military operations, offensive and defensive, in Virginia," under the control of the Confederate President, troops from the other Southern States had been thrown northward with astonishing rapidity. As rapidly as they arrived, regiments were sent to the various localities where it had been thought expedient to establish a defensive force. These posts were distributed with a view to their strategic bearing upon particular sections of territory, which it was deemed necessary to defend, and also with reference to their strategic connection with each other, and with the chain of combinations making the general plan of defense.

In the early summer, the distribution of the Southern forces in Virginia was as follows: At Manassas Junction, thirty-five miles south-west from Washington, and the point of intersection of the lines of railroad running southward to Richmond, and to the Shenandoah Valley, was a force, to the command of which General Beauregard was transferred from the charge of the defenses of Charleston. Manassas Junction was obviously a strategic point of the first importance, as the centre of the railroad system of Northern Virginia, and as a base of operations threatening Washington, and immediately across the path of any overland expedition against Richmond. The favorable estimate of General Beauregard's abilities entertained by the President, added to the popularity which followed his services at Charleston, occasioned his assignment to what was obviously to be the most important theatre of operations.

Auxiliary to the command of Beauregard, but operating independently of that officer, was a force at Harper's Ferry, on the Potomac, commanded by General Joseph E. Johnston, an officer of reputed skill, who had earned honorable distinction in Mexico, and enjoyed high rank and reputation in the Federal service. This force had a mission second in value only to that of the army at Manassas. It was charged with the defense of the rich and populous Shenandoah Valley, teeming with supplies, and inhabited by a hardy and patriotic population. Its position was intermediate between the forces operating in Western Virginia, and those in front of Washington, and threatening to the enemy's line of communication westward *via* the Baltimore and Ohio Railroad.

In Western Virginia were the commands of Generals Wise and Garnett, respectively, in the Kanawha Valley, and upon the main line of communication between the sections east and west of the Alleghany mountains. The forces of Wise and Garnett were designed for the double purpose of defending the sections of territory in which they were respectively located, and for the aid and encouragement of the patriotic portion of the population, then under the joint domination of the Union men and Federal soldiers.

Under Magruder, promoted for his victory at Bethel, was a comparatively small force, holding the peninsula of James and York Rivers, the direct route to Richmond from the coast; and at Norfolk were several thousand men, under command of General Huger.

No very acute analysis is required to penetrate the motives

of this distribution of forces in the face of the plain necessities of the situation. Yet a vast amount of conceit has been expended in glittering verbiage, aiming to exhibit the early partiality of President Davis for the weak policy of dispersion, and that aversion to the "concentration" of troops, for overwhelming victories, to be followed by decisive results, which, it is alleged, adhered to his military policy to the last. To this cant about "concentration," a sufficient answer relative to this disposition of troops is, that it has the sanction of Lee's great name, to say nothing of the complete success that followed it. There was no phase of the situation, either then or for months afterward, which could have justified for any result, then attainable by "concentration," the surrendering to the enemy of vast sections of country, which, then and subsequently, fed the army and supplied thousands of soldiers. Popular confidence, so indispensable to a government under such circumstances, was not to be won by such a policy, at the very incipiency of the contest. Were the patriots of Western Virginia, thousands of whom made heroic sacrifices, to be abandoned without an effort for their rescue? Magruder and Huger, too, had duties of no insignificant character to perform. Fortress Monroe, commanding the tributaries of the Chesapeake—the avenues leading to the very heart of Virginia, to the doors of Richmond, and the rear of the armies upon the northern borders—presented, during the entire war, an insuperable difficulty in the defense of Virginia. More than once it was the impregnable asylum for discomfited Federal hosts; and as a base of operations for the enemy, there was no period of the war when it did not challenge a vigilant observation from Richmond. To the efficient, bold, and skillful defense of the peninsula, by Magruder, the Confederate capital owed its safety for twelve months, not less than to the successful defense made upon the Potomac border. Dependent upon the command of Huger was the defense, not only of Norfolk and Portsmouth, but of an extensive back country, besides the naval defenses then in preparation at Gosport.

But in addition to these important objects, is to be remembered the inexperience of both officers and men, totally disqualifying them for those prompt and vigorous movements for which they were subsequently distinguished. Discipline and organization were yet to be supplied. The army at Manassas in July, 1861, at Centreville, in the ensuing autumn, or even in front of Richmond, in the summer of 1862, was altogether a different instrument from that compact force, which the genius of Lee had welded, when he threw it, with crushing impetus, upon the columns of Hooker at Chancellorsville. But, after all, as will be abundantly exhibited hereafter, concentration was preëminently the characteristic of the Confederate military policy. Especially did the present campaign, in all its parts, hinge upon the successful execution of this principle.

Confronting the command of Beauregard, at Manassas, was a considerable Federal army, under General McDowell, covering Washington, and threatening an advance along the line of the Orange and Alexandria and Virginia Central Railroads. Under General Patterson another large Federal force confronted General Johnston, and threatened the Shenandoah Valley. General McClellan, with a force greatly outnumbering the small commands opposed to him, operated in Western Virginia—the common name of the section of country embraced between the Ohio and Cheat Rivers, and the Baltimore and Ohio Railroad and the Great Kanawha and Gauley Rivers.

A heavy force at Fortress Monroe, threatening, with incursions, the entire tide-water section of the State, sufficiently occupied the commands of Magruder and Huger.

The Confederate plan of campaign, approved in the early summer, in its leading features was adhered to with pertinacity and success. This plan, jointly approved by the Government and the two commanders upon whom its execution devolved, contemplated defensive operations, and the union, at the critical moment, of the forces of Beauregard and Johnston, for the destruction of McDowell's command, whenever it should begin its march southward. President Davis and General Lee, at Richmond, were in regular communication with the two commanders in the field, and all operations were directed with a view to the destruction of the main body of the enemy.

General Scott, upon the Federal side, also looked to the coöperation of Patterson with McDowell, and expected him either to defeat Johnston, or to so employ him as to prevent his reinforcement of Beauregard, when the latter should be assailed by the overwhelming force of McDowell. The remoteness of Magruder and Huger, and the impossibility of sufficient secrecy in the transfer of any portion of their commands to the theatre of operations, placed them outside of the calculation. The same may be said of the Confederate forces in Western Virginia. Apprehension of danger from the command of McClellan was experienced by the Confederate authorities, especially after the disastrous defeat of General Garnett. There can be little doubt, however, that the Government and people of the North considered their army, immediately upon the ground, ample for the contemplated work, and did not feel the necessity of looking elsewhere for reinforcements.

The small force at Manassas, when General Beauregard assumed command, was increased by subsequent accessions, until, by the middle of July, it numbered about twenty thousand men. His duties were a vigilant observation of the enemy and such defensive preparations as were necessary. The pivot of the campaign was elsewhere. If Patterson could successfully occupy Johnston until the crisis at Manassas was passed, the result was doubtful, at least; but if Johnston, at the required moment, could elude his adversary, and reinforce Beauregard, the probabilities were most promising to the Confederates. In the sequel, this proved a result far more easily attained than had been hoped for. The campaign thus became a series of maneuvres, with the Confederates in possession of the decided advantage of an interior line.

General Patterson, apparently imbecile or bewildered, committed a series of blunders, to be accounted for upon no possible hypothesis accrediting to him even ordinary acquaintance with the palpable principles of the science of war. What his repeated advances, retreats, and flank movements could have been designed to accomplish, it is difficult to imagine, as his situation plainly prevented his escape from Johnston and reinforcement of McDowell, before Johnston could reach Beauregard. General Patterson's failure to *attack* Johnston preordained the disaster to McDowell on the 21st of July. Johnston, aided by the vigilance and daring of the "indefatigable" Stuart, was fully apprised of every movement of his adversary. With comparatively little difficulty he escaped from his front, and, in accordance with the plan previously indicated, reinforced Beauregard with the greater portion of his force.

With the details of the overwhelming disaster to the Feb-eral arms, at Manassas, on the 21st of July, we are not here interested. Our aim has been to glance briefly at the relations sustained by President Davis to the preliminary campaign which culminated in success so brilliant and valuable. In accordance with his preconceived purpose to be present, if possible, at the consummation of plans in which he felt so profound an interest, President Davis left Richmond on Sunday morning, July 21st, for the scene of the expected battle. Reaching the battle-field while the struggle was still in progress, it was his privilege to witness the flight, in utter confusion and dismay, of the Federal hosts in their first serious conflict with the patriot army. His presence upon the field was the inspiration of unbounded enthusiasm among the troops, to whom his name and bearing were the symbols of victory. His dispatch from the battle-field, on Sunday night, will long be remembered by those who gathered from it their first intelligence of the great victory:

"MANASSAS JUNCTION, Sunday Night.

"Night has closed upon a hard-fought field. Our forces were victorious. The enemy were routed, and precipitately fled, abandoning a large amount of arms, knapsacks, and baggage. The ground was strewn for miles with those killed, and the farm-houses and ground around were filled with the wounded. Pursuit was continued along several routes towards Leesburg and Centreville, until darkness covered the fugitives. We have captured many field batteries and stands of arms, and one of the United States flags. Many prisoners have been taken. Too high praise can not be bestowed, whether for the skill of the principal officers, or the gallantry of all our troops. The battle was mainly fought on our left. Our force was 15,000; that of the enemy estimated at 35,000.

JEFF'N DAVIS."

He remained at Manassas, in consultation with Generals Beauregard and Johnston, until the morning of Tuesday, July 23d. The return of the President to Richmond was the occasion of renewed patriotic rejoicings. An immense crowd awaited at the railroad depot, in expectancy of his arrival, and both there and at his hotel occurred most enthusiastic demonstrations of popular delight at the success of the army, and of public regard for himself.* At night Mr. Davis addressed, with thrilling effect, an immense audience, from a window of the Spottswood Hotel, recounting some of the in-

*The speech made by Mr. Davis at the depot of the Virginia Central Railroad was not reported in the newspapers. The writer, in company with two friends, was in the crowd which greeted the return of Mr. Davis to the capital, and such was the effect of the scene and the glowing words of the speaker, that neither can ever be forgotten. A few hours subsequently to the scene at the depot, the words, as given below, were repeated, in the presence of several persons who heard Mr. Davis, and were pronounced by them the identical language used by him. They were preserved in writing, and are now published for the first time. Apart from its historical interest, the speech is a remarkable specimen of spontaneous, sententious eloquence, eminently appropriate to the occasion:

"*Fellow-citizens of the Confederate States:*

"I rejoice with you, this evening, in those better and happier feelings which we all experience, as compared with the anxiety of three days ago. Your little army—derided for its want of numbers—derided for its want of arms—derided for its lack of all the essential material of war—has met the grand army of the enemy, routed it at every point, and it now flies, in inglorious retreat, before our victorious columns. We have taught them a lesson in their invasion of the sacred soil of Virginia; we have taught them that the grand old mother of Washington still nurtures a band of heroes; and a yet bloodier and far more fatal lesson awaits them, unless they speedily acknowledge that freedom to which you were born."

cidents of the battle, which he declared to be a decisive victory, if followed by energetic measures, and counseled moderation and forbearance in victory, with unrelaxed preparations for future trials. It was upon this occasion that he uttered the memorable injunction, "Never be haughty to the humble, or humble to the haughty."

The immediate and palpable consequence of the victory of Manassas was the rescue of the Confederacy from the peril by which, for weeks, it had been threatened. The South was now plainly a power, capable of fighting ably and vigorously, and with greatly improved prospects of success, for the independence which it had asserted. Time was to develop a far greater value in this wonderful success than was then made available. A few days only were required to exhibit, what at first appeared merely a thorough repulse of the Federal army, as an overwhelming rout, capable of being followed to such results as might have changed even the fate of a nation. Not many weeks sufficed to convince the Southern people of the fact which must ever dwell among their saddest associations, that an opportunity, inestimable in value, and almost unparalleled in its flattering inducements to a people situated as they were, had been utterly unappreciated and irrevocably lost.

In the numerous accounts which have been written, representing all shades of opinion from different stand-points on both sides, and from the wide discussion which has resulted, history can be at no loss for material upon which to base an intelligent estimate of this battle, and of the extent to which the victors reaped the advantages of success. Differences of opinion have prevailed, and will, in all probability, continue to prevail, respecting the purely military questions involved in the discussion of the absence of such a vigorous, pertinacious, and unrelenting pursuit by the Confederates as was necessary to secure the fruits of a decisive victory. But the stubborn conviction, nevertheless, remains, and will never be eradicated from the Southern mind—that, barring the immediate security to the Confederate capital, Manassas was but a barren victory, where results of a most decisive character were within easy reach. Nor is this popular impression unsustained by such competent military authority, as will command respect for its judgment, upon those aspects of the question, upon which a military judgment is alone valuable.

So emphatic became the public condemnation of the inactivity of the army, and especially when, by subsequent information, was revealed the real condition of the enemy after his overwhelming disaster, that inquiry was naturally made as to the authorship of such an erroneous policy. The presence of President Davis, both during a portion of the battle and during the day following, was promptly seized upon as affording a clue to the mystery. For months he rested under the suspicion of having, by peremptory order, stopped the pursuit of the enemy, in the face of the protestations of his generals, who would have pressed it to the extent of attainable results.

How such an impression—*so utterly in conflict with the facts*—could have obtained, by whom, or for what purpose it was disseminated, it is now needless to inquire. The slander was, at length, after having been circulated to the injury of Mr. Davis throughout the country, so conclusively answered as to receive not even the pretense of belief, save from an unscrupulous partisanship, at all times deaf to facts which could not be perverted injuriously to the President. It nevertheless had served a purpose, in preparing the popular mind for those constantly iterated charges of "executive interference," in the plans and dispositions of the armies of the Confederacy, which followed at subsequent stages of the war.

It may be asked, Why did Mr. Davis suffer this suspicion, when the proof of its injustice might have been so easily adduced? This inquiry would indicate an imperfect acquaintance with that devoted patriotism and knightly magnanimity which belong to his character. Any explanation acquitting himself, must have thrown the responsibility upon Generals Johnston and Beauregard, and he preferred rather to suffer an undeserved reproach, than to excite distrust of two officers, then enjoying the largest degree of popular confidence. With him, selfish considerations were never permitted to outweigh the interests of the country. Actuated by this impulse, he, in more than one instance, where the names of men high in public favor were used in his disparagement, refused, even in self-defense, that retaliation, which must have hurt the cause in proportion as it diminished confidence in its prominent representatives. Mr. Davis, with that decorum which has equally illustrated his public and private life, recognized the special propriety of a denial of these injurious rumors *from other sources,* fully apprized of their falsity, and from which such an acquittal of himself would have come with becoming candor and grace.

Justice, proverbially slow, has been tardy indeed in its awards to Mr. Davis; but in this instance, as it must inevitably in others, it has come time enough for his historical vindication. The reader, uninformed as to the merits of this question, will be content with a limited statement from the mass of testimony, which has ultimately acquitted Mr. Davis of having prevented the pursuit of the Federal army after its overthrow upon the field of Manasses. In a publication, presenting an elaborate indictment against Mr. Davis, as the main instrument of the downfall of the Confederacy, written since the war, is found the following admission: "As is known, he (President Davis) was at Manasses the evening of the 21st July, 1861. Until a late hour that night he was engaged with Generals Johnston and Beauregard, at the quarters of the latter, in discussing the momentous achievements of the day, the extent of which was not as yet recognized at all by him or his generals. Much gratified with known results, his bearing was eminently proper. He certainly expressed no opposition to any forward movement; nor at the time displayed a disposition to interpose his opinion or authority touching operations and plans of campaign."*

General Johnston, in a communication published since the war, assumes the responsibility of the failure to pursue, and, with the advantage of retrospect, defends that course with cogent reasoning and an interesting statement of facts. Says General Johnston: "'The substantial fruit' of this victory was the preservation of the Confederacy. No more could have been hoped for. The pursuit of the enemy was not continued because our cavalry (a very small force) *was driven back* by the 'solid resistance' of the United States infantry. Its rear-guard was an entire division, which had not been engaged, and was twelve or fifteeen times more numerous than our two little bodies of cavalry. The infantry was not required to continue the pursuit, because it would have been harassing it to no purpose. It is well known that infantry, unencumbered by baggage trains, can easily escape pursuing cavalry."

That no farther results were to be hoped for than the arrest of the Federal advance toward Richmond, he endeavors to de-

* The *Harper's Magazine* article of General Jordan.

monstrate as follows: "A movement upon Washington was out of the question. We could not have carried the intrenchments by assault, and had none of the means to besiege them. Our assault would have been repulsed, and the enemy, then become the victorious party, would have resumed their march to Richmond; but if we had captured the intrenchments, a river, a mile wide, lay between them and Washington, commanded by the guns of a Federal fleet. If we had taken Alexandria, which stands on low and level ground, those guns would have driven us out in a few hours, at the same time killing our friends, the inhabitants. We could not cross the Potomac, and therefore it was impracticable to conquer the hostile capital, or emancipate oppressed Maryland."

But these statements, ample, as far as they go, in the vindication of Mr. Davis, only partially tell the story of Manassas. They do not fully describe his real relation to the question, though we are far from imputing to General Johnston an intentional omission. A statement of Mr. Davis' views was not necessarily germane to General Johnston's explanation of his own conduct. His purpose is to establish the reasons which induced him to decline pursuit of the enemy, or rather, which, in his judgment, made pursuit impracticable. Nor is it germane to our purpose to discuss these reasons; to attempt either a demonstration of their fallacy or an argument in their support. They have not been accepted as conclusive either by the public, or by unanimous military judgment.

The great name of Stonewall Jackson, himself an actor in the most thrilling scenes of that wonderful triumph of Southern valor, and dating from that day his record upon the "bead-roll of fame," is authoritatively given in opposition to the policy which General Johnston approves. In this connection, we can not forbear to quote the biographer of that illustrious man, in passages showing that wondrous intuition of great soldiership, more distinctive, perhaps, of Jackson, than of any commander of the present century, excepting only Napoleon. Professor Dabney says: "Jackson, describing the manifest rout of the enemy, remarked to the physicians, that he believed 'with ten thousand fresh men he could go into the city of Washington.'" Again, after a most graphic picture of the condition of the Federal army, its demoralization, panic, and utter incapacity to meet an attack by the victorious Confederates, and an able statement of the inducements to a vigorous pursuit, the biographer of General Jackson makes this impressive statement: "With these views of the campaign, General Jackson earnestly concurred. His sense of official propriety sealed his lips; and when the more impatient spirits inquired, day after day, why they were not led after the enemy, his only answer was to say: 'That is the affair of the commanding generals.' But to his confidential friends he afterward declared, when no longer under the orders of those officers, that their inaction was a deplorable blunder; and this opinion he was subsequently accustomed to assert with a warmth and emphasis unusual in his guarded manner."*

Mr. Davis was far from approving the inaction which followed Manassas. He confidently expected a different use of the victory. When called away by the pressing nature of his official duties at Richmond, he left the army with a heart elastic with hope, at what he considered the certainty of even

* The Federal official reports are overwhelmingly in confirmation of these views of General Jackson. General McClellan stated that "in no quarter were the dispositions for defense such as to offer resistance to a respectable body of the enemy."

more glorious and valuable achievements. His speech at the depot in Richmond, which we have given elsewhere, is evidence of his exultant anticipations. The speech at the Spottswood, entering more into details, still better authenticates his hopes of an immediate and successful advance.* There could be no misinterpretation of the ardor with which, in glowing sentences, he predicted the immediate and consecutive triumphs of what he proudly termed the "gallant little army."

Indeed, before leaving Manassas, President Davis favored the most vigorous pursuit practicable. On the evening of the battle, while the victory was assured, but by no means complete, he urged that the enemy, still on the field, (Heintzelman's troops, as subsequently appeared,) be warmly pressed, as was successfully done. During the night following the engagement he made a disposition of a portion of the troops, with a view to an advance in the morning. These troops were removed, but not by himself, to meet an apprehended attack upon the head-quarters of the army. An advance on Monday, the 22d July, was out of the question, in consequence of the heavy rain.

It is not to be understood that President Davis fully appreciated, on Sunday night, the 21st, the overwhelming rout of the Federal army, nor that he advocated, as practicable, an immediate movement in pursuit, by the entire army. No one could have anticipated the utter disorganization attending the flight of the Federals. He had, too, positive evidence of the confusion prevailing among portions of the Southern troops.

*The writer heard this speech of Mr. Davis, and his recollection is positive of the encouragement extended by the President to the hope of an immediate forward movement. The recollection of the author of "The Diary of a Rebel War Clerk" seems to be substantially the same.

Summoned by a message from a youthful connection, who was mortally wounded, Mr. Davis rode over a large portion of the field, in a vain search for the regiment to which the young man was attached. Upon his return, he accidentally met an officer who directed him to the locality of the regiment, where he found the corpse of his relative. The evidences of disorganization, upon which General Johnston dwells with so much force and emphasis, were indeed palpable, but Mr. Davis confidently believed that an efficient pursuit might be made by such commands as were in comparatively good condition. Such were his impressions then, and that he contemplated immediate activity as the sequel of Manassas, is a matter of indisputable record.

That Mr. Davis did not insist upon the undeferred execution of his own views, is proof less of his approval of the course pursued, than of an absence of that pragmatic disposition with which he was afterwards so persistently charged. His subsequent hearty tributes to Beauregard and Johnston, and prompt recognition of their services, show how far he was elevated above that mean intolerance, which would have made him incapable of according merit to the opinions and actions of others, when averse to his own conclusions.

This determined spirit of misrepresentation of the motives and conduct of the President, beginning thus early—respecting the origin of which we shall have more to say hereafter—was to prove productive of the most serious embarrassments to the Confederate cause. The first great success in arms achieved by the South, was to originate questions tending to excite distrust in the capacity of the Executive, and subsequently distrust of his treatment of those who were under his authority. Misrepresentation was not to cease with the attempt already mentioned to impair public confidence in Mr. Davis. A pragmatic interference with the plans of his generals was persistently charged upon him. The almost uninterrupted inactivity of the main army in Virginia, following the battle of Manassas, by which the enemy was permitted, without molestation, to organize a new army—a subject of constant and exasperated censure by the public—was falsely attributed to Mr. Davis' interference with Generals Johnston and Beauregard. It is a sad evidence of the license characteristic of a purely partisan criticism, that this falsely alleged interference has even been ascribed to the instigations of a mean envy of the popularity of those officers.

The purely personal differences of public men are not the proper subject-matter of historical discussion. In the prosecution of our endeavor to give an intelligent and candid narrative of the events of the war, in so far as President Davis was connected with them, we shall have occasion to dwell upon those differences between himself and others respecting important questions of policy which are known to have existed. We do not see that the personal relations of President Davis with Generals Johnston and Beauregard, are here a subject of appropriate inquiry. Nor are those minor questions of detail as to the organization of the army, which arose between them, of such significance as to justify elaborate discussion here. That President Davis chose to exercise those plain privileges with which the Constitution invested him; that he should have consulted that military knowledge which his education and service had taught him; that he should make available his valuable experience as Minister of War; and that he should have failed to interpret the acts of Congress agreeably to the tastes of generals in the field, rather than according to his own judgment, is certainly singular evidence upon which to base charges of "pragmatism," "persecution," and "envy" of those generals.*

* One evidence of this "persecution" would appear to consist in the fact that the President, having reluctantly commissioned Generals Lovell and G. W. Smith, upon the recommendations of Generals Beauregard and Johnston, chose also to commission, at the same time, with a similar rank, General Van Dorn, giving the latter a senior commission. Smith and Lovell had but recently come to the South, both being residents of New York, before the war, while Van Dorn had promptly sought service in the Confederate army before hostilities commenced, had done excellent service, and been constantly in front of the enemy. Another proof of "persecution" is that the President refused to permit such an organization of the army as he believed to be in conflict with the laws of Congress.

The commonly assigned origin of the difference between President Davis and General Beauregard, which gave rise to so much scandal and falsehood during the war, was the suppression of the preliminary portion of General B.'s report of the battle of Manassas. The correct version of that matter is now well known. President Davis did not suppress any portion of Beauregard's report. He did object to certain preliminary statements of the report, and requested that they should be altered or omitted. When this was declined, the President sent the report to Congress, accompanied by an indorsement of his own, correcting what he conceived to be errors. General Beauregard's friends in Congress, unwilling that these comments of the President should be published, suppressed both the objectionable passages and the executive indorsement. So that they, and not the President, occasioned that "suppression," from which arose much gossip and mystery. A sufficient answer to these charges of personal antagonism by the President to these two officers, should be the fact that he retained them in command of the two largest armies of the Confederacy, until relinquished by them, in the one case, because of sickness, and in the other, in consequence of a wound which caused disability.

While the main struggle in Virginia was yet undecided, the Confederate force, under General Garnett, in Western Virginia, had been disastrously defeated by the Federal army of General McClellan. The Confederate commander, a brave and promising officer, was killed, in a gallant endeavor to protect the retreat of his command. This achievement of General McClellan, though attributable mainly to his vastly superior force, was attended by evidences of skill, which indicated him as a prominent figure in the events of the immediate future. In the midst of the gloom and disappointment consequent upon the disaster at Manassas, General McClellan appeared to the Northern Government and masses to be an officer specially recommended, by his late success, for the important charge of the army designed to protect the capital. He was immediately summoned to Washington, and placed in charge of its defenses. With rare capacity for general military administration, and with especial aptitude for organization, General McClellan addressed himself with vigor and success to the work assigned him. Under his direction, the defenses of Washington were speedily put in admirable condition, and within a few months, he had created an army which, in discipline, organization, and equipment, would have compared favorably with the best armies of the world.

General McClellan was too sagacious and prudent a commander to repeat the errors of his predecessor. He was evidently determined not to undertake an aggressive campaign until his preparations were completed. During the progress of those preparations, he endeavored also to provide against those aggressive movements which he evidently anticipated from his adversaries. But the autumn and winter were to pass away without any serious demonstration by the Confederate commanders, and with but one important movement of the enemy.

In the early fall, Generals Johnston and Beauregard advanced to a position in close proximity to the Federal capital. Unable, however, to provoke an engagement with the Federal commander, whose present purposes were purely defensive and preparatory, the Confederate army withdrew from the front of Washington, and retired within its former lines about Manassas and Centreville.

In the latter part of October, an engagement of some importance occurred near Leesburg, occasioned by an attempt of General McClellan to throw a force across the Potomac, doubtless with the view of an advance on the Confederate left wing. The numbers engaged in this engagement were comparatively small, which rendered more remarkable its sanguinary character. Nearly the entire Federal force, though outnumbering more than two to one the Confederate force, was captured or destroyed. There was good reason to regard this movement as preliminary to a general advance of the Federal army. The battle of Leesburg was very dispiriting in its effects upon the North, and equally re-assuring to the Southern Government and people. No other operations of note occurred during the autumn and winter upon the lines of the Lower Potomac.

General Jackson, who by a circumstance which is now well known to the world, had acquired at Manassas the *sobriquet* of "Stonewall," in September, 1861, was made a Major-General. Late in December, in charge of a considerable force, he executed, with indifferent success, a movement against detachments of the enemy in the neighborhood of Romney, and other points along the Upper Potomac.

The disasters sustained by the Confederates in Western Virginia, in the early summer, were not repaired by the transfer of General Lee to that quarter. A large and valuable section of country remained as the enemy's trophy, almost undisputed at the termination of the campaign. The reputation of General Lee suffered severely from the absence of that success which was anticipated from his presence in command. It is a noteworthy circumstance that when, a few months afterward, the President placed Lee in command of the main army of Virginia, his ill-success in Western Virginia was alleged as conclusive evidence of his unfitness for the position to which "executive partiality" had assigned him.

In the meantime, upon the distant theatre of Missouri, the war had assumed a most interesting phase. Many months before the legally-elected legislature of that State adopted an ordinance of secession, Missouri was contributing valuable aid to the struggling Confederacy. Driven by the oppressive course of the Federal Government into resistance, in spite of their efforts to save their State from the destructive presence of war, the Southern men of Missouri organized under the leadership of General Sterling Price and Governor Jackson. Accessions of men from all portions of the State were constantly made to the patriot forces, and, within a few weeks, a large force was upon the southern border, animated by an enthusiastic desire to undertake the redemption of their homes.

But the Missourians, though sufficiently numerous to constitute an effective army, were confronted by difficulties which would have appalled men of less heroic purpose, or enlisted in an inferior cause. Hostilities had been precipitated upon them while they were entirely unprepared—wanting arms, ammunition, and other indispensable material of war.

The remoteness of Missouri from the seat of government, and the inadequate transportation, prevented that prompt and efficient aid by the Confederate authorities which it was equally their interest and inclination to afford. Nevertheless, with almost miraculous rapidity, the army of General Price was organized, and supplied with such material as he could obtain.

The Federal commander, in his march southward from St. Louis, pursued, with considerable vigor, the various detachments of the patriots who were hastening to the standards of Price. After several minor engagements, in which the Missourians displayed the most devoted heroism, a considerable battle was fought, early in August, near Springfield, in the south-western corner of the State, in which the Federal army was disastrously defeated, and its commander killed. In this battle, the Missouri forces were aided by a Confederate force, under General McCulloch, which had advanced northward from Arkansas. Later in the year, General Price advanced through the central portion of the State, receiving large additions to his army, and captured the largest garrison of Federal troops in Northern Missouri. Having accomplished these valuable aims, he, with great skill and daring, effected a safe retreat to the south-western frontier. President Davis, in a message to Congress, echoed the hearty appreciation of the Southern people, in a special tribute to the valor and devotion of the southern population of Missouri.

Kentucky also had become the theatre of hostilities. The Federal Government, recognizing the neutrality of Kentucky so long as was necessary to mature their plans for her subjugation, finally insisted upon making her a party to the war, and invaded her territory with a view to operations against the Confederacy. President Davis thus stated the motives of the policy adopted by the Confederate Government respecting Kentucky:

"Finding that the Confederate States were about to be invaded through Kentucky, and that her people, after being deceived into a mistaken security, were unarmed, and in danger of being subjugated by the Federal forces, our armies were marched into that State to repel the enemy, and prevent their occupation of certain strategic points, which would have given them great advantages in the contest—a step which was justified, not only by the necessities of self-defense on the part of the Confederate States, but also by a desire to aid the people of Kentucky. It was never intended by the Confederate Government to conquer or coerce the people of that State; but, on the contrary, it was declared by our Generals that they would withdraw their troops if the Federal Government would do likewise. Proclamation was also made of the desire to respect the neutrality of Kentucky, and the intention, by the wishes of her people, as soon as they were free to express their opinions.

"These declarations were approved by me; and I should regard it as one of the best effects of the march of our troops into Kentucky, if it should end in giving to her people liberty of choice, and a free opportunity to decide their own destiny, according to their own will."

Not long after the occupation of various points in Kentucky, by the respective armies, an engagement occurred at Belmont, on the Missouri shore, near Columbus, resulting in the defeat of the Federal force engaged. The Confederate forces engaged were a portion of the command of General Polk, and the defeated Federal commander was General U. S. Grant.

Before the first year of the war terminated, the Confederates experienced reverses resulting from the naval superiority of the enemy. Expeditions were undertaken against the Carolina coast, and were successful to the extent of securing a permanent lodgment of the Federal forces.

In the month of November the forcible seizure, by a Federal naval officer, of the persons of Messrs. John Slidell and James M. Mason, commissioners, respectively, from the Confederate States to France and England, and, at the time, passengers on an English steamer, excited strong hope of those complications between the United States and European powers which were reasonably anticipated by the South. This act was a palpable outrage and violation alike of international law and comity. It was, nevertheless, indorsed by public sentiment at the North, in manifold forms of expression.

In England, the intelligence of an outrage upon the national flag was received with outbursts of popular indignation, which compelled the Government to make a resentful demand upon the United States. The course of the English Government was characteristic of the nation which it represented. There was neither discussion nor parley, but a simple imperative demand for the surrender of the commissioners and their attachès.

Never was so deep a humiliation imposed upon a people as that imposed by the course of the Federal authorities upon the North. The prisoners, over whose capture the whole North had but recently exulted, as at the realization of the fruits of a brilliant victory, were surrendered immediately. Mr. Seward even declared that they were surrendered "cheerfully," and in accordance with the "most cherished principles of American statesmanship," and advanced an argument in favor of complying with the demands of the British Government, far more to have been expected from a British diplomatist, than from the leading statesman of a people who had promptly indorsed the outrage.

This concession of the Federal Government was the first of numerous disappointments in store for the Southern people, in the hope, so universally indulged, of foreign intervention. Expectation of immediate complications between England and the United States, received great encouragement from the earlier phase of the "Trent affair," as was called the seizure of Messrs. Mason and Slidell. Consequent upon the correspondence between the Governments of England and the United States, growing out of the "Trent affair," were announcements in Parliament, which should have discouraged the anticipation of interference by England, at least with the cabinet then in power. Lord John Russell declared that the blockade of the Southern ports was effective, in spite of abundant evidence, and in spite, even, of the declarations of the British consul at Charleston to the contrary. This concession was intended, doubtless, as a salvo to the North for its deep humiliation, and was, indeed, rightly construed as an evidence of the real sympathies of the British cabinet in the American struggle. In this aspect, it was an assurance of no little significance.

At the election, in November, Mr. Davis, without opposition, was chosen the first President of the Confederacy, under the permanent government, which was soon to succeed the provisional organization. Mr. Stephens was reëlected Vice-President.

In his message to the provisional Congress, at the beginning of its last session, the President thus sketched the situation at the close of the first year of the war:

"*To the Congress of the Confederate Sates:*

"The few weeks which have elapsed since your adjournment have brought us so near the close of the year, that we are now able to sum up its general results. The retrospect is such as should fill the hearts of our people with gratitude to Providence for his kind interposition in their behalf. Abundant yields have rewarded the labor of the agriculturist, whilst the manufacturing interest of the Confederate States was never so prosperous as now. The necessities of the times have called into existence new branches of manufactures, and given a fresh impulse to the activity of those heretofore in operation. The means of the Confederate States for manufacturing the necessaries and comforts of life, with inthemselves, increase as the conflict continues, and we are rapidly becoming independent of the rest of the world, for the supply of such military stores and munitions as are indispensable for war.

"The operations of the army, soon to be partially interrupted by the approaching winter, have afforded a protection to the country, and shed a lustre upon its arms, through the trying vicissitudes of more than one arduous campaign, which entitle our brave volunteers to our praise and our gratitude.

"From its commencement up to the present period, the war has been enlarging its proportions and extending its boundaries, so as to include new fields. The conflict now extends from the shores of the Chesapeake to thé confines of Missouri and Arizona; yet sudden calls from the remotest points for military aid have been met with promptness enough, not only to avert disaster in the face of superior numbers, but also to roll back the tide of invasion from the border.

"When the war commenced, the enemy were possessed of certain strategic points and strong places within the Confederate States. They greatly exceeded us in numbers, in available resources, and in the supplies necessary for war. Military establishments had been long organized, and were complete; the navy, and, for the most part, the army, once common to both, were in their possession. To meet all this, we had to create, not only an army in the face of war itself, but also military establishments necessary to equip and place it in the field. It ought, indeed, to be a subject of gratulation that the spirit of the volunteers and the patriotism of the people have enabled us, under Providence, to grapple successfully with these difficulties.

"A succession of glorious victories at Bethel, Bull Run, Manassas, Springfield, Lexington, Leesburg, and Belmont, has checked the wicked invasion which greed of gain, and the unhallowed lust of power, brought upon our soil, and has proved that numbers cease to avail, when directed against a people fighting for the sacred right of self-government and the privileges of freemen. After seven months of war, the enemy have not only failed to extend their occupancy of our soil, but new States and Territories have been added to our Confederacy; while, instead of their threatened march of unchecked conquest, they have been driven, at more than one point, to assume the defensive; and, upon a fair comparison between the two belligerents, as to men, milita[illegible] means, and financial condition, the Confederate States are relatively much stronger now than when the struggle commenced."

CHAPTER XI.

PROSPECTS AT THE BEGINNING OF 1862—EXTREME CONFIDENCE OF THE SOUTH—EXTRAVAGANT EXPECTATIONS—THE RICHMOND EXAMINER ON CONFEDERATE PROSPECTS—WAR BETWEEN ENGLAND AND THE UNITED STATES PREDICTED—THE BLOCKADE TO BE RAISED—THE SOUTHERN CONFEDERACY DECREED BY HEAVEN—RESULT OF THE BOASTFUL TONE OF THE SOUTHERN PRESS—THE CONFEDERATE GOVERNMENT NOT RESPONSIBLE FOR THE DISASTERS OF 1862—PRESIDENT DAVIS URGES PREPARATION FOR A LONG WAR—HIS WISE OPPOSITION TO SHORT ENLISTMENTS OF TROOPS—PREMONITIONS OF MISFORTUNES IN THE WEST—THE CONFEDERATE FORCES IN KENTUCKY—GENERAL ALBERT SIDNEY JOHNSTON—HIS CAREER BEFORE THE WAR—CHARACTER—APPEARANCE—THE FRIEND OF JEFFERSON DAVIS—MUTUAL ESTEEM—SIDNEY JOHNSTON IN KENTUCKY—HIS PLANS—HIS DIFFICULTIES—THE FORCES OF GRANT AND BUELL—CRUEL DILEMMA OF GENERAL SIDNEY JOHNSTON—A REVERSE—GRANT CAPTURES FORTS HENRY AND DONELSON—LOSS OF KENTUCKY AND TENNESSEE—FEDERAL DESIGNS IN THE EAST—BURNSIDE CAPTURES ROANOKE ISLAND—SERIOUS NATURE OF THESE REVERSES—POPULAR DISAPPOINTMENT—ORGANIZED OPPOSITION TO THE CONFEDERATE ADMINISTRATION—CHARACTER AND MOTIVES OF THIS OPPOSITION—AN EFFORT TO REVOLUTIONIZE PRESIDENT DAVIS' CABINET—ASSAULTS UPON SECRETARIES BENJAMIN AND MALLORY—CORRECT EXPLANATION OF THE CONFEDERATE REVERSES—CONGRESSIONAL CENSURE OF MR. BENJAMIN—SECRETARY MALLORY—CHARACTERISTICS OF THE SOUTHERN MIND—THE PERMANENT GOVERNMENT—SECOND INAUGURATION OF MR. DAVIS—SEVERITY OF THE SEASON—THE CEREMONIES—APPEARANCE OF PRESIDENT DAVIS—HIS INAUGURAL ADDRESS—ITS EFFECT—POPULAR RE-ASSURANCE—MESSAGE TO CONGRESS—COMMENTS OF RICHMOND PRESS.

WHEN President Davis held his first New-Year's reception, as the chief magistrate of the infant Confederacy, there were not wanting signs of the approaching shadows, which were to throw in temporary eclipse the brilliant foreground of the first year of the war. Richmond was then in its exultant spirit, its gayety, festivity, and show, the type of that fatal confidence in Southern invincibility, which, in a few weeks of disaster, was brought to grief and humiliation.

In that numerous and brilliant assemblage, representing the various branches of the new government, civil, naval, and military, members of Congress and of State Legislatures, and admiring citizens, eager to make formal tender of their esteem to the first President of the South, there were few who discerned the omens of the coming storm, which was to shake its foundation, the power of which that occasion was an imposing symbol. Perhaps there were as few who could penetrate his assuring exterior of grace, gentleness, and dignity, and share the anxiety with which, even in the midst of popular adulation, he contemplated the approach of that stern trial for which the country was so deficient in preparation.

With singular accord of opinion, writers, who had an *inside* view of the Southern conduct of the war, have commented upon the disasters consequent upon the period of fancied security and relaxed exertions which followed the battle of Manassas. We can not share, however, the shallow and unphilosophical conclusion which pronounces the glorious triumph of Manassas a calamity to the South. The temporary salvation of the Confederacy, guaranteed by that victory, was not its only fruit. Manassas gave a stamp of *prestige* to Southern valor and soldiership, which not even a deluge of subsequent disasters could efface. It gave an imperishable record and an undying incentive to resolution.

Yet it is not to be questioned that the public apathy, engendered by an exaggerated estimate of the value of the numerous and consecutive triumphs of the preceding summer and autumn, was measurably productive of evil consequences. Encouraged by the press, in many instances, the Southern people saw, in the comparatively easy triumphs of their superior valor over undisciplined Northern mobs—for which Manassas, Belmont, Leesburg, and similar engagements constituted the mere apprenticeship of war—the auguries significant of a speedy attainment of their independence. Inflated orators and boastful editorials proclaimed the absolute certainty of early interference of foreign powers, in behalf of the South, as the source of the indispensable staples of cotton and tobacco. In the face of the enormous preparations of the enemy, his monster armies, numbering, in December, 1861, more than six hundred thousand men; his numerous fleets for sea-board operations, and iron-clad floating batteries for the interior streams, comparatively insignificant successes were pointed to as sufficient proofs of the inability of the enemy to make any serious impression upon Southern territory.

The Richmond *Examiner*, which had early evinced a disposition hostile to President Davis and his administration, the ablest and most influential journal of the South, destined to furnish both the brains and inspiration in support of future opposition, was conspicuous in its contempt for the fighting qualities of the North, and vehement in its prophesies of good fortune for the Confederacy. Late in December, the *Examiner*, commenting upon recent intelligence from the North, said: "All other topics become trifles beside the tidings of England which occupies this journal, and all commentary that diverts public attention from that single point is impertinence. The effect of the outrage of the Trent on the public sentiment of Great Britain more than fulfills the prophesy that we made when the arrest of the Confederate ministers was a fresh event. All legal quibbling and selfish calculation has been consumed like straw in the burning sense of incredible insult. The Palmerston cabinet has been forced to immediate and decisive measures; and a peremptory order to Lord Lyons comes with the steamer that brings the news to the American shore. He is directed to demand the unconditional surrender of Messrs. Mason and Slidell, to place them in the position they were found beneath the British flag, and a complete disavowal of their seizure as an authorized act. *Now, the Northern Government has placed itself in such a position that it can do none of these things. The Abolitionist element of the Northern States would go straight to revolution at the least movement toward a surrender of the captives;* the arrest was made by the deliberately written orders of the Government, already avowed and published beyond the hope of apology or possibility of retraction.

"The United States can do absolutely nothing but refuse the demands of Great Britain, and abide the consequences of that refusal. What they will be can be clearly foretold: *first, there will be the diplomatic rupture; Lord Lyons will demand his passports, and Mr. Adams will be sent away from London; then will follow an immediate recognition of the Southern Confederacy, with encouragement and aid in fitting out its vessels, and supplying their wants in the British ports and islands. Lastly, a war will be evolved from these two events.*"

Continuing its comments upon what it terms the "raving madness" of the North, the *Examiner* says: "Then came the proclamation of Lincoln. Nothing but insanity could have dictated it; and without it the secession of Virginia was impossible. *Then their crazy attempt to subdue a country not less difficult to conquer than Russia itself, with an armed mob of loafers.*"

In the contemplation of the pleasing sketch which its imagination had executed, the *Examiner* asks: "*Spectators of these events, who can doubt that the Almighty fiat has gone forth against the American Union, or that the Southern Confederacy is decreed by the Divine Wisdom?*" It declares that the "dullest worldling, the coolest Atheist, the most hardened cynic, might be struck with awe by the startling and continued interposition of a power beyond the control or cognizance of men in these affairs;" and triumphantly asks: "Who thought, when the Trent was announced to sail, that on its deck, and in the trough of the weltering Atlantic, the key of the blockade would be lost?"

The natural and inevitable result of the assurances tendered to the people, was to lull the patriotic ardor which marked the first great uprising for defense, when two hundred thousand men sprung to arms. There can be no justice in holding the Confederate Government responsible for the popular apathy, which it had no agency in producing, or for the weakness of the armies, which, next to the naval weakness of the South, was the immediate cause of the disasters of the early months of 1862.

Since the commencement of hostilities, the Government had been indefatigable in its efforts to promote enlistments of *volunteers for the war*, instead of the twelve-months' system, which could be adequate for the demands of a temporary exigency only, and not for such a terrific struggle as must result from the temper and resources of the two contestants. Volunteering was as yet the only method of raising troops sanctioned by law, or likely to meet popular approval. The country was not yet prepared for an enforced levy of troops; and it is only necessary to remember the opposition, in certain quarters, to the execution of the subsequent conscription law, adopted under the pressure of disasters which made its necessity plain and inevitable, to conjecture the temper in which such a measure would have been met, in the over-confident and foolishly exultant tone of the press and public in the winter of 1861.

Mr. Davis especially sought to disabuse the public mind of its fallacious hope of a short contest, by his efforts to place the military resources of the South upon a footing capable of indefinite resistance to an attempt at conquest, which was to end only with the success or exhaustion of the North. Conscious of the perpetual disorganization and decimation of the armies which must result from the system of short enlistments, he had, early in the war, attracted unfriendly criticism by his refusal of any more six or twelve-months' volunteers than were necessary to meet the shock of the enemy's first advance. It was clear to his mind that, under the wretched system of short enlistments, which he characterized as a "frightful cause of disaster," the country must, at some period of the war, be virtually without an army. Such was the case in January and February, 1862, when the enemy eagerly pressed his immense advantage while the process of furloughs and reënlistments was in progress, and the army almost completely disorganized.

Such a crisis was inevitable, and had it not occurred then, it would merely have been deferred, to be encountered at a period when the capacity of the Confederacy was even less adequate for its perils. The lesson was not without its value, since it drove the country and the press to a recognition of the fact that independence was not to be won by shifts and dalliance, by temporary expedients, and by spasmodic popular uprisings for temporary exigencies.

The efforts of the Government were unceasing to prepare for the tremendous onset of the enemy in almost every quarter of the Confederacy, which it must have been blind, indeed, not to anticipate. The responses to the calls of the Government were neither in numbers nor enthusiasm encouraging. The people were blind in their confidence, and deaf to appeals admonishing them of perils which, in their fancied security, they believed impossible of realization. But this soothing sense of security was soon to have a terrible awakening. The Confederate Government had recognized the peculiar perils menacing the western section of its territory. There for weeks rested the anxious gaze of President Davis, and thence were to come the first notes of alarm—the immediate premonitions of disaster.

Immediately, upon the occupation of Kentucky by the Confederate forces, had begun the development of a plan of defense by the Southern generals. The command of General Polk, constituting the Confederate left, was at Columbus. On the upper waters of the Cumberland River, in South-eastern Kentucky, was a small force constituting the Confederate right, commanded first by General Zollicoffer, and afterward by General Crittenden. At Bowling Green, with Green River in front, and communicating by railway with Nashville and the South, was the main Confederate force in Kentucky, commanded by General Buckner until the arrival of General Albert Sidney Johnston, whom President Davis had commissioned a full general in the Confederate service, and assigned to the command of the Western Department.

Apart from the historical interest which belongs to the name of Albert Sidney Johnston, and from the dramatic incident of his death at the very climax of a splendid victory, which immediately paled into disaster upon his fall, as the long and valued friend of Jefferson Davis, he is entitled to special mention in the biography of the latter.

Albert Sidney Johnston was born in Mason County, Kentucky, in 1803. He graduated at West Point in 1826; was commissioned as Lieutenant of infantry; served in the Black Hawk war with distinction; resigned and settled in Texas in 1836. He volunteered as a private in her armies soon after the battle of San Jacinto. His merit soon raised him from the ranks, and he was appointed senior Brigadier-General, and succeeded General Houston in the command of the Texan army. In 1838 he was appointed Texan Secretary of War, and in 1839 organized an expedition against the hostile Cherokees, in which he routed them completely in a battle on the river Neches. He warmly advocated the annexation of Texas to the United States, and after this union was effected, he took part in the Mexican war. His services at the siege of Monterey drew upon him the public favor and the thanks of General Butler. He continued in the army, and in 1857, was sent by President Buchanan as Commander-in-Chief of the United States Army to subdue the Mormons. His successful advance in the Great Salt Lake City, and the skill and address with which he conducted a difficult enterprise, largely increased his fame. When the war commenced between the North and South, he was in California, but when he learned the progress of the revolution, he resigned his commission and set out from San Francisco, to penetrate by land to Richmond, a distance of two thousand three hundred miles.

The safe arrival of General Albert Sidney Johnston, within the lines of the Confederacy, was greeted with a degree of public acclamation hardly less enthusiastic than would have signalized the intelligence of a great victory. It was known that the Federal authorities, anxious to prevent so distinguished and valuable an accession to the generalship of the South, were intent upon his capture. For weeks popular expectation had been strained, in eager gaze, for tidings of the distinguished commander, who, beset by innumerable perils and obstacles, was making his way across the continent, not less eager to join his countrymen, than were they to feel the weight of his noble blade in the unequal combat.

Few of the eminent soldiers, who had sought service under the banners of the Confederacy, had a more brilliant record of actual service; and to the advantages of reputation, General Johnston added those graces and distinctions of person with which the imagination invests the ideal commander. He was considerably past middle age; his height exceeded six feet, his frame was large and sinewy; his every movement and posture indicated vigorous and athletic manhood. The general expresion of his striking face was grave and composed, but inviting rather than austere.

The arrival of General Johnston in Richmond, early in September, was a source of peculiar congratulation to President Davis. Between these illustrious men had existed, for many years, an endearment, born of close association, common trials and triumphs, and mutual confidence, which rendered most auspicious their coöperation in the cause of Southern independence.

"Albert Sidney Johnston," says Professor Bledsoe, in a recent publication, "who, take him all in all, was the simplest, bravest, grandest man we have ever known, once said to the present writer: 'There is no measuring such a man as Davis;' and this high tribute had a fitting counterpart in that which Davis paid Johnston, when discussing, in the Federal Senate, the Utah expedition. Said he . . . . . . 'I hold that the country is indebted to the administration for having selected the man who is at the head of the expedition; who, as a soldier, has not a superior in the army or out of it; and whose judgment, whose art, whose knowledge is equal to this or any other emergency; a man of such decision, such resolution that his country's honor can never be tarnished in his hands; a man of such calmness, such kindness, that a deluded people can never suffer by harshness from him.'"

President Davis immediately tendered to General Johnston the command of one of the two grand military divisions of the Confederacy, and he as promptly repaired to the scene of his duties.

The general features of General Johnston's policy contemplated a line of defense running from the Mississippi through the region immediately covering Nashville to Cumberland Gap—the key to the defense of East Tennessee and Southwestern Virginia, and thus to the most vital line of communication in the South. It is easy to conceive the large force requisite for so important and difficult a task, against the immense armies of Grant and Buell, numbering, in the aggregate, more than one hundred thousand men. Despite the earnest appeals of General Johnston, and notwithstanding that upon the successful maintenance of his position depended the successful defense of the entire southern and south-western sections of the Confederacy, his force, at the last of January, 1862, did not exceed twenty-six thousand men. Informed of his perilous situation, the Confederate Government could do no more than second the appeals and remonstrances of General Johnston. Slight accessions were made to his force from the States which were menaced, but, as results speedily demonstrated, he was unable to meet the enemy with an adequate force at any one of the vital points of his defensive line.

In the immediate front of General Johnston's position was the army of Buell, estimated at forty thousand men, which, during the entire winter, was in training for its meditated advance along the line of the railroad in the direction of Nashville. Under Grant, at Cairo, was an army of more than fifty thousand men, which, in coöperation with a formidable naval force, was designed to operate against Nashville, and, by securing possession of the line of the Tennessee and Cumberland Rivers, to hold Kentucky and West Tennessee. General Johnston's position was indeed a cruel dilemma, and was sufficiently explained in a letter to President Davis, representing the inadequacy of his force, for either front of attack, upon a line whose every point demanded ample defense. Only a self-denying patriotism could have induced General Johnston to occupy his false position before the public, which accredited to him an army ample even for aggressive warfare. With an almost certain prospect of disaster, he nevertheless resolved to make the supreme effort which alone could avert it.

His plan was to meet Grant's attack upon Nashville with sixteen thousand men, hoping, in the meanwhile, by boldly confronting Buell with the residue of his forces, to hold in check the enemy in his immediate front. During the winter, by a skillful disposition of his forces and adroit maneuvers, he deceived the enemy as to his real strength, and thus deferred the threatened advance until the month of February.

The month of January, 1862, was to witness the first check to the arms of the Confederacy, after seven months of uninterrupted victory. The scene of the disaster was near Somerset, Kentucky. The forces engaged were inconsiderable as compared with the conflicts of a few weeks later, but the result was disheartening to the impatient temper of the South, not yet chastened by the severe trials of adversity. General Crittenden was badly defeated, though, as is probable, through no erroneous calculation or defective generalship on his part. A melancholy feature of the disaster was the death of General Zollicoffer. With the repulse and retreat of the Confederate forces after the battle of Fishing Creek, as the action was called, followed the virtual possession of South-eastern Kentucky by the Federal army. The Confederate line of defense in Kentucky was thus broken, and the value of other positions materially impaired.

Early in February the infantry columns of Grant and the gunboats of Commodore Foote commenced the ascent of the Tennessee River. The immediate object of assault was Fort Henry, an imperfectly constructed fortification, on the east bank of the river, near the dividing line of Kentucky and Tennessee. After a signal display of gallantry by its commander, General Tilghman, the fort was surrendered, the main body of the forces defending it having been previously sent to Fort Donelson, the principal defense of the Cumberland River. The capture of Fort Henry opened the Tennessee River, penetrating the States of Tennessee and Alabama, and navigable for steamers for more than two hundred miles, to the unchecked advance of the enemy.

General Grant promptly advanced to attack Fort Donelson. After a series of bloody engagements and a siege of several days, Fort Donelson was surrendered, with the garrison of more than nine thousand men. This result was indeed a heavy blow to the Confederacy, and produced a most alarming crisis in the military affairs of the Western Department. General Johnston was near Nashville, with the force which had lately held Bowling Green, the latter place having been evacuated during the progress of the fight at Fort Donelson. Nashville was immediately evacuated, and the remnant of General Johnston's army retreated southward, first to Murfreesboro', Tennessee, and afterwards crossed the Tennessee, at Decatur, Alabama.

In January, General Beauregard had been transferred from Virginia to Kentucky, and, at the time of the surrender of Nashville, was in command of the forces in the neighborhood of Columbus, Kentucky, which protected the passage of the Mississippi. The entire Confederate line of defense in Kentucky and Tennessee having been lost with the surrender of Forts Henry and Donelson, its various posts became untenable. In a subsequent portion of this narrative, we shall trace the results of the Confederate endeavor to establish a new line of defense in the West by a judicious and masterly combination of forces.

Meanwhile, the preparations of the enemy in the East were even more formidable and threatening than in the West. It was in Virginia that the "elastic spirit" of the North, as the Richmond *Examiner* termed the alacrity of the consecutive popular uprisings in favor of the war at the North, was chiefly ambitious and hopeful of decisive results in favor of the Union. Here was to be sought retrieval of the national honor lost at Manassas; here was the capital of the Confederacy, which, once taken, the "rebellion would collapse." The energy and administrative ability of General McClellan had accomplished great results in the creation of a fine army and the security of the capital. But, with the opening of the season favorable to military operations, he was expected to accomplish far more decisive results—nothing less than the capture of Richmond, the expulsion of the Confederate authority from Virginia, and the destruction of the Confederate army at Manassas.

Until the opening of spring, military operations in Virginia were attended by no events of importance. But the East was not to be without its contribution to the unvarying tide of Confederate disaster. In the month of February, Roanoke Island, upon the sea-line of North Carolina, defended by General Wise, with a single brigade, was assaulted by a powerful combined naval and military expedition, under General Burnside, and surrendered, with its garrison. This success opened to the enemy the sounds and inlets of that region, with their tributary streams, and gave him easy access to a productive country and important communications.

It was not difficult to estimate correctly the serious nature of these successive reverses covering nearly every field of important operations. They were of a character alarming, indeed, in immediate consequences, and, necessarily, largely affecting the destiny of the war in its future stages. Retreat, evacuation, and surrender seemed the irremediable tendency of affairs every-where. Thousands of prisoners were in the hands of the enemy, the capital of the most important State in the West occupied, the Confederate centre was broken, the great water-avenues of the south-west open to the enemy, the campaign transferred from the heart of Kentucky to the northern borders of the Gulf States, and hardly an available line was left for the recovery of the lost territory.

Within a few weeks the extravagant hopes of the South were brought to the verge of extreme apprehension. The public mind was not to be soothed by the affected indifference of the press to calamities, the magnitude of which was too palpable, in the presence of actual invasion of nearly one half the Southern territory, and of imminent perils threatening the speedy culmination of adverse fortune to the Confederacy. Richmond, which, during the war, was at all times the reflex of the hopes and aspirations of the South, was the scene of gloom and despondency, in painful contrast with the ardent and gratulatory tone so lately prevalent.

Popular disappointment rarely fails in its search for scape-goats upon which to visit responsibility for misfortunes. A noticeable result of the Confederate reverses in the beginning of 1862 was the speedy evolution of an organized hostility to the administration of President Davis. The season was eminently propitious for outward demonstrations of feeling, heretofore suppressed, in consequence of the brilliant success, until recently, attending the movement for Southern independence. The universal and characteristic disposition of the masses to receive, with favor, censure of their rulers, and to charge public calamities to official failure and maladministration, was an inviting inducement, in this period of public gloom, to the indulgence of partisan aspirations and personal spleen.

To one familiar with the political history of the South during the decade previous to secession, there could be no difficulty in penetrating the various motives, instigating to union, for a common purpose, the heterogeneous elements of this opposition. Prominent among its leaders were men, the life-long opponents of the President, notorious for their want of adhesion to any principle or object for its own sake, and especially lukewarm, at all times, upon issues vitally affecting the safety of the South. These men could not forget, even when their allegiance had been avowed to the sacred cause of country and liberty, the rancor engendered in the old contests of party.

Some, in addition to disappointed political ambition, arising from the failure of the President to tender them the foremost places in the Government, had personal resentments to gratify. Much the larger portion of the opposition, which continued, until the last moments of the Confederacy, to assail the Government, had its origin in these influences, and they speedily attracted all restless and impracticable characters—born Jacobins, malcontents by the decree of nature, and others of the class who are "never at home save in the attitude of contradiction."

At first feeble in influence, this faction, by pertinacious and unscrupulous efforts, eventually became a source of embarrassment, and promoted the wide-spread division and distrust which, in the latter days of the Confederacy, were so ominous of the approaching catastrophe. Its earliest shafts were ostensibly not aimed at the President, since there was no evidence that the popular affection for Mr. Davis would brook assaults upon him, but assumed the shape of accusations against his constitutional advisers. A deliberate movement, cloaked in the disguise of respectful remonstrance and petition, sustained by demagogical speeches—which, though artfully designed, in many instances revealed the secret venom—was arranged, upon the assembling of the First Congress under the permanent Government, to revolutionize the cabinet of President Davis.

Mr. Benjamin, the Secretary of War, and Mr. Mallory, Secretary of the Navy, were the objects of especial and most envenomed assault. They were assailed in Congress, and by a portion of the Richmond press, as directly chargeable with the late reverses. Yet it should have been plain that the most serious of these disasters were attributable chiefly to the overwhelming naval preponderance of the enemy—an advantage not to have been obviated entirely by any degree of foresight on the part of the Confederate naval secretary—and by a deficiency of soldiers, for which the country itself, and not Mr. Benjamin, was to be censured.

The indisputable facts in the case were ample in the vindication of Mr. Mallory, as to the insufficient defenses of the Western rivers, now in Federal possession. The obvious dangers of the Cumberland and Tennessee Rivers, as an avenue of access to the heart of the South, were not overlooked by the Government. The channels of these rivers are navigable during a large portion of the year, and the two streams gradually approach each other, as they pass from Tennessee into Kentucky, on their course to the Ohio, coming at one point within less than three miles of each other, and emptying their waters only ten miles apart. The facilities afforded by their proximity for combined military and naval operations, were necessarily apparent. The Government contemplated the defense of these streams by floating defenses the only means by which they could be debarred to the enemy. The Provisional Congress, however, by a most singular and fatal oversight of the recommendation of the Government, made no appropriation for floating defenses on the Tennessee and Cumberland, until the opportunity to prepare them had passed.

It authorized the President to cause to be constructed thirteen steam gunboats *for sea-coast defense*, and such floating defenses for the Mississippi River as he might deem best adapted to the purpose; but no provision was made for armed steamers on the large Western interior rivers until the month of January, 1862, when an act was approved appropriating one million of dollars, to be expended for this purpose, at the discretion of the President, by the Secretary of War, or of the Navy, as he might direct. This was less than *four weeks* before the actual advance of the Federal gunboats, and was, of course, too late for the needed armaments. The appropriation of one hundred thousand dollars, for equipment and repairs of vessels of the Confederate navy, hardly sufficed to enable the Secretary of that department to maintain a few frail steamers on the Tennessee, hastily prepared from commercial or passenger boats, and very imperfectly armed.

A congressional investigating committee censured Mr. Benjamin and General Huger as responsible for the capture of Roanoke Island and its garrison. The latter affair was indeed a disaster not to be lightly palliated, and was one of those inexplicable mishaps, which, upon retrospection, we see should have been avoided, though it is at least doubtful who is justly censurable. It is, however, only just to state that no view of the Roanoke Island disaster has ever been presented to the writer, which did not acquit General Wise of all blame. His exculpation was complete before every tribunal of opinion.

Whatever may have been the real merit of these issues made against Secretaries Mallory and Benjamin, it is very certain that those two gentlemen continued to be the objects of marked disfavor from those members of Congress, and that portion of the Richmond press known to be hostile to the administration of Mr. Davis. Popular prejudice is proverbially unreasoning, and it was indeed singular to note how promptly the public echoed the assaults of the hostile press against these officials, upon subsequent occasions, when they were held accountable for disasters with which they had no possible connection.*

This period of Confederate misfortunes gave the first verification of a fact which afterward had frequent illustration, that the resolution of the South, so indomitable in actual contest, staggered under the weight of reverses. The history of the war was a record of the variations of the Southern mind between extreme elation and immoderate depression. Extravagant exultation over success, and immoderate despondency over disaster, usually followed each other in prompt succession. Overestimating, in many instances, the importance of its own victories, the South quite as frequently exaggerated the value of those won by the enemy. There was thus a constant departure from the middle ground of dispassionate judgment, which would have accurately measured the real situation; making available its opportunities, by a vigorous prosecution of advantage, and overcoming difficulties by energetic preparation.

But this despondency happily gave place to renewed determination, as the success of the enemy brought him nearer the homes of the South, and made more imminent the evils of subjugation. A grand and noble popular reanimation was the response to the renewed vigor and resolution of the Government.

When the Confederate Government was organized at Montgomery, the operation of the provisional constitution was

* The friends of Mr. Mallory, in illustration of this unreasoning prejudice, were accustomed to declare that, "were a Confederate vessel to sink in a storm, in the middle of the ocean, the Richmond *Examiner* and Mr. Foote would advocate the censure of the Secretary of the Navy, as responsible for her loss."

limited to the period of one year, to be superseded by the permanent government. No material alteration of the political organism was found necessary, nor was there any change in the *personnel* of the administration—Mr. Davis having been unanimously chosen President at the election in November, and retaining his administration as it existed at the close of the functions of the provisional constitution. Though the change was thus merely nominal, the occasion was replete with historic interest to the people whose liberties were involved in the fate of the government, now declared "permanent." It was, indeed, an assumption of a new character—a declaration, with renewed emphasis, of the high and peerless enterprise of independent national existence; an introduction to a future, promising a speedy fulfillment of inestimable blessings or "woes unnumbered."

On the 18th of February, 1862, the first Congress, under the permanent constitution of the Confederate States, assembled in the capitol at Richmond. On the 22d occurred the ceremony of the inauguration of President Davis.

To the citizens of Richmond and others who were spectators, the scene in Capitol Square, on that memorable morning, was marked by gloomy surroundings, the recollection of which recalls, with sad interest, suggestive omens, which then seemed to betoken the adverse fate of the Confederacy. The season was one of unusual rigor, and the preceding month of public calamity and distress had been fitly commemorated by a protracted series of dark and cheerless days. Never, within the recollection of the writer, had there been a day in Richmond so severe, uncomfortable, and gloomy, as the day appointed for the ceremony of inauguration. For days previous heavy clouds had foreshadowed the rain, which fell continuously during the preceding night, and which seemed to increase in volume on the morning of the ceremony. The occasion was in singular contrast with that which, a year previous, had witnessed the installment of the provisional government—upon a day whose genial sunshine seemed prophetic of a bright future for the infant power then launched upon its voyage.

But however wanting in composure may have been the public mind, and whatever the perils of the situation, the voice of their twice-chosen chief quickly infused into the heart of the people, that unabated zeal and unconquerable resolution, with which he proclaimed himself devoted anew to the deliverance of his country. The inaugural address was a noble and inspiring appeal to the patriotism of the land. Its eloquent, candid, and patriotic tone won all hearts; and even the unfriendly press and politicians accorded commendation to the dignity and candor with which the President avowed his official responsibility; the manly frankness with which he defended departments of the government unjustly assailed; and the assuring, defiant courage, with which he invited all classes of his countrymen to join him in the supreme sacrifice, should it become necessary.

The inaugural ceremonies were as simple and appropriate as those witnessed at Montgomery a year previous. The members of the Confederate Senate and House of Representatives, with the members of the Virginia Legislature, awaited in the hall of the House of Delegates the arrival of the President. In consequence of the limited capacity of the hall, comparatively few spectators—a majority of them ladies—witnessed the proceedings there. Immediately fronting the chair of the speaker were the ladies of Mr. Davis' household, attended by relatives and friends. In close proximity were members of the cabinet.

A contemporary account thus mentions this scene: "It was a grave and great assemblage. Time-honored men were there, who had witnessed ceremony after ceremony of inauguration in the palmiest days of the old confederation; those who had been at the inauguration of the iron-willed Jackson; men who, in their fiery Southern ardor, had thrown down the gauntlet of defiance in the halls of Federal legislation, and in the face of the enemy avowed their determination to be free; and finally witnessed the enthroning of a republican despot in their country's chair of state. All were there; and silent tears were seen coursing down the cheeks of gray-haired men, while the determined will stood out in every feature."

The appearance of the President was singularly imposing, though there were visible traces of his profound emotion, and a pallor, painful to look upon, reminded the spectator of his recent severe indisposition. His dress was a plain citizen's suit of black. Mr. Hunter, of Virginia, temporary President of the Confederate Senate, occupied the right of the platform; Mr. Bocock, Speaker of the House of Representatives, the left. When President Davis, accompanied by Mr. Orr, of South Carolina, Chairman of the Committee of Arrangements, on the part of the Senate, reached the hall and passed to the chair of the Speaker, subdued applause, becoming the place and the occasion, greeted him. A short time sufficed to carry into effect the previously arranged programme, and the distinguished procession moved to the Washington monument, where a stand was prepared for the occasion.

Hon. James Lyons, of Virginia, Chairman of the House Committee of Arrangements, called the assemblage to order, and an eloquent and appropriate prayer was offered by Bishop Johns, of the Diocese of Virginia. The President, having received a most enthusiastic welcome from the assemblage, with a clear and measured accent, delivered his inaugural address:

FELLOW-CITIZENS: On this, the birthday of the man most identified with the establishment of American independence, and beneath the monument erected to commemorate his heroic virtues and those of his compatriots, we have assembled, to usher into existence the permanent government of the Confederate States. Through this instrumentality, under the favor of Divine Providence, we hope to perpetuate the principles of our revolutionary fathers. The day, the memory, and the purpose seem fitly associated.

It is with mingled feelings of humility and pride that I appear to take, in the presence of the people, and before high Heaven, the oath prescribed as a qualification for the exalted station to which the unanimous voice of the people has called me. Deeply sensible of all that is implied by this manifestation of the people's confidence, I am yet more profoundly impressed by the vast responsibility of the office, and humbly feel my own unworthiness.

In return for their kindness, I can only offer assurances of the gratitude with which it is received, and can but pledge a zealous devotion of every faculty to the service of those who have chosen me as their Chief Magistrate.

When a long course of class legislation, directed not to the general welfare, but to the aggrandizement of the Northern section of the Union, culminated in a warfare on the domestic institutions of the Southern States; when the dogmas of a sectional party, substituted for the provisions of the constitutional compact, threatened to destroy the sovereign rights of the States, six of those States, withdrawing from the Union, confederated together to exercise the right and perform the duty of instituting a government which would better secure the liberties for the preservation of which that Union was established.

Whatever of hope some may have entertained that a returning sense of justice would remove the danger with which our rights were threatened, and render it possible to preserve the Union of the Constitution, must have been dispelled by the malignity and barbarity of the Northern States in the prosecution of the existing war. The confidence of the most hopeful among us must have been destroyed by the disregard they have recently exhibited for all the time-honored bulwarks of civil and religious liberty. Bastiles filled with prisoners, arrested without civil process, or indictment duly found; the writ of *habeas corpus* suspended by executive mandate; a State Legislature controlled by the imprisonment of members whose avowed principles suggested to the Federal executive that there might be another added to the list of seceded States; elections held under threats of a military power; civil officers, peaceful citizens, and gentle women incarcerated for opinion's sake, proclaimed the incapacity of our late associates to administer a government as free, liberal, and humane as that established for our common use.

For proof of the sincerity of our purpose to maintain our ancient institutions, we may point to the Constitution of the Confederacy and the laws enacted under it, as well as to the fact that, through all the necessities of an unequal struggle, there has been no act, on our part, to impair personal liberty or the freedom of speech, of thought, or of the press. The courts have been open, the judicial functions fully executed, and every right of the peaceful citizen maintained as securely as if a war of invasion had not disturbed the land.

The people of the States now confederated became convinced that the Government of the United States had fallen into the hands of a sectional majority, who would pervert the most sacred of all trusts to the destruction of the rights which it was pledged to protect. They believed that to remain longer in the Union would subject them to a continuance of a disparaging discrimination, submission to which would be inconsistent to their welfare and intolerable to a proud people. They, therefore, determined to sever its bonds, and establish a new confederacy for themselves.

The experiment, instituted by our revolutionary fathers, of a voluntary union of sovereign States, for purposes specified in a solemn compact, had been prevented by those who, feeling power and forgetting right, were determined to respect no law but their own will. The Government had ceased to answer the ends for which it had been ordained and established. To save ourselves from a revolution which, in its silent but rapid progress, was about to place us under the despotism of numbers, and to preserve, in spirit as well as in form, a system of government we believed to be peculiarly fitted to our condition and full of promise for mankind, we determined to make a new association, composed of States homogeneous in interest, in policy, and in feeling.

True to our traditions of peace and love of justice, we sent commissioners to the United States to propose a fair and amicable settlement of all questions of public debt or property which might be in dispute. But the Government at Washington, denying our right to self-government, refused even to listen to any proposals for a peaceful separation. Nothing was then left to us but to prepare for war.

The first year in our history has been the most eventful in the annals of this continent. A new government has been established, and its machinery put in operation, over an area exceeding seven hundred thousand square miles. The great principles upon which we have been willing to hazard every thing that is dear to man have made conquests for us which could never have been achieved by the sword. Our Confederacy has grown from six to thirteen

States; and Maryland, already united to us by hallowed memories and material interests, will, I believe, when able to speak with unstifled voice, connect her destiny with the South. Our people have rallied, with unexampled unanimity, to the support of the great principles of constitutional government, with firm resolve to perpetuate by arms the rights which they could not peacefully secure. A million of men, it is estimated, are now standing in hostile array, and waging war along a frontier of thousands of miles; battles have been fought, sieges have been conducted, and, although the contest is not ended, and the tide for the moment is against us, the final result in our favor is not doubtful.

The period is near at hand when our foes must sink under the immense load of debt which they have incurred—a debt which, in their efforts to subjugate us, has already attained such fearful dimensions as will subject them to burdens which must continue to oppress them for generations to come.

We, too, have had our trials and difficulties. That we are to escape them in the future is not to be hoped. It was to be expected, when we entered upon this war, that it would expose our people to sacrifices, and cost them much both of money and blood. But we knew the value of the object for which we struggled, and understood the nature of the war in which we were engaged. Nothing could be so bad as failure, and any sacrifice would be cheap as the price of success in such a contest.

But the picture has its lights as well as its shadows. This great strife has awakened in the people the highest emotions and qualities of the human soul. It is cultivating feelings of patriotism, virtue, and courage. Instances of self-sacrifice and of generous devotion to the noble cause for which we are contending are rife throughout the land. Never has a people evinced a more determined spirit than that now animating men, women, and children in every part of our country. Upon the first call, the men fly to arms; and wives and mothers send their husbands and sons to battle without a murmur of regret.

It was, perhaps, in the ordination of Providence that we were to be taught the value of our liberties by the price which we pay for them.

The recollections of this great contest, with all its common traditions of glory, of sacrifices, and of blood, will be the bond of harmony and enduring affection amongst the people, producing unity in policy, fraternity in sentiment, and joint effort in war.

Nor have the material sacrifices of the past year been made without some corresponding benefits. If the acquiescence of foreign nations in a pretended blockade has deprived us of our commerce with them, it is fast making us a self-supporting and an independent people. The blockade, if effectual and permanent, could only serve to divert our industry from the production of articles for export, and employ it in supplying commodities for domestic use.

It is a satisfaction that we have maintained the war by our unaided exertions. We have neither asked nor received assistance from any quarter. Yet the interest involved is not wholly our own. The world at large is concerned in opening our markets to its commerce. When the independence of the Confederate States is recognized by the nations of the earth, and we are free to follow our interests and inclinations by cultivating foreign trade, the Southern States will offer to manufacturing nations the most favorable markets which ever invited their commerce. Cotton, sugar, rice, tobacco, provisions, timber, and naval stores will furnish attractive exchanges. Nor would the constancy of these supplies be likely to be disturbed by war. Our confederate strength will be too great to attempt aggression; and never was there a people whose interests and principles committed them so fully to a peaceful policy as those of the Confederate States. By the character of their productions, they are too deeply interested in foreign commerce wantonly to disturb it. War of conquest they can not wage, because the Constitution of their Confederacy admits of no coerced association. Civil war there can not be between States held together by their volition only. This rule of voluntary association, which can not fail to be conservative, by securing just and impartial government at home, does not diminish the security of the obligations by which the Confederate States may be bound to foreign nations. In proof of this, it is to be remembered that, at the first moment of asserting their right of secession, these States proposed a settlement on the basis of a common liability for the obligations of the General Government.

Fellow-citizens, after the struggles of ages had consecrated the right of the Englishman to constitutional representative government, our colonial ancestors were forced to vindicate that birthright by an appeal to arms. Success crowned their efforts, and they provided for their posterity a peaceful remedy against future aggression.

The tyranny of an unbridled majority, the most odious and least responsible form of despotism, has denied us both the right and the remedy. Therefore we are in arms to renew such sacrifices as our fathers made to the holy cause of constitutional liberty. At the darkest hour of our struggle, the provisional gives place to the permanent government. After a series of successes and victories, which covered our arms with glory, we have recently met with serious disasters. But, in the heart of a people resolved to be free, these disasters tend but to stimulate to increased resistance.

To show ourselves worthy of the inheritance bequeathed to us by the patriots of the Revolution, we must emulate that heroic devotion which made reverse to them but the crucible in which their patriotism was refined.

With confidence in the wisdom and virtue of those who will share with me the responsibility, and aid me in the conduct of public affairs; securely relying on the patriotism and courage of the people, of which the present war has furnished so many examples, I deeply feel the weight of the responsibilities I now, with unaffected diffidence, am about to assume; and, fully realizing the inadequacy of human power to guide and to sustain, my hope is reverently fixed on Him, whose favor is ever vouchsafed to the cause which is just. With humble gratitude and adoration, acknowledging the Providence which has so visibly protected the Confederacy during its brief but eventful career, to Thee, O God! I trustingly commit myself, and prayerfully invoke Thy blessing on my country and its cause.

The effect of this address upon the public was electrical. The anxious and dispirited assemblage, which, for more than an hour previous to the arrival of the President, had braved the inclement sky and traversed the almost impassable avenues of Capitol Square, in eager longing for re-assuring words from him upon whose courage and will so much depended, was not disappointed. A consciousness of a burden removed, of doubts dispelled, of the re-assured feeling, which comes with strengthened conviction that confidence has not been misplaced, animated and thrilled the crowd as it caught the impressive tones and gestures of the speaker. In the memory of every beholder must forever dwell the imposing presence of Mr. Davis, as, with uplifted hands, he pronounced the beautiful and appropriate petition to Providence, which forms the peroration.

The message sent by President Davis to Congress, a few days after the inauguration, is hardly inferior in importance, as a historical document, to the inaugural address. In view of its explanations of the earlier policy of the Confederate

Government, of the causes of recent disasters, and indications of important changes in the future conduct of the war, we present entire this first message of Mr. Davis to the First Congress assembled under the permanent Constitution:

To the Senate and House of Representatives of the Confederate States—

In obedience to the constitutional provision, requiring the President, from time to time, to give to the Congress information of the state of the Confederacy, and recommend to their consideration such measures as he shall judge necessary and expedient, I have to communicate that, since my message at the last session of the Provisional Congress, events have demonstrated that the Government had attempted more than it had power successfully to achieve. Hence, in the effort to protect, by our arms, the whole of the territory of the Confederate States, sea-board and inland, we have been so exposed as recently to encounter serious disasters. When the Confederacy was formed, the States composing it were, by the peculiar character of their pursuits, and a misplaced confidence in their former associates, to a great extent, destitute of the means for the prosecution of the war on so gigantic a scale as that which it has attained. The workshops and artisans were mainly to be found in the Northern States, and one of the first duties which devolved upon this Government was to establish the necessary manufactories, and in the meantime to obtain, by purchase from abroad, as far as practicable, whatever was required for the public defense. No effort has been spared to effect both these ends, and though the results have not equaled our hopes, it is believed that an impartial judgment will, upon full investigation, award to the various departments of the Government credit for having done all which human power and foresight enabled them to accomplish.

The valor and devotion of the people have not only sustained the efforts of the Government, but have gone far to supply its deficiencies.

The active state of military preparations among the nations of Europe, in April last, the date when our agents first went abroad, interposed unavoidable delays in the procurement of arms, and the want of a navy has greatly impeded our efforts to import military supplies of all sorts.

I have hoped for several days to receive official reports in relation to our discomfiture at Roanoke Island, and the fall of Fort Donelson. They have not yet reached me, and I am, therefore, unable to communicate to you such information of those events, and the consequences resulting from them, as would enable me to make recommendations founded upon the changed condition which they have produced. Enough is known of the surrender of Roanoke Island to make us feel that it was deeply humiliating, however imperfect may have been the preparations for defense. The hope is still entertained that our reported losses at Fort Donelson have been greatly exaggerated, inasmuch as I am not only unwilling, but unable to believe that a large army of our people have surrendered without a desperate effort to cut their way through investing forces, whatever may have been their number, and to endeavor to make a junction with other divisions of the army. But in the absence of that exact information which can only be afforded by official reports, it would be premature to pass judgment, and my own is reserved, as I trust yours will be, until that information is received. In the meantime, strenuous efforts have been made to throw forward reinforcements to the armies at the positions threatened, and I can not doubt that the bitter disappointments we have borne, by nerving the people to still greater exertions, will speedily secure results more accordant with our just expectation, and as favorable to our cause as those which marked the earlier periods of the war.

The reports of the Secretaries of War and the Navy will exhibit the mass of resources for the conduct of the war which we have been enabled to accumulate, notwithstanding the very serious difficulties against which we have contended.

They afford the cheering hope that our resources, limited as they were at the beginning of the contest, will, during its progress, become developed to such an extent as fully to meet our future wants.

The policy of enlistment for short terms, against which I have steadily contended from the commencement of the war, has, in my judgment, contributed, in no immaterial degree, to the recent reverses which we have suffered, and even now renders it difficult to furnish you an accurate statement of the army. When the war first broke out, many of our people could with difficulty be persuaded that it would be long or serious. It was not deemed possible that any thing so insane as a persistent attempt to subjugate these States could be made—still less that the delusion would so far prevail as to give to the war the vast proportions which it has assumed. The people, incredulous of a long war, were naturally averse to long enlistment, and the early legislation of Congress rendered it impracticable to obtain volunteers for a greater period than twelve months. Now, that it has become probable that the war will be continued through a series of years, our high-spirited and gallant soldiers, while generally reënlisting, are, from the fact of having entered the service for a short term, compelled, in many instances, to go home to make the necessary arrangements for their families during their prolonged absence.

The quotas of new regiments for the war, called for from the different States, are in rapid progress of organization. The whole body of our new levies and reënlisted men will probably be ready in the ranks within the next thirty days. But, in the meantime, it is exceedingly difficult to give an accurate statement of the number of our forces in the field. They may, in general terms, be stated at four hundred regiments of infantry, with a proportionate force of cavalry and artillery, the details of which will be shown by the report of the Secretary of War. I deem it proper to advert to the fact that the process of furloughs and reënlistment in progress for the last month had so far disorganized and weakened our forces as to impair our ability for successful defense; but I heartily congratulate you that this evil, which I had foreseen and was powerless to prevent, may now be said to be substantially at an end, and that we shall not again, during the war, be exposed to seeing our strength diminished by this fruitful cause of disaster—short enlistments.

The people of the Confederate States, being principally engaged in agricultural pursuits, were unprovided at the commencement of hostilities with ships, ship-yards, materials for ship-building, or skilled mechanics and seamen, in sufficient numbers to make the prompt creation of the navy a practicable task, even if the required appropriations had been made for the purpose. Notwithstanding our very limited resources, however, the report of the Secretary will exhibit to you a satisfactory progress in preparation, and a certainty of early completion of vessels of a number and class on which we may confidently rely for contesting the vaunted control of the enemy over our waters.

The financial system, devised by the wisdom of your predecessors, has proved adequate to supplying all the wants of the Government, notwithstanding the unexpected and very large increase of expenditures resulting from the great augmentation in the necessary means of defense. The report of the Secretary of the Treasury will exhibit the gratifying fact that we have no floating debt; that the credit of the Government is unimpaired, and that the total expenditure of the Government for the year has been, in round numbers, one hundred and seventy millions of dollars—less than one-third the sum wasted by the enemy in his vain effort to conquer us—less than the value of a single article of export—the cotton crop of the year.

The report of the Postmaster-General will show the condition of that department to be steadily improving—its revenue increasing, and already affording the assurance that it will be self-sustaining at the date required by the Constitution, while affording ample mail facilities for the people.

In the Department of Justice, which includes the Patent Office and Public Printing, some legislative provision will be required, which will be specifically stated in the report of the head of that department.

I invite the attention of Congress to the duty of organizing a Supreme Court of the Confederate States, in accordance with the mandate of the Constitution.

I refer you to my message communicated to the Provisional Congress in November last, for such further information touching the condition of public affairs, as it might be useful to lay before you; the short interval which has since elapsed not having produced any material changes in that condition, other than those to which reference has already been made.

In conclusion, I cordially welcome representatives who, recently chosen by the people, are fully imbued with their views and feelings, and can so ably advise me as to the needful provisions for the public service. I assure you of my hearty coöperation in all your efforts for the common welfare of the country.

JEFFERSON DAVIS.

The message, not less than the inaugural address, was received with many evidences of public reanimation. The following extracts indicate the state of feeling in Richmond at this period:

THE PRESIDENT'S MESSAGE.

(From the Richmond Whig, Feb. 26, 1862.)

The President makes a candid and frank confession of our recent reverses. Very justly, he does not regard them as vital to our cause; but they will entail a long war upon us. That long war ensures our independence, and the ultimate confusion and ruin of the Yankees. . . . .

The *Examiner*, of the same date, in the opening paragraph of its leader, said:

The President's Message is a manly and dignified document, but, like the inaugural, it contains not a solitary word indicating the plan or policy of the Government. Far from objecting to this characteristic, we think it eminently proper that the executive should keep its counsels from the public eye, and that the Congress should withdraw its deliberations from the public ear. What is wanted from the one is distinct and peremptory *orders;* and from the other, decisive and adequate provisions for the public safety. The duty of the country is unhesitating obedience; of the soldiers, the courage that prefers death in glory, like Jennings Wise. . . . .

CHAPTER XII.

POPULAR DELUSIONS IN THE EARLY STAGES OF THE WAR—A FEW CONFLICTS AND SACRIFICES NOT SUFFICIENT—MORE POSITIVE RECOGNITION OF MR. DAVIS' VIEWS—HIS CANDID AND PROPHETIC ANNOUNCEMENTS—MILITARY REFORMS—CONSCRIPTION LAW OF THE CONFEDERACY—THE PRESIDENT'S VIEWS AND COURSE AS TO THIS LAW—HIS CONSISTENT REGARD FOR CIVIL LIBERTY AND OPPOSITION TO CENTRALIZATION—RECOMMENDS CONSCRIPTION—BENEFICIAL RESULTS OF THE LAW—GENERAL LEE COMMANDER-IN-CHIEF, "UNDER THE PRESIDENT"—NATURE OF THE APPOINTMENT—FALSE IMPRESSIONS CORRECTED—MR. DAVIS' CONFIDENCE IN LEE, DESPITE POPULAR CENSURE OF THE LATTER—CHANGES IN THE CABINET—MR. BENJAMIN'S MANAGEMENT OF THE WAR OFFICE—DIFFICULTIES OF THAT POSITION—THE CHARGE OF FAVORITISM AGAINST MR. DAVIS IN THE SELECTION OF HIS CABINET—HIS PERSONAL RELATIONS WITH THE VARIOUS MEMBERS OF HIS CABINET—ACTIVITY IN MILITARY OPERATIONS—THE TRANS-MISSISSIPPI—BATTLE OF ELK HORN—OPERATIONS EAST OF THE MISSISSIPPI—GENERALS SIDNEY JOHNSTON AND BEAUREGARD—ISLAND NO. 10—CONCENTRATION OF TROOPS BY THE CONFEDERATE AUTHORITIES—FAVORABLE SITUATION—SHILOH—A DISAPPOINTMENT—DEATH OF SIDNEY JOHNSTON—TRIBUTE OF PRESIDENT DAVIS—POPULAR VERDICT UPON THE BATTLE OF SHILOH—GENERALS BEAUREGARD, BRAGG, AND POLK ON THE BATTLE—THE PRESIDENT AGAIN CHARGED WITH "INJUSTICE" TO BEAUREGARD—THE CHARGE ANSWERED—FALL OF NEW ORLEANS—NAVAL BATTLE IN HAMPTON ROADS—NAVAL SUCCESSES OF THE ENEMY.

WE have briefly indicated the causes which now elevated the Southern people to a more intelligent appreciation of the nature and necessities of the struggle in which they were engaged. There was reason for the congratulation which President Davis experienced at the unmistakable evidences of the awakening of the public mind to the stern duties which, from the beginning, he had sedulously inculcated.

The progress of the war had already developed the existence of numerous errors upon both sides, and had exploded many cherished theories having possession of the popular mind of each section, with reference to the power, resources, and spirit of its antagonist. Both parties had entered into the contest with the firm conviction of certain triumph, and with the purpose to make the struggle as short as possible. The war-cry of the North was "Let it be short, sharp, and decisive;" and they appealed to their numbers, wealth, and sectional hatred, as elements of superiority, which would inevitably end the war in their favor in a few months. The South was equally disposed to a speedy conclusion. With the masses of the South and the majority of their advisers, the predominant idea and aspiration was to teach the enemy, by prompt and heavy blows, the impossibility of successful invasion, and thus shorten the period of bloodshed. Thus both, from a necessity which neither was able to avoid, began with gigantic preparations, hoping, by a few mighty conflicts of arms, and one lavish sacrifice of life and treasure, to bring to prompt arbitrament an issue which was the growth of a century.

But the aroused spirit of sectional strife was not to be appeased by a single holocaust. The American people, a youthful giant, totally uneducated in the experience of war, having never yet tested their strength and dimensions, would not consent that the game of empire should be decided by a single dramatic *denouement*, a Waterloo, a Solferino, or Sadowa. Manassas had been the bitter but beneficent chastisement of the North, and the reproof was accepted with that wonderful elasticity, which afterwards amazed the world with its manifestations after the most disheartening failures. A rebuke no less signal waited upon the South, and its correcting influence immediately exhibited a temper which was the temporary salvation of the Confederacy, and the inspiration to a series of campaigns among the most memorable in the annals of warfare.

With the inauguration of the permanent government came not only renewed resolution in the prosecution of the war, but a more positive recognition and adoption of the views of President Davis. We have elsewhere described the antagonism between those views and the theory of the leaders at Montgomery, shared by the press and people of the South, which derided any other hypothesis than a six-months' war, with the certainty of independence. Whatever weight may be accredited to the statements which we have made in demonstration of Mr. Davis' conviction, that the war would be one of unexampled magnitude and long duration; whatever may be the rational inference from his opposition to a military system contemplating a war lasting six or twelve months; whatever the credence extended to his own subsequent declarations of the difficulties preventing the complete preparation for the emergency, which he contemplated,* at least there was no

* The careful reader will hardly have overlooked the passage, in the Message to Congress, in the preceding chapter, in which Mr. Davis thus alludes to this subject: "The active state of military preparation among the nations of Europe, in April last, the date when our agents first went abroad, interposed unavoidable delays in the procurement of arms, and the want of a navy has greatly impeded our efforts to obtain military supplies of all sorts."

A few months later, he said, speaking with characteristic candor: "I was among those who, from the beginning, predicted war as the consequences of secession, although I must admit that the contest has assumed proportions more gigantic than I had anticipated. I predicted war, not because our right to secede and to form a government of our own was not indisputable and clearly defined in the spirit of that declaration,

room for misconception of his expectations as to the war in its future stages.

Congratulating the Confederate Congress upon the auspicious awakening of the popular mind from dangerous delusions, even through the hard experience of adversity, he admonishes Con-

which rests the right to govern on the consent of the governed, but saw that the wickedness of the North would precipitate a war upon us."—*Address before Mississippi Legislature, December*, 1862.

Mr. Davis here candidly admits that the "gigantic proportions" of the war exceeded his expectations, as they did also the expectations of the whole country and of the world. He did foresee a *great war*, and prepared for it; but he was not guilty of the foolish pretension that the war simply realized his expectations, when every statesman of Europe and America was deceived, both as to its duration and magnitude. Who believes that Napoleon the First, equally the unrivaled master of war and diplomacy, would pretend that he foresaw the extent and duration, or the results, of the wars of the empire? that he realized the inextinguishable nature of English hostility, or anticipated the numerous perfidies of Austria? Mr. Seward, who is likely to be remembered, with some distinction, in connection with the diplomacy and statesmanship of the late war, constantly predicted its termination in "ninety days." *No opinion can be truthfully ascribed to Mr. Davis indicating a light estimate of the struggle either before or during the war.* Yet there is a retrospective statesmanship in the South which now claims that he should have been lifted to its own preternatural powers, and from the first have seen every phase and incident. How absurd must this pretension appear to the sober judgment of fifty years hence.

Mr. Davis was even accredited in Richmond, by an extravagant and unfounded popular report, with the prophecy that "children then (1862) unborn would be soldiers in the war between the North and South." People in those days saw nothing in the action of the Government indicating its faith in a short war. Their only consolation was found in the editorials of Richmond newspapers predicting foreign intervention should McClellan be defeated.

gress and the country to prepare for a "*war lasting through a term of years.*" But a few weeks later and he invited the Legislature of Virginia to contemplate a possible duration of the war for twenty years upon the soil of that State. In all his declarations, public and private, was evidenced the adherence to that original conviction of a struggle long, bloody, and exhaustive, and with varying fortune, which had prompted the heroic assurance, at his first inauguration at Montgomery, of an "inflexible" pursuit of the object of independence.

President Davis sufficiently exposed, in his first message to the new Congress, the evil consequences of the pernicious military system under which the war had thus far been conducted. Indeed, its evils were apparent, and the country responded to the urgent appeals of the President for a more efficient organization of the armies of the Confederacy—one that should insure a force sufficient to meet the present exigency and to provide for future defense. It was with considerable reluctance that he finally recommended the adoption of the act of conscription. Constitutional scruples were at least debatable, but there could be no question as to the appearance of bad faith by the Government, with the patriotic volunteers, who had responded at the first call to arms, and who were now compelled to remain in the field, by a law adopted, just as their term of service was expiring. Yet this was the class necessarily constituting the majority of those who would be subject to the operation of the law, as they were a majority, or an approximate majority, of the arms-bearing population.

To one so peculiarly jealous of encroachments by the central power upon the privileges of the States, the proposition had additional objections. Mr. Davis had hoped to avoid the necessity of a measure, so much after the manner of military despotism, and sought to take advantage of the patriotic ardor exhibited upon the first rush to arms, by inducing enlistments for the war. Especially distasteful was a resort to compulsion into the ranks, in a war the success of which necessarily depended upon the voluntary and patriotic aid of the people, while the enemy, without difficulty, raised a half million of men for their schemes of conquest.

Second to the object of independence only, the controlling aspiration of President Davis was, that the war might not terminate in the destruction of civil liberty. With evident pride, he proclaimed the honorable fact that, "through all the necessities of an unequal struggle, there has been no act on our part to impair personal liberty or the freedom of speech, of thought, or of the press."* His consistent regard for civil liberty was preserved even in instances where additions to the executive authority would result. The rôle of Louis Quatorze, of Frankenstein, or of Cæsar, presented no attractions to the republican executive, whose position and authority were, themselves, a protest against the exercise of arbitrary and ungranted powers.

It is a striking evidence of the contempt for consistency, manifested by Mr. Davis' assailants, that these virtues, so commendable in the executive of a free people, should then have actually constituted the ground of accusation, by those who subsequently charged him with an ambition to unite in himself all the departments of the Government. There arose, at this time, a demagogical demand for a "Dictator"—that morbid aspiration characteristic of men of weak nerve and deficient

* Inaugural Address, February 22, 1862.

fortitude, which vainly seeks to make Government more powerful for good purposes, by removing all restraints upon its power to do evil.

Emphatic in the assertion of the authority conferred by the Constitution upon his position, President Davis was no less persistent in his refusal to countenance the investiture of himself with dictatorial powers.

But the stern and pressing exigencies of the times outweighed considerations of even the gravest import, and induced a resort to that measure which the President had hoped to avoid, but upon which now depended the salvation of the country. In accordance with the recommendation of the President, Congress, on the 16th of April, 1862, adopted the conscription law, which was thenceforward, with many material modifications rendered necessary by circumstances, the basis of the military system of the Confederacy. This law placed at the disposal of the President, during the war, every citizen not belonging to a class exempted, between the ages of eighteen and thirty-five, thus annulling all contracts made with volunteers for short terms. By this act, the States surrendered their control over such of their citizens as came within the terms of the act, and in each State were located camps of instruction, for the reception and training of conscripts. There were other features of the conscription law, having in view an increased solidity and harmony of the army organization.

It is impossible to overestimate the immediate benefits realized to the Confederacy from this legislation. The incipient disorganization of the army, consequent upon the numerous furloughs granted to such of the men as would reënlist for the war, was instantly checked; large additions were made to commands already in the field, and the discipline and general frame-work of the army greatly improved.

Second in importance to the adoption of the act of conscription only, among the accessions of strength to the military system of the Confederacy at this period, was the appointment of General Lee to the general command of the armies, "under the direction of the President."*

The nature of the position thus assigned to one whom the concurrent criticism of his age pronounces the most eminent of American commanders, has been much misunderstood, and with its discussion has been associated much injurious misrepresentation of President Davis.

General Lee, after the failure of his campaign in North-western Virginia, in the autumn of 1861, became the object of a vast amount of disparaging criticism. His case was, indeed, in marked coincidence with that of Sidney Johnston. Both were distinguished in the Federal service; previous to the war they were generally conceded to be the ablest officers of that service; both were known to have been the classmates of Jefferson Davis and his intimate friends. In their first campaigns, both were adjudged, by the hot and impulsive temper of the time, to have committed gross and signal fail-

* The order was in these terms:

" WAR DEPARTMENT,
"ADJUTANT AND HIS INSPECTOR-GENERAL'S OFFICE,
" March 13, 1862.

General Orders,
No. 14.

"General Robert E. Lee is assigned to duty at the seat of Government; and, under the direction of the President, is charged with the conduct of military operations in the armies of the Confederacy.

" By command of the Secretary of War.

"S. COOPER,
"*Adjutant and Inspector-General.*"

ure. Neither had many apologists. Johnston was declared an imbecile—a mere martinet, without any of the qualities of true generalship; and Lee was pronounced incompetent for higher duties than the clerical performances of the War Office.

President Davis alone remained firm in behalf of these two men, whom a few months sufficed to triumphantly vindicate. What nobler vindication should he himself claim than that, through his firmness and discernment, was given the needed opportunity to the three great soldiers—Lee, Sidney Johnston, and Stonewall Jackson—who, above all others, have illustrated American warfare.*

It has been erroneously supposed and asserted, that General Lee was assigned the position of commanding general at the special instance of Congress, and in obedience to the proclaimed will of the people. Whatever may have been the concurrence of the Confederate Congress in the selection made by President Davis of Lee for that position, there is no ground for the hypothesis that the Southern people welcomed this promotion of General Lee as an assurance of good fortune in the future conduct of the war.

Indeed, the act of Congress, creating the office of commanding general, was adopted at the special suggestion of the President, who immediately assigned Lee to the discharge of its duties. Congress designed General Lee to be Minister of War, and, with a view to the promotion of that purpose, repealed a provision which deprived of his rank in the army, a general

* The fact is not generally known that the President was, upon two occasions, assailed with urgent petitions for the removal of Stonewall Jackson, which he peremptorily rejected on both occasions; first, after the campaign about Romney, in December, 1861, and again, after the battle of Kernstown, March, 1862.

assigned to the control of the War Office. But President Davis clearly understood the broad and palpable distinction, between the talents requisite for successful administration of that department of the Government, and the genius of a great soldier. He had too just an appreciation of the high military qualities of Lee, to consent to their virtual entombment in a civil position. In accordance with these suggestions, the President obtained the adoption of the necessary legislation, and conferred upon General Lee the control and supervision of the purely military affairs and operations of the war administration. Thus it was neither in compliance with the action of Congress, nor in deference to the popular will, that President Davis selected an appropriate sphere for the genius of Lee, where it "soon dawned upon the admiration of mankind, and retained its effulgence undimmed to the last."*

The terms of the order assigning General Lee to duty, "under the direction of the President," have been construed to signify, that it was not designed that he should exercise those appropriate functions which obviously appertain to the position of commanding-general. It has been argued that the President thus created Lee a sort of "chief of staff," or ornamental attaché of his military household, with a purely complimentary and meaningless title. The selections made by Mr. Davis, of Lee first, and, subsequently, of Bragg, as incumbents of the position, sufficiently repel this absurd conclusion. It is true that the President did not delegate to these officers his constitutional functions as commander-in-chief, but to assist and advise him, in the discharge of those arduous and laborious functions, required no ordinary skill and experience. The

*I am mainly indebted for these facts to a recent publication by Professor Bledsoe, late Assistant Secretary of War of the Confederate States.

well-known confidence, reposed by the President in General Lee, may accurately measure the influence of the latter, upon the Confederate military administration.

In the progress of those events, which have thus far engrossed our attention, notable changes had occurred in the cabinet. Early in the summer of 1861, Mr. Toombs had surrendered the portfolio of State, and Mr. Hunter, a former United States Senator from Virginia, whose name was prominently associated with the political history of the Union for more than twenty years, was placed at the head of the Confederate administration. During the ensuing winter, Mr. Hunter retired from the cabinet, and was transferred to the Confederate Senate.

Mr. Benjamin, originally Attorney-General, had been temporarily assigned to the War Department, upon the resignation of Mr. Walker, who was the first incumbent. The connection of Mr. Benjamin with the War Office continued for several months, when he was transferred to the Department of State, where he remained until the overthrow of the Confederacy. The period of his administration of the War Department measures an important space in the history of the Confederacy. It was a period marked by numerous, consecutive, and appalling disasters, and, as has been already seen, Mr. Benjamin did not escape the penalty of official position during a season of public calamity. We have glanced briefly at the question of his official responsibility, not with a view of his vindication, though we have denied the justice of the unlimited reproach, which pursued both himself and Secretary Mallory, long after even the pretext had disappeared.

The censure of Mr. Benjamin was based upon the assumption that he was responsible for reverses, which a more skillful and attentive management would have avoided. Yet the facts establish the declaration of Mr. Davis that those reverses were unavoidable. They, indeed, simply foreshadowed the fact, which the country soon after realized, of the immense disadvantage of the Confederate forces in all cases where the naval facilities of the enemy could be made available. Can it be successfully maintained that another in the place of Mr. Benjamin would have prevented the fall of Forts Henry and Donelson, of Roanoke Island, of Newbern, of Memphis, of Island No. 10, and of New Orleans? General Randolph, the successor of Mr. Benjamin, is universally conceded to have made a competent secretary of war during his brief term; yet will it be maintained that had General Randolph, instead of Mr. Benjamin, been the successor of Mr. Walker, that all, or any of those disasters would have been prevented?

Mr. Benjamin can hardly be deemed less fortunate than his successors. Messrs. Randolph and Breckinridge were, perhaps, fortunate in the brief period of their responsibility, or they, too, might have shared the public censure so freely lavished upon Messrs. Walker, Benjamin, and Seddon.

Perhaps no more thankless position was ever assumed by an official than the management of the War Department of the Confederate States. The difficult problem propounded by Themistocles—"to make a small state a great one"—was of easy solution, compared to that presented the luckless incumbent of an office, in which the abundance of responsibilities and embarrassments was commensurate only with the poverty of resources with which to meet them. To create an army from a population of between five and six millions, able to successfully cope with an adversary supported by a home population of twenty-five millions, aided by the inexhaustible reserves of Europe; with blockaded ports, a newly-organized Government, and a country of limited manufacturing means; to match in the material of war the wealthiest and most productive nation in the world; to maintain the strength and efficiency of an army decimated by its own unnumbered victories, and from a population depleted by successive conscriptions, was the encouraging task devolving upon President Davis and his Secretary of War. It is, at least, reasonable to doubt whether even the genius of Napoleon, or of Carnot, was ever summoned to such an enterprise.

No allegation was made more freely and persistently against Mr. Davis than that of favoritism. At times he was represented as a merciless, inexorable, capricious master, who would tolerate neither intelligence nor independence in his subordinates, who were required to be the subservient agents of his will. Again, he was declared an imbecile puppet in the hands of Mr. Benjamin, who, with an amazing protean adaptability, assumed the character of Richelieu, Mazarin, Wolsey, or Jeffreys, as might meet the convenience of the censors. At all times, however, the public was urged to believe Mr. Davis was engaged in devising rewards for unworthy favorites, who, while obsequious to his whims, insolent in the enjoyment of his bounty, and secure under the executive ægis, were surely carrying the cause to perdition.

This allegation of favoritism was assumed to have a conspicuous illustration in the case of Mr. Benjamin, for whom the President retained his partiality even after he had been censured by Congress, and when his unpopularity was not to be concealed. The same motive was affirmed, however, in the selection of his other advisers; and to obviate the necessity of detail hereafter, we will dispose of this subject at once.

Despite the persistent assertion to the contrary, the fact is indisputable, that, in the selection of no single member of his cabinet, did Jefferson Davis make use of the opportunity to reward either a friend or a partisan. In no case did personal favor even remotely influence his choice, save in the appointment of Mr. Seddon as Secretary of War—an appointment made with the universal acclaim of the public and the newspapers. James A. Seddon and Jefferson Davis were, indeed, friends of twenty years' standing; but, besides, Mr. Seddon was recommended not more by the confidence of the President, than by the unlimited confidence of the country in his intellect, integrity, and patriotism.

Personal details are frequently not to be denied an important historical bearing, and the motives of Mr. Davis, in the choice of his cabinet, claim no insignificant page in his official history. We have briefly adverted elsewhere to some of these considerations.

When the Confederate cabinet was organized at Montgomery, Robert Toombs was placed at its head; yet between Davis and Toombs there had not been close intimacy, hardly mutual confidence—certainly nothing like ardent friendship. But Mr. Toombs represented an overwhelming majority of the people of Georgia, the wealthiest and largest State of the Confederacy at that period, as determined at their last election. He was peculiarly the representative public man of Georgia; the most prominent citizen of his State, repeatedly selected for its highest honors, and then a reputed statesman. When Mr. Toombs resigned, his successor was Mr. Hunter, who had served with Mr. Davis in the Senate, and in whose qualifications the President had confidence. They had both been friends of Mr. Calhoun, and disciples of his political school.

Political accord by no means signifies personal intimacy, and while Mr. Hunter has many admirers, and was greatly respected in Virginia and in the Senate, he has not been generally accredited with marked sympathetic tendencies.

Mr. Benjamin was originally made Attorney-General, because of his high legal reputation, and because Louisiana was entitled to a representative in the cabinet, but not because of personal considerations, since his relations with Mr. Davis were neither intimate nor cordial. The partiality of the President for Mr. Benjamin was, indeed, an after-thought—the result of observation of his wonderful mental resources, his unequal capacity for labor and zealous devotion to the cause.

Mr. Mallory was recommended for the Navy Department by his previous experience. There had been mutual kind feeling between himself and Mr. Davis as Senators, but nothing like close association. Mr. Davis had never seen Mr. Walker until he was appointed Secretary of War, in accordance with the emphatic choice of Alabama. General Randolph was appointed solely in consequence of Mr. Davis' convictions of his fitness. Previous to the war General Randolph was undistinguished, save in Virginia, where his fine capacity and exalted worth were becomingly appreciated. General Breckinridge, the last Confederate Secretary of War, was sufficiently recommended by his talents and position. Mr. Memminger was made Secretary of the Treasury, not as the friend of Mr. Davis, but as the choice of South Carolina. With Mr. Trenholm, his successor, the President had no personal acquaintance, until he became a member of the cabinet. Mr. Davis, the last Attorney-General, was originally neither a personal friend nor a party associate of the President; nor was Mr. Watts, his predecessor.

With the favorable response of Congress and the people to the vigorous and timely suggestions of the President, began a more spirited prosecution of the war, though the season of peril was not yet tided over, nor the current of adversity exhausted. Already there were numerous indications of the increased scale, and enlarged theatre of operations, which the war now demanded.

At the conclusion of active operations in the Trans-Mississippi district, in the autumn of 1861, the State forces of Missouri, still retaining their separate organization, under General Price, and the Confederate forces of McCulloch, were located south of Springfield, near the Arkansas line. An unfortunate phase of the Southern conduct of the war in this quarter, and one from which arose no little apprehension, was the apparently irreconcilable difference between Generals Price and McCulloch. With a view to secure the indispensable element of harmony, President Davis, during the winter, appointed Major-General Earl Van Dorn, an able and gallant officer, to the supreme command of military operations in the Trans-Mississippi department. General Van Dorn was a favorite with the President, and his services had already been of a character to justify the high expectations, indulged not less by himself than by the public, of fortunate results of the unanimity, at last secured in a quarter where its absence had been severely felt.

The result of the enemy's movements, begun early in January, 1862, was the retreat of the weak column of Price to the Boston Mountains, in Arkansas, where McCulloch was encamped. This junction of the two commands did not result in coöperation until the arrival of General Van Dorn, early in March. With a vigor characteristic of this officer's career,

Van Dorn advanced against the enemy, advantageously posted, and with numbers superior to his own force. The result was the battle of Elk Horn, a brilliant but fruitless engagement, in which the Southern commander, in consequence of the want of discipline among his soldiers, and partially through the effects of those earlier dissensions with which he had no connection, failed to realize the ends at which he aimed.*

Elk Horn was probably the most considerable engagement, in point of the numbers engaged, fought during the war, west of the Mississippi. Unimportant in its bearing upon the general character of the war, it was a decided check upon the aspiration of the Confederate Government to recover Missouri, and to give its authority a solid establishment in the Trans-Mississippi region. This was afterward the least important theatre of the war, though subsequent events there were by no means unworthy of record. Even at this early stage, the war was rapidly tending to a concentration of the energies of both parties, upon the more vital points of conflict in Virginia, and the central zone of the Confederacy. A few weeks later Generals Van Dorn and Price, with the major portion of the Trans-Mississippi army, were transferred to the scene of operations east of the great river.

General Albert Sidney Johnston, after his retreat from Nashville, consequent upon the fall of Fort Donelson, paused at Murfreesboro', Tennessee, for a sufficient period to receive accessions to his force, which increased it to the neighborhood of twenty thousand men. These accessions were portions of the command lately operating in South-eastern Kentucky, and remnants of the forces lately defending Fort Donelson. Gen-

* In this engagement General Benjamin McCulloch, of Texan fame, a brave and efficient soldier, was killed.

eral Beauregard, having evacuated Columbus, which, in common with the other posts of the former Confederate line of defense in Kentucky and Tennessee, became untenable with the loss of the Tennessee and Cumberland Rivers, concentrated his forces at Corinth, in the northern part of Mississippi.

The evacuation of Columbus did not necessarily give the enemy control of the Mississippi above Memphis. A strong position was taken by the Confederate forces at Island No. 10, forty-five miles below Columbus. Considerable anticipation was indulged by the Southern public, of a successful stand at this point for the control of the Mississippi. It was, however, captured by the enemy; and in the loss of two thousand men and important material of war by its surrender, the Confederacy sustained another severe blow, and the Federal Secretary of the Navy justly congratulated the North, upon a "triumph not the less appreciated because it was protracted and finally bloodless."

The retirement of the forces of General Albert Sidney Johnston south of the Tennessee River, and the location of General Beauregard's command at Corinth, readily suggested the practicability of a coöperation, by those two commanders, for the defense of the valley of the Mississippi, and the extensive railroad system, of which Corinth is the centre. With the approbation of President Davis, a concentration of troops, from various quarters, ensued, and, about the first of April, an admirable army of forty thousand men was assembled in the neighborhood of Corinth, and upon the railroads leading to that point. There was no situation during the war more assuring of good fortune to the Confederates, than that presented in Northern Mississippi in the early days of April, 1862. President Davis indulged the highest anticipations from this grand combination of forces which he so cordially approved. He confidently expected a victory from the Western army, led by that officer whose capacity he trusted above all others, which should more than compensate for the heavy losses of the previous campaign. General Johnston was no less hopeful of the situation. The conjuncture was indeed rare in its opportunities. The exposed situation of General Grant, whose command lay upon the west bank of the Tennessee River, with a most remarkable want of appreciation of its precarious position by its commander, and a total absence of provision for its safety, invited an immediate attack by the Confederate commander, before the Federal column could be reinforced by Buell, then making rapid marches from Nashville.

The incidents of the battle of Shiloh are familiar to the world. It constitutes, perhaps, the most melancholy of that series of "lost opportunities" in the Confederate conduct of the war, upon which history will dwell with sad interest. The first day's victory promised fruits the most brilliant and enduring. The action of the second day can only be construed as a Confederate disaster. Such was the sentiment of the South, and such must be the verdict of history.

Shiloh was, perhaps, the sorest disappointment experienced by the South, until the loss of Vicksburg, and the defeat of Gettysburg threatened the approaching climacteric of the Confederacy. The public grief at the death of General Johnston was tinged with remorse, for the unmerited censure with which the popular voice, encouraged by the press, had previously assailed him. Not until his death did the South appreciate the worth of this great soldier. Never, perhaps, had there been a more sublime instance of self-abnegation than was displayed by Sidney Johnston.

All through the autumn and winter of 1861 he had maintained his perilous position in Kentucky, confronted by forces quadruple his own, and yet assailed by an impatient and ignorant public, for not essaying invasion, with a force which subsequent events proved inadequate for defense. But not even the hideous array of facts following the reverses of February secured his vindication; still he was assailed by an unreasoning public, instigated by a carping, partisan press. He was ridiculed as incompetent—as one who had traversed the curriculum of West Point, only to become educated in the frippery of military etiquette. For the first time, President Davis was charged with a desire to reward favorites, even at the risk of the public welfare, as illustrated by his retention in high command, of one whom actual trial had proven incapable, and undeserving of his previous reputation.

But President Davis, happily for his own fame, not less than for the fame of this illustrious victim of popular clamor, was unmoved by the censures of the public, and the invectives of the newspapers. He did not permit the confidence which, upon deliberate judgment, and upon a long and intimate acquaintance, he had reposed in General Johnston, to be shaken, and sternly repelled the clamor against him, as he afterwards did in the case of Lee, and even of Stonewall Jackson. His habitual reply to importunate petitions for the removal of Johnston was: "If Sidney Johnston is incompetent to command an army, then the Confederacy has no general fit for that position."

Humanity rejoices in no attribute more noble than the capacity for warm and enduring friendship; and there is nothing more exalted in the character of Jefferson Davis than his devotion to his friends. At all times as true as steel to those for whom he professes attachment, he knows no cold medium, cherishes no feeling of indifference, but his nature kindles responsively to the warmth in the bosom of others. A like enthusiasm towards himself has usually been the reward of his heroic constancy. In Sidney Johnston there was that touching union of chivalric generosity and tender sympathy, which peculiarly qualified him for fellowship with Jefferson Davis. Such friendship, as that which united them, rises to the sublimity of the noblest virtue, and presents a spectacle honorable to human nature.

President Davis commemorated the death of General Johnston in a communication to Congress, and in terms of touching and appropriate feeling. Said he:

"But an all-wise Creator has been pleased, while vouchsafing to us His countenance in battle, to afflict us with a severe dispensation, to which we must bow in humble submission. The last, long, lingering hope has disappeared, and it is but too true that General Albert Sidney Johnston is no more. My long and close friendship with this departed chieftain and patriot forbid me to trust myself in giving vent to the feelings, which this intelligence has evoked. Without doing injustice to the living, it may safely be said that our loss is irreparable. Among the shining hosts of the great and good who now cluster around the banner of our country, there exists no purer spirit, no more heroic soul, than that of the illustrious man whose death I join you in lamenting. In his death he has illustrated the character for which, through life, he was conspicuous—that of singleness of purpose and devotion to duty with his whole energies. Bent on obtaining the victory which he deemed essential to his country's cause, he rode on to the accomplishment of his object, forgetful of self, while his very life-blood was fast ebbing away. His last breath cheered his comrades on to victory. The last sound he heard was their shout of victory. His last thought was his country, and long and deeply will his country mourn his loss."

The battle of Shiloh was an incident of the war justifying more than a passing notice. Never since Manassas, and never upon any subsequent occasion, had the Confederacy an opportunity so abundant in promise. The utmost exertions of the Government had been employed to make the Western army competent for the great enterprise proposed by its commander. The situation of Grant's army absolutely courted the tremendous blow with which Johnston sought its destruction, a result which, in all human calculation, he would have achieved had his life been spared. At the moment of his death a peerless victory was already won; the heavy masses of Grant were swept from their positions; before nightfall his last reserve had been broken, and his army lay, a cowering, shrunken, defeated rabble, upon the banks of the Tennessee. That, at such a moment, the army should have been recalled from pursuit, especially when it was known that a powerful reinforcement, ample to enable the enemy to restore his fortunes, was hastening, by forced marches, to the scene, must ever remain a source of profound amazement.

It was the story of Manassas repeated, but with a far more mournful significance. It was not the failure to gather the fruits of the most complete victory of the war, nor the irreparable loss of Sidney Johnston, which filled the cup of the public sorrow. Superadded to these was the alarming discovery that the second great army of the Confederacy, in the death of its commander, was deprived of the genius which alone had been proven capable of its successful direction. Johnston had no worthy successor, and the Western army discovered no leader capable of conducting it to the goal which its splendid valor deserved.

A very perceptible diminution of what had hitherto been unlimited confidence, not only in the genius, but even in the good fortune of Beauregard, was the result of his declared failure at Shiloh. Not even his distinguished services, subsequently, were sufficient to entirely efface that unfortunate record. Military blunders, perhaps the most excusable of human errors, are those which popular criticism is the least disposed to extenuate. The reputation of the soldier, so sacred to himself, and which should be so jealously guarded by his country, is often mercilessly mutilated by that public, upon whose gratitude and indulgence he should have an unlimited demand. We shall not undertake to establish the justice of the public verdict, which has been unanimous, that the course of General Beauregard involved, at least, an "extraordinary abandonment of a great victory." It only remains to state the material from which a candid and intelligent estimate is to be reached.

General Beauregard has explained his course, in terms which, it is to be presumed, were at least satisfactory to himself. His official report says: "Darkness was close at hand; officers and men were exhausted by a combat of over twelve hours without food, and jaded by the march of the preceding day through mud and water."

General Bragg, who conspicuously shared the laurels of the first day's action, has recorded a memorable protest against the course adopted at its close. Says General Bragg. . . . "It was now probably past four o'clock, the descending sun warning us to press our advantage and finish the work before night should compel us to desist. Fairly in motion, these commands again, with a common head and a common purpose, swept all before them. Neither battery nor battalion could withstand their onslaught. Passing through camp after camp, rich in military spoils of every kind, the enemy was driven headlong from every position, and thrown in confused masses upon the river bank, behind his heavy artillery, and under cover of his gunboats at the landing. He had left nearly the whole of his light artillery in our hands." . . . . . *The enemy had fallen back in much confusion, and was crowded, in unorganized masses, upon the river bank, vainly striving to cross.* They were covered by a battery of heavy guns, well served, and their two gunboats, now poured a heavy fire upon our supposed position, for we were entirely hid by the forest. *Their fire, though terrific in sound, and producing some consternation at first, did us no damage, as the shells all passed over, and exploded far beyond our position.* . . . . The sun was about disappearing, so that little time was left us to finish the glorious work of the day. . . . . Our troops, greatly exhausted by twelve hours' incessant fighting, without food, *mostly responded to the order with alacrity, and the movement commenced with every prospect of success.* . . . . . *Just at this time, an order was received from the commanding general to withdraw the forces beyond the enemy's fire.*

The testimony of General Polk, also a distinguished participant in the battle, was concurrent with that of General Bragg, and no less emphatic in its suggestions. In his report is to be found the following passage:

"The troops under my command were joined by those of Generals Bragg and Breckinridge, and my fourth brigade, under General Cheatham, from the right. The field was clear. The rest of the forces of the enemy were driven to the river and under its bank. We had one hour or more of daylight still left; were within from one hundred and fifty to four hundred yards of the enemy's position, and nothing seemed wanting to complete the most brilliant victory of the war, but to press forward and make a vigorous assault on the demoralized remnant of his forces.

"At this juncture his gunboats dropped down the river, near the landing, where his troops were collected, and opened a tremendous cannonade of shot and shell over the bank, in the direction from which our forces were approaching. The height of the plain on which we were, above the level of the water, was about one hundred feet, so that it was necessary to give great elevation to his guns, to enable him to fire over the bank. The consequence was that shot could take effect only at points remote from the river's edge. They were comparatively harmless to our troops nearest the bank, and became increasingly so to us as we drew near the enemy and placed him between us and his boats.

"Here the impression arose that our forces were waging an unequal contest—that they were exhausted, and suffering from a murderous fire, and by an order from the commanding general they were withdrawn from the field."

President Davis could only share the universal dissatisfaction with the unfortunate termination of the battle of Shiloh. A conclusive evidence of his forbearance and justice is seen in the fact, that he did not avail himself of the opportunity to displace an officer, toward whom he was charged with entertaining such bitter and implacable animosity, when public sentiment would, in all probability, have approved the expediency of that step. But General Beauregard was in no danger of mean resentment from President Davis, who so frequently braved the anger of the public against its distinguished serv-

25

ants. General Beauregard retained the control of the Western army, without interference from the executive, and within a few weeks, by the successful execution of his admirable retreat from Corinth, which he justly declared "equivalent to a brilliant victory," did much to repair his damaged reputation.* So eminent, in its perfection and success, was the

* When General Beauregard had eluded Halleck at Corinth, and brought his army to Tupelo, he turned over the command to General Bragg, and sought repose and recuperation at Bladon Springs, Alabama. Those who assume to be the friends and admirers of General Beauregard, but who are far more anxious to establish a mean malignity in the character of Mr. Davis, than to exalt their favorite, have laid great stress upon the fact, that the President then placed Bragg in command of the army for the ensuing campaign, thus placing Beauregard in retirement. There can be little difficulty in comprehending the commendable motives which prompted Mr. Davis to this course. The period of General Beauregard's absence from his command (three weeks, it is understood) would protract the period of inactivity until midsummer. Time was precious. The Western army had done nothing but lose ground all the current year, and, meanwhile, Lee was preparing his part of the operations, by which the Government hoped to throw the enemy back upon the frontier. Was, then, the Western army to lie idle, awaiting the disposition and convenience of one man? With the approval of the army and the country, the President appointed to the vacated command, an able and devoted soldier, whose reputation and service justified the trust. The writer has seen nothing from General Beauregard approving the assaults of his pretended admirers upon Mr. Davis, and it is not unreasonable to suppose that he does not indorse them.

It is also urged that Mr. Davis, when pressed to remove Bragg and replace Beauregard, declared that he would not, though the whole world should unite in the petition. Very likely, and altogether proper that he should not remove an officer while in the actual execution of his plans of campaign. But there can be no better explanation than that given by Mr. Davis: "The President remarked, that so far as giving Beauregard

retreat of Beauregard with his little army from the front of Halleck, who had more than one hundred thousand men, that a portion of the Northern press admitted that while Shiloh made Grant ridiculous, Corinth made a corpse of Halleck's military reputation.

As yet there had been no compensating advantage gained by the Confederacy to repair the disasters sustained in the early part of the year. Indeed, the train of reverses had hardly been more than temporarily interrupted, when a calamity hardly less serions than the loss of Tennessee happened in the loss of New Orleans, the largest, most populous, and most wealthy city of the Confederacy. This event was speedily followed by the calamitous results which were to be expected. It was the virtual destruction of Confederate rule in Louisiana. It cut off the available routes to Texas, so inestimable in its impor-

command of Bragg's army is concerned, that was out of the question. *Bragg had arranged all his plans*, and had co-intelligence with the Department, with Kirby Smith, and Humphrey Marshall; and *to put a new commander at the head of the army would be so prejudicial to the public interests, he would not do it if the whole world united in the petition.*"

But President Davis never designed that General Beauregard should be without a command. With that just appreciation of the real merits of his generals, apart from the cheap applause or unmerited censure of the crowd, which distinguished most of his selections, he placed General Beauregard in charge of the coast defenses, where his reputation was certainly múch enhanced. In this oft-repeated and unfounded charge of "injustice" and "persecution," in the case of General Joseph E. Johnston, as in that of General Beauregard, there is no specification, more awkwardly sustained, than that which denies the abundant opportunity enjoyed by each of those officers, for the display of the superior genius asserted for them by their admirers. The slightest acquaintance with the history of the war will verify this statement.

tance as a source of grain and cattle; gave the enemy a base of operations against the entire gulf region, and was altogether disheartening to the South.*

Some time previous to the fall of New Orleans, which occurred in the latter days of April, the Confederacy had made its most serious effort to dispute the hitherto absolute naval supremacy of the North. On the 8th of March, 1862, occurred the famous naval engagement in Hampton Roads, between the Confederate iron-clad Virginia, and the Federal Monitor. Ever since the summer of 1861, the Navy Department had been preparing, at Gosport Navy-yard, a formidable naval contrivance—a shot-proof, iron-plated steam battery. The result of the experiment was a success, which did much to relieve the Navy Department of undeserved reproach, and to produce a revolution in theories relating to naval science and architecture all over the world.

About this period the activity of the naval forces of the enemy was rewarded by additional successes. The towns of

* Much crimination and recrimination followed the fall of New Orleans. It is, at least, safe to say, that public opinion in the South was much divided, as to where the burden of censure for this dire and unexpected calamity should properly rest. The intelligence of the capture of the city was an appalling surprise, not only to the public in Richmond, but to the Government. President Davis declared that the event was totally unexpected by him. The fall of New Orleans was one of those instances, in which the Confederates had decided for them, in a most unsatisfactory manner, the long disputed question as to the efficiency of shore batteries against vessels of war. Precedents established, when sailing vessels were used in warfare, were overthrown by the experience of steam vessels, especially when iron-plated. Commodore Farragut, with perfect success and comparative ease, passed the forts below New Orleans, after the chief of the naval force had despaired of their reduction.

Newbern, Washington, and other places of less note in North Carolina, were captured by naval expeditions in conjunction with detachments from the army of General Burnside. The successes of the Burnside expedition, which had been prepared by the North with such large expectations, were by no means inconsiderable; but they were soon lost sight of in the presence of the more absorbing operations in the interior. The naval resistance of the South had thus far necessarily been feeble. In the subsequent progress of the war, except in rare instances, it disappeared altogether as an element in the calculation of means of defense.

The vulnerability of the South upon the sea-coast, and along the lines of her navigable rivers, measured the extent of the good fortune of the enemy. The North was shortly to yield a reluctant recognition of the comparatively insignificant influence of its long train of triumphs in the promotion of subjugation. Upon the soil of Virginia—classic in its memories of contests for freedom, the chosen battle-ground of the Confederacy—was soon to be shed the effulgence of the proudest achievements of Southern genius and valor—a radiance as splendid as ever shone upon the blazing crest of war.

CHAPTER XIII.

THE "ANACONDA SYSTEM"—HOW FAR IT WAS SUCCESSFUL—TERRITORIAL CONFIGURATION OF THE SOUTH FAVORABLE TO THE ENEMY—ONE THEATRE OF WAR FAVORABLE TO THE CONFEDERATES—THE FEDERAL FORCES IN VIRGINIA—THE CONFEDERATE FORCES—THE POTOMAC LINES—CRITICAL SITUATION IN VIRGINIA—EVACUATION OF MANASSAS—TRANSFER OF OPERATIONS TO THE PENINSULA—MAGRUDER'S LINES—EVACUATION OF YORKTOWN—STRENGTH OF THE OPPOSING FORCES BEFORE RICHMOND—DESTRUCTION OF THE "VIRGINIA"—PANIC IN RICHMOND—MR. DAVIS' CALMNESS AND CONFIDENCE—HE AVOWS HIMSELF "READY TO LEAVE HIS BONES IN THE CAPITAL OF THE CONFEDERACY"—REPULSE OF THE GUNBOATS—"MEMENTOES OF HEROISM"—JACKSON'S VALLEY CAMPAIGN—A SERIES OF VICTORIES, WITH IMPORTANT RESULTS—BATTLE OF "SEVEN PINES"—A FAILURE—GENERAL JOHNSTON WOUNDED—PRESIDENT DAVIS ON THE FIELD—PRESIDENT DAVIS AND GENERAL JOHNSTON—AN ATTEMPT TO FORESTALL THE DECISION OF HISTORY—RESULTS OF LEE'S ACCESSION TO COMMAND—JOHNSTON'S GENERALSHIP—MR. DAVIS' ESTIMATE OF LEE—LEE'S PLANS—THE ADVISORY RELATION BETWEEN DAVIS AND LEE—THEIR MUTUAL CONFIDENCE NEVER INTERRUPTED—CONFEDERATE STRATEGY AFTER M'CLELLAN'S DEFEAT BEFORE RICHMOND—MAGICAL CHANGE IN THE FORTUNES OF THE CONFEDERACY—THE INVASION OF MARYLAND—ANTIETAM—TANGIBLE PROOFS OF CONFEDERATE SUCCESS—GENERAL BRAGG—HIS KENTUCKY CAMPAIGN—CONFEDERATE HOPES—BATTLE OF PERRYVILLE—BRAGG RETREATS—ESTIMATE OF THE KENTUCKY CAMPAIGN OF 1862—OTHER INCIDENTS OF THE WESTERN CAMPAIGN—REMOVAL OF M'CLELLAN—A SOUTHERN OPINION OF M'CLELLAN—BATTLE OF FREDERICKSBURG—BATTLE OF MURFREESBORO'—BATTLE OF PRAIRIE GROVE—THE SITUATION AT THE CLOSE OF 1862—PRESIDENT DAVIS' RECOMMENDATIONS TO CONGRESS—HIS VISIT TO THE SOUTH-WEST—ADDRESS BEFORE THE MISSISSIPPI LEGISLATURE.

THE Federal Government frankly accepted the true teachings of the war in its earlier stages, and no feature of the lesson was more palpable than the inferiority of the North in the art of war and military administration. No longer trusting, to any extent whatever, to a contest of prowess with an enemy whose incomparable superiority was already established, Mr. Lincoln, his cabinet, and his military advisers, were concurrent in their convictions of the necessity of a policy which should make available the numerical superiority of the North. The "anaconda system" of General Scott, adhered to by General McClellan, and sanctioned by the Government and the people, though by no means new in the theory and practice of war, was based upon a just and sagacious view of the situation.

To overwhelm the South by mere material weight, to crush the smaller body by the momentum of a larger force, comprehends the Federal design of the war, undertaken at the inception of operations in 1862. The success attending the execution of this design we have described in preceding pages. We have accredited to the enemy the full extent of his successes, and endeavored to demonstrate that they resulted not from Confederate maladministration, but from a vigorous and timely use of his advantages and opportunity by the enemy. But while according to the North unexampled energy in preparation, and an unstinted donation of its means to the purpose, which it pursued with indomitable resolution, no concession of an improved military capacity is demanded, from the fact that use was made of obvious advantages not to be overlooked even by the stupidity of an Aulic council.

We have shown that the preponderating influence in the achievement of the enemy's victories in the winter and spring of 1862, was his naval supremacy. Even at that period it was palpable that, without his navy, his scheme of invasion would be the veriest abortion ever exposed to the ridicule of mankind. The maritime facilities of the enemy were, in the end, decisive of the contest in his favor.

Upon those fields of military operations which have thus far occupied our attention, we have seen how propitious to the enemy's plans, in every instance, was the geographical configuration. Wherever a navigable river emptied into the sea, which was the undisputed domain of the North, or intersected its territory, a short and, in many instances, almost bloodless struggle had ended in the expulsion or capture of the Confederates defending its passage. Yet, in many instances, these results had a most serious bearing upon the decision of the war. It was impossible for Sidney Johnston to hold Kentucky and Tennessee unless the Mississippi, running parallel with his communications, and the Cumberland and Tennessee, running in their rear, should remain sealed to the enemy. It was equally impracticable to hold the region bordering upon the North Carolina sounds after the fall of Roanoke Island. After the fall of New Orleans, the entire avenue of the Mississippi, except the limited section between Vicksburg and Port Hudson, was open to the enemy, giving him bases of operations upon both its banks, and opening to his ravages vast sections of the Confederacy.

Thus had the naval supremacy of the enemy brought him, in a few days, to the very heart of extensive sections of territory, which never could have been reduced to his sway, had he been compelled to fight his way overland from his frontiers. Thus was the great element of *space*, usually so potent in the defense of an invaded people, annihilated, almost before the struggle had been fairly begun.

The upper regions of Eastern Virginia, remote from the

navigable tributaries of the Atlantic and the larger rivers, was the only theatre of war, where the superior valor and skill of the Confederates could claim success from the Federal hosts, deprived of their gunboats and water communications. Here, though not entirely neutralized, his water facilities did not at all times avail the enemy; here the struggle was more equal, and here was demonstrated that superior manhood and soldiership of the South, which, not even an enemy, if candid, will deny.

Of the seven hundred thousand men, which were claimed as under arms for the preservation of the Union, in the beginning of 1862, it is reasonably certain that more than a half million were actually in the field, and of these at least one-half, were operating in Virginia, with Richmond as the common goal of their eager and expectant gaze. The army of McClellan, numbering little less than two hundred thousand men, in the vicinity of Washington, was entitled to the lavish praise, which he bestowed upon it, in his declaration, that it was "magnificent in material, admirable in discipline and instruction, excellently equipped and armed." In the valley of the Shenondoah was the army of Banks, more than fifteen thousand strong. General Fremont, with about the same force, commanded the "Mountain Department," embracing the highland region of Western Virginia. By the first of March these various commands, with other detachments, had reached an aggregate of quite two hundred and fifty thousand men.

We have sufficiently described those causes, by which the already disproportionate strength of the Confederates, previous to the adoption of the conscription act, and the inception of the more vigorous and stringent military policy of the Confederate Government, was reduced to a condition in most alarming contrast with the enormous preparations of the enemy.

General Joseph E. Johnston still held his position, with a force which, on the first of March, barely exceeded forty thousand men. The command of General Stonewall Jackson, in the Shenandoah Valley, did not exceed thirty-five hundred, embracing all arms. General Magruder held the Peninsula of York and James Rivers, covering the approaches to Richmond in that direction, with eleven thousand men, and General Huger had at Norfolk and in the vicinity not more than ten thousand. The Confederate force in Western Virginia was altogether too feeble for successful defense, and indeed, the Government had some months previous abandoned the hope of a permanent occupation of that region.

The Confederate authorities had long since ceased to cherish hope of offensive movements upon the line of the Potomac. Circumstances imposed a defensive attitude, attended with many causes of peculiar apprehension for the fate of the issue in Virginia. Weeks of critical suspense, and vigilant observation of the threatening movements of the Federal forces, were followed by the transfer of the principal scene of operations to the Peninsula.

The evacuation of the position so long held by General Johnston at Manassas, executed with many evidences of skill, but attended with much destruction of valuable material, was followed immediately by an advance of General McClellan to that place. The necessity of a retirement by General Johnston to an interior line had been duly appreciated by the Confederate Government, though there were circumstances attending the immediate execution of the movement, which detracted from its otherwise complete success. The destruction of valuable material, including an extensive meat-curing establishment, containing large supplies of meat, and established by the Government, which ensued upon the evacuation of Manassas, elicited much exasperated censure. Similar occurrences at the evacuation of Yorktown, a few weeks later, revived a most unpleasant recollection of scenes incident to the retreat from Manassas. The extravagant destruction of property, in many instances apparently reckless and wanton, marking the movements of the Confederate armies at this period, was a bitter sarcasm upon the practice, by many of its prominent officers, of that economy of resources which the necessities of the Confederacy so imperatively demanded.

Not only the weakness of his forces indicated to General Johnston the perils of his position, but the territorial configuration again came to the aid of the enemy, and gave to General McClellan the option of several avenues to the rear of the Confederate army. It is not improbable that McClellan appreciated the extremity of Johnston's situation, and has, indeed, assigned other reasons for his advance upon Manassas than the expectation of an engagement, where the chances would have been overwhelmingly in his favor. At all events, the retirement of General Johnston to the line of the Rapidan, imposed upon the Federal general an immediate choice of a base from which to assail the Confederate capital. Originally opposed to an overland movement *via* Manassas, McClellan was now compelled to abandon his favorite plan of a movement from Urbanna, on the Rappahanock, by which he hoped to cut off the Confederate retreat to Richmond, in consequence of Johnston's retirement behind the Rappahanock. General McClellan promptly adopted the movement to the peninsula, a plan which he had previously considered, but which he regarded "as less brilliant and less promising decisive results." *

When General Johnston left Manassas, it is probable that he was not fully decided as to the position which he should select. Receiving a dispatch † from President Davis, he halted the army, and immediately the President left Richmond for Johnston's head-quarters, for the purpose of consultation. General Johnston's position now was simply observatory of the enemy. It was yet possible that McClellan might undertake an overland movement; and, indeed, a portion of his force had followed the retreating Confederates. In that event Johnston would occupy the line upon which Lee subsequently foiled so many formidable Federal demonstrations. From his central position he could also promptly meet a serious demonstration against Richmond from the Chesapeake waters or the Shenandoah Valley. When the numerous transports at Fortress Monroe, debarking troops for the peninsula, revealed the enemy's real purpose, the army of General Johnston was carried to the lines of Magruder, at Yorktown. Johnston was, however, decidedly opposed to the movement to the Peninsula, declaring it untenable, and urging views as to the requirements of the situation, which competent criticism has repeatedly commended.

* These revelations of the designs of McClellan are derived from the admirable work of Mr. Swinton—the "History of the Army of the Potomac"—perhaps the ablest and most impartial contribution yet made to the history of the late war.

It is noteworthy that General Grant attempted nearly the same approach to Richmond and was signally foiled—a fact which he promptly recognized, by his change of plan, after his bloody repulse at Cold Harbor, June 3, 1864.

† This dispatch was in substance: "Halt the army where it is."

While the transfer of Johnston's army to the Peninsula was in process of execution, the situation in Virginia was, in the highest degree, critical. The strength of Magruder was necessarily so divided, that the actual force, defending the line threatened by McClellan with eighty thousand men, was less than six thousand Confederates. Meanwhile the various Federal detachments in other quarters were coöperating with the main movement of McClellan. Banks and Shields were expected, by their overwhelming numbers, to crush Jackson in the Shenandoah Valley, and then, forming a junction with the large force of Fremont, who was required to capture Staunton, it was designed that these combined forces should unite with the army of McDowell, advancing from the direction of Fredericksburg, at some point east of the Blue Ridge. Thus a force, aggregating more than seventy thousand men, threatening Richmond from the north, was to unite with McClellan advancing from the east. Such was, in brief, the Federal plan of campaign, which the North expected to accomplish the reduction of Richmond and the total destruction of the Confederate power in Virginia. It does not devolve upon us to discuss, in detail, the defects of this faulty combination, but the sequel will show how promptly and triumphantly the Confederate leaders availed themselves of the opportunity presented by this crude arrangement of their adversaries.

Happily the bold attitude and skillful dispositions of Magruder were aided by the over-tentative action of his antagonist. The latter, greatly exaggerating the force in his front, and convinced of the hopelessness of an assault upon the Confederate works, permitted the escape of the golden moment, and prepared for a regular siege of Yorktown. In the meantime General Magruder describes his situation to have been as follows: "Through the energetic action of the Government, reënforcements began to pour in, and each hour the Army of the Peninsula grew stronger and stronger, until anxiety passed from my mind as to the result of an attack upon us."

The untenability of the Peninsula was very soon made apparent, and the important advantage of *time* having been gained, and the escape of General Huger's command from its precarious position at Norfolk secured, General Johnston abandoned the works at Yorktown, retreating to the line of the Chickahominy, near Richmond. This movement was made in obedience to the necessities of the situation, and was in accordance with his original desire for a decisive engagement with McClellan, at an interior point, where a concentration of the Confederate forces would be more practicable. General McClellan did not pursue the retreating column with much energy after the decisive blow given his advance at Williamsburg, by Longstreet.

With the arrival of Johnston upon the Richmond lines, the Confederate Government began, with energy and rapidity, the concentration of its forces. The superb command of Huger was promptly transferred to Johnston, and troops from the Carolinas were thrown forward to Richmond as rapidly as transportation facilities would permit. By the last of May the Confederate forces in front of Richmond reached an aggregate of seventy-five thousand men. McClellan had sustained losses on the Peninsula which reduced his strength to the neighborhood of one hundred and twenty thousand.

A cruel necessity of the evacuation of Norfolk and Portsmouth was the destruction of the Confederate iron-clad "Virginia," which had so long prevented the ascent of James River by the Federal gunboats. So invaluable was this vessel in the defense of Richmond, that McClellan had named, as an essential condition of a successful campaign on the Peninsula, that she should be "neutralized." It was found impossible to convey the Virginia to a point unoccupied on either shore of the river by the enemy's forces, and, by order of her commander, the vessel was destroyed. Immediately a fleet ascended the river for the purpose of opening the water highway to the Confederate capital.

The intelligence of the destruction of the "Virginia," and the advance of the Federal fleet, was received, in Richmond, with profound consternation. No one, unless at that time in Richmond, can realize the sense of extreme peril experienced by the public. There were few who dared indulge the hope of a successful defense of the city against the dreaded "gunboats" and "monitors" of the enemy, which, the people then believed, were alike invulnerable and irresistible.

The wise precautionary measures of the Government, in preparing its archives for removal, in case of emergency, to a point of safety, greatly increased the panic of the public. Rumors of a precipitate evacuation of the city, by the Confederate authorities, were circulated, and there was wanting no possible element which could aggravate the public alarm, save the calm demeanor of President Davis, and the deliberate efforts of the authorities—Confederate, State, and municipal—to assure the safety of the city. The courage and confidence of the President, in the midst of this almost universal alarm, in which many officers of the Government participated, quickly aroused an enthusiastic and determined spirit in the hearts of a brave people. Knowing the critical nature of the emergency, he was nevertheless resolved to exhaust every expedient in the defense of Richmond, and then to abide the issue. His noble and defiant declaration was: "I am ready and willing to leave my bones in the capital of the Confederacy." In response to resolutions from the Virginia Legislature, urging the defense of the city to the last extremity, he avowed his predetermined resolution to hold Richmond until driven out by the enemy, and animated his hearers by an assurance of his conviction, that, even in that contingency, "the war could be successfully maintained, upon Virginia soil, for twenty years."*

The accounts of the enemy were required to demonstrate to the citizens of Richmond, that, by the obstructions in the channel of the river, and the erection of the impregnable batteries at Drewry's Bluff, their homes were again secured from

*The incidents of this trying period, when Richmond was doubly threatened by the hosts of McClellan, and the gunboats in the river, are "mementoes of heroism," proudly illustrating the unconquerable spirit of that devoted city and its rulers. We give the resolution passed by the Legislature on the occasion referred to—May 14, 1862:

"*Resolved by the General Assembly*, That this General Assembly expresses its desire that the capital of the State be defended to the last extremity, if such defense is in accordance with the views of the President of the Confederate States; and that the President be assured, that whatever destruction or loss of property, of the State, or individuals shall hereby result, will be cheerfully submitted to."

Two days after, at a public meeting of the citizens of Richmond, Governor Letcher said, that under no circumstances would he approve the surrender of the city, and avowed his readiness to endure bombardment, if necessary. In the same stout spirit spoke Mayor Mayo:

"I say now—and I will abide by it—when the citizens of Richmond demand of me to surrender the capital of Virginia, and of the Confederacy, to the enemy, they must find some other man to fill my place. I will resign the mayoralty. And when that other man elected in my stead shall deliver up the city, I hope I may have physical courage and strength enough left to shoulder a musket and go into the ranks."

the presence of the invaders. The significance of that brief engagement, during which the guns were distinctly audible in Richmond, was very soon made evident in the loss of their terrors by the Federal gunboats. President Davis was a spectator of the engagement, by which the Confederate capital was rescued from imminent peril of capture.

But the repulse of the gunboats in James River, with its assuring and significant incidents, was the precursor of far more brilliant successes, which, it was evident, would largely affect the decision of the general issue in Virginia. In the months of May and June, 1862, was enacted the memorable "Valley campaign" of Stonewall Jackson—a campaign which, never excelled, has no parallel in brilliant and accurate conception, celerity, and perfection of execution, save the Italian campaign of Napoleon in 1796. General Jackson's exploits in the Valley of the Shenandoah present an aggregate of military achievements unrivaled by any record in American history.

On the 23d of March, Jackson fought the battle of Kernstown, near Winchester, with three thousand Virginians against eighteen full Federal regiments, sustaining, throughout an entire day, an audacious assault upon Shields' force, and at dark leisurely retiring with his command, after having inflicted upon the enemy a loss nearly equal to his own strength. Elsewhere has been mentioned the effort made to induce President Davis to remove Jackson, in compliance with the popular dissatisfaction at his failure to achieve, against such overwhelming odds, more palpable fruits of victory. The immediate consequence of Kernstown was the check of Banks' advance in the Valley, and the recall of a large force, then on the way from Banks to aid McClellan's designs against Johnston.

Leaving General Ewell, whose division had been detached from Johnston, to intercept any demonstration by Banks in the Valley, or across the Blue Ridge, Jackson united his command with that of General Edward Johnson, a full brigade, and defeating the advance of Fremont, under Milroy, at McDowell, compelled a disorderly retreat by Fremont through the mountains of Western Virginia. Returning to the Valley, he assaulted, with his united force, the column of Banks, annihilated an entire division of the enemy, pursued its fugitive remnants to the Potomac, and threatened the safety of the Federal capital. Alarmed for Washington, Mr. Lincoln halted McDowell in his plans of coöperation with McClellan, and for weeks the efforts of the Federal Government were addressed to the paramount purpose of "catching Jackson." Eluding the enemy's combinations, Jackson turned upon his pursuers, again defeated Fremont at Cross Keys, and immediately crossing the Shenandoah, secured his rear, and destroyed the advance of Shields within sight of its powerless confederate. Resuming the retreat, Jackson paused at Weyer's Cave, and awaited the summons of his superiors to enact his thrilling rôle in the absorbing drama at Richmond. Within the short period of seventy days, Jackson achieved at Kernstown, McDowell's, Front Royal, Winchester, Strasburg, Harrisonburg, Cross Keys, and Port Republic, eight tactical victories, besides innumerable successful combats. But he had done more. He had wrought the incomparable strategic achievement of neutralizing sixty thousand men with fifteen thousand; he had recalled McDowell, when, with outstretched arm, McClellan had already planted his right wing, under Porter, at Hanover Court-house, to receive the advance of the coöperating column from Fredericksburg.

Meanwhile the lines of Richmond had been the scene of no incident of special interest until the battle of "Seven Pines," on the 31st of May. After his arrival upon the Chickahominy, McClellan had been steadily fortifying his lines, and wherever an advance was practicable, preparing approaches to Richmond. His line, extending over a space of several miles, was accurately described by the course of the Chickahominy, from the village of Mechanicsville, five miles north of Richmond, to a point about four miles from the city, in an easterly direction. Having partially executed his design of bridging the Chickahominy, McClellan had crossed that stream, and in the last days of May, his left wing was fortified near the locality designated the "Seven Pines." This initiative demonstration by McClellan, which placed his army astride a variable stream, was sufficiently provocative of the enterprise of his antagonist. To increase the peril of the isolated wing of the Federal army, a thunder-storm, occurring on the night of the 29th of May, had so swollen the Chickahominy as to render difficult the accession of reënforcements from the main body.

Such was the situation which invited the Confederate commander to undertake the destruction of the exposed column of his adversary—a movement which, if successful, might have resulted in the rout of the entire left wing of the enemy, opening a way to his rear, and securing his utter overthrow. Seven Pines was an action, in which the color of victory was entirely with the Confederates, but it was the least fruitul engagement fought by the two armies in Virginia. There was no engagement of the war in which the valor of the Confederate soldier was more splendidly illustrated, though happily that quality then did not require so conspicuous a test. However able in design, it was in execution a signal failure—a series of loose, indefinite and disjointed movements, wanting in coöperation, and apparently in able executive management.

President Davis, in company with General Lee, was present during most of the engagement. Frequently under fire, and in consultation with his generals in exposed positions, he was conspicuous chiefly by his efforts to animate the troops, and his presence was greeted with evidences of the enthusiasm and confidence which it inspired.

The battle of "Seven Pines," in itself barren of influence upon the decision of the campaign, was nevertheless attended by an incident—the painful and disabling wound received by General Johnston, in all probability decisive of the future history of the Army of Northern Virginia. Leading to an immediate and positive change of policy, it is hardly a bold declaration that this incident determined the future of the war in Virginia.

A disposition has been freely indulged to influence the sentence of history, by placing President Davis and General Johnston in a sort of antithetical juxtaposition, as exponents of different theories as to the proper conduct of the war by the South. In view of the failure of the Confederacy, it has been ingeniously contended that the result vindicated the wisdom of General Johnston's views. But besides its evident unfairness to Mr. Davis, no criticism could be founded less upon the intrinsic merits of the case. Overzealous and intemperate partisans generally evince aptitude in the exaggeration of minor differences between the leaders, whose interests they profess to have at heart. Such results are not unfrequent in the lives of eminent public men. In the case of General Beauregard, the unhappy effects of officious intermeddling and misrepresentation, from such sources, between the President and that distinguished officer, are especially notable.

But the assumption that events have indicated the wisdom of General Johnston's views, in their declared antagonism to those of Mr. Davis, is altogether unsustained. The immediate results of a change of commanders, and a consequent inauguration of a different policy*—a policy in accordance with Mr. Davis' own views, may, with far more reason, be alleged in support of a contrary theory. The vigorous and aggressive policy adopted and executed by Lee not only accorded with the wishes of the President, but fulfilled the long-deferred popular expectation, and agreeably disappointed the public in Lee's capacity. For despite the general disappointment at the absence of decisive achievements by the Army of Northern Virginia, General Johnston commanded far more of public confidence, than did General Lee at the period of the latter's accession to command.

Nothing could have been more disadvantageous to Lee, than the contrast so freely indicated between himself and other officers. Johnston was criticised merely because of the absence of brilliant and decisive achievements. Lee was assumed to have proven his incompetency by egregious failure. He was ridiculed as a closet general. His campaigns were said to exist only on paper—to consist of slow methodical tactics, and incessant industry with the spade, and he was pronounced

* It is only fair to state that General Johnston proposed operations, similar in their main features to those of Lee, though it does not therefore follow that they would have been equally successful. Johnston's ability as a strategist can not be questioned, and to those who closely and intelligently studied his campaigns, there can be little doubt as to his aggressive qualities, though in this respect, *results* were not in his favor.

totally deficient in aggressive qualities. A prominent Richmond editor, criticising his North-western Virginia campaign, asserted that the unvarying intelligence from Lee was that he was "hopelessly stuck in the mud," and an officer was heard to compare him to a terrapin, needing the application of a hot coal to his back to compel him to action. But with the lapse of a fortnight that army, which received the intelligence of Lee's appointment to command with misgiving and distrust, began to experience renewed life and hope. It was not the few additional brigades given to that army which so soon started it upon its irresistible career of victory. A mighty hand projected its impetus, and directed its magnificent valor against those miles of intrenchments which it had seen grow more and more formidable, itself meanwhile an inactive spectator.

Lee found the army within sight of Richmond; he lifted it from the mud of the Chickahominy, defeated an enemy intrenched and in superior force; pursued the panting and disheartened fugitives to the shelter of their shipping; defeated a second army—then both together—within hearing of the Federal capital; fought an indecisive battle upon the enemy's soil, and reëstablished the Confederate line upon the frontier. Is it a matter of wonder that the President, the army, and the people recognized the significance of these results, and applauded the substitution of the new system and the new status for the old? A better explanation of so pronounced a contrast is needed than that the "prejudice" or "injustice" of Davis withheld from Johnston, five or even ten thousand men, which he gave to Lee.

Yet there could be no hypothesis more presumptuous, in view of the abundant testimony of competent military judgment, and none more palpably untenable, than that which would deny greatness as a soldier to Johnston. As a consummate master of strategy, in that sense which contemplates the movements of heavy masses, and looks to grand ultimate results, Johnston has probably few equals. His sagacity in the divination of an enemy's designs is remarkable; and if he be considered as having marked deficiencies, they must be counted as a lack of Jackson's audacity, of Lee's confident calculation and executive perfection. The South regards Lee as beyond criticism. Jefferson Davis is accustomed to say "the world has rarely produced a man to be compared with Lee." Yet in mere intellectuality, it is at least questionable whether Johnston had his superior among the Southern leaders.

But it often happens that qualities, however great, are not those which the occasion demands. That marvelous union of qualities in Lee, which has placed him almost above parallel, probably made him alone adequate to the hazardous posture of affairs at Richmond in the summer of 1862. The result, at least, made evident to the world, the wisdom of the President, in that choice, which was at first declared the undeserved reward of an incompetent favorite.

Whatever may be alleged to the contrary, President Davis at all times, to the full extent of his power, aided General Johnston in the consummation of his designs. To assert that, upon any occasion, he either interposed obstacles to Johnston's success, or denied him any means in his power to confer, is to question that personal fidelity of Jefferson Davis, which his bitterest enemy should be ashamed to deny. Few Southern men, at least, have yet attained that measure of malignity, or that hardihood of mendacity.

General Lee was not dilatory in his preparations to gratify that longing aspiration which the President, on his own behalf, and in the name of the country, briefly expressed, that "something should be done." Lee had a *carte blanche*, but frequent and anxious were the consultations between the President and himself. The world now knows what followed those days and nights of anxious conference, in which were weighed the chances of success, the cost of victory, and the possibilities of defeat. The plan executed by General Lee was one of the most hazardous ever attempted in war, but it was not less brilliant than bold, and at least one precedent had been furnished by the great master of the art of war at Austerlitz. Its perils were obvious, but the sublime confidence of Lee in the success of his combinations went far to secure its own justification.

During the week of engagements which followed, the President was constantly with the army and fully advised of its movements.* The cordial recognition of this advisory relation between himself and Lee, is indicated by the natural pride, and becoming sense of justice, with which the latter, in the report of his operations against McClellan, mentions the approving presence of the President, during the execution of

* Mr. Davis was every day upon the battle-field, and from this circumstance the impression prevailed in Richmond that he was directing the army in person. A common report, which I have never seen contradicted, was that the President narrowly escaped death during the progress of the battles. As related to the writer, the circumstance was as follows: The President, in company with General Magruder and other officers, was at a farm-house, upon which one of the Federal batteries was preparing to open. General Lee, apprised of the President's whereabouts, sent a courier to warn him of his danger, and he and his companions escaped without injury, just as the Federal battery opened fire.

his plans. This noble harmony between Davis and Lee, equally creditable to each, was never interrupted by one single moment of discord. It was never marred by dictation on one side, or complaint on the other. Unlike other commanders, Lee never complained of want of means, or of opportunity for the execution of his plans. Satisfied that the Government was extending all the aid in its power, he used, to the best advantage, the means at hand and created his opportunities. Lee never charged the President with improper interference with the army, but freely counseled with his constitutional commander-in-chief, whom he knew to be worthy of the trust conferred by the country in the control of its armies. President Davis fully comprehended and respected the jealous functions of military command, and in the exercise of that trust no one would have more quickly resented unauthorized official interference. A soldier himself, he recognized freedom of action as the privilege of the commander; as a statesman, he rendered that cordial coöperation, which is the duty of government.

When Lee had driven McClellan from his position along the Chickahominy, he had raised the siege of Richmond. The retreat of McClellan to the James River, conducted with such admirable skill, and aided by good fortune, placed the Federal army in a position where, secure itself, another offensive movement against the Confederate capital might, in time, be undertaken. Confederate strategy, however, soon relieved Richmond from the apprehension of attack, and in less than two months from the termination of the pursuit of McClellan, Lee, by a series of masterly strokes, demolished the armies under Pope, united for the defense of Washington, and was preparing an invasion of Maryland.

An almost magical change in the fortunes of the Confederacy was wrought by these active and brilliant operations, embracing so short a period, and marked by results of such magnitude.

Not only were the two main armies of the enemy defeated, but the entire Federal campaign in the East had been entirely disconcerted. Richmond was saved, Washington menaced, and McClellan forced back to the initial point of his campaign. Western Virginia, the Carolina coast, and other localities, for months past in Federal occupation, were almost divested of troops to swell the hosts gathering for the rescue of Washington, and to meet the dreaded advance, northward, of Lee's invincible columns. From the heart of Virginia the cloud of war was again lifted to the Potomac frontier; the munificent harvests of the valley counties, of Fauquier, Loudon, and the fertile contiguous territory, were again in Confederate possession, and a numerous and victorious army was now anxious to be led across the Rubicon of the warring sections.

From harrowing apprehension, from vague dread of indefinable but imminent peril, the South was transported to the highest round of confident expectation. The North, which, in the last days of June, eagerly awaited intelligence of McClellan's capture of Richmond, now regarded its own capital as doomed, and did not permit itself to breathe freely until McClellan announced the *safety of Pennsylvania,* when Lee had retired to Virginia.

The inducements which invited a movement of the Confederate forces across the Potomac were manifold. Whatever judgment the result may now suggest, the invasion of Maryland was alike dictated by sound military policy and justified by those moral considerations which are ever weighty in war. The overwhelming defeat of Pope more than realized the hope of President Davis and General Lee, when the strategic design of a movement northward was put in execution, by which was sought the double purpose of withdrawing McClellan from James River and effectually checking the advance of Pope. The successive and decisive defeats of Pope offered the prospect of an offensive by which the splendid successes of the campaign might be crowned with even more valuable achievements. Demoralized, disheartened, in every way disqualified for effectual resistance, the remnants of the armies which Lee had beaten, each in succession, and then combined, would be an easy prey to his victorious legions, could they be brought to a decisive field engagement. There yet remained time, before the end of the season of active operations, for crushing blows at the enemy, which would finish the work thus far triumphantly successful.

To inflict still greater damage upon the enemy—to so occupy him upon the frontier as to prevent another demonstration against Richmond during the present year—to indicate friendship and sympathy for the oppressed people of Maryland—to derive such aid from them as their condition would enable them to extend, were the potent inducements inviting the approbation of the Confederate authorities to a movement across the Potomac. President Davis was pledged to an invasion of the enemy's country whenever it should prove practicable. Now, if ever, that policy was to be initiated. Hitherto the enemy's power, not the will of the Confederate Government, had prevented. Now that power was shattered. The mighty fabric trembled to its base, and who would now venture to estimate the consequences of a brilliant victory by Lee, on Maryland soil, in September, 1862? What supporter of the Union can now dwell, without a shudder, upon the imagination, even, of a repetition, at Antietam, of the story of the Chickahominy, or Second Manassas?

The climax of the Maryland campaign was the battle of Antietam—a drawn battle, but followed by the early withdrawal of the Confederate army into Virginia. It is unnecessary to dwell upon the causes conspiring to give this portion of the campaign many of the features of failure. With a force greatly reduced by the straggling of his weary and exhausted troops, Lee was unable to administer the crushing blow which he had hoped to deliver.* As a consequence, the people of Maryland, of whom a large majority were thoroughly patriotic and warm in their Southern sympathies, were not encouraged to make that effective demonstration which would inevitably have followed a defeat of McClellan.

Nevertheless, there was some compensation in the terrible punishment inflicted upon the enemy at Antietam; and there was the heightened prestige, so greatly valued by the South at this period, in the eyes of Europe, arising from the temper and capacity of the weaker combatant to undertake so bold an enterprise. In the tangible evidences of success afforded by the capture of Harper's Ferry, with its numerous garrison supplies of arms and military stores, was seen additional compensation for the abandonment of the scheme of invasion.

* A serious disadvantage suffered by General Lee was the capture of his plan of battle by General McClellan. Completely informed as to his adversary's movements, and with ninety thousand men against thirty-three thousand, the wonder is, that McClellan did not overwhelm the Confederate army. The means by which the enemy obtained this important paper was a subject of much gossip in the Confederacy.

An interval of repose was permitted the Army of Northern Virginia, after its return from Maryland, in its encampments near Winchester, during which it was actively strengthened and recruited to the point of adequate preparation for expected demonstrations of the enemy.

The operations of the Western army, in many respects, were a brilliant counterpart to the campaign in Virginia, though lacking its brilliant fruits. We have mentioned the circumstance which placed General Braxton Bragg in command of the Western army, after its successful evacuation of Corinth. General Bragg was equally high in the confidence of the President and the Southern people. Greatly distinguished by his services in Mexico, his skillful handling, at Shiloh, of the magnificent corps of troops, which his discipline had made a model of efficiency, more than confirmed his Mexican fame.

Space does not permit us to follow, in detail, the execution of the able and comprehensive strategy, by which General Bragg relieved large sections of Tennessee and Alabama from the presence of the enemy, penetrated the heart of Kentucky, maintained an active offensive during the summer, and transferred the seat of war to the Federal frontier. A part of these operations was the hurried retreat of Buell's immense army, from its posts in Alabama and Tennessee, for the defense of Louisville and Cincinnati; large captures of prisoners, horses, arms and military stores; and the brilliant progress and successive victories of Kirby Smith and Morgan. For weeks the situation in Kentucky seemed to promise the unqualified success of the entire Western campaign. There was, indeed, reasonable hope of a permanent occupation of the larger portion of Kentucky and Tennessee by the Confederate forces.

But the battle of Perryville—an engagement not unlike Antietam in its doubtful claim as a Federal victory—was followed by the retreat of General Bragg, which was executed with skill, and with results going far to relieve the disappointment of the popular hope of a permanent occupation of Kentucky. Buell, on his arrival at Louisville, whither he had retreated, received heavy reënforcements, which greatly increased his already superior numbers; and Perryville, a battle which General Bragg fought, rather to secure his retreat than with the expectation of a decisive victory, would have been an overwhelming Confederate success, had Bragg been sufficiently strong to follow up his advantage.

No Confederate commander, save Lee and Jackson, was ever able to present a claim of a successful campaign so well grounded as the Kentucky campaign of Bragg. With a force of forty thousand men, he killed, wounded, and captured more than twenty thousand of the enemy; took thirty pieces of artillery, thousands of small arms; a large supply of wagons, harness, and horses; and an immense amount of subsistence, ample not only for the support of his own army, but of other forces of the Confederacy. During the succeeding autumn and winter, Bragg's army was conspicuous for its superior organization, admirable condition and tone; was abundantly supplied with food and clothing, and in larger numbers than when it started upon its campaign in August. Moreover, General Bragg redeemed North Alabama and Middle Tennessee, and recovered possession of Cumberland Gap, the doorway, through the mountains, to Knoxville and the Virginia and Tennessee Railroad—the main avenue from Richmond to the heart of the Confederacy. Evincing his determination to hold the recovered territory, General Bragg, within a month from his return from Kentucky, was confronting the principal army of the enemy, in the West, before Nashville.

Incidental to the movement of Bragg into Kentucky, and constituting a part of the programme, attempted upon the large theatre of the Western campaign, were the repulse of the first attack of the enemy upon Vicksburg, the partial failure of General Breckinridge's expedition to Baton Rouge, and the serious reverse sustained by Van Dorn at Corinth. In connection with the more important demonstration into Kentucky, these incidents of the Western campaign may be briefly aggregated as the recovery of the country between Nashville and Chattanooga, and the important advantage of a secure occupation of Vicksburg and Port Hudson, thus closing the Mississippi to the enemy for two hundred miles.

Subsequent operations in Virginia, at the close of 1862, were entirely favorable to the Confederacy. While the two armies were confronting each other, with the imminent prospect of active and important operations, General McClellan was relieved, and one of his corps commanders, General Burnside, assigned to the command of the Federal army of the Potomac. As is now universally acknowledged, General McClellan was sacrificed to the clamor of a political faction. By this act Mr. Lincoln became responsible for much of the ill-fortune which awaited the Federal arms in Virginia.

Perhaps among his countrymen, a Southern tribute to General McClellan may constitute but feeble praise. He was unquestionably the ablest and most accomplished soldier exhibited by the war on the Northern side. "Had there been no McClellan," General Meade is reported to have said, "there would have been no Grant." In retirement, if not exile, General McClellan saw the armies which his genius created, achieve undeserved distinction for men, his inferiors in all that constitutes true generalship. He saw the feeble and wasted remnant of an army, with which he had grappled in the day of its glory and strength, surrender to a multitudinous host, doubly as large as the army with which he had given Lee his first check at Antietam. A true soldier, McClellan was also a true gentleman, an enemy whose talents the South respects none the less, because he did not wantonly ravage its homes, nor make war upon the helpless, the aged, and infirm. President Davis, who, while Federal Secretary of War, conferred upon McClellan a special distinction, held his genius and attainments in high estimation. He received the intelligence of his removal with profound satisfaction.

The North was not required to wait long for a competent test of the new commander's capacity. Foiled and deceived by Lee, in a series of maneuvres, the results of which made him only less ridiculous than the gasconading Pope among Federal commanders, Burnside finally assailed Lee, on the 13th December, at Fredericksburg. The result was a bloody slaughter, unequaled in previous annals of the war, an overwhelming repulse, and a demoralized retreat across the Rappahannock.

The Western campaign terminated with the battle of Murfreesboro'. The Federal commander, Rosecrans, the successor of Buell, advanced from Nashville to drive Bragg from his position. A brilliant and vigorous attack by Bragg, on the 31st December, routed an entire wing of the Federal army; on the second day the action was more favorable to Rosecrans, who had retreated, after his reverse on the first day, to stronger positions. Receiving information that the enemy was strongly reënforcing, General Bragg fell back to Tullahoma, a position more favorable for strategic and defensive purposes.

The transfer, after the battle of Shiloh, of the troops of Price and Van Dorn to the army east of the Mississippi, had almost divested the Trans-Mississippi Department of interest in the public mind. After Elk Horn, there was but one considerable engagement, in 1862, west of the Mississippi. This was the battle of Prairie Grove, a fruitless victory, won by General Hindman, about the middle of December. The country north of the Arkansas River continued to be nominally held by the Federal forces.

Thus, in nearly every quarter, the second year of the war terminated with events favorable to the prospects of Southern independence. Though the territorial jurisdiction of the Confederacy was contracted, the world was not far from regarding the task of subjugation as already a demonstrated and hopeless failure. All the invasive campaigns of the enemy, save the first shock of his overwhelming onsets against weak and untenable posts, in the winter and early spring, had been brought to grief, and nowhere had he maintained himself away from his water facilities. An unexampled prestige among nations now belonged to the infant power, which had carried its arms from the Tennessee to the Ohio, had achieved a week of victories before its own capital, and carried the war back to its threshold. After such achievements the Southern Confederacy rightly claimed from those powers which have assumed to be the arbiters of international right an instant recognition upon the list of declared and established nationalities.

In our brief and cursory glance at military operations, we have omitted to mention the action of the Government designed to promote the successful prosecution of the war.

27

This action is mainly comprehended by the various suggestions of the President's messages to Congress. These recommendations related chiefly to measures having in view the increased efficiency of the service. He invited the attention of Congress, especially, to the necessity of measures securing the proper execution of the conscription law, and the consolidation of companies, battalions and regiments, when so reduced in strength as to impair that uniformity of organization, which was necessary in the army. Legislation was urged, having in view a better control of military transportation on the railroads, and the improvement of their defective condition. The President also recommended various propositions relating to organization of the army, and an extension of the provisions of the conscription law, embracing persons between the ages of thirty-five and forty-five years.

About the middle of December President Davis visited the camps of the Western Department, spending several weeks in obtaining information as to the condition and wants of that section of the Confederacy, and devising expedients for a more successful defense in a quarter where the Confederate cause was always seriously menaced. His presence was highly beneficial in allaying popular distrust, founded upon the supposition that Virginia and the Atlantic region engrossed the attention of the Government to the exclusion of concern for the West and the Mississippi Valley. When the President returned to Richmond, there were signs of popular animation in the South-west, which justified a more confident hope of the cause, than the South was permitted to indulge at any other period of the struggle.

An incident of this visit was the address of the President before the Mississippi Legislature. The warm affection of

Mr. Davis for Mississippi is more than reciprocated by the noble and chivalrous people of that State. He was always proud of the confidence reposed in him by such a community, and Mississippi can never abate her affection for one who so illustrated her name in the council chamber and upon the field of battle. In this address he alluded, with much tenderness, to this reciprocal attachment, declaring, that though "as President of the Confederate States, he had determined to make no distinction between the various parts of the country—to know no separate State—yet his heart always beat more warmly for Mississippi, and he had looked on Mississippi soldiers with a pride and emotion, such as no others inspired."

Declaring that his course had been dictated by the sincere purpose of promoting the cause of independence, he admonished the country to prepare for a desperate contest, with a power armed for the purposes of conquest and subjugation. He characterized severely the conduct of the war by the North. Reviewing its progress, and recounting the immense disadvantages, with which the South contended, he maintained that the South should congratulate itself on its achievements, and not complain that more had not been accomplished. The conscription law was explained and defended as to many of its features not clearly understood by the people. We give an extract from Mr. Davis' remarks as to the Confederate conscription, a subject of vast misrepresentation during the war, and of much ignorant censure since:

"I am told that this act has excited some discontentment, and that it has provoked censure far more severe, I believe, than it deserves. It has been said that it exempts the rich from military service, and forces the poor to fight the battles of the country. The poor do, indeed, fight the battles of the country. It is the poor who save nations and make revolutions. But is it true that, in this war, the men of property have shrunk from the ordeal of the battle-field? Look through the army; cast your eyes upon the maimed heroes of the war whom you meet in your streets and in the hospitals; remember the martyrs of the conflict; and I am sure you will find among them more than a fair proportion drawn from the ranks of men of property. The object of that portion of the act which exempts those having charge of twenty or more negroes, was not to draw any distinction of classes, but simply to provide a force, in the nature of a police force, sufficient to keep our negroes in control. This was the sole object of the clause. Had it been otherwise, it would never have received my signature. As I have already said, we have no cause to complain of the rich. All our people have done well; and, while the poor have nobly discharged their duties, most of the wealthiest and most distinguished families of the South have representatives in the ranks. I take, as an example, the case of one of your own representatives in Congress, who was nominated for Congress and elected, but still did a sentinel's duty until Congress met. Nor is this a solitary instance, for men of largest fortune in Mississippi are now serving in the ranks."

The President strongly and eloquently recommended the provision by the Legislature for the families of the absent soldiers of Mississippi. Said he: "Let this provision be made for the objects of his affection and his solicitude, and the soldier, engaged in fighting the battles of his country, will no longer be disturbed in his slumbers by dreams of an unprotected and neglected family at home. Let him know that his mother Mississippi has spread her protecting mantle over those he loves, and he will be ready to fight your battles, to protect your honor, and in your cause to die."

The address concluded with an earnest appeal for unrelaxed exertion, and the declaration that, "in all respects, moral as well as physical, the Confederacy was better prepared than it was a year previous"—a declaration verified not less by the favorable situation than by the evident apprehension of the North and the expectations of Europe.

CHAPTER XIV.

RESPECT OF MANKIND FOR THE SOUTH—THE MOST PROSPEROUS PERIOD OF THE WAR—HOW MR. DAVIS CONTRIBUTED TO THE DISTINCTION OF THE SOUTH—FACTION SILENCED—THE EUROPEAN ESTIMATE OF JEFFERSON DAVIS—HOW HE DIGNIFIED THE CAUSE OF THE SOUTH—HIS STATE PAPERS—HIS ADMINISTRATION OF CIVIL MATTERS—THE CONTRAST BETWEEN THE TWO PRESIDENTS—MR. DAVIS' OBSERVANCE OF CONSTITUTIONAL RESTRAINTS—ARBITRARY ADMINISTRATION OF MR. LINCOLN—MR. DAVIS' MODERATION—HE SEEKS TO CONDUCT THE WAR UPON CIVILIZED IDEAS—AN ENGLISH CHARACTERIZATION OF DAVIS—COLONEL FREEMANTLE'S INTERVIEW WITH HIM—MR. GLADSTONE'S OPINION—THE PURELY PERSONAL AND SENTIMENTAL ADMIRATION OF EUROPE FOR THE SOUTH—INCONSISTENT CONDUCT OF THE EUROPEAN GREAT POWERS—THE LONDON "TIMES" BEFORE M'CLELLAN'S DEFEAT—THE CONFEDERACY ENTITLED TO RECOGNITION BY EUROPE—ENGLAND'S SYMPATHY WITH THE NORTH—DIGNIFIED ATTITUDE OF PRESIDENT DAVIS UPON THE SUBJECT OF RECOGNITION—HIS EARLY PREDICTION UPON THE SUBJECT—FRANCE AND ENGLAND EXPOSED TO INJURIOUS SUSPICIONS—TERGIVERSATIONS OF THE PALMERSTON CABINET—THE BROAD FARCE OF "BRITISH NEUTRALITY"—ENGLAND DECLINES TO UNITE WITH FRANCE IN AN OFFER OF MEDIATION BETWEEN THE AMERICAN BELLIGERENTS—ENGLAND'S "POLICY"—SHE SOUGHT THE RUIN OF BOTH SECTIONS OF AMERICA—CULMINATION OF THE ANTISLAVERY POLICY OF THE NORTH—MR. LINCOLN'S CONVERSATION WITH A KENTUCKY MEMBER OF CONGRESS—THE WAR A "CRIME" BY MR. LINCOLN'S OWN SHOWING—VIOLATION OF PLEDGES AND ARBITRARY ACTS OF THE FEDERAL GOVERNMENT—THE MASK REMOVED AFTER THE BATTLE OF ANTIETAM—THE REAL PURPOSE OF EMANCIPATION—MR. DAVIS' ALLUSION TO THE SUBJECT—INDIGNATION OF THE SOUTH AT THE MEASURE—MILITARY OPERATIONS IN TEXAS AND MISSISSIPPI—VICKSBURG—PORT HUDSON—LOSS OF ARKANSAS POST—FEDERAL FLEET REPULSED AT CHARLESTON—PREPARATIONS FOR THE CAMPAIGN—UNITY AND CONFIDENCE OF THE SOUTH—MR. DAVIS' ADDRESS TO THE COUNTRY—IMPORTANT EXTRACTS—GENERAL LEE PREPARES FOR BATTLE—HIS CONFIDENCE—CONDITION OF HIS ARMY—BATTLE OF CHANCELLORSVILLE—JEFFERSON DAVIS' TRIBUTE TO STONEWALL JACKSON.

THERE is much justice in the sentiment that declares that there can be magnificence even in failure. Men often turn to the contemplation of rôles enacted in history, ending in disaster and utter disappointment of the originating and vitalizing aspiration, with far more of interest than has been felt in following records marked by the palpable tokens of complete success.

It may well be doubted, whether the Confederate States of America, even had victory crowned their prolonged struggle of superhuman valor and unstinted sacrifice, could have commanded more of the esteem of mankind, than will be awarded them in the years to come. Retrospect of the most prosperous period of the fortunes of the Confederacy—the interval between the battle of Fredericksburg, December, 1862, and the ensuing midsummer—reveals a period in which there was wanting no element of glory, of pride, or of hope. Many a people, now proudly boasting an honored recognition at the council-board of nations, might envy the fame of the meteor power which flashed across the firmament, with a glorious radiance that made more mournful its final extinguishment.

A notable feature of the distinction which the South, at that time especially, commanded in the eyes of the world, was the enthusiastic and universal tribute of mankind to the leader, whose genius, purity, dignity, and eloquence so adorned the cause of his country. The North sought to console its wounded national pride by accounting for the crushing and humiliating defeats of the recent campaign, by contrasts between the able leadership of its antagonist, and its own imbecile administration. At the South faction was silenced, in the presence of the wondrous results achieved in spite of its own outcries and prophecies of failure. Demagogues, in such a season of good fortune, ceased their charges of narrowness, of rash zealotry, of favoritism, of incompetency, seemingly conscious, for once, of the praise which they bestowed upon the Executive, whom they accused of usurping all the authority of the Government, in ascribing such results to his unaided capacity.

From Europe, in the beginning, so prejudiced against the South and its cause, so misinformed of Southern motives, and unacquainted with Southern history, came the tribute of disinterested eulogy, the more to be valued, because reluctantly accorded, to the Confederacy and its ruler. To Europe the South was now known not only through a series of unparalleled victories; as a people who had successfully asserted their independence for nearly two years, against such odds as had never been seen before; as a land of valiant soldiers, of great generals, and of large material resources. If possible, above these, the statesmen and politicians of Europe admired the administrative capacity, which, they declared, had given a superior model and a new dignity to the science of statesmanship. To the educated circles of Europe the new power was introduced by State papers, which were declared to be models, not less of skilled political narration and exposition, than of literary purity and excellence. Accustomed to hear the South twitted as a people dwarfed and debased by the demoralization of African slavery, the educated classes of England acknowledged the surprise and delight they experienced from the powerful and splendid vindications of the cause of the Confederacy, in the messages of Mr. Davis. It has been truthfully remarked that there could be no better history of the war than that contained in his numerous state papers. They are the exhaustive summary, and unanswerable statement of the imperishable truths which justify the South, and overwhelm her enemies with the proof of their own acts of wrong and violence.

Under the new light given to mankind, as to the origin, nature, and purposes of the American Union, which Mr. Davis so lucidly explained, Europe soon recognized his position as something else than that of a ruler of an insurgent district. But not only as the chosen Executive of eleven separate communities, several of which European governments had previously recognized as sovereign; as one who had organized great armies, maintained them in the field, and selected leaders for their command already illustrious in the annals of war; not for these and other features of enduring fame, alone, was Jefferson Davis admired in Europe. The contrast between the civil administrations of the hostile sections was viewed as, perhaps, the chiefly remarkable phase of the struggle.

President Lincoln, beginning the war with usurpation, had committed, in its progress, every possible trespass upon the Federal Constitution, and was now under the influence of a faction whose every aim contemplated the overthrow of that instrument. President Davis, supported by a confiding people, and an overwhelming majority of every Southern community, ruled in strict conformity with the laws of the land and its Constitution. In the midst of a revolution, unexampled in magnitude, in fierceness, and vindictiveness on the part of the enemy, and of difficulties in his own administration, he furnished an example of courage, humanity, and magnanimity, together with the observance of order, civil freedom, and legal and constitutional restraints unexampled in history. In the Confederacy, the Roman maxim, *Inter arma silent leges*, universally recognized and practiced among nations, had an emphatic repudiation, so far as concerned the exercise of power by the executive department. Whatever may have been the exceptional cases of unauthorized oppression or violence, there was always redress in the judiciary department of the Government, which continued in pure and dignified existence until the end.

The President, obeying the dictates of exalted patriotism—acting always for the public good, if not always with unimpeachable wisdom, at least with incorruptible integrity—made no attempt at improper interference with Congress, nor sought to exercise undue influence over its deliberations. The press, usually the first bulwark of the public liberties to attract the exercise of depotism, so trammeled at the North, was free in the South every-where; in some instances, to the extent of licentiousness, and to the positive injury of the cause.

In marked contrast with these exhibitions were the evidences of coming despotism at the North. The Federal judiciary was rapidly declining from its exalted purity, before the exactions of military power; the Federal Congress was charged by the press with open and notorious corruption, and was aiding Mr. Lincoln in usurpations which startled the despotisms of Europe, and have since led to the annihilation of the republican character of the Government.

Conspicuous, too, was the desire of Mr. Davis to conduct the war upon a civilized and Christian basis. His forbearance, his moderation, and stern refusal to resort to retaliation, under circumstances such as would have justified its exercise in response to the cruelties and outrages of the enemy, amazed the European spectator, and at times dissatisfied his own countrymen. "Retaliation is not justice," was his habitual reply to urgent demands, and again and again did he decline to "shed one drop of blood except on the field of battle." Never forgetting the dignity of the contest, he, up to the last moment of his authority, redeemed the pledge which he had made in the first weeks of the war: "to smite the smiter with manly arms, as did our fathers before us."

There have been few spectacles presented to the admiring gaze of mankind, more worthily depicted than that union of capacities and virtues in Jefferson Davis, which so eminently qualified him, in the opinion of foreigners, for the position he held. An English writer has eloquently sketched him as "one of the world's foremost men, admired as a statesman, respected as an earnest Christian, the Washington of another generation of the same race. A resolute statesman, calm, dignified, swaying with commanding intellect the able men that surrounded him; eloquent as a speaker, and as a writer giving state papers to the world which are among the finest compositions in our time; of warm domestic affections in his inner life, and strong religious convictions; held up by vigor of the spirit that nerved an exhausted and feeble frame—such was the chosen constitutional ruler of one-fourth of the American people."

Colonel Freemantle, a distinguished English officer, whose faithful and impartial narrative of his extended observations of the American war, commended him to the esteem of both parties, thus concludes an account of an interview with President Davis, in the spring of 1863:

"During my travels many people have remarked to me that Jefferson Davis seems, in a peculiar manner, adapted to his office. His military education at West Point rendered him intimately acquainted with the higher officers of the army; and his post of Secretary of War, under the old Government, brought officers of all ranks under his immediate personal knowledge and supervision. No man could have formed a more accurate estimate of their respective merits. This is one of the reasons which gave the Confederates such an immense start in the way of generals; for, having formed his opinion with regard to appointing an officer, Mr. Davis is always most determined to carry out his intention in spite of every obstacle. His services in the Mexican war gave him the prestige of a brave man and a good soldier. His services as a statesman pointed him out as the only man who, by his unflinching determination and administrative talent, was able to control the popular will. People speak of any misfortune happening to him as an irreparable evil too dreadful to contemplate."

Mr. Gladstone, a member of the British cabinet, the eminent leader of a party in English politics, and a sympathizer with the objects of the war as waged by the North, avowed his enthusiastic appreciation of the lustre reflected upon the new Government, by its able administration, in the assertion that "Mr. Jefferson Davis had created a nation."

But the admiration of Europe was to prove a mere sentiment, unaccompanied by any practical demonstration of sympathy. In view of the course so persistently adhered to by the great powers of Europe, it is curious to note the purely sentimental and personal character of their professed sympathy for the South. The earliest expression of foreign opinion indicated a reluctant recognition of the valor and devotion of a people, from whom they had not expected the exhibition of such qualities. When, by the protraction of the struggle, the brilliant feats of arms executed by the Southern armies, the indomitable resolution of the South, and its evident purpose to encounter every possible sacrifice for sake of independence, there was no longer ground for misapprehension, they still disregarded all the precedents and principles which had goverend their course respecting new nationalities.

Applauding the valor of the Southern soldiery, the heroism, endurance, and self-denial of a people whom they repeatedly declared to have already established their invincibility; rapturous in their panegyrics upon the genius, zeal, and Christian virtues of the Confederate leaders; they never interposed their boasted potentiality in behalf of justice, right, and humanity. English writers were eloquent in acknowledgment of the additional distinction conferred upon Anglo-Saxon statesmanship and literature by Davis; diligent in tracing the honorable English lineage of Lee, and establishing the consanguinity of Jackson; but English statesmen persistently disregarded those elevated considerations of humanity and philanthropy, which they have so much vaunted as prompting their intercourse with nations. Confessing a new enlightenment from the expositions of Mr. Davis, and from diligent inquiry into the nature of the Federal Government, Europe soon avowed its convictions in favor of the legal and constitutional right of secession asserted by the South. It declared that it but awaited the exhibition of that earnestness of purpose, and that capacity for resistance, which should establish the "force and consistency" which are the requisite conditions of recognized nationality.

The London *Times*, while the army of McClellan was still investing Richmond, used language which the North and the South accepted as significant and prophetic. Said the *Times:*

"It can not be doubted that we are approaching a time when a more important question even than that of an offer of mediation may have to be considered by England and France. *The Southern Confederacy has constituted itself a nation for nearly a year and a half.* During that time the attachment of the people to the new Government has been indubitably shown; immense armies have been raised; the greatest sacrifices have been endured; the persistence of the South in the war, through a long series of battles—some victories, some defeats—has shown the 'force and consistency' which are looked upon as tests of nationality. Wherever the Government is unmolested, the laws are administered regularly as in time of peace; and wherever the Federals have penetrated, they are received with an animosity which they resent, as at New Orleans, by a military rule of intolerable brutality. The vision of a Union party in the South has been dispelled, as the Northerners themselves are compelled, with bitterness and mortification, to admit.

"All these circumstances point but to one conclusion: Either this war must be brought to an end, or the time will at last come when the South may claim its own recognition by foreign nations as an independent power. The precedents of the American colonies, of the Spanish colonies, of Belgium, and of Tuscany, and of Naples the other day, forbid us to question this right when asserted by the Confederate States. It is our duty *to anticipate* this possible event, and it may be wise, as well as generous, for statesmen on this side of the ocean to approach the American Government in a friendly spirit, with the offer of their good offices, at this great crisis of its fortunes."

If such a statement of the question was just and truthful, when a numerous and confident army, under a leader of proven skill, was engaged in close siege of the capital of the Confederacy, how much more unanswerable were its conclusions when McClellan was defeated? What were the evidences of "force and consistency" demanded after the combined armies of McClellan and Pope were hurled back upon the Potomac; after Bragg had forced Buell to the Ohio; and when Fredericksburg had crowned six months of success with a victory that inevitably imposed a defensive attitude upon the North during the entire winter?

When Chancellorsville inflicted a defeat, the most decisive

and humiliating of the war, upon the North, there was indeed no longer even a pretext, by which could be disguised the evident purpose of England not to interfere in behalf of a cause with which she had no sympathy, whatever her constrained respect for its champions and defenders. The loss of Vicksburg and Gettysburg in the ensuing summer, so productive of distrust in Europe of the Confederate cause, was quickly followed by developments which dispelled nearly all remaining hope of that recognition which it was equally the right of the Confederacy to hope, and the duty of Europe to render.

The attitude of the Confederate Government, in its relations with European governments, was ever one of imposing dignity. President Davis contented himself with calm and statesmanlike presentation of the claims of the cause which he represented. His unanswerable exposition of the position of the Confederacy, and lucid discussions of international jurisprudence, never took the semblance of supplication, and were accompanied by dignified remonstrance, even, only when it became evident that the Confederacy was excluded from the benefits of that policy which the laws of nations and every precedent demanded. Hope of foreign assistance unquestionably constituted a large share of that confidence of success which, until the later stages of the war, continued to animate the South. Her people hoped for foreign aid in some shape, because they were confident of their ability to demonstrate their *right* to it; and they *expected* it only when they *had* demonstrated that right. But never was there any abatement or relaxation of effort by the Confederate Government because of this just right and expectation. In the midst of the most cheering events, and when recognition appeared certain, President Davis declared his conviction of the necessity of such effort as should secure independence without aid from any quarter. In his address to the Mississippi Legislature, December, 1862, from which we have already quoted, he said:

"In the course of this war our eyes have been often turned abroad. We have expected sometimes recognition and sometimes intervention at the hands of foreign nations, and we had a right to expect it. Never before, in the history of the world, had a people so long a time maintained their ground, and showed themselves capable of maintaining their national existence, without securing the recognition of commercial nations. I know not why this has been so, but this I say, 'Put not your trust in princes,' and rest not your hopes on foreign nations. This war is ours; we must fight it out ourselves; and I feel some pride in knowing that, so far, we have done it without the good-will of any body."

It seems, indeed, difficult to explain the course of Europe, especially of England and France, in the American war, upon any hypothesis consistent with either courage, humanity, or the usages of nations. Delay, caution, and attendance upon results were becoming in the beginning; but, after the defeat of McClellan upon the Chickahominy, and, still more, at the close of operations in 1862, they were no longer exacted by moral obligation or international comity. Having all the attributes of an independent power—a power at war with a neighbor, assailed by its armies, blockaded by its fleets, as had been numerous other independent powers—there was nothing whatever anomalous in the situation of the Confederate States forbidding the practice of plain justice towards them. Recognition was not only warranted by the facts of the case, but by immemorial usage in Europe, especially by the apposite precedent of the separation of Belgium from Holland. The existence of slavery in the South, even though sanctioned by law and the religious convictions of her people, is an altogether insufficient explanation of a policy which has exposed the European great powers to the suspicion of having been actuated by the most unworthy motives.

Especially does the course of England seem indefensible towards a people, with whom the war developed so much of common instinct, so many appeals of sympathy and evidences of identity with herself—a people whose ancestors were the uncompromising enemies of regicides, and had maintained their loyalty to the crown of England in spite of the power and threats of Cromwell, whose Puritan dominion New England acknowledged.

The injustice of England did not end with her refusal of recognition. In the beginning she promptly proclaimed "strict neutrality," and her Premier declared the Confederates "belligerents." This phrase, apparently a just concession of the declared independence of the South, was gratefully acknowledged by a struggling people, and evoked the fierce indignation of the North. It was, however, designedly ambiguous, and to be interpreted, philologically and practically, as the prospects of the controversy or the wishes of the Palmerston cabinet might dictate. The English cabinet did not necessarily mean a recognition of a divided sovereignty, justifying suspension of relations with both sections, until the question of sovereignty should be settled. The phrase "belligerents" was subsequently declared to mean, merely, that the "two sections were at war"—a fact which the participants felt to have already had ocular demonstration. Meanwhile, relations between London and Washington were not interrupted, and commercial intercourse continued as before. But England not only ignored the South, and denied the Confederate commissioners a formal and official audience—her vessels respected the Federal blockade, while Confederate vessels were warned from her coasts. Such is only a limited statement of features which made "English neutrality" the broadest farce and severest irony of the age.*

Early in 1863, or late in 1862, the Emperor Napoleon proposed to England to join France and other powers in a joint mediation, to suggest an armistice and a conference. This humane proposition England refused, declining to take any step which might aid pacification, and thus did both North and South finally comprehend what was meant by the "duty and policy" of that power, which had so industriously propagated American dissensions for her own aggrandizement. An editorial in the Richmond *Enquirer*, written, probably, by John Mitchel, pithily described the motives of England in the remark: "In short, the North is not yet bankrupt enough, the South not yet desolated enough, to suit the 'policy' of England." France saved her reputation, upon the score of humanity and justice, by evincing at least a right disposition, though it is difficult to reconcile her continued dalliance upon England, respecting the American question, with that bold policy, which usually characterizes the great master of European diplomacy. France had, however, less of interest and of expectation than England, from the dissolution of the Union; less motive for desiring its downfall, and the exhaustion of both combatants.

* A sufficient proof of the injury done the South by the pretended neutrality of England was the confession of the British Foreign Secretary. Said he: "The impartial observance of neutral obligation by Her Majesty's Government has thus been exceedingly advantageous to the cause of the more powerful of the two contending parties."

Such, however, was the policy, adhered to by England and France, in defiance of legal and moral obligation, and to the mortal injury of the South, in her brave and defiant struggle with that power, which history may yet declare, the "great powers" of Europe dared not defy.

An interesting phase of the war, in the beginning of 1863, was the culmination of the policy of the Federal Government respecting the subject of slavery. A brief space will suffice to exhibit a record of violated pledges, of constitutional infractions, and abuse of power by the Federal Government, altogether unexampled in a war to be hereafter noted for its arbitrary measures.

In the early stages of the war the North assumed, as the justification of coercive measures, not only the purpose of preserving the Union, but the relief of a "loyal party" in the South, who were oppressed by a violent minority having "command of the situation." Of this theory of the war, as waged by the North, the conversation of President Lincoln with a Kentucky member of Congress, in the presence of Senator Crittenden, was sufficiently declaratory:

"'Mr. Mallory, this war, so far as I have any thing to do with it, is carried on on the idea that there is a Union sentiment in those States, which, set free from the control now held over it by the presence of the Confederate or rebel power, will be sufficient to replace those States in the Union. If I am mistaken in this, if there is no such sentiment there, if the people of those States are determined with unanimity, or with a feeling approaching unanimity, that their States shall not be members of this Confederacy, it is beyond the power of the people of the other States to force them to remain in the Union; and,' said he, 'in that contingency—in the contingency that there is not that sentiment there—THIS WAR IS NOT ONLY AN ERROR, IT IS A CRIME.'"

Mr. Lincoln was probably not a very close student of the philosophy of history, or he would hardly have thus emphatically committed himself to a pledge, which, if observed, would have inevitably ended the war in a few weeks. The teachings of history were valueless, without their unvarying testimony to the potency of the sword of the common enemy in healing the divisions of an invaded country. It would be difficult, too, to imagine what he would have deemed that approximation to unity in the South, which would render a further prosecution of the war a crime. A faction of "Union men," truculent, treacherous, and insidious, in their hostility to the Confederate Government, unquestionably existed in the South during the entire progress of the war, but they were few in numbers, and their recognized leaders were, with hardly a single exception, men of abandoned character, notoriously without influence, save with their ignorant and unpatriotic followers. But this pretense of a Union party in the South, which the North, at first, declared a majority, was conveniently abandoned, when other pretexts were sought. In the face of evidence not to be denied, of the profound and sincere purpose of separation, entertained by more than seven-eighths of the citizens of the seceded States, the Northern conscience easily overcame its scruples as to a war which the Northern President had, by anticipation, pronounced a "Crime."

Palpable violations of vows were, indeed, marked characteristics of the conduct of the war as justified by the facile and pliant conscience of the North. The paramount purpose of coercion was to maintain the authority and dignity of the Constitution, assailed by "rebels in arms." No theory was avowed contemplating any other termination of the war, than a simple restoration of the "Union under the Constitution." The assertions of the Northern press, and the resolutions of mass meetings were re-affirmed by the most solemn enactments of the Federal Congress, and public declarations of Mr. Lincoln, that the North sought merely to save the Union, with the form and spirit of the Constitution unimpaired. In view of subsequent events, it is almost incredible that in Mr. Lincoln's first inaugural address should be found this passage:

"I declare that I have no purpose, directly or indirectly, to interfere with the institution of slavery in the States where it exists. I believe I have no lawful right to do so, and I have no inclination to do so. . . . . The right of each State to order and control its own domestic institutions according to its own judgment exclusively, is essential to the balance of power on which the perfection and endurance of our political fabric depended."

Then, after the defeat at Bull Run, Congress passed the following resolution, which was signed by Mr. Lincoln as President:

"*Resolved*, That this war is not waged upon our part with any purpose of overthrowing or interfering with the rights or established institutions of these States, but to defend and maintain the supremacy of the Constitution, and to preserve the Union, with all the dignity, equality, and rights of the several States unimpaired; that, as soon as these objects are accomplished, the war ought to cease."

As if to give every possible form of assurance of the legitimate and constitutional objects of the war, and leaving no room for doubt in the mind of posterity, of complete and unredeemed perfidy, the Federal authorities were at especial pains to declare their policy to foreign governments.

Mr. Seward, as Mr. Lincoln's Secretary of State, in his instructions to Mr. Dayton, Minister to France, says:

"The condition of slavery in the several States will remain just the same, whether it (the rebellion) succeed or fail. There is not even a pretext for the complaint that the disaffected States are to be conquered by the United States, if the revolution fail; for the rights of the States, and the condition of every human being in them, will remain subject to exactly the same laws and form of administration, whether the revolution shall succeed or whether it shall fail."

There was little room to doubt the purpose of the North to emancipate the slaves of the South, if at any period of the war such action could be advantageously taken. Mr. Lincoln always manifested great timidity and reluctance in approaching the subject, and it was observable that, at critical moments of the war, he courted the sympathy of the Democratic party, which was opposed to the policy of emancipation, so importunately urged upon him by the radical wing of the Republican party.

General McClellan had, with noble firmness, refused to countenance the revolutionary designs of the radical faction, and his removal from command after his repulse at Richmond was the palpable and decisive triumph of the emancipation policy in the sympathies of Mr. Lincoln. Restored to command, in order that he might save Washington from capture, no other officer being deemed to have the requisite ability and confidence of the army, he retained his position but a few weeks after that object was accomplished. By successive steps,

Mr. Lincoln was finally brought to issue a preliminary proclamation of emancipation, in September, 1862, which went into effect January 1, 1863. After the battle of Antietam, no farther necessity for concealment was deemed necessary, and to the design of subjugation was now added the proclaimed purpose to destroy the organic existence of the States and two thousand millions of Southern capital.

Emancipation was justified by the Federal administration as a "military necessity"—a wretched explanation from those who had boasted their ability to "exterminate the South" in a few months. Since the war, a claim of philanthropy, as the motive of emancipation, has been falsely asserted. Reckless of the fate of the slave, the North sought only vengeance against his master. In the sequel, each step of despotism becoming easier than its predecessor, malice against the master has been still the motive which instigated the enfranchisement of his former slave.

The New-Year's proclamation of Mr. Lincoln, reaching the Confederacy at the most auspicious period of its fortunes, was received with evidences of just indignation, and of a more stern purpose in the conduct of the war. President Davis thus referred to the subject in his message to Congress:

"The public journals of the North have been received, containing a proclamation, dated on the first day of the present month, signed by the President of the United States, in which he orders and declares all slaves within ten of the States of the Confederacy to be free, except such as are found within certain districts now occupied in part by the armed forces of the enemy. We may well leave it to the instincts of that common humanity which a beneficent Creator has implanted in the breasts of our fellow-men of all countries to pass judgment on a measure by which several millions of human beings of an inferior race—peaceful and contented laborers in their sphere—are doomed to extermination, while, at the same time, they are encouraged to a general assassination of their masters by the insidious recommendation 'to abstain from violence unless in necessary self-defense.' Our own detestation of those who have attempted the most execrable measure recorded in the history of guilty man, is tempered by profound contempt for the impotent rage which it discloses. So far as regards the action of this Government on such criminals as may attempt its execution, I confine myself to informing you that I shall—unless in your wisdom you deem some other course more expedient—deliver to the several State authorities all commissioned officers of the United States that may hereafter be captured by our forces, in any of the States embraced in the proclamation, that they may be dealt with in accordance with the laws of those States providing for the punishment of criminals engaged in exciting servile insurrection. The enlisted soldiers I shall continue to treat as unwilling instruments in the commission of these crimes, and shall direct their discharge and return to their homes on the proper and usual parole."

Mr. Davis urged upon the people the evidence, given by this measure, of the utterly ruthless and unscrupulous character of the war waged upon the South, and counseled the resolution of "absolute and total separation of these States from the United States." The eloquent appeals of Mr. Davis were sustained by the united press of the Confederacy, and by unmistakable indications of a thoroughly aroused popular indignation.

The results of military operations, in the winter months of 1863, were of a character altogether favorable and re-assuring to the Confederates. Movements on a large scale were prevented by the heavy rains and extreme rigor of the season, though there were many incidents evincing activity and enterprise on both sides. Early in January occurred the recapture of Galveston, Texas, by General Magruder. This exploit, marked by a display of energy, daring, and skill, was a handsome vindication of a most meritorious officer, who, for some months previous, had suffered unmerited censure. General Magruder had commanded a portion of the Army of Northern Virginia, in the assault upon McClellan, at Malvern Hill. The partial failure of the attack secured the Federal retreat, and the public, impatient at the check sustained at a moment of so much promise, visited an unwarranted censure upon Magruder. President Davis acknowledged, in a most flattering letter to his former classmate, the brilliant achievement of his command at Galveston.

After the battle of Murfreesboro', the more important operations, in the West, were enacted in the State of Mississippi. The successful defense of Vicksburg, in the summer of 1862, effectually closed the Mississippi to the Federal fleets. To reduce this stronghold became an object of prime importance to the Federal Government, the North-western States being especially interested in securing the unobstructed navigation of the great river. The Confederate Government, equally apprized of the value of Vicksburg, concentrated forces for its defense, and made the maintenance of that position one of the leading features of its designs in the West.

A second attempt, under the auspices of General Sherman, was made against Vicksburg, in December, 1862. The signal failure attending this expedition brought upon Sherman a degree of reproach, at the North, in singular contrast with the applause which he received twelve months later. A few weeks later, the third attempt against Vicksburg was undertaken by

General Grant, who sought to turn the Confederate defenses, through the smaller rivers connecting the Yazoo and Mississippi. This attempt was doomed to a failure no less decided and humiliating than that of its predecessor. On the 14th of March the Confederate batteries at Port Hudson, the lower defense of the Mississippi, repulsed the fleet of Farragut, who sought, by passing the batteries, to coöperate with Porter's fleet above.

These repeated failures of the Federal demonstrations against the Confederate strongholds on the Mississippi, were accepted as auspicious indications of continued successful defense in a vital quarter of the Confederacy. The loss of Arkansas Post, with a garrison of three thousand men, somewhat diminished the ardor of the congratulations experienced by the South from the successes on the Mississippi, and General Beauregard's signal defeat of the Federal fleet at Charleston.

At the opening of spring, there was wanting no indication of the gigantic struggle which was to make memorable the third year of the war. By common consent it was declared that this, if not the last, would, at least, be the decisive year of the struggle. An imperative necessity impelled the Federal administration to the most powerful efforts. Without brilliant and decided military results, the party in opposition to the war would inevitably gain possession of a sufficient number of States, to enable them to enter the next Presidential contest with fair prospects of success. The approaching expiration of the terms of service of large numbers of his veteran troops, also impelled the enemy to early activity.

On the part of the Confederates, there was apparently nothing left undone which could increase the chances of success. This period is remarkable in the history of the war, not less for its auspicious signs for the Confederacy, than for the union and coöperation every-where observable. It was equally a period encouraging hope and inviting effort to wring from the reluctant North confession of final defeat, and to inflict a just punishment upon an enemy, who had but lately proclaimed his purpose to use even the slaves of the South for the subjugation of her citizens. Extraordinary activity was displayed, during the winter and spring, in strengthening the army and adding to its efficiency, by the execution of the recent legislation of Congress recommended by President Davis. The utmost exertions of the Government were, of course, insufficient to strengthen the armies to the point of equality with the enormous array presented by the enemy on every theatre of operations. Yet the Government, the people, and the army, with calmness and confidence, awaited the issue, in the conviction that every preparation had been made which the resources of the country admitted.

Early in April, President Davis, in compliance with a request of Congress, addressed an eloquent invocation to the country, in behalf of the duties of patriotism at so critical a moment of the struggle. Stating his concurrence in the views of Congress, he declared his confidence in the patriotic disposition of the people to carry into effect the measures devised for the deliverance of the country.

"Alone, unaided," said he, "we have met and overthrown the most formidable combinations of naval and military armaments that the lust of conquest ever gathered together for the conquest of a free people. We began this struggle without a single gun afloat, while the resources of our enemy enabled them to gather fleets which, according to their official list, published in August last, consisted of four hundred and thirty-seven vessels, measuring eight hundred and forty thousand and eighty-six tons, and carrying three thousand and twenty-six guns. . . . . . To oppose invading forces composed of levies which have already exceeded thirteen hundred thousand men, we had no resources but the unconquerable valor of a people determined to be free."

Mr. Davis alluded encouragingly to the immediate prospects of the war:

"Your devotion and patriotism have triumphed over all these obstacles, and calling into existence the munitions of war, the clothing and the subsistence, which have enabled our soldiers to illustrate their valor on numerous battle-fields, and to inflict crushing defeats on successive armies, each of which our arrogant foe fondly imagined to be invincible.

"The contrast between our past and present condition is well calculated to inspire full confidence in the triumph of our arms. At no previous period of the war have our forces been so numerous, so well organized, and so thoroughly disciplined, armed, and equipped, as at present. The season of high water, on which our enemies relied to enable their fleet of gunboats to penetrate into our country and devastate our homes, is fast passing away; yet our strongholds on the Mississippi still bid defiance to the foe, and months of costly preparation for their reduction have been spent in vain. Disaster has been the result of their every effort to turn or storm Vicksburg and Port Hudson, as well as every attack on our batteries on the Red River, the Tallahatchie, and other navigable streams."

In this address President Davis did not fail to rebuke that tendency to excessive confidence from which relaxed exertion is ever apt to follow. Albeit he has been so freely charged with entertaining excessive confidence himself, and encouraging others to share his over-sanguine and exaggerated hopes, he yet never lost an opportunity of rebuking it as a dangerous error.

The most important feature of the address is the earnest and admonitory appeal, for immediate exertion, to obviate the difficulty of obtaining supplies for the army, already becoming a question of alarming concern. Mr. Davis even then avowed his conviction that, in such a contest as the war had then become, the question of food was the "one danger which the Government of your choice regards with apprehension." Earnestly appealing to the "never-failing patriotism" of the land, he said: "Your country, therefore, appeals to you to lay aside all thought of gain, and to devote yourselves to securing your liberties, without which these gains would be valueless."

Reminding the country of embarrassments, already encountered, he indicated the only method of avoiding similar difficulties in future:

> "Let your fields be devoted exclusively to the production of corn, oats, beans, peas, potatoes, and other food for man and beast. Let corn be sowed broadcast, for fodder, in immediate proximity to railroads, rivers and canals; and let all your efforts be directed to the prompt supply of these articles in the districts where our armies are operating. You will then add greatly to their efficiency, and furnish the means without which it is impossible to make those prompt and active movements which have hitherto stricken terror into our enemies and secured our most brilliant triumphs."

Those who witnessed the operation of causes which eventually brought the country to the verge of starvation, and made Lee's army—whose proud array of "tattered uniforms and bright muskets" had never yet yielded to the onset of the enemy—the *victim of famine,* can attest the fidelity of this graphic and prophetic sketch:

"It is known that the supply of meat throughout the country is sufficient for the support of all; but the distances are so great, the condition of the roads has been so bad during the five months of winter weather, through which we have just passed, and the attempt of groveling speculators to forestall the market, and make money out of the life-blood of our defenders, have so much influenced the withdrawal from sale of the surplus in hands of the producers, that the Government has been unable to gather full supplies.

"The Secretary of War has prepared a plan, which is appended to this address, by the aid of which, or some similar means to be adopted by yourselves, you can assist the officers of the Government in the purchase of the corn, the bacon, the pork, and the beef known to exist in large quantities in different parts of the country. Even if the surplus be less than believed, is it not a bitter and humiliating reflection that those who remain at home, secure from hardship, and protected from danger, should be in the enjoyment of abundance, and that their slaves also should have a full supply of food, while their sons, brothers, husbands, and fathers are stinted in the rations upon which their health and efficiency depend?"

The concluding paragraph of this address, so remarkable for its eloquence, and for its frank and powerful statement of the condition and necessities of the Confederacy, in one of the most thrilling moments of its fate, is as follows:

"Entertaining no fear that you will either misconstrue the motives of this address, or fail to respond to the call of patriotism, I have placed the facts fully and frankly before you. Let us all unite in the performance of our duty, each in his sphere; and with concerted, persistent, and well-directed effort, there seems little reason to doubt that, under the blessings of Him to whom we look for guidance, and who has been to us our shield and strength, we shall maintain the sovereignty and independence of the Confederate States, and transmit to our posterity the heritage bequeathed to us by our fathers."

Late in March, General Lee intimated his convictions, to the Government, of an early resumption of active movements by the enemy. The disparity between the main armies in Virginia was even greater than in previous campaigns. General Hooker, the Federal commander, had, under his immediate direction, more than one hundred thousand men, while General Lee—in consequence of the necessary withdrawal of Longstreet, with two divisions, to meet a threatened movement by the enemy from the south of James River, and to secure the supplies of an abundant section, open to Federal incursions—had less than fifty thousand.* But Lee manifested his characteristic confidence and self-possession in the presence of the perilous crisis. Having adequately represented the situation to

* General Lee stated the proportion of the Federal strength to his own as *ten to three.* Mr. Swinton states Hooker's force at one hundred and twenty thousand infantry, twelve thousand cavalry, and four hundred guns. Lee's effective force was considerably less than fifty thousand.

The absence of Longstreet was severely felt by General Lee in his operations against Hooker. The presence of a force was absolutely indispensable upon the south side of James River, in the early spring, to meet the formidable Federal force in the neighborhood of Suffolk. An impression, altogether erroneous, however, prevailed, that Longstreet's detention from Lee was caused by President Davis. The President eventually ordered Longstreet to Lee, after his delay at Richmond.

his Government, he was aware of the cordial coöperation, to the extent of its ability, which had been extended. During the suspension of active hostilities, his every wish for the increased efficiency of his command was promptly fulfilled, and at the opening of the campaign he lacked no element of readiness, save *numbers*, that which the country could not supply, and of the absence of which, Lee, therefore, *never complained*. In every other element of efficiency, the army of Northern Virginia was never in better condition, than when it eagerly awaited the advance of Hooker across the Rappahannock.

The battle of Chancellorsville is memorable as the most decisive triumph of the Army of Northern Virginia, and from the mournful incident of the extinction of that noble life which was identified with its highest glory. The culmination of Lee's superb strategy, the most splendid illustration of his master-genius, was sadly emphasized by the irreparable loss of Stonewall Jackson.

Commemorating, by a letter of special thanks to the army, a victory which baffled the most perilous and boastful attempt yet made upon the Confederate capital, President Davis shared the grief of a stricken country for the loss of one of its most illustrious champions. In that procession of mourners which followed, through the streets of Richmond, the bier of the fallen hero, there was not one who felt anguish more acute than that of the chief who had so honored and sustained Jackson when living.*

* "Of Stonewall Jackson, Mr. Davis spoke with the utmost tenderness, and some touch of reverential feeling, bearing witness to his earnest and pathetic piety, his singleness of aim, his immense energy as an executive officer, and the loyalty of his nature, making obedience the first of all duties. . . . . . He had the faculty, or, rather, gift of exciting and

holding the love and confidence of his men to an unbounded degree, even though the character of his campaigning imposed on them more hardships than on any other troops in the service. Good soldiers care not for their individual sacrifices, when adequate results can be shown, and these General Jackson never lacked. . . . . . 'For glory he lived long enough,' continued Mr. Davis, with much emotion; 'and if this result had to come, it was the Divine mercy that removed him. He fell like the eagle, his own feather on the shaft that was dripping with his life-blood. In his death, the Confederacy lost an eye and arm; our only consolation being that the final summons could have reached no soldier more prepared to accept it joyfully.' "—*Craven's Prison Life of Jefferson Davis*, pp. 180, 181.

CHAPTER XV.

CONFEDERATE PROSPECTS AFTER THE BATTLE OF CHANCELLORSVILLE—THE MILITARY SITUATION—PRIMARY OBJECTS OF THE CONFEDERATES—AFFAIRS IN THE WEST—A BRIEF CONSIDERATION OF SEVERAL PLANS OF CAMPAIGN SUGGESTED TO THE CONFEDERATE AUTHORITIES—VISIONARY STRATEGY—AN OFFENSIVE CAMPAIGN ADOPTED—THE INVASION OF PENNSYLVANIA JUSTIFIED—CONDITION OF THE ARMY OF NORTHERN VIRGINIA AT THIS PERIOD—THE MOVEMENT FROM THE RAPPAHANNOCK—LEADING FEATURES OF THE CONFEDERATE PLAN—LEE'S STRATEGY AGAIN ILLUSTRATED—GETTYSBURG—A FATAL BLOW TO THE SOUTH—LEE RETURNS TO VIRGINIA—THE SURRENDER OF VICKSBURG—OTHER REVERSES—EXULTATION OF THE NORTH—THE CONFEDERATE ADMINISTRATION AGAIN ARRAIGNED BY ITS OPPONENTS—THE CASE OF GENERAL PEMBERTON—POPULAR INJUSTICE TO A GALLANT OFFICER—A BRIEF REVIEW OF THE SUBJECT—PEMBERTON'S APPOINTMENT RECOMMENDED BY DISTINGUISHED OFFICERS—HIS ABLE ADMINISTRATION IN MISSISSIPPI—HIS RESOLUTION TO HOLD VICKSBURG, AS THE GREAT END OF THE CAMPAIGN—HIS GALLANTRY AND RESOURCES—NOBLE CONDUCT OF THIS PERSECUTED OFFICER—A FURTHER STATEMENT—THE MISSION OF VICE-PRESIDENT STEPHENS—ITS OBJECTS—PRESIDENT DAVIS SEEKS TO ALLEVIATE THE SUFFERINGS OF WAR—MAGNANIMITY AND HUMANITY OF THE OFFER—PROUD POSITION IN THIS MATTER OF THE SOUTH AND HER RULER—THE FEDERAL GOVERNMENT DECLINES INTERCOURSE WITH MR. STEPHENS—EXPLANATION OF ITS MOTIVES—CORRESPONDENCE BETWEEN MESSRS. DAVIS AND STEPHENS.

THE situation of affairs, so eminently favorable to the Confederacy, after the victory of Chancellorsville, admitted no doubt that the opportune occasion would be promptly seized, for the delivery of a telling blow, which should hasten an acknowledgment of Southern independence. A brief summary of the military situation, at the opening of summer, 1863, will show the simple and judicious policy, by which the Confederate administration proposed to make efficient use of its advantages.

The battle of Chancellorsville, followed by the disorganized retreat of the largest force yet consolidated for the capture of Richmond, and the signal failure of an attempt, which, at its outset, the North declared to be conclusive of the fate of the Confederacy, secured the safety of the Confederate capital, at least, until another campaign could be organized. Moreover, it tendered to the Confederate authorities the choice of a vigorous offensive, holding out tempting inducements; or a detachment of a portion of Lee's army for the relief of other sections of the Confederacy. With two-thirds of his own force, Lee had repulsed and crippled the enormous army of Hooker, and it appeared reasonably certain, that the same force could maintain a successful defensive, while the segment, or its equivalent, which was absent at Chancellorsville, might be sent, for a temporary purpose, to Bragg, in Tennessee, or to the relief of Pemberton in Vicksburg.

At the opening of spring the primary objects of the Confederacy were the safety of Richmond, the safety of Vicksburg—the key to its tenure of the Mississippi Valley—and the holding of its defensive line in Middle and East Tennessee, the barrier between the enemy and the vitals of the Confederacy. The first of these objects was amply secured by the victory of Chancellorsville, leaving to the main Confederate army, its own choice of the field of future operations.

In the Western Department, commanded since December, 1862, by General Joseph E. Johnston, the situation was less promising, though by no means forbidding hope of a favorable solution. General Bragg maintained a somewhat precarious defensive against Rosecrans, who confronted the Confederate commander, with an army much larger than that with which he had fought the battle of Murfreesboro'. General Pemberton, after a series of actions, had retired within the lines of Vicksburg, where he was closely besieged by General Grant with a numerous army—the Federal fleet in the river, meanwhile, continuing its bombardment. The characteristic stubbornness of Grant, aided by his ample force, made evident the ultimate fate of Vicksburg and Pemberton's army, either by famine, or the assaults of the enemy, unless succor should come in the shape of a demonstration against the besieging army, with which the garrison might be expected to coöperate. Not long after Pemberton's retirement into Vicksburg, General Johnston reached Mississippi and began the collection of a force, by which it was expected that the besieged stronghold and its garrison would be relieved.

But while the situation in the West thus seemed to invite the presence of a portion of the army of Northern Virginia, relieved of any immediate danger from its antagonist, there were cogent considerations in behalf of another policy which was adopted. Two weeks, at least, would have been required, in the indifferent condition of the Southern railroads, for the transportation of a force from Virginia, competent to enable Bragg to assume the aggressive. A much longer period would have been required to transfer to Jackson, such a force as General Johnston would have deemed sufficient to justify an attack upon Grant. Besides, the government was fully satisfied, that the reënforcements sent to Johnston would soon enable him to make an effective demonstration against the besieging army, which, sustained by a simultaneous attack by Pemberton in front, would have a reasonable prospect of success.

The project of a direct reënforcement to Johnston, from Lee's army, was speedily abandoned, and the more practicable plan of reënforcing Bragg was also dismissed. Nothing whatever was to be expected from a victory by Bragg over Rosecrans, unless it could be made a *decisive* victory, ensuring either the destruction of the Federal army, or the complete abandonment of its advanced line in Tennessee, for which it had paid such heavy toll. Such a result, necessitating the reënforcement of Rosecrans from Grant, meanwhile, after the victory had been won, troops being sent to Johnston from Bragg, was indeed brilliant to contemplate. Or there was another prospect equally agreeable. When Rosecrans had been defeated troops might be sent to capture Fort Pillow, on the Mississippi, which, cutting off Grant's supplies from the North, as did Port Hudson from the South, would compel the Federal army at Vicksburg to fight for its subsistence, and under most discouraging circumstances. In addition to these prospects, there was also the choice of a movement for the complete redemption of Kentucky and Tennessee.

These brilliant designs of a visionary and vaporing strategy, abundant in the Confederacy during the war, and now ostentatiously paraded by the cheap wisdom of retrospection, lacked, however, the essential feature of practicability. To have reënforced Bragg sufficiently from Lee's army, to have enabled him to undertake the offensive, with any prospect of the complete success necessary, would have weakened the army in Virginia to such an extent, as to seriously endanger Richmond. Even though Bragg were thus sufficiently reënforced to defeat a numerous army, led by an able commander, and occupying a position of great strength, a full month would have been required to accomplish the results indicated. Waiving all consideration of the incertitude of battle, and assuming that success would attend every movement of the Confederate army, what reasonable calculation would enable Bragg to have gotten his forces in readiness, and marched them either into Kentucky to Fort Pillow, or to Jackson, in time to have saved Vicksburg? But, apart from the folly of so weakening Lee, as to endanger Richmond (which would have been immediately assailed by Hooker, with his command of ninety thousand men, in coöperation with the forces at Suffolk, Fortress Monroe, and Winchester—an aggregate of more than forty thousand more), to undertake operations so doubtful and hazardous, was the consideration of the promising inducements for an offensive campaign in the East.

President Davis and General Lee were concurrent in their convictions of the wisdom of a campaign which should drive the enemy from Virginia, locate the army in an abundant and hostile country, and compensate for any disasters which might be sustained in the West, by an overwhelming defeat in the enemy's country of his main army, which at once covered his capital. and the approaches to his large cities.

This bold and brilliant conception was equally justified by the situation, and consistent with that able military policy which was throughout characteristic of the Confederate authorities, and based upon the only theory on which a weak power can be successfully defended against invasion.

The strategic theory which dictated the invasion of Pennsylvania was that of the "defensive, with offensive returns," made forever famous by its triumphant practice by Frederick the Great—the favorite theory of Napoleon—not less signally illustrated by Jackson's Valley campaign, and grandly executed by Lee in his irresistible onset upon Pope.

Twitted by the newspapers for their infatuation with the

defensive attitude, and condemned by the voice of the public, for the maintenance of a policy which continually subjected the soil of the South to the devastations of the enemy, the Confederate authorities, neither in the invasion of Maryland, in 1862, nor in the invasion of Pennsylvania, yielded merely to public clamor. In both instances President Davis and General Lee were governed by the sound military considerations, which in each case justified the assumption of the offensive. Nothing is more universally conceded than the ultimate subjection of a people who permit themselves to be forced always on the defensive. On the other hand, no blows have been so telling in warfare, as those delivered by an antagonist who, lately on the defensive, at the opportune moment, when the foe is stunned by defeat, assumes a skillful and vigorous offensive.

It was now the third year of the war, and for more than twelve months no considerable success had rewarded the enormous sacrifices and expenditures of the North. The fluctuating sentiment, characteristic of that section, had settled down into a feeling of indifference and distrust, beyond which there was but one step to the abandonment of the war as a hopeless experiment. The evident apprehension, by the Federal Government, of an invasion of Pennsylvania, attended by a ruinous defeat of Hooker's army, a result which both sides considered probable, plainly demonstrated, that the virtual termination of the war would be the reward of a successful assumption of the offensive by the Confederates.

A more favorable conjuncture, for a final trial with its old antagonist, could not have been desired by the Army of Northern Virginia. The invincible veterans of Longstreet, oftener victors than the Tenth Legion of Cæsar, had rejoined their companions, who boasted the additional honors of Chancellorsville. Reënforcements from other quarters were added,* and the Army of Northern Virginia, a compact and puissant force, seventy thousand strong, which had never yet known defeat, instinctively expected the order for advance into the enemy's country. Never was the *morale* of the army so high, never had it such confidence in its own prowess, and in the resources of its great commander, and never was intrusted to its valor a mission so grateful to its desires, as that tendered by President Davis, "to force the enemy to fight for their own capital and homes."

Under Lee were trusted lieutenants, whose fame, like that of their followers, was world-wide, and whose laurels were a part of the unnumbered triumphs of the matchless valor of that noble army. Longstreet, the Lannes of the South, was again at the head of his trained corps—the assembled chivalry of the South, in whose exploits every State of the Confederacy claimed a glory peculiarly its own. The bronzed veterans of Jackson, who had shared the glory of their immortal leader from Manassas to Chancellorsville, now followed Ewell, the maimed hero, whom Jackson had named as his successor. Under Hill, the youngest of the corps commanders, were men worthy of a leader who, in twelve months, had filled the successive grades from Colonel to Lieutenant General. The cavalry was still intrusted to Stuart, that bold, able chief, and "rarely gallant and noble gentleman, well supporting by his character the tradition that royal blood flowed in his veins." With such leaders, and with thoroughly tried and efficient subordinate officers, improved transportation, equipment and clothing, and with numbers approaching nearer an equality

* Chiefly conscripts.

with the Federal army, than at any other period, the Army of Northern Virginia no more doubted, than did its commander and the Government, that it was at the outset of a campaign brilliant and decisive beyond parallel in its history.

About the middle of May, General Lee visited Richmond, when the general features of the campaign were determined. The movement from the camps near Fredericksburg and the Rapidan, commenced early in June. The incipient feature of General Lee's plan was a flank movement, while still confronted by the army of the enemy—perhaps the most delicate and difficult problem in war—by which, leaving the south bank of the Rappahannock, he sought to draw the Federal army away from its position. To meet the contingency of a movement by the enemy in the direction of Richmond, A. P. Hill, with his *corps d'armée*, was left near Fredericksburg. That skillful officer ably executed his instructions, checking the Federal demonstrations near his lines, and concealing the absence of the main body of the army until the advance was well under way. General Stuart fully performed his important part of covering the movements of the infantry, by seizing the mountain passes, and detaining the advance of the enemy, in the execution of which he fought several fierce cavalry engagements, winning them all with inferior forces. The army was marched through an abundant country, not desolated by war, and affording good roads. Important incidents of the advance were the capture of Winchester, Berryville, and Martinsburg, by the forces of Ewell, with their garrisons, aggregating seven thousand men, and considerable material of war.

These brilliant results of Lee's strategy were accomplished with wonderful regularity and promptitude, and were attended with inconsiderable loss.

Crossing the Potomac, the second stage of the campaign was the occupation of Western Maryland—the least friendly section of the State—where the army could be abundantly supplied, and the important objects of destroying the Baltimore and Ohio Railroad, and the Cumberland Canal, so valuable to the enemy, could be accomplished. The next step was to advance into Pennsylvania, capturing large supplies much needed by the army, occupying several large towns of that State, and destroying communications—meanwhile the army living on the enemy, and kept well in hand for a general engagement, *whenever battle could be advantageously offered.* In the execution of this portion of the plan, an extensive and fertile section of Pennsylvania was occupied, strong detachments were pushed far into the interior, and a movement against Harrisburg was in preparation, when the advance of the Federal army induced General Lee to concentrate his forces for battle.

The consummate strategy of Lee had now made him apparently master of the situation, and gave him the option of tendering or declining a grand and decisive engagement. It is impossible to overestimate the generalship, which, within twenty-five days, had transferred an army, in the presence of the enemy, from the Rappahannock to the interior of Pennsylvania, making large captures *en route,* and inflicting heavy damage upon the Federal communications, without being even momentarily arrested. Never once had been relaxed the grasp of that master-hand which controlled the army in all its movements. Its various parts, within easy supporting distance, were clearly so disposed, as to be readily assembled, to meet the exigency that was inevitable. When Lee drew in his several columns around Gettysburg, the South confident in the invincibility of the army, and in the genius of its leader, never doubted the issue of the grand trial of arms which was at hand. With more than apprehension the North awaited the fate of the army, upon which its last hope of security rested. A defeat of the Army of the Potomac now would signify, not a check in a boastful advance upon Richmond, but the capture of Washington, the presence of the avenging columns of Lee upon the banks of the Delaware—perhaps of the dreaded Stuart upon the Hudson.

It was contemplated that the invasion of Pennsylvania would result in a decisive battle. Indeed, that result was inevitable, unless the Federal authorities should unresistingly submit to the invasion—an event not for a moment to be anticipated. But a vital feature in the theory of the invasion was that the position of Lee would necessitate an advance against him by the Federal commander, leaving to Lee the choice of time and place for giving battle. The calculation was that Lee would be master of the situation at all times, as indeed he undoubtedly was until the engagement of Gettysburg was joined. We are not here at liberty to discuss the details of that battle, or to consider how far it was a departure from, or in pursuance of the original design of the Confederate campaign.* If competent criticism shall condenmn the

*It has been generally assumed that General Lee committed grave errors at Gettysburg. The following explanation by Lee shows the extreme caution with which such a judgment should be pronounced: "*It had not been intended to fight a general battle at such distance from our base unless attacked by the enemy;* but, finding ourselves unexpectedly confronted by the Federal army, it became a matter of difficulty to withdraw through the mountains with our large trains. At the same time, the country was unfavorable for collecting supplies, while in the presence of the enemy's main body, as he was enabled to restrain our foraging parties by occupying the passes of the mountains with regular and local troops. A bat-

tactics of Lee at Gettysburg, he has yet disarmed censure by the surpassing magnanimity with which he assumed the responsibility.

The great joy of the North did not exaggerate the terrible blow sustained by the Confederacy in the failure of the Pennsylvania campaign. It was the last serious demonstration upon Federal soil undertaken by the South—all movements of an offensive character subsequently undertaken being merely raids or diversions, designed to give relief to the sorely-pressed Confederate capital. It imposed upon the South the cruel necessity of a continuation of the war upon its own soil—a precarious defensive, with a capacity of resistance greatly diminished.

Gettysburg marked the most serious step in that decline of Confederate fortunes which the fall of Jackson, in the moment of his greatest triumph, so ominously presaged.*

Yet the condition of Lee's army was far from desperate on the morning of the 4th of July, when it still confronted its

tle thus became, in a measure, unavoidable. Encouraged by the successful issue of the first day, and in view of the valuable results which would ensue from the defeat of the army of General Meade, it was thought advisable to renew the attack."

Mr. Swinton, who derived his information from General Longstreet, makes a statement which throws much light upon the theory with which this campaign was undertaken: "Indeed, in entering upon the campaign, General Lee expressly promised his corps commanders that *he would not assume a tactical offensive, but force his antagonist to attack him.*"—*Campaigns of the Army of the Potomac.*

*Major John Esten Cooke justly says: "Gettysburg was the Waterloo—Cemetery Hill the Mount St. Jean of the war. . . . . . Not without good reason is the anniversary of this great battle celebrated at the North with addresses and rejoicings—with crowds, and brass bands, and congratulations. The American Waterloo is worth making that noise over; and the monument proposed there is a natural conception.

antagonist, neither evincing a disposition to attack. Retiring in perfect order, and bringing off his extensive trains and seven thousand prisoners, he tendered the enemy battle at Hagerstown, while making preparations to recross the Potomac. General Meade, an able and prudent soldier, made as vigorous a pursuit as the crippled condition of his army would permit. In a short time General Lee was once more upon the lines of the Rapidan, and General Meade soon took position upon the Rappahannock. Here the campaign terminated, and the two armies, like giants exhausted by a mighty wrestle, gladly availed themselves of a season of repose.

But Gettysburg did not complete the agony of the South. The disastrous failure of the most prodigious and promising enterprise, undertaken by its largest, and heretofore invincible army, was simultaneous with an event hardly less fearful in its consequences. On the fourth of July, the garrison of Vicksburg, reduced to the point of starvation, surrendered to the persevering and indomitable Grant. This event signified the loss of an army of twenty-five thousand men, the possession by the enemy of the Confederate Gibraltar of the Mississippi Valley, the loss of all tenure upon the great river by the South, and the severance of the Confederacy. Port Hudson, with its garrison of five thousand men, being no longer tenable, after the fall of Vicksburg, was immediately surrendered to the besieging army of General Banks. The sum of Confederate disasters in the summer of 1863, was completed by the failure of the attempt to capture Helena, Arkansas, followed by the capture of Little Rock, and Federal control of the important valley in which it is situated.

Within ninety days the South was brought from the hope of almost instant independence to the certainty of a long, bitter, and doubtful struggle. Its armies terribly shattered, its resources in men and means apparently almost exhausted, it seemed for a time doubtful whether the Confederacy was capable of longer endurance of the terrible ordeal. The exultation of the North was proportionate to the extent of its victories. A new lease was given to the war. Confidence was fully restored, and the Federal Government could now make no demand, that would be thought extravagant, upon the energies of the North, for the promotion of the object it had so much at heart. But a few months sufficed to show that the constancy and fortitude of the South was still capable of a desperate struggle with the power and determination of the North.

This period of misfortune and apprehension was signalized by a most determined arraignment of the Confederate administration. It is worthy of remark, however, that in all the embittered censure visited upon President Davis, for his alleged responsibility for the crushing reverses of the summer campaign, there was avowed but little censure of the most fatal of those disasters—the failure of the movement into Pennsylvania. The privilege of assailing Mr. Davis with or without reason, did not include the privilege to condemn Lee and his army.

In the case of Vicksburg circumstances were assumed to be different. Without even waiting for the facts, or for any explanation of that terrible calamity, General Pemberton was accused of having betrayed his command. He was of Northern birth, and he had surrendered on the fourth of July—such was the evidence of Pemberton's treason. Despite the fact that Johnston was known to be in the neighborhood with a force collected for the relief of Vicksburg, and though it had been plain to the country for weeks, that Vicksburg could not be saved, except by a successful demonstration by that force, it was not admitted among the possibilities of the case, that Johnston* shared the responsibility for the disaster.

When, however, the Federal accounts revealed the gallant defense made by Pemberton, and thus put to shame the unworthy insinuation of treachery, the censure of that unfortunate commander and the President assumed another direction. Pemberton, it was asserted, was notoriously incompetent, so proven, and so represented to the President before his assignment to command in Mississippi; and the indignation of the country was invoked upon the most signal instance of favoritism yet exhibited. The extent to which this censure of Mr. Davis was successful, may be estimated, when it is stated that no act of his administration so imperiled his popularity as did the appointment of General Pemberton. Yet it is undeniable that this was the result of the unfortunate sequel at Vicksburg, and dictated by popular passion in a moment of terrible disappointment, rather than by any sufficient reason ever urged to show that the appointment was unwise and undeserved.

Sustained by the recommendations of several of the first officers in the Confederate army, President Davis made Pemberton a Lieutenant-General, and assigned him to the command of the Department of Mississippi. The command was

* General Johnston, whether willingly or unwillingly, it is not necessary for us to inquire, was the favorite of the anti-administration faction. His name and opinions were, upon all occasions, quoted to aid in the disparagement of the administration. This faction was as blind in its zealotry in favor of Johnston, as in its prejudice against Davis. The motive of this zealous championship of Johnston was, however, to offset the well-known confidence of General Lee in the President.

one of vital importance to the country, and within its limits were the home and all the possessions of Mr. Davis. In October, 1862, General Pemberton took charge of his department, finding it in a most disordered and embarrassing condition. His administration was of a character to give great satisfaction to the Government, and its fruits were speedily realized in the thorough and efficient reorganization of an army, but lately defeated, the improved efficiency of its various departments, and the successful defense of an extensive district, with forty thousand men, against the armies of Grant and Banks, the smallest of which nearly equaled the entire force of Pemberton. Indeed, it can hardly be alleged that the administration of General Pemberton, previous to the siege of Vicksburg, was faulty or unsatisfactory. With what justice, then, can it be charged that Mr. Davis retained in command an officer proven to be incompetent?

In the reports of Generals Johnston and Pemberton, written from different stand-points, and each with the object of vindicating its author, the operations which led to the retirement of the latter within the lines of Vicksburg were elaborately discussed. It is at least safe to state that General Pemberton's reasons are as forcibly stated in explanation of his own conduct, as are General Johnston's in demonstration of the errors of his subordinate. Pemberton was controlled in all his movements by the paramount purpose of holding Vicksburg, the last obstruction to the enemy's free navigation of the Mississippi, and the connecting link between the two great divisions of the Confederacy. If he had abandoned Vicksburg, with a view to save his army, and refused to stand a siege, can it be reasonably supposed that his assailants would have been more merciful? His mission was to save Vicksburg and the Valley of the Mississippi, and, when forced back by the overwhelming numbers of Grant, he preferred even to risk his army, rather than to surrender the objects of the whole campaign without an effort.

During the siege, the engineering skill of General Pemberton, and his fertility of expedients were conspicuously displayed. Works, which, under the unceasing and concentrated fire of hundreds of guns, were demolished, re-appeared, in improved forms, which only consummate ingenuity could have devised. Works built to withstand guns used in ordinary warfare were found wholly inadequate to resist the heavy metal of the enemy; and, subjected to the incessant and galling fire of musketry, the artillery could with difficulty be worked. But the energy and resources of General Pemberton met even these difficulties. The position of the pieces was constantly changing; embankments disappeared under the enemy's fire; but the Confederate artillery would still be found in position, and stronger than before.

But the skill of the commander and the heroic endurance of the garrison were unavailing. From the first, relief from without was expected. For forty-eight days this hope stimulated the commander and the garrison, and General Pemberton subsequently declared that he "would have lived upon an ounce a day, and have continued to meet the assaults of all Grant's army, rather than have surrendered the city, until General Johnston had realized or relinquished that hope." When the hope of aid was finally abandoned, the surrender of Vicksburg was simply a question of time and honor. The alternative was either to capitulate or attempt to cut through the enemy's lines. In a council of his officers, Pemberton favored the latter plan, but yielded to the views of the majority.

The case of General Pemberton was a striking instance of public ingratitude. Vindicating his devotion to the cause of the South, by surrendering his commission in the Federal service, turning his back upon his kindred, and leaving a large property in the country of the enemy, he was stigmatized by the very people in whose cause he had made these sacrifices. His loyalty, capacity, and fidelity were questioned, even while he was in the front of death. His noble reply to these accusations can never be forgotten. Said he to his troops: "You have been told that I was disloyal and incompetent, and that I would sell Vicksburg. *Follow me*, and you shall see *at what price* I shall sell it." The story of the devotion shown at Vicksburg is no mean one in the history of the Confederacy. But the great qualities of this abused man have even a nobler testimony than the gallantry of that defense. Convinced that the cloud of prejudice and misrepresentation which followed him, rendered useless to the cause his services in high position, he tendered his resignation as a Lieutenant-General, and requested to be ordered to duty with his original rank of Lieutenant-Colonel of Artillery.*

When the facts belonging to the unfortunate campaign in Mississippi were made known, the censure of Pemberton was rather for what he *failed to do*, than *what he had done.* But suppose the same test should be applied to General Johnston; would there not be found an equal wanting of *results?* If Johnston was powerless to make even a diversion with more than twenty thousand men, (his force at the time of Pember-

* The President ordered a Court of Inquiry for investigation of the facts of the campaign in Mississippi. General Pemberton requested that the most searching inquiry should be made, and that the court be allowed to *invite all attainable testimony against him.*

ton's surrender,) how much more helpless was Pemberton to check Grant?

A dispassionate and careful inquiry will demonstrate that the operations of General Pemberton, antecedent to the siege of Vicksburg, are far less censurable than was assumed by his assailants. There can be no manner of doubt, that if worthy of blame, he should not be visited with the whole responsibility. It is difficult to imagine how Pemberton could have adopted a different course, consistently with the main purpose of the campaign—which was to prevent the capture of Vicksburg. It is certain that he would have been doubly condemned, if he had executed a safe retreat, and abandoned the stronghold without an effort to save it.

A sufficient reply to the statement that Pemberton was appointed without the desirable evidence of fitness, is that the occasion was one precluding the employment of any officer whose capacity for such a command had been proven by ample trial. Every officer of established merit was then in a position from which he could not be spared. The presence of Lee in Virginia was deemed necessary by the whole country. The most popular of his lieutenants (Longstreet) was then freely criticised for an assumed failure in a recent independent command; and, besides, he was obviously needed in the Pennsylvania campaign. Beauregard was also thought to be in his appropriate place, in charge of the coast defenses; and, indeed, it was next to impossible to avoid the employment of a comparatively untried commander in some important position. The confidence of Mr. Davis in Pemberton, too, was amply sustained by the testimony of officers, in whose judgment the country confided.

But Pemberton *failed*, and it was the misfortune of the

President to have conferred distinction upon an unsuccessful commander. Waiving all discussion of the extent to which Pemberton may be justified, and even conceding the appointment to have been a bad one, let us remember how few really capable commanders are produced by even the greatest wars. Was President Davis to call twenty into existence, fit to command armies, when Napoleon declared his armies did not afford half a dozen? Let it be remembered, too, that it was his penetration that sustained Lee, Sidney Johnston and Jackson, in the face of popular clamor; that *he* rewarded, with suitable acknowledgment, the skill and gallantry of Ewell, Early, Stuart, Gordon, Longstreet, and Hood; of Breckinridge, Cleburne, Magruder, Morgan, and others whose names make up the brilliant galaxy of Confederate heroes.*

That President Davis was tenacious of his opinions is unquestionably true, and his firm grasp of his purposes was the explanation of his ascendancy over other minds, and a leading attribute of his fitness for his position. But this strenuous

* It is noteworthy that when trial vindicated the confidence of Mr. Davis in an officer, of whose capacity the critics were doubtful (as was the case in numberless instances), they made no acknowledgment of error. For example, the President was accused of the most unworthy nepotism in his appointment of General "Dick" Taylor, who was a brother of Mr. Davis' first wife. Yet that appointment was insisted upon by Stonewall Jackson, in whose army Taylor commanded a brigade. The President made Taylor a Brigadier, because he thought him competent; and afterward a Major-General, because Jackson *knew* him to be worthy of it. Did Taylor's subsequent career vindicate the President or the critics?

The case of the brave and efficient Early was another instance in which Mr. Davis was at variance with the newspaper and congressional censors, and in which, as usual, the President was sustained by Lee. It is needless to multiply examples.

adhesion to a settled aim, characteristic of all men born for influence, is a very different quality from that unreasoning zealotry which belongs to weak minds. If, indeed, the favoritism of Mr. Davis *lost* Vicksburg, with equal justice, it may be claimed that it *won* the Seven Days' victories, Manassas, Fredericksburg, and Chancellorsville.

An interesting event in the history of this period of the war, was the unsuccessful mission of Vice-President Stephens, to the Federal authorities, designed, as explained by President Davis, "to place the war upon the footing of such as are waged by civilized people in modern times." The annexed correspondence requires hardly a word of explanation. Consistent with the forbearance and humanity, with which Mr. Davis had endeavored to prevent war, by negotiation, was this effort to soften its rigors and to abate the bitterness which it had then assumed.

Recent atrocities of the Federal authorities* had compelled

*One of the worst of these proceedings of the enemy, was the execution of Captains Corbin and McGraw. On hearing of their fate, the Confederate Government inquired of the Federal authorities the reason of their actions. The response was, that they were executed as spies. The record of their trial was then demanded. In answer to this request, the Federal Government furnished a copy of the charges and specifications against them, and of the sentence of the court which condemned them, *but none of the evidence.*

From the papers thus furnished, it appears that it was not true that they had been accused or tried as spies—that the sole charge against these unfortunate gentlemen was, that they had recruited soldiers for the Confederacy in Kentucky, a State embraced in our political system and represented regularly in the Confederate Congress by Senators and Representatives. Nor was the evidence of this charge supplied. Not a scintilla of proof appeared that these men were spies. The sole pretext for their execution was the technical one that these officers were recruiting in

the Confederate Government to seriously entertain the purpose of retaliation. Reluctant to adopt a course which would remove the last restraint upon the spirit of cruelty and revenge, making the war a system of unmitigated barbarism upon both sides, President Davis determined to make an earnest appeal to the humanity of the Federal authorities. In addition to this object the mission of Mr. Stephens sought the arrangement of all disputes between the governments, respecting the cartel of exchange, upon a permanent and humane basis, by which the soldiers of the two armies should be sent to their homes, instead of being confined in military prisons.

To make the mission more acceptable to the Federal Government, President Davis removed every obstacle to intercourse upon terms of equality, and selected a gentleman of high position, of known philanthropy and moderation, and from several reasons likely to obtain an audience of the Federal authorities. The choice of time was not less indicative of the magnanimity of Mr. Davis. The Confederate army was then in Pennsylvania, apparently upon the eve of a victory already assured, and which, if gained, would have placed it in possession of the Federal capital and the richest sections of the North. At such a moment, so promising in opportunity of ample vengeance for the ravages and desolation, which everywhere marked the presence of the Federal armies, the Confederate President tendered his noble plea in behalf of civilization and humanity. With rare justice has it been said, that this

one of the States claimed by the enemy, as one of the United States, a principle which applies equally to Virginia or South Carolina, and which would, if carried out, sentence to the gallows every officer and private we had in our service.

position of Mr. Davis "merited the applause of the Christian world."

Mr. Stephens was contemptuously denied even a hearing. The sequel soon revealed the explanation of the conduct of the Federal Government, by which it became doubly chargeable for the sufferings of a protracted war, in declining to aid in the abatement of its horrors, and by abruptly closing the door against all attempts at negotiation. General Meade had repulsed General Lee at Gettysburg, while Mr. Stephens was near Fortress Monroe. Flushed with triumph and insolent in the belief that Lee's army could not escape destruction, the Federal authorities declared such intercourse with "rebels" to be "inadmissable." In other words, detention of the Confederate prisoners, and outrages upon the Southern people, were part of a political and military system at Washington, and *would be persisted in.* At subsequent stages of the war were seen the objects of this policy, which the Federal Government virtually proclaimed, and which it persistently adhered to.

The correspondence between President Davis and Vice-President Stephens proudly vindicates the humanity and magnanimity of the South. It is alone a sufficient reply to the cant of demagogues and the ravings of conscience-stricken fanatics, over the falsely-called "Rebel barbarities."

OFFICIAL CORRESPONDENCE.

RICHMOND, July 2, 1863.

Hon. Alexander H. Stephens, Richmond, Va.—

SIR: Having accepted your patriotic offer to proceed, as a military commissioner, under flag of truce, to Washington, you will receive herewith your letter of authority to the Commander-in-chief of the army and navy of the United States.

This letter is signed by me as Commander-in-chief of the Confederate land and naval forces.

You will perceive, from the terms of the letter, that it is so worded as to avoid any political difficulties in its reception. Intended exclusively as one of those communications between belligerents, which public law recognizes as necessary and proper between hostile forces, care has been taken to give no pretext for refusing to receive it, on the ground that it would involve a tacit recognition of the independence of the Confederacy.

Your mission is simply one of humanity, and has no political aspect.

If objection is made to receiving your letter, on the ground that it is not addressed to Abraham Lincoln, as President, instead of Commander-in-chief, etc., then you will present the duplicate letter, which is addressed to him as President, and signed by me, as President. To this latter, objection may be made, on the ground that I am not recognized to be President of the Confederacy. In this event, you will decline any further attempt to confer on the subject of your mission, as such conference is admissable only on the footing of perfect equality. My recent interviews with you have put you so fully in possession of my views, that it is scarcely necessary to give you any detailed instructions, even were I, at this moment, well enough to attempt it.

My whole purpose is, in one word, to place this war on the footing of such as are waged by civilized people in modern times; and to divest it of the savage character which has been impressed on it by our enemies, in spite of all our efforts and protests.

War is full enough of unavoidable horrors, under all its aspects, to justify, and even to demand, of any Christian rulers who may be unhappily engaged in carrying it on, to seek to restrict its calamities, and to divest it of all unnecessary severities.

You will endeavor to establish the cartel for the exchange of prisoners on such a basis as to avoid the constant difficulties and complaints which arise, and to prevent, for the future, what we deem the unfair conduct of our enemies, in evading the delivery of the prisoners who fall into their hands; in retarding it by sending them on circuitous routes, and by detaining them, sometimes for months, in camps and prisons; and in persisting in taking captives non-combatants.

Your attention is also called to the unheard-of conduct of Federal officers, in driving from their homes entire communities of women and children, as well as of men, whom they find in districts occupied by their troops, for no other reason than because these unfortunates are faithful to the allegiance due to their States, and refuse to take an oath of fidelity to their enemies.

The putting to death of unarmed prisoners has been a ground of just complaint in more than one instance, and the recent execution of officers of our army in Kentucky, for the sole cause that they were engaged in recruiting service in a State which is claimed as still one of the United States, but is also claimed by us as one of the Confederate States, must be repressed by retaliation, if not unconditionally abandoned, because it would justify the like execution in every other State of the Confederacy; and the practice is barbarous, uselessly cruel, and can only lead to the slaughter of prisoners on both sides—a result too horrible to contemplate, without making every effort to avoid it.

On these and all kindred subjects, you will consider your authority full and ample to make such arrangements as will temper the present cruel character of the contest; and full confidence is placed in your judgment, patriotism, and discretion, that while carrying out the objects of your mission, you will take care that the equal rights of the Confederacy be always preserved.

Very respectfully,

[Signed] JEFFERSON DAVIS.

RICHMOND, 8th July, 1863.

His Excellency Jefferson Davis—

SIR: Under the authority and instructions of your letter to me of the 2d instant, I proceeded on the mission therein assigned, without delay. The steamer Torpedo, commanded by Lieutenant Hunter Davidson, of the navy, was put in readiness, as soon as possible, by order of the Secretary of the Navy, and tendered for the service. At noon, on the 3d, she started down James River, hoisting and bearing a flag of truce after passing City Point. The next day, the 4th, at about one o'clock P. M., when within a few miles of Newport News, we were met by a small boat of the enemy, carrying two guns, which also raised a white flag before approaching us. The officer in command informed Lieutenant Davidson that he had orders from Admiral Lee, on board the United States flag-ship Minnesota, lying below, and then in view, not to allow any boat or vessel to pass the point near which he was stationed, without his permission. By this officer, I sent to Admiral Lee a note, stating my objects and wishes, a copy of which is hereto annexed, marked A. I also sent to the admiral, to be forwarded, another note, in the same language, addressed to the officer in command of the United States forces at Fort Monroe. The gunboat proceeded immediately to the Minnesota with these dispatches, while the Torpedo remained at anchor. Between three and four o'clock P. M., another boat came up to us, bearing the admiral's answer, which is hereunto annexed, marked B. We remained at or about this point in the river until the 6th instant, when, having heard nothing further from the admiral, at 12 o'clock M., on that day, I directed Lieutenant Davidson again to speak the gunboat on guard, and to hand the officer in command another note to the admiral. This was done. A copy of this note is appended, marked C. At half past two o'clock P. M., two boats approached us from below, one bearing an answer from the admiral to my note to him of the 4th. This answer is annexed, marked D. The other boat bore the answer of Lieutenant-Colonel William H. Ludlow, to my note of the 4th, addressed to the officer in command at Fort Monroe. A copy of this is annexed, marked E. Lieutenant-Colonel Ludlow also came up in person in the boat that brought his answer to me, and conferred with Colonel Ould, on board the Torpedo, upon some matters he desired to see him about in connection with the exchange of prisoners.

From the papers appended, embracing the correspondence referred to, it will be seen that the mission failed from the refusal of the enemy to receive or entertain it, holding the proposition for such a conference "inadmissable."

The influences and views that led to this determination, after so long a consideration of the subject, must be left to conjecture. The reason assigned for the refusal by the United States Secretary of War, to wit: "that the customary agents and channels are considered adequate for needful military communications and conferences," to one acquainted with the facts, seems not only unsatisfactory, but very singular and unaccountable, for it is certainly known to him that these very agents, to whom he evidently alludes, heretofore agreed upon in a former conference, in reference to the exchange of prisoners, (one of the subjects embraced in your letter to me,) are now, and have been for some time, distinctly at issue on several important points. The existing cartel, owing to these disagreements, is virtually suspended, so far as the exchange of officers on either side is concerned. Notices of retaliation have been given on both sides.

The efforts, therefore, for the very many and cogent reasons set forth in your letter of instructions to me, to see if these differences could not be removed, and if a clearer understanding between the parties, as to the general conduct of the war, could not be arrived at, before this extreme measure should be resorted to by either party, was no less in accordance with the dictates of humanity than in strict conformity with the usages of belligerents in modern times. Deeply impressed as I was with these views and feelings, in undertaking the mission, and asking the conference, I can but express my profound regret at the result of the effort made to obtain it; and I can but entertain the belief, that if the conference sought had been granted, mutual good could have been effected by it; and if this war, so unnatural, so unjust, so unchristian, and so inconsistent with every fundamental principle of American constitutional liberty, "must needs" continue to be waged against us, that at least some of its severer horrors, which now so eminently threaten, might have been avoided.

Very respectfully,

ALEXANDER H. STEPHENS.

CHAPTER XVI.

OPERATIONS OF GENERAL TAYLOR IN LOUISIANA—THE MISSISSIPPI VALLEY IRRECOVERABLY LOST TO THE CONFEDERACY—FEDERALS FOILED AT CHARLESTON—THE DIMINISHED CONFIDENCE OF THE SOUTH—FINANCIAL DERANGEMENT—DEFECTIVE FINANCIAL SYSTEM OF THE SOUTH—MR. DAVIS' LIMITED CONNECTION WITH IT—THE REASONS FOR THE FINANCIAL FAILURE OF THE CONFEDERACY—INFLUENCE OF SPECULATION—ANOMALOUS SITUATION OF THE SOUTH—MR. DAVIS' VIEWS OF THE FINANCIAL POLICY OF THE SOUTH AT THE BEGINNING OF THE WAR—MILITARY OPERATIONS IN TENNESSEE—BRAGG RETREATS TO CHATTANOOGA—MORGAN'S EXPEDITION—SURRENDER OF CUMBERLAND GAP—FEDERAL OCCUPATION OF CHATTANOOGA—BATTLE OF CHICKAMAUGA—BRAGG'S EXPECTATIONS—GRANT'S OPERATIONS—BRAGG BADLY DEFEATED—PRESIDENT DAVIS' VIEW OF THE DISASTER—GENERAL BRAGG RELIEVED FROM COMMAND OF THE WESTERN ARMY—CENSURE OF THIS OFFICER—HIS MERITS AND SERVICES—THE UNJUST CENSURE OF MR. DAVIS AND GENERAL BRAGG FOR THE REVERSES IN THE WEST—OPERATIONS IN VIRGINIA IN THE LATTER PART OF 1863—CONDITION OF THE SOUTH AT THE CLOSE OF THE YEAR—SIGNS OF EXHAUSTION—PRESIDENT DAVIS' RECOMMENDATIONS—PUBLIC DESPONDENCY—THE WORK OF FACTION—ABUSE OF MR. DAVIS IN CONGRESS—THE CONTRAST BETWEEN HIMSELF AND HIS ASSAILANTS—DEFICIENCY OF FOOD—HOW CAUSED—THE CONFEDERACY EVENTUALLY CONQUERED BY STARVATION.

THOUGH indicating that stage of the war, when began the steady decline of the Confederacy, the summer of 1863 was not wholly unredeemed by successes, which, however transient in significance, threw no mean lustre upon Southern arms.

A series of brilliant operations marked the career of General Richard Taylor in Lower Louisiana. Preceded by a successful campaign in the Lafourche region, an expedition was undertaken by General Taylor against Brashear City, in the latter days of June. A strong and important position was carried, and eighteen hundred prisoners, with over five millions of dollars worth of stores, were captured. For some time the hope was indulged, that this success of General Taylor would compel the abandonment of the Federal siege of Port Hudson, and that Taylor could also make a successful diversion in favor of Vicksburg. This hope was disappointed, and Taylor, not having the strength to cope with the large force of the enemy sent against him, after the fall of the Mississippi strongholds, was forced to abandon the country which he had so gallantly won. The valley of the Mississippi was irrecoverably in Federal possession, and the Confederacy was able at no subsequent stage of the war, to undertake any serious enterprise for its redemption.

At Charleston the Federal fleet and land forces continued, during the summer, their fruitless and expensive attacks. The skill of General Beauregard, and the firmness of his small command, made memorable the siege of that devoted city, so hated and coveted by the North, yet among the last prizes to fall into its hands.

But momentary gleams of hope were insufficient to dispel the shadow of disaster, which, by midsummer, seemed to have settled upon the fate of the Confederacy. The violent blow dealt the material capacity of the South by the surrender of Vicksburg; the diminished prestige, from the serious check at Gettysburg, in its wondrous career of victory, and the frightful losses of the Army of Northern Virginia, were immediately followed by a marked abatement of that unwavering confidence in the ultimate result, which had previously so stimulated the energy of the South.

The material disability and embarrassment resulting from the possession, by the enemy, of large sections of the Confederacy, and consequent contraction of its territorial area; the destruction of property; the serious disturbance of the whole commercial system of the South, by the loss of Vicksburg; and the diminished confidence of the public, were attended by a fatal derangement of the already failing Confederate system of finance.

In the American war, as in all wars, the question of finance entered largely into the decision of the result. At an early period many sagacious minds declared that the contest would finally be resolved into a question as to which of the belligerents "had the longer purse." In acceptance of this view, the belief was largely entertained that the financial distress in the South, consequent upon the heavy reverses of this period, clearly portended the failure of the Confederacy.

President Davis, since the war, has avowed his appreciation of the financial difficulties of the South, as a controlling influence in the failure of the cause. By unanimous consent, the management of the Confederate finances has been declared to have been defective. The universal distress attendant upon a depreciated currency, which rarely improved in seasons of military success, and grew rapidly worse with each disaster, rendered the financial feature of Mr. Davis' administration, peculiarly vulnerable to the industry of a class ever on the alert for a pretext available to excite popular distrust of the President. With entire justice, we might dismiss this subject, claiming for Mr. Davis the benefit of the plea which always allows a ruler some exemption from responsibility for the errors of a subordinate. We have rarely sought to fasten culpability upon those who differed with him, in some instances, perhaps where it would have more clearly established his own exculpation. No act or utterance of Mr. Davis could be urged to show that *he* ever claimed for himself the benefit of such a plea. Fidelity to his friends is a trait in his character, not less worthy of admiration than magnanimity and forbearance to his foes. His ardent and sympathetic nature doubtless often condoned the errors of those whose motives he knew to be good; but his friends can testify that he far more frequently overlooked the asperities of his enemies.*

*General D. H. Hill has given a most manly exhibition of feeling toward Mr. Davis, in an article published, some months since, in his magazine. We quote from General Hill, who alludes, at length, to the alleged rancor of Mr. Davis toward his opponents. General Hill prefaces his remarks with the declaration, that he "has never been among the personal friends of Mr. Davis;" that he was "at no time an admirer of his executive abilities;" and further declares himself to have been the recipient of an "unexplained, and perhaps unexplainable wrong," at the hands of Mr. Davis. Says this gallant soldier:

"It was said of Mr. Davis that he could see no good in his enemies and no evil in his friends. I know of one instance, at least, of incorrectness of the former statement. I was present when a discussion took place in regard to the suppression of a newspaper because of the disloyal character of its articles, which were producing desertion in the army, and disaffection among the people at home. The editor had been converted to Unionism by the battle of Gettysburg and fall of Vicksburg, and, like all new-born proselytes, was fiery in his zeal. A cabinet officer present said: 'This man is not more disloyal than ——' (naming a well-known editor, whose assaults upon Mr. Davis at this time were very virulent.) 'I don't see how one paper can be suppressed without suppressing the other.' To this a gentleman replied: 'You are unjust. Mr. ——, though an enemy of the President, yet shows by his abuse of the Yankees that he has no love for them. The other editor betrays hatred of the President and of his own people.' Mr. Davis immediately assented to this, saying: 'You have exactly described the difference between the two men.' . . . . . But

We have elsewhere explained the appointment of Mr. Memminger, as having been dictated by other considerations than that of a reliance upon his special fitness. But while doubting his capacity for his difficult and anomalous situation, we are not so sure that he exhibited such marked unfitness as should have forbidden his retention in office, and called for the appointment of another, with the expectation of a more satisfactory administration. In the end, yielding to the vast pressure against him, Mr. Memminger left the cabinet, and Mr. Davis appointed, as his successor, a gentleman unknown to himself, but recommended as the possessor of financial talents of a high order. When Mr. Trenholm became Secretary of the Treasury, the opportunity for reform had long since passed, if, indeed, such an opportunity existed after the repulse at Gettysburg and the surrender of Vicksburg. It is hardly within the range of probability, that, after those reverses, any conceivable ingenuity could have arrested the downward tendency of Confederate finances. In the history of Confederate finance, before those disasters, is to be found much extenuation, if not ample

it *is not* true that he could see no good in his enemies, and that he pursued them with rancorous hate. I do not doubt that in the comparison with his supposed friends, they were in his estimation both intellectually weak and morally perverse. But, apart from this, he could be just and appreciative of their merits. I saw him several times during the session of a Confederate Congress in which he had been harshly assailed. Once he alluded incidentally to his troubles, but without the least resentment in language or manner. I think that there was no instance of the supression of a newspaper, though several editors were notoriously disloyal to the Confederate cause, and still more of them intensely hostile to the Confederate President. Like Washington, Mr. Davis held 'error to be the portion of humanity, and to censure it, whether committed by this or that public character, to be the prerogative of a freeman.'"

apology, for a system which was imposed by the force of circumstances and the novelty of the situation, rather than by the errors of one man, or a number of men.

In his message of December, 1863, Mr. Davis reviewed the subject in all its phases, as it had been presented up to that period, and sketched the plan, afterwards adopted by Congress, but without the result hoped for of increasing the value of the currency, by compulsory funding and large taxation. His discussion of this subject was always characterized by perspicuity and force, but finance was that branch of administration with which he affected the least familiarity, and which he least assumed to direct. Knowing the profound and unremitting attention which the subject required, he sought the aid of others competent for the inquiry, which he had little leisure to pursue.

This subject, during the entire war, was a fruitful theme for the disquisitions of charlatans. Finance is a subject confessedly intricate, and but few men in any country are capable of able administration of this branch of government. Yet the Confederacy swarmed with pretenders, advocating opposing theories, which their authors, in every case, declared to be infallible. The Confederate administration neither wanted for advisers, nor did it fail to seek the advice of those who were reputed to have financial abilities. Its errors were, to a large degree, shared by the ablest statesmen of the South.

Criticism is proverbially easy and cheap, after the result is ascertained, and we now readily see the leading causes of the depreciation of Confederate money. In the last twelve months of the war, the rapid and uninterrupted depreciation was occasioned by the want of confidence in the success of the cause, on the part of those who controlled the value of the money.

Such was the alarm and distrust consequent upon the disasters of July, 1863, that the Confederate currency is stated to have declined a thousand per cent., within a few weeks. Previous to that period the decline was gradual, but far less alarming in its indications. The plan adopted by the Government, partly in deference to popular prejudice against direct taxation by the general Government, and partly as a necessity of the situation—that of credit in the form of paper issues, followed by the enormous issues necessary to meet the expenses of a war, increasing daily in magnitude—pampered the spirit of speculation, which, by the close of the second year, had become almost universal. This latter influence may safely be declared to have greatly accelerated the unfortunate result, and the extent of its prevalence reflects an unpleasant shadow upon the otherwise unmarred fame of the South for self-denying patriotism.

It is customary to speak of the financial management of the Confederacy in especial disparagement, when contrasted with that of the North. The injustice of this contrast, however, is palpable. We are not required to disparage the Federal financial system—which was, indeed, conducted with consummate tact and ingenuity—to extenuate the errors, in this respect, of the Confederacy. The circumstances of the antagonists were altogether different; the position of the South financially, as in other respects, was peculiar and anomalous. Completely isolated, with a large territory, with virtually no specie circulation,* hastily summoned to meet the exigencies of the most gigantic war of modern times, the South had no alternative but to resort to an entirely artificial, and, to some extent, un-

*At the beginning of the war, the South had only fifty millions of coin, and had a paper circulation of about the same amount.

tried system of finance. From the outset, the basis of the Confederate system was the patriotism and the confidence of the people. The first was nobly steadfast, but the second was necessarily dependent upon military success. When at last the virtual collapse of the credit indicated the increasing public despondency, it was plain that a catastrophe was near at hand.

It has been generally agreed that the only scheme by which the South could have assured her credit, was to have sent large amounts of cotton to Europe, during the first year of the war, while the blockade was not effective. This plan, if successfully carried out, would have given the Confederacy a cash basis in Europe of several hundred millions in gold, in consequence of the high prices commanded by cotton afterwards. With even tolerable management, the Confederacy would thus have been assured means to meet the necessities of the war. The merit of this plan depended largely upon its practicability. Mr. Davis approved it, but it is easy to imagine how—engrossed with his multifarious cares, and occupied in meeting the pressing exigencies of each day—he lacked opportunity to mature and execute a measure of so much responsibility.

While the campaign in Mississippi, which terminated so disastrously, was still pending, General Bragg continued to occupy his position in Southern Tennessee. Too weak to attack Rosecrans, because of the reduction of his army, by the reënforcements sent to the Mississippi, Bragg was able merely to maintain a vigilant observation of his adversary. After the fall of Vicksburg General Rosecrans received reënforcements sufficient to justify an advance against the Confederates. After an obstinate resistance the Confederate commander was flanked by a force, which the superior strength of his antagonist enabled him to detach, and abandoned a line of great natural strength, and strongly fortified. This was an important success to the enemy, who were hereafter able, with much better prospects, to undertake expeditions against the heart of the Confederacy. General Bragg extricated his army from a perilous position, and made a successful retreat to Chattanooga. Auxiliary to the retreat of Bragg was the diversion made by General John Morgan, which occasioned the detachment of a portion of Burnside's forces from East Tennessee, which threatened Bragg's rear. The expedition of Morgan was pushed by that daring officer through Kentucky and across the Ohio, to the great alarm of the States upon the border of that river, but ended in the capture of Morgan and nearly all his command.

A most painful surprise to the South was the surrender of Cumberland Gap, early in September. This was a serious blow at the whole system of defense in Tennessee and the adjacent States. A Richmond newspaper declared that the possession of Cumberland Gap gave the enemy the "key to the back-door of Virginia and the Confederacy." The officer in command of the position was severely censured by the country, and though he has since explained his conduct in terms, which appear to be satisfactory, the impression prevailed until the end of the war, that the loss of this most important position was caused by gross misconduct. The comment of President Davis explains the serious nature of this affair: "The entire garrison, including the commander, being still held prisoners by the enemy, I am unable to suggest any explanation of this disaster, which laid open Eastern Tennessee and South-western Virginia to hostile operations, and broke the line of communication between the seat of government and Middle Tennessee. This easy success of the enemy was followed by the advance of General Rosecrans into Georgia, and our army evacuated Chattanooga."

Thus the coöperating movements of Rosecrans in Middle Tennessee, and of Burnside in East Tennessee, had the ample reward of expelling the Confederates from their strong lines of defense in the mountains. Cumberland Gap controlled the most important line of communication in the Confederacy. Chattanooga was the portal from which the enemy could debouch upon the level country of the Gulf and Atlantic States. The capture of Vicksburg and seizure of the Mississippi Valley, by which the Confederacy was sundered, was the first stage of conquest. Chattanooga was now the base from which was to be attempted the next great step of Federal ambition—the second *bisection* of the Confederacy.

When Rosecrans advanced into Georgia, after his occupation of Chattanooga, the aspect of affairs was exceedingly threatening, and it became necessary to strengthen Bragg sufficiently to enable him to give battle, and thus check the advance of the enterprising Federal commander. With this view the corps of Longstreet was temporarily detached from Lee, and sent to Bragg. This accession to his forces gave General Bragg the opportunity of winning one of the most brilliant victories of the war. The signal defeat of Rosecrans was followed by his precipitate retreat into Chattanooga, closely pressed by Bragg.

For weeks the Federal army was besieged with a good prospect for its ultimate surrender. The imperiled position of Rosecrans had the effect of relieving the pressure of invasion at other points, forcing the concentration, for his relief, of large bodies of troops withdrawn from the armies in the Mississippi Valley and in Northern Virginia. General Bragg made an able disposition of his forces in the neighborhood of

Chattanooga, and awaited with confidence the surrender of Rosecrans. He subsequently said: "These dispositions, faithfully sustained, ensured the enemy's speedy evacuation of Chattanooga for want of food and forage. *Possessed of the shortest road to his depot, and the one by which reënforcements must reach him, we held him at our mercy, and his destruction was only a question of time.*"

The situation fully justified this statement. So crippled was Rosecrans by his defeat at Chickamauga, that an attack upon Bragg was out of the question. The alternative of starvation, or retreat, seemed forced upon the Federal army. The roads in its rear were in a terrible condition, and the distance over which its supplies had to be drawn, was sixty miles. At this critical moment, General Grant, whose command had been enlarged, after his success at Vicksburg, and now embraced the three main Federal armies in the West, reached the field of operations. Grant immediately executed a plan of characteristic boldness, by which he effected a lodgment on the south side of the Tennessee River, and secured new lines of communication, thus relieving the beleaguered army. General Longstreet, to whom the holding of this all-important route was confided, made an unsuccessful night attack designed to defeat Grant's movement.

Having relieved the Federal army of the apprehension of starvation or a disastrous retreat, Grant now meditated operations, which, however hazardous, or however in violation of probability may have been their success, were fully vindicated by the result. Waiting until he thought his accumulation of forces sufficient to justify an assault upon the strong positions of the Confederates, Grant finally made a vigorous and well-planned attack with nearly his entire force. The result was a disastrous defeat and retreat of Bragg's army. General Grant claimed, as the fruits of his victory, seven thousand prisoners and nearly fifty pieces of artillery.

There were circumstances attending this battle peculiarly discouraging to the South. These circumstances were thus commented upon by President Davis:

"After a long and severe battle, in which great carnage was inflicted on him, some of our troops inexplicably abandoned positions of great strength, and, by a disorderly retreat, compelled the commander to withdraw the forces elsewhere successful, and finally to retire with his whole army to a position some twenty or thirty miles to the rear. It is believed that if the troops who yielded to the assault had fought with the valor which they had displayed on previous occasions, and which was manifested in this battle on the other parts of the line, the enemy would have been repulsed with very great slaughter, and our country would have escaped the misfortune, and the army the mortification of the first defeat that has resulted from misconduct by the troops.

With this disastrous battle terminated the connection of General Bragg with the army, which he commanded during a large portion of its varied career. Fully acknowledging his defeat, General Bragg candidly avowed to the Government the extent of a reverse, which he declared disabled him from any serious resistance, should the Federal commander press his success. At his own request he was relieved, and, seeking recuperation for his shattered health, was not assigned to duty until February, 1864, when President Davis ordered him to the discharge of the duties of "Commanding General," at Richmond, the position held by General Lee before his transfer to the command of the Army of Northern Virginia.

No commander was more harshly criticised than Bragg, and the unfortunate career of the Western army, under his command, was an inexhaustible theme for diatribe and invective from the opponents of the Confederate administration. Bragg was often declared to be, at once the most incompetent and unlucky of the "President's favorites." Yet nothing is more certain than that an impartial review of his military career will demonstrate General Bragg to have been a soldier of rare and superior merit. It certainly can not be claimed that his campaigns exhibited the brilliant and solid achievements of several of those conducted by Lee, or of the Valley campaigns of Jackson. The great disparity of numbers and means of the two sections, enabled few Confederate commanders to achieve the distinction of unmarred success, even before that period of decline when disaster was the rule, and victory the exception with the Confederate forces.

But Bragg can not justly be denied the merit of having, with most inadequate means, long deferred the execution of the Federal conquest of the West. At the time of his assumption of command, in June, 1862, the armies of Grant and Buell, nearly double his own aggregate of forces, were overrunning the northern borders of the Gulf States, and threatening the very heart of the Confederacy. His masterly combinations, attended by loss altogether disproportioned to the results accomplished, recovered large sections of territory, which had been for months the easy prey of the enemy, and transferred the seat of war to Middle Tennessee. Here he maintained his position for nearly a year, vigorously assailing the enemy at every opportunity, constantly menacing his communications, and firmly holding his important line, in the face of overwhelming odds, while the Confederate armies in every other quarter were losing ground. Finally, when forced back by the concentration of Federal forces, released by their successes elsewhere, Bragg skillfully eluded the combinations for his destruction, and, at an opportune moment, delivered Rosecrans one of the most timely and stunning blows inflicted during the war. No fact of the war is more clearly established than Bragg's exculpation from any responsibility for the escape of the Federal army from the field of Chickamauga. His positive commands were disobeyed, his plan of battle threatened with entire derangement by the errors of subordinates, and the escape of Rosecrans secured by the same causes. But still more cruel was the disappointment of Bragg's well-grounded expectation of a successful siege of Chattanooga. So clear is his exculpation in this case, that no investigation of facts, severely reflecting upon others, is required.

While the controversy between Bragg and Longstreet was pending, some disposition was manifested to censure the former for his rejection of a plan of campaign proposed by Longstreet after the victory of Chickamauga. The latter officer suggested crossing the Tennessee above Chattanooga, and then moving upon the enemy's rear, with a view to force him back upon Nashville. The pregnant criticism of General Bragg quickly disposes of the suggestion. Said he: "The suggestion of a movement by our right, immediately after the battle, to the north of the Tennessee, and thence upon Nashville, requires notice only because it will find a place on the files of the department. Such a movement was utterly impossible for want of transportation. Nearly half our army consisted of reënforcements just before the battle, without a wagon or an artillery horse, and nearly, if not quite, a third of the artillery horses on the field had been lost. The railroad bridges, too, had been destroyed to a point south of Ringgold, and on all the road from Cleveland to Knoxville. To these insurmountable difficulties were added the entire absence of means to cross the river, except by fording at a few precarious points too deep for artillery, and the well-known danger of sudden rises, by which all communication would be cut off, a contingency which did actually happen a few days after the visionary scheme was abandoned." General Bragg continues a recitation of cogent considerations in support of his objections to a plan which he declares utterly wanting in "military propriety."

The culmination of Bragg's unpopularity was his defeat at Missionary Ridge. No officer, save Lee, could, by any possibility, have hoped for a dispassionate judgment by the public, at this desperate stage of the war, of an affair so calamitous. The real explanation of that battle was unquestionably contained in the extract from President Davis' message previously given. Although Bragg could oppose but little more than thirty thousand troops to the eighty thousand which Grant threw against him, the strength of his position would have compensated for this disparity, had his troops fought with the usual spirit of Confederate soldiers.

It was not to be anticipated that the enemies of the President in Congress and the hostile press would fail to find a pretext upon which to throw the responsibility upon Mr. Davis. The disaster was declared to have resulted from the detachment of Longstreet for an expedition into East Tennessee. It is only necessary to state the facts of the case to show the falsity and injustice of this criticism. In the first place, as we have already stated, Bragg's force was sufficient to hold his tremendously strong position without Longstreet, should his army fight with its usual spirit. Secondly, Longstreet's corps was a part of Lee's army, detached for a purely temporary purpose with Bragg, and its absence was a source of constant anxiety to General Lee. This temporary purpose was well served at the battle of Chickamauga, which Bragg designed to be a destructive blow, and which failed in a part of its purpose, through no fault of that commander.

It was never intended to leave Longstreet in the West any longer than was necessary to relieve Bragg in his great exigency after the evacuation of Chattanooga. That result being accomplished, Longstreet was detained for a few weeks, in the expectation that Rosecrans, driven to desperation by his necessities, would attempt to retreat, in which event, Longstreet could perform valuable service in aiding to destroy the Federal army. When Grant, however, opened the Federal communications, and Longstreet was foiled in his effort to prevent it, there was no longer a sufficient reason for his detention so far from Lee. Accordingly, he was sent through East Tennessee, with the double design of opening communication with Virginia, where, at any moment, he might be needed, and of clearing East Tennessee of the forces of Burnside.

Had Longstreet's expedition been successful, it can not be doubted that the pressure against Bragg would have been immediately relieved, and a vital section restored to the Confederacy. We can not pause, however, to review the incidents of General Longstreet's movement, nor to revive the controversy between himself and a subordinate, evoked by an expedition whose results exhibited few features of success.

President Davis, better acquainted with the facts of the war than the critics who so often mislead the public, held General

Bragg in that high estimation to which his unquestioned patriotism and his military qualities entitled him. Of General Bragg it may be fairly said that he made the most of his opportunities and his means. If he made retreats, they were always preceded by bloody fights, and marked by obstinate resistance. If his constrained and sullen retreats lost territory, they were not comparable in that respect with that mysterious "strategy" of other commanders in high favor with the opponents of Mr. Davis, which eventually threatened to "toll" the enemy to the Atlantic coast, or the Gulf of Mexico, without once bringing him to a general engagement.

Bragg never feared to stake his fame on the gage of battle, and, if he sustained reverses, he won many more victories. An educated soldier, he was also a rigid disciplinarian, and had little toleration for the demagogism so conspicuous in volunteer armies. This was the occasion of much of the personal enmity by which he was embarrassed both in and out of the army. But, whatever the justice of the public condemnation of Bragg, his period of usefulness in the Western army was at an end. Very soon afterwards General Joseph E. Johnston took command of the army in Northern Georgia.

The two armies in Virginia, weakened by the detachments from each sent to the West, continued inactive until autumn. In October, General Lee prepared a brilliant campaign, the object of which was to place his army between General Meade and Washington. Meade, though forced back to the neighborhood of Manassas and Centreville, had become apprized of Lee's movement in time to prevent the consummation of the strategy of the Confederate commander. An incident of the expedition was the severe repulse of a part of General Hill's command, attended with considerable loss. Meanwhile, General

Imboden, coöperating with the movements of the main army, captured several hundred prisoners and valuable stores in the Shenandoah Valley. Early in November, nearly two thousand Confederates were captured at Rappahannock Station by a movement marked by skill and gallantry on the part of General Sedgwick. The campaign in Northern Virginia terminated with a handsome success by the division of General Edward Johnson over a large detachment from Meade's army at Mine Run. In December, General Averill, with a force of Federal cavalry, made a destructive raid into South-western Virginia, and destroyed portions of the Virginia and Tennessee Railroad.

At the close of 1863, there were many signs of the approaching exhaustion of the South, yet there was good reason to hope that, by a vigorous use of means yet remaining, the war might be brought to a favorable conclusion. The peace party of the North, despite the increased strength and popularity of Mr. Lincoln's administration, resulting from the Federal successes of the summer, was evidently becoming more bold and defiant. The whole North, too, was disappointed at the prospect of an indefinite resistance by the South. Gettysburg and Vicksburg were not followed, as had been anticipated, by the immediate collapse of the Confederacy. Under such circumstances, the South had much to anticipate from a bold and defiant front at the opening of the next campaign. Unquestionably its resources were less adequate than before, but there was evidently capacity to prolong the war for an almost indefinite period. Thus, while the Confederacy could not cherish the hope of daring exploits at the opening of the campaign, which should again make the enemy apprehensive for his own homes, there was a well-grounded anticipation of a successful defensive, which should wear out the enemy's ardor, and again present opportunities for bold enterprise.

The message of President Davis to Congress, which met early in December, was one of his ablest productions. Reviewing the entire field of the war, in its more important phases, it was equally remarkable for its frank statement of the situation, and for the energetic policy recommended.

There could be no difficulty in comprehending the needs of the Confederacy at this distressing period. The three great elements of war—men, money, and subsistence—were now demanded to a greatly increased extent. In nothing was the campaign of 1863 more fatal, than in the terrible losses inflicted on the armies of the Confederacy. At the close of the year, the Army of Northern Virginia, including the absent corps of Longstreet, was weaker, by more than a third of the force carried into Pennsylvania. The losses of the Western army had fearfully diminished its strength, and its frequent disasters had greatly impaired its *morale.* Measures were now required which should repair the losses, and, if possible, increase the army beyond its strength at the opening of the previous campaign, in order to meet the enormous conscription preparing at the North.

President Davis indicated the following methods of adding to the army: "Restoring to the army all who are improperly absent, putting an end to substitution, modifying the exemption law, restricting details, and placing in the ranks such of the able-bodied men now employed as wagoners, nurses, cooks, and other employés as are doing service, for which the negroes may be found competent."

These were evidently the last expedients by which the Confederate armies could be recruited from the white population.

By successive enactments Congress had empowered the President to call into the field all persons between the ages of eighteen and forty-five. The exigency consequent upon the reverses of the summer had necessitated the requisition of the last reserves provided by Congress—the class between forty and forty-five. Conscription had failed to give the effective strength calculated upon. Each extension of the law exhibited, in the result, an accession of numbers greatly below the estimate upon which it was based. This was largely due to the inefficient execution of the law, and to the opposition which it encountered in many localities. But the results also indicated a most exaggerated estimate of the available arms-bearing population of the South. In the latter part of 1863, the rolls of the Adjutant-General's office in Richmond showed a little more than four hundred thousand men under arms; and Secretary Seddon stated that, from desertions and other causes, "not more than a half—never two-thirds—of the soldiers were in the ranks."

The message of Mr. Davis indicated defective features in the system of conscription, and suggested improvements as follows:

"On the subject of exemptions, it is believed that abuses can not be checked unless the system is placed on a basis entirely different from that now provided by law. The object of your legislation has been, not to confer privileges on classes, but to exonerate from military duty such number of persons skilled in the various trades, professions, and mechanical pursuits, as could render more valuable service to their country by laboring in their present occupation than by going into the ranks of the army. The policy is unquestionable, but the result would, it is thought, be better obtained by enrolling all such persons, and allowing details to be made of the number necessary to meet the wants of the country. Considerable numbers are believed to be now exempted from the military service who are not needful to the public in their civil vocation.

"Certain duties are now performed throughout the country by details from the army, which could be as well executed by persons above the present conscript age. An extension of the limit, so as to embrace persons over forty-five years, and physically fit for service in guarding posts, railroads, and bridges, in apprehending deserters, and, where practicable, assuming the place of younger men detailed for duty with the nitre, ordnance, commissary, and quartermaster's bureaus of the War Department, would, it is hoped, add largely to the effective force in the field, without an undue burden on the population."

The message further recommended legislation replacing "not only enlisted cooks, but wagoners, and other employés in the army, by negroes." From these measures the President expected that the army would be "so strengthened, for the ensuing campaign, as to put at defiance the utmost efforts of the enemy."

But the meagre results of conscription revealed not only an excessive calculation of the numerical strength of the Confederacy; they indicated the reluctance with which the harsh necessities of the war, in its later stages, were met. As the war was protracted, popular ardor naturally waned, and in the presence of losses and reverses, the spirit of voluntary sacrifice gradually disappeared. Draft and impressment were now required to obtain the services and the means, which, in the beginning, were lavishly proffered.

Partially the result of a natural popular weariness of the increasing exactions of a long and exhaustive struggle, these were also the legitimate fruits of the distrust so assiduously inculcated by the fault-finders. When reverses to their armies came with appalling rapidity, and, in many instances, in spite of the exertions of their ablest and most popular leaders, the people saw confidence and industry only in their Government, and that Government they were constantly taught to believe grossly incompetent and unworthy. Under such circumstances, how could there be that unity and coöperation, without which the cause was preordained to failure? In that industry which sought every possible occasion for censure, that ingenuity which exaggerated every error, that intemperance which filled the halls of Congress with denunciation, and the land with clamor and discontent, the North at last found allies which ably assisted its armies.

More violent, intemperate, and unscrupulous than ever, were the assaults upon the administration, in that long period of agony which followed the disasters in Mississippi and Pennsylvania. Such was an appropriate occasion, when a grief-stricken country implored the unanimity which alone could bring relief, for agitation, revenge, and invective. In Congress Mr. Davis was assailed with furious vituperation, because he had refused, at the instance of a member, to remove Bragg, and place Johnston in command of the Western army. Yet General Johnston, after a visit to Tennessee, earnestly advised the President *not* to remove Bragg, as the *public interests would suffer by that step.* Almost daily Mr. Davis was assailed for not having properly estimated the war, in the diatribes of an able editor, who himself, but a few weeks before hostilities opened, declared *there would be no war.* Of such a character were the accusers and the accusations.

If Jefferson Davis courted revenge, he could find ample satisfaction in the contrast between himself and some of his foremost accusers, which the sequel has drawn. *He* fell at last, but only when that cause was lost, which he unselfishly loved, and which his heart followed to its glorious grave. His name is already immortal—the embodiment of the heroism, the virtues, the sufferings, the glory of a people who revere him and scorn his persecutors. Nor can the South forget that many, who, during her arduous struggle, constantly assailed her chosen ruler, have since taken refuge in the camp of those who first conquered, and now seek to degrade her people.

A source of universal alarm in the South, at this period, was the deficiency of food. We have elsewhere quoted freely the admonitions of President Davis respecting the question of supplies, and indicating the cause which led to so much suffering in the armies of the Confederacy. Ever since the loss of large sections of Tennessee, in the spring of 1862, this subject had occasioned anxiety. Without entering into details, it may be briefly stated, that, with the loss of Kentucky and the larger portion of Tennessee, the Confederacy lost the main source of its supplies of meat. As other sections were occupied by the enemy, and communications were destroyed, the area of the Confederacy became more and more contracted, and its sources of supply still more limited. Even when supplies were abundant in many quarters, the armies in the field suffered actual want, in consequence of the want of transportation, and of the remoteness of the supplies from the lines of the railroads.

But while the meat in the Confederacy was rapidly diminishing in quantity, as the Federal armies advanced, and seized or destroyed every thing in the shape of subsistence, the army was still deprived of supplies which should have been made available. The unpatriotic practice of hoarding supplies—a temptation suggested by the rife spirit of speculation, arising from a redundant and depreciated currency—necessitated the passage of impressment laws. These laws were practically rendered nugatory by the inadequate provisions for their execution. In no respect was the timid and demagogical legislation of the Confederate Congress, so illustrated as by its adoption of a system of impressment, which aggravated the very evil it was designed to remedy.

Various expedients were attempted, with partial success, for obtaining subsistence beyond the limits of the Confederacy. It will be readily seen, however, how precarious was this dependence. It was impossible for the Confederacy to maintain its armies, while its resources in every other respect were rapidly reaching the point of exhaustion. In the end the want of food proved the most efficient adversary of the South. The final military catastrophe made the Federal army master of a country already half conquered by starvation.*

* My limited space has prevented the extended account of the Confederate Commissary Department, which was originally designed. The history of its commissariat is an important chapter in the history of the Confederacy. President Davis was much abused for his retention of Colonel Northrop, who has been charged, both during and since the war, with incompetency, corruption, and every conceivable abuse of his office. The amount of truth, in the charge of corruption against Colonel Northrop, may be estimated, when we state a fact known almost universally in Richmond, that few persons suffered the privations of the war more severely than he. Hundreds of the most respectable gentlemen in the South willingly testify to the unimpeachable patriotism and purity of Colonel Northrop. Equally false was the statement that Mr. Davis gratified merely his personal partiality in appointing Commissary-General a man who had given no previous evidence of fitness. Colonel Northrop, when in the regular Federal army, had seen extensive service in that department, where he was detailed, after having been disabled. His services were

amply testified to by his superiors, who regarded him as having peculiar qualifications for the duties of the commissariat. Of these facts Mr. Davis had *personal knowledge*, though, when he placed Colonel Northrop at the head of the Confederate commissariat, they had not met for more than twenty years.

Again, when commissioned by Mr. Davis, Colonel Northrop was the Commissary-General of South Carolina—a position to which he would hardly have been invited, without at least some conviction, by the authorities of that State, of his fitness. It is well known, too, that a committee of the Confederate Congress investigated the affairs of the Commissary Department, and made a report which amply and honorably vindicated Colonel Northrop. Indeed, a member of that committee, one of the ablest men in Virginia, and not friendly to Mr. Davis, declared it to be the best managed department of the Confederate Government.

Editors perpetually clamored against Colonel Northrop for issuing *half rations* to the army, who daily issued *half sheets* to their subscribers—refusing to understand that in each case the cause was the same, viz., an exhaustion of supply, resulting from the depletion of the resources of the country.

CHAPTER XVII.

AN EFFORT TO BLACKEN THE CHARACTER OF THE SOUTH—THE PERSECUTION OF MR. DAVIS AS THE SUBSTITUTE FOR THE ASSUMED OFFENSES OF THE SOUTH—REPUTATION OF THE SOUTH FOR HUMANITY—TREATMENT OF PRISONERS OF WAR—EARLY ACTION OF THE CONFEDERATE GOVERNMENT UPON THE SUBJECT—MR. DAVIS' LETTER TO MR. LINCOLN—THE COBB-WOOL NEGOTIATIONS—PERFIDIOUS CONDUCT OF THE FEDERAL AUTHORITIES—A CARTEL ARRANGED BY GENERALS DIX AND HILL—COMMISSIONER OULD—HIS CORRESPONDENCE WITH THE FEDERAL AGENT OF EXCHANGE—REPEATED PERFIDY OF THE FEDERAL GOVERNMENT—SUSPENSION OF THE CARTEL CAUSED BY THE BAD FAITH OF THE FEDERAL ADMINISTRATION, AND THE SUFFERING WHICH IT CAUSED—EFFORTS OF THE CONFEDERATE AUTHORITIES TO RENEW THE OPERATION OF THE CARTEL—HUMANE OFFER OF COMMISSIONER OULD—JUSTIFICATION OF THE CONFEDERATE AUTHORITIES—GUILT OF THE FEDERAL GOVERNMENT—MR. DAVIS' STATEMENT OF THE MATTER—COLONEL OULD'S LETTER TO MR. ELDRIDGE—NORTHERN STATEMENTS: GENERAL BUTLER, NEW YORK TRIBUNE, ETC.—THE CHARGE OF CRUELTY AGAINST THE SOUTH—A CONTRAST BETWEEN ANDERSONVILLE AND ELMIRA—IMPOVERISHMENT OF THE SOUTH—DISREPUTABLE MEANS EMPLOYED TO AROUSE RESENTMENT OF THE NORTH—THE VINDICATION OF THE SOUTH AND OF MR DAVIS—HIS STAINLESS CHARACTER, HIS HUMANITY AND FORBEARANCE—AN INQUIRY OF HISTORY.

IT is in vain to invoke the admiration of mankind for qualities of greatness, displayed either in the history of a nation or the life of an individual, unless those qualities shall have been adorned by the practice of humanity and the observance of high moral obligation. Since the political fabric of the South has been overthrown, a brave and virtuous people cherish with a more tenacious affection than ever, that honorable reputation which was their birthright, and which they worthily illustrated during the late war. The violent commotion with which the American Union was but lately convulsed has renewed the historical analogy of revolutions, not less in the sequel than in its progress. When the strife of arms was ended, and the two great armies ceased their death struggles, and parted with that mutual respect which is characteristic of brave antagonists, events were far from encouraging the cessation of sectional bitterness which was to be hoped for.

The dominant party at the North, apparently not satisfied with the political overthrow of the South, and the complete extinction of its social system, has followed up the triumphs of the Federal armies with a persistent and implacable war upon the character and reputation of the South. To affix a stigma upon a conquered foe, to brand with infamy a class of their own countrymen—the descendants of the compatriots of Franklin, Hancock, and Adams—and to consign to perpetual obloquy a cause which enlisted the sympathies of five millions of people, are the aims of a malignant and remorseless faction. These are the motives which have instigated the effort to frame an indictment against the Christianity, the morality, and the humanity of the South, and to visit every form of degradation, to practice every refinement of cruelty upon its most distinguished representative.

It is impossible to explain, upon any other theory, the exceptional rigor with which, since the termination of the war, Mr. Davis has been pursued. As the most honored by the South, he has been selected as the proper substitute upon whom to visit the offenses of his people. To convict Jefferson Davis of heinous offenses against humanity is to blacken the cause which he represented—to degrade the people of whom he was the chosen ruler. The North should have been admonished, by previous examples, of the futility of its attempts to prejudge historical questions of such moment. Of what avail were the malignity, the misrepresentation, and the unrelenting vindictiveness of England against Napoleon?

As yet, the North has been unable, even by *ex parte* evidence, to obtain a pretext for the arraignment of Jefferson Davis for those atrocious crimes of which it was pretended he was guilty. Even perjury has proven inadequate to the invention of material with which to sustain a complicity in guilt, from which his previous character alone should have vindicated him. Who can doubt the inevitable recoil when the investigations of history, unobstructed by prejudice and passion, shall lay bare the *facts* upon which posterity will render its verdict? History, in such a question, will know neither North nor South, nor will it accept all testimony as *truth* which comes under the guise of "*loyalty,*" nor reject as *falsehood* all upon which has been placed the odium of "*disloyalty.*"

In this volume, we could not, even if so disposed, avoid reference to that question which so involves the honor and humanity of the South—*the extent of her regard, in the conduct of the late war, for those moral obligations which are recognized by all Christian and civilized communities.* The course of her enemies has left the South no alternative, and she can not be apprehensive of the result when the record is fairly consulted.

We have now reached, with a due regard for chronological order, a point where naturally arises the subject of the treatment of prisoners, which, in the later months of 1863, assumed its most interesting phase. We approach the subject not with any expectation of enlightenment of the Northern mind. Upon this subject a large portion of the Northern people have resolutely turned their backs upon all statements which do not favor their sectional prejudices. Calumnies are often believed by mere force of iteration; and so persistent has been the effort to poison the Northern mind with falsehood that at least a generation must pass away before the South can expect an impartial hearing. Nevertheless, by grouping together, in these pages, important testimony from various sources, and *confined to neither section,* we hope to promote, however feebly, the great end of historic truth.

At an early period of the contest, the Confederate Government recognized its obligation to treat prisoners of war with humanity and consideration. Before any action was taken by Congress upon the subject, the executive authorities provided prisoners with proper quarters and barracks, and with rations —the same in quantity and quality as those furnished to the Confederate soldiers who guarded them. The first action of Congress with reference to prisoners was taken on the 21st of May, 1861. Congress then provided that "all prisoners of war taken, whether on land or at sea, during the pending hostilities with the United States, shall be transferred by the captors from time to time, and as often as convenient, to the Department of War; and it shall be the duty of the Secretary of War, with the approval of the President, to issue such instructions to the Quartermaster-General and his subordinates as shall provide for the safe custody and sustenance of prisoners of war; *and the rations furnised prisoners of war shall be the same in quantity and quality as those furnished to enlisted men in the army of the Confederacy.*" This declared policy of the Confederate authorities was adhered to, not only in the earlier months of the war, when provisions were abundant, but was afterwards pursued as far as possible under the *peculiar style of warfare waged by the North.* Even amid the losses and privations to which the enemy subjected them, they sought to carry out the humane purpose of this solemn declaration.

The first public announcement by President Davis, with respect to prisoners, was made in a letter to President Lincoln, dated July 6th, 1861. This letter was called forth by the alleged harsh treatment of the crew of the Confederate vessel *Savannah,* then prisoners in the hands of the enemy. We extract a paragraph of this letter:

"It is the desire of this Government so to conduct the war now existing, as to mitigate its horrors as far as may be possible; and, with this intent, its treatment of the prisoners captured by its forces has been marked by the greatest humanity and leniency consistent with public obligation; some have been permitted to return home on parole, others to remain at large under similar condition within this Confederacy, and all have been furnished with rations for their subsistence, such as are allowed to our own troops. It is only since the news has been received of the treatment of the prisoners taken on the *Savannah,* that I have been compelled to withdraw these indulgences, and to hold the prisoners taken by us in strict confinement."

In his message, dated July 20th, 1861, he mentioned this letter, and thus alluded to the expected reply from President Lincoln:

"I earnestly hope this promised reply (which has not yet been received) will convey the assurance that prisoners of war will be treated, in this unhappy contest, with that regard for humanity, which has made such conspicuous progress in the conduct of modern warfare."

Several months elapsed, after the beginning of hostilities, before the captures on either side were sufficiently numerous to demand much consideration. A proposition was even made in the Confederate Congress, to return the Federal prisoners, taken at the first battle of Manassas, without any formality whatever.

In February, 1862, negotiations occurred between the two governments, with a view to the arrangement of a system of exchange. In these negotiations Generals Howell Cobb and Wool represented their respective Governments. The result was a cartel, by which prisoners of either side should be paroled within ten days after their capture, and delivered on the frontier of their own country. A point of difference was, however, raised, as to a provision requiring each party to pay the expense of transporting their prisoners to the frontier. This difference General Wool reported to the Federal Government, which refused to pay these expenses. At a second interview, March 1st, 1862, this action of the Federal authorities being made known to General Cobb, the latter immediately conceded the point, and proposed to make the cartel conform in all its features to the wishes of General Wool. The latter declined any arrangement, declaring "that his Government had changed his instructions," and abruptly terminated the negotiations.

The explanation of this conduct was apparent. While the negotiations between Generals Wool and Cobb were pending, Fort Donelson had fallen, reversing the previous state of things, and giving the North an excess of prisoners. These prisoners, instead of being sent South on parole, were carried into the interior of the North, and treated with severity and indignity. Repudiating this agreement, just as soon as it was ascertained that their captures at Donelson placed the South at disadvantage, the Federal authorities foreshadowed that "consistently perfidious conduct," which President Davis declared to be characteristic of their entire course upon the subject.

It was impossible to bring the Federal Government to any arrangement, until the fortune of war again placed the Confederates in possession of the larger number of prisoners. An immediate consequence of the Confederate successes in the summer of 1862, was the indication of a more accommodating spirit by the enemy. Negotiations between General D. H. Hill, on behalf of the Confederate authorities, and General John A. Dix, on behalf of his Government, resulted in the adoption of a new cartel of a completely satisfactory and humane character. Under this cartel, which continued in operation for twelve months, the Confederate authorities restored to the enemy many thousands of prisoners in excess of those whom they held for exchange, and encampments of the surplus paroled prisoners were established in the United States, where the men were able to receive the comforts and solace of constant communication with their homes and families. In July, 1863, the fortune of war again favored the enemy, and they were enabled to exchange for duty the men previously delivered to them, against those captured and paroled at Vicksburg and Port Hudson. The prisoners taken at Gettysburg, however, remained in their hands, and should have been at once returned to the Confederate lines on parole, to await exchange. Instead of executing a duty imposed by the plainest dictates of justice and good faith, pretexts were instantly sought for holding them in permanent captivity. General orders rapidly succeeded each other from the bureau at Washington, placing new constructions on an agreement which had given rise to no dispute while the Confederates retained the advantage in the number of prisoners. With a disregard of honorable obligations, almost unexampled, the Federal authorities did not hesitate, in addition to retaining the prisoners captured by them, to declare null the paroles given by the prisoners captured by the Confederates in the same series of engagements, and liberated on condition of not again serving until exchanged. They then openly insisted on treating the paroles given by their own soldiers as invalid, and those of Confederate soldiers, given under precisely similar circumstances, as binding. A succession of similar unjust pretensions was maintained in a correspondence tediously prolonged, and every device employed, to cover the disregard of an obligation, which, between belligerent nations, is only to be enforced by a sense of honor.

We have not space sufficient for even a sketch of the protracted correspondence, which ensued between the commissioners of exchange, respecting the suspension of the cartel. In its progress Commissioner Ould triumphantly vindicated the action of the Confederate Government, in every instance meeting in an unanswerable manner, the counter-charges of the Federal authorities. The South can require no better record of its honorable and humane conduct, than is furnished by this correspondence. The Confederate Government was singularly fortunate in the selection of Mr. Ould, who unites to a most honorable and amiable character, an intellect of unusual vigor and astuteness, as was abundantly shown in his conclusive demonstrations of the perfidious conduct of the authorities at Washington.

For twelve months after the date of the cartel (that is, until after the battle of Gettysburg), the Confederates held a considerable excess of prisoners. It has never been alleged, amid all the calumny which has assailed the South, that during this period, the Federal prisoners (unless held on serious charges), were not promptly delivered. Commissioner Ould several times urged the Federal authorities to send increased transportation for their prisoners. On the other hand, numbers of Confederate officers and soldiers were kept in irons and dungeons, in many instances without even having charges preferred against them.

On the 26th July, 1863, Commissioner Ould said in a letter to the Federal Agent of Exchange: "Now that our official connection is being terminated, I say to you in the fear of God—and I appeal to him for the truth of the declaration—that there has been no single moment, from the time we were first brought together in connection with the matter of exchange, to the present hour, during which there has not been an open and notorious violation of the cartel, by your authorities. Officers and men, numbering over hundreds, have been, during your whole connection with the cartel, kept in cruel confinement, sometimes in irons, or doomed to cells, without charges or trial. . . . . . The last phase of the enormity, however, exceeds all others. Although you have many thousands of our soldiers now in confinement in your prisons, and especially in that horrible hold of death, Fort Delaware, you have not, for several weeks, sent us any prisoners. . . . . For the first two or three times some sort of an excuse was attempted. None is given at this present arrival. I do not mean to be offensive when I say that effrontery could not give one."

In reply to these and similar charges by Commissioner Ould, which he, in repeated instances, substantiated by naming the Confederate officers and soldiers thus shamefully treated, the enemy retorted with a charge of similar treatment of Federal prisoners. Yet the prison records of the Confederacy, in no instance, show the detention of prisoners while the cartel was in operation, unless held under grave charges. Commissioner Ould, in his letter of August 1, 1863, effectually silenced this replication. Said he: "You have claimed and exercised the right to retain officers and men indefinitely, not only upon charges actually preferred, but upon mere suspicion. You have now in custody officers who were in confinement when the cartel was framed, and who have since been declared exchanged. Some of them have been tried, but most of them have languished in prison all the weary time without trial or charges. *I stand prepared to prove these assertions.* This course was pursued, too, in the face not only of notice, but of protest. Do you deny to us the right to detain officers and men for trial upon grave charges, while you claim the right to keep in confinement any who may be the object of your suspicion or special enmity?"

The paroles issued after capture were respected by both parties, until, about the middle of 1863, the Federal authorities declared void the paroles of thousands of their soldiers, who had been sent North by the Confederate Government. At that time, it is noteworthy, the Federal Government had no lists of paroled prisoners to be charged against the Confederacy. The latter had previously discharged all its obligations from its large excess of prisoners, leaving still a large balance in their favor unsatisfied. In this condition of affairs, Commissioner Ould was notified that "exchanges will be confined to such equivalents as are held in confinement on either side." After such a display of perfidy, no surprise should be occasioned by the subsequent action of the Federal authorities. This announcement, in unmistakable phraseology, meant simply that, as the Confederates had returned equivalents for all paroles held against them, and the Federals held no paroles to be charged against the Confederacy, hereafter no exchange would be made except for men actually in captivity. In other words, having received all the benefits which they could from the observance of the cartel, the Federal Government openly repudiated it, the moment that its operation would favor their antagonists. Commissioner Ould promptly declined the perfidious proposition of the enemy, which would have continued thousands of Confederate soldiers in prison, after their Government had returned all prisoners in their possession, and yet held the paroles of Federal soldiers, largely exceeding in number the Confederate soldiers held captive by the enemy. Subsequently the Federal officers and soldiers, in violation of their paroles, and without being declared exchanged, were ordered back to their commands. Commissioner Ould then very properly declared exchanged an equal number of Confederate officers and men, who had been paroled by the enemy at Vicksburg.

With these transactions ended all exchanges under that provision of the cartel which provided the delivery of prisoners within ten days. All subsequent deliveries of prisoners were made by special agreement. The facts which we have stated, showing the suspension of the cartel to have been occasioned by the *bad faith of the Federal Government, are upon record*, and can not be disputed. They are accessible to every Northern reader, who may feel disposed to satisfy his judgment, *by facts*, rather than to foster prejudices based upon the most monstrous falsehoods, ever invented in the interest of fanaticism and hate. The suspension of the cartel was the direct cause of those terrible sufferings which were afterwards endured by the true men of both sides. It led directly to the hardships, the exposure, and hunger of Andersonville, the cruelties of Camp Douglas, the freezing of Confederate soldiers upon the bleak shores of the Northern lakes, and those countless woes which are endured by the occupants of military prisons, even when conducted upon the most humane system. Having been guilty of a shameful violation of faith, the Federal Government persisted in a policy, which was not only cruel to the South, but brought upon the brave men who were fighting its battles, the sufferings which the North has falsely pictured with every conceivable feature of horror and atrocity.

Until the end of the war, the Confederate Government continued its efforts to secure the renewed operations of the cartel—a policy which humanity to its own defenders demanded. Why it was not renewed, the motives which dictated a policy which occasioned an almost unexampled degree of human suffering, is a question abundantly answered in the testimony here adduced, the most conclusive portions of which comes from Northern sources.

In January, 1864, it was plain from the disposition of the enemy that the majority of the prisoners of both sides were doomed to confinement for many weary months, if not until the end of the war. Under this impression, Commissioner Ould wrote the following letter, which was promptly delivered to the Federal Agent of Exchange:

"CONFEDERATE STATES OF AMERICA, WAR DEPARTMENT,
"RICHMOND, VA., January 24, 1864.

"*Major-General E. A. Hitchcock, Agent of Exchange*—

"SIR: In view of the present difficulties attending the exchange and release of prisoners, I propose that all such on either side shall be attended by a proper number of their own surgeons, who, under rules to be established, shall be permitted to take charge of their health and comfort. I also propose that these surgeons shall act as commissaries, with power to receive and distribute such contributions of money, food, clothing, and medicines as may be forwarded for the relief of the prisoners. I further propose that these surgeons shall be selected by their own Government, and that they shall have full liberty, at any and all times, through the Agents of Exchange, *to make reports not only of their own acts, but of any matters relating to the welfare of the prisoners.*

"Respectfully, your obedient servant,

"ROBERT OULD,

"*Agent of Exchange.*"

To this humane proposition *no answer was ever made.* It is needless to depict the alleviation of misery which its adoption would have secured. Can there be but one interpretation of the motives of those who rejected this noble offer? These propositions are indeed extraordinary, in view of the obloquy heaped upon the Confederate authorities for their alleged indifference to the health and comfort of their prisoners. Most noticeable, however, is the invitation extended to the Federal authorities to investigate, and report to the world, the treatment and condition of Federal soldiers in Southern prisons.

But this is far from completing the evidence which convicts the Federal Government of a purpose to trade upon the sufferings of their prisoners, and thus inflame the resentment of the North during the war, and shows the malignant purpose of a faction to establish a foul libel upon the South in the mind of posterity. On the 10th of August, 1864, Commissioner Ould wrote as follows:

"*Major John E. Mulford, Assistant Agent of Exchange*—

"SIR: You have several times proposed to me to exchange the prisoners respectively held by the two belligerents, officer for officer, and man for man. The same offer has also been made by other officials having charge of matters connected with the exchange of prisoners. This proposal has heretofore been declined by the Confederate authorities, they insisting upon the terms of the cartel, which required the delivery of the excess on either side upon parole. In view, however, of the very large number of prisoners now held by each party, and the suffering consequent upon their continued confinement, I now consent to the above proposal, and agree to deliver to you the prisoners held in captivity by the Confederate authorities, provided you agree to deliver an equal number of Confederate officers and men. As equal numbers are delivered from time to time, they will be declared exchanged. This proposal is made with the understanding that the officers and men, on both sides, who have been longest in captivity, will be first delivered, where it is practicable. I shall be happy to hear from you as speedily as possible, whether this arrangement can be carried out.

"Respectfully, your obedient servant,

"ROBERT OULD,

"*Agent of Exchange.*"

It will be seen that the Confederate authorities, by this proposition, consented to waive all previous questions, to concede every point to the enemy, that could facilitate the release from captivity of its own soldiers and those of the North. As an inducement to action by the Federal authorities, this letter was accompanied by a *statement exhibiting the mortality among the prisoners at Andersonville.* Receiving no reply, Commissioner Ould made the same proposition to General Hitchcock, in Washington. The latter making no response, application was made again to Major Mulford, who replied as follows:

"*Hon. R. Ould, Agent of Exchange—*

"SIR: I have the honor to acknowledge the receipt of your favor of to-day, requesting answer, etc., to your communication of the 10th inst., on the question of the exchange of prisoners, to which, in reply, I would say, I have no communication on the subject from our authorities, nor am I yet authorized to make any.

"I am, sir, very respectfully, your obedient servant,

"JOHN E. MULFORD,

"*Assistant Agent of Exchange.*"

Nothing could exceed the generosity of this offer. When it was made, the North had a large excess of prisoners. By this arrangement every Federal soldier would have been released from captivity, while a large surplus of Confederates would have remained in the enemy's hands. The brutal calculation of the Federal authorities was that an exchange would add so many thousands of muskets to the depleted ranks of the Confederacy, and would, besides, deprive them of every pretext for the manufacture of chapters of "rebel barbarities."

It was known to the world that the means of subsistence in the South was so reduced—chiefly through the cruel warfare waged by the North—that Confederate soldiers were then subsisting upon a third of a pound of meat, and a pound of indifferent meal or flour each day. Upon such rations, half naked, thousands of them barefooted, Confederate soldiers were exposed to sufferings unexampled in history. How could it be possible, under such circumstances, to prevent suffering among the prisoners? Military prisons, under the most favorable circumstances, are miserable enough, but the Federal prisoners in the South were compelled to endure multiplied and aggravated miseries, imposed by the condition of the South—shared by their captors, and by the women and children of the country which they invaded. But what possible palliation can there be for the guilt of a Government which willfully subjected its defenders to horrors which it so blazoned to the world? Declaring that "rebel pens" were worse than Neapolitan prisons and Austrian dungeons, the Federal authorities yet persistently rejected offers of exchange.

There could be no more forcible presentation of the question than that made by President Davis:

"In the meantime a systematic and concerted effort has been made to quiet the complaints in the United States of those relatives and friends of the prisoners in our hands, who are unable to understand why the cartel is not executed in their favor, by the groundless assertion that we are the parties who refuse compliance. Attempts are also made to shield themselves from the execration excited by their own odious treatment of our officers and soldiers now captive in their hands, by misstatements, such as that the prisoners held by us are deprived of food. To this last accusation the conclusive answer has been made, that, in accordance with our laws and the general orders of the department, the rations of the prisoners are precisely the same, in quantity and quality, as those served out to our own gallant soldiers in the field, and which have been found sufficient to support them in their arduous campaign, while it is not pretended by the enemy that they treat prisoners by the same generous rule. By an indulgence, perhaps unprecedented, we have even allowed the prisoners in our hands to be supplied by their friends at home with comforts not enjoyed by the men who captured them in battle. In contrast to this treatment, the most revolting inhumanity has characterized the conduct of the United States towards prisoners held by them. One prominent fact, which admits no denial nor palliation, must suffice as a test: The officers of our army—natives of southern and semi-tropical climates, and unprepared for the cold of a northern winter—have been conveyed for imprisonment, during the rigors of the present season, to the most northern and exposed situation that could be selected by the enemy. There, beyond the reach of comforts, and often even of news from home and family, exposed to the piercing cold of the northern lakes, they are held by men who can not be ignorant of—even if they do not design—the probable result. How many of our unfortunate friends and comrades, who have passed unscathed through numerous battles, will perish on Johnston's Island, under the cruel trial to which they are subjected, none but the Omniscient can foretell. That they will endure this barbarous treatment with the same stern fortitude that they have ever evinced in their country's service, we can not doubt. But who can be found to believe the assertion that it is our refusal to execute the cartel, and not the malignity of the foe, which has caused the infliction of such intolerable cruelty on our own loved and honored defenders?"

Since the war, Commissioner Ould has given testimony of the most conclusive character. While the subject of the treatment of prisoners was pending in Congress, during the past summer, he wrote the following letter. It will be observed that he offers to *prove his statements by the testimony of Federal officers.*

"WASHINGTON, July 23, 1867.

"*To the Editors of the National Intelligencer*—

"I respectfully request the publication of the following letter, received by me from Colonel Robert Ould, of Richmond. It will be perceived that it fully sustains my statement in the House, with the unimportant exception of the number of prisoners offered to be exchanged, without equivalent, by the Confederate authorities. Very respectfully,

"CHARLES A. ELDRIDGE."

"RICHMOND, July 19, 1867.

"*Hon. Charles A. Eldridge*—

"MY DEAR SIR: I have seen your remarks as published. They are substantially correct. Every word that I said to you in Richmond is not only true, but can be proved by Federal officers. I did offer, in August, to deliver the Federal sick and wounded, without requiring equivalents, and urged the necessity of haste in sending for them, as the mortality was terrible. I did offer to deliver from ten to fifteen thousand at Savannah without delay. Although this offer was made in August, transportation was not sent for them until December, and during the interval, the mortality was perhaps at its greatest height. If I had not made the offer, why did the Federal authorities send transportation to Savannah for ten or fifteen thousand men? If I made the offer, based only on equivalents, why did the same transportation carry down for delivery only three thousand men?

"Butler says the offer was made in the fall (according to the newspaper report), and that seven thousand were delivered. The offer was made in August, and they were sent for in December. I then delivered more than thirteen thousand, and would have gone to the fifteen thousand if the Federal transportation had been sufficient. My instructions to my agents were to deliver fifteen thousand sick and wounded, and if that number of that class were not on hand, to make up the number by well men. The offer was made by me in pursuance of instructions from the Confederate Secretary of War. I was ready to keep up the arrangement until every sick and wounded man had been returned.

"The three thousand men sent to Savannah by the Federals were in as wretched a condition as any detachment of prisoners ever sent from a Confederate prison.

"All these things are susceptible of proof, and I am much mistaken if I can not prove them by Federal authority. I am quite sure that General Mulford will sustain every allegation here made.

"Yours truly, R. OULD.

"P. S.—General Butler's correspondence is all on one side, as I was instructed, at the date of his letters, to hold no correspondence with him. I corresponded with Mulford or General Hitchcock. "R. OULD."

In another letter, written about the same time, Colonel Ould thus invites investigation:

"General Mulford will sustain every thing I have herein written. He is a man of honor and courage, and I do not think will hesitate to tell the truth. I think it would be well for you to make the appeal to him, as it has become a question of veracity."

But though President Davis and Colonel Ould are known by thousands of people, North and South, to be men of unimpeachable truthfulness, and though no *honorable* enemy would question their statements, we can not hope that their testimony will make headway against the intolerant prejudices and passions of faction. General B. F. Butler is doubtless sufficiently orthodox, and, besides, his testimony is voluntary. Says this exponent of latter-day "loyalty:"

"The great importance of the question; the fearful responsibility for the many thousands of lives which, by the refusal to exchange, were sacrificed by the most cruel forms of death; from cold, starvation, and pestilence of the prison-pens of Raleigh and Andersonville, being more than all the British soldiers killed in the wars of Napoleon; the anxiety of fathers, brothers, sisters, mothers, wives, to know the exigency which caused this terrible—and perhaps as it may have seemed to them useless and unnecessary—destruction of those dear to them, by horrible deaths, each and all have compelled me to this exposition, so that it may be seen that these lives were spent as a part of the system of attack upon the rebellion, devised by the wisdom of the General-in-Chief of the armies, to destroy it by depletion, depending upon our superior numbers to win the victory at last.

"The loyal mourners will doubtless derive solace from this fact, and appreciate all the more highly the genius which conceived the plan and the success won at so great a cost."

The New York *Tribune* will also be accepted as competent authority. Referring to the occurrences of 1864, the *Tribune* editorially says:

"In August the rebels offered to renew the exchange, man for man. General Grant then telegraphed the following important order: 'It is hard on our men, held in Southern prisons, not to exchange them, but it is humanity to those left in the ranks to fight our battles. Every man released on parole or otherwise becomes an active soldier against us at once, either directly or indirectly. *If we commence a system of exchange* which liberates *all prisoners* taken, we will have to fight on till the whole South is exterminated. If we hold those caught, they amount to no more than dead men. At this particular time, to release all rebel prisoners North would insure Sherman's defeat, and would compromise our safety here.'"

Here is even a stronger statement from a Northern source:

"NEW YORK, August 8, 1865.

"*Moreover, General Butler, in his speech at Lowell, Massachusetts, stated positively that he had been ordered by Mr. Stanton to put for-*

ward the negro question to complicate and prevent the exchange. . . . . . Every one is aware that, when the exchange did take place, not the slightest alteration had *occurred* in the question, *and that our prisoners might as well have been released twelve or eighteen* months before as at the resumption of the *cartel, which would have saved to the Republic at least twelve or fifteen thousand* heroic lives. That they were not saved is due *alone to Mr. Edwin M. Stanton's peculiar policy and dogged obstinacy;* AND, AS I HAVE REMARKED BEFORE, HE IS UNQUESTIONABLY THE DIGGER OF THE UNNAMED GRAVES THAT CROWD THE VICINITY OF EVERY SOUTHERN PRISON WITH HISTORIC AND NEVER-TO-BE-FORGOTTEN HORRORS.

"I regret the revival of this painful subject, but the gratuitous effort of Mr. Dana to relieve the Secretary of War from a responsibility he seems willing to bear, and which merely as a question of policy, independent of all considerations of humanity, must be regarded as of great weight, has compelled me to vindicate myself from the charge of making grave statements without due consideration.

"Once for all, let me declare that I have never found fault with any one because I was detained in prison, for I am well aware that that was a matter in which no one but myself, and possibly a few personal friends, would feel any interest; that my sole motive for impeaching the Secretary of War was that the people of *the loyal North might know to whom they were indebted for the cold-blooded and needless sacrifice of their fathers and brothers, their husbands and their sons.*

"JUNIUS HENRI BROWNE."

Now, what is the "inexorable logic" of this train of evidence? Either the calumnies against the South stand self-convicted, or those who have uttered them show themselves to have been worse fiends than they pretend to believe the Confederate authorities to have been.

But can a candid world credit the charge of cruelty against the South? Honorable enemies, even, will scorn the allegation of torture, of designedly inflicting suffering upon helpless men, against a people who, within the past six years, have so honorably illustrated the American name. Brave men are never cruel—cowards only delight in torture of the helpless. Cruelty to prisoners would be inconsistent not only with the known generosity of the Southern character, but with that splendid courage which the North will not dishonor itself by calling in question.

Until the suspension of the cartel, the Federal prisoners, even at the risk of their recapture, were kept in Richmond convenient for exchange. Confederate prisoners, on the other hand, were hurried to the Northern frontier, where the rigor of the climate alone subjected them to the most cruel sufferings. Driven by the course of the Federal Government, respecting the subject of exchange, the Confederate authorities selected a site for the quartering of prisoners, whom it was impossible to subsist in Richmond or its neighborhood. Andersonville was selected, in accordance with an official order contemplating the following objects: "A healthy locality, plenty of pure, good water, a running stream, and, if possible, shade trees, and in the immediate neighborhood of grist and saw-mills." Such were the "horrors of Andersonville," which the world has been urged to believe the Confederate Government selected with special view to the torment and death of prisoners.

The terrible mortality among the prisoners at Andersonville was not due either to starvation or to the unhealthiness of the locality. Federal soldiers were unaccustomed to the scanty and indifferent diet upon which the Confederates were fed, and which caused the death of thousands of delicate youths in the Southern armies. By this single fact may be explained much of the mortality at Andersonville. When to scurvy and other fatal forms of disease, produced by inadequate and unwholesome diet, are added the mental sufferings, which are peculiarly the lot of a prisoner, the despondency, and, in the case of the Andersonville prisoners, the despair occasioned by the refusal of their own Government to relieve them, we have abundant explanation of the most shocking mortality.

But the statement that the mortality of Andersonville was in excess of that of all other military prisons, is a willful falsehood. We present the following extracts from a letter to the New York *World*, by a gentleman, whose integrity will be vouched for by thousands of the best people in Virginia:

PRISON MORTALITY—ANDERSONVILLE AND ELMIRA.

"RICHMOND, VA., August 14.

"*To the Editor of the World*—

"SIR: I have just seen, in a city paper, a paragraph, credited to the *World*, alleging that among the Confederate prisoners at Elmira, during the last four or five months of the use of that prison, the deaths only amounted to a few individuals out of many thousand prisoners. I am not able to controvert that fact, as I left there on the 11th of October, 1864; but if the impression desired to be produced is that the general mortality at that pen was slight, I can contradict it from *the record.* During a portion of the period of my incarceration in the Elmira pen, it was my duty to receive, from the surgeon's office, each morning, the reports of the deaths of the preceding day, and embody them in an official report, to be signed by the commandant of the prison, and forwarded to the commandant of the post. I entered, each morning, in a diary, which now lies before me, the number of reported deaths; and the facts demonstrate that, in as healthy a location as there is in New York, with every remedial appliance in abundance, with no epidemic, and with a great boast of humanity, the deaths were relatively larger than among the Federal prisoners at Andersonville among a famished people, whose quartermaster could not furnish shelter to its soldiers, and whose surgeons were without the commonest medicines for the sick. The record shows that at Andersonville, between the 1st of February and 1st of August, 1864, out of thirty-six thousand prisoners, six thousand, or one-sixth, died—a fearful rate unquestionably. But the official report of the Elmira pen shows, that during the month of September, 1864, which was the first month after the quota of that prison was made up, *out of less than nine thousand five hundred prisoners*, the deaths were THREE HUNDRED AND EIGHTY-SIX. In other words, the average mortality at Andersonville, during that period, was one thirty-sixth of the whole per month, while at Elmira it was *one twenty-fifth* of the whole. At Elmira it was *four per cent.;* at Andersonville, less than *three per cent.* . . . . .

"Another item, which I gather from my diary, will indicate the manner in which the medical officer at Elmira discharged his functions. The hospitals began to be filled, in the latter part of August, with obstinate cases of scurvy. Men became covered with fearful sores, many lost their teeth, and many others became cripples, and will die cripples from that cause. The commandant of the post ordered a report to be made of all the scorbutic cases in prison, grave and trifling; and on the morning of Sunday, September 11, the lists were added up, when it was found that of nine thousand three hundred prisoners examined, *eighteen hundred and seventy* were tainted with scurvy.

"The Federal Government, as one of its measures of reconstruction, is officially and expensively engaged in traducing the Southern people, and the facility with which it procures all necessary evidence, whether the object be to hang or to calumniate, warrants the belief that we shall have a couple of volumes a year for the rest of the century, demonstrating the barbarity of the rebels. Against so admirable a system of manufacturing evidence, it is, of course, idle to oppose the feeble efforts of individuals, but I regard the duty none the less binding on such of us as know the truth to declare it; and I hope that, throughout the Southern States, intelligent and credible men are now putting into authentic form, the evidences of Federal outrages, the exploits of the Shermans and Sheridans, and Milroys and Butlers, one day to be published by general subscription of our people, that the world may judge between us and the spoon thieves, the furniture thieves, the barn-burners, the bummers, and the brutes who too often wore the uniform of the Federal army.

"A. M. K."

Can the North expect impartial history to accept its miserable subterfuge of "disloyalty," by which such testimony as this is now excluded?

Any reference to this subject must be wholly inadequate which does not describe the condition of the South at the period when she is alleged to have been guilty of unexampled atrocities. The blockade of the South by the North was stringent beyond any precedent in modern warfare. *Medicines* were held as contraband. Southern hospitals were not supplied, for that reason, with all the medicaments that were needed by sick and wounded soldiers; and those who were prisoners in our hands necessarily shared, in this respeet, the privations of the Confederate soldiers. But if there was any thing "cruel and inhuman" in this deficiency, *whose fault* was it? Of *whom* is the cruelty and inhumanity to be alleged? The South searched her forests and meadows for restoratives. She ran in medicines, as far as practicable, at great cost and hazard. We shared our stores with our prisoners. If the supply was inadequate or ill-assorted, we again ask, are *we* to be charged with cruelty and inhumanity?

The same observations are applicable as to supplies of food and clothing. The war was waged, by the North, on the policy of unsparing devastation. Mills were burnt, factories demolished, barns given to the flames, and the means of comfort and of living destroyed on system. What the South was able to save, she shared with her prisoners. We gave them such rations as we gave our own soldiers. Does any one suspect the Confederate Government of deliberately stinting its own soldiers? How, then, can it be pretended that it was "cruel and inhuman" to prisoners whom it fed as well? If we could not maintain them as well as we wished, it was through the success of those who wasted our subsistence, for the purpose of reducing us to that precise condition of inability. It is obviously *monstrous* to charge the fact, and to charge it as blame, upon *us*—to accuse the South of "cruelty and inhumanity."*

* We present two resolutions of a series adopted by Federal prisoners of war:

"*Resolved*, That whilst allowing the Confederate authorities all due praise for the attention paid to our prisoners, numbers of our men are daily consigned to early graves in the prime of manhood, far from home and kindred, and this is not caused intentionally by the Confederate Government, but by the force of circumstances; the prisoner is obliged to go without shelter, and, in a great portion of cases, without medicine.

. . . .

"*Resolved*, That whereas, in the fortune of war, it was our lot to become prisoners, we have suffered patiently, and are still willing to suffer, if by

But there is still another revelation to be added to the overwhelming evidence which demonstrates the murderous purpose of the Federal authorities, equally toward their own men and toward Confederate soldiers, by which they adroitly sought to cover the Confederate Government with accusing blood. A marked feature in the policy of the Lincoln cabinet was, at concerted intervals, to inflame the heart of the North by appeals to passion and resentment. The supreme excellence of the Federal administration, in this respect, was, indeed, its substitute for statesmanship. To conceal its own iniquitous course, with reference to the exchange of prisoners, the administration successfully sought to frenzy the Northern masses by the most ingenious misrepresentations of the condition of their men in the Southern prisons.

To this end the foul brood of pictorial falsifiers—the Harpers, Leslies, etc.—gave willing and effective aid. Men in the most horrible conditions of human suffering—ghastly skeletons, creatures demented from sheer misery—a set of wretched, raving, and dying creatures—were photographed, the pictures reduplicated to an unlimited extent, and scattered broadcast over the North, as evidence of the brutality practiced upon

so doing we can benefit the country, *but we would most respectfully beg to say that we are not willing to suffer to further the ends of any party or clique*, to the detriment of our own honor, our families, and our country; and we would beg this affair be explained to us, that we may continue to hold the Government in the respect which is necessary to make a good citizen and a soldier.

BRADLEY,

"*Chairman of Committee, on behalf of Prisoners.*"

These resolutions were adopted at a meeting of prisoners in Savannah, September 28, 1864, and sent to President Lincoln.

Federal prisoners in the South. In view of the well-known and designed influence of these appeals upon Northern sentiment, what must be the scorn of the civilized world for the perfidy which used the means which we here relate, to accomplish its iniquitous ends?

Immediately preceding the return of these prisoners, the Federal Agent applied for the delivery of the *worst* cases of *sick* Federal prisoners. Said he: "Even in cases where your surgeons think the men too ill to be moved, and not strong enough to survive the trip, if *they* express a desire to come, let them come." At this time, it should be remembered, regular exchanges were intermitted. Commissioner Ould, consistently with his known humanity and the humane disposition of his Government, consented to send the *worst* cases of their prisoners, provided that they would not be accepted as representatives of the average condition of the Federal prisoners in the South, and used as a means to inflame Northern sentiment. This condition was sacredly pledged.

With this understanding, Commissioner Ould prepared a barge adapted specially to the purpose, and, with the aid of the Richmond Ambulance Committee, carefully and tenderly delivered the prisoners. The Federal vessel that received them sailed immediately to Annapolis, where, instead of receiving the tender treatment that their pitiable condition required, they were made a spectacle of for an obvious purpose. Photographic artists made portraits of them; a committee of Congress was sent to report upon their condition; in short, they had been obtained for a purpose; and, how well that purpose was subserved, the South, at least, well knows. These miserable wrecks of humanity, specially asked for, specially selected as the *worst* cases, were pointed to as representatives of the average state of Federal prisoners in the South, although the most sacred assurances had been given that they would be used for no such purpose.

History will be searched in vain for such an example of mingled wickedness, perfidy, and cruelty. Yet the faction that could practice such treachery and barbarity has dared to impeach the honor and humanity of the South. Through such means, it, of course, can easily be proven that the South "starved and tortured" thousands of Union prisoners. Nor can Stanton, Holt, and Conover have difficulty in proving that these cruelties were by direct order of President Davis.

Need we pursue this subject further? We have not adduced one-tenth of the evidence which completes the record of Southern justice and humanity, yet what candid mind will deny that this testimony is ample? The vindication of the South, too, is the assured defense of Jefferson Davis. Nay, more: the exceptional victim of Northern malice is known to his countrymen to have a special record of humanity which should have claimed a special consideration from the enemy. Upon no subject was President Davis more censured in the South than for what was termed his "ill-timed tenderness" for the enemy. Stung to madness by the devastations and cruelties attending the invasion of their country, the people often responded to the clamor of the newspapers for retaliation against the harsh measures of the enemy. Before the writer is a Richmond newspaper, of date during the war, in which the leading editorial begins with the assertion that "The chivalry and humanity of Mr. Jefferson Davis will inevitably ruin this Confederacy," and the editor continues to reproach Mr. Davis for culpable leniency.

To the same alleged cause the *Examiner* was accustomed to

attribute what it described as the "humiliating attitude of the Confederacy. Said the *Examiner:* "The enemy have gone from one unmanly cruelty to another, encouraged by their impunity, till they are now, and have for some time, been inflicting on the people of this country the worst horrors of barbarous and uncivilized war." Yet, in spite of all this, the *Examiner* alleged, that Mr. Davis, in his dealings with the enemy, was "as gentle as the sucking dove." The same paper published a "bill of fare" provided for one of the prisons, and invoked the indignation of the country upon a policy which fed the prisoners of the enemy better than the soldiers of the Confederacy.

Never, indeed, did the ruler of an invaded people exhibit such forbearance in the face of so much provocation. When reminded of the relentless warfare of the enemy, which spared neither age, sex, nor condition, of his devastation, rapine and violence, Davis' invariable reply was: "The crimes of our enemies can not justify us in a disregard of the duties of humanity and Christianity." There can be little doubt that Mr. Davis occasionally erred in his extreme generosity to the foe. Yet, how noble must be that fame, which is marred only by such a fault. History has canonized Lamartine for preventing the re-raising of the red flag in 1848. What will be its award to the heroic firmness of Jefferson Davis, in preventing the raising of the black flag, among a people, whose dearest rights were assailed, whose homes were destroyed, and themselves subjected to the most ruthless persecutions known in modern warfare?

But apart from the perjured testimony, which has been utterly inadequate to establish the charge of "cruelty to prisoners," has the time passed, when the honorable character of a people and of an individual can be properly considered? The whole history of the United States does not exhibit a public career more stainless than that of Jefferson Davis, while in the service of the Union. Occupying almost every position of honor and trust, in both houses of Congress, member of the cabinet, and as a gallant soldier, the breath of slander never once tarnished his name. To his incorruptible official and private integrity, to the sincerity of his convictions, and the rectitude and honesty of his intentions, no men could better testify than those Republican Senators, who were, for years, his associates. Indeed, Mr. Davis has been peculiar in his complete exemption from that personal defamation, which is almost a necessity of political life.

But, impartial history will ask, whence come these calumnies against the great, pure, and pious leader of a brave people, in a struggle for liberty? Then must come that inevitable recoil, which shall bring to just judgment, a government, which destroyed the houses and the food of non-combatants; the fruits of the earth and the implements of tillage; which condemned its own defenders to imprisonment and death; which imprisoned without charges, gray-haired men, and doomed them to tortures, which brought them to premature graves; exposed helpless women and children to starvation, by depriving them of their natural protectors; which declared medicines contraband of war, and finally sought, by perjury, to justify cruelty to a helpless captive, because his people, in the midst of starvation, could not adequately feed and nurture the captive soldiers of the enemy.

CHAPTER XVIII.

DICATIONS OF POPULAR FEELING AT THE BEGINNING OF 1864—APATHY AND DESPONDENCY OF THE NORTH—IMPROVED FEELING IN THE CONFEDERACY—THE PROBLEM OF ENDURANCE—PREPARATIONS OF THE CONFEDERATE GOVERNMENT—MILITARY SUCCESS THE GREAT DESIDERATUM—A SERIES OF SUCCESSES—FINNEGAN'S VICTORY IN FLORIDA—SHERMAN'S EXPEDITION—FORREST'S VICTORY—THE RAID OF DAHLGREN—TAYLOR DEFEATS BANKS—FORREST'S TENNESSEE CAMPAIGN—HOKE'S VICTORY—THE VALUE OF THESE MINOR VICTORIES—CONCENTRATION FOR THE GREAT STRUGGLES IN VIRGINIA AND GEORGIA—FEDERAL PREPARATIONS—GENERAL GRANT—HIS THEORY OF WAR—HIS PLANS—THE FEDERAL FORCES IN VIRGINIA—SHERMAN—FEEBLE RESOURCES OF THE CONFEDERACY—THE "ON TO RICHMOND" AND "ON TO ATLANTA"—GENERAL GRANT BAFFLED—HE NARROWLY ESCAPES RUIN—HIS OVERLAND MOVEMENT A TOTAL FAILURE—SHERIDAN THREATENS RICHMOND—DEATH OF STUART—BUTLER'S ADVANCE UPON RICHMOND—THE CITY IN GREAT PERIL—BEAUREGARD'S PLAN OF OPERATIONS—VIEWS OF MR. DAVIS—DEFEAT OF BUTLER, AND HIS CONFINEMENT IN A "CUL DE SAC"—FAILURE OF GRANT'S COMBINATIONS—CONSTANTLY BAFFLED BY LEE—TERRIBLE LOSSES OF THE FEDERAL ARMY—GRANT CROSSES THE JAMES—HIS FAILURES REPEATED—HIS NEW COMBINATIONS—EARLY'S OPERATIONS IN THE VALLEY AND ACROSS THE POTOMAC—THE FEDERAL COMBINATIONS AGAIN BROKEN DOWN—FAVORABLE SITUATION IN VIRGINIA—THE MISSION OF MESSRS. CLAY, THOMPSON, AND HOLCOMBE—CORRESPONDENCE WITH MR. LINCOLN—THE ARROGANT AND MOCKING REPLY OF THE FEDERAL PRESIDENT.

DESPITE the solid advantages obtained by the North in the campaign just ended, the close of the winter developed the existence of great apprehension at Washington, and a correspondingly improved feeling in the South. It was indeed remarkable that the conviction entertained by both sides, that the struggle was now about to assume its latest and decisive phase, should have evoked such different manifestations of feeling at Washington and Richmond.

At the North was seen a singular apathy, which temporarily checked overwrought displays of popular exultation, and a mutual distrust of the Government and the public, not at all encouraging of success in designs demanding zealous coöperation. The thoughtful observer of Northern sentiment readily detected the presence of depression and suspicion—a general apprehension that the restoration of the Union was an enterprise developing new and unseen obstacles at each step, and a confusion of views as to the management of the war. But, in the violent exhibitions of party spirit, the North realized its chief cause of alarm. The peace party increased in numbers and influence with the prolongation of the war, and the preservation of power by the Government party was clearly dependent upon such military results, as should foreshadow the speedy "collapse of the rebellion." In short, the North saw that the culmination of the momentous struggle was to be reached, while it was in the throes of an embittered Presidential contest.

There was another explanation of the altered feeling in the two sections developed during the winter. Throughout the war, the Northern mind was singularly accessible to the influence of sensation and "clap-trap;" hence were always to be expected periodical galvanic excitements, followed by revulsion of feeling. The conservative instincts of the South sought repose rather than excitement; and the crippled condition of the enemy, after his achievements of the summer and fall, gave the South a sufficient respite for the recovery of much of its lost confidence. Nor was the transition of the Southern mind, within a few weeks, from depression to something like hopeful anticipation, based upon a mere presentiment of prosperous fortune. The lessons of the war, not less than the teachings of previous history, encouraged reanimation. It was contended that the conquest of a territory so extensive, and the subjection of a people numerically as strong and as courageous as those of the South, was physically impossible. It was urged that the Federal successes of the preceding summer had only placed the enemy upon the threshold of his enterprise, and that, in surmounting the resolute resistance which had almost defeated his earliest movements, he had vainly wasted the spirit and the strength which were now needed for his further progress.

From such a condition of feeling, the logical conclusion was that the war had now become a question of endurance, and that the Confederacy must now depend upon its capacity to resist until the North should abandon the war in sheer disgust. The Richmond journals pithily stated the problem as one of "Southern fortitude and endurance against Yankee perseverance."

In the meantime, the enforced quiet of the enemy was diligently improved by the Government. Probably at no period of the war did the Confederate administration exhibit more energy and skill in the employment of its limited resources, than in its preparations for the campaign of 1864. The vigorous measures of the President were, in the main, seconded by Congress, though this session was not wanting in those displays of demagogism which, throughout the war, diminished the influence and efficiency of that body. In the sequel, the expedients adopted did not realize the large results anticipated. The financial legislation of Congress did not improve the value of the currency, nor did the various expedients resorted to for strengthening the army obtain the desired numbers. It was calculated that the Confederate armies would aggregate, by the opening of spring, something like four hundred thousand men, of which the repeal of the substitute law alone was expected to furnish seventy thousand. The real strength of all the Confederate armies, however, did not exceed two hundred thousand men when the campaign was entered upon. The execution of the conscription law was a subject of sore perplexity to the administration, and, though President Davis made strenuous exertions to remedy the difficulty, the system continued defective until the end.

The army was, nevertheless, strengthened both in numbers and material, while its spirit, as shown in the alacrity and unanimity of reënlistment, was never surpassed. Military success was now the end to which the Government devoted its whole energies, as the real and only solution of its difficulties. In time of war military success is the sole nepenthe for national afflictions. Without victories the Confederacy would seek in vain a restoration of its finances through the expedients of legislation. Equally necessary were victories for relief of the difficulty as to food. Should the spring campaign be successful, the Confederacy would recover the country upon which it had been mainly dependent for supplies, and such additional territory as was required to put at rest the alarming difficulty of scarcity.

The expectation of the South was much encouraged by a series of successes upon minor theatres of the war, during the suspension of operations by the main armies. A signal victory was won late in February, by General Finnegan, at Ocean Pond, Florida, the important event of which was the decisive failure of a Federal design to possess that State.

The most serious demonstration by the enemy, during the winter months, was the expedition of Sherman across the State of Mississippi. This movement, undertaken with all the vigor and daring of that commander, was designed to capture Mobile and to secure the Federal occupation of nearly the whole of Alabama and Mississippi. It was the second experiment, undertaken by Federal commanders, during the war, of leaving a regular base of operations, and seeking the conquest of a large section of territory, by penetrating boldly into the interior. The first similar attempt was made by Grant, from Memphis into the interior of Mississippi. It is notable that both these expeditions were marked by shameful failure. They signally illustrated the military principle of the impossibility of successful penetration of hostile territory, even when held by a greatly inferior force, and, moreover, clearly indicate the fate that would inevitably have overtaken Sherman, in his "march to the sea," had there been an opposing army to meet him. When Van Dorn captured Grant's supplies at Holly Springs, in the autumn of 1862, the Federal commander had no alternative but to make a rapid retreat to his base. A similar experience awaited Sherman, who, leaving Vicksburg with thirty thousand men, marched without opposition through Mississippi—General Polk, with his corps of ten thousand men, falling back before him. Coöperating with Sherman was a large cavalry force, which, leaving North Mississippi, was to unite with him at Meridian, and upon this junction of forces depended the success of the entire expedition. But General Forrest, a remarkably skillful and energetic cavalry leader, attacked the Federal column, utterly routing and dispersing it, though not having more than one-third the force of the enemy. This necessitated the retreat of Sherman, with many circumstances indicating demoralization among his troops. His expedition terminated with no results sufficient to give it more dignity, than properly belonged to at least a dozen other plundering and incendiary enterprises, undertaken by Federal officers who are comparatively without reputation. The exploits of Sherman in Mississippi gave him a "bad eminence," which he afterwards well sustained by the burning of Rome and Atlanta, the sack of Columbia, and his career of pillage and incendiarism in the Carolinas.

A notable event of the winter was the raid of Dahlgren, an expedition marked by every dastardly and atrocious feature imaginable. When this expedition of "picked" Federal cavalry had been put to ignominious flight by the departmental clerks at Richmond, its retreat was harassed by local and temporary organizations of farmers, school-boys, and furloughed men from Lee's army. Not until its leader was killed, however, was revealed the fiendish errand which he had undertaken. Upon his person was found ample documentary evidence of the objects of the expedition, viz.: *to burn and sack the city of Richmond, and to assassinate President Davis and his cabinet.** Yet this man, killed in honorable combat, after

*Upon the person of Dahlgren was found the address, from which extracts relative to the purpose of the expedition are given. The portions which we omit are mainly exhortations to the courage of the men in a desperate enterprise:

"*Officers and men*—

"You have been selected from brigades and regiments, as a picked command, to attempt a desperate undertaking—an undertaking, which, if successful, will write your names on the hearts of your countrymen in letters that can never be erased, and which will cause the prayers of your fellow-soldiers, now confined in loathsome prisons, to follow you wherever you may go.

his cut-throat mission had failed, was apotheosized by the North as a "hero," who had been "assassinated" while on an errand of patriotism and philanthropy. The shocking details of this diabolical scheme, substantiated by every necessary proof of authenticity, were published in the Richmond journals, and instead of provoking the condemnation of the

"We hope to release the prisoners from Belle Island first, and, having seen them fairly started, we will cross the James River into Richmond, destroying the bridges after us, and exhorting the released prisoners to destroy and burn the hateful city; and do not allow the rebel leader, Davis, and his traitorous crew to escape," etc. The conclusion of this remarkable order is, "Ask the blessing of the Almighty, and do not fear the enemy."

We have not space for the indisputable testimony which has established the authenticity of the "Dahlgren Papers"—a subject upon which there is no longer room for doubt. The writer, at the time of this raid, had full descriptions of them from persons who saw the originals. They were found upon Dahlgren's body by a school-boy thirteen years old, who could not write, and were immediately placed in the hands of his teacher. The soiled folds of the paper were plainly visible. The words referring to the murder of President Davis were a part of the regular text of the manuscript. Additional proof of the authenticity of the papers was furnished by the note-book, also found upon the person of Dahlgren, containing a rough draft of the address to the troops, and various memoranda. The address was written in pencil in the note-book, and differs very slightly from the copy, containing, however, the injunction that the Confederate authorities be "*killed on the spot.*" The statement of Mr. Halbach, who is still living, supported by the testimony of a number of persons, must be deemed conclusive of the genuineness of the documents published in the Richmond journals.

Hon. Stephen R. Mallory, late Confederate Secretary of the Navy, has recently made the following statement of Mr. Davis' course concerning this matter:

"An expedition directed avowedly against the lives of the heads of the

hypocritical "humanity" of the North, with characteristic effrontery were ridiculed as "rebel forgeries."

The Trans-Mississippi region was, in the early spring, the scene of brilliant and important Confederate successes. About the middle of March, the famous "Red River Expedition" of General Banks, contemplating the complete subjugation of Louisiana, and the occupation of Western Texas, was undertaken. The result was, perhaps, the most ignominious failure of the war. Defeated by General Taylor, in a decisive engagement at Mansfield, General Banks, with great difficulty, effected his retreat down Red River, and abandoned the enterprise, which he had undertaken with such extravagant anticipations of fame and wealth.

In the month of April, Forrest executed a brilliant campaign among the Federal garrisons in Tennessee, capturing

Government, and aiming at firing an entire city, was deemed so violative of the rules of war as to demand a retribution of death upon all concerned in it.

"The subject was one of universal discussion in Richmond; excitement increased with what it fed upon; Congress participated in it; and a pressure was brought to bear upon Mr. Davis to order the execution of some of the captured.

"He entertained no doubt that justice, humanity, and policy equally forbade this cruel measure, and refused to sanction it; and at the same time referred the subject to General Lee, then near Petersburg, for immediate attention. The General's answer promptly came, asserting, without having been apprized of them, the views already presented by Mr. Davis; and the chief of which was, that the men, having surrendered with arms in their hands, and been accepted and treated as prisoners of war, could not, in retaliation for the unexecuted designs of their leader, be treated otherwise. This disposed of the case, and satisfied the people, who were ever ready to recognize the wisdom and policy of General Lee's judgment."

several thousand prisoners and adding large numbers of recruits to his forces. With a force mainly organized within three months, this dashing officer penetrated the interior of Tennessee, which the enemy had already declared "conquered," capturing garrisons and stores, and concluded his campaign by penetrating to the Mississippi River, and successfully storming Fort Pillow.* The most encouraging event of the spring was the capture of Plymouth, North Carolina, by General Hoke. This enterprise, executed with great gallantry and skill, had the tangible reward of a large number of prisoners, many cannon, and an important position with reference to the question of supplies.†

The aggregate of these Confederate successes was not inconsiderable. Expectation was strengthened by them at the South, and proportionately disappointed at the North. It was chiefly in their influence upon public feeling that these minor victories were valuable, as they in no way affected the main current of the war, and were speedily overlooked at the first sound of the mighty shock of arms along the Rapidan and in Northern Georgia. Indeed, the actors in these

*The "Fort Pillow massacre" was a fruitful theme for new chapters of "rebel barbarities." Forrest was charged with indiscriminate slaughter of a captive garrison, when, in fact, he only continued to fight a garrison which had not surrendered. After the Confederates had forced their way into the fort, the flag was not taken down, nor did the garrison offer to surrender. The explanation obviously was that the enemy relied upon their gunboats in the river to destroy Forrest's forces after they had entered the fort.

†In the last two years of the war, there were few more promising officers than General Hoke. Mr. Davis thought very highly of his capacity, and, upon one occasion, alluded to him as "that gallant North Carolinian, who always did his duty, and did it thoroughly."

preliminary events were, in most instances, themselves shifted to these two main theatres, upon which the concentrated power of each contestant was preparing its most desperate exertions. Troops on both sides were recalled from South Carolina, and even Florida, to participate in the great wrestle for the Confederate capital, and the impending struggle in Georgia absorbed nearly all the forces hitherto operating west of the Alleghanies and east of the Mississippi.

However discouraged may have been the public mind of the North at the beginning of the year, the preparations of the Federal Government, for the spring campaign, indicated no abatement of energy or determination. Well aware of the diminished resources of the South, and of the political necessities which imperatively demanded speedy and decisive successes, the Federal administration prepared a more vigorous use of its great means than had yet been attempted. The draft was energetically enforced, and volunteering was stimulated by high bounties. At no period of the war were the Federal armies so numerous, so well equipped and provided with every means that tends to make war successful. Their *morale* was better than at the outset of any previous campaign. The Federal armies were now inured to war, composed mainly of seasoned veterans, and commanded by officers whose capacity had been amply tested in battle.

The agents selected by the Federal Government, to carry out its designs, were men whose previous career justified their selection. The sagacity of the North had, at length, realized the one essential object, to the accomplishment of which all its efforts must contribute. This object was the destruction of Lee's army. Virginia was justly declared the "backbone" of Confederate power; Lee's army was the pedestal of the edifice.

It was in the clearer appreciation of this object, and in the determination to subordinate every concern of the war to its accomplishment, that Northern sentiment made a step forward, that was, of itself, no insignificant auxiliary to ultimate success. The blows which Sherman prepared to deliver upon the distant fields of Georgia, were aimed at Lee's army, not less than were those of Grant. While the latter "hammered away continuously" in Virginia, to pulverize, as it were, the column from which so many Federal endeavors had been forced to recoil, Sherman was expected to pierce the very centre of the Confederacy, and seize or destroy every remaining source of sustenance.

The presence in Virginia of the General commanding all the Federal forces, was sufficiently indicative of his recognition of the supreme object of the campaign. The successful career of this officer was the recommendation which secured for him the high position of Commander-in-Chief of the armies of the Union. He was the most fortunate officer produced by the war—fortunate not less in having won nearly every victory which could promote the successful conclusion of the war, but fortunate in having won victories where defeat was the result to be logically expected.

It is not at all necessary to weigh, in detail, the merits of General Grant as a soldier. With the overwhelming argument of *results* in his favor, there would be little encouragement, even if there could be strict justice, in denying superior ability to Grant. His campaigns have contributed nothing to military science, in its correct sense, and the military student will find in his operations few incidents that illustrate the art or economy of war. In discarding the formulas of the schools, and condemning the theories upon which the best of his predecessors had conducted the war, Grant, by no means, proved that he was not a good soldier. But his independence in this respect did not establish his claim to genius, since his contempt for military rules and theories was not followed by the display of any original features of true generalship. His name was coupled with a great disaster at Shiloh, where he was rescued from absolute destruction by the energy of Buell, and the delay of his adversary. At Donelson, at Vicksburg, and at Missionary Ridge, he had succeeded by mere weight of numbers; and, indeed, in no instance had he exhibited any other quality of worth, than boldness and perseverance. But his success was a sufficient recommendation to the material mind of the North, which did not once pause to consider how far Grant's victories were due to his military merit.

But whatever the defects of Grant in the higher qualities of generalship, he was preëminently the man for the present emergency. If the Federal Government saw the necessity of vigorous warfare, looking to speedy and final results, General Grant knew how to conduct the campaign upon that idea, provided the Government would give him unlimited means, and the Northern people would consent to the unstinted sacrifice. Grant knew no other than an aggressive system of warfare, and contemplated no other method of destroying the Confederacy, than by the momentum of superior weight—by heavy, simultaneous and continuous blows. The plans of Grant were remarkable for their simplicity, and contemplated merely the employment of the maximum of force against the two main armies of the Confederacy, keeping the entire force of the South in constant and unrelieved strain. By "continuous hammering" he thus hoped eventually to destroy or exhaust it.

General Grant was again fortunate in having the unlimited

confidence of his Government, which placed at his disposal a million of soldiers, and was prepared to accede to his every demand. To the most trusted of his lieutenants—Sherman—Grant intrusted the conduct of operations against the centre of the Confederacy, reserving for himself the control of the campaign against Richmond, and Lee's army. His plan of operation was to *destroy*, not to *defeat*, an army which he knew could not be conquered, so long as its vitality remained. The military talent of the North had been already exhausted against Lee, and its largest army too often baffled by the Army of Northern Virginia, to admit the hope of defeating it in battle. To *outgeneral* Lee, Grant well knew required a greater master of the art of war than himself. To *conquer* the Army of Northern Virginia, he, not less than his army, knew to be impossible. His calculation was to wear it out by the "attrition" of successive and remorseless blows. This theory was based upon the plain calculation that the North could furnish a greater mass of humanity for the shambles, (as was afterward calculated it could spare a greater mass for the prisons,) than the South, and that thus when the latter should be exhausted, the former would still have left abundant material for an army. Such was Grant's theory of the war. Whatever may be thought of it as a military conception, the theory was one that must succeed in the end, provided the perseverance of the North should hold out.

General Grant determined upon a direct advance with the Army of the Potomac against Richmond, by the overland route from the Rapidan. The frame-work of his plan, however, embraced coöperating movements in other quarters, which should, at the same time, occupy every man that might be available for the reënforcement of Lee. Grant was embarrassed by no lack of the men who were needed to make each one of these movements formidable. The most important of these was that designed to occupy the southern communications of Richmond, thus at once making the Confederate capital untenable, and cutting off the retreat of Lee. This operation was intrusted to General Butler, who, with thirty thousand men, was to ascend James River, establish himself in a fortified position near City Point, and invest Richmond on its south side. The other auxiliary movements were designed against the westward communications of Richmond, and were to be undertaken by Generals Sigel and Crook—the former, with seven thousand men, moving up the Shenandoah Valley, and the latter, with ten thousand, moving against the Virginia and Tennessee Railroad. The force immediately under General Grant was one hundred and forty thousand men of all arms. Thus the grand aggregate of the Federal armies now threatening Richmond reached the neighborhood of one hundred and ninety thousand men. In addition to these was a force at Washington, equal in strength to the whole of Lee's army.

The Federal Government was hardly less lavish in the distribution of its enormous resources to Sherman than to Grant. Sherman had proven himself an officer of much enterprise. Intellectually he was the superior of Grant, but not less than other Federal commanders he relied upon superior numbers to overcome the skill and valor of the Confederate armies. Physical momentum was needed to overwhelm Johnston, and was amply supplied. Sherman demanded one hundred thousand men to capture Atlanta, and, by the consolidation of the various armies which had hitherto operated independently in the West, his force attained within a few hundreds of that number.

In painful contrast with this enormous outlay of forces, were the feeble means of the Confederacy. When the season favorable for military operations opened, General Lee confronted Grant upon the Rapidan, and General Johnston faced Sherman near Dalton, in Northern Georgia. Neither of these armies reached fifty thousand men. The undaunted aspect and mien of firm resistance, with which both awaited the perilous onset of the enemy, were, however, assuring of the steady determination which still defended the Confederacy. Critical as was the emergency, the Government and the country yet believed the strength of these two armies equal to the great test of endurance, at least beyond the perils of the present campaign. *To hold its own* was the primary hope of the Confederacy. If autumn could be reached without decisive victories by the North, and the great Federal sacrifices of spring and summer should then have proven in vain, there was ample ground for hope of those dissensions among the enemy, which, throughout the struggle, constituted so large a share of Confederate expectation.

On the 3d of May, 1864, General Grant initiated the campaign in Virginia, by crossing the Rapidan with his advanced forces; on the 5th, the correspondent movement of Sherman, a thousand miles away, was begun. By the morning of the 5th, one hundred thousand Federal soldiers were across the Rapidan, and on the same day, the first round of the great wrestle occurred. Entertaining no doubt of his capacity to destroy Lee, Grant imagined that his adversary would seek to escape. Having, in advance, proclaimed his contempt for "maneuvres," he was solicitous only for an opportunity to strike the Confederate army before it should elude his grasp. But Hooker had made the same calculation a year before, and was disappointed, and a like disappointment was now in store for Grant.

Lee had no power either to prevent the Federal crossing of the Rapidan, nor to prevent the turning of his right. Instead of retreating, he immediately assumed the aggressive, and dealt the assailant one of the most effective blows ever aimed by that powerful arm. Three days sufficed to reveal to the Federal commander his miscalculations of his adversary's designs, and, baffled in all his operations, he already indicated distrust of his system of warfare, and was compelled to attempt by "maneuvre," what he had failed to effect by brute force. The events of the 5th and 6th of May clearly demonstrated that strategy could not yet be dispensed with in warfare. Indeed, nothing but Lee's extreme weakness and the untoward wounding of Longstreet, in just such a crisis, and in exactly the same manner as marked the fall of Jackson, prevented the defeat of the Federal campaign in its incipiency. But for these circumstances the Federal Agamemnon would have been completely unhorsed on the 6th of May, and would have added another name to the list of decapitated commanders whom Lee had successively brought to grief. But the luck of Grant did not forsake him, and he still had numbers sufficient to attempt the "hammering" process again. Grant's first attempt at "maneuvre" was a movement upon Spottsylvania Court-house, a point south-east of the late battle-fields, by which he sought to throw his army between Lee and Richmond. Again he was to be disappointed, and again did the Confederate commander prove himself the master of his antagonist, in every thing that constitutes generalship. The Confederate forces were already at Spottsylvania, when the Federal column reached the neighborhood, and Lee, so cautious in his words, announced to his Government that the enemy had been "repulsed with heavy slaughter."

But Lee had done far more than foil Grant. He had secured an impregnable position upon the Spottsylvania heights, against which Grant remorselessly, but vainly, dashed his huge columns for twelve days. At the end of that period Lee's lines were still intact, his mien of resistance still preserved, and the "hammering" generalship of Grant had cost the North nearly fifty thousand veteran soldiers. Men already began to ask the question, to which history will find a ready answer: "*What would be the result if the resources of the two commanders were reversed?*" Not even the North could fail to see how entirely barren of advantage was all this horrible slaughter. The "shambles of the Wilderness" became the popular phrase descriptive of Grant's operations, and the Northern public was rapidly reaching the conclusion that the "hammer would itself break on the anvil."

While the dead-lock at Spottsylvania continued, and Lee held Grant at bay, Richmond was seriously threatened by coöperating movements of the enemy. General Grant had organized a powerful cavalry force under Sheridan, for operations against the Confederate communications. Sheridan struck out boldly in the direction of Richmond, followed closely by the Confederate cavalry. For several days he hovered in the neighborhood of the city, unable to penetrate the line of fortifications, and eventually retired in the direction of James River.

A melancholy incident of this raid of Sheridan was the death, in an engagement near Richmond, of General J. E. B. Stuart, the renowned cavalry leader of the Army of Northern Virginia. This was a severe bereavement to the South, and a serious loss to the army. Stuart's exploits fill a brilliant chapter of the war in Virginia, and he was probably the ablest cavalry chieftain in the Confederate army. President Davis, who was constantly on the field during the presence of Sheridan near Richmond, deeply deplored the loss of Stuart. The President, not less than General Lee, reposed great confidence in Stuart's capacity for cavalry command, and the noble character and gallant bearing of Stuart enlisted the warm personal regard of Mr. Davis—a feeling which was heartily reciprocated. Upon the day of his death, Mr. Davis visited the bedside of the dying chief, and remained with him some time. In reply to the question of Mr. Davis, "General, how do you feel?" Stuart replied: "Easy, but willing to die, if God and my country think I have fulfilled my destiny and done my duty."

The important correspondent movement of Butler upon the south side of James River, began early in May. Ascending the river with numerous transports, Butler landed at Bermuda Hundreds, and advanced against the southern communications of Richmond. The force near the city was altogether inadequate to check the army of Butler, and almost without opposition he laid hold of the Richmond and Petersburg Railroad, and advanced within a few miles of Drewry's Bluff, the fortifications of which commanded the passage of the river to the Confederate capital. Troops were rapidly thrown forward from the South, and by the 14th May, General Beauregard had reached the neighborhood of Richmond, from Charleston.

Probably at no previous moment of the war was Richmond so seriously threatened, as pending the arrival of Beauregard's forces. Mr. Davis was, however, resolved to hold the city to the last extremity. Though much indisposed at the time, he was every morning to be seen, accompanied by his staff, riding in the direction of the military lines. Superintending, to a large extent, the disposition of the small force defending the city, he was fully aware of the extreme peril of the situation, but nevertheless determined to share the dangers of the hour. When Beauregard reached the scene the crisis had by no means passed. Unless Butler should be dislodged, not only was Richmond untenable, but it was impossible to maintain Lee's army north of James River. Yet the force available seemed very inadequate to any thing like a decisive defeat of the enemy. The aggregate of commands from the Carolinas, added to the force previously at Richmond, did not exceed fifteen thousand men, while Butler, with thirty thousand, held a strongly intrenched position.

Immediately upon his arrival, General Beauregard suggested a plan of operations, by which he hoped to destroy Butler, and, without pausing, to inflict a decisive defeat upon Grant. The plan he proposed was that Lee should fall back to the defensive lines of the Chickahominy, even to the intermediate lines of Richmond, temporarily sending fifteen thousand men to the south side of the James, and with this accession of force he proposed to take the offensive against Butler. Pointing out the isolated situation of Butler, he urged the opportunity for his destruction by the concentration of a superior force. Under the circumstances General Beauregard thought the capture of Butler's force inevitable, and the occupation of his depot of supplies at Bermuda Hundreds a necessary consequence. When these results should be accomplished, he proposed, at a concerted moment, to throw his whole force upon Grant's flank, while Lee attacked in front. General Beauregard was confident of his ability to make the attack upon Butler, in two days after receiving the desired reënforcements, and was equally confident of the result both against Butler and Grant. His proposition concluded with the declaration that Grant's fate could not be doubtful if the proposed concentration should be made, and indicated the following gratifying results: "The destruction of Grant's forces would open the way for the recovery of most of our lost territory."

Whatever his views as to its feasibility, the President could not refuse a careful consideration of a plan, whose author, in advance, claimed such momentous results. Upon reflection President Davis declined the plan as involving too great a risk, not only of the safety of Richmond, but of the very existence of Lee's army. The proposition of Beauregard was submitted on the 14th May. At that time the grapple between Grant and Lee was still unrelaxed. Twelve days of battle had cost Lee fifteen thousand men. Meanwhile he had not received *a single additional musket*, while Grant had nearly supplied his losses by reënforcements from Washington. Thus, while Lee's force did not reach forty thousand, Grant's still approximated one hundred and thirty thousand. The President also knew that Grant was at that moment closely pressing Lee, moving toward his left, and seeking either to overlap or break in upon the right flank of Lee.

The proposed detachment of fifteen thousand men from Lee, leaving him not more than twenty-five thousand, in such a crisis, would have been simply madness. Butler, it is possible, might have been destroyed, but the end of the Confederacy would have been hastened twelve months. It is questionable whether, at any moment after Grant crossed the Rapidan, the overmatched army of Lee could have been diminished without fatal disaster. The timely arrival of Longstreet had prevented a serious reverse on the 6th May. Is it reasonable to suppose that Lee could have detached one-third of his army, without Grant's knowledge, or that the energy of the Federal commander would have permitted an hour's respite to his sorely-pressed adversary after the discovery? The case would have been altogether different, had Lee been already safe within his works at Richmond. Under the circumstances proposed, he had before him a perilous retrograde, followed by a force four times his own strength, and commanded by the most unrelenting and persistent of officers.

But there was another view of the proposition not to be overlooked by the President in his perilous responsibility. It is true Beauregard promised grand results—nothing less than the total destruction of nearly all the Federal forces in Virginia. In brief, his plan proposed to destroy two hundred thousand men with less than sixty thousand. Again it was true the enemy was to be destroyed in detail—Butler first, and Grant afterwards. There were precedents in history for such achievements. But it should be remembered that *if* Butler should be immediately destroyed, and *if* Lee should be guaranteed a safe retrograde, Beauregard would still be able to aid Lee to the extent of but little more than twenty thousand men. This would give Lee less than fifty thousand with which to take the offensive against more than twice that number. Against just such odds Lee had already tried the offensive, and failed because of his weakness. He had assailed Grant under the most favorable circumstances, effecting a complete surprise when the Federal commander believed him already retreating, but was unable to follow up his advantage. Was there reason to believe that any better result would follow from a repetition of the offensive?

Believing himself not justified in hazarding the safety of

the Confederacy upon such a train of doubtful conditions, and agreeing with General Beauregard, that Butler could be dislodged from his advanced positions, so menacing to Richmond, Mr. Davis rejected a plan which, under different circumstances, he would have heartily and confidently adopted.

With remarkable promptitude, Beauregard conceived a brilliant plan of battle, and within twenty-four hours had already put it in virtual execution. With fifteen thousand men, he drove Butler from all his advanced works, and confined him securely in the *cul de sac* of Bermuda Hundreds, where, in a few months, ended the inglorious military career of a man who, in every possible manner, dishonored the sword which he wore, and disgraced the Government which he served. The brilliant conception of Beauregard merited even better results, which were prevented not less by untoward circumstances than by the weakness of his command.

While Beauregard thus effectually neutralized Butler, Grant's combinations, elsewhere, were brought to signal discomfiture. The expedition from the Kanawha Valley had been, in a measure, successful in its designs against the communications of South-western Virginia, but did not obtain the coöperation designed, by the column moving up the Shenandoah Valley. Sigel, in his advance up the Valley, was encountered at Newmarket by General Breckinridge, who signally defeated him, capturing artillery and stores, and inflicting a heavy loss upon the enemy. Sigel retreated hastily down the Valley.

General Grant, on the 11th of May, proclaimed to his Government his purpose "to fight it out on this line if it takes all summer," yet, within a week afterwards, he was already meditating another plan of operations. Forty thousand of the bravest soldiers of the Federal army had been vainly sacrificed, and yet the Confederate line remained intact upon the impregnable hills of Spottsylvania. A week was consumed in fruitless search for a weak point in the breastplate of Lee. Grant was again driven to "maneuvre." Foiled again and again by the great exemplar of strategy, with whom he contended, Grant at no point turned his face towards Richmond without finding Lee across his path. Moving constantly to the left, the 3d of June—exactly one month from the crossing of the Rapidan—found Grant near the Chickahominy, and Lee still facing him. The fortune of war again brought the belligerents upon the old battle-ground of the Peninsula. Just before Lee reached the defenses of Richmond, for the first time during the campaign, he received reënforcements.* Grant also was strengthened, drawing sixteen thousand men from Butler at Bermuda Hundreds.

On the 3d of June occurred the second battle of Cold Harbor. It was the last experiment of the strictly "hammering" system, unaided by the resources of strategy. It cost Grant thirteen thousand men, and Lee a few hundred. Such was a fitting *finale* of a campaign avowedly undertaken upon the brutal principle of the mere consumption of life, and in contempt of every sound military precept. Cold Harbor terminated the overland movement of Grant, and he speedily abandoned the line upon which he had proposed "to fight all summer." Not that he willingly abandoned his "hammering" principle after this additional sacrifice of lives, for he would still have dashed his army against the impregnable wall in

* At Hanover Junction, on the 23d of May, General Lee was joined by Breckinridge's division, numbering less than three thousand muskets, and by Pickett's division of perhaps three thousand five hundred muskets. General Lee was compelled, very shortly afterwards, to send Breckinridge's division back to the Valley.

his front, but his men recoiled, in the consciousness of an impotent endeavor. They had done all that troops could accomplish, and shrank from that which their own experience told them was *impossible*. And there should be no wonder that the Federal army was reluctant to be vainly led to slaughter again. For forty days its proven mettle had been subjected to a cruel test, such as even Napoleon, reckless of his men's lives as he was, had never imposed upon an army. It is safe to say that no troops but Americans could have been held so long to such an enterprise as that attempted by Grant in May, 1864, and none but Americans could have withstood such desperate assaults as were sustained by Lee's army.

In one month, from the Rapidan to the Chickahominy, more than sixty thousand of the flower of the Federal army had been put *hors du combat*, and many of the best of its officers, men identified with its whole history, were lost forever. In one month Lee had inflicted a loss greater than the whole of the force which he commanded during the last year of the war! Yet this was the "generalship" of Grant, for which a meeting of twenty-five thousand men in New York returned the "thanks of the nation." The world was invited, by the sensational press of the North, to admire the "strategy" which had carried the Federal army from the Rapidan to the James, a position which it might have reached by transports without the loss of a man.

For a brief season, hope, positive and well-defined, dawned upon the South. Thus far the problem of *endurance* was in favor of the Confederacy. Grant's stupendous combinations against Richmond had broken down. The spirit of the North seemed to be yielding, and again the Federal Government encountered the danger of a collapse of the war.

The battle of Cold Harbor convinced General Grant of the futility of operations against Richmond from the north side of James River. He therefore determined to transfer his army to the south side of the river, and seek to possess himself of the communications southward, and to employ coöperative forces to destroy or occupy the communications of Richmond with Lynchburg and the Shenandoah Valley. This involved new combinations, and Grant still had abundant means to execute them. If successful, this plan would completely isolate Richmond, leaving no avenue of supplies except by the James River Canal, which also would be easily accessible.

Lee could not prevent the transfer of Grant's army to the south side. Petersburg and Richmond were both to be defended, and his strength was too limited to be divided. Grant made a vigorous dash against Petersburg. He had anticipated an easy capture of that city by a *coup de main*, but in this he was disappointed. Petersburg was found to be well fortified, and the desperate assaults made by the Federal advanced forces were repulsed. In a few days Lee's army again confronted Grant, and Richmond and Petersburg were safe.

Thus the system of rushing men upon fortifications failed on the south side not less signally than in the overland campaign. The Federal commander had no alternative but a formal siege of Petersburg. Driven by circumstances beyond his control, General Grant thus assumed a position which, in the end, proved fatal to the Confederacy, and the results of which have exalted him, in the view of millions, to rank among the illustrious generals of history. The south side of James River was always the real key to the possession of Richmond. Sooner or later the Confederate capital must fall, if assailed from that direction with pertinacity, and with such ample means as were given to Grant.

The new Federal combination was in process of execution by the middle of June. After the defeat of Sigel, a large force was organized in the lower valley, and intrusted to the direction of General Hunter, an officer distinguished by fanatical zeal against the section of which he was a native, and by the peculiar cruelty of a renegade. Breckinridge had been withdrawn from the Valley, to Lee's lines, immediately after his defeat of Sigel, and Hunter without difficulty overwhelmed the small force left under General Jones. Forming a junction with Crook and Averill from North-western Virginia, at Staunton, Hunter advanced upon Lynchburg, meanwhile destroying public and private property indiscriminately, and practicing a system of incendiarism and petty oppression against which even Federal officers protested.

It was necessary to detach a portion of the army from the lines of Richmond to check the demonstration of Hunter. Accordingly, General Early, who had acquired great reputation in the battles upon the Rapidan, was sent with eight thousand men to the Valley. Uniting his forces to those already on the ground, General Early made a vigorous pursuit of Hunter, whose flight was as dastardly as his conduct had been despicable. Retreating with great precipitation through the mountains of Western Virginia, Hunter's force, for several weeks, bore no relation to operations in Virginia. With the Shenandoah Valley thus denuded of invaders, Early rapidly executed a movement of his forces down the Valley, with a view to a demonstration beyond the Potomac frontier, which was entirely uncovered by Hunter's retreat. The movement of Early into Maryland caused, as was anticipated, a detachment from Grant's forces, for the defense of the Federal capital. Advancing with extraordinary vigor, General Early pursued the retreating enemy, defeating them in an engagement near Frederick City, and arrived near Washington on the 10th of July. Warned of the approach of heavy reënforcements from Grant, which must arrive before the works could be carried, Early abandoned his design of an attack upon Washington, and retired across the Potomac, with his extensive and valuable captures.

Signal failure attended the cavalry expeditions sent by Grant against the railroads. Sheridan, while moving northward against Gordonsville and Charlottesville, from which points, after inflicting all possible damage upon the railroads to Richmond, he was to join Hunter at Lynchburg, was intercepted by Wade Hampton, the worthy successor of Stuart, and compelled to abandon his part of the campaign. An extended raid, under Wilson and Kautz, on the south side, also terminated in disaster. The expedition of Burbridge against South-western Virginia was baffled by a counter-movement of Morgan with his cavalry, into Kentucky, the Federal forces following him into that State.

Thus again were all of General Grant's plans disappointed, and by midsummer the situation in Virginia was altogether favorable to the Confederacy. There was indeed good reason for the evident apprehension of the North, that, after all, Grant's mighty campaign was a failure. His mere proximity to the Confederate capital signified nothing. All his attempts against both Petersburg and Richmond, whether by strategy or *coups de main*, had ended in disaster; the Confederate lines were pronounced impregnable by the ablest Federal engineers, and after the ridiculous *fiasco* of "Burnside's mine," the capture of Richmond seemed as remote as ever. To increase public alarm at the North, was added the activity of Lee, his evident confidence in his ability to hold his own, with a diminished force, and even to threaten the enemy with invasion.

The Confederate Government, fully apprized of the momentous results, with which the present year was pregnant, and of the increased peril which assailed the Confederacy, in consequence of its diminished resources, depended upon other influences, than an exhibition of military strength, to promote its designs. The cause of the South could no longer be submitted, unaided, to the arbitrament of battle. At other periods, while freely avowing his desire for peace, and offering to the Federal authorities, opportunity for negotiation, President Davis had relied almost solely upon the sword, as the agency of Southern independence. The opening of the spring campaign of 1864 was deemed a favorable conjuncture for the employment of the resources of diplomacy. To approach the Federal Government directly would be in vain. Repeated efforts had already demonstrated its inflexible purpose not to negotiate with the Confederate authorities. Political developments at the North, however, favored the adoption of some action that might influence popular sentiment in the hostile section. The aspect of the peace party was especially encouraging, and it was evident that the real issue to be decided in the Presidential election, was the continuance or cessation of the war.

A commission of three gentlemen, eminent in position and intelligence, was accordingly appointed by Mr. Davis to visit Canada, with a view to negotiation with such persons in the North, as might be relied upon, to facilitate the attainment of peace. This commission was designed to facilitate such preliminary conditions, as might lead to formal negotiation between the two governments, and their intelligence was fully relied upon to make judicious use of any political opportunities that might be presented in the progress of military operations

The Confederate commissioners, Messrs. Clay, of Alabama, Holcombe, of Virginia, and Thompson, of Mississippi, sailed from Wilmington at the incipiency of the campaign on the Rapidan. Within a few weeks thereafter they were upon the Canada frontier, in the execution of their mission. A correspondence with Horace Greeley commenced on the 12th of July. Through Mr. Greeley the commissioners sought a safe conduct to the Federal capital. For a few days Mr. Lincoln appeared to favor an interview with the commissioners, but finally rejected their application, on the ground that they were not authorized to treat for peace. In his final communication, addressed "To whom it may concern," Mr. Lincoln offered safe conduct to any person or persons having authority to control the armies then at war with the United States, and authorized to treat upon the following basis of negotiation: "the restoration of peace, the *integrity of the whole Union, and the abandonment of slavery*."

Upon this basis, negotiation was, of course, precluded, and peace impossible. Mr. Lincoln was perfectly aware that the commissioners had no control of the Confederate armies, and that the Confederate Government alone was empowered to negotiate. He therefore did not expect the acceptance of his passport, and added to the mockery an arrogant statement, in advance, of the conditions upon which he would consent to treat. Even if the commissioners had been empowered to treat, Mr. Lincoln's terms dictated the surrender of every thing for which the South was fighting, and more than the North professed to demand at the outset. Abolition was now added to the conditions of re-admission to the Union. Mr. Lincoln's proposition was a cruel mockery, an unworthy insult to the manhood of a people, whom his armies, at least, had learned to respect.

CHAPTER XIX.

DISAPPOINTMENT AT RESULTS OF THE GEORGIA CAMPAIGN—HOW FAR IT WAS PARALLEL WITH THE VIRGINIA CAMPAIGN—DIFFERENT TACTICS ON BOTH SIDES—REMOVAL OF GENERAL JOHNSTON—THE EXPLANATION OF THAT STEP—A QUESTION FOR MILITARY JUDGMENT—THE NEGATIVE VINDICATION OF GENERAL JOHNSTON—DIFFERENT THEORIES OF WAR—THE REAL PHILOSOPHY OF THE SOUTHERN FAILURE—THE ODDS IN NUMBERS AND RESOURCES AGAINST THE SOUTH—WATER FACILITIES OF THE ENEMY—STRATEGIC DIFFICULTIES OF THE SOUTH—THE BLOCKADE—INSIGNIFICANCE OF MINOR QUESTIONS—JEFFERSON DAVIS THE WASHINGTON OF THE SOUTH—GENERAL JOHN B. HOOD—HIS DISTINGUISHED CAREER—HOPE OF THE SOUTH RENEWED—HOOD'S OPERATIONS—LOSS OF ATLANTA—IMPORTANT QUESTIONS—PRESIDENT DAVIS IN GEORGIA—PERVERSE CONDUCT OF GOVERNOR BROWN—MR. DAVIS IN MACON—AT HOOD'S HEAD-QUARTERS—HOW HOOD'S TENNESSEE CAMPAIGN VARIED FROM MR. DAVIS' INTENTIONS—SHERMAN'S PROMPT AND BOLD CONDUCT—HOOD'S MAGNANIMOUS ACKNOWLEDGMENT—DESTRUCTION OF THE CONFEDERATE POWER IN THE SOUTH-WEST.

GENERAL JOHNSTON had failed to realize either the expectations of the public, or the hope of the Government, in his direction of the campaign in Georgia. His tactics were those uniformly illustrated by this officer in all his operations, of falling back before the enemy, and seeking to obviate the disadvantage of inferior numbers by partial engagements in positions favorable to himself. There was, indeed, some parallel between his campaign and that of Lee, between the Rapidan and James, but the results in Virginia and Georgia were altogether disproportionate. The advance of Sherman was slow and cautious, but nevertheless steady;

and when the campaign had lasted seventy days, he was before Atlanta, the objective point of his designs, and in secure occupation of an extensive and important section of country, heretofore inaccessible to the Federal armies. Not only were Sherman's losses small, as compared with those of Grant, but his force was relatively much weaker.

There can be no just comparison of these two campaigns, either as illustrating the same system of tactics, or as yielding the same results. The aggregate of Federal forces in Georgia did not exceed, at the beginning of the campaign, one hundred thousand men, if indeed it reached that figure. To oppose this, Johnston had forty-five thousand. We have already stated the aggregate of Federal forces in Virginia to have been at least four times the force that, under any circumstances, Lee could have made available. The public did not interpret as *retreats*, the parallel movements by which Lee successively threw himself in the front of Grant, wherever the latter made a demonstration. Not once had Lee turned his back upon the enemy, nor abandoned a position, save when the baffled foe, after enormous losses, sought a new field of operations. At its conclusion, Grant had sustained losses in excess of the whole of Lee's army, abandoned altogether his original design, and sought a base of operations, which he might have reached in the beginning, not only without loss, but without even opposition.

Some explanation of the widely disproportionate results achieved in Virginia and Georgia, is to be found in the different tactics of the Federal commanders. Sherman, whose nature is thoroughly aggressive, yet developed great skill and caution. Instead of fruitlessly dashing his army against fortifications, upon ground of the enemy's choosing, he treated the positions of Johnston as fortresses, from which his antagonist was to be flanked.

But while this explanation was appreciated, the public was much disposed to accept the two campaigns as illustrations of the different systems of tactics accredited to the two Confederate commanders. It was seen that in Virginia the enemy occupied no new territory, and, at the end of three months, was upon ground which he might easily have occupied at the beginning of the campaign, but to reach which, by the means selected, had cost him nearly eighty thousand men.* In Georgia, on the other hand, Sherman had advanced one hundred miles upon soil heretofore firmly held by the Confederacy, and without a general engagement of the opposing forces. In Virginia, the enemy had no difficulty as to his transportation, and the farther Grant advanced towards James River, the more secure and abundant became his means of supply. In Georgia, Sherman drew his supplies over miles of hostile territory, and was nowhere aided by the proximity of navigable streams.

When in a censorious mood, the popular mind is not over-careful of the aptness of the parallels and analogies, wherewith to justify its carping judgments. Without denying his skill, or questioning his possession of the higher qualities of generalship, people complained that "Johnston was a retreating general." Whatever judgment may have arisen from subsequent events, it can not be fairly denied that when Johnston

* This estimate includes Grant's losses in his assaults upon the fortifications of Petersburg, immediately after his passage of the James River. I have seen his total losses from the Rapidan, until the siege of Petersburg was regularly begun, estimated by Northern writers, at over ninety thousand.

reached Atlanta, there was a very perceptible loss of popular confidence, not less in the issue of the campaign than in General Johnston himself. It was in deference to popular sentiment, as much as in accordance with his views of the necessity of the military situation, that President Davis, about the middle of July, relieved General Johnston from command. Sympathizing largely with the popular aspiration for a more bold, ample, and comprehensive policy, and appreciating the value of unlimited public confidence, Mr. Davis had lost much of his hope of those decisive results, which he believed the Western army competent to achieve.

The dispatch relieving General Johnston was as follows:

"RICHMOND, VA., July 17, 1864.

"*To General J. E. Johnston:*

"Lieutenant-General J. B. Hood has been commissioned to the temporary rank of General, under the law of Congress. I am directed by the Secretary of War to inform you, that as you have failed to arrest the advance of the enemy to the vicinity of Atlanta, and *express no confidence that you can defeat or repel him,* you are hereby relieved from the command of the Army and Department of Tennessee, which you will immediately turn over to General Hood.

"S. COOPER,

"*Adjutant and Inspector-General.*"

This order sufficiently explains the immediate motive of Johnston's removal, but there was a train of circumstances which, at length, brought the President reluctantly to this conclusion. The progress of events in Georgia, from the beginning of spring, had developed a marked difference in the views of General Johnston and the President. Early in the year Mr. Davis had warmly approved an offensive campaign against the Federal army, while its various wings were not yet united. The Federal force, then in the neighborhood of Dalton, did not greatly exceed the Confederate strength, and Mr. Davis, foreseeing the concentration of forces for the capture of Atlanta, believed the opportunity for a decisive stroke to exist before this concentration should ensue. General Hood likewise favored this view of the situation. He urged that the enemy would certainly concentrate forces to such an extent, if permitted, as would gradually force the Southern army back into the interior, where a defeat would be irreparable, with no new defensive line, and without the hope of rallying either the army or the people. General Johnston opposed these views, on the ground that the enemy, if defeated, had strong positions where they could take refuge, while a defeat of the Confederate force would be fatal. This difference of opinion is to be appropriately decided only by military criticism, but it can not be fairly adjudged that an offensive in the spring would not have succeeded, because it failed in the following autumn. Circumstances were altogether different.

General Johnston's operations between Dalton and Atlanta were unsatisfactory to Mr. Davis. Here again arises a military question, which we shall not seek to decide, in the evident difference as to the capacity of the Army of Tennessee, for any other than purely defensive operations. It was, indeed, not so much an opposition on the part of the President, to Johnston's operations, as the apprehension of a want of ultimate aim in his movements. Whatever the plans of General Johnston may have been, they were not communicated to Mr. Davis, at least in such a shape as to indicate the hope of early and decisive execution. Alarmed for the results of a policy having seemingly the characteristics of drifting, of waiting upon events, and of hoping for, instead of *creating opportunity*, Mr. Davis yet felt the necessity of giving General Johnston an ample trial. During all this period strong influences were brought to bear against Johnston, and upon the other hand, he was warmly sustained by influences friendly both to himself and the President.

For weeks the President was importuned by these conflicting counsels, the natural effect of which was to aggravate his grave doubts as to the existence of any matured ultimate object in General Johnston's movements. Upon one occasion, while still anxiously deliberating the subject, an eminent politician, a thorough patriot, a supporter of Mr. Davis, and having to an unlimited extent his confidence, called at the office of the President, with a view to explain the situation in Georgia, whence he had just arrived. This gentleman had been with the army, knew its condition, its enthusiasm and confidence. He was confident that General Johnston would destroy Sherman, and did not believe that the Federal army would ever be permitted to reach even the neighborhood of Atlanta. Mr. Davis, having quietly heard this explanation, replied by handing to his visitor a dispatch just received from Johnston, and *dated at Atlanta*. The army had already reached Atlanta, before the gentleman could reach Richmond, and he acknowledged himself equally amazed and disappointed.

Despite his doubts and apprehensions, however, Mr. Davis resisted the applications of members of Congress and leading politicians from the section in which General Johnston was operating, for a change of commanders, until he felt himself no longer justified in hazarding the loss of Atlanta without a struggle. There appeared little ground for the belief that

Johnston would hold Atlanta, nor did there appear any reason why his arrival there should occasion a departure from his previous retrograde policy. Of the purpose of General Johnston to evacuate Atlanta the President felt that he had abundant evidence. Not until he felt fully satisfied upon this point, was the removal of that officer determined upon. Indeed, the order removing Johnston sets forth as its justification, that he had expressed no confidence in his ability to "repel the enemy." If Atlanta should be surrendered, where would General Johnston expect to give battle?*

Subsequently to his removal, General Johnston avowed that his purpose was to hold Atlanta; and, therefore, we are not at liberty to question his purpose. But this does not alter the

*President Davis regarded the security of Atlanta as an object of the utmost consequence, for which, if necessary, even great hazards must be run. His frequent declaration was that the Confederacy "*had no vital points.*" This theory was correct, as there was certainly no one point, the loss of which necessarily involved the loss of the cause. Yet it was obvious in the beginning that certain sections, either for strategic reasons, or as sources of supply, were of vast importance for the prosecution of the war to a speedy and successful conclusion. The value of Richmond and Virginia was obvious. Equally important was a secure foothold in the Mississippi Valley, and the possession of the great mountainous range from Chattanooga to Lynchburg, the "backbone region" of the South. Mr. Davis regarded each one of these three objects as justifying almost any hazard or sacrifice. Under no circumstances could he approve a military policy which contemplated the surrender of either of these objects, without a desperate struggle. He had wanted Vicksburg defended to the last extremity, and now desired equal tenacity as to Atlanta. This city was a great manufacturing centre; the centre of the system of railroads diverging in all directions through the Gulf States, and it was the last remaining outpost in the defense of the central section of the Confederacy.

legitimate inference drawn by Mr. Davis at the time of his removal. Can it be believed that the President would have taken that step, if satisfied of Johnston's purpose to deliver battle for Atlanta?

This entire subject belongs appropriately only to military discussion, and no decision from other sources can possibly affect the ultimate sentence of that tribunal. Yet the most serious disparagement of Mr. Davis, by civilian writers, has been based upon the removal of Johnston from the command of the Western army. Granting that General Johnston would have sought to hold Atlanta, can it be believed that the ultimate result would have been different? When Sherman invested Atlanta, the North found some compensation for Grant's failures in Virginia; and even though his force should have been inadequate for a siege, can it now be doubted that he would have been reënforced to any needed extent? The mere presence of Sherman at Atlanta was justly viewed by the North as an important success. He had followed his antagonist to the very heart of the Confederacy, and was master of innumerable strong positions held by the Confederates at the outset of the campaign. To suppose that he would, at such a moment, be permitted to fail from a lack of means, is a hypothesis at variance with the conduct of the North throughout the war.

General Johnston has that sort of negative vindication which arises from the disasters of his successor, though, as we shall presently show, Mr. Davis was nowise responsible for the misfortunes of General Hood.* The question is one which must

* Yet the argument that General Hood's errors establish the wisdom of General Johnston's policy, can hardly be deemed fair by an intelligent and impartial judgment. A more competent commander than Hood might have more ably executed an offensive campaign, even after the fall of

some day arise as between the general military policy of the Confederacy, and the antagonistic views which have been so freely ascribed to General Johnston by his admirers. We have no desire to pursue that antagonism, which, if it really existed, can hardly yet be a theme for impartial discussion. Towards the close of the war, it was usual to accredit Johnston with the theory that the Confederacy could better afford to *lose territory than men*, and that hence the true policy of the South was to avoid general engagements, unless under such circumstances as should totally neutralize the enemy's advantage in numbers. We are not prepared to say to what extent these announcements of his views were authorized by General Johnston, or to what extent they were based upon retrospection. Some confirmation of their authenticity would seem to be deducible from General Johnston's declaration since the war, that the "Confederacy was too weak for offensive war." Certainly there could be no theory more utterly antagonistic to the genius of the Southern people, and that is a consideration, to which the great commanders of history have not usually been indifferent. Nor was it the theory which inspired those achievements of Southern valor, which will ring through the centuries. It was not the

Atlanta; or, again, other tactics than those of Johnston, from Dalton to Atlanta, might have had better results.

After Johnston's removal, the President received numerous letters from prominent individuals in the Cotton States, heartily applauding that step. The condemnation of the President, for the removal of Johnston, came only after Hood's disasters; and it must be remembered that Hood's later operations were not in accordance with Mr. Davis' views.

The writer remembers a pithy summary of the Georgia campaign, made by a Confederate officer, shortly before the end of the war. Said he: "While Johnston was in command there were *no results at all;* when Hood took command, *results came very rapidly.*"

theory which Lee and Jackson adopted, nor, we need hardly add, that which Jefferson Davis approved.

Indeed, the philosophy of the Southern failure is not to be sought in the discussion of opposing theories among Confederate leaders. The conclusion of history will be, not that the South accomplished less than was to be anticipated, but far more than have any other people under similar circumstances. Southern men hardly yet comprehend the real odds in numbers and resources which for four years they successfully resisted. Other questions than those merely of aggregate populations and material wealth, enter into the solution of the problem.

By the census of 1860, the aggregate free population of the thirteen States, which the Confederacy claimed, was 7,500,000, leaving in the remaining States of the Union a free population of over twenty millions. This statement includes Kentucky and Missouri as members of the Confederacy; yet, by the compulsion of Federal bayonets, these States, not less than Maryland and Delaware, were virtually on the side of the North. Kentucky proclaimed neutrality, but during the whole war was overrun by the Federal armies, and, with her State government and large numbers of her people favoring the North, despite the Southern sympathies of the majority, her moral influence, as well as her physical strength, sustained the Union. The legitimate government of Missouri, and a majority of her people, sided with the South; but early occupied and held by the Federal army, her legitimate government was subverted, and her moral and physical resources were thrown into the scale against the Confederacy.

To say nothing of the large numbers of recruits obtained by the Federal armies from Kentucky, Maryland and Missouri, (chiefly from their large foreign populations,) their contributions to the Confederate army were nearly, if not quite, compensated by the accessions to Federal strength from East Tennessee, Western Virginia, and other portions of the seceded States. It would be fair, therefore, to deduct the population of these two States from that of the South, and this would leave the Confederacy five and one-half millions. Dividing their free populations between the two sections, and the odds were six and a half millions against twenty and a half millions. This is a liberal statement for the North, and embraces only the original populations of the two sections at the beginning of hostilities. There can hardly be a reasonable doubt, that had the struggle been confined to these numerical forces, the South would have triumphed. But hordes of foreign mercenaries, incited by high bounty and the promise of booty, flocked to the Federal army, and thus was the North enabled to recruit its armies to any needed standard, while the South depended solely upon its original population. As the South was overrun, too, negroes were forced or enticed into the Federal service, and thus, by these inexhaustible reserves of foreign mercenaries and negro recruits, the Confederate army was finally exhausted.

The following exhibition of the strength of the Federal armies is from the report of the Secretary of War, at the beginning of the session of Congress in December, 1865:

Official reports show that on the 1st of May, 1864, the aggregate national military force of all arms, officers and men, was nine hundred and seventy thousand seven hundred and ten, to-wit:

Available force present for duty	662,345
On detached service in the different military departments	109,348
In field hospitals or unfit for duty	41,266
In general hospitals or on sick leave at home	75,978
Absent on furlough or as prisoners of war	66,290
Absent without leave	15,483
Grand aggregate	970,710

The aggregate available force present for duty May 1st, 1864, was distributed in the different commands as follows:

Department of Washington	42,124
Army of the Potomac	120,386
Department of Virginia and North Carolina	59,139
Department of the South	18,165
Department of the Gulf	61,866
Department of Arkansas	23,666
Department of the Tennessee	74,174
Department of the Missouri	15,770
Department of the North-west	5,295
Department of Kansas	4,798
Head-quarters Military Division of the Mississippi	476
Department of the Cumberland	119,948
Department of the Ohio	35,416
Northern Department	9,540
Department of West Virginia	30,782
Department of the East	2,828
Department of the Susquehanna	2,970
Middle Department	5,627
Ninth Army Corps	20,780
Department of New Mexico	3,454
Department of the Pacific	5,141
Total	662,345

And again:

Official reports show that on the 1st of March, 1865, the aggregate military force of all arms, officers and men, was nine hundred and sixty-five thousand five hundred and ninety-one, to-wit:

Available forces present for duty	602,598
On detached service in the different military departments	132,538
In field hospitals and unfit for duty	35,628
In general hospitals or on sick leave	143,419
Absent on furlough or as prisoners of war	31,695
Absent without leave	19,683
Grand aggregate	965,591

This force was augmented on the 1st of May, 1865, by enlistments, to the number of one million five hundred and sixteen, of all arms, officers and men (1,000,516).

And again he says:

The aggregate quotas charged against the several States under all calls made by the President of the United States, from the 15th day of April, 1861, to the 14th day of April, 1865, at which time drafting and recruiting ceased, was	2,759,049
The aggregate number of men credited on the several calls, and put into service of the United States, in the army, navy, and marine corps, during the above period, was	2,656,553
Leaving a deficiency on all calls, when the war closed, of	102,596

This statement does not include the regular army, nor the negro troops raised in the Southern States, which were not raised by calls on the States. It may be safely asserted that the "available force present for duty," of the Federal armies at the beginning or close of the last year of the war, exceeded the entire force called into the service of the Confederacy during the four years. The aggregate of Federal forces raised during the war numbered more than one-third of the free population of the Confederate States, including men, women, and children.*

*It has been contended that the odds against the South in numbers and resources were compensated by the advantages of her defensive position, and by the strong incentives of a war for her homes and liberties. An ingenious argument in demonstration of the assumed defective administration of the Confederacy has been deduced from various historical examples of successful resistance against overwhelming odds. The most plausible citation has been the success of Frederick the Great, in his defense of Prussia against the coalition of Russia, Austria, and France. This illustration has no value, as it does not at all meet the case.

Waiving all consideration of the peculiar strategic difficulties of the South, Frederick first had the advantage of his English alliance. Frederick never fought odds greater than two to one, while the South fought three, four, sometimes five to one—but never equal numbers. Again, Prussia was inaccessible except by overland marches—not penetrated, like the South, in every direction by navigable rivers, and nearly surrounded by the sea. Frederick, too, was absolute in Prussia, and had the lives and property of all his subjects at his control. Mr. Davis, on the other hand, never could consolidate the resources of the South as he

But this disparity of numbers, apparently sufficient of itself to decide the issue against the South, was by no means the greatest advantage of the North. When it is asserted that the naval superiority of the North decided the contest in its favor, we are not limited to the consideration merely of that absolute command of the water, which prevented the South from importing munitions of war, except at enormous expense and hazard, which made the defense of the sea-coast and contiguous territory impossible, and which so disorganized the Confederate finances. The Confederacy encountered strategic difficulties, by reason of the naval superiority of the North, which, at an early period of the war, counter-balanced the advantages of its defensive position.

In the beginning the enemy had easy, speedy, and secure access to the Southern coast, and wherever there was a harbor or inlet, was to be found a base of operations for a Federal army. Thus, at the outset, the Confederacy presented on every side an exposed frontier. In every quarter, the Federal armies had bases of operations at right angles, each to the other, and thus, wherever the Confederate army established a

desired, being constantly hampered by demagogism in Congress, which could at all times be coerced by the press hostile to the administration, or influenced by the slightest display of popular displeasure. Pretending to place the whole means of the country at the disposal of the President, Congress yet invariably rendered its measures inoperative by emasculating clauses providing exemptions and immunities of every description. President Davis was too sincere a republican, and had too much regard for the restraints of the Constitution to violently usurp ungranted powers.

It is to be remembered, too, that the South received no foreign aid, while Frederick was at last saved by the accession of Peter to the Russian throne, which event dissolved the coalition against Prussia.

defensive line, it was assailable by a second Federal army advancing from a second base. The advantage of rapid concentration of forces, usually belonging to an interior line, was obviated by the easy and rapid conveyance of large masses by water.

Probably the most serious strategic disadvantage of the South was its territorial configuration, through the intersection of its soil in nearly every quarter by navigable rivers, either emptying into the ocean, of which the North, at all times, had undisputed control, or opening upon the Federal frontier. In all the Atlantic States of the Confederacy navigable streams penetrate far into the interior, and empty into the sea. The Mississippi, aptly termed an "inland sea," flowing through the Confederacy, was, both in its upper waters and at its mouth, held by the North. The Tennessee and Cumberland Rivers, with their mouths upon the Federal frontiers, navigable in winter for transports and gunboats, in the first twelve months of the war, brought the Federal armies to the centre of the South-west. In the Trans-Mississippi region, the Arkansas and Red Rivers gave the enemy convenient and secure bases of operations along their margins. Each one of these streams having inevitably, sooner or later, become subject to the control of the Federal navy, afforded bases of operations against the interior of the South, while it was likewise threatened from the Northern frontier.

The difficulty of *space*, which defeated Napoleon in his invasion of Russia, and which has baffled the largest armies led by the ablest commanders, had an easy solution for the North. Remarkable illustrations of the extent to which these water facilities aided the North, were afforded by the signal failure attending every overland advance of the Federal armies so long as the Confederates could raise even the semblance of an opposing force. Besides the innumerable Federal failures in the Appalachian region of Virginia, Sherman and Grant, the most successful of Northern commanders, illustrated this military principle in instances already noted. When Sherman finally marched from the Confederate frontier to the ocean, General Grant's policy of "attrition" had virtually destroyed the military strength of the South, and Sherman simply accomplished an unopposed march through an undefended country. There can be no better illustration of these strategic difficulties of the Confederacy, than that afforded by the train of disasters in the beginning of 1862, each of which was directly and mainly attributable to the naval advantages of the enemy and the geographical configuration.

A candid review of the events of the first two years of the war will demonstrate the inevitable failure of subjugation of the South, but for these advantages of her invaders. Not only are the facilities of transportation possessed by the North to be considered, but the further advantage extended by its fleet in the event of military reverse. The shipping constituted an invulnerable defense and convenient shelter for the fugitive Federals. Upon at least two occasions, the two main Federal armies were rescued from destruction by the gunboats—in the case of Grant at Shiloh, and of McClellan on James River.

Nor was it possible for the South to make adequate provision to meet the naval advantages of the North. The Federal Government retained the whole of the navy. The North was manufacturing and commercial, while the South was purely agricultural in its means; hence the incomparable rapidity with which the Federal Government accumulated shipping of every character. The initial superiority of the North in naval resources prevented the South from obtaining from foreign sources the men and the material for the equipment of vessels of war. Then, again, the disputed question of the capacity of shore batteries to resist vessels of war, had a most inopportune solution for the South, and in cases where great interests were involved. We have already noted one instance where this question had a fatal solution—that of New Orleans. And in this instance, too, the want of time for preparation was a fatal difficulty. But for the unfinished condition of the iron-clads at New Orleans, the possession of the Mississippi by the enemy would have been greatly deferred, though, with the head-waters and mouth of the great river in Federal control, it was hardly more than a question of time, should the North skillfully employ its superior manufacturing resources and preponderant population.

The special weapon of the North, from which no amount of victories ever brought the Confederacy one moment's relief, was the blockade—a weapon which the injustice of foreign powers placed in the grasp of our adversaries. The blockade ruined the Confederate finances and, by preventing the importation of military material, weakened the Confederate armies to the extent of thousands of men who were detailed for manufacturing and other purposes. It was the blockade, too, which caused the derangement of the internal economy of the South, creating the painful contrast in the effects of the war upon the two sections. The North, with its ports open, the abundant gold of California, and petroleum stimulating speculation, found in the war a mine of wealth. Patriotism and profit went hand in hand. The vast expenditures of Government created a lucrative market; the enormous transportation demanded made the railroads prosperous beyond parallel; and the sources of popular prosperity and exhilaration were inexhaustible. The condition of the South was the exact reverse. With its commerce almost totally suspended; frequently in peril of famine; whole States, one after another, occupied or devastated by the enemy, so that when the Confederate armies expelled the enemy they could not maintain themselves, and were compelled to retreat; deprived of every comfort, and nearly of all the necessaries of life, the history of the war in the South is a record of universal and unrelieved suffering.

It must be apparent that we have here given but a superficial review and imperfect statement of the obstacles with which the South contended. But, assuredly, before even this array of odds, such minor questions as the removal of one officer and the retention of another sink into utter insignificance. As we have before intimated, many of the most important incidents in the conduct of the war must be reserved for the decision of impartial military judgment. What if it should be granted that the appointment of Pemberton and the removal of Johnston were fatal blunders, were they compensated by no acts of judicious selection of other officers for promotion and reward? Is the firm and constant support of Lee, of Sidney Johnston, of Jackson, and of Early to be accounted as nothing? Are we to accept the imputation of error to Mr. Davis alone? We need not pursue the career of General Johnston much farther than its beginning to discover what his countrymen unanimously deplored as an error, what Stonewall Jackson declared a fatal blunder. General Lee confessed his error at Gettysburg. Beauregard, too, has been generally adjudged to have seriously erred at Shiloh. Yet how easy would it be to construct a plausible theory, demonstrating the seriously adverse influence upon the fortunes of the Confederacy, from each one of those errors. And we could extend the parallel much farther. Napoleon estimated the merits of different generals by the comparative number of their faults and virtues. Perhaps that is even a better philosophy which urges us to measure the reputations of men, "not by their exemption from fault, but by the size of the virtues of which they are possessed." Assuredly, the South can never demur to the application of this test either to herself or her late leader. Judged by such a standard of merit, neither can be apprehensive for the award of posterity. Two generations hence, if not sooner, Jefferson Davis, not less for his wisdom than for his virtues, will be commemorated as the Washington of the South.

With a view to dramatic unity, we shall disregard somewhat of chronological order, and follow, with a rapid summary, the movements of the ill-starred Western army of the Confederacy, to the point where its existence virtually terminated. The successor of General Johnston, General John B. Hood, embodied a rare union of the characteristics of the popular ideal of a soldier. He was the noblest contribution of Kentucky chivalry to the armies of the South, and his record throughout the war, even though ending in terrible disaster, was that of a gallant, dashing, and skillful leader. Identified with the Army of Northern Virginia from an early period of its history, he shared its dangers, its trials, and its most thrilling triumphs. "Hood and his Texans" were household words in the Confederacy, and the bulletins from every battle-field in Virginia were emblazoned with their exploits. Few commanders have possessed to a greater extent than Hood that magnetic mastery over troops, which imbues them with the consciousness of irresistible resolution. Of conspicuous personal gallantry and commanding *physique*, he united to fiery energy, consummate self-possession and excellent tactical ability. A favorite with General Lee and President Davis, he had also received the warm commendation of Stonewall Jackson for his distinguished services at Cold Harbor, in 1862.

Painfully wounded and disabled at Gettysburg, he accompanied his old division to Georgia, and, while his previous wound was yet unhealed, he lost a leg at Chickamauga. After months of painful confinement, he was again in Richmond, soliciting the privilege of additional service to his country. His conspicuous devotion challenged equally the admiration of the people and the Government, and President Davis was universally declared never to have conferred a more deserved promotion than that by which he made Hood a Lieutenant-General. General Hood was assigned to the command of a *corps* under Johnston, and accompanied the army in its movements from Dalton to Atlanta.

The appointment of Hood as the successor of Johnston was the occasion of renewed anticipation to the South. His aggressive qualities, it was thought, would supply that bold and energetic policy which the country believed to be the great need of the situation in Georgia. Nor was there any thing in the record of Hood, to cause apprehension that his possession of these qualities excluded such an equipoise of mental faculties, as should ensure a sound and discreet system of operations.

We shall not discuss in detail the operations which General Hood so speedily inaugurated. They were necessitated, to a large extent, by a situation of affairs for which he was not responsible. The one object of Hood, and the one hope and necessity of the Confederacy, was the expulsion of Sherman from a vital section. Sherman had not delayed an hour in his purpose of securing possession of the Macon road, and severing the communications of Atlanta. Already he was preparing operations similar to those by which Grant sought the isolation of Petersburg; and if his strength was not then adequate, there could be no question of his capacity to obtain ample means from his Government to secure the great results of his skillfully conducted and successful campaign. The situation required precisely that immediate execution of a vigorous policy by which Lee had relieved Richmond of the presence of McClellan.

While thus foreseeing the fatal result of permitting himself to be besieged in Atlanta, General Hood did not rashly assail the enemy. A favorable opportunity was presented, by a gap between two of Sherman's columns, for a concentrated assault upon that which was most exposed. Though the Confederate forces were admirably massed and skillfully led, they were eventually repulsed by the murderous fire of the Federal artillery, which was concentrated with signal promptitude and served with rare ability. This demonstration was a failure, though it had promised favorably, and, for a time, exposed the entire Federal army to serious danger. A series of subsequent engagements, fought by Hood to prevent the consummation of Sherman's design to isolate Atlanta, left the enemy in possession of the Confederate line of supply, and Atlanta was evacuated on the 1st of September.

Such was the melancholy conclusion, for the Confederacy, of the first stage of the Georgia campaign. Military judgment must decide, how far an able offensive policy, at the outset of the campaign would have delayed, if not entirely checked the march of Sherman to Atlanta; how far an offensive was then practicable; to what extent Hood's course was imposed upon him by a situation which he did not create, and whether his accession to command, either altered or hastened the ultimate fate of Atlanta.

The emergency consequent upon the fall of Atlanta, summoned President Davis to Georgia. His visit was dictated by the double purpose, of healing dissensions in that State, and of devising measures for the restoration of the campaign. The perverse course of Governor Brown had proven successful in the dissemination of disaffection, and his teachings were beginning to mature those fruits of demoralization in Georgia, which the subsequent march of Sherman abundantly developed. It would be impossible to characterize the conduct of this official in terms of extravagant severity. Capricious and perverse in his hostility to the Confederate Government, while yet professing fealty to the cause, he contrived, in the most distressing exigencies, to paralyze the energies of Georgia, and finally to create a feeling bordering closely upon open disaffection.

The conduct of Governor Brown, acceptable only to the clique of malcontents who followed him, was the subject of criticism throughout the Confederacy, and of suspicion by a large portion of the public. It is a matter of record that after the fall of Atlanta he refused to coöperate with the Confederate authorities for the defense of Georgia, and *demanded* the return of the Georgia troops in Virginia, unless the President would send reënforcements. Yet he was perfectly aware that the Confederate Government then, had not one man to spare in any quarter, and was in a crisis, produced solely by the want of numbers. His communications to the Confederate Government were usually splenetic assaults upon the President, whose military administration he offensively criticised, and whom he charged with an ambition to destroy every protection to the reserved rights of the States. There is no point of view in which the course of Governor Brown is not equally incomprehensible and indefensible. It was freighted with disaster and defeat to the cause which he professed to serve. Considered in the aspect of partisan administration, or the indulgence of personal spleen, its inconsistency was paralleled only by its folly. It demoralized public sentiment, and tended largely to that corruption of the public and the army which, in the last stage of the war, was so palpable. Not the least injurious feature of Governor Brown's official policy was the unpropitious seasons which he selected for the indulgence of his capricious and splenetic moods. Upon the heels of crushing military disasters, and when the Confederate authorities were most helpless, Governor Brown was most exacting.

The purposes of his persistent and vindictive impeachments of the Confederate Government, at such periods, must remain a subject of speculation. Certainly he did not exalt his dignity as a statesman, nor approve his earnestness as a patriot, by giving precedence to his personal animosities over his official duties, and by substituting for coöperation in support of a cause to which he protested his devotion, a system of malignant controversy with the national authorities.

The interviews of President Davis, with Governor Brown, during his visit to Georgia, in September, failed, as had all previous efforts to that end, to effect an accommodation of differences. Governor Brown was determined not to be satisfied, and though Mr. Davis, having made nearly every concession demanded, left him under the impression that Brown was at last prepared to coöperate with him heartily and zealously, he was speedily convinced of the error of such a calculation.

While on his way to Hood's army Mr. Davis addressed the citizens of Macon, and spoke with great candor, concerning the perils of the situation, which, though serious, he believed, might be repaired. Alluding to the demand made upon him for reënforcements from Virginia, he said that the disparity in Virginia was greater than in Georgia; the army under Early had been sent to the Valley, because the enemy had penetrated to Lynchburg; and now should Early be withdrawn, there would be nothing to prevent the Federal army from forming a complete cordon of men around Richmond. He had counseled with General Lee upon all these points; his mind had sought to embrace the entire field, and the necessities of every quarter, and his conclusion was, that "if one-half of the men now absent from the field, would return to duty, we can defeat the enemy. With that hope, I am now going to the front. I may not realize this hope, but I know that there are men there, who have looked death too often in the face to despond now."

On the 18th September, the President reached Hood's headquarters, and on the following day reviewed the whole army. He addressed the troops in terms of encouragement, and his promise to them of an advance northward, was received with unbounded enthusiasm. The situation in Georgia admitted a very limited consideration of expedients, by which to obtain compensation for the loss of Atlanta. Sherman's presence, unmolested, in the interior of Georgia, during the autumn and winter, would be fatal. He would then be in a position to assail, at leisure, the only remaining source of supplies for the Confederate armies. His cavalry could safely penetrate in every direction, destroying communications and supplies, and producing universal demoralization.

Hood was confident that his army was capable of better fighting than it had performed against Sherman, provided it could meet the enemy under such circumstances as should promise the recovery of the ground lost, in the event of victory. To attack Sherman in Atlanta was not to be considered, and to await the development of the enemy's plan would be dangerous. Sherman had already announced his purpose to rest his army at Atlanta, with a view to its preparation for the arduous enterprises yet before it. Hence, it became necessary to adopt a plan, which should draw him away from his defenses, and compel him to fight upon equal ground.

It may be briefly stated that the subsequent operations of General Hood, when they ceased to menace the enemy's flank, and assumed the character of a mere detachment upon the Federal rear, was not the plan of campaign which Mr. Davis expected to be carried into execution. He approved a concentration upon the Federal flank, which it was not likely Sherman would permit to be endangered. Seeing, however, the exposed situation of the country south of Atlanta, in consequence of the movement into Alabama, Mr. Davis opposed any operations which should place Hood's army *beyond striking distance of Sherman, should the latter move southward from Atlanta.*

It is remarkable to what extent the movements of Sherman demonstrated the judicious character of the Confederate movement, so long as it was in conformity with these views of Mr. Davis. Puzzled, at first, as to Hood's purposes, Sherman was no longer perplexed as to what his own course should be, when it was evident that Hood was making a serious demonstration for the recovery of Tennessee, meanwhile giving up Georgia entirely to Federal possession. When these larger and more doubtful enterprises were added to the original scope of the Confederate movement, Mr. Davis was too remote from the scene to assume the responsibility of recalling the army from an enterprise which he felt assured would not be attempted without justifying information by the commander.*

But, after all, the disastrous consequences, following the uncovering of Georgia, are to be attributed less to the intrinsically erroneous strategy of Hood, than to the consummate vigor and promptitude of Sherman. Odious to the South as Sherman is, by reason of his cruelties and barbarities, he can not be denied the merit of an immediate grasp of the critical situation, and a no less prompt execution. A commander of less self-possession, and less audacity, would have been bewildered by the transfer of an army from his immediate front to his rear, and placed astride his communications. The "march to the sea" was no military exploit, and only a brazen charlatanism could exalt it as an illustration of genius. The proof of

* General Hood's magnanimous acknowledgment is sufficient for the acquittal of Mr. Davis from any responsibility for this ill-starred movement. On taking leave of his army, in January, 1865, Hood said, speaking of the late campaign: "*I am alone responsible for its conception, and strove hard to do my duty in its execution.*"

But in addition to this, there was a correspondence, between Mr. Davis and a Confederate officer of high rank, which *completely exculpated Mr. Davis.* In accordance with Mr. Davis' accustomed magnanimity and regard for the public welfare, this correspondence was never published. The facts in this matter conspicuously illustrate the persistent and reckless misrepresentation, which has not ceased with the termination of the war. With a class of writers, the *facts* regarding Mr. Davis are things least to be desired. In many instances, their attacks upon his fame are puerile, but in others, where facts are either distorted or wantonly disregarded, the object seems to be merely to gratify a wicked spirit of detraction.

Sherman's merit is to be seen in the quick determination and execution of his purpose, when the real significance of Hood's operations was revealed. His telegram to Washington fully described the situation and prophesied the sequel: "Hood has crossed the Tennessee. Thomas will take care of him and Nashville, while Schofield will not let him into Chattanooga or Knoxville. *Georgia and South Carolina are at my mercy, and I shall strike.* Do not be anxious about me. I am all right."

We are not permitted to trace the unfortunate Tennessee campaign of General Hood, culminating in his disastrous defeat at Nashville, in December, and in the virtual destruction of the gallant but ill-starred army, upon whose bayonets the Confederate power, west of the Alleghanies, was so long upheld. It was the final campaign of the Confederacy in that quarter, and, with its failure, perished forever the hope of defending the western and central sections of the South.* Meanwhile, Sherman, unopposed, had marched like Fate through Georgia, to Savannah, realizing Grant's assertion that the Confederacy was a mere shell, and revealing a fact, until then not clearly appreciated, of the exhaustion and demoralization of its people.

*In the autumn of 1864, General Price advanced into Missouri, proclaiming his purpose to be a permanent occupation. The expedition ended in disaster. Defeated in an engagement on the Big Blue, Price retreated into Kansas, and finally into Southern Arkansas. The campaign did not affect the current of the war elsewhere, and was a failure.

CHAPTER XX.

INCIDENTS ON THE LINES OF RICHMOND AND PETERSBURG DURING THE SUMMER AND AUTUMN—CAPTURE OF FORT HARRISON—OTHER DEMONSTRATIONS BY GRANT—THE SITUATION NEAR THE CONFEDERATE CAPITAL—EARLY'S VALLEY CAMPAIGN—POPULAR CENSURE OF EARLY—INFLUENCE OF THE VALLEY CAMPAIGN UPON THE SITUATION NEAR RICHMOND—WHAT THE AGGREGATE OF CONFEDERATE DISASTERS SIGNIFIED—DESPONDENCY OF THE SOUTH—THE INJURIOUS EXAMPLES OF PROMINENT MEN—THE PRESIDENT AND GENERAL LEE—MR. DAVIS' POPULARITY—WHY HE DID NOT FULLY COMPREHEND THE DEMORALIZATION OF THE PEOPLE—HE HOPES FOR POPULAR REANIMATION—WAS THE CASE OF THE CONFEDERACY HOPELESS?—VACILLATING CONDUCT OF CONGRESS—THE CONFEDERATE CONGRESS A WEAK BODY—MR. DAVIS' RELATIONS WITH CONGRESS—PROPOSED CONSCRIPTION OF SLAVES—FAVORED BY DAVIS AND LEE—DEFEATED BY CONGRESS—LEGISLATION DIRECTED AGAINST THE PRESIDENT—DAVIS' OPINION OF LEE—RUMORS OF PEACE—HAMPTON ROADS CONFERENCE—THE FEDERAL ULTIMATUM—THE ABSURD CHARGE AGAINST MR. DAVIS OF OBSTRUCTING NEGOTIATIONS—HIS RECORD ON THE SUBJECT OF PEACE—A RICHMOND NEWSPAPER ON THE FEDERAL ULTIMATUM—DELUSIVE SIGNS OF PUBLIC SPIRIT—NO ALTERNATIVE BUT CONTINUED RESISTANCE—REPORT OF THE HAMPTON ROADS CONFERENCE.

MEANWHILE the siege of Petersburg had progressed drearily through the months of summer and autumn. The "hammering" principle was abandoned by General Grant, for a series of maneuvres having in view the possession of the railroads extending southward and eastward.

About the middle of August a portion of Grant's army was established upon the Weldon road. This was by no means a line of communication vital to General Lee, though several heavy engagements ensued from its disputed possession. The

Federal losses in these engagements were very heavy, and were hardly compensated by any immediate advantage following the permanent acquisition, by General Grant, of the Weldon Railroad. The location of the Federal army gave ample opportunity for the transfer of forces to either side of the river, and General Grant did not fail to avail himself of his facilities, for aiding the more important operations before Petersburg, by numerous diversions in the direction of Richmond. One of these movements upon the north side of James River, in the last days of September, resulted disastrously to the Confederates, in the loss of Fort Harrison, a position of great importance in the defense of that portion of the Confederate line. Efforts to recapture it were unavailing, and attended with heavy loss. The enemy was left in secure possession of a position from which Richmond could be seriously menaced. The last serious demonstration by General Grant, before winter, was the movement of a heavy force, with the view of turning the Confederate position, and obtaining the possession of Lee's communications with Lynchburg and Danville. Though sustained by a strong diversion on other portions of the line, this demonstration was barren of results.

Thus, the beginning of winter found the Confederate forces still safely holding the lines of Richmond and Petersburg. The situation near the Confederate capital was encouraging, and indicated an almost indefinite resistance. But nearly every other quarter of the Confederacy was darkened by the shadow of disaster.

The campaign of Hood in Tennessee had its counterpart in the Valley campaign of General Early. This campaign, the original design of which was the expulsion of Hunter, was doubly important afterwards in the design to secure the harvests of the Shenandoah Valley, and to continue the diversion of a large Federal force from the front of Richmond. The earlier movements of General Early were attended with success, and the Confederacy had the promise of a campaign, which should renew the glories of Stonewall Jackson, in a district which his exploits had made forever famous. In its conclusion was revealed, perhaps more strikingly than upon any other theatre of the war, the overwhelming odds and obstacles, with which the Confederacy contended in this desperate stage of its history. The activity of General Early in the summer months, and his well-earned reputation as an officer of skill and daring, induced the enemy to concentrate a heavy force to protect the Potomac frontier, and, if possible, to overwhelm the Confederate army in the Valley. In the months of September and October, several engagements occurred, in which General Early was badly defeated, and his army at the close of autumn exhibited so many evidences of demoralization, as to occasion apprehension for its future efficiency.

The censure of General Early by the public and the newspapers was unsparing. Most unworthy allegations, totally unsupported, were circulated in explanation of his disasters. That such a man as Early, whose every promotion had been won by a heroism and efficiency inferior to those of none of Lee's subordinates, should have been recklessly condemned for reverses, which were clearly the results of no errors or misconduct of his own, is now a striking commentary upon that sullen despondency into which the Southern mind was fast settling. A victory, in any quarter, was now almost the last expectation of the public, and still Early was recklessly abused for not winning victories, with a demoralized army, against forces having four times his own strength. Neither President

Davis nor General Lee ever doubted General Early's efficiency; and the letter of the commanding general to Early, written in the last hours of the Confederacy, constitutes a tribute to patriotic and distinguished services, which the old hero may well cherish in his exile, as a worthy title to the esteem of posterity.

The defeat of Early at Cedar Creek, late in October, was the decisive event of the last campaign in the Shenandoah Valley. In December nearly all Early's forces were transferred to General Lee's lines, and the bulk of the Federal army in the Valley returned to General Grant. General Early remained in the Valley with a fragmentary command, which Sheridan easily overran on his march from Winchester to the front of Petersburg.

Events in the Valley had a marked influence upon the situation near Richmond. The Confederate authorities had hoped for such a successful issue in the Valley as should relieve Richmond of much of Grant's pressure. The disappointment of this hope left the Federal frontier secure, and gave Grant a large accession of strength, for which Lee had no compensation, except the *débris* of a defeated and dispirited army.

The aggregate of military disasters with which the year 1864 terminated, established the inevitable failure of the Confederacy, unless more vigorous measures than the Government had ever yet attempted should be adopted, and unless the people were prepared for sacrifices which had not yet been exacted. The reserves of men, which the various acts of conscription were designed to place in the field, were exhausted, or beyond the reach of the Government, and the supplies of the army became more and more precarious each day. There was, indeed, nothing fatal as affecting the ultimate decision of the contest, in the military events of the past year, if unattended by a decay of public spirit. It was not until the winter of 1864–1865 that any considerable body of the Southern people were brought to the conviction that their struggle was a hopeless one. The waste of war is in nothing more continuous than in its test of the moral energy of communities. In the last winter of the war the distrust of the popular mind was painfully apparent. The South began to read its fate when it saw that the North had converted warfare into universal destruction and desolation, and when it exchanged the code of civilized war for the grim butchery of Grant, and the savage measures of Sherman and Sheridan. It was plain that while the losses of the Federal army were shocking, and were sufficient to have unnerved the army and the people of the North, the "attrition" of General Grant had caused a fearful diminution of the Confederate armies.

The facility of the Federal Government in repairing its losses of men, baffled all previous calculation in the Confederacy, and it had long since become evident that the resources of the North, in all other respects, were equal to an indefinite endurance. Indeed, it has been justly said that the material resources of the North were not seriously tested, but merely developed by the war. Peculiarly disheartening to the South was the triumph of the Republican party in the reëlection of Mr. Lincoln—an event plainly portending a protraction of the war upon a scale, which should adequately employ the inexhaustible means at the command of the Federal Government.

It would be needless to speculate now as to the material capacity of the South to have met the demands of another campaign. The military capacity of the Confederacy in the last months of the war, is not to be measured by the number of men that still might have been brought to the field, or by the material means which yet survived the consumption and waste of war. These considerations are admissible only in connection with that moral condition of the public, which fitted or disqualified it for longer endurance of the privations and sacrifices of the war. Long before the close of winter, popular feeling assumed a phase of sullen indifference which, while yet averse to unconditional submission to the North, manifestly despaired of ultimate success, viewed additional sacrifices as hopeless, and anticipated the *worst.*

Only a hasty and ill-informed judgment could condemn the Southern people for the decay of its spirit in this last stage of the war. No people ever endured with more heroism the trials and privations incidental to their situation. Yet these sacrifices appeared to have been to no purpose; a cruel and inexorable fate seemed to pursue them, and to taunt them with the futility of exertion to escape its decree. Victories, which had amazed the world, and again and again stunned a powerful adversary, and which the South felt that, under ordinary circumstances, should have secured the reward of independence, were recurred to only as making more bitter the chagrin of the present. Previous defeats, at the time seeming fatal, had been patiently encountered, and bravely surmounted, so long as victory appeared to offer a reward which should compensate for the sacrifice necessary to obtain it. But, now, even the hope of victory had almost ceased to be a source of encouragement, since any probable success would only tend to a postponement of the inevitable catastrophe, which, perhaps, it would be better to invite than to defer.

It must be confessed, too, that the people and the army of the Confederacy, in this crisis, found but little source of reanimation in the example of a majority of its public men. Long before the taint of demoralization reached the heart of the masses, the Confederate cause had been despaired of by men whose influence and position determined the convictions of whole communities. In President Davis and General Lee the South saw conspicuous examples of resolution, fortitude, and self-abnegation. It is not to be denied that the impatient and almost despairing temper of the public was visibly influenced by the persistent crimination of Mr. Davis, by the faction which sought to thwart him even at the hazard of the public welfare. But when it was discovered that the unity of counsel and purpose which had animated the President and General Lee at every stage of the struggle, was still maintained, popular sympathy still clung to the leader, whose unselfish devotion and unshaken fortitude should have been a sufficient rebuke to his accusers.

A vast deal of misrepresentation has been indulged to show that Mr. Davis had become unpopular in the last stage of the war, and that he was the object of popular reproach as chiefly responsible for the condition of the country. To the contrary, there were many evidences of the sympathy which embraced Mr. Davis as probably the chief sufferer from apprehended calamities. His appearance in public in Richmond, was always the occasion of unrestrained popular enthusiasm. Even but a few weeks before the final catastrophe, there were signal instances of the popular affection for him, and it was painfully evident to those who knew his character, that these demonstrations were accepted by him as an exhibition of popular confidence in the success of the cause. Indeed, the very confidence which these exhibitions of popular sympathy produced in the mind of Mr. Davis, has been urged as an evidence of a want of sagacity, which disqualified him for a clear appreciation of the situation of affairs.

Perhaps with more color of truth than usual, this view of Mr. Davis' character has been presented. That he did not fully comprehend the wide-spread demoralization of the South in the last months of the war, is hardly to be questioned. Judging men by his own exalted nature, he conceived it impossible that the South could ever abandon its hope of independence. He did not realize how men could cherish an aspiration for the future, which did not embrace the liberty of their country. No sacrifice of personal interests or hopes were, in his view, too great to be demanded of the country in behalf of a cause, for which he was at all times ready to surrender his life. Of such devotion and self-abnegation, a sanguine and resolute spirit was the natural product, and it is a paltry view of such qualities to characterize them as the proof of defective intellect. Just such qualities have won the battles of liberty in all ages. Washington, at Valley Forge, with a wretched remnant of an army, which was yet the last hope of the country, and with even a more gloomy future immediately before him, declared that in the last emergency he would retreat to the mountains of Virginia, and there continue the struggle in the hope that he would "yet lift the flag of his bleeding country from the dust." In the same spirit Jefferson Davis would never have abandoned the Confederate cause so long as it had even a semblance of popular support.

Almost to the last moment of the Confederacy, he continued to cherish the hope of a reaction in the public mind, which he believed would be immediately kindled to its old enthusiasm by a decided success. It was in recognition of this quality of inflexible purpose, as much as of any other trait of his character, that the South originally intrusted Davis with leadership. Fit leaders of revolutions are not usually found in men of half-hearted purpose, wanting in resolution themselves, and doubting the fidelity of those whom they govern. Desperate trial is the occasion which calls forth the courage of those truly great men, who, while ordinary men despair, confront agony itself with sublime resolution.

If ingenuity and malignity have combined to exaggerate the faults of Mr. Davis, the love of his countrymen, the candor of honorable enemies, and the intelligence of mankind have recognized his intellectual and moral greatness. The world to-day does not afford such an example of those blended qualities which constitute the title to universal excellence. For one in his position, the leader of a bold, warlike, intelligent, and discerning people, there was demanded that union of ardor and deliberation which he so peculiarly illustrated. Revolutionary periods imperatively demand this union of capacities for thought and action. The peculiar charm of Mr. Davis is the perfect poise of his faculties; an almost exact adjustment of qualities; of indomitable energy and winning grace; heroic courage and tender affection; strength of character, and almost excessive compassion; of calculating judgment and knightly sentiment; acute penetration and analysis; comprehensive perception; laborious habits, and almost universal knowledge. Of him it may be said as of Hamilton: "He wore the blended wreath of arms, of law, of statesmanship, of oratory, of letters, of scholarship, of practical affairs;" and in most of these fields of distinction, Mr. Davis has few rivals among the public men of America.

But it is altogether a fallacious supposition that the military situation of the Confederacy, in the last winter of the war, was beyond reclamation. The most hasty glance at the situation revealed the feasibility of destroying Sherman, when he turned northward from Savannah, with a proper concentration of the forces yet available. President Davis anxiously sought to secure this concentration, but was disappointed by causes which need not here be related. With Sherman defeated, the Confederacy must have obtained a new lease of life, as all the territory which he had overrun, would immediately be recovered, and the worthless title of his conquests would be apparent, even to the North. There were indeed many aspects of the situation encouraging to enterprise, could an adequate army be obtained, and the heart of the country reanimated. President Davis was not alone in the indulgence of hope of better fortune. Again he had the sanction of Lee's name in confirmation of his hopes, and in support of the measures which he recommended.

But the resolution of the President was not sustained by the coöperation of Congress. The last session of that body was commemorated by a signal display of timidity and vacillation. Congress assembled in November, and at the beginning of its session its nerve was visibly shaken. Before its adjournment in March, there was no longer even a pretense of organized opinion and systematic legislation. Its occupation during the winter was mainly crimination of the President, and a contemptible frivolity, which at last provoked the hearty disgust of the public. The calibre of the last Confederate Congress may be correctly estimated, when it is stated that as late as the 22d of February, 1865, less than sixty days before the fall of Richmond, that body was earnestly engaged in devising a *new flag for the Confederacy.*

Not a single measure of importance was adopted without

some emasculating clause, or without such postponement as made it practically inoperative. Of all the vigorous suggestions of Mr. Davis for recruiting the army, mobilizing the subsistence, and renovating the material condition of the country, hardly one was adopted in a practicable shape. Congress had clearly despaired of the cause. It had not the courage to counsel the submission, of which it secretly felt the necessity, and left the capital with a declaration that the "conquest of the Confederacy was geographically impossible," yet clearly attesting by its flight a very different view of the situation.

The history of the Congress of the Confederate States is a record of singular imbecility and irresolution. It was a body without leaders, without popular sympathy, without a single one of those heroic attributes which are usually evoked in periods of revolution. It may safely be asserted that in the history of no other great revolution does the statesmanship of its legislators appear so contemptible, when compared with the military administration which guided its armies. Whatever may be the estimate of the executive ability of the Confederate administration, it can not be denied that its courage was abundant; nor can it be questioned that the courage of Congress often required the spur of popular sentiment. In the wholesale condemnation of Mr. Davis by a class of writers, it is remarkable that the defective legislation of the Confederacy should be accredited with so little influence in producing its failure. If he was so grossly incompetent, what must be the verdict of history upon a body which, for four years, submitted to a ruinous administration when the corrective means were in its own hands?

Of Mr. Davis' relations with Congress, Ex-Secretary Mallory writes as follows:

"I have said that his relations with members of Congress were not what they should have been, nor were they what they might have been. Towards them, as towards the world generally, he wore his personal opinions very openly. Position and opportunity presented him every means of cultivating the personal good-will of members by little acts of attention, courtesy, or deference, which no man, however high in his position, who has to work by means of his fellows, can dispense with. Great minds can, in spite of the absence of these demonstrations towards them in a leader—nay, in the face of neglect or apparent disrespect—go on steadily and bravely, with a single eye to the public welfare; but the number of these in comparison to those who are more or less governed by personal considerations in the discharge of their public duties is small. While he was ever frank and cordial to his friends, and to all whom he believed to be embarked heart and soul in the cause of Southern independence, he would not, and, we think, could not, sacrifice a smile, an inflection of the voice, or a demonstration of attention to flatter the self-love of any man, in or out of Congress, who did not stand in this relation. Acting himself for the public welfare, regardless of self or the opinions of others, he placed too light a value upon the thousand nameless influences by which he might have brought others up, apparently, to his own high moral standard. By members of Congress, who had to see him on business, his reception of them was frequently complained of as ungracious. They frequently, in their anxiety amidst public disaster, called upon him to urge plans, suggestions, or views on the conduct of the war, or for the attainment of peace, and often pressed matters upon him which he had very carefully considered, and for which he alone was responsible.

"Often, in such cases, though he listened to all they had to say—why, for example, some man should be made a brigadier, major or lieutenant-general, or placed at the head of an army, etc.—and in return calmly and precisely stated his reasons against the measure, he at times failed to satisfy or convince them, simply because, in his manner and language combined, there was just an indescribable something which offended their self-esteem. Some of his best friends left him at times with feelings bordering closely upon anger from this cause, and with a determination, hastily formed, of calling no more upon him; and some of the most sensible and patriotic men of both Houses were alienated from him more or less from this cause. The counsel of judicious friends upon this subject, and as to more unrestrained intercourse between him and the members of the Senate and the House, was vainly exerted. His manly, fearless, true, and noble nature turned from what to him wore the faintest approach to seeking popularity, and he scorned to believe it necessary to coax men to do their duty to their country in her darkest hour of need."

When Congress assembled in November it was plain that the army must have other means of recruiting than from the remnant yet left by the conscription. There was but one measure by which the requisite numbers could be supplied, and that was the extension of the conscription to the slave population. Public sentiment was at first much divided upon this subject, but gradually the propriety of the measure was made evident, and something like a renewal of hope was manifested at the prospect of making use of an element which the enemy so efficiently employed. President Davis had, for months previous, contemplated the enlistment of the slaves for service in various capacities in the field. In the last winter of the war he strongly urged a negro enrollment, as did General Lee, whose letter to a member of Congress eventually convinced the country of its necessity.

Whatever may have been the merits of the proposition to arm the slaves, as a means of renovating the military condition of the Confederacy, the dilatory action of Congress left no hope of its practical execution. The discussion upon this subject continued during the entire session, and was at last terminated by the adoption of a bill providing for the reception of such slaves into the service as might be tendered by their masters. Mr. Davis and General Lee both advocated the extension of freedom to such of the slaves as would volunteer, and this was clearly the only system of enrollment upon which they could be efficiently employed. But even though the slave-holding interest had not thus emasculated the measure, by refusing emancipation, it was too late to hope for any results of importance. The bill was not passed until three weeks before the fall of Richmond.

But Congress found congenial employment in giving vent to its partisan malignity, by the adoption of measures plainly designed to humiliate the Executive, and with no expectation of improving the condition of the Confederacy, which most of its members believed to be already beyond reclamation. In this spirit was dictated the measure making General Lee virtually a military dictator, and that expressing want of confidence in the cabinet. All of this action of Congress was extra-official, and subversive of the constitutional authority of the Executive, but it utterly failed in its obvious design.

President Davis never made a more noble display of feeling, than in his response to the resolution of the Virginia Legislature recommending the appointment of General Lee to the command of the armies of the Confederacy. Said he: "The opinion expressed by the General Assembly in regard to General R. E. Lee has my full concurrence. Virginia can not have a higher regard for him, or greater confidence in his character and ability, than is entertained by me. When General Lee took command of the Army of Northern Virginia, he was in command of all the armies of the Confederate States by my order of assignment. He continued in this general command, as well as in the immediate command of the Army of Northern Virginia, as long as I could resist his opinion that it was necessary for him to be relieved from one of these two duties. Ready as he has ever shown himself to be to perform any service that I desired him to render to his country, he left it for me to choose between his withdrawal from the command of the army in the field, and relieving him of the general command of all the armies of the Confederate States. It was only when satisfied of this necessity that I came to the conclusion to relieve him from the general command, believing that the safety of the capital and the success of our cause depended, in a great measure, on then retaining him in the command in the field of the Army of Northern Virginia. On several subsequent occasions, the desire on my part to enlarge the sphere of General Lee's usefulness, has led to renewed consideration of the subject, and he has always expressed his inability to assume command of other armies than those now confided to him, unless relieved of the immediate command in the field of that now opposed to General Grant."

A striking indication of the feverish condition of the public mind of both sections, during the last winter of the war, was the ready credence given to the most extravagant and improbable rumors. Washington correspondents of Northern newspapers declared that the air of the Federal capital was "thick with rumors of negotiation." At Richmond this credulous disposition was even more marked. Men were found as late as the middle of March, who believed that President Davis had actually formed an alliance, offensive and defensive, with the French Emperor. In the month of January the rumors as to peace negotiations assumed a more definite shape, in the arrival of Mr. Francis P. Blair at the Confederate capital.

It is remarkable that the "Blair mission" and its sequel, the Hampton Roads conference, though palpably contemplating only the discussion of such mere generalities as belong to other efforts at peace at different stages of the war, and, indeed, introducing nothing in the shape of formal negotiation, should have been dignified as a most important episode. Equally remarkable, in view of the published proceedings of the Hampton Roads conference, is the disposition to censure President Davis for having designedly interposed obstacles to the consummation of peace. Mr. Blair visited Richmond by the permission of President Lincoln, but without any official authority, and without having the objects of his mission committed to paper. In short, Mr. Blair's mission had no official character, and he came to Richmond to prevail upon Mr. Davis to encourage, in some manner, preliminary steps to negotiation. In his interviews with the Confederate President, Mr. Blair disclaimed the official countenance of the Federal authorities for the objects of his visit. It was known to the world, that Mr. Davis, upon repeated occasions, had avowed his desire for peace upon any terms consistent with the honor of his country, and that he would not present difficulties as to forms in the attainment of that object, at this critical period. Hence, despite the unauthorized nature of Mr. Blair's conciliatory efforts, Mr. Davis gave him a letter, addressed to himself, avowing the willingness of the Confederate authorities to begin negotiations, to send or receive commissioners authorized to treat, and to "renew the effort to enter into a conference, with a view to secure peace between the two countries."

Mr. Lincoln, in a letter to Mr. Blair, acknowledged having read Mr. Davis' note, and avowed his readiness to receive an agent from Mr. Davis, or from the authority resisting the Federal Government, to confer with him informally, with the view of restoring peace to the people of "our common country."

The commissioners appointed by Mr. Davis, after this notification, were Vice-President Stephens, Senator Hunter, and Judge Campbell. The conference was held on a steamer lying in Hampton Roads, between the three Confederate commissioners and Messrs. Lincoln and Seward. By both sides the interview was treated as informal; there were neither notes nor secretaries, nor did the interview assume any other shape than an irregular conversation. During the four hours of desultory discussion, there was developed no basis of negotiation, no ground of possible agreement. Mr. Lincoln declared that he would consent to no truce or suspension of hostilities, except upon the single condition of the disbandment of the Confederate forces, and the submission of the revolted States to the authority of the Union. The result was simply the assertion, in a more arrogant form, of the Federal *ultimatum*—the unconditional submission of the South, its acquiescence in all the unconstitutional legislation of the Federal Congress respecting slavery, including emancipation, and the right to legislate upon the subject of the relations between the white and black populations of each State. Mr. Lincoln, moreover, refused to treat with the authorities of the Confederate States, or with the States separately; declared that the consequences of the establishment of the Federal authority would have to be accepted, and declined giving any guarantee whatever, except an indefinite assurance of a liberal use of the pardoning power, towards those who were assumed to have made themselves liable to the pains and penalties of the laws of the United States.

The statement of the Confederate commissioners, and all the known facts of the transaction, demonstrate, without argument, the injustice of holding Mr. Davis responsible, to any extent, for the results of the Hampton Roads conference. With one voice the South accepted the result as establishing the purpose of the Federal Government to exact "unconditional submission," as the only condition of peace, and scorned the insolent demand of the enemy. If the South had shown itself willing to accept the terms of the Federal Government, or if Mr. Lincoln had suggested other propositions than that of unconditional submission, then only could Mr. Davis be charged with having presented obstacles to the termination of the war.

Nor is it to be assumed that the terms of his letter to Mr. Blair, referring to his desire for peace between the "two countries," precluded negotiation upon the basis of reunion. His language was that of a proper diplomacy, which should not commit the error of yielding in advance to the demands of an enemy, then insolent in what he regarded as the assurance of certain victory. The period was opportune for magnanimity on the part of the North, but not propitious for the display of over-anxious concession by the South. Mr. Davis was at this time anxious for propositions from the Federal Government, for, while he had not despaired of the Confederacy, he was deeply impressed with the increasing obstacles to its success. His frequent declaration, at this time, was: "I am solicitous only for the good of the people, and am indifferent as to the forms by which the public interests are to be subserved." Indeed, the Federal authorities had ample assurance that Mr. Davis would present any basis of settlement, which might be offered, to the several States of the Confederacy for their individual action. Nor did he doubt the acceptance of reconstruction, without slavery even, by several of the States—an event which would have left the Confederacy too weak for further resistance.

In view of the consistent record of Mr. Davis, during the entire period of the war, to promote the attainment of peace, it is remarkable that there should ever have been an allegation of a contrary disposition. In a letter, written in 1864, to Governor Vance, of North Carolina, he conclusively stated his course upon the subject of peace. Said Mr. Davis, in this letter:

"We have made three distinct efforts to communicate with the authorities at Washington, and have been invariably unsuccessful. Commissioners were sent before hostilities were begun, and the Washington Government refused to receive them or hear what they had to say. A second time, I sent a military officer with a communication addressed by myself to President Lincoln. The letter was received by General Scott, who did not permit the officer to see Mr. Lincoln, but promised that an answer would be sent. No answer has ever been received. The third time, a few months ago, a gentleman was sent, whose position, character, and reputation were such as to ensure his reception, if the enemy were not determined to receive no proposals whatever from the Government. Vice-President Stephens made a patriotic tender of his services in the hope of being able to promote the cause of humanity, and, although little belief was entertained of his success, I cheerfully yielded to his suggestions, that the experiment should be tried. The enemy refused to let him pass through their lines or hold any conference with them. He was stopped before he ever reached Fortress Monroe, on his way to Washington. . . . .

"If we will break up our Government, dissolve the Confederacy, disband our armies, emancipate our slaves, take an oath of allegiance, binding ourselves to obedience to him and of disloyalty to our own States, he proposes to pardon us, and not to plunder us of any thing more than the property already stolen from us, and such slaves as still remain. In order to render his proposals so insulting as to secure their rejection, he joins to them a promise to support with his army one-tenth of the people of any State who will attempt to set up a government over the other nine-tenths, thus seeking to sow discord and suspicion among the people of the several States, and to excite them to civil war in furtherance of his ends. I know well it would be impossible to get your people, if they possessed full knowledge of these facts, to consent that proposals should now be made by us to those who control the Government at Washington. Your own well-known devotion to the great cause of liberty and independence, to which we have all committed whatever we have of earthly possessions, would induce you to take the lead in repelling the bare thought of abject submission to the enemy. Yet peace on other terms is now impossible."

The spirit in which the South received the results of the Hampton Roads conference is to be correctly estimated by the following extract from a Richmond newspaper, of date February 15, 1865:

"The world can again, for the hundredth time, see conclusive evidence in the history and sequel of the 'Blair mission,' the blood-guiltiness of the enemy, and their responsibility for the ruin, desolation, and suffering which have followed, and will yet follow, their heartless attempts to subjugate and destroy an innocent people. The South again wins honor from the good, the magnanimous, the truly brave every-where by her efforts to stop the effusion of blood, save the lives and the property of her own citizens, and to stop, too, the slaughter of the victims of the enemy's cruelty, which has forced or deceived them into the ranks of his armies. We have lost nothing by our efforts in behalf of peace; for, waiving all consideration of the reanimation and reunion of our people, occasioned by Lincoln's haughty rejection of our commissioners, we have added new claims upon the sympathy and respect of the world and posterity, which will not fail to be remembered to our honor, in the history of this struggle, even though we should finally perish in it. The position of the South at this moment is indeed one which should stamp her as the champion, not only of popular rights and self-government, which Americans have so much cherished, but as the champion of the spirit of humanity in both sections; for it can not be supposed that we have all the sorrows as well as sufferings of this war to endure, and that there are no desolate homes, no widows and orphans, no weeds nor cypress in the enemy's country. . . . .

"One fact is certain, that whatever Seward's design may have been, and whatever its success may be, the Confederacy has derived an immediate advantage from the visit of our commissioners to Fortress Monroe. Nothing could have so served to reanimate the courage and patriotism of our people, as his attempted imposition of humiliation upon us. Lincoln will hear no more talk of 'peace' and 'negotiation' from the Southern side, for now we are united as one man in the purpose of self-preservation and vengeance, and it may not be long before his people, now rioting in excessive exultation over successes really valueless, and easily counter-balanced by one week of prosperous fortune for the South, will tremble at the manifestation of the spirit which they have aroused."

But the evidences of popular reanimation in the South were delusive. For a brief moment there was a spirit of fierce and almost desperate resolution. At a meeting held in the African church, in Richmond, President Davis delivered one of his most eloquent popular orations, and the enthusiasm was perhaps greater than upon any similar occasion during the war. But popular feeling soon lapsed into the sullen despondency, from which it had been temporarily aroused by the unparalleled insult of the enemy. Yet the *ultimatum* of Mr. Lincoln, and the declared will of the South, left President Davis no other policy than a continuation of the struggle, with a view to the best attainable results. Upon this course he was now fully resolved, looking to the future with serious apprehension, not altogether unrelieved by hope.

The report of the Hampton Roads conference and its results, was made by President Davis, to Congress, on the 5th February:

"*To the Senate and House of Representatives*
of the Confederate States of America:

"Having recently received a written notification, which satisfied me that the President of the United States was disposed to confer, informally, with unofficial agents that might be sent by me, with a view to the restoration of peace, I requested Hon. Alexander H. Stephens, Hon. R. M. T. Hunter, and Hon. John A. Campbell, to proceed through our lines, to hold a conference with Mr. Lincoln, or such persons as he might depute to represent him.

"I herewith submit, for the information of Congress, the report of the eminent citizens above named, showing that the enemy refuse to enter into negotiations with the Confederate States, or any one of them separately, or to give our people any other terms or guarantees than those which a conqueror may grant, or permit us to have peace on any other basis than our unconditional submission to their rule, coupled with the acceptance of their recent legislation, including an amendment to the Constitution for the emancipation of negro slaves, and with the right, on the part of the Federal Congress, to legislate on the subject of the relations between the white and black population of each State.

"Such is, as I understand, the effect of the amendment to the Constitution, which has been adopted by the Congress of the United States.

"JEFFERSON DAVIS.

"EXECUTIVE OFFICE, Feb. 5, 1865."

"RICHMOND, VA., February 5, 1865.

"*To the President of the Confederate States*—

"SIR: Under your letter of appointment of 28th ult., we proceeded to seek an informal conference with Abraham Lincoln, President of the United States, upon the subject mentioned in your letter.

"The conference was granted, and took place on the 3d inst., on board a steamer anchored in Hampton Roads, where we met President Lincoln and Hon. Mr. Seward, Secretary of State of the United States. It continued for several hours, and was both full and explicit.

"We learned from them that the Message of President Lincoln to the Congress of the United States, in December last, explains clearly and distinctly, his sentiments as to terms, conditions, and method of proceeding by which peace can be secured to the people, and we were not informed that they would be modified or altered to obtain that end. We understood from him that no terms or proposals of any treaty or agreement looking to an ultimate settlement would be entertained or made by him with the authorities of the Confederate States, because that would be a recognition of their existence as a separate power, which, under no circumstances, would be done; and, for like reasons, that no such terms would be entertained by him from States separately; that no extended truce or armistice, as at present advised, would be granted or allowed without satisfactory assurance, in advance, of complete restoration of the authority of the Constitution and laws of the United States over all places within the States of the Confederacy; that whatever consequences may follow from the reëstablishment of that authority must be accepted, but the individuals subject to pains and penalties, under the laws of the United States, might rely upon a very liberal use of the power confided to him to remit those pains and penalties if peace be restored.

"During the conference the proposed amendments to the Constitution of the United States, adopted by Congress on the 31st ult., were brought to our notice. These amendments provide that neither slavery nor involuntary servitude, except for crime, should exist within the United States or any place within their jurisdiction, and that Congress should have the power to enforce this amendment by appropriate legislation.

"Of all the correspondence that preceded the conference herein mentioned, and leading to the same, you have heretofore been informed. Very respectfully, your obedient servants,

"ALEX. H. STEPHENS,
"R. M. T. HUNTER,
"J. A. CAMPBELL."

CHAPTER XXI.

MILITARY OPERATIONS IN THE EARLY PART OF 1865—LAST PHASE OF THE MILITARY POLICY OF THE CONFEDERACY—THE PLAN TO CRUSH SHERMAN—CALM DEMEANOR OF PRESIDENT DAVIS—CHEERFULNESS OF GENERAL LEE—THE QUESTION AS TO THE SAFETY OF RICHMOND—WEAKNESS OF GENERAL LEE'S ARMY—PREPARATIONS TO EVACUATE RICHMOND BEFORE THE CAMPAIGN OPENED—A NEW BASIS OF HOPE—WHAT WAS TO BE REASONABLY ANTICIPATED—THE CONTRACTED THEATRE OF WAR—THE FATAL DISASTERS AT PETERSBURG—MR. DAVIS RECEIVES THE INTELLIGENCE WHILE IN CHURCH—RICHMOND EVACUATED—PRESIDENT DAVIS AT DANVILLE—HIS PROCLAMATION—SURRENDER OF LEE—DANVILLE EVACUATED—THE LAST OFFICIAL INTERVIEW OF MR. DAVIS WITH GENERALS JOHNSTON AND BEAUREGARD—HIS ARRIVAL AT CHARLOTTE—INCIDENTS AT CHARLOTTE—REJECTION OF THE SHERMAN-JOHNSTON SETTLEMENT—MR. DAVIS' INTENTIONS AFTER THAT EVENT—HIS MOVEMENTS SOUTHWARD—INTERESTING DETAILS—CAPTURE OF MR. DAVIS AND HIS IMPRISONMENT AT FORTRESS MONROE.

MILITARY operations in the first three months of 1865 tended to the concentration of forces upon the greatly-reduced theatre of war, which was now confined mainly to Virginia and North Carolina. The developments of each day indicated the near approach of critical and decisive events. With Sherman sweeping through the Carolinas, and the Confederate forces retiring before him; with Wilmington, the last port of the Confederacy, captured, and a new base thus secured for a column auxiliary to Sherman, it was evident that but a short time would develope a grand struggle, which should not only decide the fate of Richmond, but which should involve nearly the entire force at the command of the Confederacy.

The last definite phase of the military policy of the Confederate authorities, previous to the fall of the capital, was the design of concentration for the destruction of Sherman, who was rapidly approaching the Virginia border. This would, of course, necessitate the abandonment of Richmond, with a view to the junction of the armies of Lee and Johnston. The latter officer, with the remnant of Hood's army, and other fragmentary commands, confronted Sherman's army—forty thousand strong—with a force of about twenty-five thousand men. When Lee's army should unite with Johnston's, the Confederate strength would approximate sixty thousand—a force ample to overwhelm Sherman.

The success of this design was mainly dependent upon the question of the *time* of its execution. If the concentration against Sherman should be attempted prematurely, that Federal commander would be warned of his danger in time to escape to the coast, or to retire until reënforcements from Grant should reach him. It was thus highly important that Sherman should advance sufficiently far to preclude his safe retreat, while, at the same time, the distance between Lee and Johnston should be shortened. On the other hand, if the concentration should be delayed too long, General Grant might, by a vigorous assault upon Lee, either hold the latter in his works at Petersburg, or cut off his retreat, either of which events would defeat the proposed concentration. In the sequel, the activity of Grant, his overwhelming numbers, and the timely arrival of Sheridan's cavalry, after the latter had failed in his original design against Lynchburg and the Confederate communications, precipitated a catastrophe, which not only prevented the consummation of this design, but speedily proved fatal to the Confederacy.

There was nothing in the calm exterior of President Davis, during the days of early spring, to indicate that he was then meditating an abandonment of that capital, for the safety of which he had striven during four years of solicitude, and in the defense of which the flower of Southern chivalry had been sacrificed. There was no abatement of that self-possession, which had so often proven invulnerable to the most trying exigencies; no alteration of that commanding mien, so typical of resolution and self-reliance. To the despondent citizens of Richmond, there was something of re-assurance in the firm and elastic step of their President, as he walked, usually unattended, through the Capitol Square to his office. His responses to the respectful salutations of the children, who never failed to testify their affection for him, were as genial and playful as ever, and the slaves still boasted of the cordiality with which he acknowledged their civility.

A similar cheerfulness was observed in General Lee. In the last months of the war, it was a frequent observation that General Lee appeared more cheerful in manner than upon many occasions, when his army was engaged in its most successful campaigns. Hon. William C. Rives was quoted in the Confederate Congress, as having said that General Lee "had but a single thing to fear, and that was the spreading of a causeless despondency among the people. Prevent this, and all will be well. We have strength enough left to win our independence, and we are certain to win it, if people do not give way to foolish despair."

From the beginning of winter, the possibility of holding Richmond was a matter of grave doubt to President Davis. He had announced to the Confederate Congress that the capital was now menaced by greater perils than ever. Yet a proper consideration of the moral consequences of a loss of the capital, not less than of the material injury which must result from the loss of the manufacturing facilities of Richmond, dictated the contemplation of its evacuation only as a measure of necessity. When, however, the dilatory and vacillating action of Congress baffled the President in all his vigorous and timely measures, there was hardly room to doubt that the alternative was forced upon General Lee of an early retreat or an eventual surrender. When spring opened, the Army of Northern Virginia was reduced to less than thirty-five thousand men. With this inadequate force, General Lee was holding a line of forty miles, against an army nearly one hundred and seventy-five thousand strong. A prompt conscription of the slaves, upon the basis of emancipation, the President and General Lee believed would have put at rest all anxiety for the safety of Richmond. But when the threadbare discussions and timid spirit of Congress foretold the failure of this measure, preparations were quietly begun for a retirement to an interior line of defense.

These preparations were commenced early in February, and were conducted with great caution. Mr. Davis did not believe that the capture of Richmond entailed the loss of the Confederate cause should Lee's and Johnston's armies remain intact. That it diminished the probability of ultimate success was obvious, but there was the anticipation of a new basis of hope, in events not improbable, could Lee's army be successfully carried from Petersburg. A thorough defeat of Sherman would obviously recover at once the Carolinas and Georgia, and give to the Confederacy a more enlarged jurisdiction and more easy subsistence, than it had controlled for more than a year. A reasonable anticipation was the re-awakening of the patriotic spirit of the people, and the return of thousands of absentees to the army, as the immediate results of a decisive defeat of Sherman. Then, even if it should prove that the Confederacy could not cope with the remaining armies of the enemy, it was confidently believed that the North, rather than endure the sacrifices and doubts of another campaign, would offer some terms not inconsistent with the honor of the South to accept. At all events, resistance must continue until the enemy abated his haughty demand of unconditional submission.

The movements of Sherman and Johnston reduced the theatre upon which the crisis was enacting to very contracted limits. The fate of the Confederacy was to be decided in the district between the Roanoke and James Rivers, and the Atlantic Ocean and the Alleghanies. General Grant, fully apprised of the extremities to which Lee was reduced, for weeks kept his army in readiness to intercept the Confederate retreat. It was greatly to the interest of the Federal commander that Lee should be held at Petersburg, since his superior numbers must eventually give him possession of the Southside Railroad, which was vital to Lee not only as a means of subsistence, but as an avenue of escape. But General Grant, sooner than he anticipated, found an opportunity for a successful detachment of a competent force against the Southside Railroad by the arrival of Sheridan's cavalry, ten thousand strong—as splendid a body of cavalry as ever took the field. The swollen condition of James River had prevented the consummation of Sheridan's original mission, which was, after he had effectually destroyed all Lee's communications northward and westward, to capture Lynchburg, and thence to pass rapidly southward to Sherman. Finding the river impassable, Sheridan retired in the direction of Richmond, passed Lee's left wing, crossed the Pamunkey River, and, by the 25th of March, had joined Grant before Petersburg. General Grant was not slow in the employment of this timely accession.

The fatal disaster of Lee's defeat at Petersburg was the battle of Five Forks, on the 1st of April, by which the enemy secured the direct line of retreat to Danville. For, without that event, the fate of Petersburg and Richmond was determined by the result of Grant's attack upon the Confederate centre on the 2d of April. With all the roads on the southern bank of the Appomattox in the possession of the enemy, there remained only the line of retreat upon the northern side, which was the longer route, while the pursuing enemy had all the advantage of the interior line. But for that disadvantage, Lee's escape would have been assured, and the Confederate line of defense reëstablished near the Roanoke River.

President Davis received the intelligence of the disasters while seated in his pew in St. Paul's Church, where he had been a communicant for nearly three years. The momentous intelligence was conveyed to him by a brief note from the War Department. General Lee's dispatch stated that his lines had been broken, and that all efforts to restore them had proven unsuccessful. He advised preparations for the evacuation of the city during the night, unless, in the meantime, he should advise to the contrary. Mr. Davis immediately left the church with his usual calm manner and measured tread.* The tranquil demeanor of the President conveyed no indica-

* The author has seen an absurd statement, made without any inquiry into the facts, that Mr. Davis was seen to turn "ghastly white" at the moment of receiving the intelligence of the disaster at Petersburg. It is

tion of the nature of the communication. But the incident was an unusual one, and, by the congregation, most of whom had for days been burdened with the anticipations of disaster, the unspoken intelligence was, to some extent, correctly interpreted.

The family of Mr. Davis had been sent southward some days before, and he was, therefore, under the necessity of little preparation for departure. Though his concern was obvious, his calmness was remarkable. In this trying exigency in his personal fortunes, he showed anxiety only for the fate of the country, and sympathy for that devoted community from which he was now compelled to separate

On the night of Sunday, April 2d, 1865, Mr. Davis, attended by his personal staff, members of his cabinet, and attachés of the several departments, left Richmond, which then ceased forever to be the capital of the Southern Confederacy. In a few hours after, that city, whose defense will be more famous than that of Saragossa, whose capture was for four years the aspiration of armies aggregating more than a million of men, became the spoil of a conqueror, and the scene of a conflagration, in which "all the hopes of the Southern Confederacy were consumed in one day, as a scroll in the fire."

In accordance with his original design of making a new defensive line near the Roanoke River, Mr. Davis proceeded

simply one of a thousand other reckless calumnies, with as little foundation as the rest.

We do not feel called upon here to relate the details of the evacuation of Richmond and the occupation of the city by the Federal army. They are, doubtless, known to every intelligent reader, and we are here specially concerned only in the movements of Mr. Davis.

directly to Danville. His determination was to maintain the Confederate authority upon the soil of Virginia, until driven from it by force of arms. Reaching Danville on the 3d of April, he issued, two days afterwards, the following proclamation:

"DANVILLE, VA., April 5, 1865.

"The General-in-Chief found it necessary to make such movements of his troops as to uncover the capital. It would be unwise to conceal the moral and material injury to our cause resulting from the occupation of our capital by the enemy. It is equally unwise and unworthy of us to allow our own energies to falter, and our efforts to become relaxed under reverses, however calamitous they may be. For many months the largest and finest army of the Confederacy, under a leader whose presence inspires equal confidence in the troops and the people, has been greatly trammeled by the necessity of keeping constant watch over the approaches to the capital, and has thus been forced to forego more than one opportunity for promising enterprise. It is for us, my countrymen, to show by our bearing under reverses, how wretched has been the self-deception of those who have believed us less able to endure misfortune with fortitude than to encounter danger with courage.

"We have now entered upon a new phase of the struggle. Relieved from the necessity of guarding particular points, our army will be free to move from point to point, to strike the enemy in detail far from his base. Let us but will it, and we are free.

"Animated by that confidence in your spirit and fortitude which never yet failed me, I announce to you, fellow-countrymen, that it is my purpose to maintain your cause with my whole heart and soul; that I will never consent to abandon to the enemy one foot of the soil of any of the States of the Confederacy; that Virginia—noble State—whose ancient renown has been eclipsed by her still more glorious recent history; whose bosom has been bared to receive the main shock of this war; whose sons and daughters have exhibited heroism so sublime as to render her illustrious in all time to come—that Virginia, with the help of the people, and by the blessing of Providence, shall be held and defended, and no peace ever be made with the infamous invaders of her territory.

"If, by the stress of numbers, we should be compelled to a temporary withdrawal from her limits, or those of any other border State, we will return until the baffled and exhausted enemy shall abandon in despair his endless and impossible task of making slaves of a people resolved to be free.

"Let us, then, not despond, my countrymen, but, relying on God, meet the foe with fresh defiance, and with unconquered and unconquerable hearts.

"JEFFERSON DAVIS."

Meanwhile, some semblance of order in several of the departments of government was established, though, of course, the continued occupation of Danville was dependent upon the safety of Lee's army. Days of anxious suspense, during which there was no intelligence from Lee, were passed, until on Monday, the 10th of April, it was announced that the Army of Northern Virginia had surrendered.

Leaving Danville, Mr. Davis and his party went by railroad to Greensboro', North Carolina. Here Mr. Davis met Generals Johnston and Beauregard. Consultation with these two officers soon revealed to Mr. Davis their convictions of the hopelessness of a farther protraction of the struggle.

Ex-Secretary Mallory gives the following narrative of the last official interview of President Davis with Generals Johnston and Beauregard:

"At 8 o'clock that evening the cabinet, with the exception of Mr. Trenholm, whose illness prevented his attendance, joined the President at his room. It was a small apartment, some twelve by sixteen feet, containing a bed, a few chairs, and a table, with writing materials, on the second floor of the small dwelling of Mrs. John Taylor Wood; and a few minutes after eight the two generals entered.

"The uniform habit of President Davis, in cabinet meetings, was to consume some little time in general conversation before entering upon the business of the occasion, not unfrequently introducing some anecdote or interesting episode, generally some reminiscence of the early life of himself or others in the army, the Mexican war, or his Washington experiences; and his manner of relating and his application of them were at all times very happy and pleasing.

"Few men seized more readily upon the sprightly aspects of any transaction, or turned them to better account; and his powers of mimicry, whenever he condescended to exercise them, were irresistible. Upon this occasion, at a time when the cause of the Confederacy was hopeless, when its soldiers were throwing away their arms and flying to their homes, when its Government, stripped of nearly all power, could not hope to exist beyond a few days more, and when the enemy, more powerful and exultant than ever, was advancing upon all sides, true to his habit, he introduced several subjects of conversation, not connected with the condition of the country, and discussed them as if at some pleasant ordinary meeting. After a brief time thus spent, turning to General Johnston, he said, in his usual quiet, grave way, when entering upon matters of business: 'I have requested you and General Beauregard, General Johnston, to join us this evening, that we might have the benefit of your views upon the situation of the country. Of course, we all feel the magnitude of the moment. Our late disasters are terrible, but I do not think we should regard them as fatal. I think we can whip the enemy yet, if our people will turn out. We must look at matters calmly, however, and see what is left for us to do. Whatever can be done must be done at once. We have not a day to lose.' A pause ensued, General Johnston not seeming to deem himself expected to speak, when the President said: 'We should like to hear your views, General Johnston.' Upon this the General, without preface or introduction—his words translating the expression which his face had worn since he entered the room—said, in his terse, concise, demonstrative way, as if seeking to condense thoughts that were crowding for utterance: 'My views are, sir, that our people are tired of the war, feel themselves whipped, and will not fight. Our country is overrun, its military resources greatly diminished, while the enemy's military power and resources were never greater, and may be increased to any desired extent. We can not place another large army in the field; and, cut off as we are from foreign intercourse, I do not see how we could maintain it in fighting condition if we had it. My men are daily deserting in large numbers, and are taking my artillery teams to aid their escape to their homes. Since Lee's defeat they regard the war as at an end. If I march out of North Carolina, her people will all leave my ranks. It will be the same as I proceed south through South Carolina and Georgia, and I shall expect to retain no man beyond the by-road or cow-path that leads to his house. My small force is melting away like snow before the sun, and I am hopeless of recruiting it. We may, perhaps, obtain terms which we ought to accept.'

"The tone and manner, almost spiteful, in which the General jerked out these brief, decisive sentences, pausing at every paragraph, left no doubt as to his own convictions. When he ceased speaking, whatever was thought of his statements—and their importance was fully understood—they elicited neither comment nor inquiry. The President, who, during their delivery, had sat with his eyes fixed upon a scrap of paper which he was folding and refolding abstractedly, and who had listened without a change of position or expression, broke the silence by saying, in a low, even tone: 'What do you say, General Beauregard?'

"'I concur in all General Johnston has said,' he replied.

"Another silence, more eloquent of the full appreciation of the condition of the country than words could have been, succeeded, during which the President's manner was unchanged.

"After a brief pause he said, without a variation of tone or expression, and without raising his eyes from the slip of paper between his fingers: 'Well, General Johnston, what do you propose? You speak of obtaining terms. You know, of course, that the enemy refuses to treat with us. How do you propose to obtain terms?'

"'I think the opposing Generals in the field may arrange them.'

"'Do you think Sherman will treat with you?'

"'I have no reason to think otherwise. Such a course would be in accordance with military usage, and legitimate.'

"'We can easily try it, sir. If we can accomplish any good for the country, Heaven knows I am not particular as to forms. How will you reach Sherman?'

"'I would address him a brief note, proposing an interview to arrange terms of surrender and peace, embracing, of course, a cessation of hostilities during the negotiations.'

"'Well, sir, you can adopt this course, though I confess I am not sanguine as to ultimate results.'

"The member of the cabinet before referred to as conversing with General Johnston, and who was anxious that his views should be promptly carried out, immediately seated himself at the writing-table, and, taking up a pen, offered to act as the General's amanuensis. At the request of the latter, however, the President dictated the letter to General Sherman, which was written at once upon a half sheet of letter folded as note paper, and signed by

General Johnston, who took it, and said he would send it to General Sherman early in the morning, and in a few minutes the conference broke up. This note, which was a brief proposition for a suspension of hostilities, and a conference with a view to agreeing upon terms of peace, has been published with other letters which passed between the two Generals.

"On or about the 16th of April, the President, his staff, and cabinet left Greensboro' to proceed still further south, with plans unformed, clinging to the hope that Johnston and Sherman would secure peace and the quiet of the country, but still all doubtful of the result, and still more doubtful as to consequences of failure."

Pending the negotiations between Generals Johnston and Sherman, Mr. Davis was earnestly appealed to by his attendants to provide for his own safety, in the event of the failure to obtain terms from Sherman. There would have been no difficulty in his escaping either across the Mississippi into Mexico, or from the Florida coast to the West Indies. Apparently regardless of his personal safety, he was reluctant to contemplate leaving the country under any circumstances. It is certain that he would not have entertained the idea of an abandonment of any organized body of men yet willing to continue in arms for the cause.

Accompanied by the members of his cabinet, General Cooper, and other officers, some of whom were in ambulances, and others on horseback, Mr. Davis went from Greensboro' to Lexington. Here he spent the night at the residence of an eminent citizen of North Carolina. Continuing their journey, the party reached Charlotte during the morning of the 18th of April. At this place were extensive establishments of the Confederate Government; and arrangements had already been made for the accommodation of Mr. Davis and his cabinet. During the day of his arrival at Charlotte, Mr. Davis received a dispatch from General Breckinridge—who, in company with Mr. Reagan, had returned to Greensboro' to aid the negotiations between Johnston and Sherman—announcing the assassination of President Lincoln.

In connection with this event, Mr. Mallory writes as follows:

"To a friend who met him a few minutes after he had received it, and who expressed his incredulity as to its truthfulness, Mr. Davis replied that, true, it sounded like a canard, but, in such a condition of public affairs as the country then presented, a crime of this kind might be perpetrated. His friend remarked that the news was very disastrous for the South, for such an event would substitute for the known humanity and benevolence of Mr. Lincoln a feeling of vindictiveness in his successor and in Congress, and that an attempt would doubtless be made to connect the Government or the people of the South with the assassination. To this Mr. Davis replied, sadly: 'I certainly have no special regard for Mr. Lincoln, but there are a great many men of whose end I would much rather hear than his. I fear it will be disastrous to our people, and I regret it deeply.'"

Mr. Davis remained at Charlotte nearly a week. Meanwhile the terms of agreement between Johnston and Sherman were received, and by Mr. Davis submitted to the cabinet. At a meeting of the cabinet, held on the morning after the propositions were received, the written opinions of the various members were concurrent in favor of the acceptance of the Sherman-Johnston settlement. Three days afterwards, Mr. Davis was informed by General Johnston of the rejection, by the Federal Government, of the proposed settlement, and that he could obtain no other terms than those accorded by General

Grant to General Lee. The surrender of General Johnston was, of course, conclusive of the Confederate cause east of the Mississippi. Whatever Mr. Davis' hopes might have been previous to that event, and whatever his determination had been in case of disapproval by the Federal Government of Sherman's course (a contingency which he anticipated), it was plain that Johnston's surrender made resistance to the Federal Government east of the Mississippi impracticable.

Fully recognizing this fact, Mr. Davis was yet far from contemplating surrender at discretion. His hope now was to cross the Mississippi, carrying with him such bodies of troops as were willing to accompany him; these, added to the force of Kirby Smith, would make an army respectable in numbers, and occupying a country of abundant supplies. In the Trans-Mississippi region Mr. Davis would have continued the struggle, in the hope of obtaining more acceptable terms than had yet been offered. In this expectation he was greatly strengthened by the spirit of resistance indicated by bodies of men who had refused to lay down their arms with the surrendered armies of Lee and Johnston.

We again quote from the account of Mr. Mallory:

"No other course now seemed open to Mr. Davis but to leave the country, and his immediate advisers urged him to do so with the utmost promptitude. Troops began to come into Charlotte, however, escaping from Johnston's surrender, and there was much talk amongst them of crossing the Mississippi, and continuing the war. Portions of Hampton's, Debrell's, Duke's, and Ferguson's commands of cavalry were hourly coming in. They seemed determined to get across the river, and fight it out; and, wherever they encountered Mr. Davis, they cheered, and sought to encourage him. It was evident that he was greatly affected by the constancy and spirit of these men, and that, regardless of his own safety, his thoughts dwelt upon the possibility of gathering together a body of troops to make head against the foe and to arouse the people to arms.

"His friends, however, saw the urgent expediency of getting further south as rapidly as possible, and, after a week's stay at Charlotte, they left, with an escort of some two or three hundred cavalry, and, two days afterwards, reached Yorkville, South Carolina, traveling slowly, and not at all like men escaping from the country.

"In pursuing this route, the party met, near the Catawba River, a gentleman, whose plantation and homestead lay about half a mile from its banks, and who had come out to meet Mr. Davis, and to offer him the hospitality of his house.

"His dwelling, beautifully situated, and surrounded by ornate and cultivated grounds, was reached about 4 o'clock P. M., and the charming lady of the mansion, with that earnest sympathy and generous kindness which Mr. Davis, in misfortune, never failed to receive from Southern women, soon made every man of the party forget his cares, and feel, for a time at least, 'o'er all the ills of life victorious.'

. . . . . .

"At Yorkville, Colonel Preston and other gentlemen had arranged for the accommodation of Mr. Davis and his party at private houses, and here they remained one night and part of the next day.

"A small cavalry escort scouted extensively, and kept Mr. Davis advised of the positions of the enemy's forces—to avoid which was a matter of some difficulty. With this view, the party from Yorkville rode over to a point below Clinton, on the Lawrenceville and Columbus Railroad, and thence struck off to Cokesboro', on the Greenville Railroad.

"Here the party received the kindest attention at private houses. On the evening of his arrival, Mr. Davis received news by a scout that the enemy's cavalry, in considerable force, was but ten miles off, and that he was pressing stock upon all sides; and it was deemed advisable to make but a brief stay.

"At 2 o'clock in the morning Mr. Davis was aroused by another scout, who declared that he had left the enemy only ten miles off, and that they would be in the town in two or three hours. This intelligence infused energy throughout the little party. It was composed of men, however, familiar with real, no less than with rumored perils; men who had faced danger in too many forms to be readily started from their propriety; and preparations were very deliberately made with such force as could be mustered to pay due honor to his enterprise.

"Several hours elapsed without further intelligence of the enemy's movements, and at half-past six in the morning the party rode out of Cokesboro' toward Abbeville, expecting an encounter at any moment, but Abbeville was reached without seeing an enemy.

"At Abbeville the fragments of disorganized cavalry commands, which had thus far performed, in some respects, an escort's duty, were found to be reduced to a handful of men anxious only to reach their homes as early as practicable, and whose services could not further be relied on. They had not surrendered nor given a parole, but they regarded the struggle as terminated, and themselves relieved from further duty to their officers or the Confederate States, and, with a few exceptions, determined to fight no more. They rode in couples or in small squads through the country, occasionally 'impressing' mules and horses, or exchanging their wretched beasts for others in better condition; and, outside of a deep and universal regret for the failure of their cause, usually expressed by the remark that 'The old Confederacy has gone up,' they were as gleeful and careless as boys released from school. Almost every cross-road witnessed the separation of comrades in arms, who had long shared the perils and privations of a terrific struggle, now seeking their several homes to resume their duties as peaceful citizens. Endeared to each other by their ardent love for a common cause—a cause which they deemed unquestionably right and just, and which, surrendered not to convictions of error, but to the logic of arms, was still as true and just as ever—their words of parting, few and brief, were words of warm, fraternal affection; pledges of endless regard, and mutual promises to meet again.

"From information gained here, it was evident that his cavalry was making a demonstration; but whether to capture Mr. Davis, or simply to expedite his departure from the country, could not be determined. The country, or at least those familiar with military movements at this period, have doubtless long since satisfied themselves upon this point.

"To suppose that Mr. Davis and his staff, embracing some eight or ten gentlemen, all superbly mounted, and with led horses, could ride from Charlotte, N. C., to Washington, Ga., by daylight, over the highroads of the country, their coming heralded miles in advance by returning Confederate soldiers, without the cognizance and consent of the Federal commanders, whose cavalry covered the country, would be to detract from all that was known of their activity and vigilance.

"Political considerations, adequate to account for this unmolested progress, may readily be imagined. Whether they influenced it is only known to those who had the direction of public affairs at the time. But be this as it may, Mr. Davis' progress could not well have been more public and conspicuous.

"Mr. Davis, who was more generally known by the soldiers than any other man in the Confederacy, was never passed by them without a cheer, or some warm or kindly recognition or mark of respect. The fallen chief of a cause for which they had risked their lives and fortunes, and lost every thing but honor, his presence never failed to command their respect, and to add a tone of sympathy and sadness to the expression of their good wishes for his future. They knew not his plans for the future, nor could they conjecture what fate might have in store for him; but their hearts were with him, go where he might.

"Bronzed and weather-beaten veterans, who, when other hearts were sore afraid, still hoped on and fought 'while gleamed the sword of noble Robert Lee,' grasped his hand, without the power of giving voice to thoughts which their tear-glistening eyes revealed. Of such men were the great masses of the Confederate armies composed. Firm and inflexible in their convictions of right, and yielding not their convictions, but their armed maintenance of them only, to the stern arbitrament of war, they may be relied upon to observe with inviolable faith every pledge and duty to the United States, assumed or implied, by their submission or parole.

"At Abbeville Mr. Davis was again urged by his friends to leave the country, either from the southern shores of Florida or by crossing the Mississippi and going to Mexico through Texas; but though he listened quietly to all they had to say upon the subject, and seemed to acquiesce in their views, he never expressed a decided willingness or readiness to do so.

"To some of his friends it was apparent that his capture was not specially sought by the military authorities, and that he had but to change his dress and his horse, and to travel with a single friend, to pass unrecognized and in safety to the sea-shore, and there embark. Hitherto, as has been already said, his coming along his selected route was known to the people miles in advance. Schools were dismissed that the children might, upon the road-side, greet him. Ladies, with fruits and flowers, presented with tears of sympathy, were seen at the gates of every homestead, far in advance, awaiting his approach; and it was hardly supposable that the general in command, whose spies, and scouts, and cavalry covered the country, and were heard of upon all sides, was the only person uninformed of Mr. Davis' movements.

"The assertion that General Sherman, aware of this journey, permitted it to facilitate the departure of Mr. Davis and his friends from the country, is not made or designed; for it is possible that his capture was desired and attempted; but the facts are matters of history, and are given regardless of the speculations which they may justify.

"The party left Abbeville at 11 o'clock the same night for Washington, Georgia, a distance of some forty-five miles, and by riding briskly they reached the Savannah River at daylight, crossing it upon a pontoon bridge, and rode into Washington at about 10 o'clock A. M. Just before leaving Abbeville they learned that a body of Federal cavalry was *en route* to destroy this bridge, and might reach it before them, and hence they pushed on vigorously, meeting no enemy, but delayed about an hour by mistaking the right road.

"The night was intensely dark, the weather stormy. In approaching the bridge through the river swamp the guide and Colonel Preston Johnston, and another of the party, rode a half mile in advance, and the latter encountered a mounted Federal officer. The rays of blazing lightwood within a wood-cutter's small cabin fell upon him as he stood motionless beneath a tree, and revealed his water-proof riding-coat and the gold band upon his cap. He hurriedly inquired, as he listened to the tramp of the coming horsemen:

"'What troops are these?'

"'What force is this?'

"'Is this Jeff. Davis' party?'

"'Yes,' replied the party addressed, while revolving in his mind the best course to pursue, 'this is Jeff. Davis' escort of five thousand men.'

"The officer vanished in the darkness, and no others were encountered.

"At Washington it was found that squads of Federal cavalry scouts were there. A few were in the town at the time, and Mr. Davis was again urged to consult his safety. His family and servants, with a small train of ambulances, accompanied by his private Secretary, Mr. Burton Harrison, had passed through Washington twenty-four hours before, and the enemy then only some twenty miles distant, and Mr. Davis ascertained that he might readily overtake them; and before adopting any plan to leave the country, he desired to see and confer with them.

"On the following morning, with his party somewhat reduced in numbers, he left Washington and joined his family.

"The circumstance of the capture of Mr. Davis, as given officially by General Wilson, were in harmony with that system of misrepresentation by which the popular mind was perverted as to all he said, and did, and designed. His alleged attempt to escape, disguised in female apparel—a naked fiction—served well enough for the moment to gratify and amuse the popular mind. Barnum, the showman, true to his proclivity for practical falsehood, presented to the eyes of Broadway a graphic life-size representation of Mr. Davis, thus habited, resisting arrest by Federal soldiers; and many thousands of children, whose wondering eyes beheld it will grow to maturity and pass into the grave, retaining the ideas thus created as the truth of history. Fortunately, however, history rarely leaves her verification wholly to the testimony of envy, hatred, malice, or falsehood, but contrives, in her own time and method, ways and means to bring truth to her exposition.

"It has been seen that before the President's proclamation connecting him with the assassination, with every desired opportunity, and with every means of escape from the country at his command, Mr. Davis refrained from leaving it; and it is very doubtful whether, in face of the charge of complicity with this great crime, any power on earth could have induced him to leave.

"The sentiment to which the noble Clement Clay, of Alabama, gave utterance, upon learning that he was charged as *particeps criminis* in the assassination doubtless actuated Mr. Davis. Clay was able to escape from the country, and was prepared to do so;

but when his heroic and loveable wife made known to him this charge, with indignation and scorn at its base falsehood breathing in every tone, he rose quietly, and said: 'Well, my dear wife, that puts an end to all my plans of leaving the country. I must meet this calumny at once, and will go to Atlanta and surrender myself and demand its investigation.'

"Had Mr. Davis left the country, falsehood and malignity would have multiplied asserted proofs of this black charge against him; and the shortcomings, errors, and crimes, perhaps, of others, would have been conveniently attributed to the faults of his head or heart. But his long captivity, his cruel treatment, the patient, passive heroism with which, when powerless otherwise, and strong only in honor and integrity, he met his fate, have combined, not only to seal the lips of those of his Confederate associates who had wrongs, real or fancied, to resent, but to concentrate upon him the heartfelt sympathy of the Southern people, and no little interest and sympathy wherever heroic endurance of misfortune gains consideration among men.

"His escape from the country and a secure refuge in a foreign land, sustained by the respect and affection of the Southern people, were within his own control; and he might have reasonably looked forward to a return to his native State, as a result of a change in her political status, at no distant day. But he refrained from embracing the opportunities of escape which were his by fortune or by Federal permission.

"The suggestions of friends as to his personal safety were heard with all due consideration, and he manifested none of the airs of a would-be political martyr; and yet it was evident that captivity and death had lost with him their terrors in comparison with the crushing calamity of a defeat of a cause for whose triumph he had been ever ready to lay down his life.

"The general language and bearing of the people of the country through which he passed, their ardent loyalty to the South, their profound sorrow at the failure of her cause, and their warm expressions of regard for himself—all confirmatory of the conviction that, notwithstanding the odds against her, a thorough and hearty union of the people and leaders would have secured her triumph, affected him deeply.

"Throughout his journey he greatly enjoyed the exercise of riding and the open air, and decidedly preferred the bivouac to the bed-room; and at such times, reclining against a tree, or stretched upon a blanket, with his head pillowed upon his saddle, and under the inspiration of a good cigar, he talked very pleasantly of stirring scenes of other days, and forgot, for a time, the engrossing anxieties of the situation."

The solicitude of Mr. Davis for the safety of his family led to his capture. Several weeks had elapsed since he had parted with them, and almost the first positive information that he received, made him apprehensive for their safety. In the then disorganized condition of the country through which he was passing, the inducements to violence and robbery by desperate characters were numerous. Hearing that the route which Mrs. Davis was pursuing was infested by marauders, he determined to see that his family was out of danger, before putting into execution his design of crossing the Mississippi. While with his family, Mr. Davis was surprised by a body of Federal cavalry, and at the time being unarmed and unattended by any force competent for resistance, he was made a prisoner. On the 19th May, 1865, he was placed in solitary confinement at Fortress Monroe.

CHAPTER XXII.

MOTIVE OF MR. DAVIS' ARREST—AN AFTER-THOUGHT OF STANTON AND THE BUREAU OF MILITARY JUSTICE—THE EMBARRASSMENT PRODUCED BY HIS CAPTURE—THE INFAMOUS CHARGES AGAINST HIM—WHY MR. DAVIS WAS TREATED WITH EXCEPTIONAL CRUELTY—THE OUTRAGES AND INDIGNITIES OFFERED HIM—HIS PATIENT AND HEROIC ENDURANCE OF PERSECUTION—HIS RELEASE FROM FORTRESS MONROE—BAILED BY THE FEDERAL COURT AT RICHMOND—JOY OF THE COMMUNITY—IN CANADA—RE-APPEARANCE BEFORE THE FEDERAL COURT—HIS TRIAL AGAIN POSTPONED—CONCLUSION.

ALL doubt has long since been dispelled as to the motive of the pursuit and arrest of Mr. Davis. His arrest and imprisonment were the after-thought of the saturnine Secretary of War, and his associate inquisitors of the Bureau of Military Justice, at Washington. The details given by Mr. Mallory, of the circumstances of Mr. Davis' progress through North Carolina, South Carolina, and a part of Georgia, added to facts which are yet fresh in the public memory, fully justify the conclusion that the Federal authorities connived at his supposed purpose to escape the country. The reputation of Mr. Lincoln among his countrymen, for humanity as well as good sense, renders it extremely probable that such would have been his method of avoiding the perplexity which must arise from the capture of Mr. Davis.

Well understanding that the inflamed public sentiment of the North, regarding Mr. Davis as a political offender of the worst possible character, would not tolerate his immediate release, the Federal Government would have served the ends of humanity and sound policy by encouraging his escape. On the other hand the laws of the United States tolerate prolonged imprisonment only after trial and sentence. Hence the arrest of Mr. Davis must open an endless perspective of embarrassments. He could not be tried simply as an individual, nor could his punishment for any alleged crime of his own, be the sole object to be sought. His arraignment before a judicial tribunal, would be the arraignment of the principle of State Sovereignty, of the States which had sought to put that principle in practice, of the five millions of American citizens who had supported it, and who had cheerfully risked their lives and earthly possessions for its maintenance.

Nay, more, the trial of Jefferson Davis, upon a charge of treason, meant the trial of the North also. Should all efforts to convict the South in the person of Mr. Davis, of treason, fail, the recoil might well be dreaded by those who instigated the war upon the rights and existence of the States. It was not to be safely assumed that the legal decision of a constitutional question, which divided the framers of the Federal Constitution, would necessarily affirm the party and sectional dogmas upon which the North waged the war. Should secession be legally justified, what justification could the North claim, that is rightfully denied to Russia in her conduct towards Poland? What plea should England need for her outrages upon Ireland? With Jefferson Davis acquitted of treason, what could the conduct of the North for four years have been, but a revelry in blood—the wanton perpetration of a monstrous crime?

In this dilemma the industry of the Bureau of Military

Justice, which afterwards achieved an immortality of infamy, by its record of judicial murders, aided by the ingenuity of Stanton, devised a scheme for the arrest of Mr. Davis, upon charges designed to cover him and the cause which he represented, with everlasting obloquy. Not content with having triumphed by superior numbers, in a war of political opinions, which in the beginning was declared not to be waged for social or political subversion; not content with having settled a grave constitutional question, by brute force, in a government founded upon the idea of popular consent, the Federal authorities were now made a party to infamous falsehoods, the circumstances and results of which have fixed a stigma upon the American name.

Contemporary with the announcement of events, which proclaimed the irretrievable downfall of the Confederacy, were the calumnies of the Northern press, under the alleged inspiration of Stanton, representing that Mr. Davis was escaping with wagons filled with plunder, and with the gold of the Richmond banks; and that he had endeavored to escape in the concealment of female apparel. No one knew better than those who promulgated this paltry defamation, its utter falsity, and we would not insult Mr. Davis and the Southern people by bestowing consideration upon such palpable calumnies. It was not calculated that such a portraiture of one, whose personal honor, courage, and manhood had triumphantly endured every test, would be accepted by the intelligence even of the North. But it nevertheless had an obvious purpose, which was well answered. It imposed upon the weak and credulous. The besotted and cowardly mobs of the Northern cities, who filled the air with clamor for the "blood of traitors," while the men who had conquered the South, were touched with sympathy for the misfortunes of foes whom they respected, of course eagerly accepted any caricature of Mr. Davis agreeable to their own vulgar imaginations. In this manner was consummated the first step in the object of delaying the feeling of personal respect, and of sympathy for misfortunes, which eventually assert themselves in the masses, for a fallen foe, whom it was already resolved to persecute with oppression and cruelty previously unknown under the American political system.

Next came the atrocious proclamation charging Mr. Davis with complicity in the assassination of President Lincoln. It is safe to say that incidents hitherto prominent by their infamy, will be forgotten by history, in comparison with the dastardly criminal intent which instigated that document. Circumstances warrant the belief that not one of the conspirators against the life and honor of Mr. Davis, believed either then or now, that the charge had one atom of truth. Had the charge been honestly made, it would have been disavowed, when its falsity became apparent. But this would not have subserved the end of the conspirators, and the poison was permitted to circulate and rankle, long after the calumny had been exploded during the investigations of the military commission, in the cases of Mrs. Surratt and Captain Wirz. At length justice was vindicated by the publication of the confidential correspondence between Holt and Conover, which disclosed the unparalleled subornation and perjury upon which the conspirators relied. Well has it been said that the world will yet wonder "how it was that a people, passing for civilized and Christian, should have consigned Jefferson Davis to a cell, while they tolerated Edwin M. Stanton as a Cabinet Minister."

We have no desire to dwell upon the details of Mr. Davis' long and cruel imprisonment. The story is one over which the South has wept tears of agony, at whose recital the civilized world revolted, and which, in years to come, will mantle with shame the cheek of every American citizen who values the good name of his country. In a time of profound peace, when the last vestige of resistance to Federal authority had disappeared in the South, Mr. Davis, wrecked in fortune and in health, in violation of every fundamental principle of American liberty, of justice and humanity, was detained for two years, without trial, in close confinement, and, during a large portion of this period, treated with all the rigor of a sentenced convict.

But if indeed Mr. Davis was thus to be prejudged as the "traitor" and "conspirator" which the Stantons, and Holts, and Forneys declared him to be, why should he be selected from the millions of his advisers and followers, voluntary participants in his assumed "treason," as the single victim of cruelty, outrage, and indignity? What is there in his antecedents inconsistent with the character of a patriotic statesman devoted to the promotion of union, fraternity, harmony, and faithful allegiance to the Constitution and laws of his country? We have endeavored faithfully to trace his distinguished career as a statesman and soldier, and at no stage of his life is there to be found, either in his conduct or declared opinions, the evidence of infidelity to the Union as its character and objects were revealed to his understanding. Nor is there to be found in his personal character any support of that moral turpitude which a thousand oracles of falsehood have declared to have peculiarly characterized his commission of "treason."

No tongue and pen were more eloquent than his in describing the grandeur, glory, and blessings of the Union, and in invoking for its perpetuation the aspirations and prayers of his fellow-citizens. In the midst of passion and tumult, in 1861, he was conspicuous by his zeal for compromise, and for a pacific solution of difficulties. No Southern Senator abandoned his seat with so pathetic and regretful an announcement of the necessity which compelled the step. The sorrowful tone of his valedictory moistened the eye of every listener, and convinced even political adversaries of the sincerity and purity of his motives. His elevation to the Presidency of the Confederacy was not dictated by the recognition of any supposed title to leadership in the secession movement. His election was indeed a triumph over the extreme sentiment of the South, and was declared by those who opposed it to involve a compromise of the exclusive sectionalism which was the basis of the new government. His administration of the Confederate Government exhibited the same unswerving loyalty to duty, to justice and humanity, which his previous life so nobly exemplified. The people of the South alone know how steadfastly he opposed the indulgence of vengeance; how he strove, until the last moments of the struggle, to restrain the rancor and bitterness so naturally engendered under the circumstances. Yet, when Jefferson Davis lay a helpless prisoner in the strongest fortress of the Union, with "broad patches of skin abraded" by the irons upon his limbs, men were practically pardoned who had devoted years of labor to the purpose of disunion, and had reproached him for not unfurling the "black flag." Is not the inference, then, justified that all of these tortures and indignities were aimed at the people and the cause which his dignity, purity, and genius had so exalted in the eyes of mankind?

But how impotent are falsehood and malignity to obstruct the illumination of truth! As subornation and perjury proved unavailing to convict him of atrocious guilt, so equally has persecution failed to accomplish its purpose. To all that shameful picture of barbarous violence and gratuitous insult; of insolent *espionage* and vulgar curiosity; of the illustrious leader of a brave people, whose whole life does not exhibit one act of meanness or shame, or one word of untruth, crushed by disaster, and prostrate with disease, fettered as if he were a desperate felon; restricted in his diet, and not even permitted a change of linen, except by the authority of a military jailer; an object of unrelaxed scrutiny, often driven to his cell by the peering curiosity of vulgar men and unsexed women—to all this there was but one relief—the patient and constant heroism of the sufferer, giving heart to his despairing countrymen, and ennobling his own captivity. History furnishes no similar instance of patient and dignified endurance of adversity and persecution.

The incidents of Mr. Davis' history since his release from Fortress Monroe, do not require detailed narration. For the most part they are confined to that domain of privacy which decency holds to be inviolable. When two years—wanting a few days—from the date of his incarceration had elapsed, Mr. Davis was transferred by the military authorities to the custody of the Federal civil authorities at Richmond. Here, amid the congratulations of friends, and the rejoicings of the community, which loves him as it loves but one other—his constant friend and compeer in fame—he was released from custody under circumstances which are well known. The interval between his release in May, 1867, and his re-appearance before the Federal court, at Richmond, in the ensuing

November, was passed by Mr. Davis in Canada. There he was the recipient of the respect and sympathy which his character and his sufferings might have been expected to elicit from a humane people. At the November term of the Federal court, Mr. Davis was again present, with his eminent counsel, awaiting trial, and was again released upon recognizance to appear on the 25th March, 1868.

In the face of the close proximity of the event, it would be unprofitable to speculate as to the sequel of this third appearance of Jefferson Davis before a judicial tribunal, to answer the charge of treason. Nor do we propose to add to the brief consideration, which has already been given in this volume, of the legal and historical question involved in the case of Mr. Davis. The subject has been exhausted. The masterly expositions by Mr. Davis of the theory of the Federal Government (some of which we have given), are at once the complete vindications of himself and his countrymen, and the sufficient monuments of his fame.

But are the issues of the war to be subjected to candid and impartial legal adjudication? Will the North approve this raising of a doubt as to its own justification, merely in the hope of vengeance upon one who is powerless for injury? But if there is to be admitted another jurisdiction than that of War; if the arbitrament of battle is to be carried to the higher tribunal of Law and Public Opinion; if there is to be a trial and not a judicial farce, with a foregone conclusion and a prejudged sentence, the South and its late leader will not shrink from the verdict. Of this, the world requires no more emphatic iteration than that furnished by past events.

But the decision of this question, whatever it may be, can not recover the wager which the South gallantly staked and irretrievably lost. Time will show, however, the amount of truth in the prophecy of Jefferson Davis, made in reply to the remark that the cause of the Confederacy was lost: "*It appears so. But the principle for which we contended is bound to re-assert itself, though it may be at another time and in another form.*"

www.ingramcontent.com/pod-product-compliance
Lightning Source LLC
LaVergne TN
LVHW021053110826
845150LV00001B/62

* 9 7 8 1 4 2 5 5 6 7 5 8 3 *